HOMING INSTINCT

HOMING INSTINCT

Using Your Lifestyle to Design and Build Your Home

JOHN CONNELL

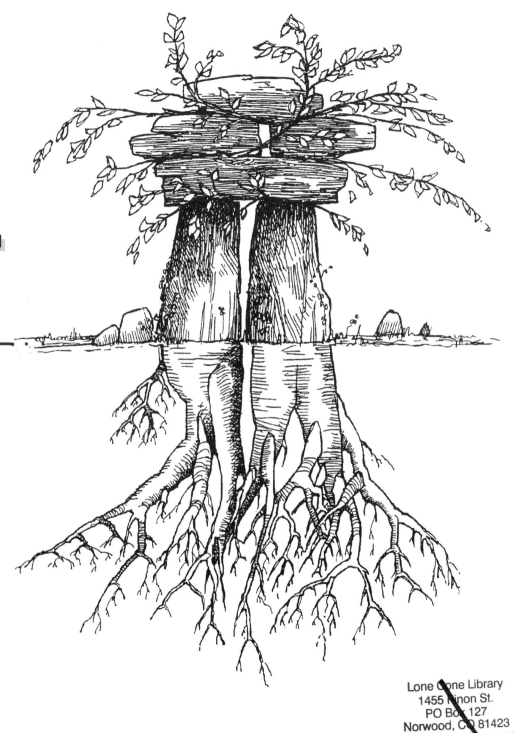

McGraw-Hill

New York   San Francisco   Washington, D.C.   Auckland   Bogotá
Caracas   Lisbon   London   Madrid   Mexico City   Milan
Montreal   New Delhi   San Juan   Singapore
Sydney   Tokyo   Toronto

McGraw-Hill

A Division of The **McGraw·Hill** Companies

1 2 3 4 5 6 7 8 9 0   KGP/KGP   9 0 3 2 1 0 9 8

ISBN 0-07-012346-2

The sponsoring editor for this book was Wendy Lochner and the production supervisor was Pamela A. Pelton. It was set in New Aster by North Market Street Graphics.

Printed and bound by Quebecor/Kingsport.

 This book is printed on recycled, acid-free paper containing a minimum of 50% recycled, de-inked fiber.

Contents

List of Appendices   vi
Foreword by Michael J. Crosbie   vii
Acknowledgments   ix
Introduction: Your *First* How-To Book   1

BEFOREGROUND AND BACKGROUND

1   The Story of How Vernacular Architecture Was Run Over by Henry Ford's Assembly Line   5

2   The History and Philosophy of the Yestermorrow School   19

3   The Grand Design: Site, Studio, and You   27

THE SITE

4   Your Place in the World   35

5   Site Design and Development   55

THE PROGRAM

6   The Endless Questions   69

7   Bubbles and Storyboards: Diagramming Your Program   81

THE BUILDING

8   Foundations and Liquid Stone   93

9   Walls and Wallness   119

10   Frames, Framing, and Skeletons   133

11   What Works and What Doesn't: Looking at the Interconnected Effects of Gravity, Temperature, Moisture, and Ethics   163

12   Masonry: Piling Things Up   191

13 The Roof and the Sky   217

14 A Window for Your Spirit,
A Door for the Dance   235

15 Understanding the Thermal Comfort of Your
Building's Envelope   257

16 Energy, Choices and Heating Systems   279

17 Plumbing and DWV (Drainage, Waste,
and Venting)   303

18 Power and Lights   329

19 Finishes, Finishing and Punchlist   355

Epilogue: You & Yestermorrow   361

Appendices   367

Glossary   419

Bibliography   433

Index   439

LIST OF APPENDICES

APPENDIX 1   Program Questionnaire   369

APPENDIX 2   National Weather Information:
Degree Days   372

APPENDIX 3   Heat Loss Calculation Example   380

APPENDIX 4   Drafting Conventions   386

APPENDIX 5   Foundation Design Guide   391

APPENDIX 6   Earthquake Basics   401

APPENDIX 7   Structures for Everyone:
Beams and Span Charts   404

APPENDIX 8   Structures for the Brave: Deflection,
Columns, Modulus of Elasticity, and
Moment of Inertia   408

APPENDIX 9   Framing Square Basics:
Laying Out a Rafter   412

APPENDIX 10   Count Rumford's Basic Relationships
for Fireplace Design   416

APPENDIX 11   Building Codes and Your Friend
the Inspector   417

Foreword

You're about to embark on a fantastic journey. Along the way you will see and learn things that will surprise you. There will be occasional moments of despair, crisis, frustration, anger, and humiliation. But more often there will be exhilarating experiences of great accomplishment, pride, joy, and self-satisfaction. You will do things that you never dreamed you could do. And in the process you will create something that will reflect the person you are and the values you hold dear. You're about to design and build your own home.

You have picked up the right book to prepare yourself for this journey. It's written by a master tour guide, the Eugene Fodor of home design and building—and a renegade architect. John Connell has chosen for his profession, and demonstrates on every page of this book, the demystification of architecture—an activity which, among most professional architects, is regarded with a great deal of suspicion. Why should an architect reveal his secrets of home design and building to nonarchitects? Because as the person who will dwell in the home you build, there is no architect in the world who knows as much as you do about how you want to live. John has created a path—the Yestermorrow Design/Build School and this book—that will allow you to design and build a home that is a portrait of yourself.

I first became aware of Yestermorrow while a doctoral student in architecture school working on a dissertation about owner homebuilding and improvement. I thought this was a worthy subject for architects to understand, in the hope that they could help guide those who had never designed or built a house. In conventional architectural practice, the potential homeowner (what we call "the client") hires an architect to design a house, based on long conversations about what the client wants in the house, how they like to entertain guests, how big the kitchen should be, what hobbies they pursue, etc. The architect then translates these needs and wishes (what we call "the program") into a building. This process is not cheap, and house clients are usually people of means. At the other end of the scale, folks of little or moderate means build their own houses, their initial motivation often being to save money. They rarely, if ever, consider designing the house themselves, but pull floor plans out of a book. This is what you might call the "helicopter school of design"—just pick the plan up off the page and drop it onto your site.

In my doctoral work I searched for ways that architects could break down the barriers of "boutique" design and help those of the helicopter school to design their own homes. I found the key at Yestermorrow, where architects and builders work together with people from all walks of life and awaken them to the possibilities of good home design, allay their fears that it is mysteriously incomprehensible, and instill a passion for good design that is a reflection of their lives.

In our culture, the idea that houses can communicate the dreams of their occupants is not given much attention. But when we look at houses in other cultures we find that our emphasis on the house as a "commodity" is the exception rather than the rule. In cultures around the world, many of which we erroneously refer to as "primitive," the community builds in unison and the houses reflect the values and beliefs of the builders. This is accomplished without professionals. Everyone who builds and dwells is an architect, and the house undergoes transformations over time, keeping it in rhythm with the dweller, the community, and the natural world.

As members of an industrialized culture, however, we gave up our birthright to design and build our own homes as our lives became more complicated and the work of our society was divided up among specialists. There are professional designers and professional builders who churn out houses for professional accountants, computer programmers, airline pilots, teachers, firemen, social workers, or whatever your path in life. Because all of us do not belong to one faith or political persuasion—and there are thousands of facets of modern life that define who we are—our culture is fractured. We don't share a common language for design and building as do smaller communities that are insulated from each other. Mass communications may connect us as a global village, but they do not provide a shared set of "dwelling beliefs." What we believe in and hold valuable is up to us to choose from our cultural smorgasbord—it is not handed down to us as unquestioned tradition, as it is in smaller communities.

What does this mean for you, the person who wants to design and build your own home? It means that to do so honestly and to revel in the result, you must answer questions about what your home will look like, how it will function, what it will be made of, where it will be located, and how it will be lighted, heated, and cooled. If you do not provide an answer, someone else will—the window salesman, the backhoe operator digging your foundation, or the plumber—people who hardly have an interest in making your home a reflection of your life. That's your job.

If you don't think it really matters where the windows go, how the floor plan is worked out, or what the pitch of the roof is, you should be aware (and warned) that the cumulative effect of overlooking these items might be harmful. At the very least, you will lose a huge, perhaps once in a lifetime, opportunity to make your home your own. Richard Neutra, an architect who designed many homes in California during the first half of this century, claimed that he could design a house in such a way that would land a happily married couple in divorce court within six months of moving in. His point was that design is not benign. Where you locate rooms, what views you have within the house and out, the quantity of privacy, the materials used, the choice of lighting—all of it affects your interaction with the built environment and the people you live with. Design can enhance that relationship—smoothing the path of your life—or the lack of carefully considered design can just as easily make your home an obstruction to living well.

You may also be familiar with Winston Churchill's observation that "We shape our buildings and they thereafter shape us." When you design and build a home you enter into a symbiotic relationship with it. You act upon the built environment and it in turn shapes your life. If you ignore it, it deteriorates, and with it the quality of your life. You are what you build.

Fortunately, mass communication now makes it possible for every one of us to have access to information, almost instantaneously. Living in the Information Age allows you to gain knowledge about design and building that was previously the closely guarded secret of professional designers and builders. As a casual perusal of the books at your local home center or hardware store will reveal, there are literally tons of tomes that tell you *how* to build virtually anything. But they never address *what* to build, or *why* to build it, which are much harder questions to answer. Only you can provide that information, because you're the expert on your life.

John Connell provides in this book a way of thinking about what you might want in the design of your home, and good questions to help you discover the house inside you. But he won't tell you what you should do (and as an architect myself, I understand the superhuman effort it takes for John not to tell you). That choice is up to you.

—MICHAEL J. CROSBIE
Essex, Connecticut
May 1992

Acknowledgments

Books, like buildings, are never made by just one person. Although buildings have their architects and books have their authors, the reality of complex things is that they come into being through team effort.

Only because of the constant and skillful urging of my friend, Joann Davis, did I even attempt to assemble such a team.

"Me write a book? Is this a good idea?" I asked. I was doubtful, so I asked friend and author Michael Crosbie.

"Of course, it's long overdue," he urged. Michael has been a constant support.

But Joanne and Michael, as supportive as they were, could not really be trusted to give me honest feedback. I felt they were just sparing my feelings when they kept saying the book was looking great. So I turned to that reliable source of unconditional, sometimes brutal, truth—the family. My brother, Flip, has been a writer in several professional capacities; certainly he would give me straight feedback. My sister, Laurie, a paralegal, is even less given to sugarcoating the truth. Their feedback, along with Diane Lisevick's and Kincaid Connell's, has been more than helpful; it has been essential. As "test" readers with little or no prior knowledge of the subject, they helped me purge incomprehensible passages and let me know where more explanation or a picture was needed. To read and comment on a book about something of which you have no knowledge is a truly daunting task—especially a book this long. Not only am I personally grateful, but I want to thank the test readers on behalf of all future readers.

Technical editing of special chapters required specialists. It takes a professional to review a chapter on structural mechanics or photovoltaic design. I would be nervous, to say the least, if Martin Gehner of Yale's Architecture School had not reviewed the sections on concrete and structures. Similarly, I am only comfortable that the sections on wind and solar power are state-of-the-art because Jito Coleman from Northern Energy Systems took the time to review them. Then Mac Rood, Keith Giamportone, and Jim Edgcomb, all architects and Yestermorrow instructors, read the entire book looking for misleading or poorly formated information. This was a humbling experience. They found and corrected numerous passages; they suggested additions and deletions. In large measure it can be said that this book was formed by the Yestermorrow staff.

Finally, in the "trenches" where the book, bibliography, glossary, and appendices were finally assembled, edited, and re-edited, I had the constant help of Joan Heaton and James Burde.

And that was just the first edition. In this new edition, which has been updated, corrected and expanded, I've had to chase hundreds of literary, figurative, and technical details to ground. Without the tireless help of my wife April, this one-of-a-kind design book would never have made deadline. Thank you one and all!

HOMING INSTINCT

Introduction: *Your* First *How-To Book*

SCENE: THE AUTHOR DISCUSSES THE BOOK WITH A WOULD-BE BUYER

"Hmmm, another how-to book, right?"

"Well, no. Not exactly. Sure, there's a lot of nuts and bolts in here, but that's not really my focus. This is more of a design/ build book. Are you familiar with that term, design/build?"

"No, I don't think so. Is it the same as *owner*/build? I'm really just interested in making a house, you know. I want a well-built place that I can afford and that works for me. I'm willing to do a lot of the work myself, but I need to learn how to do it first."

"Exactly. That's what this book is all about. You can do much more than most people imagine. To be honest, even I was surprised in the beginning. As a licensed architect I never imagined nonprofessionals could be as successful at making great residential architecture as trained architects and builders. But like all teachers, I've learned just as much as the students. For the last eighteen years I've been helping people like you take on the design and construction of their own homes. This book is a compilation of what I've learned that works. It won't be the *only* book you need, but it should be the *first book.*"

"Why?"

"Well, which book were you going to use?"

"I don't know. It's sort of a catch-22. Not knowing much about the subject, I'm not really prepared to evaluate all these how-to books. They all have so much information in them. This one has great charts, that one has great pictures, and I've heard this other one is supposed to be good. But I really don't know."

"That's why you should read this book *first.* We will start with what you already know the most about—*yourself.* Then we will take you through the design of your house. We will ask the same questions and use the same process as a professional architect. After that, we will discuss the construction of your design. As you can see from the table of contents, we touch on everything from foundation to final finishes. Of course, we can't cover everything, so at the end we will list a number of other good books for further reading."

"So I'll know where to go next. O.K., that sounds good."

"Yes, but here is the most important part. The design and construction of your house must be reintegrated into *one process,* the way it used to be. Remember, I said this is a book about design/build."

"Reintegrated? I'm not sure I understand."

"Well, for silly reasons explained in the first chapter, architects and builders parted company many years ago. The two professions always seem to be pointing their fingers at each other, screaming 'It's *their* fault!!' whenever anything goes wrong. For years the poor homeowner has been adrift in the confusion this generated.

"Actually, the architects and builders have also been a bit confused. The architects have been trying to design buildings without really understanding how they are built. Most architects have never been involved in the construction process first hand. Sometimes they draw up plans that *can't* be built. Besides suffering ridicule from the builders, they have missed the design inspiration latent in the act of building. It's a two-way street. The materials and methods inform the design process; then the design process explores fascinating new ways to use the materials and methods. Meanwhile, builders have been trying to build without really understanding the architectural intentions of the design. They have merely been 'assembling.' Decisions made on site are always made to expedite assembly, sometimes to the considerable detriment of the project. If the builder understands and supports the design concept, he will be able to take it into consideration as he makes the hundreds of small, unforeseen decisions that must be made during the construction of a house. The architect will adore him and so will the client. But, of course, this is rarely the case. So all this confusion needs to be sorted out before you start on your own house.

"How-to books often present design and construction the way they have been practiced (*mal*practiced?) for the last century—separately. The books on design merely give instruction on how to organize information, draft, build models, and, sometimes, present compelling images. The books on construction present a partial list of techniques and procedures without suggesting when to use them or how to think about them. They are mere cookbooks.

"In this book I have tried to integrate the two. The construction chapters may sound a bit heady and the design chapters just a bit technical. But, throughout, the information has been presented as different aspects of *one* process—design/build. I'll admit it's an awkward label and often misused. Nevertheless, when it means the fullest integration of the design and con-

struction processes, it refers to the best approach for anyone serious about making their own place. So that's another key reason that you should make this your first book. It's the only book that will show you how to *think* about design and construction—as design/build. After you have read this, you will have a unified overview. You will then be able to read any of the hundreds of other 'how-to' books and know where the specific information fits into the big picture."

"The big picture?"

"Yes, you know, the Big Picture, the Grand Design . . . This is Your Life!"

"Ahh, right."

"Seriously, if you want to design/build your own place, you had better get self-directed. No book can tell you how to live your life. After all, isn't that what a house is all about? It's the place where you live *your life.*"

"Well, how about if I take one of those courses at that Yestermorrow School up in Vermont?"

"I thought you would never ask! Yes, that would help. The architects and builders who teach there take you through the process of designing and building your home. Nevertheless, the answers to the important questions are determined by you, not them. They can ask the questions and direct you to resources. They can discuss your responses and offer alternatives. They help give you confidence and discover the instinct every human has for making a home. But in the end, the cor-

rect way to do things will depend on you. This really *is your life.*"

"Yeah, I'd like to take that course someday. Someday I may have the time and money. But not this year."

"Pluck up, friend. This book was written as a sort of *Cliff Notes* for those who don't have the time or money to attend the Yestermorrow School. It covers the big picture and gives you a context from which to proceed. Most importantly, it gives you a way to approach and think about this whole endeavor."

"Is it a step-by-step type of thing? Does it tell me what to do first, second, etc.?"

"No."

"So how does this book help me? I need to know where to start, what to do first. I need to know what's important and what's trivial. I need to know who to turn to for help and how the pros do it."

"Great. It's all here. But it isn't a step-by-step sort of thing. It's reiterative. You will find yourself coming back to this book many times to get your bearings. It is organized from the largest considerations to the smallest. It asks the big questions first. You might do well to follow the same sequence. I'll try to summarize. There are four basic parts:

"The first three chapters give you some background. They explain why people are rediscovering the rewards of making their own homes. All across the country, people of every background are solving their 'housing problem(s)' by returning to the American tradition of self-reliance. This is not hollow patriotic hoopla I'm talking about. At the core of our society is a do-it-yourself tradition that stretches back to the pioneers. This tradition was temporarily obscured by an era of specialists. But today people are starting to remember that they don't need a professional to tell them what they should like, what they can afford, or how they should live. So we start with a little history.

"The second part of this book, Chapters 4 and 5, begins to focus on your site. Regardless of whether your site is in the city or country or still just a dream, you have to know what to look for. This part shows you what's important and how to lay out your site.

The third part is about your design program. In these chapters we lead you through a series of design queries that help you avoid forgetting something important. Also, it is here that we present an approach to design/building that will serve as a guide throughout your entire project. It's called the Design Helix.

"Finally, in Chapters 6 through 19 we present alternatives and options in all the basic areas of construction. While these chapters explain all the underlying principles, they don't go into endless technical detail (we have appendices for that). The purpose of these chapters is to inform your design decisions with an understanding of how buildings go together. What are the differences between masonry and wood? Timber frame or balloon frame? Gas heat or solar heat? We go beyond just nuts and bolts issues here. We explore questions of cost, durability, intention, ethics, and most importantly—self-expression."

"O.K., but why read this book if I'm just going to use an architect?"

"Would you know how to shop for an architect? Do you know what an architect does? Do you think you could work *with* an architect?"

"Uh, let's see. I guess, maybe no and yes . . . I'm not sure."

"Right. Even if you plan to employ professional design talent, it is still essential that you understand where they fit in. Architects can be very helpful if used knowledgeably. They can also take your money and run amok if you let them."

"I see. And I suppose it's the same with a builder."

"Sure. Whether you use an architect, builder, plumber, mason, excavator—whoever—*communication is the key*. If you want to be involved and in control, you must be able to communicate with a lot of different people. It's unlikely that you will cut every board or place every tile, but you need to be able to speak meaningfully with those who will. You must understand the context in which they work. If you do, it's easy to get them to produce the results you want. If you don't, you will have only yourself to blame for the consequences.

"So, in short, this book should put you back in control of your house and home. It will enable you to follow your own personal homing instinct. Whether you're working with an architect and builder or pounding every nail yourself, this book will help you get the house that's right for you."

"Hmmm. So I guess it's not just another how-to book. Maybe it's a design/build fairy tale where the architects and builders make up, the owners get the house they want, and everyone lives happily ever after."

"Now you're talking!"

BEFOREGROUND AND BACKGROUND

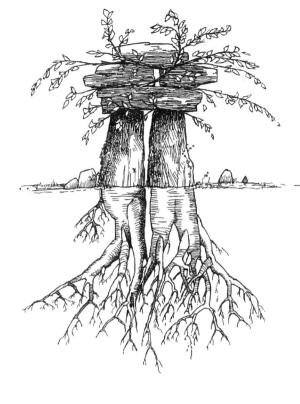

The Story of How Vernacular Architecture Was Run Over by Henry Ford's Assembly Line

IIII **The Human Quality of Making a Home**

People need homes. Although this seems obvious, Son Bao Vong reminded me that this apparent truth can be considered in several different ways. Son is Chinese by birth, but she was raised in Vietnam. Her father ran the Saigon newspaper until the Vietcong took over. Son became one of the Vietnam refugees who fled to America. When she arrived she was fourteen years old with no clothes, no family, and unable to speak English. Today she is an architect in Seattle promoting social responsibility through architecture. In 1988, Son was one of my design/build students at Yestermorrow.

"People in the city need bathrooms, maybe more than houses," Son remarked one day.

"People? Oh, you mean the homeless," I answered. I wasn't thinking about it that way. "Yes, of course the homeless need bathrooms . . . *in* their homes, ideally. But c'mon Son, that's a tall order for our little school to fill. Before anything can be done about the homeless, something must be done about basic American values, the cost of living, and many other basic urban issues."

"You think it's a matter of money?" she challenged.

"Well, not entirely, I guess." I didn't want to be specific. One develops a sixth sense for when Son is about to make a point. "But Son, you've got to agree that the homeless don't have the money to buy a house. Separation of wealth in this country is becoming an outrage. Certainly effective programs could be developed to provide shelter for the homeless with a mere fraction of our defense budget." Standard wisdom, I figured.

"Sure, housing," she answered, "but you're missing the point. Of course. This is America. You think of money and things to buy. What the homeless really need is a *place* where they can feel they belong. In China even beggars have a 'home.' They live outdoors, all about the market square. No walls and roof for them. Roof over-hangs and alleyways are their shelters. They survive on handouts, for sure, but everyone accepts them. They *belong* there. That is where the beggars live. When one dies, he or she is missed. If one were mur-dered, there would be fear and outrage, same as for you or me. In that culture, beg-gars aren't homeless, they are just '*house-less*.' Lacking a house, they do not become invisible as they do in this country."

"Ahh!" The light bulb finally came on. "I see. You're talking about a sense of place in their society, a sense of belonging."

This is very true, of course, and terribly overlooked in the way Americans think about their homes. In our material society "home" usually means "house," which usually means "investment," and the big-ger the better. Thus "home" has become an object or product much more than a place or state of belonging. In America, pursuit of property seems to have eclipsed the "pursuit of happiness." While this is an important issue, it only scratches the sur-face of what's implied by the statement: "People *need* homes."

At the time of my discussion with Son, I had been thinking in more fundamental terms. I didn't mean it was "right" or "appropriate" or "fair" that all people need homes. I simply meant the human species requires homes, or houses, to survive. People need houses biologically. As ani-mals we need shelter the same way we need food and water. Without homes, the human species is a failure, kaput, extinct.

As we think about designing our own homes, it is enlightening to look at humanity as just another species in Dar-win's dog-eat-dog world. Evolutionary theory assumes that it is natural for species to compete for resources and habi-tat. Food and predators are the daily rou-tine. Speed, strength, or other physical endowments can make the difference between the dinosaurs' fate or the rabbits' proliferation. (Actually, the roach has a better track record than the rabbit.)

On first inspection, human beings might not seem too promising. At the dawn of time, if the gods invited you to make a little wager, would you seriously consider placing your money on the human beings? Physically they are frail and very slow. They have no wings, claws, or barbs. Their teeth start falling out around middle age. They have no scales or hide for protection and no fur or feathers for warmth. Indeed, if you leave an unpro-tected human being out in the wild, he will usually perish within a day or two. That is, if another animal doesn't get him first.

What, then, can explain the obvious success of this awkward creature? Some species lacking physical strength survive through evasion. The bird, for example, survives all land-based predators by sim-ply taking to the air. Such an ecological fit means the species is given a protective advantage by the very surroundings in which it lives. The fish is ideally suited for the water; the bird is perfectly designed for the air. Indeed, most animals are appropriately configured to fit into the particular ecosystem in which they sur-vive. If they wander out of their habitat, chances for survival go down precipi-tously. It is exactly here that we start to understand the awesome ability of the human species to survive. The human being can survive in just about any ecosys-tem, any habitat. In the mountains, on the shoreline, in the woods or desert, on the water, even under the water; people have been pushing back the boundaries of their habitat for centuries. It is our very success in this regard that is responsible for our despoiling many delicate regions of the earth. Today our species inhabit the polar ice cap, the ocean floor, and we're even looking at outer space!

With such a vulnerable physical consti-tution, there can be only one explanation for this unequaled proliferation. *People make shelter.* Indeed, human beings make shelter the way birds fly or fish swim. It's our evolutionary thing.

Our ability to make houses stems from our highly touted opposable thumb and our ability to reason. Human beings are toolmakers; tools give us the physical abilities that our bodies lack, these tools enable us to make shelter. With no fur, claws, fangs, or wings, what other choice have we? This is the primitive essence in the act of making shelter. It is the survival instinct of our species. People need houses just as we need food. Think about that when you're feeling as if you'd really like to make your own place. It's not a weird desire. It's a homing instinct and, for a human being, the most natural thing in the world.

But this is only the starting point. Above all, the human being is a social animal. We live in groups and develop cultures. Shelter is collective. Making shelter is essential to making communities and establishing security. Making shelter is a basic human behavior that has evolved with our different cultures over the millennia. In every culture, making buildings allows us a measure of physical security while helping us resolve spiritual questions concerning our place in the universe. In many ways, making a house is an act of marking our existence. It becomes a container for our traditions and our personal ceremonies. For me, this is the foundation of what we mean by "culture."

Making shelter is only the precondition for making *homes*. Homes are shelters that reflect the attitudes and ways of life of the people who create them. A home is different from a house, which is just physical geometry. (Note that we have the term "housing" not "homing" for those multi-unit communities designed for statistically average occupants: affordable housing, worker housing, housing for the elderly, etc.) Anthropologists study the homes of a people to get a detailed and subtle impression of how they lived, their traditions, and what was important to them. But natural environment has an equal hand with culture in determining a people's approach to house building. Resources, climate, and geography each leave their mark on a vernacular architecture.

Local materials were the obvious choice for early builders. If a people lived in a wooded area, it was natural to use wood in their homes. If wood was scarce, perhaps rock was not, but the building season had to be long enough to assemble the rocks. If rock was unavailable, sometimes the very earth could be made into bricks. Here again, climate was a factor. The innate qualities of local materials suggested appropriate technologies for assembling them. Building traditions grew out of the local materials as used within the constraints of local weather conditions. Today we refer to structures built in this regional tradition as vernacular architecture.

Vernacular means native or local. It also means "of the local culture." Vernacular architecture, then, refers to a tradition of building done by the people who are native to an area. This is a very interesting concept for modern Americans. We are such a footloose people that traditions of any sort, least of all building traditions, have a hard time surviving. That's not to say, however, that there aren't very real vernacular traditions across this vast country. Indeed, America is like a laboratory example of the way vernacular housing develops in response to both the natural environment and a people's way of life.

Vernacular Architecture in America

There are precious few examples of the original vernacular architecture that was found by the Puritans when they colonized the Americas. The varied and wonderfully appropriate cultures of the Native Americans proved to be the first casualty of what would later become the Great Throwaway Society. It is a cultural embarrassment.

Ironically, the early settlers were highly concerned about moral righteousness. They had endured danger and deprivation to be able to settle in this New World just to be free to follow their own religious and social beliefs. While much in early American vernacular can be traced to English society, the settlers' primary reason for being here was to be rid of it. They, like so many immigrants since, were seeking a more perfect society.

The Puritan English were not the only group to settle in the New World. The Spanish set up many missions and military installations. Nevertheless, the Spanish settlements were simple extensions of European society. The Puritans, Separatists, and unlanded farmers in the Massachusetts Bay Colony hoped to create a totally new societal order. They did.

The Puritans tried to demonstrate their values and beliefs in every aspect of their new lives. Even today, this effort can easily be seen in the architecture and planning of their settlements. Consider the meeting house and church. These reflect the belief that everyone must stand together in the face of God. No individuals could exist outside the church or the community. Indeed, bachelors and widows were made to live with other families. And the town law required that everyone live within one and a half miles of the meeting house. In fact, sometimes people were required to move closer to town just to satisfy this requirement. Such practices determined the organization of early town plans just as profoundly as the town green or "commons."

Individual pride or personal expression was squelched. The architecture of the individual house or home had to express the equality (sameness) and spiritual humility of each settler. Regardless of personal resources, it was understood that most had come to the New World to escape the inequities of a class-based society. Here, everyone would have a fair and equal life in the eyes of God. And "faire" was a word that could handily be used to describe architecture. "Faire" meant

square, regular, and of a straightforward design. No large or expressive architecture will be found in the early vernacular of our country, even though (and maybe a little because) the Baroque style was blossoming in Europe. Given the climate and the abundance of timber, it is hardly surprising that early settlers developed their own version of the timber frame, with shingles on the roof and clapboards on the exterior walls. The exterior and size were likely constrained by the shortness of the building season and the severity of the winters. The interiors further reinforced the Puritans' beliefs and covenants. Small and simple rooms insured that one was always in the presence of others, constantly under mutual surveillance lest the basically sinful human nature get the upper hand. All this demonstrates how powerfully-built form can express values.

Even today these early vernacular structures have a strong effect on contemporary Americans. While not every region of America is a direct architectural descendent of the Massachusetts Bay Colony, the Puritans have left a cultural heritage that still subtly affects much of our nation's attitudes about work, play, and wealth. Especially in the area of domestic architecture, we find a direct line back to colonial insistence on simplicity and equality. Today this is still behind most Americans' desire for a "normal" house. The normal house that sits at the center of our American Dream is still a

"faire house." It still traces much of its meaning and origins to the early settlers' vernacular architecture and town planning. Perhaps all too often, "normal" still means "colonial."

By the early 1800s the ideal American home was a single-family detached dwelling that expressed family pride at the same time as being unpretentious and economical. Here we can see the beginnings of a tradition of values and beliefs that has evolved uninterrupted to the present day. This is consensus shaped by many voices.

By the 1830s ministers, schoolteachers, physicians, poets, and jurists all over the country were instructing their fellow citizens about good homes. These were not architectural suggestions. These were moral instructions. This practice of defining a "proper home" is continued today in magazines such as *House Beautiful, Better Homes and Gardens, Architectural Digest, Home,* and numerous other publications. Each publication brings a slightly different harmony to the ongoing opera: *The American Dream House.* Upon closer inspection, each opinion about what makes a proper house reveals itself to be a thinly masked commentary on societal values.

In the 1800s writers such as Henry Thoreau, James Fenimore Cooper, and Washington Irving were all using architectural references to articulate their moral advice to readers. Defining the American home had become a national mission. It correlated with the mission to define the American family.

At this time more attention was given to improving the individual, especially the individual child. A home was increasingly understood to be a place that would influence the moral and spiritual makeup of a child. Greater emphasis on private spaces arose. In 1843 Catherine Beecher wrote "Treatise on Domestic Economy" in which spatial specialization was highlighted. Writers of the day insisted increasingly that each house was to have separate areas for family social life, personal privacy, and household production. Kitchens, dining rooms, living rooms, bedrooms, and parlors all became de rigueur.

Such individualization was in sharp contrast to the Puritan "all equal in the eyes of God" approach. Now comes the idea that a child will grow to be an adult, an individual, and both will be affected by the spaces they inhabit.

The mid-1800s saw the widespread use of "pattern books." These books, published by the builders of the day, contained illustrated floor plans, elevations, and details accompanied by text extolling the virtues of a "perfect house." This was an important chapter in the development of the American vernacular. With the continued emphasis on specialized use of space, the simple symmetrical layout of a few general rooms gave way to more var-ied floor plans with each room having a distinct shape and function. This translated into more variety in the outward appearance of the homes. Usually a pattern book would include a house for the mountains, the plains, the seacoast, the town, and the farm. Many were by landscapers, the most famous of whom was Andrew Jackson Downing. Each different house design would be shown in its setting with appropriate landscaping. Here were examples of Gothic Revival, Lombard, Norman, Tudor Revival, Byzantine Revival, and Italianate, in addition to the more common Greek Revival- and colonial-style cottages. This was the arrival of diversity. After decades of narrowly defined "normal" homes, citizens could now choose between several different patterns. Builders actually spoke of "styles" and sought to create a mood using certain architectural motifs. The box shape was cast aside and the creative carpenter discovered gingerbread.

It is at just about this time that we see the first publications aimed squarely at the "owner/builder." In 1859 Charles Dwyer published *The Immigrant Builder* in which he described inexpensive dwellings of sod blocks, rammed earth, adobe, and lightweight wood frame. These plans were provided so the homesteader could build from local materials. The homesteader, it should be remembered, is the true forerunner of today's owner/builder. Americans have always pursued home and happiness through the act of settling. Squatter rights were originally based on the notion that anyone who builds a home and works the land is entitled to possession of the fundamental happiness associated with same. (And as we all know, "possession is nine-tenths of ownership.")

It wasn't long before builders were mixing styles and inventing their own decorative motifs. Stylistic inventiveness was seen as a way to cultivate independence and national identity. The idea that national unity resulted from artistic freedom was frequently found in the latest pattern books. But this was still a very modern notion and only a small percentage of the population embraced it. Though less likely to sell books, the equal-in-God's-eyes architecture was still the majority position. Normal.

In 1846 Louis Godey of Philadelphia decided to promote an "own-your-own-home" movement by publishing American cottage plans in his monthly women's fashion journal. Godey's *Lady's Book* published 450 model house designs between 1846 and 1898. These plans are said to be the basis for over four thousand homes built during a single decade. Architectural diversity became more than just a response to the site or the latest revival going on in Europe. In Godey's publications sentimental poetry, prose, feminine fashion, and idealized American homes were all brought together into one domestic dialogue.

This dialogue, sometimes boiling over into a debate, has continued and deepened over the years. It goes on today, and this very book is but a small part of it. Many have contributed to what they hoped would be the definitive American residential architecture. Basic values and standards have been established, challenged, and reestablished. But through it all, certain themes have persisted. Families are still seen as the center of American life. Children are the reason for embracing the American Dream. They are still the best hope for the future. And each child is an individual with a unique but alterable disposition. So by the mid-1800s it was generally agreed that a healthy family could only be found in a proper house.

Every social communicator of the time insisted that healthy families should settle in the country. Nathaniel Willis took it a step further. In his book *Out-Doors at Idle-wild** he made a connection between rural virtues and republican values. Living in the country was becoming American. Rural life was romanticized. Living in the city was considered an unfortunate necessity.

Pattern-book authors insisted on local materials and that led to the championing of primitive aesthetics and rustic simplicity. Emerson exalted the "common . . . the familiar" as did others holding up the rugged log cabin as our national cultural

* *Out-Doors at Idlewild, or, The Shaping of a Home on the Banks of the Hudson* by N. Willis (New York: Charles Scribner, 1855).

heritage. This rustic romanticism took on its largest form in the great Adirondack camps built from 1870 to 1930. It is still very much with us today in the current flurry of "log homes" being built in every climate and region of America.

These manufactured log homes are an interesting snapshot of how past vernacular styles are being repackaged in this country. With all the latest conveniences and gadgets, they are truly modern. Indeed, rather than a response to site or climate, they are manufactured in a factory—like cars! But unlike cars, the owner assembles them. After all, we are still, as always, a nation of do-it-yourselfers. This may have come from our early Puritan values of economic restraint and moderation. Or it may reflect the American tradition of self-reliance and independence. Unfortunately, it also reflects our long tradition of picking aesthetics out of a book or magazine.

After two hundred years it would seem that Americans might look more deeply into their landscape and culture for vernacular inspiration. How might we think about our homes today? What is the local way of doing things? From what materials do we want to make our homes? What values and beliefs are expressed in the way we make our homes—and communities? In a nation as large and cross cultural as ours, the answers to these questions are complex and changing.

Sadly, the architectural responses

haven't been. Because of the homogenizing effect of television and other mass media, we can expect to see the same ranch or colonial in every corner of our nation. Normal. Normal expectations for a house can be found in magazines and in plan books found in your local grocery store. Some books have over two hundred different plans. Nevertheless, each one is a cookie-cutter design. We are a culture that values the individual; why do we continue to live in houses that were designed to mute individual expression?

Shopping for the American Dream

The family home, sweet home (where the heart is, every man's castle) has been at the center of the American Dream since before the first Americans even got off the boat. It has always been a central symbol of what is enviable in American culture. The house symbol evokes many issues beyond the basics of shelter and protection. Issues like freedom, self-determination, privacy, and status are all resident in the idealized American home. More than a dream, for most Americans it is considered a fundamental right.

Of course, that is not how most people actually think of their homes. We are, by our own admission, a nation of shoppers, not a nation of sociologists. This nation-of-shoppers mentality has been particularly intrusive since the Second World War.

When the troops returned from Europe, there was a terrible housing shortage. On the other hand, the government had just successfully saved the world for democracy. It had done so using crisis management and the famous *ninety-day wonders*. This refers to the three-month officer training period during the Second World War. Civilians became commanding officers in ninety days of intensive training that had previously taken *years* at military academies. In other words, we were in the habit of solving problems quickly, and often with the help of impressive industrialization.

Architects in Europe had been promoting the use of industrial methods since the middle twenties. Ludwig Mies van der Rohe had declared ornament and style obsolete. Walter Gropius, founder of the Bauhaus, advised that the housing "problem should be attacked at its roots. The real solution," he claimed, was that houses should "not be built at the site, but in specialized factories by serial manufacturing of mountable elements." Corbusier announced that the modern world needed "a machine for living." In 1928 Bucky Fuller came close to realizing this machine with his Dymaxion Dwelling. Yet for all this, mass-produced housing saw little success during the period between the wars. Rather it was a time of attitude shift. People started to accept the assembly-line aesthetic as something modern and superior. "Custom crafted" became an unaffordable reference to the past.

It was during and after the Second World War that mass-produced housing really took off. The government had constructed over 190,000 prefabricated units during the war. By the end of the war there were over seventy-five manufacturers tooled up and ready to supply assembly-line housing for the returning troops. It was now widely accepted that homes should be designed, assembled, marketed, and sold like any other expensive product, most specifically like the automobile. The failure of the Lustron Home and other highly publicized prefabrications did little to disabuse the housing industry of this seductive notion. While factory-built housing didn't really revive until the fifties, the postwar housing crisis saw large-scale-housing developers building thousands of cookie-cutter homes on site. Lacking the factory pedigree certainly didn't prevent these units from being built, marketed, and sold as products.

As our society of shoppers became more and more mobile, the idea of buying and selling a house became more commonplace, even expected. It became symbolic of moving up the ladder of success. A promotion often meant relocation. The new house was always bigger than the last. Buying a house started to become more like buying a car. One certainly had to consider function and utility, but just as important were the implicit connotations of status and investment. Where you lived and what your house looked like have long been indicators of material success. In this way location was still somewhat important, but creating a sense of place became secondary. Remember that this was during the full blossom of America's love affair with the automobile, the road, and even the mobile home. The notion of place had taken a backseat to the thrill of motion and the lure of the future, the technological factory-built future.

Let's take a moment here to really understand what "sense of place" is. Why is it so important? Can't we buy it or otherwise locate it according to some formula? Must it be so elusive? What is it?

Ironically, a sense of place has become one of the rarest as well as one of the most sought after qualities in a house. It's not elusive but neither can it be packaged and sold. A place develops a special quality as a result of ongoing human activity. Part of the allure of an older home is this palpable history of human activity. It validates the location. (In the sixties we might have said, "It's where it's *at*." Obviously.) To establish this sense of place needn't take generations; it can be developed within one lifetime. It starts with a level of commitment. As you live in one location your habits, traditions, and ceremonies become a part of the place. Without asking, visitors can sense that you belong there.

Perhaps the easiest way to understand this sense of place is to look at where it's missing. Today, most occupants stay in their homes for less than five years on average. This is not enough time to raise a family, watch a tree mature, or even worry about the interior decoration. The idea of *making* a home (formerly "homemaking") is less applicable. If you might be moving within a few years, how excited can you get about personalizing the house?

So you won't find a "sense of place" in a housing development or a tract house, regardless of size or price. You won't find a sense of place in a shopping mall or a trailer park or a condo, or in student housing or elderly housing or any kind of "housing." In general, you won't find a sense of place in urban or rental situations. These are all places that are designed to accommodate movement. These are transition points, not destinations. Although the American Dream is about a destination, the American way of life is about movement. We see ourselves as jet-setters, headed up the corporate ladder, always acquiring the latest thing. And until recently, we've had the cheap energy to make such a wasteful life-style possible (for some). Nevertheless, when they finally arrive at the top, most successful Americans want to settle down. A home in the country is still the central altar at which we praise the American Dream. Furthermore, it is one of the most symbolic rewards for having "made it" in our society. So in the meantime, while still on the treadmill, most people shop for their homes like any other commodity. You get the best you can afford, and take comfort in the knowledge that you can trade up later. Nothing need be permanent.

The noted architect Charles Moore elegantly describes why a sense of place is a key ingredient in his work. In his *The Place of Houses* he explores some of the ways in which houses contribute to the creation of a memorable place:

> To our minds, the legitimate purpose of architecture, to lay special claim to parts of the world ("insides"), has turned about on us. We have overbuilt, and often built so badly that instead of having what, for instance, the Middle Ages had (where most of what was built was secure and everything outside the walls was scary), we have now made a world in which the most alien things are what we have built for ourselves, while nature by contrast looks good.
>
> What we have built does scare us. Most of it has no message for us. We can't claim it as our own, and we can't comfortably inhabit it. Thus the legitimate search for roots has become frantic, as people seek to anchor themselves in an increasingly bland and undifferentiated geography.

ⅢⅢ Building Houses, not Homes

The early settlers designed and built their own homes. As our society evolved and specialization developed, people with the means had their homes built for them. Architects would design them; builders would construct them. This is still how many larger homes and commercial buildings are brought into existence. But generally, this has become too expensive and time consuming for all but a few. Now we just shop for and purchase our homes. For the last fifty years or so, we have developed a vital marketplace for buying and selling homes. There have never been so many choices available to the house shopper.

Developers and builders have produced a wide variety of "units" resulting from research, marketing, and sometimes even the advice of architects. Today we still have the custom-built home, but now it can be panelized, modularized, factory-built, and delivered. The marketplace also offers a wide variety of mobile homes, trailer homes, and other manufactured housing.

All of these options can be had at a wide variety of prices and corresponding levels of quality; it should be a shoppers' paradise. Increasingly, however, it isn't. Today, fewer and fewer people can afford the house of their dreams. Indeed, fewer can afford any house at all.

The cost of the American Dream has just plain risen out of sight. And for the few who can afford something, the options are disappointing. This isn't a sudden development; we have been watching this trend for the last few decades. It is only the most recent chapter in a story that started when manufacturers discovered that "appearance" could be marketed as easily as "substance." As corners were cut and quality reduced, only the *appearance* of quality ("the look and feel of real leather") was actually improved. Indeed, a generation of TV watchers are frequently confused by the disparity between what they see on the tube and the reality in which they live. Increasingly, this same generation is now aspiring to the illusion of success rather than the real thing. Who and what they really are has become less important than who they appear to be. This is a very nervous and empty existence; it can only last a little while. In time, the pendulum must swing the other way. People are beginning to miss the substance and meaning of former days. They sense the flimsiness of their lives in which nothing is made to last and everything is disposable. The cult of "newness" is still at large and current talk of recycling seems merely another way to perpetuate it. Even our buildings are now designed to have an average life span of only twenty-five years.

This sociocultural harangue is well outside the scope of this book (lucky for you!), but it has an important impact on what we are talking about here. At the Yestermorrow School, where we teach all sorts of people to design and build their own homes, a substantial percentage of our students can easily afford what's available in the middle and even the upper market. Saving money is not why they are learning to do it themselves. Rather, they have decided that this is the only way to get what they want into a house.

What each student wants varies. Some simply want an affordable home. Others are looking for a particular look or layout.

Some have been told they need an architect but are unsure of how to use one. And many have already tried architects and don't want to repeat the experience. This also applies to the assembly of the house. Some students simply want to learn a straightforward method for building a house. Others are looking for a level of quality or special skills not covered in a basic do-it-yourself primer. Many have heard horror stories concerning professional contractors and they want to avoid being victimized by their lack of knowledge.

Most people simply don't understand how the buildings in which they live work. I have had students without a clue as to the operating relationship between a wall switch and the overhead light, where the water goes down the drain, or why we have basements. In addition, consider the sad fact that more and more buildings simply *don't work*. They don't work mechanically, spiritually, ethically, or socially. Even uneducated occupants know that their homes don't "work." They may not be able to point to specific errors or omissions, but they can genuinely feel that their house lacks a critical energy. It has no spirit; no sense of place.

Traditional methods using professionals, experts, and specialists are losing credibility. People want more direct involvement and control. Irrespective of socioeconomic status, people want to reconnect with their built environment.

This is why the Yestermorrow School was started and has flourished.

▥ The Pitch: Design Your Home, Build Your House . . . Save the World!

Owner/building is hardly a new phenomenon. It's an age-old practice that lost popularity with the advent of the Industrial Revolution. Specialization, industrialization, and the god of convenience all conspired to retire the tradition of owner/building prematurely. But today the Industrial Revolution is over and people have developed a more cynical attitude toward promises from the assembly line. These promises have been compromised by a generation of stupendous failures, most notably in the house-building industry.

People are dissatisfied with the housing provided by the developers, the panelizers, the industrialists, and the professionals. The reasons vary: cost is too high, quality is too low, location is wrong, design is too impersonal, or, increasingly, the design doesn't accommodate modern life-styles. Distrust of big industry coupled with dissatisfaction with available options is leading increasing numbers of people back to the practice of doing it for themselves. When you elect to design and build your own house, you are doing much more than saving some money or pursuing a hobby. You're setting up a *home base*. A home base is a place in the world with your name written indelibly all over it. By investing your personal time and effort into this place, it necessarily becomes much more than a financial investment: It becomes the center of your life. The community and your neighbors automatically become part of your concern, part of your "site." The assumption that you won't be moving out in the next few years is a comfort and an inspiration to everyone in the community. Indeed, this action is likely to have a ripple effect. When you demonstrate that you're willing to place your money on the table and commit to a home base, it's much easier for others to do likewise.

If you're a family, the benefits of establishing a home base increase exponentially. For children a house isn't just a metaphor or symbol for the universe—it *is* the universe. It is the center of their world. Everything else relates to this reliable, enduring piece of geography. School, friends, camp, summer jobs, vacation trips—everything revolves around the locus of home. It's funny how readily we understand the importance of such stability when it comes to our children, but how easily we ignore it when it comes to ourselves. The truth is that we *all* do better with a secure home base. Before you start thinking about exceptions and why this doesn't apply to your situation, let's consider a few implications. Settling down in one place often raises concerns about work, money, vacation, and play.

Work comes in many different forms. But implicit in every job is the idea of advancement and that can often mean relocation. For the past several decades large corporations have been moving people here and there as if they were some type of equipment. Even small companies and the self-employed up and move to follow the best work opportunities. If you want to make more money or stay with the corporation, the thinking goes, you have to be mobile. Recently, however, increasing numbers of employees are saying "no thanks." Today there are more options. For the desk worker, electronic communications has allowed everything from presentations to conferences to take place over the telephone lines. If it requires paper it can be faxed or mailed overnight. And when the situation absolutely requires a warm body, the plane or train is usually available and affordable.

People with a trade or nondesk-based skill face a different situation. If you produce a hard product, it must be brought to market. Nevertheless, the means now exist for reaching world markets without actually being there. Living in Vermont, I see this demonstrated all the time. Our rural state is mostly inhabited by people who make things that are purchased elsewhere. Many craftspeople, as well as professionals, work for companies or clients that are out of state. When they must travel for work, they don't move their homes. They refuse to make their homes

hostage to how much money is being made in some other part of the nation. They have made their homes where they want to live their lives.

Recreational travel has become even better. When I was younger, traveling was a huge logistical drag. Every time I moved I had to carry everything I owned with me. Though I gave plenty of lip service to "traveling light" and the freedom of "knapsack living," the truth was I traveled very little. Packing and/or moving share a place with root canal work on my list of personal pleasures. That's now all in the past. Today I have a home base. I am totally invested in this place and it is the center of my world. When I travel, I take only what I need; I travel more now because of it. More importantly, there's a different feeling about traveling now that I know there is a home somewhere to which I will be returning. More than a repository for material possessions, my home base allows me to keep memories and images I bring back from my travels. It's a walk-through scrapbook or museum of my family's lives.

Some people will only make this kind of commitment to their second home. These people expect to move around and so they are reluctant to put too much of their personal lives into their primary residence. For these folks, relocation is the unavoidable price of "making it."

The problem with this approach is that life is too short. Why put the best of my life into something I only visit for two weeks a year? What if I never make a million or win the lottery? I want my primary residence to have the special feeling of a vacation home—*every day of the year.* I'm going to put my money and effort into the place where I spend the most time. That way my family and I can make lasting friendships, plant trees, raise children, and get involved with the community. I guess I'm impatient, but I want to invest in my own universe, my own world, and I want to do it in the present.

There is no better way to explore all the possibilities in life than designing your own home. Even if you don't build it. Design lets you explore your world view and what you want in your life. Design allows you to custom tailor a place for all your physical and spiritual needs: It's the ultimate fantasy. You can change your world again and again for the cost of paper and pencils. Imagine your life over time. Add a room for kids, for a hobby, for a business, for retirement, for anything. Shape the outdoors as well as the indoors. Create fantastical walks, wonderful patios, perfect barbecues. Design for a life after you've won megabucks, then reduce it to reflect current reality. Keep the best, phase in the rest. And when you finally hit on the perfect design, you'll not only be ready to build, but you will have a deeper understanding of exactly what makes up your life.

Yestermorrow

Talking about the future used to feel like speculation on the distant world of our not-yet-born grandchildren. These days, we discuss it one day and it appears by the end of the month! It's not always so wonderful, either. More and more we have learned to fear the future as it increasingly reveals itself to be the offspring of poor decisions from our past. But I still find the future of our homes and houses to be promising, even exciting. We may have to go through a traumatic change in the way we have been thinking for the last seventy years and I admit that could be harrowing. But the dawn of a major shift in the way we make our homes is already upon us. Many of today's settlement trends recall values left behind when energy was cheap and we became a footloose society. Other trends reflect a limited-resource future where high technology and electronic information redefine where and how we dwell. This is what I call "yestermorrow":

YESTERMORROW =
VALUES FROM PAST + BLDG. TECH FROM FUTURE

I think a few general observations will demonstrate that yestermorrow is not a proposal; it's here today.

I want to bring your attention to six well-documented trends that have come to an interesting focus: house quality, energy, disposable income, global intercommunication, family demographics, and general education. Now don't lose courage, this is not a form letter. Get another cup of coffee and stay with me on this.

House Quality: Since the late thirties, when the assembly line was seen as the solution to our housing shortage, the quality of available housing stock has slowly but steadily declined. Whether built one at a time on speculation or in dozens by developers, today's homes have never been less satisfactory to the potential buyers.

Income: Along with the quality, the ability of most people to buy a house has also declined. Particularly in the last ten to fifteen years, the separation of wealth has rendered the vast majority unable to afford a home. So most people can't afford what's on the market and they wouldn't choose to buy it if they could.

Global Communication: The evening news and other mass media have made the global village a reality. Most people are now aware of how other people are living in different parts of the world. It should surprise no one that building your own home is the global norm, hardly the exception. Only in our industrialized culture do we hand this primary human activity over to others.

Education: Never in the history of this nation have so many been so educated. The majority of our median-aged adults have a better education than their parents and probably better than will be available for their children. In the absence of hard cash, knowledge has become the alternative currency. This highly educated generation is used to learning whatever they need to know. They assume that they can, and must, learn whatever is needed to overcome the current housing situation.

Families: The baby boomers are now parents. While single or empty-nested, the idea of moving around from job to job made pretty good sense. But now children, schools, and length of commutes play a larger role in defining the "quality of life" for this biggest demographic group.

Energy: Though we're reluctant to admit it, the writing is on the wall. Cheap energy is a thing of the past. In particular, cheap petroleum and the attendant lifestyle is destined for the "tar pits." The highly mobile, disposable American Dream will have to be replaced with something that takes less energy and lasts longer.

These six trends, taken together with everything they imply, suggest that we are on the threshold of yestermorrow. It is a time when much of the way our forebearers thought about making a house will be reformated to embrace tomorrow's lifestyles, materials, and politics. People and families haven't changed as much as was once predicted. The American Dream still has healthy roots buried in the soils of individual effort and self-actualization. What has changed (petered out) is the postwar promise of the industrialized future.

Increasing numbers of individuals are taking back the responsibility for making their homes. After half a century, it is clear that homes cannot be satisfactorily produced with an assembly-line mentality. Technology is still a powerful tool and will obviously play a role in heightening the quality of our future homes. Today's owner/builders are quickly assimilating the potential of modern materials and methods. But how and where they use them is now something they want to determine for themselves. What this new generation of owner/builders will make with their latest tools is still evolving. Vision and design are needed to help with the next era of vernacular building.

This is what the Yestermorrow School is all about. It's a place where we are reconsidering yesterday's building *attitudes* while redirecting the use of tomorrow's building *technologies*. We are reinspecting the basic assumptions about how we make our homes. The protective enclave of a school is the perfect format for this exploration. It keeps special interests and short-term considerations from truncating the process. With some luck, we may see the resurgence of a rich and regional tradition of vernacular architecture in this country. Homes designed and built by their occupants will find new expression and communities will reflect the way people want to live.

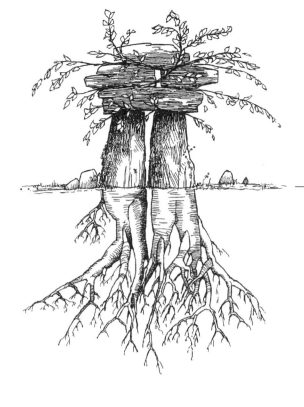

2

The History and Philosophy of the Yestermorrow School

⫼ Getting It All Together

I asked one of my students why she was taking the Yestermorrow design/build course:

"Because it's cheaper than an architect and I'll get what I want instead of what they want me to have."

After further questioning I learned that this woman had already talked with several architects and they all said that a 10 to 15 percent fee is standard. "I have $180,000 for my budget," she said. "If I pay $18,000 (10 percent) for my architect, I'm not going to have enough money for my garage. Moreover, their fee is based on construction costs, so the more the project goes over budget, the more they get paid. I heard that and immediately decided I wanted no part of it."

"But don't you think a professional will save you more money than they cost?" I asked. No, no, she insisted. Everyone knows that architect-designed homes cost more than others. Everyone knows that architects will spend your money for you but not always on what you want. Everyone knows how costly and *optional* a design professional is. Yikes, architects have a bad rep. As we shall see a bit later, the client isn't the only one with complaints about the architect. Wait until we hear from the builders.

But before we let anyone else take a shot at the professionals, let's give them a little consideration. Ten percent may seem like a large fee, but what is it supposed to buy? Well, according to the American Institute of Architects, it will cover five services: preliminary design and programming; design development; construction documents; budget analysis and bid supervision; site inspections and review.

A brief elaboration of each area will be helpful.

Preliminary Design and Programming

The initial design concept must be developed from a consideration of client needs and site requirements. Often the architect must organize and articulate this program before starting the actual design work. The program states the design problem to be solved and the preliminary design is where the solutions take their first form. Many consider this to be the most creative phase of the work. Certainly it has the fewest constraints on "what's possible." Incidentally, this may be why many architects would like to do nothing else—just design.

Design Development

After the preliminary design has been discussed with the client there are usually changes to be made. Even if the client is satisfied, there are other issues that will influence it. The mechanical, structural, code, and site conditions may dictate considerable redesign. By the end of this phase the building should be a solid possibility, with no loose ends or soft edges. The client must sign off on the design and the architect should feel confident that it can be constructed pretty much exactly as depicted. Architects enjoy this phase of the work less than preliminary design but still a good deal more than what follows.

Construction Documents

If buildings were toy models, the construction documents would be the assembly instructions. Everything required to build the design must be brought together in the drawings and specifications. Each joint, dimension, material, and technology must be researched and explained for the builder. In short, the building must be "constructed" on paper. This is time consuming and very demanding work. Errors during this phase of the job can cost hundreds of thousands of dollars. Naturally, the associated lia-

bility of this work makes it the least popular phase of the project. However, it is the surest demonstration of what most clients think is invaluable about having an architect involved in the first place. They're supposed to know how it goes together!

Budget Analysis and Bid Supervision

This is shopping. The architect has had an eye on the cost of things throughout the design process (supposedly). Who better to oversee the bids and quotes given by the various contractors wishing to build the project? In this phase the architect works closely with the client, acting a bit like a coach. Different strategies are discussed for structuring the job and the many contracts that will be let. This is all meant to control cost, quality, and schedule. In the end the client will sign a contract with the builder and the architect will become the arbiter of same.

Site Inspections and Review

Here the architect is both policeman and problem solver. Once the building is under construction, the architect must make regular visits to the site to answer questions and insure that the project is being built as depicted in the construction documents. In recent years the architect has lost popularity among the building trades because there have been many more problems as a result of the architect's inadequate understanding of the construction process. Builders and the trades often refer to site blueprints as the "funny papers."

"Hey! Who has the funny papers? I need to get the pitch for this roof."

"I don't know, Don was looking at them. Check in the Port-a-Let."

Funny or not, I think "complete architectural services" is a fabulous value if you can actually get it all for a mere 10 percent. A realtor will get almost that much just for showing the building. The developer gets several times that much for organizing the financing. In residential design it is often more profitable to be the electrician than the architect!

This is not because all architects are interested in missionary work (though I've sometimes wondered). Architects have configured their profession so they simply can't make a proper profit on a small building. By linking their fee to the cost of the project, they have determined that a 1,000-square-foot room will net them more than a 500-square-foot room. While this is a generalization, it is basically true that architects can't make even 10 percent on most residential-size jobs.

Nevertheless, architects *love* designing homes (here's where the missionary work comes in). The home is perhaps the most fundamental type of building, and all other types of space must take their cues from residential space. We are born in homes, not schools, museums, office towers, or commercial plazas. As children we come to understand the palpable qualities of three-dimensional space in bedrooms, attics, basements, under the stairs, in window seats, and in countless other small-scale spaces that make up residential architecture. Later in life our needs may be provided for by different types of space: commercial, municipal, sporting, theatrical, etc. Yet through it all, the human animal understands and navigates these manifold spatial experiences by referring back to original residential space. So, naturally, architects love to design homes. When residential clients arrive in the office, they are told that the architect can do wonderful things for them but it will be costly. This is hardly a good way to make a sale. When the client demurs, the architect often suggests an abbreviated arrangement: "How about if we take you through design and design development for only 5 percent? Then you can work with your builder. He will know how to build it so there's less need for construction documents, bid supervision, or site visits."

Notice that the fee has been reduced somewhat while the task at hand has been reduced radically. Although the abbreviated arrangement may vary a bit, the basic concept doesn't change. The architect will do the part he enjoys while the client is left to figure out the rest. This usually comes with disastrous consequences in terms of cost, schedule, and quality. The builder is trying to make sense of plans that have never been distilled in the construction document phase. So he's mad. The client is told that some of these things are going to cost more because of unforseeables. So he's mad. The architect learns that the design has been changed to accommodate the cost of these unforeseeables. So he's mad. Everyone's mad and the job is costing more, taking longer, and suffering in quality.

Well, I guess I've made my point. Architects have trouble servicing the residential sector. So what can be done? Should all houses be built from plan books or by rote? Should the government subsidize architects the way they do artists and farmers? Is creativity and expressiveness just too costly?

No, the problem is not with the product, it's with the process. Architectural services are just as important in the design of a house as they are in a skyscraper. It's the format of the profession that causes these problems, not the architects. We need to find a new way to configure these services so that they are affordable and properly used. And this, of course, is exactly what Yestermorrow School has taken as its point of departure.

Underlying Yestermorrow's educational philosophy is the assumption that the knowledge and methods used by architects would be invaluable to those contemplating a house. At the same time, we realize that we must separate this information from the framework of the profession. While our students need what the architect knows, they may not necessarily need the professional architect. (And we *know* they can do without the professional price tag.)

Surprisingly, this would not be considered renegade thinking by most architects. They are confident that they can design better houses, but they also know (from experience) that there are few who can afford their fee, small as it is. Traditionally architects have had a very high opinion of what they do and its usefulness in varied situations. Indeed, it has long been assumed that there are few problems that wouldn't eventually succumb to the skillful application of design thinking. This is part of what gives architecture its potential as an art form. Architects know that a culture's essential personality can be read in the forms built by the people. Furthermore, architects can express specific political, spiritual, or personal themes with buildings the same way a sculptor or painter expresses such themes with their respective media. Architects have long felt that they might solve most of society's ills if only they could arrive at the proper design principles. And so it has been since time out of mind that architects dogmatically announce such a set of design principles (their own) with the arrival of each new trend in style. Vitruvius, Palladio, Downing, Corbusier, Gropius, Breuer, Mies, Wright, Johnson, Moore, Alexander—the list goes on and on (see Glossary for the short who's who of architectural history). Each valiantly attempting to explain once and for all how architectural design can be used to make a better world . . . if only everyone would listen.

With a tradition of problem-solving confidence behind them, most architects have little trouble with Yestermorrow's premise that architectural information and methodology would be invaluable to those making a home. The problem for architects has always been how to make a living providing this information. For Yestermorrow, however, this problem is unimportant. We are a school. So our first task is to separate the very important substance of architectural design from the irrelevant format of the profession. In short, we traded in architects for teachers, and clients for students.

Our next challenge is to make the students aware of the value of this fabulous information. Generally we find students consider architectural design expensive, confusing, elitist, and, in any event, optional. What isn't realized by many people (including quite a few architects) is that the essentials of architecture are not comprised simply of what they see in the design magazines.

Architecture has much to do with site, program, and occupant. It results from choreographed problem-solving. Figuring out where the driveway goes, proportioning the rooms, understanding the natural lighting, selecting the materials, the colors, the proportions—these are only *part* of architecture. It is also about the structural and mechanical systems, the energy consumption, the costing, the different foundation options, roofing options, siding options, and all the transitions between materials. Architectural design is where building starts; it's the basics. But it's also much more; ultimately, it's where building ends up. Residential architecture

is to building what haute cuisine is to cooking; tailored fashion is to clothing; and the automobile is to mass transit. It's *expressive,* personally expressive.

During Yestermorrow's early years our students arrived eager to "hit the site." However, when we invited them into the design studio there was often hesitation:

"No thanks, I think my brother's wife can design this for me. She knows about these things. She's in the flower club and . . ."

"Oh, I didn't know we were going to be doing studio work. Listen, I'm not too good at math, can I just work on the site . . ."

"Say, I came here to learn how to build, not draw pretty pictures. Besides, I think I'm going to send away for some plans from one of those magazines at the grocery store check-out line . . ."

"Do we *have* to do this to learn how to build . . . ?"

The answer is "no" you don't need to understand "design" to learn *how* to build, but "yes" you must understand it to know *what* and *why* to build. If you are learning how to build just so you can take a job building for someone else, I guess you don't need to know much more than how it's done. A little routine training will make you a useful tool in someone else's grand design. On the other hand, if you want to be involved in making your own place, then you had better "get architecture," as the Bible Belters might say.

Residential architecture, remember, is not necessarily elitist or trendy. If it looks elitist or confusing it's because people are letting it be done *for* them, done *to* them.

A nice analogy can be found in the world of high fashion, which often seems ridiculous.

"Wouldn't catch me dead in that getup!" someone says.

Well, why not? What would we catch you in? Most people have pretty good answers. They have accepted the responsibility for dressing themselves. Sure, they look at fashions. Who doesn't? In the end, however, they choose their own. Dressing is very personal; it expresses much about who and what you are. Those who dress strictly from the fashion magazines are either nervous about who they are or very involved in the fashion industry. The vast majority of us, however, pick and choose our own look. Many alter (renovate) what's available off the rack. Some tailor their own (new construction). And everyone looks in the mirror to assess how they look (the design) before leaving the house.

If every individual had the same comfortable understanding of home design as they do of their own dress habits, our built environment would be less bewildering. More importantly, societal ills formally addressed by a few utopian theorists would be open to the problem-solving abilities of the masses—the very people who are enduring these ills.

Whether designing a house, a dress, or a

city, the process is basically the same. At the start one must have an attitude and a value system with which to navigate among the options. This is sometimes referred to as the designer's *vision*. If the vision is clear and strong, the problems associated with realizing it will be solvable.

Therefore, we decided that the two most important issues facing Yestermorrow students were: understanding and clarifying their vision; and learning how to solve design and construction problems.

These are the two areas that can't be addressed by reading a book or watching a videotape. To understand your vision requires time with paper and pencil. It requires dialogue. Instructors must be both supporting and critical. Essentially our students are asked to answer the questions "Who are you?" and "What do you really want?" These are profound questions. Most people don't think about them as often or as deeply as they are asked to at Yestermorrow. We are asking students to *define and build their reality*.

The trouble with reality is that it comes with gravity, moisture, temperature, and a price tag. Therefore, problem solving is the second fundamental skill that Yestermorrow addresses. Again, it can't be learned from reading a book or listening to a lecture. The only way to learn how to solve a problem is by *doing it*. There is often conflict between what a person wants and what is possible. These problems are appropriately addressed in the design studio, where different solutions can be tested out inexpensively in the abstract. Students need help finding the information required to solve their problems. Then, once they have access to the data, they need some help organizing it and thinking about it. In the studio students learn to represent design solutions (drafting and model building) in a dimensionally accurate way that allows the staff and other students to discuss the merits of the solution. In this way strengths and weaknesses can be identified and further design work can be undertaken.

While some of this is technical, many design problems must be solved in the context of the original vision. If the vision is not clearly understood, there will be no way of knowing if one solution is any better than another.

So the Yestermorrow educational philosophy, which will be presented throughout this book, starts by asking the students, "What do you want? What is your personal vision?" Then we give the students tools to explore different answers to this query. Finally, we show them where they can obtain technical information that will help define their solutions. Then they must make a few trial attempts at putting all this information together in an elegant, affordable, architectural solution. The first solutions are rarely perfect. Instead, they serve to illustrate what needs to be added, modified, or eliminated. Then, just like professional architects, the students go back to the drawing boards, and do it all again. Architectural design is complex; to some degree the solutions must be arrived at through trial and error.

Through this reiterative process students come to understand what they are striving for and how the problem-solving process works. By doing it, they get better at it.

The same method works on site. Since there are endless material and technology choices, we can't hope to cover them all in any comprehensive way. Moreover, our students come from many different parts of the country and building practices and traditions will often reflect the local environment and climate. Teaching how to build a stick frame- or shingle-style house will be of little use to a student interested in adobe; presenting the details of an asphalt roof will do little for someone interested in standing seam.

Knowing how to build is not simply knowing how to cut a rafter, or how to lay up bricks, wire a light, plumb a toilet, or some other particular skill; these are just the methods that are involved. Building requires an understanding of materials, weather, gravity, and, above all, standards of quality. You can't learn how to build a house the way you learn how to overhaul a car engine. An engine is comprised of many pieces, each of which has a very specific size and place. A building also has many pieces, but each can be devised in a variety of ways from many different materials and in many different shapes. This is what makes building so creative. It is also why you must know *what* you are building before you can know *how* to build it.

On site, then, our problem is even more difficult than in the studio. What can we teach that is relevant for all students from all over the country with different programs, budgets, and different local building traditions? Why, *problem solving*, of course.

If a student learns about a method or technology as a specific solution to a general problem, then it becomes an example. Shingles are only one kind of roofing, but they address all the basic problems of any roof covering; concrete block is only one kind of foundation, but you will address most of the same problems when you design and build a poured concrete foundation. Framing out for a door in a 2 × 6 frame wall will tell you a lot about what must be considered if you were putting the same door in an 8″ brick wall. In short, learning how to build means understanding the general issues at hand, not executing a series of specific moves learned by rote. And the most important single skill of the experienced builder is his ability to solve problems that are unforeseeable in the studio.

Yestermorrow has been guiding students through increasingly complex building situations since its first class. We've found repeatedly that the only way to gain expertise in solving construction prob-

lems is to experience them. This is at the heart of why students come to Yestermorrow. They are paying for the opportunity to solve real problems with real materials on real buildings. We try to condense a few years of experience in the trades into a few weeks of concentrated building in the field.

Design/Build

Once a year the Yestermorrow staff reviews what we are doing at a weekend-long faculty meeting. Many of our teachers are practicing architects, many are professional builders, a few are artists. We're trying to find a middle path where design and assembly are fully integrated— call it "making." This is what arts or crafts schools teach: full integration of mind and body. This is design/build.

When I was in architecture school I knew I wanted to build something, and quite a few of my classmates shared the feeling. I remember being surprised by how much "architecture" was decided in the field. In school we were learning about coherent design. This was total design control from site plan all the way down to the tiniest details. Real design decisions were being made by a couple of guys wearing tool belts standing around scratching their heads. But they weren't thinking about the design philosophy or the overall concept. They were simply trying to finish the job. As I proceeded along

in my professional training I began to work in offices. Here I heard the architects complain about what the builders were doing to "their design."

"Cretins! How *could* they have thought it went that way?? Anybody can see how it *should* have been done."

Not true. Without the proper explanation, builders will not see how it should be done. Just as architects seem to work from the neck up, builders are often guilty of working from the neck down. The two live in different worlds, thinking and acting by different means; construction documents are their only common language. These constitute the instruction book for what the builders are making and is written by the architects who are working from the "big concept." The builders are following step-by-step instructions; they are definitely *not* working with the big concept.

Given a typical commission, however, the majority of the fee must go toward preparing the construction documents. However, architects frequently prefer to work on the ideas, the design, the image, or the look. They often use up time revising the design, leaving insufficient time to properly detail and document it. Since innovative designs often push materials and technologies into new areas, the need for instructions is more important than ever. But, since architects work from the neck up, they have little hands-on experience with the materials and methods. Knowing this, they rely on the builder to make it work. There are always several ways to make it work, however, and the best one depends on the overall design concept. Clearly architects need more hands-on experience with the materials they choose for their designs. At the same time, builders need a better sense of design theory and its importance. Finally, if these two groups are going to continue to specialize, the construction documents will need to be reconsidered. In their current form they simply won't support coherent design.

Imagine going to a music school for music theory only, never picking up an instrument. The constant presentation of others' work tempts the students to play, but the teachers insist that they must wait. Imagine going to an art school to learn about seeing and vision but never stretching a canvas, mixing paint, using clay, or carving wood. Imagine attending a school of dance where you learn choreography but never take *your* body through the moves.

The higher art forms are all characterized by the integration of mind and body. The artist works from the neck up *and* the neck down. Where this is not the case art seems contrived and confusing. Architecture that confuses is simply bad architecture.

Yestermorrow has embraced an integrated design/build approach for making houses. By fully engaging the mind and the body (and by this I mean the heart and soul as well), the resulting structure can't help but be a more coherent expression of those who are making it. This approach has antecedents among traditional art schools as well as the old housewrights; it is clearly the best way to make buildings, when feasible.

Unfortunately, it isn't always feasible. Design/build as practiced at the scale of a house would never work at the scale of our great commercial structures. We are a culture of specialists and our "pyramids" (the interstate system?) will appropriately be the product of several key people—designers, engineers, and builders. Even the fairly small buildings found in most communities—schools, churches, offices, theaters—are unlikely to be constructed by their architects. Perhaps only the house is of the right size and program to be designed and built by the same person.

Design/build seems unlikely to replace conventional professional practice, in the architect's office or on the construction site. So why get students involved?

Because assembling just one structure of your own design will acquaint you with such a rich world of information that it will serve as a wellspring for the rest of your architectural endeavors. With the human component of technology clearly experienced, we might cease designing spaces and environments that are a confusing insult to the human condition. Our cities and communities might become less intimidating, our workplaces more appropriate.

Just as the artist knows his palette, the designer must know his media. The warmth and human dimension of any technology can only be understood after the maker has been in it up to the elbows. Weld one joint, pour one foundation, set one piece of glass, and these basic ingredients of building will never be the same for you.

Cycle, Cycle, Cycle

The organization of information and the making of critical decisions is crucial to the process of designing and building your home. There are no easy formulas. Even where to begin poses a problem:

> Should I study construction technology first so that my house design will be buildable?
>
> Should I design what I want in the house first and then figure out how to build it?
>
> Maybe I should look at the site first and just see what's possible?

Hopefully, this book should make things easier. The order of the following chapters breaks the process into three major enterprises: the site, the program, and the building. Each of these will be discussed in depth. You should expect to consider and reconsider each area several times. Consider and reconsider. Cycle, cycle, cycle. This is at the heart of design/building.

This book doesn't have all the answers to every conceivable design/build question—no book does. Instead, I have attempted to supply a direction and an attitude for your own personal process. Think of it as an underlying skeleton or structure on which to assemble all the special information that is relevant to your unique project. But more important than the technical facts and figures, this book seeks to cultivate your attitude. I want you to have the whole picture and I want you to make personal choices from the fullest spectrum of alternatives. You aren't just learning how to draft, nail, saw, plumb, wire, etc. You're learning how to *think about making . . .* your house.

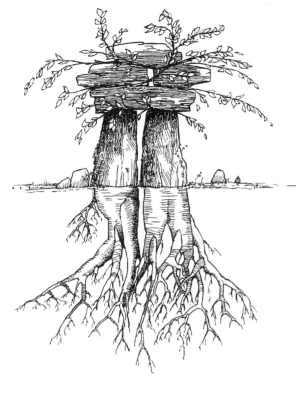

The Grand Design: Site, Studio, and You

It's the morning of the first day of school at Yestermorrow. I call this the Period of Huh. Breakfast is over and all the students are guided into the design studio. When they are all set up with drafting equipment we start to explain design and architecture. Indeed, we spend each morning and evening for the entire course focused on design and architecture. About the second day a student corners me and the "huhs" begin.

"Excuse me, but can we talk? You see, when I enrolled I didn't think I was going to learn all this design stuff. I don't need it. I really just need to know how to build. Can I skip the morning studios and go to the site?"

"No."

"Why not?"

"What are you going to do on the site?"

"Oh, I don't care. Whatever is planned will be fine. I'll just help out."

"No, I mean *what* will you build when you're finished with Yestermorrow? Why did you come here? What is it that you want to learn to build? What will you do on *your* site?"

"Oh. Well, I just came here to learn how to build."

Students are often determined that they want to learn *how* but not *what* or *why*. To our way of thinking, this is very strange. It's like wanting to eat dinner without dessert. No, it's worse. It's like wanting to do the dishes without eating anything!

Even more to the point, it's not possible. One doesn't just learn "how to build." One learns to build a particular thing and in a particular way.

There is no limit to the different materials and methods with which we can build: brick, adobe, stone masonry, log, timber frame, steel frame, rammed earth, reinforced concrete, cob, geodesic domes, tents—more are being developed all the time. Each methodology has its own logic and traditions. Each is well suited to certain situations and certain tastes, but not all. So why (and here comes the "huh") learn to build anything until you know where, why, and what you're going to build? Especially if you're only building *one* structure.

Imagine learning how to build a frame house for New England only to be transferred to a hot, dry climate in the Southwest. Or what if you learned to build a contemporary-style house and then fell in love with a building lot in a restored historic neighborhood. What good is that?

"Huh. I never thought of it that way."

Similarly, what good is it to know how to build a flat (one-story) house if your site is steep? If you're building where there is a lot of sun, you want to know about solar design and construction, but if you're settling where there isn't enough sun, you better know about the latest windows and insulation systems. If you're building in flood-plain, you'd better know how to build with poles. If you end up in the city, knowledge of pole construction will be useless.

"Huh, I guess so."

But let's not be all negative. We're not interested in showing you that you can't do this here or that there. Rather we're *only* interested in showing you what you *can* do where *you will be building.*

"Uh huh."

Note the italics. The point is that different people in different situations will build differently. Building isn't something one learns like engine repair. We're not talking about a process of assembly where each part has a unique place or function. Different cultures have been building in many varied ways all over the world using different materials and methodologies. Even within one area, the use of the same palette of materials can be found configured in a variety of ways. That's vernacular architecture—people making shelter for themselves using whatever is close at hand in ways that reflect their personal needs, rituals, traditions, and natural surroundings.

In the past, people didn't move around so much and they could learn how to build just by looking around and listening to their elders. But in today's jet-setting "global village," your home-building years may find you far from familiar territory. You must ask many questions before you can understand how you will build. Many of the answers are available in weather patterns, building codes, land values, and job markets, but the most important answers will not come from without. They will come from within!

Dramatic pause.

"So," says my student, "I guess you're telling me I have to participate in the studio to learn anything. What exactly will I learn in the studio?"

Actually, one doesn't learn in the design studio so much as explore and discover. You will discover what your dream house looks like, how it works, where it sits on the land, what it is made of, and if it will stand up for more than a week. It often shocks people to hear that the critical information concerning their future home will not be found in the studio. It will only be organized there. What makes this seem like such a massive task is the complexity of the process. Program, site, structure, weather, budget, codes, foundation, heating, cooling, style, look. It goes on seemingly without end! Who can blame those who opt for the short cuts:

"Well, we looked at a lot of plans. Finally we found these in the magazine section of our grocery store."

"This kit is so affordable and everything is included."

"We've decided to buy. We can renovate later if we don't like something. Right?"

"We worked with our builder. He drew up the plans. I think he has already built this house a few times. Everything's worked out."

Beware! False gods! Nothing is "all worked out" until *you* have worked it out. And this is exactly what you *start* to do in the studio.

▐ **The Design Helix:**
A Round Triangle

I like to think of the design process as a helical conversation. The same familiar subjects are brought up time after time. Each time around, you add another layer of complexity. For instance, you start with the site, then you consider your life-style, then the building, then back to the site, etc. Before long you discover things about the building or your life-style that conflict with what you have decided about the site. Perhaps you can resolve these conflicts by moving the building, changing the driveway, or planting some trees. These changes, however, are likely to produce a series of new problems with aspects of the design. These must then be addressed and further changes considered. Round and round you go, it seems, never getting to an end. But you are not going in circles; you are moving in a helix. (See Figure 1.)

A helix is a spring-shaped sequence—like a DNA molecule or a circular stair. From one perspective it looks like you're traveling over the same ground from time after time. However, you're actually moving up (or down) with each lap. Each time you go around, modifying this to accommodate that, your overall design is becoming more resolved, more sophisticated. There will be times when things seem hopelessly confused (or maybe just plain hopeless), and then, "Aha!" You break

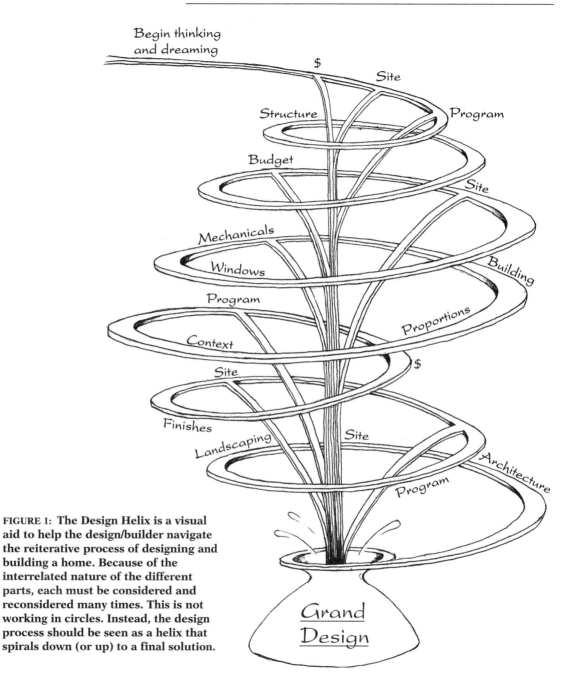

FIGURE 1: The Design Helix is a visual aid to help the design/builder navigate the reiterative process of designing and building a home. Because of the interrelated nature of the different parts, each must be considered and reconsidered many times. This is not working in circles. Instead, the design process should be seen as a helix that spirals down (or up) to a final solution.

through, seeing the building with a startlingly new clarity.

I call the Design Helix a round triangle because there are basically three areas of consideration in the design of your house: the site, your program, and the building. Obviously these are not separate considerations; they overlap and intertwine. For instance, you might locate the house to maximize solar gain (site), but that might not allow you to take full advantage of the excellent view to the west. You love views (program). Originally, you had assumed you would build a one-story house (building). To get the view without losing solar gain, you decide to build a *two*-story house (building) and put the living functions—living room, kitchen, den, etc.—upstairs (program). But building two stories means the neighbors can see you from the east (site). Besides upsetting your neighbors who don't want to see your house, you lose much cherished privacy (program). But by planting the right kind of trees along the eastern boundary (site), you still get your privacy and your solar gain.

As you can see, each of the three areas of the Design Helix is a special aspect of your grand design. Rather than three competing agendas, they are actually different perspectives on the same endeavor: designing your home. It's a complicated undertaking, no question. The Design Helix is a way to make coherent design decisions in the midst of the ever-expanding consid-

erations that must be addressed. Each time you circulate on the helix there will be new issues, new conflicts, and new compromises. The priorities you use for solving these conflicts will depend on which perspective you are favoring at that point in the process. Is the site more important? Should the program take precedence? Or the building? If the front yard is really important, you may just have to pay for a long driveway (and save the hot tub with deck for another year). At different times along the helix each of the three perspectives will become temporarily paramount.

Also, if the truth be known, things don't always proceed in a nice orderly sequence of site, program, building, site, program, etc. You will jump from one to another throughout the entire process. You will lay out the house a dozen times, you will create endless kitchen designs, the landscaping will fluctuate along with the interior plan, and the finishes will change constantly. Just when you think everything is finally worked out, the budget constraints will pull you back into the soup. Don't worry. This is exactly the way the professionals work. In fact, it's this repeated cycling that gives birth to the richness of architectural design.

Now for the most important part. Throughout the entire process the guiding light is you. The answers to what will be included are answers only *you* can provide. There is no book or formula. There is

no right or wrong. The "either/or" decisions that come with a fixed budget force us to consult our personal priorities. If we can't have everything (immediately), what do we want most (first)? It's really up to you.

"But," we hear so often, "my budget won't allow any freedom of choice at all. I have to do whatever is cheapest. Period."

What a waste to willingly constrain yourself so. Anyone considering the construction of a house has options. Nothing is ever as black and white as the bottom line. Consider color, for example. Different colors may cost exactly the same amount and make a radical difference in the feeling of the house. A peak and a flat roof can often cost about the same. Which is best for you? What about doors, windows, plumbing and light fixtures? For the same price there are always several different choices. We've found that students who say their budget doesn't allow them any latitude are often rationalizing their nervousness about making decisions. Relax. You can't make a "wrong" decision when it's your home.

One of the unexpected benefits derived from designing in the classroom is that different students can give convincing voices to different choices. Bill wants a very energy-efficient house. He has a tight budget but has read that low-E, argon-filled Thermopane windows will pay for themselves over time. In presenting his project to the class this way, everyone had to agree: saving energy is worth spending a little more up front. Another student, Jessie, concurred, but windows were not her highest priority. Jessie was after "the feel of quality." She had a special distaste for hollow-core doors and cheap hardware. The additional cost of quality hardware turned out to be just about the same as that for low-E glass on her storm windows. She was confronted with the ubiquitous budget question: How should I apportion my limited budget?

Now the answer to this question is not in a book. It's in the designer. Jill, a potter from Virginia, decided that she really wanted the front door hardware to be solid.

"This is the first tactile impression one gets," Jill said. "I know you can't see or photograph it. But for me, it sets up everything else experienced in the house. I'll wear an extra sweater when it's really cold if that's what I must do to feel solid brass at my front door."

Bill is a forester who lives in Winnipeg, Manitoba, in Canada. He usually opens his door with gloves on. Standard-duty hardware is fine with him.

Which approach is correct? Both!

Few of us have unlimited budgets, and decisions like these must be made at every level of the building design. Concrete or block, timber frame or stick built, plaster or gypsum, designer lights or porcelain fixtures, wood floors or carpet, shingles or shakes—every decision you make is part of the design of your house. Every decision has the capacity to strengthen or sabotage your design. How can anyone assume they have no choice or just blindly turn these matters over to another?

Well, in fact, very few actually do. Everyone wants their home to reflect who they are. While some are afraid to talk about it, most will attempt to discuss tastes or otherwise influence their architect or builder. The problem is often one of learning how to articulate your wants and wishes. The difference between owner/builders and those who take what they're given is not a question of influence, it's a question of communication and control.

Where the vast majority of our society has grown used to shoehorning their lives into whatever is available, the owner/builder seeks to take direct control of the entire process—including the design. In a 1984 study of owner/builders it was found that 90 percent of them chose to design their own home. While they sought consultants and training for all the how-to aspects of the job, they harbored almost no doubt that they could design it themselves. I couldn't agree more.

Design, however, is more than a floor plan and a kitchen layout. Properly understood, the design of a house should be like a portrait of all who will be using it. Furthermore, it should reflect their means, habits, hopes, and rituals. Every stick and pipe must be choreographed to support this program. Plus, it must fit properly in its surroundings.

Happily, this is all possible. Moreover, most anyone can do it. All that's needed is an orderly method that will keep the thousands of issues and decisions coherent. The following chapters will take you through such a methodology one step at a time. This methodology is the very same used by big-time architects. It has been streamlined a little for the residential scale, but the process is essentially the same. The big difference is that *you* will be making the decisions. You don't have to be an artist or "creative"; all you have to be is honest.

Be true unto yourself and like the day following the night, your owner-built home will be coherent and beautiful.
    —Shakespeare's design/builder brother

It is very important to understand and keep in mind what we mean by *the design*. It is much, much more than that little space of time in the studio spent laying out where the rooms go. That's just the architectural floor plan. We're talking about the "grand design," that overarching master plan that will make this site and house uniquely yours.

In the largest sense, the design of your house encompasses all your intentions, hopes, and dreams. Some of these may be ethereal and difficult to express. Others will be quite solid and down-to-earth. Because they're easy to explain, the down-to-earth issues usually get more emphasis. For instance, the budget, schedule, and square footage are usually discussed more than ritual, spiritual, or ceremonial needs. Grampa's hat collection and the sense of family history it carries may have a tough time getting equal time with the Minimum Housing Standards found in local codes. But which is the more essential ingredient in your home?

These, and many other hard to explain needs, are all part of your grand design. The design should reflect your attitudes about the site, the neighbors, the building, the finishes, and everything else that makes up your cosmos. Even the process by which you construct your house is part of the design, part of the drama.

"Too much!" you scream.

"But why settle for anything less?" we wonder.

"I don't care about *all* that. I *can't* care about all that."

Ah! That's a very important point. What you do and don't care about is exactly what we are talking about. No one finds everything equally important. Some things will be less critical in your design and some more. None of it, however, is optional. If you think the height of the electrical outlets above the floor is unimportant, they will simply be designed by default; the electrician will be your architect here. Similarly, maybe you haven't given any thought to the relationship your house will have with the road, the neighbors, the sun, the wind—even Mecca. That doesn't eliminate these considerations

from the design. Rather it means the foundation contractor will be your architect here (don't worry, he'll probably consult with the backhoe operator). Just because you don't give a hoot about the orientation of your home with respect to the north star, that doesn't mean it won't have one. And if you don't consider it, someone else will: design by default.

The idea, therefore, is to **include** the widest spectrum of considerations in your design. Think about them and figure out how they affect the visual, functional, and budgetary aspects of your home. Above all, think about how they will reflect the personal or expressive side of your life. Good architecture results when the greatest array of considerations have been choreographed into a coherent solution that says something about *who you are* and how *you* live. Alas, *everything* seems to be part of the design.

In general, the design process proceeds from large to small. My recommendation is that you start with your biggest decisions and then work toward smaller and smaller ones; let the larger decisions drive the smaller ones. Decide where the house will be located before worrying about what the front door will look like. Figure out how many bedrooms you will need before deciding on bathroom fixtures. Resolve the relationship between the kitchen and the eating area before insisting on an island counter. Above all, think

about function before form. And if that makes "function" sound too dry, remember that the function of a house is to cater to your personal needs and life-style preferences. This means figuring out how you want to live before deciding what it has to look like. Some life-styles just don't fit in a colonial.

Earlier we spoke of the design process as a helical conversation. As we move along the helix, we resolve ever smaller portions of the project. We can divide that cyclical path into three basic stops or arcs, each having precedence in its time and place. These three arcs are the site, the program, and the building. As you make design decisions in each of these areas there will be ramifications in the others. The design process is the act of bringing all these considerations into a coherent balance.

The Rest of the Story . . .

Books these days often seem to have a section entitled "How to Use this Book." Side-stepping the obvious potential for wise-cracks here, I would like to offer a few thoughts in this vein.

I have organized the remainder of the book about the three areas of consideration that make up the Design Helix. They are presented somewhat chronologically. The site was there first and then you and your program came along; this resulted in the design of a building. Now the building is part of the site, and as you reconsider the program you're already off and running. Site, program, building, site, program—the order isn't that crucial, but there is an order. You and the site exist before the building. You and the site are to be reflected in and expressed by the building. But once you've gone around the helix a few times, the building will start to have increasing status. It will start to have needs and rules of its own.

Each of the three agendas—site, program, building—must be thoroughly inventoried and assimilated before the design/builder can hope for a successful process.

The remaining chapters of this book will take you through this process at the first level of the Design Helix. It will be up to you to repeat and reiterate the process as you move along it toward your final design. At the end of the book I have included several appendices to serve as references. These contain much of the data and many rules of thumb that will be helpful as your design process moves toward ground breaking.

THE SITE

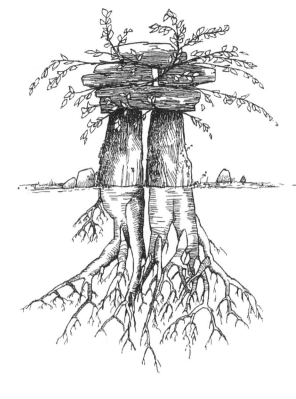

Your Place in the World

Irrespective of whether you dwell in the city or country, your site will have been there long before you. You must get to know it before you can work with it intelligently. The next two chapters should help you ask the right questions. This chapter, which explores site analysis, is considerably biased toward rural sites. Although the examples might differ, the same issues would be considered in the city: topography, noise, weather, vegetation, views, zoning, taxes, neighbors, and access. Additionally you might want to consider parking and public transportation.

Chapter 5 explores site design. There we will discuss some of the design decisions you might consider, based on what was discovered during analysis. Site design covers a lot of ground (forgive the pun). It starts as basic site development (well and septic-field design), then it expands into site design (house and driveway placement), then landscape design (gardens, lawns, patios, and walkways), and finally, landscape architecture (the whole shootin' match, including topography modifications, parking lots, curb cuts, ponds, etc.). The examples discussed here come from Yestermorrow's own history and should not be considered exhaustive.

Site Analysis

If you are going to build a house, you must have a site. With the exception of mobile homes and houseboats, all sites consist of a piece of land. Your site, however, is more than just a piece of land. City sites, rural sites, temperate sites, arctic sites, even subdivision sites—each will be different. Think of your site as your place in the world. This small corner of the world is yours alone to explore and make special. It consists of everything that's happening on and to that piece of land. You must take careful inventory.

The difficulty in assessing different sites comes from the contiguous quality of land. Each and every parcel is connected on all sides with its neighbors; a hedge or a wall can't change this. The water and air from uphill parcels will trespass on lower ones. Indeed, weather patterns are now transporting all sorts of "stuff" from one piece of land to another, sometimes from hundreds of miles away. If that's not enough, there are also sounds and smells that refuse to be constrained by our surveyed boundaries. In urban situations these conditions are intensified. One site might exist *over* another site. Car and street lights invade our little landholdings. The noise and dust from traffic penetrate our toughest defenses.

Let's face it: owning land is more like owning a ticket at the game. You have certain rights to a seat in the stadium, but your control over who sits around you and the general experience you're having in that spot is limited. You can negotiate with your neighboring fans, but they may not see things your way. Your best move is to buy a ticket in the right section of the stadium to begin with. This is why realtors chant "location, location, location" when listing the three most important considerations in evaluating a piece of property.

Irrespective of where you dwell, your site will be a constellation of possibilities and liabilities. This unique geometry of climate, natural resources, man-made resources, and spiritual energy is what you must inventory and understand. It is the first step in transforming a mere building lot into your place in the world.

What follows is a lengthy (but hardly exhaustive) discussion of things you should consider in analyzing your site. This is where you inventory the resources, weather, topography, and juxtapositions inherent to your location. The two-step process of inventory and then design is familiar to every architect or landscape designer. Nevertheless, one person's methodology can be another's miasma. For those who find the following too formulaic, I offer Witold Rybczynski's anecdote as an alternative. In his book *The Most Beautiful House in the World* he tells of the Nabdam farmer living in northern Ghana. Before building a house the farmer would have a soothsayer consult his ancestors. If the ancestors gave the green light the farmer would then sacrifice a chicken on the proposed building site. In a circle formed by all the farmer's relatives the struggling body of the sacrificed bird would be watched as it expired. In the end, if the beak pointed down it was no dice. But if the fowl died with its beak toward the heavens, the friends and relatives could break ground immediately. I have very little experience with this approach to site analysis, but I admire its conciseness and suspect it would work if you didn't mind getting all your relatives together in one place.

TOPOGRAPHY

This is the so-called "lay of the land." It is the shape, slope, or geography of your site. You must understand it. Among other things, it will affect the flow of water, the ease of circulation, and the behavior of the elements across your site. You can change the nature of small areas of topography, but anything large becomes prohibitively expensive and is usually a mistake. The shape of the land is usually the result of natural forces that have moved over it for centuries; any radical change in the shape will have to accommodate these forces. Not a task to enter into lightly.

In your study of topography I suggest building a site model as early as possible (Figure 2). If your site is an inner-city lot or a dead-flat subdivision lot, topography may (I say *may*) not need to be modeled. Elsewhere, however, the topography should be known quite accurately, at least in the immediate area around the proposed buildings. If you're building on a large parcel (several acres), a more general understanding of the topography is adequate for the areas not immediately contiguous to the building.

To build a site model you must have a topographical survey. This is a survey with elevation contours. If your site is very

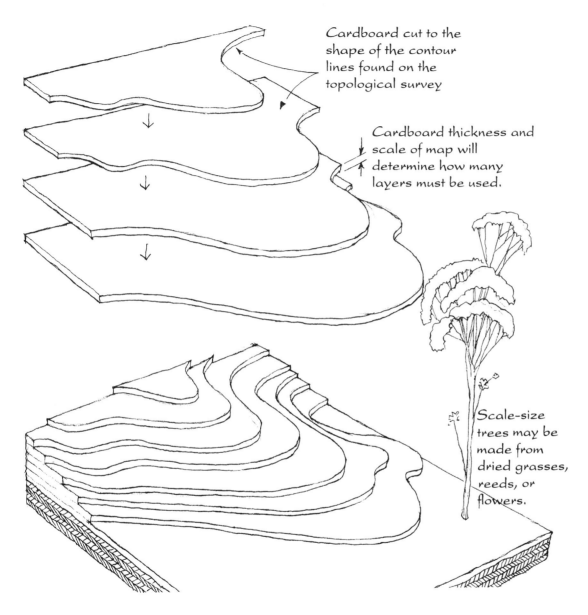

Cardboard cut to the shape of the contour lines found on the topological survey

Cardboard thickness and scale of map will determine how many layers must be used.

Scale-size trees may be made from dried grasses, reeds, or flowers.

FIGURE 2: If a topological survey is available, a simple site model can be made by cutting sheets of cardboard to the shape of the contour lines. Piling these up according to the scale on the survey will give a rough idea of the "lay of the land."

large, you may be able to get this information from geodetic survey maps. These government-prepared maps contain detailed geographical information, including contour lines that indicate the shape of the land. They are usually available from your local bookstore or stationery supplier. Alternately, you can order them directly from: U.S. Geological Survey; Box 25286; Federal Center, Bldg. 4; Denver, CO 80225.

If your site is smaller, you can hire a surveyor to draw up the elevation contours. Better still (and cheaper), you can shoot your own elevations. This is not difficult. Every Boy Scout must demonstrate this ability on his way to becoming an Eagle Scout. Indeed, the Scouts of America publishes a sixty-page booklet that explains the entire procedure very nicely. (*Surveying*, a Merit Badge Book, is available from B.S.A.; P.O. Box 909; Pineville, NC 28134-0909.)

Assuming a surveyor is too expensive and you can't find an Eagle Scout, your first task will be to rent a surveying instrument called a transit. Any place that rents tools should carry them. On a scale drawing of your site, draw lines indicating where you would like to measure the rise and fall of the land.

Figure 3 illustrates a typical line and profile. If these profile lines are arranged in a grid, the measurements taken allow the mapping of contours.

To start with, you must understand the phenomenal power and simplicity of the

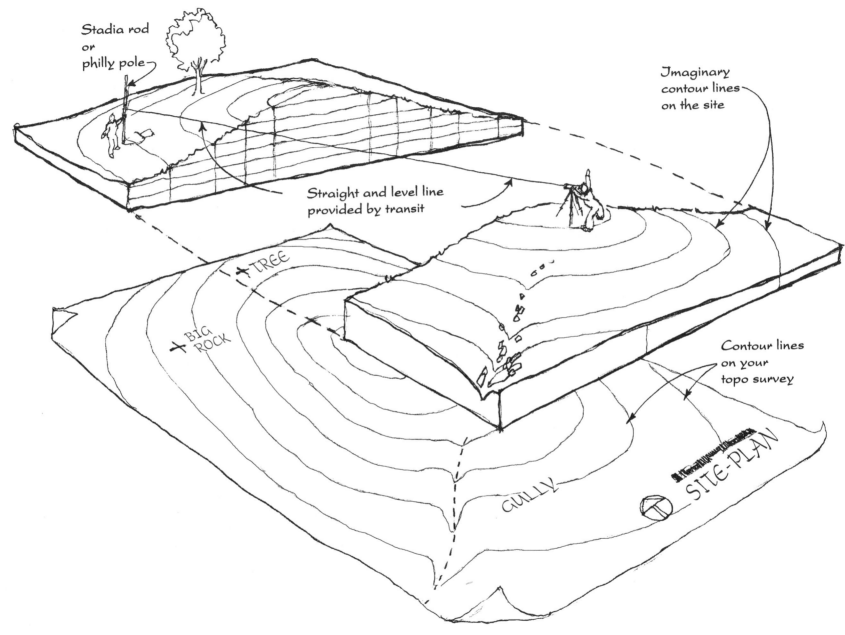

Stadia rod or philly pole

Imaginary contour lines on the site

Straight and level line provided by transit

+ TREE

+ BIG ROCK

Contour lines on your topo survey

GULLY

SITE-PLAN

FIGURE 3: Shooting elevations to make your own topographical survey.

transit. This device provides you with a straight line several hundred feet long anywhere you want. It's a reference line. This straight line can be leveled or inclined at a known angle to level (level means perfectly horizontal, like the surface of water). Either way, it becomes a powerful reference line from which we can measure the undulations of the land over long distances. Moreover, straight lines can be configured into grids and coordinates. Once that's understood, all of geometry is at your service in the measuring of your land. It is this simple straight line that allows the surveyor to capture the vagaries of the landscape and bring them accurately to the drafting board.

In Figure 2 the transit is set up "level." This means the telescopic eyepiece through which you look will show cross hairs on anything positioned at the same elevation as the transit.

Elevation is not the same as *height*. Height is a relative term that usually refers to the distance above the ground. Elevation, however, refers to the distance above (or below) a fixed point, usually sea level. Since sea level isn't that close or important for all sites, surveyors often establish their own point within the boundaries of the site. This is called a *benchmark*. The benchmark should be marked on something immovable, such as a rock or a massive tree. In the city you will sometimes find markers on large masonry buildings where surveyors have established benchmarks. Once you've established your benchmark, let's say on a tree with a nail, you will be able to take down and set up your transit without fear of losing your measurements. Whenever you set up, you simply shoot back to the benchmark and measure the distance between the new elevation of the transit and the elevation of the benchmark. The difference must be added to all the height measurements taken from the second position of the transit.

In all this you must understand that what we're really interested in is the difference in height, not in the elevations. By measuring the height of a level reference line above different areas we can learn their dispositions with respect to one another. That's what topography is all about.

Now here is the confusing part, so pay attention. The greater the height measurement, the lower the ground. Look at Figure 4.

As the ground goes down, the distance or height of the level line seen through the transit will become larger. If the land rises, the distance becomes smaller. To measure this distance you will need a stadia rod, sometimes called a "philly" pole (I don't know why). You can rent these or simply affix a tape measure to a straight board. A friend (brought along on the promise of a fine day in the open air with a beer at the end) stands at the point to be measured and holds the pole as straight as possible.

This is his only task. You will look through the transit and record the measurement seen at the cross hairs: let's say 6'6". Then the person holding the philly pole moves to the next point and you site (or shoot) the rod again. This time the cross hairs mark 6'8". The ground has fallen off 2" because the height measurement has increased by 2". The greater the height measurement, the lower the ground.

Confusion is the single biggest obstacle to successful surveying. You could have your friend wander all over the site while you take random measurements. This will give you a rather nebulous understanding of the topography. Also, it will be hell to draft up. A better idea is to use Cartesian or polar grids to locate points that you will shoot. Prior to visiting the site, number all the points and make up a chart that will allow you to record the height measurements in an orderly fashion. After you return from the field, you will be able to record all the relative heights on your drawing. Some extrapolation may be needed, but then one can draw the contour lines from these numbers.

After all the heights have been adjusted for different transit positions, they should be recorded on your plot plan. The numbers alone will give you a pretty accurate sense of the topography. An even better picture will result from constructing the contour lines, which run along the site at one level only; every point on a given contour line will be at the same elevation. The

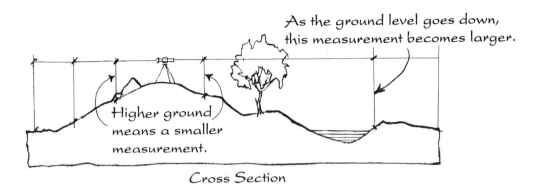

As the ground level goes down, this measurement becomes larger.

Higher ground means a smaller measurement.

Cross Section

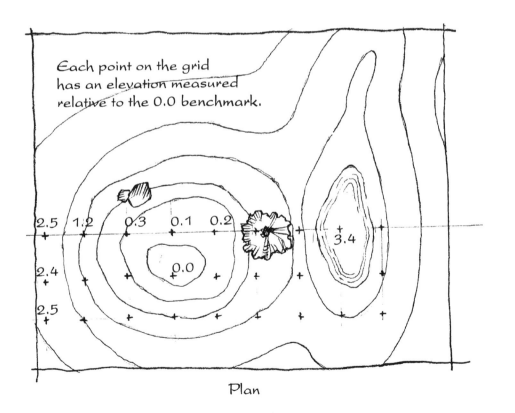

Each point on the grid has an elevation measured relative to the 0.0 benchmark.

2.5 / 1.2   0.3   0.1   0.2

3.4

2.4   0.0

2.5

Plan

FIGURE 4: Laying out a grid of elevations allows you to draw in the contours.

difference in elevation between any two adjacent contour lines is a constant, say 1'0". This means that the closer together the lines, the steeper the slope, and the further apart, the milder the slope. It is unlikely that your measurements will be in exactly 1'0" increments. This is where the strength of the grid comes in. Use the surrounding numbers to find the approximate location of the contour line (Figure 4). If more information is needed, return to the site.

Naturally, there is much more to topographical surveying than what's presented here. Accuracy and speed can be improved in a variety of ways. With this in mind, I have listed several books in the bibliography that can help.

I don't pretend that the first time you try this everything will go without a hitch. Indeed, you may have to return to your site several times to check or retake measurements. That's fine. One of the benefits of doing your own surveying is that it affords you many hours on the site, *studying* it.

WATER

With an understanding of the topography, we can now study water and how it will move across your land. Water must be considered in many forms: rain, runoff, surface water, humidity, and the water table. In some situations you will be collecting, even hoarding, the water. In others you will have to provide drainage in order to avoid being destroyed by it.

Strange as it seems, one of the biggest water considerations isn't usually visible (unless you're building a bridge). Under your site, the water table ebbs and flows with the seasons, the weather, and the subterranean soil conditions. We will discuss the water table in more detail later. For now, think of it as the surface plane of a vast underground reservoir that spreads as far as the eye can see. Though invisible, the water table will have profound effects on the vegetation, your well, and surface drainage.

Bill, one of our students from Vermont, was impressed with the relative flatness of an area on his site along the Mad River. It was inviting because it provided a nice view of the river and appeared to be an easy place for construction. He dug some test pits about 8′ deep to explore the soils where he planned his basement and his leaching field. The soil from these pits was "bony" gravel. Usually called "bank run gravel" (mostly sand and small stones with some clay), this type of soil type has good drainage characteristics and ample bearing capacity (the ability to support loads). Generally it's a fine soil on which to build. It was late autumn at the time. There was no water in Bill's pit and the vegetation was sparse. Nevertheless, with a little sod and some fertilizer, Bill imagined a fine lawn. He had visited the site several times during hard rains and was convinced that drainage would be no problem. The water seemed to disappear as soon as it hit the porous ground.

Fortunately, Bill never built in this location. While at Yestermorrow, Bill asked us to visit his site and look at his test pit. It was still dry. What Bill had failed to notice, however, was the "staining" along the pit walls about 18″ below the surface. Staining is your best indicator of high water table.

In order to see this, Bill needed to understand the basics of the hydrologic cycle (Figure 5).

The rain and snow that falls on the ground percolates down to a certain depth below which the soil is completely saturated. This saturated plane is called the *water table* and its depth varies from season to season depending on the weather. After spring thaw the rain and melt-off will combine to bring the water table closer to the surface. This is called "high water table." After a long hot summer of little rain, the plane of saturated soil will descend several feet. This is low water table. When water exists year round below the lowest level of the water table, it is referred to as an aquifer. We will come back to aquifers when we consider the well for your house (see Chapter 17). For the present it is enough that you see how the water moves through the atmosphere as weather and then through the soil as runoff.

Water is a powerful solvent. It dissolves many chemicals from both the atmosphere and the soil. These dissolved substances leave staining at high water table just like the ring in a bathtub. Thus, we can guess the high water table by studying the staining on the walls of the test pit. Had Bill built where he originally intended, his basement would have been submerged in water to within a few feet of the surface each spring.

That wouldn't have been the worst part, though. Eventually, he would have faced something far more serious than a wet basement. The flat terrain and gravelly soils on which Bill hoped to have his lawn made me nervous. Bank run gravel is so named because it usually exists along the banks of rivers. It's left there by past meanderings of the water. It all made me think we should check the town office for records of the one-hundred-year floodplain. This is the area covered by flooding at least once in every one-hundred-year period. Sure enough, Bill almost became Noah II without realizing it. His proposed building location was right in the one-hundred-year floodplain. (And the last flood of that magnitude had been ninety-two years earlier!)

One lesson here has to do with what you *can't* see by visiting your land. Not every building department will have a floodplain map, but they may have something similar. In Connecticut they have inland wetlands. In Texas they have gumbo clay. Along the coastlines they

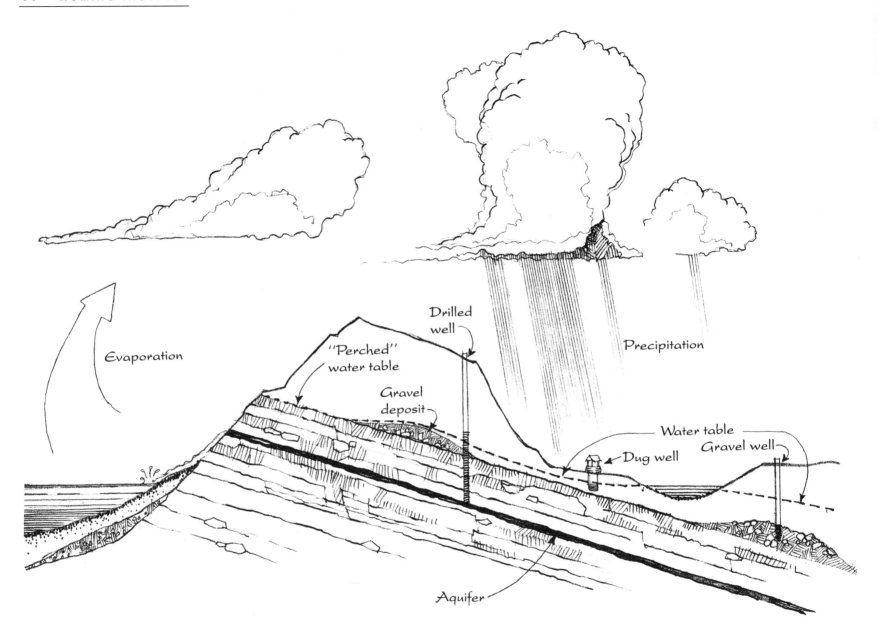

FIGURE 5: **The basic phases of the hydrologic cycle.**

have endangered dunes. Out west they have riparian laws. And almost everywhere they now have zoning, which we will discuss later. When analyzing your site, therefore, don't forget to talk with the building officials. They will help you attend to things that you might otherwise overlook.

Water table and floodplain are large-scale conditions. At a smaller, but no less important, scale is the study of surface water. When it rains, where does the water travel or collect? What aspects of the vegetation or terrain affect these conditions or will be altered by them?

Picture your site (and the surrounding landscape) from the air. With the topography in mind, try to imagine a rainstorm. What paths does the water follow and where will it collect? While walking on the site, study the vegetation and soils to see if they support your suspicions. Observing the runoff during one or two rains will be incredibly helpful. If you're in the snowbelt, try to visit the site during spring thaw. You want to consider all the different weather that visits a site over the course of four seasons.

When surface water moves, it erodes the soil. When it's stationary, it pools. Nature is incredible at bringing these two states into balance. Plant life tends to moderate the flow of surface water, reducing the erosive effects. Leaves break up the rain and roots consolidate the soil. Where water pools, plants will grow in abundance. Over countless yearly cycles they will die and compost until that low spot is leveled out with topsoil. In contrast to nature, humans have a really poor track record in dealing with surface water.

When we build, we are often forced to remove protective vegetation and soils. Roofs and paved surfaces collect and concentrate the rain. Downspouts, swales, and drainage pipes promote erosive damage where vegetation formerly handled the surface water gently. This is why we must take the time to really understand how water moves over the surface of our site. Any building, any road, any pathway concentrates water. Even a very shallow slope will be robbed of its top soils if the water running over it is concentrated. Water should be dispersed gently and evenly.

Of course, no one wants puddling and ponding around their home. What if your chosen site, perfect in every other way, is wet? Well, I guess you could just bring in the 'dozers and build swales, curtain drains, and new topography. This often works, but at considerable expense. Wouldn't it make better sense to work with the existing terrain? If you study your site carefully, it is usually possible to site your house in a harmonious way that minimizes the impact of the collected water. Consider the high—and dry—section of your property. Perhaps the driveway can be configured to divert surface runoff from the house and gently redistribute it elsewhere. If all else fails, think about building on piers.

WIND, NOISE, AND VEGETATION

You may stomp about your site for days and still not have a clue about what the wind is like at that location. Since it's invisible, you will only really know about the wind after you have experienced it for several seasons. Unfortunately, this is not a realistic contingency in most purchase and sales agreements: "Buyer will pay aforesaid amount for the parcel herein described contingent on the wind." Hmmm.

Figure 6 shows average wind directions across the nation. The actual situation on your site, however, will depend on local topography and may be quite different. Mountains, for instance, can reverse the prevailing wind direction as it curls over the ridge and eddies into the valley. Pairs of hills or mountain passes can create a venturi that will concentrate and accelerate the wind. River valleys, of course, will also direct the wind.

The local direction of the wind is usually different from winter to summer; on your site you must know which is which. In the summer, wind is a source of cooling and comfort. In the winter, it will rob your house of heat and blow snow in drifts across entries. To properly site your house and plan the surrounding landscaping, you simply must know which way the wind is blowing (Figures 7 and 8).

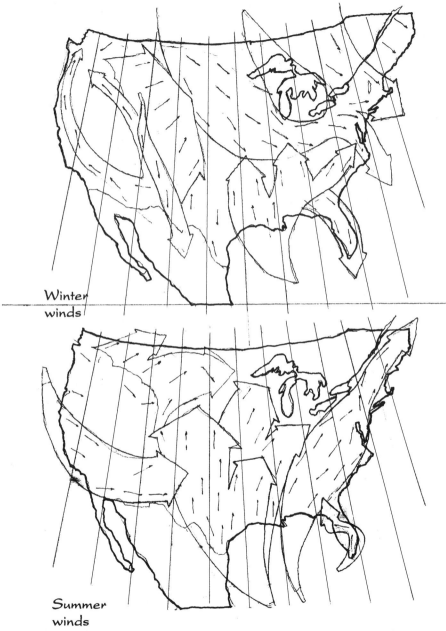

Winter
winds

Summer
winds

FIGURE 6: Average prevailing wind direction for summer and winter.

Trees and shrubs are among the best methods for moderating the wind. They will also filter noise, weather, and glare. The deciduous hardwood tree provides the classic example. In the summer its leaves form a canopy that blocks the sun while concentrating the breezes at ground level. Trees also have a cooling effect by using up heat in their respirational process. In the winter, the absence of leaves lets the beneficial sunlight through. Additionally, the dense cover of evergreens can serve as a protective wind block all year round (Figures 9a and 9b).

In thickly settled areas, vegetation also helps filter the air of dust and odors. Densely planted tree lines are frequently used to absorb noise. It should be noted that noise appears to travel up better than down. For example, a site located down-hill from a highway will experience much less noise than one located uphill.

At this point, it should be dawning on the precocious student that planting trees and shrubs is a good idea. Vegetation seems to fix everything. The only catch is that plant materials cost money and they take years to mature. Though not always an alternative, it's clearly better if you can work with the existing plants and trees. If you need further cover, plant new vegetation in harmony with what's already there. Extend the natural ground cover.

Lastly, it is important to understand that vegetation is a living resource. More than just pleasant to look at, it provides

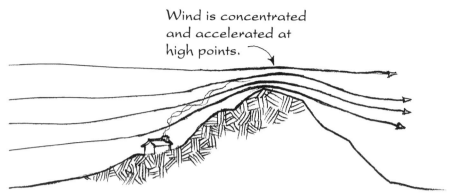

Wind is concentrated and accelerated at high points.

FIGURE 7: **The concentration and acceleration of wind by narrow passages is called the "venturi effect."**

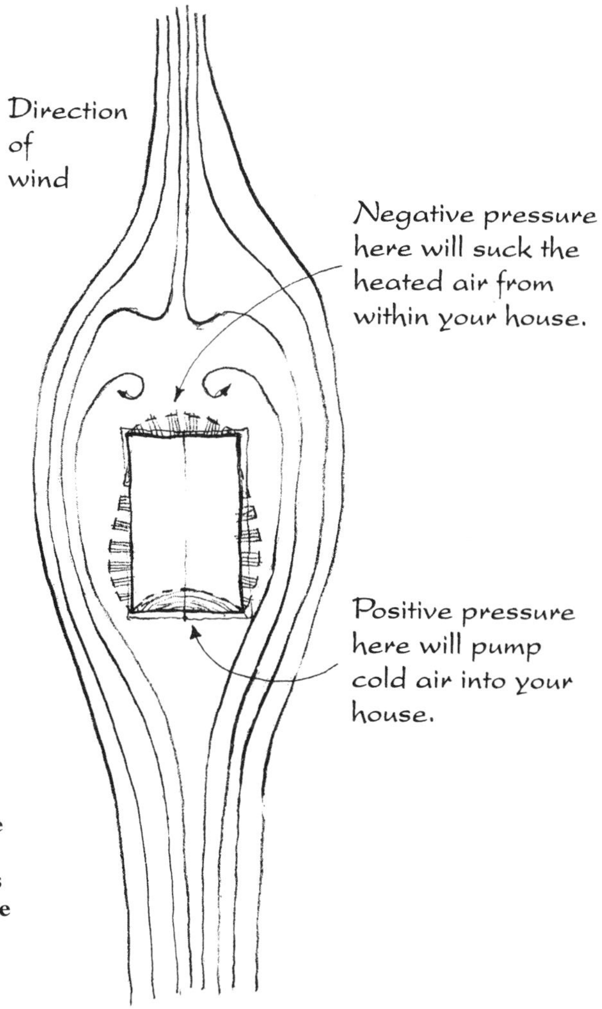

Direction of wind

Negative pressure here will suck the heated air from within your house.

Positive pressure here will pump cold air into your house.

protection, habitat, and food. Orchards, nut trees, and vegetable gardens are some of the most satisfying additions to any landscape. The animals that live among the vegetation add an incalculable richness to your site. As you inventory your site, you must endeavor to understand this habitat well. For we now know that the web of life woven by plants, bugs, birds, and animals determines our future just as surely as it does theirs. Build "lightly" on the earth and repair what you disarrange.

FIGURE 8: **Cold air is pumped into a house along the windward surfaces. Warm air is sucked out of a house along the leeward surfaces.**

VIEWS—SOLAR AND SCENIC

You mustn't spend all your time looking down at the ground. (I think my grandmother told me that.) Site analysis also includes a study of the sky and your view resources: scenic and solar. There are many opinions about scenic views but about solar views there are only facts.

Your solar view is strictly determined by the path of the sun above your site. This and the shape of the land will determine how much solar energy arrives on your site. Strictly numbers. Scenic views, however, are more varied and personal. Some sites are rich in close intimate views while others hold the possibility for panoramic vistas. When considering any scenic view, it is well to remember that it's a two-way street. Whatever can be seen *from* your site can also see *into* your site.

As you tramp about your site measuring topography and digging test pits, you

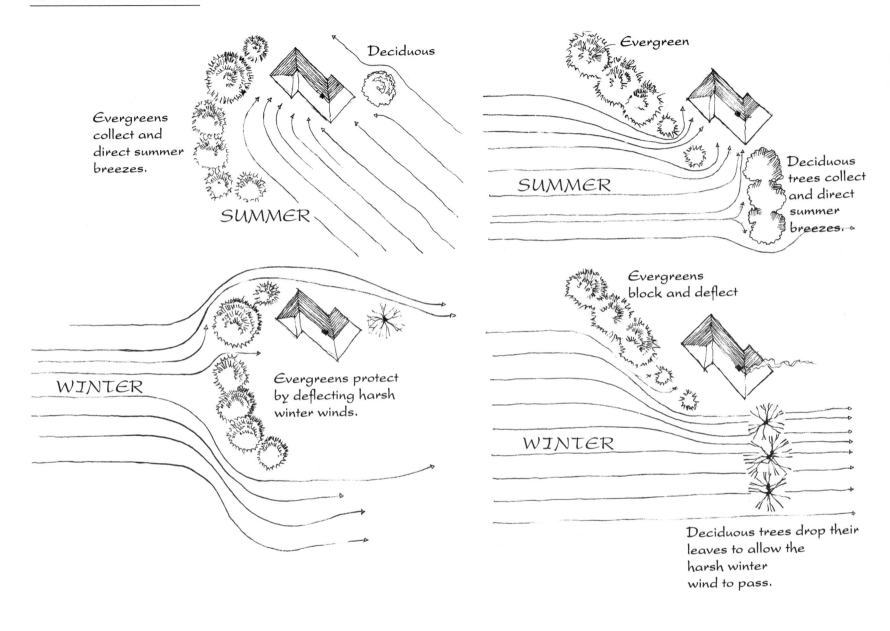

Deciduous

Evergreens collect and direct summer breezes.

SUMMER

Evergreen

SUMMER

Deciduous trees collect and direct summer breezes.

WINTER

Evergreens protect by deflecting harsh winter winds.

Evergreens block and deflect

WINTER

Deciduous trees drop their leaves to allow the harsh winter wind to pass.

FIGURE 9a: **When landscaping to enhance microclimate, remember that the prevailing winds may change directions with the seasons.**

FIGURE 9b: **For constant year-round wind direction, use deciduous trees to achieve the desired seasonal effect.**

will stand up from time to time just to take in the view. Really you're taking in much more. You're getting a sense of different places on your land. There's much more than just the view at any given point on your property, yet that's what most people use to characterize one place as opposed to another.

Keep in mind that there are different kinds of views. In addition to the long view, you should also be aware of the short and middle views. While the long view lets your eyes stretch for miles, the short view of your gardens offers richness of detail. The middle view has a bit of both. There is no "best" view; it's all a matter of taste. Since no site will have perfect panoramic views on all sides, it is important to understand the strengths of these alternatives.

Everyone is fond of the distant panoramic view. It's sort of classically American: big and majestic. It gives a sense of the geography and atmosphere.

Perhaps because of their densely settled towns, I think the Japanese have done the most with the short view. Their miniature landscapes and rock gardens are short-view configurations composed to have the same dramatic impact as a sweeping vista. I'm not suggesting that you bonsai your side yard; it's not necessary. Any study of landscape and garden design will give you access to some of the same effect. This is definitely the way to go if visual boundaries are tight.

The middle view seems to be English, if I were to generalize. It's a wonderful view but one that is largely overlooked in this country. Typically, if there's middle view potential, the designer goes for a long view. 'Tis a shame, really, and the English know it.

Well, regardless of your cultural preferences, it is important to be aware of all the views and how you came to enjoy them. That is, *without* a building. No view experienced while standing in the open will be the same when experienced from within a house. Try this. Spread your hands far enough apart so that you can't see them when facing straight ahead. Now slowly bring them together and stop when you can just see them. The angle between your arms represents what you see when outside. For most people the angle is close to 180 degrees, or a straight line. Not even a large picture window will give you the same breadth of vision. It's not supposed to.

A window frames a specific portion of the view, but never the whole thing. Remember this trade-off when analyzing the views on your site. If you build your home on the spot with the best view, you will no longer have the best view. Moreover, when you build your house where you can see the broadest view, it will became narrower and result in the largest number of people looking back and thinking, "What insensitive idiot built that monstrosity right in the middle of that fabulous landscape?"

The Zen thinking I've heard goes as follows. First: Find the single best spot on your site. Second: Build your home anywhere else. Why? It's the combination of the view with the land, the vegetation, and the approach. It's the experience. Once you build a house, garage, and driveway on the best spot, it won't be there anymore. You'll never get to experience it fully again.

Fortunately, a house has many rooms and many sides. For instance, the bedrooms and breakfast area want a good eastern exposure. The kitchen may want a southern view and the living areas perhaps a western one. Each space can only embrace a fraction of the vista you experience while standing on the undeveloped site. These views are part of the design work you have ahead. A big part of designing each room is to decide what the windows will look out on. At this point you should be taking inventory of *all* the views, not just the best one. You will need them all. Later, when you're looking at the different information that affects your site design, you may just decide to save the best view. It might become a destination in your landscaping. A tiny gazebo or bench could be placed there so that you could take a walk, relax, and enjoy the view. Ahhh, now doesn't that sound nice?

In contrast to the personal vagaries of scenic views, solar views are nicely empirical. The sun follows precisely known paths year after year. Its position and path can be calculated easily for any location at any time of year. Mountains, trees, and other physical features will modify how much sunlight you receive, i.e., create shadows. But even if you're directly exposed to high south-facing sun, you will still receive only a fraction of its energy.

A fraction? If not in the shadows, you ask, why just a fraction? Well don't complain, if we received it all we'd all have skin cancer in a week. Even as it is, sunlight cracks paint, bakes out colors, and destroys the roofs on buildings. The sun sends an incredible amount of energy toward the earth. The atmosphere reflects about a third and absorbs about a fifth. Well, at least that's the situation if we don't destroy the ozone layer. More on that later. Meanwhile, what doesn't get absorbed or reflected gets through. In terms of BTUs (British Thermal Units), which is the unit by which we measure our home heating needs, the sun sends us about 430 BTUs per square foot each hour. About 160 BTUs gets through to our site, mostly as diffuse sunlight. That's an average, of course. In the South and West there is a good deal more usable solar energy than in the Northeast. Moreover, that's a year-round average. Most places have an abundance of solar energy in the summer and less in the winter. Generally, this is precisely the reverse of how we'd like to schedule it. Nevertheless, we can't complain: it's all free!

Let's make a rough but interesting "guestimation" here. A single-family house during a typical Vermont winter will need about 60,000 BTUs each hour to stay warm. Presuming that an energy conscious Yestermorrow graduate built it, let's say only 55,000 BTUs. If we could collect all 160 BTUs coming from the sun, we would only need 344 square feet of collector. That's a surface less than $18' \times 20'$!

Unfortunately, we don't receive that much sunlight at all times and even the best collectors can't catch it *all*. Nevertheless, depending on where you live and the time of the year, the sun that falls on your site is a very real resource. It needs to be understood and worked with just like the topography, wind, and water.

Happily, there are a couple of simple (and inexpensive) devices that can help give you a clear picture of the sun's impact on your site. One is called the Solar Site Selector (available from Lewis & Assoc.; 105 Rockwood Dr.; Grass Valley, CA 95945). As shown in Figure 10, you just look at the proposed site through a wide-angle peephole and observe the horizon's profile superimposed through a transparent diagram of the sun's paths throughout the year.

Now you know where the sun will be and when. To find out how much usable heat it will bring involves further calculations and data that can be found in Appendix 2. This information will make a lot more sense when you have read the chapter on windows and glazing (Chapter 14).

At this point you need only record which parts of your site get the most sun at different times of the year.

Solar design is a powerful form-giver. By this I mean that it can be used to organize the shape and placement of everything on your site. During the 1970s interest in this "new" approach, along with the oil shortage, generated some fascinating new designs. These were pioneering efforts and some were architecturally unattractive or just plain didn't work. So when oil prices dropped in the 1980s, most people (and the government) abandoned solar design. But today we are happy to see it making a strong return, and this time the buildings are architecturally refined and work very well at reducing fuel costs. Today, any house that doesn't take advantage of solar design principles is obsolete before it leaves the drawing board. It would be like leaving the insulation out of the walls.

ZONING

Almost every community has a local zoning ordinance (or soon will have). These are the rules and guidelines that tell us where we can do what. In general, zoning is a rather new practice in this country. Although its origins go back centuries, it is still somewhat unreliable in achieving its stated goals.

Most cities and towns have a Town Plan. This document describes the vision

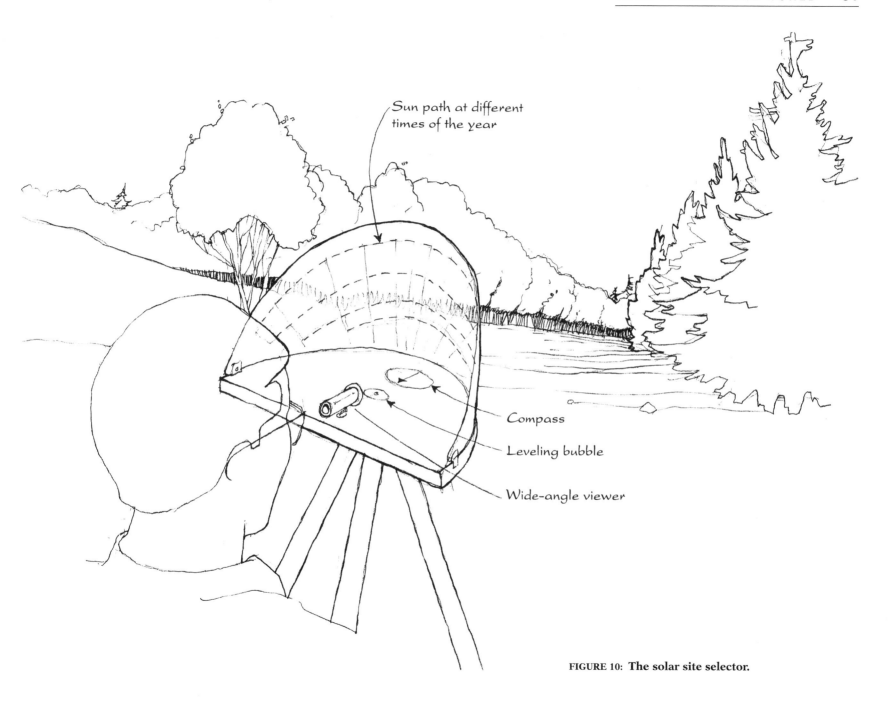

Sun path at different times of the year

Compass

Leveling bubble

Wide-angle viewer

FIGURE 10: The solar site selector.

a community holds for itself. It describes what qualities should be preserved and promoted in different areas of the town. The plan describes intentions and aspirations as well, so it is necessarily fuzzy in some respects. The Zoning, however, is quite specific. It is the Zoning ordinance that enforces the Town Plan's vision. Zoning laws tell us what type of buildings may be built where. Businesses in commercial zones. Factories in industrial zones. Bed and breakfasts in mixed-use zones. Houses in residential zones.

Zoning also tries to legislate quality at the site level. Zoning laws tell us how close we can build to the street or the edge of our lot. These are called "setbacks." For instance, in a residential zone you might be required to leave 75' in the front, 25' in the back, and 12' on either side. These are "minimum setback requirements," and every municipality has them. In the city the setbacks will be much less. If there are no setbacks, it's called "zero lot line" zoning. Obviously, you should *never* buy a piece of land without first checking the local zoning ordinance.

Among other things, the local zoning will stipulate lot size. Specifying lot size controls density and property values—theoretically. The idea is to promote neighborhood quality and protect resale value. That is, people want to live in a sparsely settled neighborhood for the quality of life, and they also want to preserve the market value of their biggest single invest-

ment. By keeping one's neighbors at a distance, one reduces the chance that they might build or do something that could reduce a neighboring home's market value. In the past this market value aspect of housing has led many developers to configure their subdivisions to maximize the number of lots. This bottom-line approach is often reflected in the quality of the houses built on these lots as well. While the developer may get away with his profits, the community is left with dozens of poorly built homes overcrowded into poorly considered neighborhoods. This can become a seed bed for "the bad side of town."

Ironically, zoning can't really guarantee the double benefit of neighborhood quality and protected property values. Large lots and vast separations destroy the essential neighborliness of a community. People become isolated and impersonal. Moreover, the large houses built on these large lots are often as poorly conceived as the smaller ones.

An illuminating contrast can be found in the densely settled but very successful towns found in rural New England or medieval Europe. Today's zoning laws would never allow such settlement patterns. Early settlers built close to the road, close to the river, and close to each other. But most of these buildings were owner-built and -occupied. They were making a place in the community that they expected to inhabit for the foreseeable future. So of

course they did their best to insure that everything was worked out as well as possible. They strove to site their buildings well not only in terms of their neighbors, but the whole community. Today, these towns and small cities are the very ideal that we strive to protect with our zoning.

ACCESS

How people and things get to and from the site is of tremendous importance. Entering the site and moving toward the house can be choreographed to heighten the sense of arrival and destination. Alternately, a poorly considered access will rudely juxtapose your house and property with the public way. When developing your site, don't overlook this opportunity to make the most of the arrival sequence leading to your house.

Since many regard privacy as a high priority, we see a lot of site plans with long driveways. City dwellers seek a building's upper floors for the same reason. But I think there are more skillful ways to attain a feeling of privacy.

Long driveways cost a lot to build and a lot to maintain. In Vermont, the plowing costs alone may give you pause. Moreover, they need to be located over reasonably sloped terrain; less than 12 percent grade. There are serious erosion problems connected with an overly steep or long drive.

Most utilities will follow your driveway and they too are priced by the foot. Rural sites are likely to have water from a well and a septic system on site, but electricity and phone must be installed along the road. In suburban and city communities everything will come from the street: phone, electricity, gas, water, septic, even cable. Each of these may require a separate trench or line of poles.

Now before I give the wrong impression, let me say that a mindlessly short driveway is no better than a mindlessly long one. Indeed, the savings in short driveways have been known to developers and spec builders for years. That's why a house right on the road (or the minimum front-yard setback) always looks like it was built on "spec"—even if it wasn't.

The message here is the same as it is throughout the book: *think* about what you're doing. The access to your site should be a comfortable sequence of unfolding views supplying adequate privacy and allowing the house to be in the best spot on the site. In the city you simply want the drive to be easily navigated and have good sight lines. Every site will be slightly different. Look at *your* site and inventory all the options.

Consider the story of Dona. As a retired military officer, Dona was comfortable speaking her mind. It was a no-nonsense mind and she wanted to design a no-nonsense house. Though her site was ample, zoning left her only one place to build (see Figure 11). But zoning didn't constrain her approach.

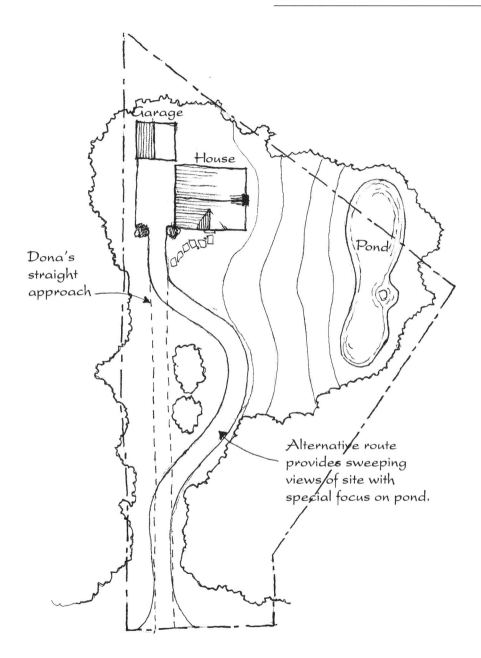

FIGURE 11: **A slight variation in alignment can make a big difference in the arrival experience.**

"Straight in. I want the house in my sights from the minute I leave the road." No nonsense.

"How about a tree-lined alley?" I suggested.

"Nope. There's a pond to the south and all the surrounding ground is pretty wet. I think we'll take it in on the high ground. Straight in. Besides, trees are expensive and take a long time to grow."

"Dona, how about a big S-turn or a diagonal drive?" I confess, I always try to push beyond the student's first idea.

"I don't think so; curves mean cash."

"But you won't even see your beautiful pond. The site is so deep and narrow, you will be right by it in a blink. Why not put the slightest inflection in your otherwise very straight driveway? This could be a no-cost option and really change the approach. It would make the driver see all parts of your property, not just the house."

"Hmmm. What would it cost? Do you think it would cost much more?"

"Well," I pondered, "my guess is it will cost an extra $700. On the other hand, it will also increase the experience of your site one hundred percent. It means you will see and experience the pond ($10,000 value man-made) and five acres ($30,000 present real estate value)."

"But I can see those anytime," she countered.

"Yes, but you won't. And if you don't see them, they might as well not be there. Even if you walk out there to experience them once a month—or even once a week—you're not getting full value. I'm talking about experiencing most of the best parts of your property *every time you use the driveway*. I'm talking about getting $40,000 worth of experience for $700!" Using this kind of logic is really awful, but over the years I've gotten pretty good at it.

"Forty thousand dollars? Do you think so? Would I get it back at resale? Hmmm. For $700 it's a good gamble."

Two years later Dona sent us a picture of her new home. It was quite a bit different from the one she started on at Yestermorrow, but I could see how it had evolved. It was still a no-nonsense dwelling. She wrote that the pond was beautiful and she enjoyed looking at it a couple of times every day. In the end, she wrote, it cost more like $1,000 extra. Nevertheless, she figured the added value was more like $500,000!

REALITY

Analyzing a site takes time. You will want to visit during several different weather conditions and as many seasons as possible. Maybe you will spend time camping on it (yes, even in town). Certainly you will spend more than a day or two there if you survey the topography. All the while you will be experiencing views, solar, access, topography, etc. Most interestingly, you will start to have feelings about certain spots. Initially you may enjoy the familiarity that develops around where you leave the car. This is the first "place" that you've made on your site. Then, perhaps that special spot where you have lunch or coffee break becomes a favorite. You may record that some spots have a certain quality of sunlight. In general, the more you actively do on your site, the more associations and feelings you will develop for different areas.

It is natural to gravitate toward the places you like on your site. You will find yourself imagining site plans with things laid out so that you are near your favorite spots. While measuring solar access you will be sure the house should go thus. Then, while doing the topo survey, it will seem obvious that it should go somewhere else. Views may suggest a further change, and drainage dictate still another. Wandering around from spot to spot, you may feel each is best at the instant you're standing there. Make no decisions! Record your observations and feelings. Be thorough. Come back often. Now it's time to go to the studio.

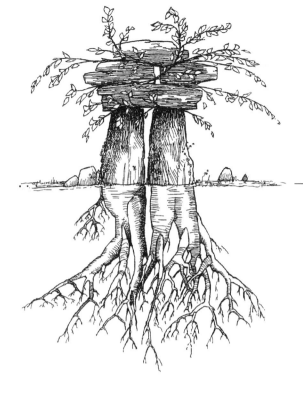

Site Design and Development

After weeks and months of visiting your site, you are now sitting at your drafting table studying a topographical site plan. On it are notations about water, soils, vegetation, prevailing winds, scenic and solar views, and possibly certain other information that is particular to your area. You may be building in a floodplain or an historic district. There may be special zoning restrictions. Perhaps your site has easements, covenants, or right-of-ways. At this point in the process you will have discovered all (or nearly all) of the important preconditions existing on your site. In addition, you will add your own list of conditions:

- a view that stops the heart!
- privacy from the train tracks
- a vast vegetable garden
- easy access and an attached garage
- a pool, hot tub, or putting green

Over your annotated topo you will place sheets of tracing paper in an endless series of experimental layouts and arrangements.

Perhaps you've known from the first time you set foot on the site exactly where the house might go. Now's your chance to test it out. On your first piece of trace you sketch in the rough scale square of a house. From your study of the site you know that the views are fantastic. But, uh oh, you will have to clear two acres of woods and build a small bridge to get your driveway in. This also means twice or three times the cost of putting in utilities. Well, it seems like an acceptable trade-off—until you realize you will have to walk up and down a hill to get to your preferred garden spot.

Next sheet of tracing paper!

THE MEADOW

I don't know why, but it seems that the most natural thing in the world for many people is to place their new home right smack in the middle of a meadow. I've seen it a hundred times. Perhaps meadow just says "yard" to people who are moving back to the country. Or maybe it's the ease of access or the facility with which the backhoe can put in a cellar hole. Whatever the reason, it's a big mistake and all too common.

Open land—meadows and fields—establishes the primary geographical quality of the rural countryside. These generous open spaces are what give us the feeling of being "on the land" as we drive out to the farms. If the fields are fully planted or the meadows teaming with livestock, so much the better. But even if the open spaces are fallow or unused, the essential character of the countryside is maintained by the mere expanse of the meadow. This is the sine qua non of the rural landscape.

So if you purchase a piece of property with open land on it, don't build in the middle of it. You will be destroying one of the great features that originally attracted you to the property. Instead, build along the edge.

The edge is really where it's all happening. In the middle of a field all views are very similar. But if your house is just inside the tree line, it will have a variety of long and short views. The driveway will also be more interesting as it makes its way along the trees. And, should you decide to fence your meadow and keep animals, you will save hundreds of dollars on fence. By preserving your meadow, you have something to anchor and orient your house design. At the edge of the forest your home will be less vulnerable to the wind and weather. The microclimate will be better for recreating in the yard.

Clearing the forest to open a field is some of the hardest labor you can imagine. The early settlers did it with little if any labor-saving technology. Even with today's heavy equipment, it's tough work. Once a meadow is open and cultivated, it's a thing to be cherished. If you own one, you will likely have your hands full just keeping it open. Trees and shrubs start to grow in. Rocks and boulders seem to come from nowhere after each spring thaw. Whether you raise livestock, keep horses, or plant crops, a field is easier to keep if you work it.

With all this in mind I hope you can see that a meadow is a valuable feature in the landscape, like a waterfall or a special vista. If you have open land on your property, treat it as something of value, not something to be used up.

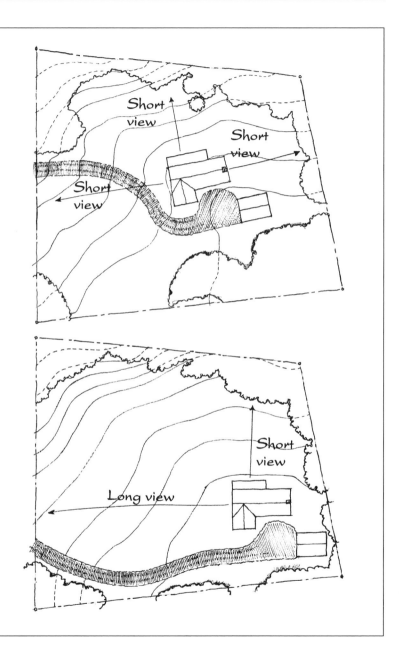

FIGURES 12a AND 12b:
Building in the middle destroys the meadow, with no significant gain in views.

This time you move the house and the garden closer together. This reduces the length of your drive but also constrains your view. Hmmm. It's time to *prioritize*.

Priorities help determine which of two equally good solutions is best for you. Some people call this the art of compromise, but I've come to hate that word. I am a confirmed "have-your-cake-and-eat-it-too" designer. Priorities allow me to know where to place my emphasis, but I'm very reluctant to actually give up one design intention for another.

Ask yourself what and why you want the things you do. What do you want from a garden, a view, a driveway? Why do you want privacy from your neighbors, the road, the train tracks? Then factor in the element of time. How much time will you spend looking at the view, working in the garden, motoring up the driveway? Finally, it's important to discover different ways to have what you want. Must the entire view be seen from your kitchen window? Perhaps you can enjoy the view better if you walk up to a gazebo at the end of the day. Won't this make the view all the more special? Maybe the sound of the train tracks could be romantic—if they were muted by a tall hedgerow. Of course some things are nonnegotiable. The sun is unlikely to change its path in the sky, and the climate will only change slightly over the course of your lifetime (if at all). The soils on your site should pretty much be accepted.

While you can truck in different types of earth (see "engineered septic systems" in Glossary), local vegetation usually does best in local soils.

In the previous chapter you indicated all nonnegotiable conditions on your site plan. These might be called constraints. At the same time you will be dealing with a wish list of items that vary in importance. These are your priorities, both high and low. Ever mindful of your constraints, site design is the art of arranging your priorities in the best possible way on your particular site.

So get out the tracing paper and go to it. Don't expect to get it right on the first try. Each attempt will likely reveal relationships and considerations that you had completely overlooked. Indeed, you should expect your site plan to change again later. After the house starts to be designed, it is normal for the site considerations to shift and change. A bathroom-window placement might alter the location of the garden. The kitchen window may affect the location of the driveway. The rooms and circulation within the house should harmonize seamlessly with the spatial arrangements out of doors. Think of the spaces immediately next to the house as the "outdoor rooms." Consider the architectural and functional qualities of these spaces the same way you would your kitchen, living or dining rooms. Be mindful of which outdoor activities need to be close to which indoor activities. As with all preliminary design,

proper configuration will only come after many iterations of design and redesign.

Remember the cyclical nature of the Design Helix. Now we are looking mostly at the site; next we will consider your program; finally we will consider the building. Then we will do it all over again, incorporating the new considerations we discovered in each preceding phase. The site design will be modified by the perspective of the program, the program modified by the building, the building by the site. Cycle, cycle, cycle.

When we started Yestermorrow, it was obvious that we needed somewhere to build. I was constantly looking at land, usually damaged or otherwise undesirable land. A knowledge of design and construction allows one to build on and improve sites that conventional spec builders wouldn't consider. While keeping the price down, this approach also repairs the environment and reduces development on precious open land.

I shopped with real estate professionals and I shopped with home/land owners. I found the owners to be more helpful. There was often a history or at least a story about their land. Realtors, in contrast, view land as a commodity. They will only spend as much effort getting to know the land as they think necessary to sell it. Whenever possible, buy from the owner. It's cheaper and they're less practiced at the art of deception. But keep in mind that

A hand-held sight level.

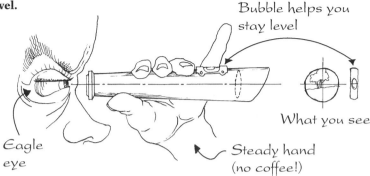

Bubble helps you
stay level

What you see

Eagle
eye

Steady hand
(no coffee!)

ignorance can be even more dangerous than a sales pitch.

A survey and title search should be considered nonnegotiable preconditions for any sale. Time and again I have discovered the unimaginable by having a survey done on a potential site. And my experiences are hardly unique. I was discussing this with John Ringel, one of Yestermorrow's design/build instructors, who says he's amazed at the cavalier manner in which some people purchase property.

Ringel is flabbergasted when he hears something like this: "I think this is the corner here, and it runs about 250 feet along the road that way. It goes back into the woods about 750 feet. It's about 4.5 acres and we think it has been perc-tested." This is not an unusual description. John tries to imagine buying something in a store like that: "Imagine if the seller kept the item behind and under the counter while telling you only the price and that it was about 2″ wide, 12″ long, it's red and more than likely working."

"Nobody would buy that, would they? Yet, they will pay large sums of money based on no more concrete or helpful information than a label 'piece of land.' Apparently," rolling his eyes to the heavens, "all rules of reason are suspended in the real estate market."

John Ringel prides himself on his site visits. He takes a compass, a hand-held site level (see illustration above), a 36″ pace, and a lot of curiosity. The client is supposed to provide the survey maps, metes and bounds, and any other relevant land descriptions. Ideally, these are provided before the visit. If the site is large enough and the description clear enough, he will start by locating it on a United States Geological Survey (USGS) map. This can only provide very general contour and topographic information. On a scale designating one inch equal to 2,000′, an acre (44,000 square feet) is about a fifth of an inch square. The contour lines are every 20′, so at best you can only find the general orientation of the slope.

Bringing together available data from several sources is always important at the outset of any project. And a survey is rarely if ever optional. Even if the land has been in the family for generations, a survey should be conducted before design or construction is begun.

An Enlightened Example

Creative site design and problem solving are second nature at Yestermorrow. Whether a renovation in the city or raw land in the country, when you're looking for property, you want to take the largest perspective possible. Consider how the property fits into its overall context. How will your intended design affect the neighborhood, the community, the world? What will be the energy costs to build and dwell in this location? Will you be destroying anything in the process of realizing your dreams? These sorts of concerns separate sustainable vernacular architecture from shortsighted cookie-cutter subdivisions.

The land I purchased for school projects was an abandoned gravel pit. It was surveyed and I bought it through a real estate agent. This realtor had done significant research on the piece and was trying to figure out how to make it attractive. She wasn't really succeeding. But I was fascinated with the idea of a gravel pit. As I shopped around, it occurred to me that my intentions were not much different from those of every other small-time developer. I was looking for a beautiful piece of land that we could subdivide into several smaller lots. Yestermorrow would then have a variety of spec building projects. As I looked at one piece after another, I found increasingly that the more beautiful the land, the more reticent I was to develop it. I assumed that development of a piece of land guaranteed degradation. I don't know where this assumption came from; maybe from fast-track developers putting up condominiums in Vermont. But it was an odd attitude for someone like me. As an architect and builder, land development was a precondition for new work. (See Figure 13.)

Well, I decided to challenge this assumption. There must be ways of putting buildings and human activity on the landscape that are not destructive. This meant that I should be able to develop a piece of beautiful land without ruining it. But even better would be to improve, even rehabilitate, a piece of already damaged land through the act of developing it. I began looking at gravel pits, swamps, and fire sites. When I found our 10-acre gravel pit sandwiched between the Mad River and Route 100 I bought it without hesitation. It was perfect. Poor soils, difficult access, floodplain; I was so confident that we could fix it that I didn't even have a test pit dug. This, of course, was stupid.

The first thing I did was consult the local zoning regulations. Pleased as I was with the 1-acre zoning, I discovered that there were special flood regulations for land bordering water. In any mountainous area the rivers are likely to overflow their banks from time to time. Every so often the flooding will be quite dramatic. Records have been kept. The Flood Plain Regulations contain maps of the one-hundred-year floodplain and the five-hundred-year floodplain. These are the areas under water during the worst flooding that occurs once every one hundred or five hundred years. Building within these areas would have grave consequences— eventually. It is not allowed.

The next thing I did was have some test pits dug. In defense of my impulsive purchase I should say that some ground work had been done prior to the realtor's receiving the land for sale. It wasn't conclusive and I should have known better, but I was already on a mission to "fix the land." The more problems it had, the more interesting my task. So I optimistically arranged for a backhoe operator to dig one or two test pits. This is usually enough. But unfortunately both filled up with water. So did the next three. Undiscouraged, I retained a soils engineer and the two of us had another nine test pits dug. It was like searching for Easter eggs with a backhoe.

When you dig a test pit, the sides of the pit will provide you with a cross section of the soils. Staining in the soils indicate levels that the ground-water has reached in the past. The upper surface of the ground-water is called the water table. The water table will vary from season to season. Spring thaw and run off will produce a "high" water table while summer heat or drought will lower the water table. A river or pond is often no more than a place where the water table has come to the surface. High water table is the critical configuration for two reasons. If it's too high it will prevent your leaching field from working and it will eventually get into your basement. (This is one reason for surrounding your house with a foundation drain; see Chapter 8.)

It does not take a geological engineer to know that when your test pit fills with water, you are too close to the water table. Anyone who has built sand castles by the surf knows what happens.

The test pits also gave us information about the soils. To no one's surprise, most of what was left in this abandoned gravel pit was clay. Fortunately, before extraction, the excavators had pushed all the topsoil into large piles at the rear of the site. Then they mined the gravel to within about 2' of the water table. Twenty years had passed before I came along, happy to acquire what was formerly beautiful shoreline property but was now largely floodplain. (I guess there *is* one born every minute!).

A dozen test pits later we had finally found enough area suitable for leaching that we knew the land could accommodate three to four houses. Zoning permit-

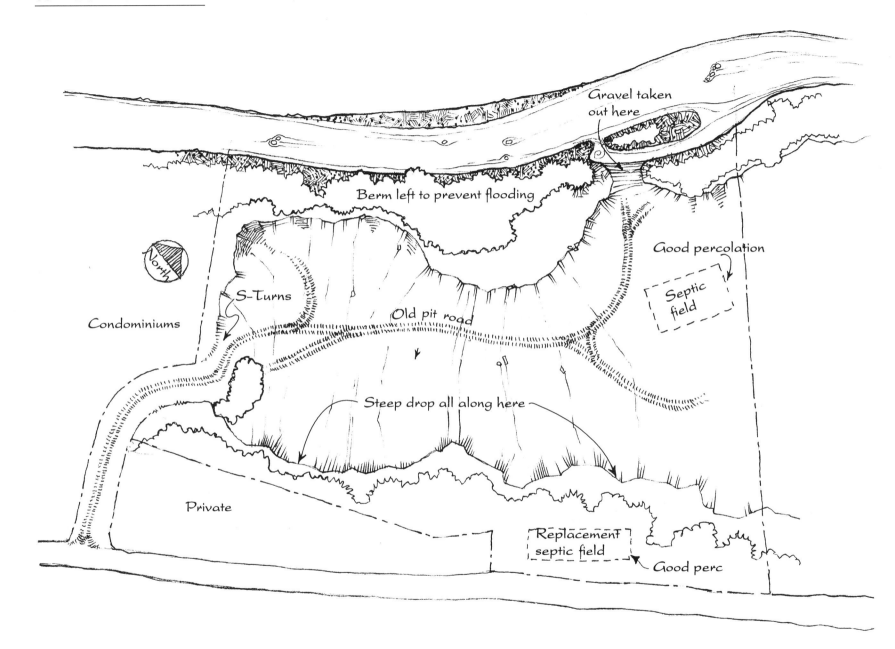

FIGURE 13: The gravel pit as we found it in 1983.

TABLE 1: PERCOLATION DATA

SOIL TYPE	TIME for water level to fall 1" in minutes	ALLOWABLE ABSORPTION in gallons per square foot per day	AREA in trenches for 100 gals of flow	COMMENTS
sand, gravelly loam	5 or less	2.5	40	
light loam	8	2.0	50	
	10	1.7	60	
loam	12	1.5	67	
	15	1.3	76	
heavy loam	22	1.0	100	
	30	.8	125	Must have an engineer
hard pan	60	.6	165	Must have an engineer
heavy clay	60	none	n/a	use alternate site

Poor soils drain slowly, requiring the added cost of an engineered septic system.

ted ten but I didn't want to crowd that many onto the site. Besides, we hadn't actually run any "perc" tests. A percolation test is required to engineer a leaching bed (see Chapter 17). It determines the speed at which water will percolate or soak into the ground. If your soils contain too much clay, the water may take hours or days to percolate—no good. On the other hand, if your soils contain too much gravel the effluent may drain through too fast—just as bad. But I am getting ahead of myself.

⦙⦙⦙⦙ Septic Considerations

Waste disposal should be one of the first things you consider when analyzing your site. If you are in a city, waste will likely be dumped into the municipal sewer, where it flows, along with millions of gallons of sewage, light industrial waste, and gray water, to the city's septic treatment plant. In the city, you just flush and forget it. For those of us living outside the reach of a centralized sewer system, we must manage our own "waste." As we shall discuss later, this waste is actually a valuable resource that we can *use*. Conventional septic treatment means losing a valuable nutrient source (see the section on Poop Plants, later). Whether you use it or lose it, if you live outside the city your septic stream must be dealt with on your own land.

Pervious soils absorb sewage more rapidly than tight ones and can handle larger quantities of effluent. Ideally, the effluent should percolate into the earth at a rate that will allow the waste to be filtered out by the soil. There it is digested by microorganisms that live in the first several inches below grade.

The size of a leaching field is calculated on the basis of volume of flow and the rate of absorption. See Table 1. Although studies indicate that an individual only generates about 50 to 60 gallons of wastewater per day, code requirements allow for 100 to 120 gallons per person per day just to be safe. These figures don't reflect any volume reductions you might accomplish by water-saver fittings or separating your gray water (all nontoilet wastewater) from your black (toilet waste). Rate of absorption is found empirically by performing percolation tests. (See Figure 14.)

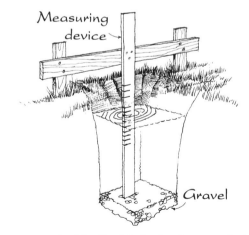

FIGURE 14: An idealized hole dug for percolation test.

In Chapter 17 we will run through a full description of percolation testing and how to size leaching fields.

All of the above is meant to help you plan the probable size and location of your septic system. This is an important criterion for site planning and can actually determine whether the site is even usable. Remember, a leaching field can't be built on, driven on, paved over or sloped. To improve land use, some septic engineers are using alternative designs, but these are still the exception. Septic tanks must be accessible so they can be pumped. These considerations exert a very real impact on your final site design.

The general method outlined above will result in an overdesigned, underenlightened, but code-acceptable system in most parts of the country. Much can be done to improve on this design, starting with the separation of gray water and ending with biological waste treatment in a greenhouse. All of this and more will be covered in Chapter 17.

THE BAD NEWS

Our test pits and perc tests were, to say the least, discouraging. So I conferred with the soils engineer. "Monitor!" he said. "We will monitor some of these test pits. Much of this staining may be 'vestigial.'" This means that the water table used to rise to this level but doesn't any more. If perc tests are unacceptable, it makes sense to moni-

tor. In our case, this meant placing a 4″ perforated drainpipe vertically in the test pits to a depth of at least 8′ and then backfilling. The pipe is then monitored for a year with special attention in the spring. If little or no water shows up in the pipe, the local codes and environmental officials may allow the design of a conventional leaching bed or grant a variance contingent on engineering a mound system.

THE GOOD NEWS

A year later we had an approved design for a septic system that would handle the waste from several (five) average-size homes (with three bedrooms). It was a tight design and there were some constraints, but we knew where the leaching bed would go and where all the tanks and pumps would be located on the site. These were largely determined by slopes and access. This gave us a good indication of how the land might be subdivided.

We had not been idle during the year of monitoring. Several classes of architecture students had spent weeks looking at different ways the site could be organized. We had looked at vehicular and utility access, topography, vegetation, solar orientation, and intralot relationships.

▥ Topography

The first thing we explored was the topography. Roaming over the site with

transits and stadia rods, students discovered that there were only two or three areas that were more than 8′ above water level. Locating buildings at these points made sense for two reasons: There was enough undisturbed soil to put in a full basement, and the slope would allow the sewage to flow to a common pumping station.

The most attractive high ground ran along the river. It was a berm of original material that the gravel operation had left intact. This was meant to protect the site from flooding during the spring thaw when the river was high. It was a tough decision, but we decided not to build there. There was plenty of soil and the best views of the river along that berm. Construction on the berm, however, would mean destruction of the original flora. The roots of the pre–gravel-pit trees and shrubs were actually reinforcing the berm against any future flooding.

There's a juvenile side of the God of Building that lives in each of us. It tempts us to believe that we can build anywhere and make it work. This is a necessary illusion if you are to be successful in your building endeavors. At the same time, it must be tempered with a bit of wisdom to avoid making a mess of every place you build. We decided to build on the highest spot that wasn't actually on the berm. Also, we configured some additional fill and the driveway to further protect the berm (Figures 15a and 15b).

FIGURE 15a: Section cut through W-10 gravel pit.

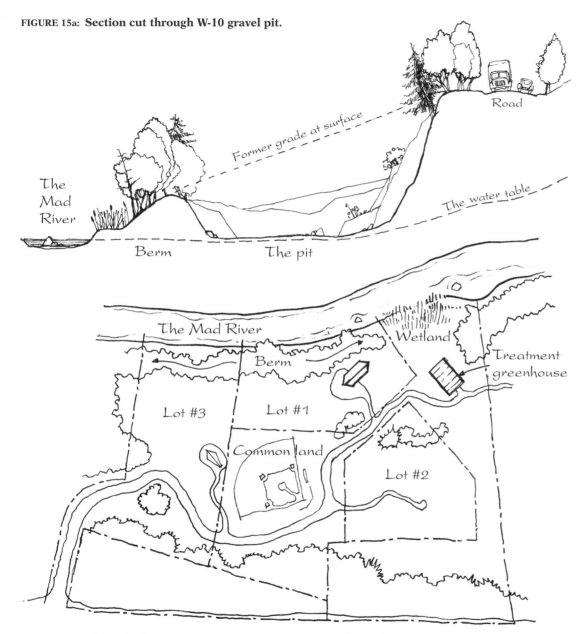

FIGURE 15b: Although the property was zoned to permit ten house lots, we felt three lots, with common land and a greenhouse, would be a better configuration.

Access(es)

Vehicular access and electrical power are two amenities that must be installed before you can begin building. Often these are poorly configured by undue concern for convenience during the construction phase. Such shortsighted decisions can be avoided through creative problem solving and temporary solutions.

The access to our gravel pit was off a right-of-way shared with some condominiums. Drivers in larger trucks (lumber, concrete, well drillers, etc.) complained about the difficulty they had navigating the tight S-turns leading from the right-of-way to the building site (see Figure 13). An even bigger problem developed when it was time to install the temporary power (an initial panel box and meter temporarily mounted on a post until the permanent ones can be installed in the building). Generally, but not without exception, power utilities will only install overhead wires along roads and driveways. This is so they can service them from boom trucks. Coming in along our circuitous drive would add a lot of length and expense.

The power company suggested we straighten our access alignment. We reviewed it. It was discovered that the double-back turns were creating important visual privacy. The ten-acre site was bounded visually on the west by the Mad River; on the east by a high, tree-covered bank; and on the north by a huge open meadow. Because of the double-back access from the south, the entire gravel pit was very enclosed and private. We certainly didn't want to lose this just to save a bit of money during the start-up phase.

At this early point in the project we knew there was still much to learn about the site and how best to configure it. So we decided to bring temporary power and telephone service to a centrally located gazebo. To save money we had the utility companies bring service only to the nearest pole along the edge of the site. This was free! From there, *we* ran it through the trees and down the steep bank to the gazebo. Because this was to be temporary, we didn't need to concern ourselves with maintenance from a boom truck.

Two years later, we installed underground power to the well-considered house sites that resulted from exhaustive site analysis and many weeks actually on the site.

▥ The Fauna

You must never forget that the reason for studying the plants, topography, water, and views on your site is because *you* want to settle there. You have decided to join the local fauna. You want to see how best to fit in. To do this you must look at your life and your needs. House, garage, garden, yards, peace, security . . . each of these things must be accommodated on your site. With this in mind, the students and I turned our attention to how the human activities might be arranged on this site.

Zoning said we could have five 2-acre lots, but site study indicated that there weren't enough appropriate soils for the septic system. Some thought the best use of the site would be just one very nice home, commanding all 10 acres. Others felt affordable housing should be built as densely as feasible. In the end, we decided on something in between. A single building would be too lonely. Cheek by jowl with a condominium complex, it could hardly pretend to be an exclusive estate. Moreover, a couple of smaller homes presented the more interesting issues of personal priorities versus public good. The site could allow several small buildings a sense of privacy at the same time as providing a sense of neighborhood or community. We realized that this sense of neighborhood was dependent on us developing a sense of place. This sense of place became our first priority (more on this when we get to Chapter 6).

A neighborhood is more than just a collection of nearby structures. The inhabitants must share some mutual interests. In this vein, we designated some common land. We decided that certain resources ought to be shared and so configured the common land to enclose them. Specifically, sewage treatment and shoreline access were seen as the major shared resources. The location of the leaching area was dictated by the few soils that percolated acceptably. As we explored the shoreline we discovered that the vestigial berm disappeared somewhat as it approached the leaching field end of the site. Therefore it made sense to collect the leaching field and the river access into a corner of the site to be held in common. This took care of the equal sharing of resources, but we felt it wouldn't necessarily pull the homeowners together. That corner of the site was remote, and it was likely that it would rarely be visited. What we wanted was a way to activate the entire site while giving every home a special place in the community.

So we added further common land in the center of the site. While surveying we had discovered that the center of the site was the lowest (closest to water table) and therefore the least desirable for building. It was also the flattest and most appropriate for a common or playing field. All the remaining land was divided into 2-plus-acre lots. Each lot allowed a variety of house placements. This meant we could later fine-tune the degree of proximity and involvement each house had with the common land.

In short, we made decisions that moved us toward our design objectives without burning too many bridges. Since this process was completed over several years by numerous students, we were able to look very carefully at the consequences of each decision. A sensitivity to the entire site developed. This was particularly evident in the placement of the greenhouse used to treat the neighborhood sewage (Figure 16).

▏▏▏▏ Poop Plants

The local ski area had run out of leaching field for their ever-multiplying condominiums, and they were exploring different methods for on-site tertiary (meaning "total") sewage treatment. One of the methods studied was biological. Using a greenhouse, John Todd and some innovative ecologists created a simulation of pond and marsh conditions. After one year of intensive experimentation, they determined that you could take raw sewage and purify it completely using only plants and marsh biota. While this has been done elsewhere for years, doing it in Vermont's cold climate was new. Unfortunately, the state of Vermont was not impressed. So the ski area reluctantly installed a mandated chemical treatment plant. The greenhouse was disassembled and donated to Yestermorrow.

We did not share the state's reservations. Suffering from a miniature version of the ski area's plight—abused soils, inadequate leaching—we decided that the greenhouse should be installed at the

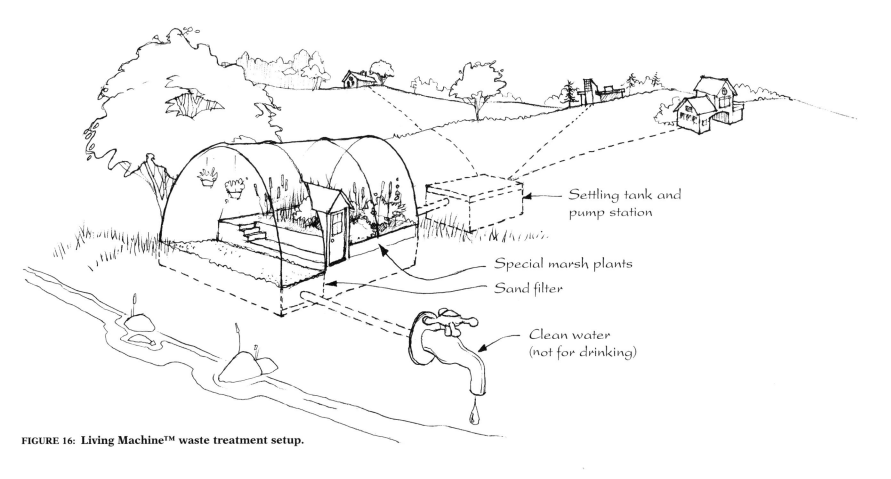

Settling tank and
pump station

Special marsh plants

Sand filter

Clean water
(not for drinking)

FIGURE 16: **Living Machine™ waste treatment setup.**

gravel pit as a demonstration of biological sewage treatment for a small subdivision. The question became where to site it.

Several students wanted to place it in the central common area and several wanted to place it by the leaching field. The different arguments revealed the subtleties of site selection.

At first we looked at five sites that were deemed possible. A Solar Path Finder was set up at each location to determine how much sun the greenhouse would receive throughout the year. Then some elevations were shot with a transit to determine where we would need effluent pumps. Some sites required more pumping than others. This data was easy to acquire and understand. It was just engineering, how much sun, how much elevation, distance from road, boundary, etc. The hard part came when we started to consider human behavior.

Placed in the central common land it was felt that the greenhouse would act as a focus for neighborhood activity, and few pumps would be needed. It would be easy to maintain and perhaps other community functions could be added: laundry, recycling bins, gardening tools, etc. But in this location very little direct sunlight would hit it between mid-October and mid-February.

The popular alternative was at the north end of the site. This had the best solar access and was closest to the leaching field. It was at the furthest end of the site from the entrance and would be unseen from any of the likely house locations. Indeed, it was quite out of the way. But was it too far? Several students thought that it was unfair to make some of the homeowners walk the entire length of the site while others would find the greenhouse relatively close. Yet this was unavoidably the case with the access to the river, which was also at this end of the site.

In the end we sited the greenhouse at the northern location. We realized that the siting of any greenhouse must be largely determined by what's good for the plants. If the plants don't thrive, the whole project becomes moot. The northernmost location provided the best solar exposure. Moreover, it was special in other ways. It bounded a huge meadow on our northern boundary and was right on the river. It was the logical place for the road, as it allowed the neighboring farmer access to his meadows. The same road would bring utilities to the greenhouse and allow vehicles to service it as needed. Rather than seeing this spot as out of the way, we started to see it as a destination. We came to realize that it would help activate the entire site. It became the reason for the road's existence. The greenhouse anchored the common area containing the leaching field and directed the circulation in the subdivision away from the condominiums, toward the open meadows to the north.

So this location became both a terminus and a transition point. It allowed our little community a sense of privacy and expansion. As a final test, we had picnic lunches there for six weeks. By the end of the summer, it felt just right.

The City

Cities and towns are energetic, stimulating, and entirely human alternatives to the natural countryside. Regardless of size, urban centers are always experiencing change: growth or decay. This continual evolution makes urban and suburban design more complicated. While you still have all the natural considerations (sun, wind, flowers, and fauna), they must now be understood in a context of manmade geometries—streets, codes, utilities, and municipal systems. Challenging they may be, but cities currently hold the most potential for the would-be home owner— Good Deals on older buildings. Moreover, densely settled cities are more environmentally sustainable than single-family homes spread all over the countryside on two- to five-acre plots.

While a city site involves all the issues found in the country, your priorities may be slightly shifted. For instance, neighbors become a more important site consideration when dwellings are closely spaced. Who will be your neighbors and for how long? Will your site compromise their privacy or will your privacy be compromised by them? This is sort of an urban corollary to the view issue in the country.

Urban views depend directly on height. Not the backyard view, of course, but the long view. Everyone wants to be higher than their neighbors. In the city you will be considering roof decks, widow walks, and cupolas. Because this is the natural reaction of anyone building in town, most cities have height regulations in their building codes. Better make a visit to the town hall.

Building codes in the city are always enforced and should be understood as initial design constraints. Their purpose is usually to protect your safety and also to provide a fair allocation of the city's resources. They will necessarily play a bigger role in your project than if you live in the country.

Another item that will play a larger role in your urban site planning is the road. Actually, automobiles will make an impact on your site design regardless of whether your project is in the city or the country. But in the city you will be closer to large numbers of cars. Traffic and the attendant noise are everywhere. Therefore, in the city, you must really deal with the street and its traffic. By locating your activities on the site cleverly, you may be able to block out much of the noise. Beyond this, however, you must provide parking or garage space for your own vehicle(s).

On the other hand, remember that public transportation can reduce or eliminate your need for a vehicle. If you locate within walking (or biking) distance of your work, you will save hundreds (possibly thousands!) of dollars each year, plus enjoy better health in the bargain. This same thinking applies to every aspect of city life. Proximity means Providence! If the perfect rural site is a south-facing slope with a view, the perfect urban counterpart must be a neighborhood with friends, markets, entertainment, and career opportunities all within walking distance.

One of the greatest qualities of any city is its history. People have been living there for generations and over time there have developed neighborhoods, parks, and special places. These constitute the urban terrain. These help establish a sense of place. History and neighborhoods. These are assets to be carefully considered in the siting of your new city home.

One last suggestion: We have quickly touched on many things that should be considered when designing your site. It may occur to you that a list of your priorities would be helpful. Indeed it would:

Dream List

1. lawn
2. side yard
3. pool
4. 2-acre garden
5.
6.

Whoa! Lists are helpful but they must be made with care and thought. Don't list *things*. List activities and adjectives. If you make a list of things, then you reduce your design process to a shopping list. Things are often symbols for personal goals. Fortunately, there are many ways to attain most goals. If you like gardening, don't simply assume that you will need a 2-acre garden. If you like swimming, don't immediately place an Olympic pool on your list. Instead, make a list of things you like doing and the qualities you feel life should have:

Dream List (take 2):

1. I enjoy working around the yard.
2. We all enjoy gardening and raising our own vegetables.
3. I like swimming. The whole family is athletic.
4. We like privacy, but we also like to socialize with our neighbors.
5. We are formal and want a formal front yard.
6. We enjoy cookouts, touch football, washing the car, building Fourth of July floats, napping, riding bikes, bringing up children, dogs, animals.
7. ???
8. ???

The point is to identify the *activities* that make up your notion of the good life. Then, in a manner consistent with a few real constraints (like your budget, codes, etc.), provide for them on your site and in your house. For instance, numbers 1 and 2 can be accommodated on a very small suburban lot or on a very large country meadow. In the city, a greenhouse or a community garden might give some satisfaction. Similarly, number 3 can be accomplished by building a lap pool and exercise room, or . . . joining the YMCA (at great savings!). Be creative in solving your design problems. Be openminded. Don't limit your design solutions to those expensive, resource-intensive ones you see in the architecture magazines.

At this point, I urge you to grab tracing paper and site plan, set up a drafting table in the busiest place in your household (to guarantee input), put on your favorite music and set out to discover your site design. The helical character of the design process will bring you back to this juncture several times, so don't feel you have to get everything right the first time. On this cycle we have yet to consider your lifestyle or building requirements. These will

undoubtedly modify any initial design decisions you make concerning the site. Still, you have to have *a starting place*, something to bounce off of. No design arrives full-blown and perfect from the designer's creative depths. So chose a house site, lay out a driveway, plant a garden, set up a tennis court . . . and don't forget to locate the well and septic field. Then cycle, cycle, cycle.

THE PROGRAM

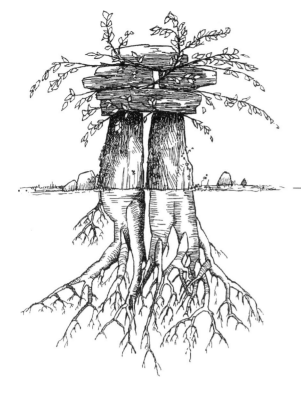

The Endless Questions

It's time to proceed with the Design Helix. Having completed an initial look at the site, we now move to the star of our story—you, and your family. In this section we will consider some basic questions that will help you better clarify *what you want*. This is an extremely important phase in the design work. It is where we establish the program for your house.

The "program" is architect jargon for "definition of the problem." Everyone knows that once a problem is adequately defined, it's already half solved. This is especially true when seeking a design solution for your house. It's such a multi-leveled puzzle and there are always many alternatives for each issue. A successful design solution must be physically durable, structurally stable, affordable, beautiful, environmentally sound, sensitively sited, and, above all—tailored to your every special need. All of these issues together comprise the program.

Although no two programs are identical, all house programs will address similar issues. That's why those plan books found in the grocery store are so popular. But as a budding design/builder, you must foreswear any such cookie-cutter approach and develop your own program. Yours will be tailored, not off the rack. To have a custom home, the first thing you must build is a custom program.

There are many ways to collect all the questions and issues to be considered; by far the most common is the questionnaire. Page upon page of questions will usually get you to think about all the issues and considerations that make the perfect house for you. Some of these questions are big: How will you heat and cool your house? Others are small: What color will the toilets be? Some are objective: How far will 2 × 12s* on 12″ centers span if there's a waterbed on the second floor? Others are subjective: Which side of the bed do you get up on? But, as we all know, there are *no* stupid questions.

Experience has shown that most people are more forthcoming with objective requirements. It's easier to specify the boiler capacity than it is to describe your tendency to get a chill. It's easier to say the kitchen must be 10′ × 20′ than it is to explain how you hate having everyone crowded in the kitchen when you're trying to cook. Many people feel that articulating a string of personal requests sounds selfish. Instead, they accept what's available and then maybe complain or whine a little.

Well now hear this all you long-suffering would-be-selfish future owner/builders: Programming means asking yourself what *you* want! Designing and building a house is like making a portrait, a *self*-portrait, in this case. You have got to be selfish. That's the whole point. A house is about the Self. Your house should be a

---

* When lumber sizes appear without unit dimensions, i.e., 2 × 4, 2 × 6, 2 × 8, 2 × 12, etc., they are nominal only. Nominal dimensions refer to the approximate unfinished sizes of lumber as it is initially sawn from the log. After planing and finishing all modern lumber is actually smaller than its nominal designation. A 2 × 12, for instance, actually measures 1½″ × 11¼″.

When lumber is designated with unit dimensions, it represents the true size. For instance a 2″ × 12″ is actually a full 2″ × 12″ in size, while a 2 × 12 is actually 1½ × 12¼.

customized stage set for the drama of your life. You are the director and all the actors (along with your family and friends, of course). There's no reward for hiding your light under a bush in this endeavor. And no professional should be called in to answer these questions for you. Designing your own house means *taking control of your life*. After all, that's what will be going on in this house you are designing. Some of the questions may be difficult, maybe never before considered. Fine, pluck up some courage and get ready for the ultimate adventure! What could be more fun than finding out how you want to live?

Since there are so many questions, and the difficult ones seem to get placed on the back burner, I have separated them out for first consideration. I call the five questions that follow "The Endless Questions." If you haven't considered these, there's little use in going on to any questionnaire. Questionnaires focus mostly on the details. (I know architects say "God is in the details," but She is also in the Big Moves.) The Big Architecture must come from the Big Questions.

Profound answers will not always turn up at the instant you ask a question. So get a pad and a small tape measure that you can keep with you at all times. As you go through your daily life, stay conscious, observe, and take notes!

Now then, you're going to love these questions. Such questions we should ask ourselves everyday. But we rarely make

the time. So even before students arrive at Yestermorrow, they're asked to consider:

- Who are you? Who would you like to be?
- How do you currently live?
- How would you prefer to live?
- What kind of world will you have, (today, and for your children)?
- What is your budget? (less cosmic but very important)
- What is your schedule?

This kind of intimate stuff makes many folks nervous. Good residential design unavoidably begs some heavy questions.

At Yestermorrow we quickly realized that we must establish a protected environment in which students can safely explore these questions. We organized studios where student designers were supported in their personal inquiries.

Who Are You?

Certain questions, such as, What is Art? and, Is there a God? can never be permanently answered. They must be asked again and again with the answer evolving a bit each time. So it is with the first and most important question in designing a house: "Who are you?"

Responding to this question will impact your final design in profound ways that go well beyond your favorite wall color or floor tile. The answers to this query won't come from a book or instructor or professional. They must come from you. So ask yourself honestly: How do you think of yourself? Are you conservative or adventuresome? Do you seek ultimate convenience or is ceremony just as important? Are you a socializer or a homebody? Do you like country or city life? What's your favorite time of the day? of the year? Virtually anything you know about yourself can be expressed in the architecture.

In addition to the present-day influence on your home design, remember also that the many answers to this question will likely change as your life unfolds. Are you single? married? employed? retired? environmentally concerned? politically indifferent? "Who are you?" is one of those questions that is never permanently answered. By embracing the roles of architect and general contractor, the owner/builder maintains the unique ability to modify his house even as his lifestyle changes.

Beyond questions of taste, there will be an examination of standards and values. How much and where will you compromise quality when the cost must be reduced? What will you do when you find a fragile ecosystem where you wanted to put your leaching field? Will you use toxic materials in the construction? How about endangered wood species? What's your feeling about union labor? Will you pay workers under the table? Should you have a security system? Will you allow your in-laws to visit? Ultimately, designing a house reveals who you are by the constellation of answers given to the many questions associated with making that house a reality.

> Some people will decide everything to accommodate future resale.
> Others will respond to every decision with, "Whatever is cheapest."
> Many insist on whatever is traditional, normal, or "correct".

If you make decisions based on what everyone else does, perhaps that's who you are. But I don't think so. People who design and build their own place are never that bland.

A note here before we go on to the other questions. As I use the word "you" I mean you *and your family*. Your family may be a goldfish or it may be a spouse, six kids, and a herd of turtles. Whatever the details, your family is everyone living in and around your house. The program must address everyone's needs, not just yours. So, while considering these questions, don't forget your roommates.

How Do You Currently Live?

Most people shoehorn their lives into whatever they can find or afford. They don't understand that they can take control. One of the simple but important goals of Yestermorrow's design training is to increase students' awareness. Understanding the effects of our built environment helps us take control on a number of different levels. Simply changing a room's color or rearranging the furniture can make a big difference. Going further, one might install a window or door, remove a wall or add a skylight. Bigger changes will have more dramatic results.

It's important to figure out which parts of your current living situation help your preferred lifestyle, and which ones hamper it. Study your current situation carefully. Are you living around your furniture and in spite of the room layout? Does the kitchen work well with the dining area? What is the typical sequence of events when you welcome a guest into your home? How about when you bring in the groceries? Are your stairs in the right location? Do you like your bedroom? Why? What's the lighting like in the different rooms? How about the acoustics? If you could move one or two rooms, which would they be and why? Could you better use your attic, basement, garage? Imagine moving any door or window in the house.

Now go outside. How many ugly places can you find about the house? What's your favorite part of the architecture? What's different since the last time you took a careful look? If you could change the relationship between the car and the house, how would you do it?

When taking control of your built surroundings, it's important not to throw the baby out with the bath. While finding what doesn't work in your house, don't forget to inventory what does. There are likely to be some very successful configurations in your current living situation. Look for them. And don't just limit your observations to your own place. Start looking at other houses. Look for design solutions and architectural preferences. Becoming conscious of architecture is the first step toward making your own.

How Would You Prefer to Live?

This one question is really what it's all about. But it's not just one question; it's a whole inquiry. There are hundreds of questions that need to be answered to fully describe how you want to live. Some of the answers are more important than others, but they all contribute. So how do we know which questions to ask? How do we give them the right emphasis? Well, there are several ways to find your way through the endless questions.

One of the best can be found in Charles Moore's *The Place of Houses*. In the chapter entitled "Yours" he suggests one possible way of listing all the many considerations that must go into defining how you want to live.

> The answers you make will not define a "plan" for your house. They will serve instead as a test to check against the ways there are of assembling rooms and machine domains and fitting them to the site. Inevitably there will be conflicts, which you can resolve in favor of whatever is more important to you. There will also be ambiguities, which you can cherish if you are of a mind to. But don't cheat on the choices, or take shortcuts. The fruit of shortcuts is stereotype.

The paths of things and of people and of the mind's eye, then, we shall list as:

Water
Air
Paper
Food
Dishes and other cooking utensils
Clothing and linen
Electricity
Dirt
Cars
Other objects
Adults
Children
Invited guests
Service people
The uninvited
Pets
Images

Moore follows this first list with a series of questions and choices representing the typical issues associated with each area. Where does water come from? Where is it used? Where does it go? Where does the dirt come from? Where does it go? What happens when a car arrives or departs? What do children and adults do together? apart? Where do they do it? As you can imagine, this list can become quite elaborate and detailed. Then it becomes a master list of things to be considered and designed for as you move around the Design Helix. While neither the master list nor the sublists should be considered exhaustive, they help you cover a lot of area in an orderly fashion.

As an alternative method, one of our instructors conducts a classwide brainstorming session. This is a little less orderly, but it sure gets things moving. Students yell out issues and considerations that will affect the way they want to live.

> I want to eliminate all heating bills! Yeah, and all maintenance! I want a widow's walk! A tower! A fireplace! I don't want to see anyone else's house from mine. I want a stream in my living room . . .

Nothing is excluded or disallowed. Negative commentary is not permitted. Each suggestion is written down on one of several large newsprint pads arranged around the studio. This is a lot of fun and very loud. As the students get into it there can be as many as three instructors feverishly writing down suggestions. After the brainstorm, the class collectively sorts and arranges the different considerations into categories and subcategories. In this way, fifteen individuals from all walks of life contribute to a master checklist that anyone could use to help organize their program.

Program requirements can include everything from the number of pegs in your coatroom to the feeling of privacy you require while communing with Nature. It need not be limited to a formulaic checklist of rooms and functions. Properly done, programming will include feelings, images, and personal preferences.

Just to get you started, let me list a few instances of very personal designs that I have come across:

- Many people include a special tree, rock, or other item from their lives. I have seen whole cars built permanently into peoples' homes.
- Hidden equipment is common. The TV or stereo that can be folded or slid back into the woodwork. Ours is hidden in the side of the chimney.
- Secret compartments and passageways come up from time to time. These are particularly popular among families with several children. I've designed a secret wine closet for one client.
- In the bathroom there are many opportunities. One of my clients designed all the tile. In the shower stall she arranged small mosaics so that they outline a man and a woman taking a shower together. The effect is striking when the translucent door is closed.
- Or consider the loft owner who really wanted to roller-skate when he returned home at night. He left out all the walls and eliminated all bumps in the floor. This meant that the marble shower floor was 14′ square to catch any splash. Also, it had to be flush with the hard maple flooring so that he could roller-skate through the shower stall when not in use.

- While we're on the shower, one of our clients by the ocean had us etch an underwater seascape on her shower door.
- When I tiled my own shower, I installed tile-size mirrors at the perfect height for each member of the family.
- Height is important. Frank Lloyd Wright was short and so all his designs had relatively low ceiling heights. He was heard to joke, "I've never met anyone taller than six feet."
- I like to take a client's measurements before designing their fireplace mantle. This allows them to lean on it comfortably while standing by the fire.
- Often the house itself becomes the personalizing image. I will always remember eating at a table where the floor plan had been carved into the tabletop. I've also seen the floor plan made into placemats. This is great fun for the kids. I've gone so far as to design a light fixture in the shape of the house I did for one client.
- Then there was the couple who asked for a pull-down map of the world in their kitchen. They liked to review different travel possibilities while eating. Apparently it was down constantly during the war in the Middle East.

- The knobs, hooks, and handles throughout the house are always fun to play with. A car enthusiast I know used hood ornaments for his cabinet pulls. Another used hammer handles. I've seen regular wooden knobs carved with initials or faces. Indeed, the builders who helped Wharton Esherick build his home carved their faces on the coat pegs by the back door.
- Faces are always great. My students cast their faces into the concrete foundation of one of our buildings at the school.
- Windows and glazing offer additional possibilities. Stained or leaded glass allows customized emblems or images. One design/builder I know included a glass slide of the family and their house within the actual stained-glass composition. Another one of our instructors double-glazed the windows in his childrens' room with little plastic animals between the inner and outer panes of glass.
- Storage and display are natural opportunities. I've seen more than a few model railroads built into the walls of enthusiasts. Collections of toys, rocks, coins, etc., can be displayed in double-function built-ins. A room divider won't seem contrived if it holds a fascinating collection of some sort.

- For raw storage, I was intrigued with a solution one of our instructors came up with: the attic drawer. He built an affordable house that can be disassembled and moved. This meant it lacked a basement and an attic. But the living room was three steps up (24″) from the entry level. So he built a massive drawer on wheels under the entire room. The stairs are connected to the front of the drawer. All the deep storage goes in this drawer.

- On a smaller scale, I have always lacked space to work at my desk comfortably. It's a secretary style, and even a moderately sized side table didn't solve the problem. So I designed and built a foldout drop-leaf table that I could attach to the adjacent wall. It makes a beautiful pattern against the wall when not in use and it affords me a large work space for those really intense bill-paying sessions.

- Customized built-ins range from little items like chess or backgammon tables, to really large items like projectors and screens. I know of at least one living room where a flick of the switch will bring down a screen, open a projector window, and bring up the sound! More useful, if less glamorous, are the many descendants from the original (and still available) Murphy bed. In addition to foldout beds, you can now have foldout ironing boards, tables, stools, food processors, etc.

Just for completeness, I have included another questionnaire in the appendix. Again, it is hardly exhaustive. It combines some of Charles Moore's approach with Yestermorrow's brainstorming technique. It's organized around the three points on the Design Helix. I encourage the reader to think of it as a starting place. Add or delete questions to suit your own particular situation. Also under consideration here are qualities—ephemeral qualities—the sort that make all the difference in the backdrop against which your life is cast. A house can take on the values, hopes, ethics, beliefs, memories, and even fears of the design/builder. I've called your house a self-portrait. Using that metaphor, then, we're now concerned with the quality of light in the painting. The implications of where it's hung or how it was executed, the mood of the subject and the artist, the time of day, the weather, and so many other intangibles, all subtly present in the final effect.

▌ What Kind of World Will You Have?

When making a house, the opportunities for this kind of expression are fantastically rich. You can literally make a world where things are exactly as you wish. Design and build your house to reflect your values, your ethics, your style, and your time. Make the very process reflect the world you wish. Design allows you to make your house a world where your deepest beliefs and values are the final word. A few examples:

- *Religious Values:* One of the best examples of designing for religious values is the Kosher kitchen maintained by orthodox Jews. Or, perhaps the front hall is designed around your Christmas tree. A special altar place can be provided for religious ceremonies or a room might be specially designed for meditation or practicing yoga.

- *Family Values:* Your home can be designed to maintain memories and reinforce personalities that might be lost in a less personal residence. If you have children, initials and names are a great way to personalize a house. Kids love a chair or stool with their name on it. Why not a stained glass window or coat hook or a tile in the bathroom wall? And don't forget the annual marking of their heights at some special doorway or corner. Remember also the gallery of photos, a museum of mementos, a sculpture or marker in the woods or even a simple bench along a special garden path. There are no limits to the opportunities for imbuing your world with a sense of the extended family.

- *Environmental Values:* Walk your talk is what the environmentalists say. Design a house that doesn't use excessive energy, pollute the groundwater, or employ toxic materials. Use only local materials and local trades. Employ water conservation measures and separate your gray water. Design an easy-to-use recycling center into your kitchen. Compost. Design for sustainable living.
- *Animal Lover:* Your design can easily express your commitment to the animal kingdom. Design special doorways, provide feeding stations or protected habitat, allow for easy access to the bed!
- *Historic Preservation:* If your passion is history, you can go much further than just renovating an old house. Besides using authentic materials and architectural detailing, you can actually build using old-fashion methods. Each room might reflect a different period. If it's the politics that are important, express the class and power struggles by letting the representative detailing clash.

A Warm-Up Exercise

At Yestermorrow students often are asked to design and build a scale model of just one room. The room is meant to be the result of a very narrow, one-word description such as: private, happy, focused, protected, scared, serene, eternal, etc. After the students have completed the rooms they exchange them with another student. Then each must alter the nature of the room using as few changes as possible. This exercise is meant to acquaint the students with the power of architectural design in determining mood, ambience, and emotional environment.

Quoting again from Charles Moore's *The Place of Houses:*

> A house is in delicate balance with its surroundings, and they with it.
> A good house is a created thing made of many parts economically and meaningfully assembled. It speaks not just of the materials from which it is made, but of the intangible rhythms, spirits, and dreams of people's lives. Its site is only a tiny piece of the real world, yet this place is made to seem like an entire world. In its parts it accommodates important human activities, yet in sum it expresses an attitude toward life.

Whether you are renovating an apartment in the city or master planning a dozen acres in the country, you are making *your own world.* Start thinking of it that way. Everything should flow from your attitudes about life and living. If play is to be part of your world, you must include it in the initial program. Celebrate the joy, sorrows, and history of *your* life in the special custom world you are designing. Make it personal.

The next question has to do with money, the big bad budget. It's important to address the first questions before this one. If you never list and prioritize all the intangible aspects of your ideal world, you may never know them. Budgets have a way of putting wonderful worlds on a diet. Most people forget to dream. Fortunately, a house lasts a long time. If you can't have everything you want right away, perhaps you can have the most important things first. Having made a list, you'll be able to plan for the rest when money permits.

What Is Your Budget?

When you design your own place, you should consider the sun, the moon, and everything between. However, if this process is to have any hope of bearing fruit, it must be grounded in the reality of your personal resources. Notice I didn't say simply "money." In establishing your budget, there are considerations that go beyond the simple question of how much money you have.

It's really no good saying, "Gee, I don't have enough for what I want." No one does; that is the nature of "wanting." Yet everyone has a budget of resources. To varying extents, everyone is capable of shaping what they have into a world that best reflects their lives. The trick needn't turn on having more. Rather, it's knowing what to do with what you have. Budgeting is the process of looking at your resources and figuring out how you want to use them.

Right off the bat you resolve to stretch your available resources as far as possible. Naturally. So what are these resources? A typical list:

- money (some)
- time (some)
- inspiration (lots)
- energy (lots)
- enthusiasm (endless)
- materials (depends)
- and friends (some)

This is truly an embarrassment of wealth, but it may not be much money. If you are to make it go the distance, you must plan for its use very carefully. This planning is all part of the design process and, remember, the design process is driven by the program.

Architectural design has earned a reputation for being very expensive. There are reasons for this. But actually it is the architects (the professionals) who are expensive, not the architecture. And I don't mean their fees. Architectural design is very much a matter of intention. If you (not an architect) are designing your house, there is no reason why it has to be designed overbudget. Indeed, the tighter your budget, the more design and planning you should employ. Most architects agree that a tight budget often produces better architecture.

Whether or not you are using a professional, architectural design is always a good investment. Paper and cardboard are always cheaper than bricks and mortar. No matter how much it costs to draw up an idea that you may ultimately discard, it is still less expensive than if you start building it and then discover it's wrong. Moreover, if you don't first explore a design on paper, you can't really know what it will take to build. Without a list of materials and a schedule of construction you run the very real risk of exceeding your resources.

Now, let's consider your time budget. If you are an internationally famous brain surgeon, it may not make good fiscal sense for you to spend your time hammering nails. On the other hand, it might make excellent spiritual sense. Nevertheless, let's be hard-nosed for a minute. While it's not very humane, every person working on your project can be seen as an hourly cost. If you earn more per hour than the person being hired, says conventional logic, it makes more sense for you to keep going to your job and hire someone else to provide the service needed. If you make less or about the same as the trade in question (e.g., I think plumbers make about the same as brain surgeons), it might make sense for you to take some time off from work and help build your house.

In reality, this question isn't entirely arithmetic. You may choose to get involved in certain parts of your house project just because that's what you want to do. Many, many people design and build their own homes despite the fact that they could easily afford to have it done for them.

There are other contributions that may be made to your budget of resources. Friends are perhaps the biggest. Building a house is pretty exciting. Also, it's the fastest way to learn how to build. If you let the word out that you're planning to build and need some help, it won't be long before you have a crew. These may not be the people to do the finish carpentry, but there's plenty of building that can be done by the novice. Vernacular methods—timber frame, straw bale, cob, etc.—require loads of voluntary labor to be affordable. Also, don't forget any friends you may have in the trades. Sometimes you can barter for your plumbing or roofing. I know at least one situation where singing lessons were traded for a kitchen.

While taking inventory of your resources, don't forget materials. The ancient vernacular building methods—adobe, timber frame, cob, thatch, straw bale, log, and so on—are all characterized by use of locally available materials. Do you have timber or stone on your land? In many parts of the country the soil may be right for making adobe or cob. Straw bale construction has been successfully used in every state. Along with inexpensive, locally available materials, these vernacular technologies presume a robust community of cheap labor. Remember, family and friends are your first wealth.

Some sites come with old or abandoned buildings. These may have timber or other materials of significant value. Also, don't forget salvage. The popularity of old doors or windows can be seen in the numerous salvage shops sprouting up around the country. You needn't pay their high prices, though. Talk to renovators in your area. Ask if they know of places where you might pick up some old building parts. Check the classifieds. I've seen windows, doors, bathtubs, toilets, floorboards, roofing—almost anything imaginable—in the classifieds. Invariably the price is low. People are usually trying to clean out their garage or shop. Often they will give stuff away just to get it out of the way.

When preparing your budget, count all your resources, not just your money. You're likely to be more wealthy than you thought.

Conclusion

This completes the short list of Endless Questions. It's likely you will be pondering them for the rest of your life. They will be your most reliable guide as you navigate the adventure of making your own place.

"But," protests the student, "what about which window to use? and, 'Should I build post and beam or platform frame?' also, 'Which is better, hydronic or forced air heat?' and—'How do I do all this the best way?'"

Yes, there are a lot of difficult choices still to make. There will be alternatives, debate, and compromise. What's perfect in one situation may be totally wrong in another. There will be technical considerations that can't be resolved just by knowing "what kind of world I want," or "who I would like to be." Yes, but having considered these big questions, you are much better able to address all the little decisions that will add up to your design. When difficult choices come up, the attitude and values revealed by your answers to the Endless Questions should keep you on track.

In the next chapter we will describe how to make a visual diagram of your answer to these and other inquiries. You are well on your way to having a personal program for the design of your house.

Do you still have that pad and tape measure?

Good.

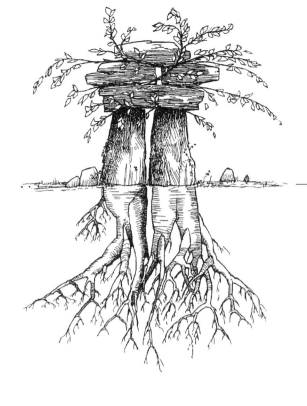

Bubbles and Storyboards: Diagramming Your Program

At this point we want to make a visual diagram of your program. Your pad should be full of observations about the way you and your family want to live. Some of these may take the form of complaints with your current home, others will be dreams for the future. Your personal program should outline your needs, attitudes, biases, and values. In numbers, charts, schedules, and lists you should see only requirements that reflect who you are, how you want to live, and what kind of world you intend to create. If your pad looks like a hopeless mess, you've proba-

bly done a thorough job. People's lives tend to be untidy. A one-page typed list suggests that you may have overlooked some of the issues in the last chapter. Reread it and then cycle back. Remember that the design process always cycles back on itself.

This next phase on the helix, Diagramming Your Design, falls between the program phase and the final design phase. Diagramming is the first effort to arrange all the program activities in real space; the diagrams are still very rough and flexible; we aren't yet dealing with joists and

plumbing. Remember that the design process moves from the largest issues toward the smallest. We are still trying to give relative locations to everything in your program, i.e., your life.

Above all, remember that the entire diagramming procedure must take place against the background of your site plan. If you are using bubbles, they should be arranged right on the site plan. Compass orientation, weather, and other site characteristics are very important when diagramming your house. For the most part, they tend to be nonnegotiable. If you want to wake up early, you better place your bedrooms to the east. If you like to cook outside, you'll place the kitchen close to the backyard. Most sites have a "best view" which may determine where the living room, dining room, or study is located. On an urban site, the location of the street often organizes everything else in the building. Even neighbors (good and bad) need to be considered when organizing your design.

Remember that many important activities take place outdoors. As you're diagramming, think about the spaces next to your house as "outdoor rooms." A barbecuing or gardening area needs to be indicated as clearly as the dining area. Where will you wash the car? Play horseshoes? Have your daughter's wedding? When you're diagramming, the building's walls do not constrain you. Diagramming focuses on behavior, not building.

With your site plan and program near at hand, get comfortable at your drafting table. There are several ways to approach the diagramming of your program. For example, at Yestermorrow we often use "bubble" diagrams. Simply draw a circle, or bubble, for each activity in your program (see Figure 17). Each bubble is sized in proportion to the needs or importance of the activity. Arrange the bubbles so that related activities overlap or share common boundaries.

Bubble diagrams are good for dia-

gramming spaces and understanding juxtapositions. They are hierarchical. The bigger or more important the activity, the bigger you make the bubble. If you want your dining room next to the kitchen, you place the appropriate bubbles next to one another. If two activities share the same space (e.g., dining room and living room), simply overlap the two bubbles.

By cutting out the bubbles with scissors you can quickly experiment with different arrangements. These diagrams allow you to see your program priorities at a glance. It's very fast, so you can discover a lot quickly. Don't settle on the first successful diagram. Keep experimenting. At Yestermorrow, this is the most popular approach, but there are certainly others.

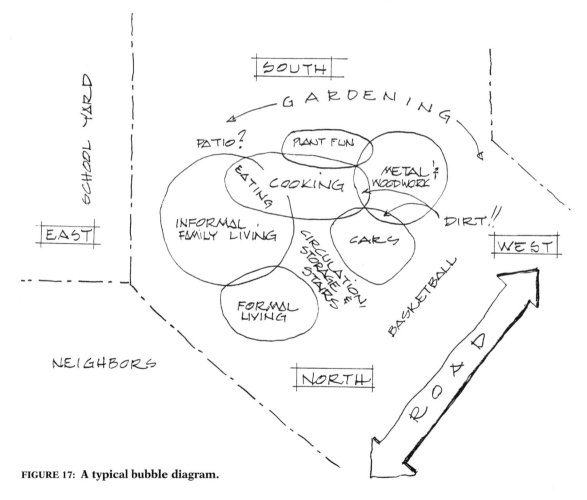

FIGURE 17: A typical bubble diagram.

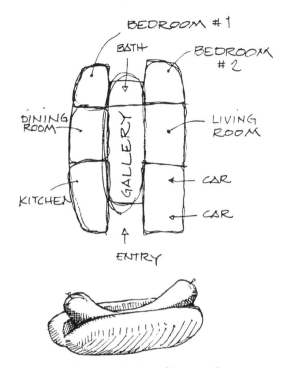

FIGURE 18: An organization diagram that uses a hotdog as the metaphor.

Metaphorical Diagrams use the essential organization of something else to establish an initial order for the building's program (Figures 18 and 19). When I was in architecture school I had a teacher who always analyzed design schemes using food metaphors.

"Ah, I see you're working on a 'hot dog' scheme. Very interesting. Don't forget to consider the symmetry of the bun and the importance of the hot dog's skin. With the right attention, this could really start to look like architecture." Then he would go to the next desk and I would overhear:

"So you're working on a lollipop scheme, I see. Well, don't overemphasize the stick. By the way, have you considered the Tootsie Roll pop as an organizing metaphor? It's very strong."

Kidding aside, metaphors of this sort can organize a complex program very quickly. The trick is to use a widely understood object for the metaphor. Hot dogs only come one way and everyone knows what it is. This arrangement allows a quick understanding of your design. However, if you use a vacuum cleaner as the organizing metaphor, little will be accomplished. Vacuum cleaners come in so many different types and styles that there are very few common denominators, and those aren't very useful. (They all suck dirt into bags?) Other proven metaphorical diagrams include fried eggs, BLT sand-

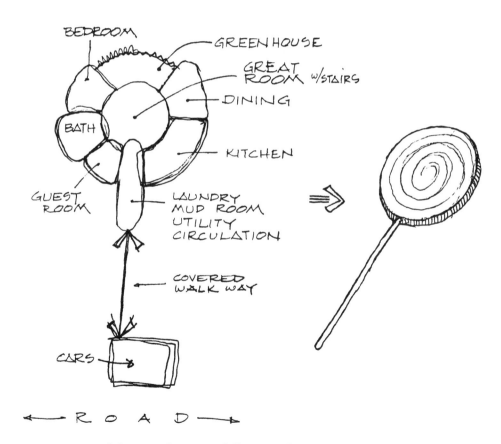

FIGURE 19: An organizational diagram that uses a lollipop as the metaphor.

wich, a hinge, a bridge, trees, geodes, and many others.

My favorite metaphor uses the human body as the organizer. Activities of mind or spirit are located up under the roof (attic), in the "head." Activities of the family are organized around the hearth, or "heart." I like the sun in my face, so I orient the front of the house to the south. My face is public, but what's behind my back is private. So this is how I arrange the front and rear yards and associated entries.

Finally, a nongraphical organizing method, the Storyboard Diagram, uses narration or a series of stories to organize the many requirements of your program. For example:

> "When I arrive at my house, I drive into the garage. As I get out of the car I can see the garden through the windows next to the doorway to the kitchen. Inspired by the fresh basil, I enter and go directly to my cookbooks. Sitting in the breakfast nook I scan the different recipes while the afternoon sun warms my back. At about this time the kids come home from school. They come in through the side door that leads to the patio. Because of the way the kitchen is laid out, they naturally end up at the counter. This is good because it keeps them out of my way. More importantly, it sets up a nice little situation where I can still work in the kitchen while they are telling me about the day's adventures. I serve them their afternoon snack."

Though essentially verbal, storyboard diagrams can be depicted graphically. Imagine a comic strip or a series of stage sets for your stories. Since most homes present several different stories on different occasions, this method of diagramming is a good way to test out different preliminary designs.

Right now I want to ask—pop quiz!— What is the point here? Why not just start experimenting with floor layouts? Must we play these games? The answer lies in the considerable complexity of building any house. Even a simple wall involves many considerations. Is it an interior or exterior wall? Insulated? Load bearing? What is the stud spacing? How about windows? How high are the headers? What about mechanicals? And code minimums? On and on it goes. With some spaces you could handle all of these considerations even while sorting out your programming requirements—but not many. Generally, it's just too much. If you start that way, you will soon be designing your kitchen to keep the plumbing runs aligned. You may size your bedroom so the floor joists can be 2 × 8s. Windows and doors will be placed to match stud spacing, and garage placement will be determined by the cost of asphalt. This is *not* the way to design a house. Yes, eventually you must work out all the technical requirements of your house. But not yet. If you start with every single consideration all at the same time, you will be overwhelmed. Worse, the specific hard-edged requirements of the technologies will likely eclipse the softer-edge human needs represented in the program.

Desperate to make sense of all this, you will likely fall back on whatever is easiest and cheapest for the technologies at hand. This is no way to organize your life!

So then, quick review. Your program should outline all the needs and wants that must be accommodated by your design. The program describes the contents, not the container. The diagram organizes the program so we can better think about the container. Once the program is organized in an appropriate diagram, we can easily figure out how to build the container. The strength of diagrams lies in their simplicity. This simplicity allows you to explore the best arrangement for your life-style on your particular site.

Diagramming a program is one of the more difficult things to describe with words. It's the sort of thing that really needs guided work in a studio. So, with that disclaimer in place, the following examples are meant to give the reader a taste of how different diagramming techniques might evolve. Let's start with bubbles:

Step 1

First I make an exhaustive attempt to answer the Endless Questions posed in the previous chapter. These may not tell me which floor tile to use in the bathroom, but they give me an excellent insight into my ultimate design goals.

WHO AM I? (ARE WE?)

I'm part of a family. I'm an experimenter. I like to try new things. She likes security. We like tradition and ceremony. We want the things we make to last. I love art over efficiency. She loves nature and the environment above everything. We like people, but need our own private spaces.

HOW DO WE CURRENTLY LIVE?

The previous owner renovated my house to be rental space for skiers and tourists. We hate the cheap finishes and poorly laid out circulation. We hate the kitchen. We're living in a building designed to make money, not house a family. The backyard is the best part of the property, but there is hardly any access to it.

HOW WOULD WE LIKE TO LIVE?

We want a place where we can raise a family. I want to set up a stage that makes our lives special, dramatic. I would like to work at home. She would rather not. We want our children to think of this as a reliable point from which to navigate. We hope they come back from time to time, with friends.

We will make a place for gatherings of friends. Also, there will be a place for a garden and some animals. The front of our house should express our membership and support of the community. The back of our house will be private.

WHAT KIND OF WORLD WILL I MAKE?

We want to make this house demonstrate the way we hope the world is headed. We will build this house from nontoxic, sustainable materials. We will heat it with renewable fuels. Independent of budget constraints, we will endeavor to keep the size of the structure as small and resource-efficient as possible. We will express exuberance for life (biodiversity), family (community) and art in the aesthetic of this house. Above all else, I want the house to accommodate adventure and fresh thinking. My world should never be predictable. Above all else, she wants the house to be a secure home.

WHAT IS MY BUDGET?

It's smaller than we need to accomplish everything at once. Still, I have an existing building to work with. I can phase in the construction. I have many friends in the trades and I have stockpiled some building materials over the years. This process may take several years. I will plan not to borrow any money until the end is in sight.

(Of course, these are summary answers merely to be used as examples. Yours should be much more deeply considered and everyone in the family should be involved.)

‖ Step 2

With the Endless Questions considered, I'm now ready to get down to more detail. Using the Site Questionnaire in Appendix 1, I develop several pages of options and preferences. These are freewheeling lists. I don't need to put them in any order or refer to any physical geometry. The important thing is that all the answers are consistent with our answers to the Endless Questions.

‖ Step 3

Ah. Now the good stuff! Looking at my program lists I see that, for me, the most important activities will center around "cross-generational socialization!" That means hanging out with the kids. O.K., so I draw my first and biggest bubble, labeling it "big kids with little kids."

The next two activities include art objects and eating. These are both important when hanging around with kids, so the next two bubbles are placed contiguous to the "kids with kids" bubble. Maybe they overlap. Eating and cooking sometimes occur outdoors, so I keep that in mind as I proceed.

Sports almost always occur outdoors (at my house), so it makes sense to place that bubble close to the outdoors side of the cooking/eating bubble. Because sports always take a lot of space, that bubble is drawn large. In my mind's eye, I see it taking up most of the backyard. A glance at my site map and I can start to see the different activities laid out on the site (Figure 20).

‖ Step 4

The bubbling of my life continues until I have a noodley shape or line for every aspect of a typical day. Then I do it over again. Usually I make about ten tries. If you've never done this before, you should give yourself about thirty tries. This is particularly important if you are a couple or

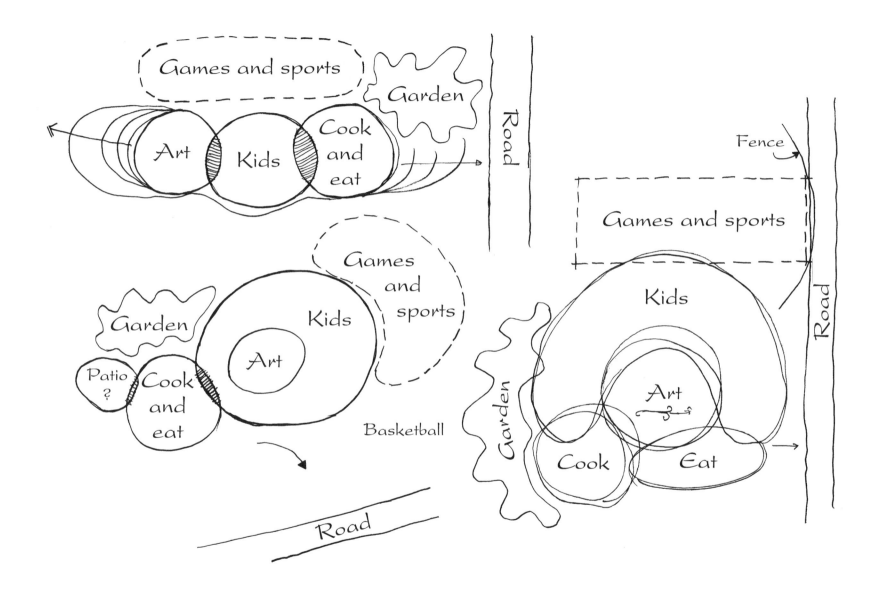

FIGURE 20: **Three different bubble diagrams that reflect my answers to "the endless questions."**

family. This phase of the design work will have ramifications all the way through the project; even after it's finished and you've moved in. You're laying out your life; don't rush it.

As the bubble diagram develops, it should start to include physical information. Imagine laying out your life on the ground plane of your actual site. You could borrow one of those boundary markers used to lay out athletic fields. Running around in circles, white powder everywhere, you could get a full-scale idea of how you would configure your life on your site. This may seem silly, but I've done almost the same thing using stakes and string. The results were very enlightening!

Step 5

The last step is review. Discuss your bubbles with the family, your friends, anyone who will listen. Garner opinions, debate, discuss. This is still a very inexpensive process. Attention here can save you thousands of dollars in later change orders. At Yestermorrow we call these "crits"—short for critiques. Each student gets a personal crit from an architect who tries to really "shake" the diagram. This helps each student produce his or her best bubbles.

This almost completes the quick example of one way to diagram your life. What's left? To cycle back to your program. What did the diagramming process remind you

to include in your program? Redo your program and then redo the diagram. Cycle, cycle, cycle.

Well, what do you think? Does this make sense? Are bubbles going to work for you? They work for most people, but not all. If you're thinking: "This is stupid. I'm not getting it," then maybe you should consider another way of diagramming your activities. I've had students say, "Look, I'm just not that graphically inclined. I don't see things that way, in bubbles. Can't I just use a house from a plan book?"

Of course not! Plan book designers don't know anything about your site or your life-style. For students who don't dig bubbles, I suggest the storyboard. Here's an example of the way it works.

Be the Building. . . .

I start with a typical day. When I open my eyes in the morning, what do I want to see? Personally, I want the light to be crashing in the window filling the room with energy. So that means the bedroom must be facing east. I want an inspiring view if possible and I want a reason to get out of the sack. Coffee! I want a coffee station right in the bedroom . . . on a timer so it's hot when I awake.

I dress quickly, taking my clothes from a specially designed set of built-in drawers that save space in the bedroom; this creates an expansive feel in the bedroom.

Oops. The shirt I want to wear this day is still in the dryer. Lucky I designed the laundry to be on the same floor as the bedrooms.

Walking down the hall that separates my bedroom from the children's, I raise my voice and announce that daybreak has officially arrived. I imagine giggling from behind closed doors and this gives me an idea. In each bedroom I will design an interior window that looks out onto the hall. That way the kids won't feel like they are shut up in their rooms; plus, it will allow me to open the shutters and wish them a good morning.

Going down the stairs I find myself . . . where? Hmmm, which room do I want to arrive in when I descend the stairs every morning? Equally important, which room would I like to ascend from? It can't be too public, but neither should it be too private. I think the kitchen is a natural for a family house, but it means a lot of traffic in the cooking area. Maybe I'll have the stairs come out on the public side of an island. That would keep the kids out of the kitchen but still maintain the connection between the bedrooms and the heart of the house. But this needs more thought. Stairs are a very important design element. They are one of the few elements that can really focus the occupant's experience of the architecture. So I will make the stairs come down in such a way that they align the occupant with a really great view of the outside. Even better, I will be looking over a slightly sunken family room at a south-facing glazed wall that opens out onto a fabulous patio and garden. (Gee, I hope someday I find a site that can accommodate this great storyline. . . .)

Before continuing with this narration, I feel the need to begin another. The kitchen has reminded me of a very important ceremony that takes place every day. We're all familiar with the return of the modern day Hunter or the Gatherer. The car arrives in the garage (from which direction? where is the road?), loaded with supplies. The Gatherer must carry bag after bag to the kitchen. What is the sequence of events? There must be enough room to open the car doors, and it must be easy to unload the car. Is there an airlock or coatroom that I will pass through? Where is the first good place to put down my load? How does this traffic interface with the other kitchen circulation? I imagine the whole sequence again, but this time with three children. And then, in a slightly different narration, I consider my return from work. The Hunter arrives home, tired from a day of survival. Home, that bastion of security and comfort. After hassling with the key for a few minutes in the evening rain (sure glad I designed a little roof and light over the rear entry), I open the door and place my coat and tools in their usual place. There is a little table on which I leave my keys, pick up mail and leave notes for the rest of my family. This is a simple ceremony, but it happens every day. It is essential to my feeling of Coming Home. That's why I've designed a special little place for the table, the keys, the tools, the coat, and the boots. Everything feels like putting on a comfortable old pair of slippers. I'm home.

Storyboard diagrams can wander all over the paper. There are no walls, simply activities. The activities that make up our lives are used to give shape to our buildings. In storylining, these activities and the sequences they generate will suggest relationships and then, finally, shapes.

This Has Been a Test

Narration is like playing house before you have one to play in. It's also effective after you've been around the Design Helix a few times. If you're trying to see how a possible floor plan will work, there's nothing better than running a few narrations. But the very best part of narration is its power to introduce fantasy into your real life. If you can imagine a story, then you can design your new house to accommodate it. It doesn't need to be a wild, fantastic story. Perhaps it's the story of how you become a famous artist or professional athlete every evening when you return from work. Maybe you've always imagined a big family with huge cookouts and banquets. Whatever the scale or character of your story, if it can be imagined, it can be designed for. Imagine your house is a boat or a train. Imagine your house is in a different time. (Colonial? Medieval? Twenty-second century?) Imagine your house blending into and healing the natural environment.

There are many ways to diagram. Some people cut up colored paper, others use clay. I've seen graph paper used (though I don't trust it) and I've seen it done on computers. The point is to see how the activities that make up your life relate to one another. After that's clear, it's much easier to design your dream house.

Schematic Building Design

So now you have a program of requirements (both physical and behavioral), several diagrams exploring relationships, and an annotated site plan. You're now ready for some serious preliminary design. This will be the first complete cycle of the Design Helix—site, program, building. It's time to take the first shot at putting your life into a buildable design.

Start freehand with only a pencil and a ¼" scale (a ruler on which ¼" equals one scale foot). Sketch different floor plans and "sections." A section is what architects call a vertical cutaway through the building. Always alternate between plan and sections for the best understanding of what you're designing. Make your walls with two lines. Indicate which way doors swing. Generally, these rough floor plans will reveal how your life will fit into the building. The sections will show how the

PLACING YOUR DOORS

Where you place a door can dramatize a room, save you money, simplify circulation, or all three. Doors modify and direct the choreography in any house. I've touched on this a bit in the sidebar called Open Plan, but the following two examples come up so often at Yestermorrow that I thought they deserved special attention.

The Kitchen

In the first layout (page 90) the bathroom is squeezed into the corner between the sink and the refrigerator. Although the sink has a nice window and the stove and refrigerator are convenient, the whole kitchen/dining set up doesn't really work.

Standard wisdom in kitchen design gives priority to the relationship between the three appliances at the points of the imaginary triangle (dashed line). In the first layout, the refrigerator opens toward the sink, but away from the stove. Moreover, the sink is too far away from the other two. The big arrow to the right indicates the dining and living rooms. People coming from these rooms to use the bathroom will collide with anyone working in the kitchen. The area designated for casual eating is also the natural place for food preparation. More conflict.

By simply moving the bathroom (and its door), all these things are fixed. The casual eating is now out of the work area and very close to the dining room. It can double as a serving area when the dining room is being used. The bathroom is also very convenient for people from other parts of the house without disrupting kitchen circulation. The relationships between the three major appliances is now vastly improved. The refrigerator opens toward both other appliances. Food can move to the sink for cleaning or to the stove for warming. The obvious areas for food preparation aren't compromised by other functions, and the kitchen sink still has a window! (See also *The Smart Kitchen* by David Golbeck, Ceres Press Inc., PO Box 87, Woodstock, NY 12498.)

The Stairs

Any house design with bedrooms upstairs must resolve the conflict between generous bedrooms and generous circulation. If your concept of a bedroom is just a room with a bed, then it needn't be a large room. If your concept of a hall is simply circulation, then it should be kept to a minimum. But if you want generous bedrooms or expansive upstairs halls, then you will have to consider your priorities.

In the first layout (page 91), there is a hallway that parallels and runs the full length of the stairwell. This upper hall is generously lit by two windows and could be regarded as a room in itself. It features some furniture, some rugs, and appointments; it might even have some storage or closets associated with it. Although the two bedroom doors are situated at one end of the hall, they might easily be separated. This would give each bedroom a section of the hall, almost like a front yard. Lastly, we shouldn't overlook the amply proportioned space of the upper stair hall. One could imagine children playing or even adults talking during a large social occasion. Its size gives the feeling, as one ascends the stairs, that the upstairs is a comfortable, generous place—even though we can't see the actual bedrooms. This is probably a bit of an illusion.

With limited funds the bedrooms will likely be just slightly smaller because of the generous hallway. In the second layout the hall has been miniaturized and the floor area gained has been added to one of the bedrooms. The stairwell is still illuminated by a window, though only one, and there is still room for at least one piece of furniture. The hall is no longer generous, but neither would we call it mean. Efficient seems to be the proper description. Meanwhile, the bedroom has benefited greatly. We know this without even seeing the entire room. It has gained a hallway worth of floor area plus a window. The window is a great improvement in that it probably means cross ventilation.

The stairs are now an efficient, almost private, means of reaching these two bedrooms.

Placing doors should be done with care and craft. If you think of your house as a three-dimensional stage set, you can test the placement of your doors by imagining the play of the actors.

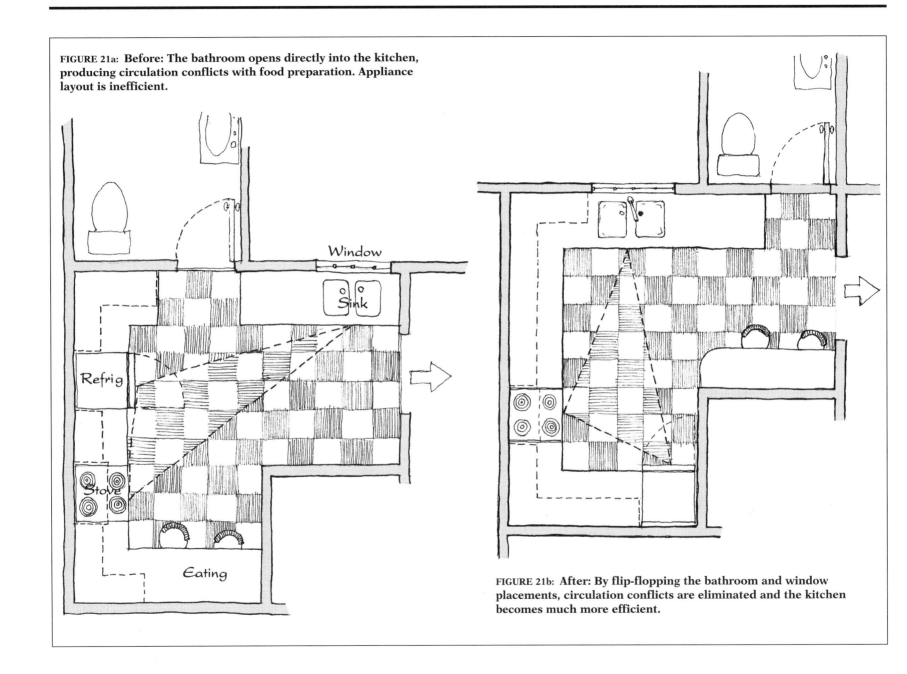

FIGURE 21a: **Before: The bathroom opens directly into the kitchen, producing circulation conflicts with food preparation. Appliance layout is inefficient.**

Window

Sink

Refrig

Stove

Eating

FIGURE 21b: **After: By flip-flopping the bathroom and window placements, circulation conflicts are eliminated and the kitchen becomes much more efficient.**

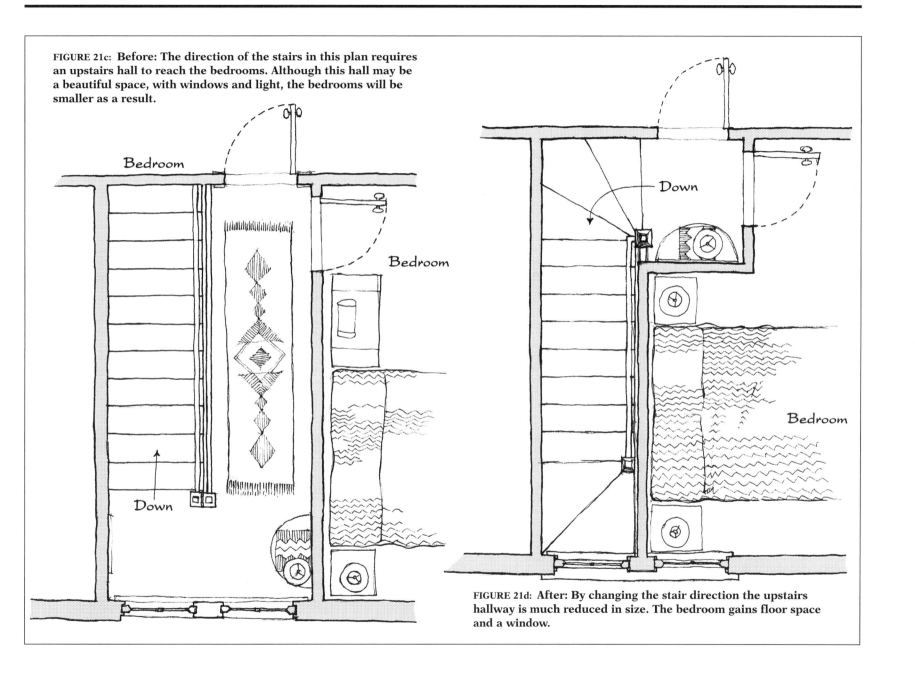

FIGURE 21c: **Before: The direction of the stairs in this plan requires an upstairs hall to reach the bedrooms. Although this hall may be a beautiful space, with windows and light, the bedrooms will be smaller as a result.**

FIGURE 21d: **After: By changing the stair direction the upstairs hallway is much reduced in size. The bedroom gains floor space and a window.**

building is structured. (See Appendix 4 for a quick, but serviceable, introduction to drafting.)

As soon as you have a rough set of scale drawings, build a scale model. This is simple. Photocopy the drawings, glue them to cardboard (with rubber cement) and then cut them out (with an Exacto knife). Then glue the walls to the floor plan using Elmer's white glue or a hot glue gun. The hard part may be the roof but you'll get it if you try (just like every Yestermorrow student for over eighteen years). Your first model may be a little slow, but don't let it become too precious. It's just a study model. Feel free to cut holes in it, change proportions, and generally modify it as you see fit. Models can tell you what to expect architecturally—proportion, scale, massing, siting, and so on.

As your design develops you will need to draw foundations, walls, floors, roofs, doors, and windows. Many of these things will end up where you always knew they would. But there will be some surprises, some discoveries. And some conflicts.

Even this preliminary design must be comprised of real world materials with very specific characteristics. Walls embody structure and insulation; doors need space to swing; and stairs require head clearance. Wood can only span so far and plumbing must be properly drained and vented. Obviously, there are many physical and technical considerations in the designing of a house. We can decide anything we want about how we choose to live, but when you start using materials, certain irreducible facts pertain. Materials have weight, strength, color, history, coefficients of expansion and cost. Cost is hardly the only concern. Some materials simply can't be used with each other; dissimilar metals for instance. If copper, aluminum, or steel are in contact, they will corrode due to galvanic action. Other materials work at their best in combinations: concrete reinforced with steel, fiberglass-reinforced epoxy, glass coated with metallic films.

The following chapters will present the materials and techniques commonly used by the owner/builder. They have been organized and thought of as an array of choices—like a Chinese menu. Rather than materials, I have arranged your choices by systems: foundations, walls, roofs, windows, doors, environmental comfort, and lighting. Though there is much technical information here, these chapters aren't meant to provide exhaustive how-to guidance. (There are better books for that listed in the bibliography.) Our purpose is to give you a feel for your choices.

You, the maker, are composing a grand piece of art—a self-portrait! Think of the different materials as colors on your architectural palette. They're all there and available for the appropriate situation. The trick is knowing which one to use when, and in combination with which others. Architectural design requires a feel for materials and *the methods they employ.* Beyond the basic materials, you must understand the methods for configuring these materials into a good roof, wall, foundation, and so on. There are fundamental considerations that underlie each part of a building, regardless of the materials chosen. What are the essential qualities of a good roof? A great window? An effective foundation? These aren't intractable philosophical questions, but the basic inquiries at the center of architectural design. What is a foundation and what must it do? What is a front door and how is it different from any other door? How do we think about walls, as structure or insulation? What's the most important thing about windows?

These next chapters give the first-time designer a guided tour through the issues and options that experienced design/builders regularly address when making houses. The danger to avoid here is that of quickly latching onto one system or approach and then letting its requirements design your house. Don't do it. You are the designer, you are the builder, and, above all, you are the client! You make the decisions. If one material or method won't serve your purposes, find another. Take a system and modify it. Be inventive. Keep looking. Everything is possible.

THE BUILDING

Foundations and Liquid Stone

Thinking About Foundations

BEARING CAPACITY

It is best to keep one very simple thing in mind when considering foundations: The foundation is *where the building meets the ground.* Obvious as this may sound, it must not be overlooked. It is an important condition that is pretty ubiquitous in our gravity-bound world. Everything and every being must deal with gravity and arrive at a suitable relationship with Mother Earth. Nature provides a wide variety of solutions to study and learn

from. Plants and animals of all types have evolved in the ever present condition of earth's gravity. Each has developed a uniquely appropriate "foundation." What aspects of these natural foundations might we imitate in order to benefit from Nature's architecture?

As a fun starting point, let's decide whether our building is like a "plant," i.e., static, or an "animal," i.e., movable. The majority will be stationary and will benefit most from a study of plants and land forms, but for those considering mobile homes, houseboats, or tents there is much

to be learned from a study of animals. This isn't meant to be silly or to trivialize the engineering aspects of foundation design. But before we deal with numbers and formulae, we must grasp the big concepts. We have been looking to Nature for an understanding of big concepts since the dawn of time.

The primary job of any foundation is to support the structure above by transferring all loads and forces to the ground. Most plants (and animals) accomplish this by getting wider at the base (Figure 22).

A big footprint spreads out the vertical

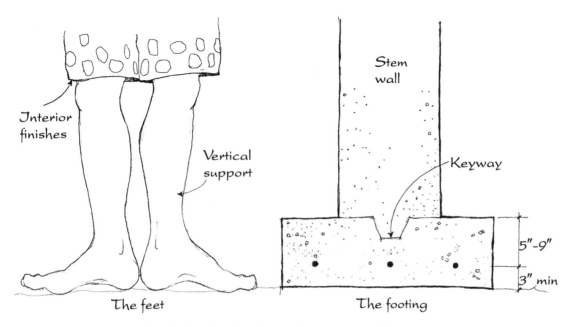

FIGURE 22: By getting wider, the footing distributes the concentrated loads over more area.

loads and resists the overturning forces of winds or earthquake. Different types of soil will require different foundation solutions. Just as certain plants can't survive in certain soils, one must remember that certain foundation types are disastrous if used in the wrong sites. It is very important to understand that the soil is an integral part of your foundation, not simply something on which it sits. Soils with different bearing or draining capacities ask for different types of foundation systems. The consequences of disregarding this requirement may be seen in the thousands of cracked, leaking, or out-of-level foundations around the country. If the founda-

tion system is properly matched to the site conditions, the resulting building will be durable and attractive at the most reasonable cost (see Table 2).

As the foundation brings the building loads down to the ground it must also hold the building away from ground-dwelling predators like termites, carpenter ants, rodents, etc. This is where the conflicting requirements of foundation design can become most irksome. The personal aesthetic of many people seeks to minimize the amount of concrete or foundation seen above the ground plane. Too little exposure, however, will result in rot and possible infestation. The answer, as

usual, is found through design. Rather than trying to hide or minimize the foundation, the designer must make it an integral part of the architectural composition. In addition to making the foundation more attractive, it will also improve the relationship between your whole house and the site.

WATER

Whether it's on or under the ground, water is almost as important as gravity in configuring your foundation. Plants, which need certain amounts of water, control this essential element with a geometry of "pipes" called roots. Animals will have a special durable skin such as hooves or callouses where they come into contact with the wet ground. Both examples provide very good lessons for the house builder: Control the water around your building and use water-impervious materials.

The first concept is particularly important. Controlling water by letting it do what water wants to do (follow gravity) is sort of the Zen way. If you provide a path for water to bypass your foundation, it will have no reason to enter. On the other hand, if you attempt to keep water out merely by using some high-powered waterproofing scheme, the results will generally be disastrous. Water *always* wins.

Water comes from all directions. It falls down out of the sky as rain and

TABLE 2: BEARING CAPACITIES OF SOILS

			Soil Type Descriptions	Bearing Capacity (psf)
Other Soils			Solid Rock	50,400
			Sedimentary rock, shale, sandstone, limestone	20,000
			Cemented gravel	15,840
			Compact sand	14,000
Coarse-Grained Soils	Gravels (more than half of coarse fraction is more than ¼")		Well-graded gravels, gravel-sand mixture, little or no fines	10,000
			Poorly graded gravels or gravel-silt mixtures, little or no fines	8,000
			Silty gravel, gravel-sand-silt mixtures	5,000
			Clayey gravels, gravel-sand-clay mixtures	4,000
	Sands (more than half of coarse fraction is less than ¼")		Well-graded sands, gravelly sands, little or no fines	7,500
			Poorly graded sands, gravelly sands, little or no fines	6,000
			Silty sands, sand-silt mixtures	4,000
			Clayey sands, sand-clay mixtures	4,000
Fine-Grained Soils	Silts and Clays	(liquid limit is less than 50%)	Inorganic silts, very fine sands, rock flour, silty, or clayey fine sands or clayey silts with slight plasticity	2,000
			Inorganic clay of low to medium plasticity, gravel clays, sandy clays, silty clays, lean clays	2,000
			Organic silts and organic silty clays of low plasticity	2,000
		(liquid limit is greater than 50%)	Inorganic silts, micaeous or diatomaceous fine sandy or silty soils, elastic silts	2,000
			Inorganic clays of high plasticity, fat clay	2,000
			Organic clays of medium to high plasticity, organic silts	2,000
			Peat and other highly organic soils	2,000

weather. It wells up under the ground as the water table. Surface runoff can come from any direction, depending on your site and the lay of the land. No matter where the water is coming from, you must design your house so that it may pass.

Proper siting is the first and best design move to prevent water problems.

Site your house where the runoff will move away from the building. If you can't get out of the path of water running along the surface, perhaps you should build on

pylons and let it flow beneath. Alternately, you may install a curtain drain along the uphill side of the building. This specially designed drainage allows the water coming down the slope to run around your house and foundation. The same principle can be used to deal with the water table or subsurface water. A "french" drain is a series of pipes that ring the foundation and sometimes go under it. Any water impinging on the house site will be drained under and around the building. It's the same basic principle in all cases: Let the water go by.

If you live in a cold climate, the moisture in the ground takes on a nasty alter ego during the winter—it becomes rock-hard ice. Ice expands, and when groundwater freezes it produces what we call a "frost heave." A frost heave has astounding force. It can move a road, it can drive a rock through a cast-iron pipe, and it can crack your foundation. The best defense is to eliminate water from around your building. If there is no water, there can be no ice. Also, if the footings are located below the frost level, then the frost can't get under them to heave the building.

The depth of frost will vary depending on your climate and soil conditions. If you have a winter without snow cover, the frost will go deeper (unless you live in a warm climate year-round). If your soil is very rocky the frost may go deeper. If you have exposed ledge the frost may go deeper. Local building codes usually designate an average frost depth that can be used in design. But to be safe, you may want to go deeper.

INSULATION, MOISTURE, ETC.

Beyond considerations of water and structure, one must also be sensitive to several other aspects of the foundation. The foundation system is a boundary between building and earth. On either side of this boundary there will be considerations that may make one foundation system preferable over another. In cold climates the insulation strategy will be important; for remote sites there will be the access problem and the availability of materials. Different architectural styles ask for different types of foundation systems. Some house plans will use the basement as living space and this will suggest further attention to moisture and thermal comfort as well as access, light, and ventilation.

Even if you don't plan on using the basement for living space, insulation and moisture control are important. If the basement is inadequately insulated, it will develop terrible moisture problems. In the summer, this is the coolest place in the house. On humid days the moisture-laden air will migrate into the basement or crawl space and condense on the cool surfaces. This can cause structural rot with alarming speed. The solution is to eliminate either the cool surfaces or the moisture, or both.

Insulating a foundation wall is always a good investment. Concrete walls are best covered on the outside with a draining insulation. This keeps the wall warm and drains any subsurface water to the foundation drain (Figure 23). I am also a fan of the *all-weather wood foundation* (AWWF). This is a treated wood foundation structured much the same way as a common stud wall (Figure 27). Consequently it can be insulated and finished with fiberglass batts and gypsum board easily. Unfortunately, the chemicals currently used to treat wood for in-ground use are unacceptably toxic. We all eagerly await the intro-

duction of an environmentally acceptable treatment to make wood rotproof.

Moisture control is equally important. Even a well-drained foundation is surrounded with moisture-laden earth. Remember that moisture is different from running water or the water table. Moisture is actually vapor or dampness in the air or the ground. This moisture will wick through any concrete structure like water through a sponge. One of my favorite fun facts illustrates this quality of concrete. If you were to place the base of a column of concrete in an adequate water supply, studies show that capillary action would

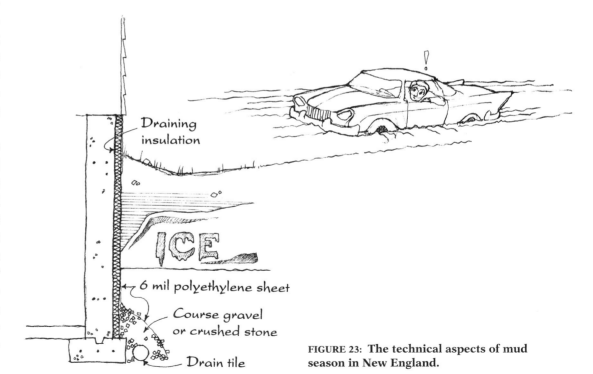

FIGURE 23: **The technical aspects of mud season in New England.**

carry the water to a height of two miles! Obviously this means it will easily get up the 8′ of your foundation wall. There it will collect under and eventually rot out your sill plate (see Figure 24).

To eliminate these problems, we spray the concrete footing and frost wall with a moisture-proofing film. Sometimes 6 ml. plastic is laid across the footing prior to forming and pouring the wall. The same

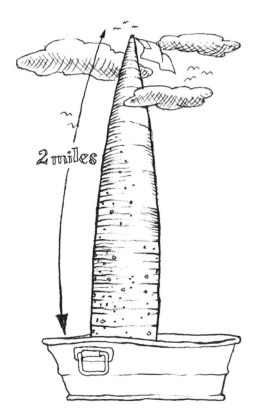

FIGURE 24: **The force of capillary action in concrete is capable of wicking water up to a height of two miles!**

precaution is taken with wood foundations.

In general, the first 5′ of earth that you place your foundation in behaves a lot like the air you place your house in—just slower. They both have temperature swings and a certain moisture content. While the air will quickly heat up in the day and cool off at night, the earth will take longer. It will still contain the day's warmth long after the sun has set and it will take a good part of the morning's heat before the night chill is burned off. Even then the earth will usually be cooler than the air. Although the daily temperature variations decrease below 5′ (it is almost constant at 8′ to 10′), there's a seasonal drift at these depths. Long after autumn has arrived, the ground will still be holding much of the summer's warmth. Conversely, when spring arrives, the air may be warm enough for T-shirts while the ground is still frozen solid. In deep frost areas this results in what New Englanders call mud season. This is the period during which the surface thaws, producing much previously frozen water, but the subsurface stays frozen. The subterranean ice keeps the water from draining back into the water table. This condition can produce dirt roads with mud so deep you can lose your car! It can also produce temporarily trapped water that will enter your foundation if it isn't properly backfilled and graded (see Figure 23).

So the earth gets cold and wet. Your

foundation should control these conditions. Generally, the earth will be cooler than the air in the summer and warmer than the air in the winter. That means in hot climates the earth's temperature is an asset in the summer; in cold climates, it's a much smaller asset in the winter. Properly configured, an earth-sheltered house can benefit extensively from the earth's temperature swings. No cheaper insulation nor finer air conditioning exist.

The big issue for earth-sheltered homes, or inhabited basements, is the moisture. In all situations, the moisture must be kept from condensing on any cooler surfaces; an uninsulated concrete wall or slab provides just such a surface. A cold-water pipe or other penetration from the outside will also "sweat." Specific strategies for controlling moisture exist for any type of foundation condition. What they all have in common is proper insulation. You can't remove the moisture from this world (nor would you want to), but without a cool surface on which to condense, it will cause little harm.

OTHER CONSIDERATIONS

Finally, there are a few other things to keep in mind when choosing and configuring a foundation. In many areas a radon test might be well advised. If the soil in your area has a high rate of emission, it is easiest and cheapest to deal with at the outset. Your local building inspector should be able to determine if it's a concern in your area. Also, inexpensive testing devices are available at most hardware stores.

It almost (but not quite) goes without saying that cost and codes must always be kept in mind while designing the foundation. There are special requirements for basement spaces in different parts of the country. These include drainage minimums, egress requirements, footing and frost wall dimensions, and special connectors for hurricanes or earthquakes. Check your local building code. As for cost, there's a foundation for every pocketbook. Your options will be limited by your site, your code, and your personal requirements. But this should not put a proper foundation outside the reach of any reasonable budget. And, I might add, economizing underground is a poor strategy. If anything goes wrong, it is one of the most expensive repairs in construction. Do it right the first time!

⠀ **The Choices**

At this point the designer has many foundation systems from which to choose. The palette of materials is also varied. Let us narrow the field.

When designing a foundation system one usually starts by selecting a geometry or shape. There are really only a few to choose from and each may be built from any number of materials:

1. Gravel trench
2. Pier: concrete, treated wood, brick, protected steel
3. Slab: concrete
4. Continuous wall: concrete, stone, block, brick, AWWF (all-weatherwood) (See illustration below and Figure 25)

These may also be combined to form numerous hybrids. The students in one advanced class built a foundation that used all three geometries (see Figure 26). Another project required that we integrate the footing and a short concrete wall called a stem wall, and a treated-wood frost wall. Other foundation designs are discussed in Appendix 5.

Assuming they are only used when and where appropriate, the list above is roughly in order of increasing cost. The gravel trench is the Volkswagen, while the continuous frost wall (with basement slab) is the Cadillac. The others fall somewhere in between. Even so, it would be misleading to think that geometry alone will determine cost. Ornate columns or piers of pressure-treated wood can be very costly compared to at least one full basement that I know of—it was built from

Stone foundations transfer the house loads by getting as wide at the base as they are tall.

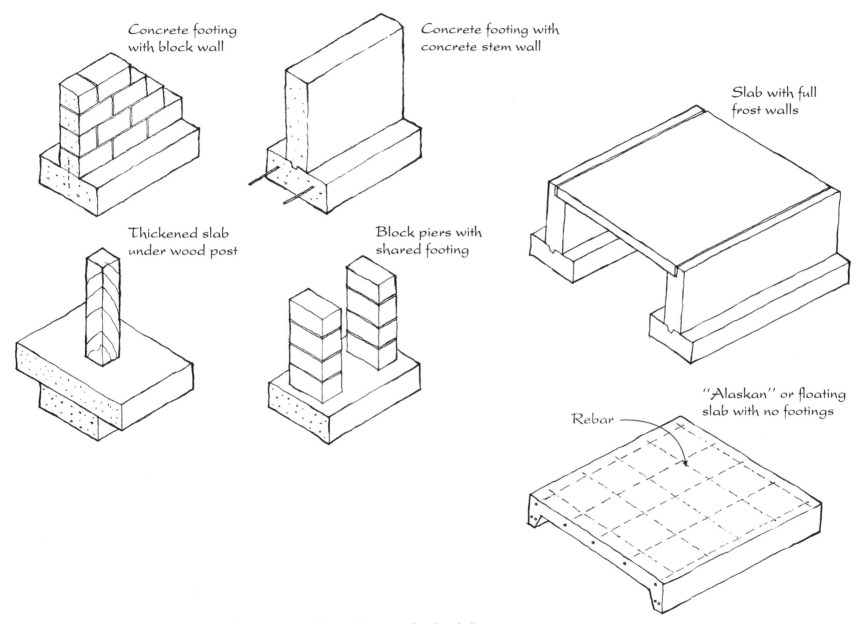

Concrete footing with block wall

Concrete footing with concrete stem wall

Slab with full frost walls

Thickened slab under wood post

Block piers with shared footing

"Alaskan" or floating slab with no footings

Rebar

FIGURE 25. A foundation solution exists for every possible combination of soil and climate.

huge bundles of old computer printouts wrapped in several layers of plastic!

The other thing to remember when choosing a foundation is *value*. As a foundation gets cheaper it gives you less per dollar. Consider the following:

> The gravel trench or pier foundation holds up the building.
>
> The slab holds up the building, and provides an insulated floor.

The frost wall holds up the building, gives you usable space, superior thermal protection, and makes it easier to install and maintain the mechanical systems.

The full basement gives you everything listed above, *plus* an additional habitable level to your house. The additional space is yours for the small difference in cost that it takes to make a 4′ frost wall into an 8′ frost wall. In general, this is very cheap space!

Again, these are generalizations that may not apply in all situations. Close to floodplains the pier foundation may be the only wise choice; in areas of deep frost the slab (sometimes called a "floating" slab) has special advantages; and in expansive clay a full basement is out of the question. But remember also, every shortcoming of any system can be overcome. If the designer understands the basic principles involved, adequate measures can usually be taken to accommodate almost any situation (see Figure 25).

As a means of illustrating the basic principles of foundation design and construction, we will next walk through each step in the pouring of a typical concrete foundation wall. As we get to each step, ask yourself: "Will this work well on my site? Is there a better way? Is there a less expensive way? What assumptions are being made? What is the purpose of each part?"

THE REINFORCED CONCRETE FROST WALL FOUNDATION

In one form or another, reinforced concrete is the most commonly used foundation material in the country. Its proper construction requires that the builder understand the fundamental principles of concrete. This is an incredible material. Liquid stone! Although used since before

FIGURE 26: The Yestermorrow students built a complex foundation for the project constructed in the Great Pit Project.

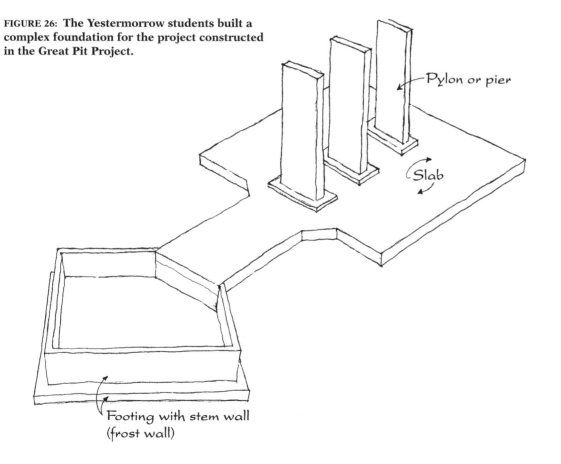

Pylon or pier

Slab

Footing with stem wall (frost wall)

FIGURE 27: **Special hybrid foundation composed of a concrete footing and a wood frost wall.**

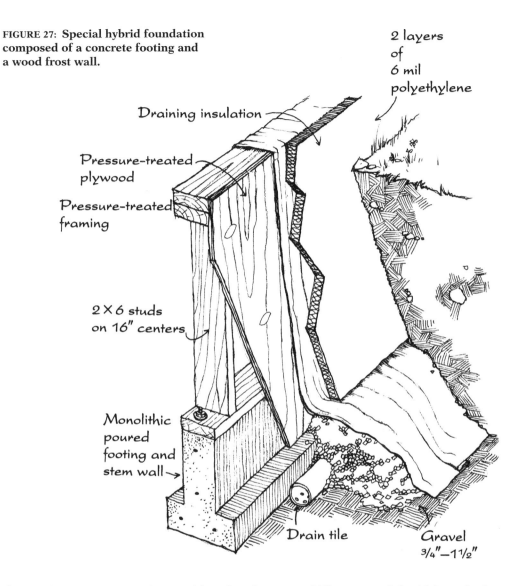

Draining insulation

Pressure-treated plywood

Pressure-treated framing

2 × 6 studs on 16" centers

Monolithic poured footing and stem wall →

2 layers of 6 mil polyethylene

Drain tile

Gravel 3/4"–1 1/2"

only a compressive strength. Concrete alone can only withstand compression loads. To handle the concomitant tensile forces we use an equally modern material—steel. Relatively small amounts of steel reinforcing, properly placed, will provide the necessary balance in tensile strength. As strong as it is, however, steel will rust away to nothing if exposed to water and sulfides. Like a car on salty roads, once the rust has started, it will move into the body of the wall. The effect of this corrosion is to expand and crack the concrete. In severe cases entire chunks of concrete will loosen and drop away. This is called spawling. Proper care in placement must be taken to prevent this. Basically, all steel should be covered by at least 1½" of concrete and if it is in direct contact with the earth a minimum of 3" is required.

Steel Reinforced Concrete

Whole books, impossibly thick, have been written about this amazing technology. Its capabilities have allowed some of the most impressive bridges and structures of our age. Here we can but touch lightly on its use in residential foundations. Although this may seem an almost trivial application, it is often undertaken too hastily with the worst results. A properly poured foundation will last hundreds of years; improperly poured, it will crack, leak, and crumble within a decade. The following steps are but an outline.

the ancient Romans, it is considered to be one of the truly "modern" materials. Reinforced concrete consists of a Portland cement–based mixture of stone and sand that hardens by chemical reaction into a

rocklike material. Although it acquires most of its strength within seven days after pouring, it continues to get a bit stronger with each passing year for the rest of eternity! This strength, however, is

STEP 1. LAYOUT

There are a variety of tools available for laying out a foundation on the site: transit, water level, string level, etc. (Proper instruction in the use of any of these instruments is best accomplished on site with the tool in hand. Written descriptions tend to sound like a freshman course in telemetry. Nevertheless, we've given it a try in Chapter 4. Regardless of the tool you use, they all provide the same thing: *a level line.* Using the level line as a reference one can stake out the footprint of the building (see Figure 28). In the course of constructing the foundation you will lay out the building at least twice if not three times. Each time must be more accurate than the time before.

The first layout will be for the excavator. Batter boards from which strings are attached will be set up around the house site. The strings outline where the foundation hole is to be dug and intersect at the corners. Since the excavator will remove the earth for several feet beyond the perimeter of the building, it is a good idea to place your batter boards at least 10' to 20' beyond the actual building footprint (see Figure 29). At this point the corners of your layout need only be accurate to within a half inch. The important thing to observe is how the building will sit on the land. Is one side sticking out of the ground excessively? Is there adequate access for automobiles and construction equipment? Are the views and solar orientation correct? These are just a few of the things that will become clear upon staking out the building for the first time.

Take some time to "live" in your house footprint after you have laid it out. This is a point at which you can make some very important adjustments in the way your building is configured on the ground plane. This must be done with great care, however, since any change in the foundation will telegraph other changes throughout the building. Still, take some time to check out and put your final decisions to bed. Because after the foundation is

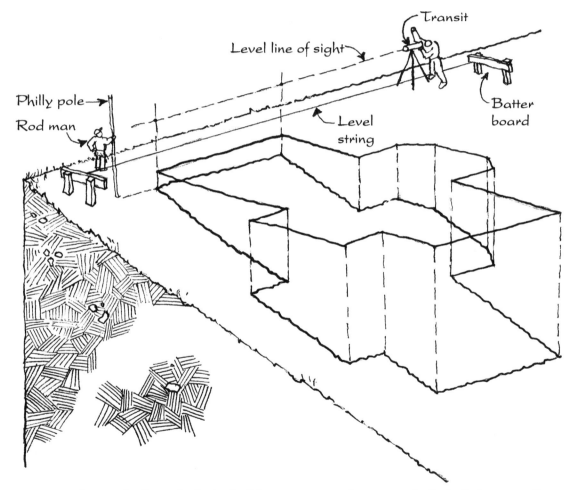

FIGURE 28: The transit allows the design/builder to transpose the accurately drafted plans onto the irregularities of the ground plane.

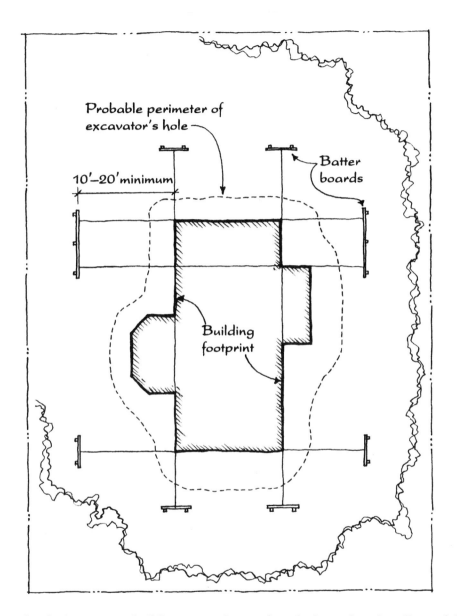

Probable perimeter of
excavator's hole

Batter
boards

10'–20' minimum

Building
footprint

FIGURE 29: When laying out your building, remember to place the batter boards well out of the excavator's way. The all-important strings will be put up and taken down several times before the foundation is completed.

poured, you will know the real meaning of "cast in stone."

STEP 2. FILL
Every foundation must sit on "undisturbed earth." This may seem like a rare commodity by the time the excavator leaves, but do not lose heart. The only situations we want to avoid are landfills, earth that has recently been dug up, or any arrangement where only a part of the building is on ledge rock (see Figure 30). All foundations settle slightly during construction except, of course, those on ledge. Ledge doesn't compress. So if part of your foundation is on ledge, that part won't settle with the rest. This unequal settlement will cause cracks and leaks. If you have ledge in your foundation hole, it is best to blast it out and then backfill with structural fill, which is anything that compacts to 100 percent of its bearing capacity upon placement and includes crushed rock, stone, and sand. If you are dealing with ledge you may want to place a 1' or 2' layer of sand over it before pouring your footings. If a section of the site under your foundation falls away, you may have to build it up with stone or crushed rock. Whatever the situation, there are two things to insist on when choosing fill for under your foundation: good drainage and good compaction.

Good drainage and compaction are assured with crushed rock or stone. Sand, however, must be used with some care. If

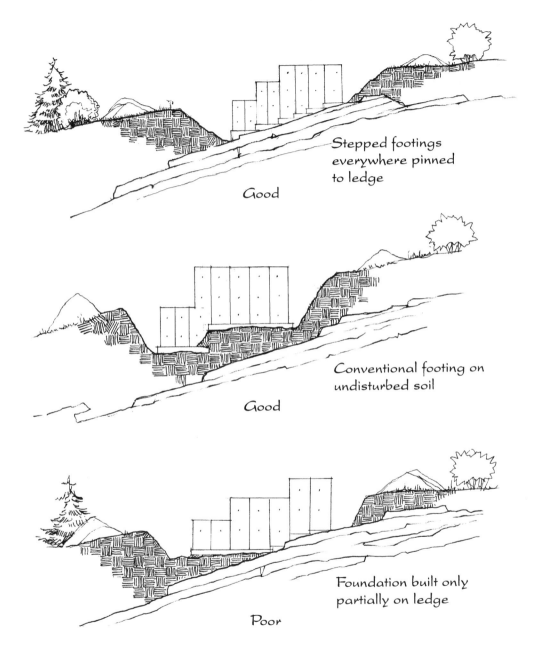

Good

Stepped footings
everywhere pinned
to ledge

Good

Conventional footing on
undisturbed soil

Poor

Foundation built only
partially on ledge

FIGURE 30: Building on ledge is an all or nothing proposition.

the sand is fine enough, it will hold the rainwater between its grains for a very long time. To avoid this, larger-grain sand sometimes mixed with small stones should be used. This is referred to as "bony" sand. As the size of the particles decreases, the material is classified as silt and then clay. Both should be avoided and under no circumstances should organic material (top soil) be used for structural fill.

One last type of fill that should be mentioned is "bank run gravel." This really isn't gravel at all but rather a mix of sand, stone, and some clay. The mix varies from location to location and consequently so do the characteristics of the gravel. Bank run gravel is very useful in the making of roads and as a porous backfill next to walls and under slabs. It is not, however, structural fill and should not be used under load-bearing foundations regardless of how much it is compacted.

All fill should be placed in 6" layers called "lifts" and compacted with a compacting machine (rentable) between each lift (see Figure 31). The amount of compaction will depend on the type of fill, the type of terrain, and the sort of building being placed on top. Structural fill is a demanding undertaking and should not be done by the novice builder without expert advice.

STEP 3. THE FOOTINGS
Now that your site has been excavated and the floor of the hole has been leveled or

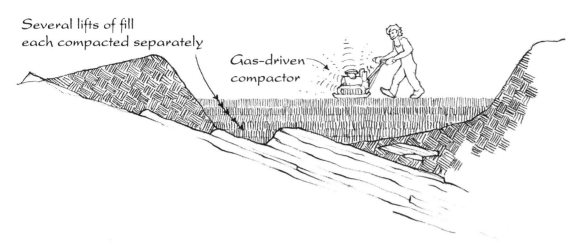

Several lifts of fill
each compacted separately

Gas-driven
compactor

FIGURE 31: Properly compacted, structural fill can be built upon without problems.

adjusted as needed, you are ready to form and pour your footings. Take a few days to do this if you haven't done it before. Get your forms all set, then order the concrete for the next day.

Remember that the function of the footing is to spread the loads developed by the building over enough "undisturbed earth" to insure little or no settling. There is nothing more complicated in this concept than the difference between high heels and snowshoes (see Figure 32).

The damage a high heel inflicts on linoleum results from concentrating all the weight of the wearer on about two square inches. The same principle leads to the design of the snowshoe. We sink down when standing in powdery snow with normal footwear because we exert about 150 pounds per square foot—too much for snow. With snowshoes on, that

same weight is spread over almost five times the area. This means we are only delivering a load of 30 pounds per square foot to the snow. The simple principle to remember is that the softer your soil is or the heavier your building becomes, the wider your footing must be. For most two-story homes and most soil conditions this means about 16″ to 20″ wide.

But how deep? The critical thing here is to be below the frost line. This varies depending on where you live. If there is never any frost where you live, the depth will be set out in the local building code.

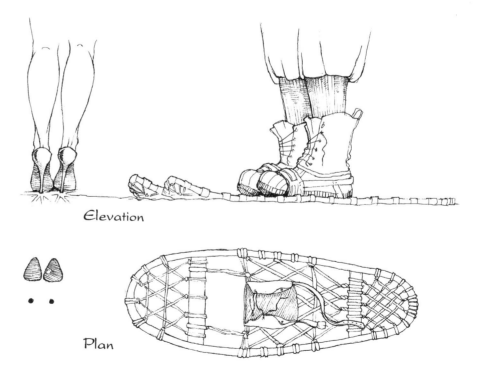

Elevation

Plan

FIGURE 32: The more you spread the load, the more stable the foundation.

At any rate, this is a good time to review what the footing is being asked to do (see Figure 33). The footing transfers the building loads to the undisturbed soil. In the illustration I have depicted the not unusual situation where soil conditions vary in a few locations over the length of the foundation wall. The footing must be able to span these soft spots, much like a beam. This would be easy to design for if the only loads were those of the building pressing down. If there's differential settling or (perish the thought) frost heaving, then the footing will be dealing with loads pressing up from below. Generally, when designing a concrete beam the reinforcing goes on the side away from the carried load. In a predictable world, we would place the steel 3″ from the underside of the footing. But in reality we might have loads coming from both sides, so the steel is often put in the middle and the thickness of the footing will be calculated so that it can act in either direction. For most two-story homes this means the footing will be about 8″ to 10″ thick with one or two number 4 reinforcing bars (½″ in diameter) placed in the middle.

All of the above will be floating through your mind as you walk about in the newly dug hole, taking compass readings, setting up the transit, and preparing for the footing layout. This is the second time you will lay out your building and it should be a bit more accurate than before. But the footing is wider than the wall, so some slack is O.K.

As a general rule, it's a good idea to minimize the amount of thinking that has to be done while looking through a transit. The footing will extend 4″ to 6″ on either side of the foundation wall. You can reduce confusion by doing a drawing of the footing and wall *before* going out to the site (see Figure 34).

Using stakes and 2 × 8s the footing can be built immediately after you lay it out (see Figure 35). The tops of all forms should be as level as possible. This makes it easy to level the concrete by running a board along the top of the forms.

Once the forms are in place, the steel rebar is tied into place. Actual placement will depend on the size of the footing and building, but generally it goes in the middle and the bars are equally spaced. If there are many bars it may be a good idea to tie in a crossbar to prevent movement during the pour. Under no conditions should the reinforcing be covered by less than 3″ of concrete. Exposed steel

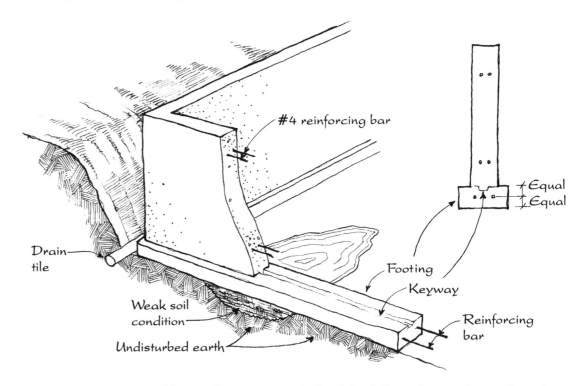

FIGURE 33: **The footing and frost wall are meant to deal with loads from above and, sometimes, from below. Also, there are considerations of moisture and frost.**

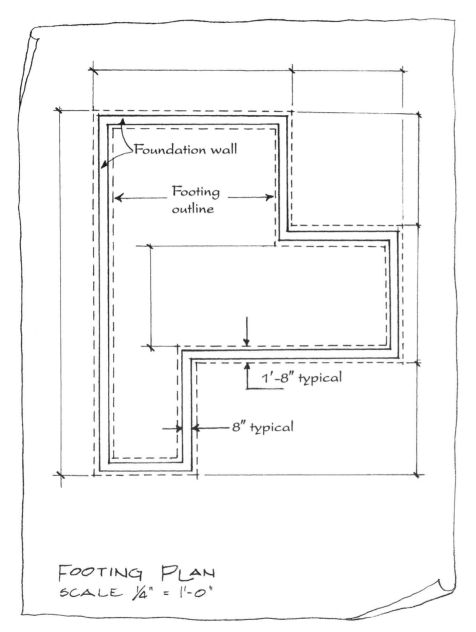

Foundation wall

Footing outline

1'-8" typical

8" typical

FOOTING PLAN
SCALE 1/4" = 1'-0"

FIGURE 34: A fully dimensioned footing plan that shows both the footing and the wall will help avoid confusion when you get to the site.

will rust and eventually break up the concrete.

Before pouring, review the other systems that will be interfacing with this part of the building.

You may need to install a number of sleeves to allow various penetrations of the foundation or footing. Sleeves allow utility lines and pipes to pass through the concrete. A section of PVC pipe or an old coffee can are two common methods for installing sleeves in your formwork. They are placed horizontally between the forms and leave a hole in the wall after the concrete is poured. Where will your power and water come from? In which direction will your septic line leave? Are there phone lines or other utilities that must enter the house underground? These important items should all be depicted on your foundation drawings.

Finally, this is a good time to gather together the materials that will be needed for the pour: anchor bolts, extra rebar, hacksaw, keyway or 2 × 4, shovels and hoes, release oil, wire and cutters, etc.

STEP 4. THE FOOTING POUR
Once everything is ready and checked, order the concrete. When it arrives, insure that it is placed carefully. Concrete is heavy, and if it is allowed to roar down a long chute, even a well-built form will move.

To distribute the cement and remove air pockets, you must "vibrate" the concrete by hitting the forms with a hammer or agitating it with a piece of rebar. Next find a piece of 2 × 4 long enough to span the two sides of the footing with a foot to spare on each side. This will be your "screed." Screed the concrete by moving the 2 × 4 along the form boards in a sawing motion that will both level it and smooth it.

After a rough screed has been completed, place the keyway in the middle of the footing (see Figure 36). The key serves two important functions. It's a water seal between the wall and footing and it's a mechanical joint that prevents the base of the wall from kicking in when backfilled. Don't omit this detail even though the "experienced" concrete truck operator may say it doesn't matter. If you don't have the keyway, at least trowel in a 3″ groove after the concrete has begun to firm up.

If you are using steel dowels to help connect the footing to the frost wall, you can interrupt the keyway when it gets to the rebar dowels. This segmented keyway combined with dowels is an extremely strong mechanical solution.

On steep sites the footing may have to be stepped (see Figure 37). This will make placing a key difficult at the step unless it is affixed to the form. This is another place where the additional use of dowels is a good idea.

Now that the forms are full, vibrated, keyed, doweled, and screeded there is nothing left to do but cover them with plastic and go home. This plastic helps the concrete cure but it may also become part of the overall moisture control strategy. Remember how moisture will "sponge" into concrete. By placing a plastic barrier between the footing and the wall, we can arrest the migration of moisture from ground toward the sill plate. It doesn't have to be plastic; a good coat of tar applied after the concrete is hard will work just as well.

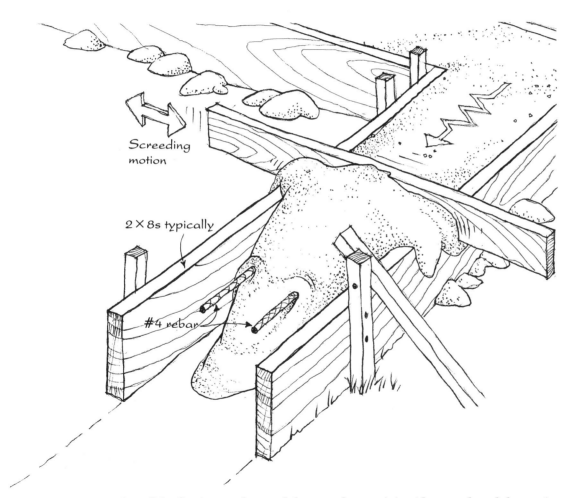

Screeding motion

2 × 8s typically

#4 rebar

FIGURE 35: Construction of the footing can be rough hewn as long as it is wide enough and the top is perfectly level.

STEP 5. LAYING OUT AND FORMING THE WALL

If you have used good lumber to form your footings, the first thing to do is strip it off for later use. Now you will proceed to lay out the building one last time on top of the footing. Fanatical accuracy is encouraged here. Check and recheck everything!

Although there are hundreds of different forming systems, all of them can be divided into two categories: custom built or modular. The custom built affords you a great deal of flexibility but it requires an understanding of form construction. For small situations this amounts to common sense and a good feel for the weight of concrete. However, anything more ambitious, say 4′ high or more, should probably be reviewed by a professional. The modular systems can be rented and are usually flexible enough. They are also a good deal cheaper to use unless you can recycle the wood needed to build custom forms. Make sure the supplier explains all the ties and supports necessary to do what you want. Usually you must supply some of your own wood for support.

If you are using rental forms, the initial setting up goes pretty quickly. The important thing is to get the corners accurately placed. Next, a string or transit can be used to straighten the walls between the corners. As the forms are supported by "strongbacks" (vertical) and "walers" (horizontal) there will be a natural tendency to climb about on this jungle gym while

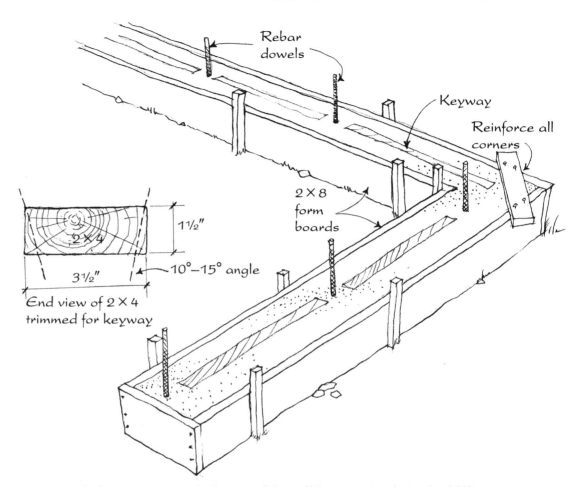

FIGURE 36: **The keyway prevents the bottom of the wall from moving during backfilling.**

working. This is O.K. as long as you check for straightness and level after you are finished.

Most walls should have at least a couple of rebars placed horizontally and low in the wall as well as a couple of similar bars at about the center. Conveniently, this is about where the "snap ties" are located

to hold the two sides of the forms together (see Figure 38). It's usually a good idea to place the lower steel before installing the upper ties. This eliminates one layer of obstacles when trying to thread the 20′ pieces of rebar into the form.

Once the forms and steel are in place it is again time to review the requirements

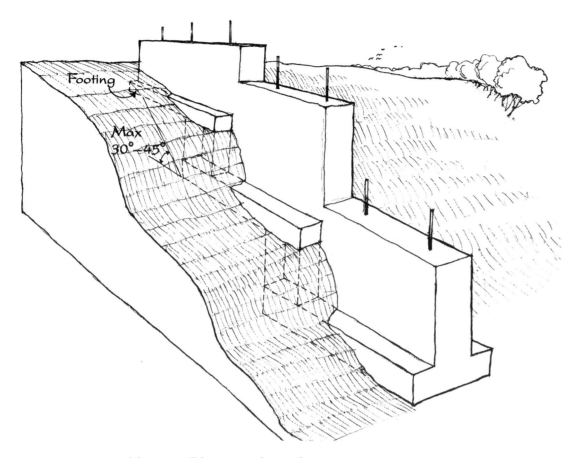

FIGURE 37: A stepped footing will be required on a sloping site.

posed concrete again and cover with plastic for another twelve hours.

A Few Notes on Formwork

The cost of concrete work is, like everything, a product of labor and materials. Unless you are building the simplest of structures, there will be occasion to construct some custom forms. The following is a list of considerations that may reduce the cost of forms.

- When planning formwork, consider the sequence of tasks. Can the formwood used on the footings be reused on the walls? Recycling of forms and materials can keep costs down. Which wall will be poured first? Will one wall get in the way of the next? Can the truck reach all the forms with its chute?
- Rent prefabricated or modular panels wherever possible.
- Consider using plywood instead of boards if the forms are to be recycled. This will reduce costly finish work. Also, consider the design possibilities of using other woods. Smaller pieces will give a nice texture to the walls. Large plywood forms can feature inlays or patterns cast with smaller cutouts.
- Use duplex or double-headed nails in order to speed stripping.
- Clean, reoil, and stack forms neatly between uses. This speeds erection and insures inventory control.

of interfacing systems. Are all the sleeves for utilities, the septic system, and vents in place? Is the waterproofing on top of the footing in place? Have you purchased the anchor bolts to be placed immediately after the pour? Were all the forms coated with release agent to facilitate later stripping?

I've seen professionals spray on the release agent after the forms are up and the rebar is in place. This is a bad practice, as the agent destroys the bond between the concrete and the reinforcing. It's much better to spray the forms prior to their assembly. If you forget, then spray them with water *only* just before the pour and then strip immediately after eighteen hours have passed. Spray the newly ex-

STEP 6. THE WALL POUR

Check the forms for straightness one more time and then order the concrete. Concrete comes in 8-yard trucks (they contain 8 cubic yards of concrete; see Appendix 5 for general foundation facts). Residential foundations usually call for 3,000 psi concrete with a 4″ to 6″ "slump." The slump refers to a test done to determine the amount of water in the mix. The greater the slump the more water in the mix. Since too much water can effect the concrete's strength, this is important. It is your prerogative to ask for a slump test to verify that you are getting the mix you ordered.

There are many options when buying concrete. You can order admixtures to help it set up in cold weather, to make it flow into the forms better, to make it waterproof, even to color it. You can also ask for it to be "pumped" if you are in a difficult spot for the truck to reach or if there is landscaping that you want to protect from the truck tires. This is expensive, however, and should be avoided if possible.

When the truck arrives you should have several friends (at least three) equipped with shovels and hoes and wearing rubber boots and gloves. Also, a wheelbarrow can be invaluable for carting concrete to those hard-to-reach corners. Build sturdy bridges over any ditches, pipes, or other obstacles. Try to imagine the entire scene *before* the truck arrives. It's very hard to concentrate when 8 yards of con-

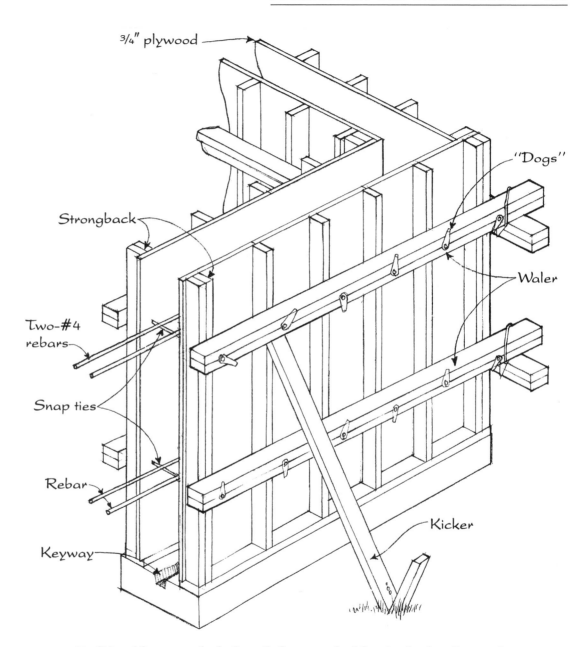

FIGURE 38: Traditional forms may be built easily from standard framing lumber. To save time, a panel-form system can be rented, but some additional wood will still be required.

crete is rumbling around in the truck, getting harder with every minute.

After the concrete is poured, vibrate it with a pencil vibrator. Screed, trowel, and level the top. Lastly, place your anchor bolts on 4′ centers per the code of the Building Officials and Code Administrators International, Inc. (BOCA) (see Figure 39).

STEP 7. CONSIDER THE WALL

So the forms are stripped and—behold!—a concrete wall! At this point much has been done, but even more remains. First, inspect the walls for flaws like entrapped air, "honeycombing," cracks, or blemishes. These need to be repaired or "parged." Locate and trim out all penetration sleeves. Many of the form systems use "snap ties," which must be snapped off after the forms are removed. Then, the end of each tie should be covered with a small amount of concrete applied with a trowel. This is very important, as it prevents rust penetration.

Your foundation seems very substantial at this point, but don't be fooled. If you were to backfill now it is likely that most of the walls would be pushed out of plumb or would fall over altogether. Although the bottom of your foundation is securely anchored to the ground, the upper edge is cantilevered into the air with little support except at the corners. What will change this delicate condition? The deck will. When the first floor deck is built you will

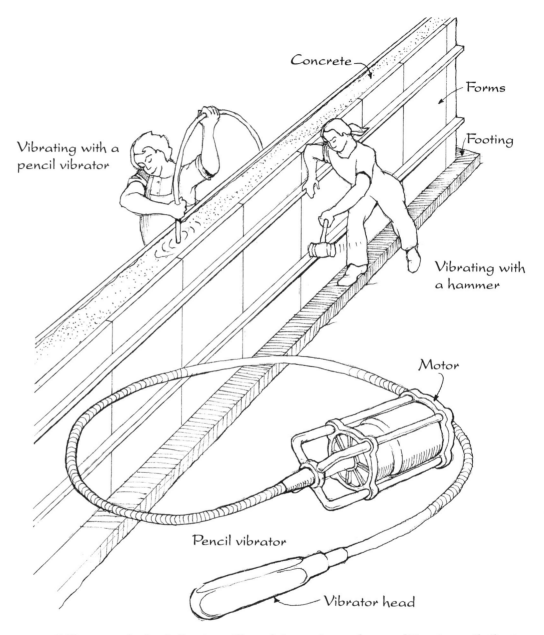

FIGURE 39: **Different methods of vibrating will result in varying surface qualities. A pencil vibrator gives the best results.**

have secured the foundation wall along its entire upper edge. This is very important, and no backfilling should be considered until the deck is in place.

It is at this point that one must protect the foundation from the ever present water in the ground. Generally there are two water paths which must be blocked.

- Water table and groundwater will enter through the construction joint between the footing and the wall, as well as through any cracks that develop later.
- Moisture or water in the ground will sponge through the foundation wall because of the porous nature of concrete.

Let's look at some of the better methods developed to deal with these conditions. We will assume that there will be heated living space in the basement formed by our foundation and that the structure above is framed in wood.

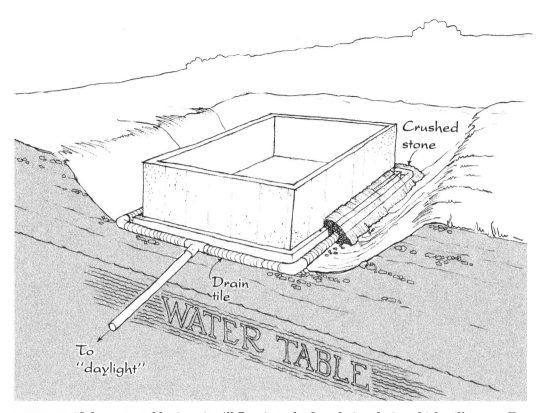

FIGURE 40: If the water table rises, it will flow into the foundation drain, which will carry off the water before it can rise further and enter the foundation.

The Foundation Drain

The most important defense against rising groundwater or hydrostatic pressure at the base of the foundation is surely the foundation or "french" drain system. This consists of a 4″ perforated pipe that runs around the entire perimeter of the building (see Figure 40). This pipe is pitched about ¼″ per foot from a high point on the uphill side of the building, around the entire perimeter, "to daylight." "To day-

light" means where it breaks out of the ground at some point downhill from the house. Alternatively, if the building is on a flat site, one must often drain the foundation into a dry well underground.

The way the french drain works is the essence of "path of least resistance." If water at the edge of a foundation has a choice between a little bitty crack or a wide open 4″ pipe, which way do you think it goes? But to make the choice even

easier, the drain must not be installed above the little bitty crack. Otherwise the water will select both paths. To be really safe, the drain should be everywhere *below* the top of the footing. This insures that the water table will always be drained to a point well below the weak point in the wall.

To be certain that the foundation drain is always working it is important to guard against clogging. This is done by setting the pipe on a bed of crushed rock and then covering the pipe with more crushed rock. The more generous you are with the crushed rock the better your drain feels, but don't make the bed so deep that it raises the drain above the top of the footing. Finally, for security, place a 2′ wide layer of filter fabric over the top of the crushed rock before backfilling. This prevents the rock from silting up. If you're still a bit nervous, backfill with gravel or other porous material.

Damp-proofing and Waterproofing the Walls

First let's clear up the difference between damp-proofing and waterproofing. Damp-proofing is a process meant to guard against the slow movement of moisture through a basement wall by means of capillary action. This should not be confused with waterproofing, which attempts (usually in vain) to prevent pressurized water from entering the basement. Generally, there should be no reason for waterproofing if your siting is at all reasonable and your foundation drain is properly installed. Damp-proofing, on the other hand, should be part of every building's vapor barrier and is very important.

The first phase of your damp-proofing goes on after the footings are stripped. A coat of Mirrorseal™, Thoroseal™, or even 6 mil. polyethylene over the top of the footing will prevent moisture from traveling up the frost wall to the building's fram-

ing. The forms for the walls are built right over the damp-proofing and the frost walls are poured as described above. After the walls have been stripped, the damp-proofing is completed. Using two coats of Thoroseal™, or some similar product, you must cover the entire foundation. If you are at all nervous about the dampness in your basement, get a professional to apply an appropriate product, or spend the extra time to do it right yourself. This is certainly not the sort of thing you want to redo after the building is backfilled.

Before leaving this section perhaps something should be mentioned for those who have an unreasonably wet site. If you are worried that there will be hydrostatic pressure against your foundation during certain times of year, there are some simple procedures that go well beyond the foundation drain and damp-proofing. Backfilling with crushed rock gives the water a better path to your drain. Covering your foundation with draining insulation—Enkadrain™, Warm 'N' Dry™—or a similar product will do the same thing.

If you're really worried, don't wait until the water gets to your foundation to deal with it. Dig a 6′ to 8′ deep curtain drain in a protective arc uphill from the building. (See illustration below.) This will take off the subsurface water. If surface runoff is

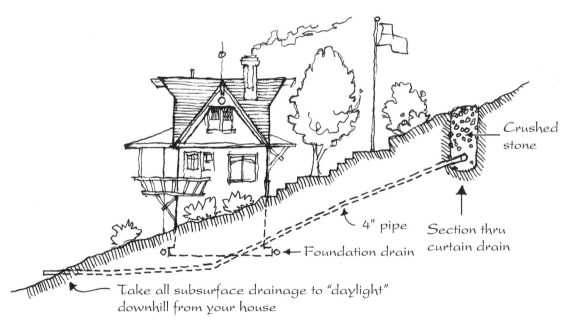

By installing an extensive curtain drain well uphill of your foundation, you can catch most surface and subsurface water before it even gets to your foundation drain.

the problem, top your backfill with about 10″ of clay graded away from the building into a swale leading around the house. Note that all these remedies consist of providing the water with an easier path to follow than the one that leads into your basement. That is as close to real waterproofing as you are likely to get (Figure 41).

The Design/Builder Attitude About Foundations

Any part of a building can be fixed after it's built. Nevertheless, the cost and impact of changing the foundation can be daunting once a house is on it. So take the necessary time to think about the design and construction logistics for your particular project. Don't just copy what others are doing. Think about your options. Any foundation system, properly considered and carefully constructed, should last a minimum of one hundred years.

Lastly, don't overlook the architectural opportunities in the foundation. The zone of transition from ground plane to building is one of the most frequently missed opportunities in residential design. How frequently I hear Yestermorrow students worry:

"I don't want to see any concrete! I hate that part of the foundation that sticks out of the ground."

And then the hopeful teacher, "Well, what can we do to make it look better? Cover it with bricks? Texture it with stone

face? Cast shape or a design into it? Paint it? Plant shrubs?"

"Shrubs! Yes. Let's hide it with shrubs."

Plants are always popular because they "hide" the foundation. But plants close to a house also provide a path for termites, carpenter ants, and other pests to get at

the wood. Try to avoid the "Let's hide it" response to those parts of a house that you haven't liked in the past. There really is no "bad" part of a house. If you are imaginative, you can find ways to include every part of the house in the overall design.

Consider the often maligned concrete

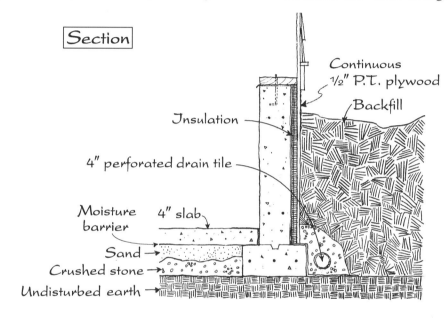

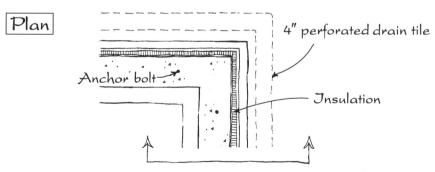

FIGURE 41: The traditional foundation uses a draining system that is simple and does little more than provide the water with an easier path around your house.

block. Common modular block (formerly "cinder block") comes in a variety of finishes and colors. So experiment! Think of those beautiful dry-laid foundations of yesteryear. Those design/builders were simply using the common block of their time. Shouldn't you try to attain something equally as successful in your own time? Perhaps the block may be intertwined with fieldstone, brick, or some other compatible material. If you approach it creatively, there's no reason why you can't make a foundation that attractively weds your house to the site as well as meeting its structural requirements.

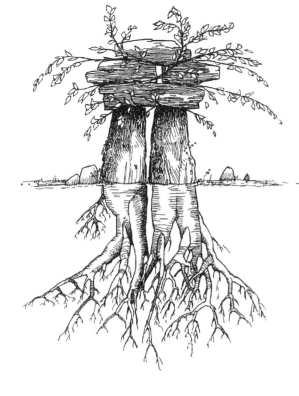

9

Walls and Wallness

⦙⦙⦙ **Introduction**

My children are arguing in their bedroom.

"This is an imaginary brick wall right along here," proclaims one of my sons, "and everything on this side of the room is mine, and everything on your side is yours—and no backs!"

What could the Great Wall of China possibly have in common with the imaginary wall used by quibbling children sharing a bedroom? For that matter, what qualities are shared by a garden wall, a curtain wall, and a bedroom wall? What, as Buddha might ask, is "wallness?"

The answer lies in the human need to lay meaningful order over the chaos of our world. Walls enclose and separate. Inside becomes differentiated from outside. Walls organize. This is truly the miracle of a simple wall. We take it for granted, naturally. But what other single device so efficiently allows us to give different meaning, and thus function, to different locations? The bedroom is for sleeping, the kitchen for cooking, the den for recreation, the garage for the car. The plants that grow inside the garden wall are the garden, those on the outside are

wildflowers. This side of the Great Wall is China, that side is the hordes. Indeed, the Great Wall of China, visible from the moon, is probably all any extraterrestrial need notice to conclude that there is intelligent life on this planet. Only intelligent life would draw a line and thus assign meaning to location. Moreover, when a location is meaningfully designated—with walls or otherwise—isn't that the first step toward making a "place"?

Among all the significant separations, there is one that is particularly crucial: Outside is the weather, inside is climate

119

control. In combination with the roof and foundation, the walls allow us to separate the vagaries and dangers of weather (and society) from our private comfort. This is very central to the making of a house.

Once inside a house, we use walls to separate the space into different zones, and the zones are divided into specific spaces or rooms. We find bedrooms and bathrooms in the private zone. Living and dining rooms are in the public zone. This may seem like basic stuff. It should. Our cultural ancestors were organizing their spaces in essentially this way centuries before they ever arrived in the New World.

This section covers the construction of walls. As we found with the foundation and will discover with the other parts of a building, understanding "how" follows most directly from an understanding of "what" and "why."

▥ Up From the Bubble Diagram

The bubble diagram allowed us to explore different spatial and functional arrangements. The interaction between rooms is controlled and moderated by walls and reflects the priorities planned for each bubble. Appropriate levels of separation/ connection are essential qualities we want to build into our walls. Walls between bedrooms should be chosen to give maximum acoustical privacy. Conversely, walls between living and dining rooms may want to be movable, half height or transparent.

Load-bearing walls must support critical loads, and if they are exterior walls they must control weather as well.

If we were to take each of the two-dimensional bubbles in our diagram and extrude it up from the paper, this might be a starting point for understanding the walls. I emphasize "starting point." All we would have at that point would be the most fundamental of wall systems. Nevertheless, it's a worthwhile exercise to cut out some strips of paper at scale dimension and "extrude" your bubble diagram (see Figure 42).

Walls, in all their glory, must organize at least four worlds for the design/builder:

Structural
Climatic
Visual
Acoustical

Depending on what is planned for the spaces within, above, or below the walls in question, one or more of these four basic concerns must be addressed. We will inspect the possibilities in each of these areas, starting with "structure." After all, if a wall can't support itself and that which is above it, all other considerations are moot.

STRUCTURE

There really aren't that many ways to organize walls into structural systems. Moreover, we usually experience all of

them by the time we're old enough to ride a bicycle. How? Snow forts, jungle gyms, tents, and card houses. Let's consider where each one leads.

Snow forts are built using one of history's most prevalent technologies: piling things on top of each other. Things to be piled up may include stones, bricks, logs, straw bales or even spare tires. The basic principles and approach are pretty much the same; we can learn a lot from building snow forts. We learn that the height of a wall is often limited by how high we can lift the building unit (snowball). We learn that the base of the wall must be thicker than the top. Going up, we find, is easier than spanning over. Windows and roofs become a problem. All the same, piling things up makes a substantial wall. Historically, this is the way most forts were built, not just those of snow. Even today we feel that a block, stone, or brick wall represents solid, built-to-last construction.

While masonry walls may carry the biggest loads, they must be constructed in a mostly vertical fashion. There is very little spanning ability in a masonry wall. Its incredible strength is a function of gravity's pull: the more mass = the more gravity's pull = the more strength. This means any horizontal configurations must be carefully corbeled or arched to insure that the vertical loads can find an adequate path to the ground (see Figure 43). Be-

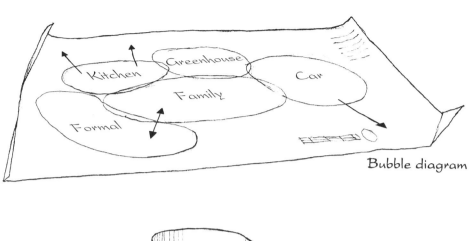

Bubble diagram

Tape some paper strips
to your bubble diagram and
you will get a rough idea
of what your rooms will
look like

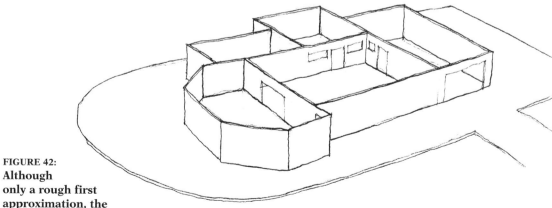

**FIGURE 42:
Although
only a rough first
approximation, the
bubble diagram can suggest much about
the ultimate wall layout. It's worth the study.**

cause masonry is so heavy, it may not be the wisest choice for very high structures. As the weight builds up, the foundation requirements can become formidable.

The other consideration with masonry construction is where to put the insulation and/or mechanicals. Double-wall masonry construction can incorporate a bit of insulation, plus it handles moisture and condensation quite well. Increase the insulation significantly, however, or try to install ducts, pipes, or vents and you end up with a very, very thick wall.

In the chapter on masonry, we will discuss masonry details and some typical wall sections (Figure 44).

The jungle gym suggests a different approach: Frame construction. As children, we encountered frames everywhere. From Tinkertoys to erector sets, from jungle gyms to tree houses, children are confronted with frames. The history of building walls with sticks and mud infill is only slightly shorter than that for piling up stones. Over the years frame construction has evolved dramatically in the regions of the world that grow timber or bamboo. Smaller and smaller sticks are used in ever more ingenious ways. Today's trees can be grown faster and harvested sooner. The results are lower costs, speedier erection, and more flexibility. One can hardly wonder that wood-frame construction is the predominant method of house building in this country. Even brick homes are gener-

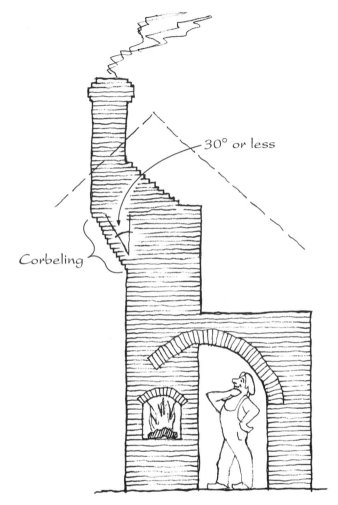

FIGURE 43: Masonry depends on gravity and weight to give it strength.

30° or less

Corbeling

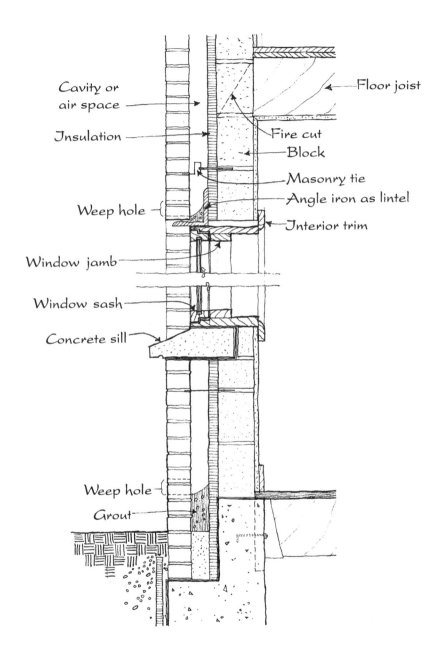

Cavity or air space

Insulation

Weep hole

Window jamb

Window sash

Concrete sill

Weep hole

Grout

Floor joist

Fire cut

Block

Masonry tie

Angle iron as lintel

Interior trim

FIGURE 44: There is much to consider in the standard masonry cavity wall.

ally just a veneer built over a wooden frame. Because this technology for making walls (and whole building envelopes) is so prevalent, I have given the subject further attention in the next two chapters.

Continuing with the child's perspective, I recall the thrill of my first tent. It was made from a bed sheet. Later I graduated to plastic tarps and then, in high school, I got my first canvas umbrella tent. Though only used in temperate climates and usually by nomadic cultures, the tent has a place in almost every culture's history. Even today, when the weather is suitable, whole segments of our society move into house tents. Fabric walls are used in voting booths, home show displays, and as windbreaks. Hospitals use fabric walls to get the most flexibility from their wards. Granted, this is still not a method of wall making that enjoys wide use in today's housing industry. As housing needs grow and affordable space becomes a priority, I anticipate more use of this ancient method for making walls. Even whole shelters.

When we built card and doll houses as children, we were foreshadowing the use of modern modular units (Figure 45). Today's industrial countries are prefabricating walls, indeed whole houses, in every conceivable form. The panelized house builder gets his walls preassembled. The concrete industry offers "tilt-up" construction and precast wall assemblies. The famous Habitat at the Montreal Expo was designed to be assembled from whole units, precast in concrete, and then piled one atop another. Contemporary timber-frame homes are commonly clad with stressed-skin panels. These wall assemblies come complete with interior finish, exterior nail base, insulation, and mechanical accommodations. The plastics industry is experimenting with modular wall units as well as prefabricated bathrooms, kitchens, and even whole living units.

FIGURE 45: Panelized and premanufactured house components are becoming a common sight as the cost of housing continues to rise.

While the industrialization of housing parts is a fact of life, I mention it with some reservation. As with any product, when you purchase the "features" you also get the shortcomings. Manufactured systems often come with unforeseen constraints. For instance, some can only be assembled in certain ways or within certain limits. It is all too common to find owner/builders embracing manufactured housing on the merits of economy while overlooking the loss of design control or site suitability. Happily, I have observed a tendency among panelizers to open their process to the custom designs of their customers. Today it shouldn't be difficult to find a panel manufacturer who will pre-build walls from your own drawings. Indeed, many will draft up your rough sketch and throw some basic engineering into the bargain.

CLIMATE

A solid, structurally secure wall may keep out the vandals, hold up the roof, and last forever. Yet to be comfortable, the walls of a house must also control temperature and moisture movement.

Eventually, heat will make its way through any wall. It's the time element that's important. A wall must be designed to control the speed with which heat moves through it. Along with the heat, moisture will be carried into a wall. Moisture must always be controlled on the warm side of the wall. Finally there's the big stuff—snow, fog, wind-driven rain, and direct sun. With the forces of Nature the question isn't control, it's survival. Depending on the climate in your region, you must choose wall technologies that will survive the brutal onslaught of rain, wind, and sun (Figure 46).

Masonry and frame-wall systems have specific advantages in different climates.

For really cold zones it is hard to beat the frame. More void than structure, the frame is ideally suited for packing the wall with loads of insulation. In very hot regions, however, one tends to find heavy masonry. The sun can beat on a thick adobe wall all day before the heat begins to get through to the interior. In many hot regions the nights are as cold as the days are hot. So when the sun goes down, the

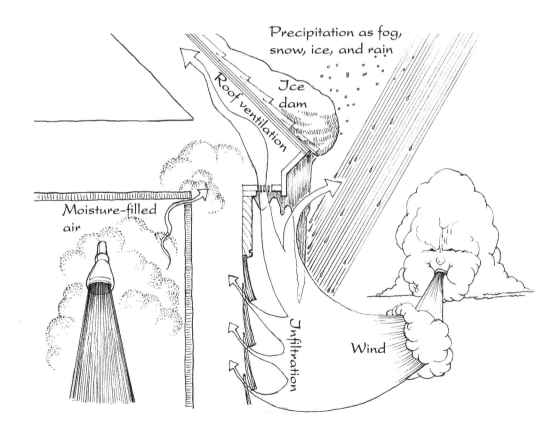

FIGURE 46: The wall must deal with moisture and temperature conditions inside as well as outside.

heated walls are just starting to give off the day's heat to the interior. They continue to do so throughout the night.

It sure would be nice if it were that simple: frame for the cold, masonry for the heat. Unfortunately, there are a great many climates that are both cold and hot, during different seasons. Moreover, many of them are humid to boot. So it is useful to understand the underlying principles that make walls successful (or not).

Let's start with heat movement. If design/build sometimes seems like an endless array of theories and systems, it is comforting to know that there are a few easy facts:

Insulation Is Good.
More Insulation Is Better.

No matter what the climate, site, program or design, the better insulated your wall, the more comfortable you will be. This is because one of the big objectives in building a house is to create a small climatic environment that is independent from the weather outside. If you live in a cold climate, you must insulate your walls to keep the heat *in*. In a hot climate the same insulation will keep the heat *out*. The more insulation between you and the outside, the less work your boiler or air conditioner must do to keep the inside temperature constant. It's simple: insulation is good.

But of course, nothing is that simple. For one thing, insulation only controls conductive heat movement. That's the heat that travels *through* the wall. Heat moves even more dramatically by means of infiltration. This is the heat that leaks through the cracks in any house. There are cracks between wall assemblies, around windows and doors, at mechanical and vent penetrations, chimneys, roof eaves, sill plates, and so forth. To give you a rough idea, a well-built home today will experience at least one full exchange of all the air in the building every hour of the day (on average). The obvious conclusion: we should build tight houses and control infiltration.

Having considered heat, let's take a look at moisture. Moisture goes wherever air goes. It can also soak into the wall materials like water into a sponge. Generally, the soaking mechanism accounts for only about 10 percent of the moisture movement; the rest follows the paths of infiltration. This seems to be yet another reason to build tight walls. Cracks and penetrations should be caulked, gypsum board well taped. Vapor barriers should always be installed on the warm side of a wall. That's the inside in a heating region, the outside in a cooling region.

Nevertheless, we know that nothing is ever perfect, and vapor barriers are no exception. Moisture-laden air will get into any wall assembly if there is space and access. This means we must be ever mindful of voids in our walls. Voids and dead air spaces should be ventilated where feasible. Moreover, we know that moisture isn't harmful until it finds a cold enough surface on which to condense. Therefore, we want to eliminate such surfaces and eliminate access to any such surfaces, within any wall or roof assembly.

But we can't eliminate the moisture itself. Humans need a certain level of moisture in the air just to feel comfortable. In arid climates, we humidify our interior spaces and in humid climates we air condition or dehumidify our spaces. Moreover, kitchens and bathrooms will always be areas of high interior humidity.

Compared to the interior, the exterior moisture conditions are far more varied from region to region. The sun, wind, and rain (and I also mean snow, fog, and sleet) will combine in very different ways depending on where you dwell. Study the local vernacular buildings to find out what works best. Generally, vernacular construction demonstrates which local materials are abundant and how to best configure them. The wind-driven rain of New England is met with shingled or tightly clapboarded walls. The moderate climate of the Mid-Atlantic permits the stately brick and stone as well as the wooden finishes. In the South and the Southwest, masonry and adobe have long been materials of choice. In the wet Northwest we mostly find wood. In temperate regions we find the widest variety of building practices.

I should add that it's not simply a matter of availability. In Vermont we have an inexhaustible supply of field stones. Vermont farmers claim it's their most successful crop, because regardless of how thoroughly they harvest the stone from their fields, there is always a new crop the next year. And yet, we have very few stone houses here. I suspect this type of wall fails on two counts. First, it's slow. Vermont has a short building season so closure must be accomplished quickly. Secondly, it's cold. A stone wall, even a thick one, will eventually become unbearably cold. And it will take a roaring fire several days to thaw it out. Just a few states south, in the Connecticut River valley, we find plenty of stone homes and by the time we get to Pennsylvania and Maryland, stone is the predominant building material. [There has always been an abundance of both stone and wood throughout New England, but the weather dictates which becomes the preferred building material (Figure 47).]

Further examples of regionally appropriate wall design can be found in Chapter 11, in which we discuss the effects of gravity, temperature, and moisture in more depth. Finally, in Chapter 15, we run through the calculations for interior climate control: heating, cooling, humidity, and ventilation. The heat gain/loss calculation described therein is the fundamental method for assessing the thermal properties of any building's envelope.

After you have completed this calculation, you will know where and how fast the heat is flowing through every wall in your house. At that juncture, sizing equipment or redesigning walls can be done knowledgeably.

VISUAL: ARCHITECTURAL APPEARANCE

Why do we find people living in contemporary glass houses in the snow belt? How can we explain log homes in the desert? What is the reason for an A-frame in Florida? These house types always look silly when we find them in the wrong climate. Historians, architects, and other keepers of "public good taste" get bent way out of shape when a transplant architecture shows up in their neighborhood.

"Why??" they all ask in chorus. "Why are you building *that*—here?"

The answer is almost always the same. Responds the innocent client: "I like it." So there you have it. After thinking about vernacular tradition, appropriate technology, durability, and common sense, people still make many very important decisions based on personal whim.

Lest there be any confusion, I'm in total support of this. I think people should be encouraged to express personal whim through their buildings. At the same time, they should educate themselves with the available information before making any hasty decisions. Many times people just

don't know what the options are or why one way is any better than another.

So, as you make your transition from bubble diagram to floor plans, be mindful of the architectural and structural aspects of your walls, roof, and other building components. If your design is traditional, you might think there is little to decide. Not so. While Spanish Colonial is almost always stuccoed masonry, New England capes come in brick as well as wood. The same is true of Italianate or Greek Revival.

An interpretive or contemporary design will always have more latitude for expression. Ask yourself which material best expresses your feelings about structure, durability, security, and strength. Masonry has the edge in this department, but I've seen some timber frames and some log homes that look solid as rock. For structural gymnastics like cantilevers, long spans, or tower spires, it's wood or steel frames that come to mind.

At this point you will also want to consider to what extent you wish to "express" the structure. Massive beams look better than little 2 × 10s when exposed. The steel ties used with brick can be very attractive when properly designed. I've seen beautiful trusses made of very small pieces of wood. Even the classic column is a form of expressed structure. Structure is a powerful form generator. If you allow it to be seen and understood, the architecture of your home will be more lucid and, thus, more successful.

FIGURE 47: The climate, as well as availability, may ultimately determine which building materials you choose.

Yestermorrow was created to help people understand how to build intelligent and appropriate—but also *expressive*—houses.

Your taste must respond to different conditions depending on whether you apply it to an exterior wall or an interior wall. Exterior walls must deal with the climate. Adobe in Seattle will be very high maintenance. Fieldstone in Minnesota will be terribly cold. And a modern glass house in Maine comes with astronomical heating bills. On the other hand, interior walls are subject to many fewer constraints. Here, the worst you could do is reduce resale value or precipitate a divorce.

Walls are vertical planes. They are like billboards or museum walls. They have terrific capacity for expression. Whatever we do with them will be highly visible and reflective of who we are. (See Figure 48.) Of course there will always be those who will tell you that it *must* be done this way or that. Not so! There's a logic behind the consensus of "good taste," but there's just as strong an argument for personal expression.

Stop for a moment and consider the human condition. We all seek two utterly contradictory situations. We want to express our *individuality* but, at the same time, we *wish to belong* to the larger group. Sometimes people hire architects or decorators to ensure that their built surroundings meet societal norms. If you design your own home, or even pick out

FIGURE 48: **External walls are like billboards; internal walls are like canvases. You may express yourself on both with a wide palette of finishes.**

the colors, there is always the risk that people may criticize or ridicule. At least, if a designer is employed, there is always someone to blame. Most people want a house that's "distinctive" but still normal. For most Americans, "normal" means colonial. The colonial "look"—rarely an authentic replication—is the design style of choice for most owner/builders. It is also the look that most spec builders and developers provide.

So what about expressing your individuality? Well, some people build excessively large colonial homes to express their wealth and prominence in the community. Some people hire historians to help them build more accurate replicas of famous colonial homes; this expresses their level of education and sophistication. Some hire architects who reinterpret past styles in a postmodern collage. This allows the client to express their appreciation of "art." Although I can appreciate these indirect modes of self-expression, they still reflect a society out of touch with its built environment. If you look at the houses that architects and builders make for themselves, you will likely be amazed. Sure, some may express formality, but many also express whimsy, craftsmanship, humor, spirituality, memory, nature, budget, materials, family, home, tradition, eccentricity, exuberance—in short, they tap and express the essence of every facet of their lives.

Architects and builders are relaxed with buildings. They do not worry so much about building it right. They're more concerned with what they will express, what they will make. Like anyone who becomes comfortable in a medium, technique becomes supportive. Content is primary.

So in this context the exterior walls become like a person's clothing; they tell something of the person within. When I design a house for someone, I think of it as a portrait. A good portrait does more than present a visual likeness, it demonstrates the subject's relationship to the family and the community. It indicates the subject's place in society and, more importantly, in history. A good portrait tells all about an individual's culture and the particular life they are living in it. This is part of what fuels our interest in historic homes. Visiting the homes of Ben Franklin, Thomas Edison, or Thomas Jefferson, we see more than just famous lifestyles. We can discern the social values, politics, education, and religion of the day. Best of all, we can see how these individuals, so famous for their personal achievements, expressed in their homes that spirit responsible for their accomplishments.

So when you are choosing a wall system, don't simply study the engineering. Don't unthinkingly settle for whatever is supposed to be "normal." Ask yourself *who you are* and what *you* want to see.

Interior walls don't have to look like those in the magazines and exterior walls needn't be just like your neighbors'. All walls don't have to be 8' high (the modular norm dictated by plywood and gyp board). Some walls need not be straight, level, or even plumb. Walls can be solid and opaque or thin and transparent. Screens and lattices allow sound transmission without full visual interaction. Half walls define boundaries without excluding joint activities.

Finally, don't forget the finishes. Walls generate radically different effects depending on their color, texture, and material from which they're made. Moreover, certain finishes come with a connotational spin. A brick wall may suggest formality while a concrete block wall suggests utility. A metal wall suggests industry. Glass-block walls take many people back to a specific era of design (but for one of my students it always reminded him of parking garages). Adobe and wood are warm organic materials that have a rural connotation, while metal and glass remind us of the city. Of course, all these associations are very general. The exceptions are almost as numerous as the examples. So what's the point? Simply to become aware of these connections for yourself. If glass block means parking garage to you, then you must design within this association. It makes no difference how many architects tell you that it is a high design material used in art deco. I had one student who associated a certain shiplap siding with the slums outside of Philadelphia. I showed her dozens of examples and endless pictures of the same siding being used in Adirondack camps of the rich and famous. This was silly. In the end I realized that she should design from her own experiences, not mine or anyone else's.

ACOUSTICS

All walls have the capacity to control sound travel. With a little attention this ability can be used to create quiet, private places even in the hubbub of a city. This is more than a subtle nuance. If you created two identical rooms with only sound deadening as the difference, you would find the feeling and human behavior exhibited in each to be dramatically different.

There are several obvious places for the use of sound deadening. A bathroom should be as acoustically hushed as it is visually private. A bedroom will provide a more restful sleep if it isn't penetrated by outside noise. Even public spaces such as a living room or den need to be considered acoustically. Listening to Brahms over the sound of the dishwasher is less than ideal.

Walls offer the first and most effective line of defense against vagrant noise transmission. What gets through and what bounces off a wall are determined by the material choice and design of the wall. Mass is the best barrier. As a wall becomes heavier, less sound gets through. Thus, a masonry wall will stop more sound than a stud wall. Underground spaces, surrounded by earth, are well known for their peace and quiet. If you live in a city, try this experiment. Take a short trip from your uppermost floor down to the basement. You will find that there is little improvement in the sound pollution from the second to the first floor, but that the basement is dramatically silent (don't forget to turn off the boiler, water pump, and washing machine).

What's happening here? Sound travels in waves. These waves propagate through different materials in proportion to their volume and pitch. Lower tones will get through where higher ones won't. Also, since it takes more energy to move heavy molecules, we find that heavy wall construction does a better job at slowing sound transmission.

"Great, but I don't want to live in my basement and I don't want to build every bathroom with concrete walls. Isn't there another way?"

It's a reasonable request, and happily the answer is "yes." Inexpensive sound deadening can be accomplished by filling your interior walls with fiberglass insulation, the more the better. Additional deadening can be had by doubling up the drywall to increase the wall's mass (keep in mind that this will change your door-jamb dimensions) or hanging the drywall from an acoustical channel, which separates the drywall from the actual framing with a thin resilient strip. Or you might even separate the two sides of the wall by staggering the studs. Special care should be taken around the waste plumbing. You don't want to pause for the sound of a toilet flushed on the second floor passing through the dining room while you're entertaining your boss for dinner. A massive cast-iron vent stack will transmit less noise than a plastic one. If you don't want to pay the extra for cast iron, secure the plastic pipe well and wrap it in insulation.

The finishes on walls (floors and ceilings, too) will have a marked effect on the acoustics of a room. Smooth, hard surfaces will reflect sound, while soft or broken surfaces will absorb it. Egg cartons are the young design/builder's affordable finish for the stereo room. I think something similar might be used in the children's playroom. Carpet on a wall will keep a room quiet, while plaster will make a room's acoustics crisp, possibly even strident.

In addition to modifying transmission of interior generated sound, properly designed walls can help reduce noise associated with a nearby highway, railroad crossing, or other exterior sources. For example, I live in a bucolic little village in Vermont—about 10 feet from a road at the bottom of a long hill. All the trucks apply their brakes just as they pass my house. When they are going up the hill, they shift into a lower (louder) gear—just as they reach my front door. In dealing with this situation I learned something about sound transmission. During the initial renovation I packed the walls with insulation and I doubled up the drywall on the inside; the results were underwhelming. The noise still filled my dining room and kitchen. Then, two years later, I invested in new windows purely for energy reasons. I took out the old single-pane double-hungs and replaced them with double-pane windows and built-in storm sashes. When I installed them, I took great pains to fill all voids around the window with insulation before replacing the trim. The trim was embedded in caulk to minimize infiltration. The acoustical effect was dramatic: The sound level inside decreased by half. I have since learned that 90 percent of audible sound will leak through the tiniest cracks, irrespective of how well the surrounding wall is insulated.

For most people, the idea of using walls to shape their acoustical environment may be new. Yet everyone responds to the types and volume of sounds around them. Evidence of this may be seen in the many "white noise" generators currently found on the market. Unfortunately, masking one sound with another doesn't produce true quiet. Use your walls to segregate, amplify, or insulate the sounds around you. It will provide an inexpensive but dramatic aspect to your home.

So, as you bring your bubbles up into walls, remember that the materials and layout of these walls will reflect the special ceremonies and daily choreography of your life. Priorities developed in your bubble diagrams become legible as the walls define the interior and exterior spaces. The materials and finishes vibrate with associations. And wherever a wall meets another assembly—ceiling, roof, foundation, etc.—you will want to detail it in an expressive way. Don't just accept the standard detail because "that's the way it's done."

Have fun with your walls and make them reflect your special lifestyle. Don't shoehorn your life into little boxes. Break open the boxes and dance with your walls!

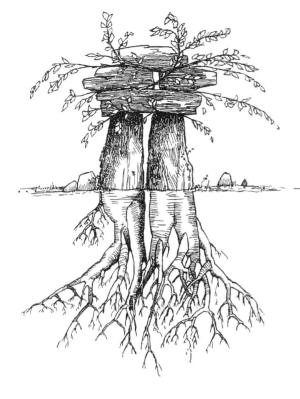

Frames, Framing, and Skeletons

The relationship between walls and roof is structurally complex and rich with design implications. As we cycle through the design helix, the interrelationship between the walls and the roof must be thoroughly understood if we want to arrive at a coherent design solution. In addition to visual content, this cohesiveness will depend on several other considerations. Structure is first, of course. Bringing the roof loads down through the walls must be done elegantly, and that means graceful transition at the eaves and gables. At this transition, we must also consider the continuity of the vapor barrier and insulation. Even roof venting can be designed. The necessary grillwork can be a key element in the successful detailing of the soffit (underside of the roof overhang). Also, the interior spaces may be affected and the size and location of windows established. Overhangs will determine the depth of the shadows and protect the walls from rain and ice. Even siting plays a role. The proportions of the walls and the pitch of your roof will visually connect (or disconnect) the building to its surroundings.

As a final incentive, let me mention this general truth. It is possible, even easy, to design a configuration of walls for which no proper roof shape exists. By contrast, any and all roof shapes, regardless of complexity, will easily accept walls beneath them. (This "general truth" will be more obvious to those who have attempted a few house designs.)

This chapter and the next will explore some of the technical aspects of wall and roof assemblies. We will start with wood frames and then look at alternatives.

Frames

To quote Danny Webster:

> **frame** (fram) n. **1.** Something composed of parts fitted and joined together; a structure, such as: a. A basic or skeletal structure designed to give shape or support: the frame of a house. b. An open structure for encasing, holding, or bordering something: a window frame. **2.** The general structure of something; system; order. Obsolete: shape, form.

In North America, wooden frames account for the vast majority of residential buildings. The following descriptions of some of the more common wood systems are presented as a design palette. Look at the different "colors"; get a feeling for which ones will best allow you to realize your personal building vision.

TIMBER FRAMES

Timber framers sometimes resent having their craft called post and beam, but that is the essence of it. Posts, beams, girts, plates, joists, and purlins make up the frame. Dimensions are large and long. It is common to see 8″ × 8″ posts, 8″ × 6″ rafters, 4″ × 4″ purlins, and spans up to 20′ and 30′! Timber frames concentrate all the loads onto relatively few posts. With such an arrangement it is important that all joints be carefully considered and executed.

Figure 49 illustrates two of the more common frame configurations. Typically they are simple but robust. The massive timbers recall the very trees from which they were cut. The clarity of the frame makes obvious what each piece is doing structurally. For this reason, timber framers are usually reluctant to see the frame hidden by the interior finishes— even though this is historically correct. (See "stress skin panels" as an alternative.) The massive pieces of wood are perfect for expressing the protective and enduring qualities of a warm shelter.

Another visual treat inherent in the timber frame is the joinery. Starting with the simple mortise and tenon, there are dozens and dozens of different joints specifically designed for particular situations. Each is an oversized version of what you might expect to find in a fine piece of furniture (Figure 50). These joints *must* be finely crafted. It is often the joinery strength that determines timber frame design. Because each stick must be interwoven with the rest, care must be taken not to carve out too much wood at a complex joint. Too many mortises close together can render the post too weak to resist the stresses converging on the joint.

And yet, structural failure of a timber frame is rare. These are sturdy buildings that resist fire and the ravages of time better than most. Because the technology was handed down through oral tradition, the designs are often conservative, both structurally and architecturally. They tend to be built with long spans allowing flexible interiors. If you trace the history of a simple barn or meeting house, you are likely to find it has accommodated a wide variety of functions over the years. Because of their flexibility and inherent durability, timber frame structures can be found that are over five hundred years old and still in use.

As the oldest uninterrupted tradition of vernacular building, timber framing is currently enjoying a renaissance. Its historic and visual appeal has overcome its disadvantages. In general, timber framing requires more material and more highly skilled labor. These are the reasons it was replaced by stick framing. But large frames are still ideal for the community construction project where "many hands make light work." Once the timbers have been cut and notched, the entire frame can be raised with the help of friends and neighbors in one or two days. I know of few things that knit people together the way a frame-raising does. And if you have no friends (a pity), a small crane will get the job done just as fast.

If you want a timber frame but lack the resources to cut and erect it, consider purchasing it. There are many outfits across the country that will cut you a custom frame. Most of these companies will travel to your site and help erect it as well. The Timber Framers' Guild of North America has a complete listing. Contact them at: Timber Framers' Guild of North America, P.O. Box 1046, Keene, NH 03431.

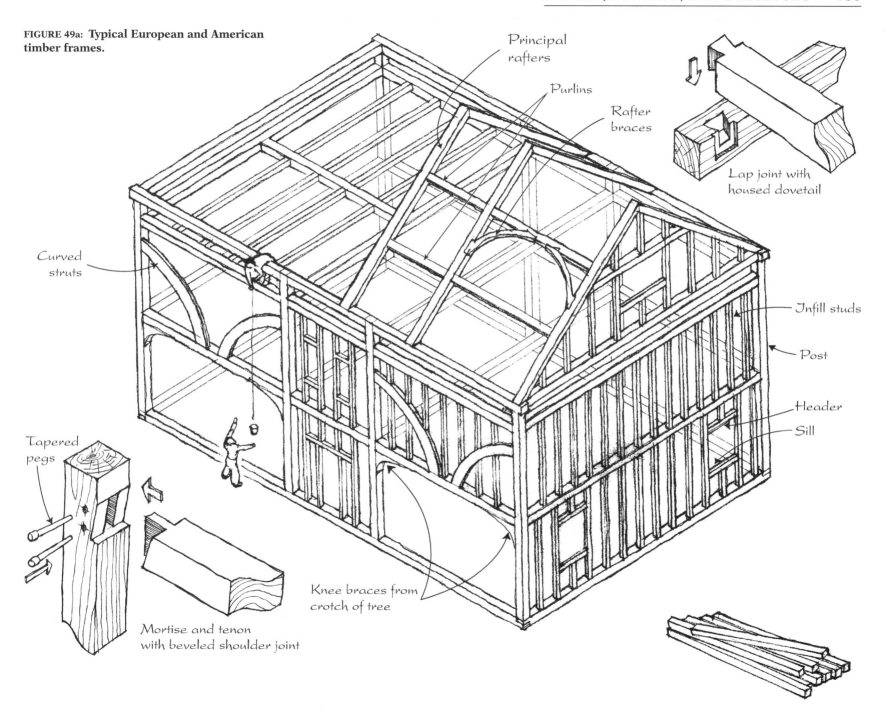

FIGURE 49a: Typical European and American timber frames.

Principal rafters

Purlins

Rafter braces

Lap joint with housed dovetail

Curved struts

Infill studs

Post

Header

Sill

Tapered pegs

Mortise and tenon with beveled shoulder joint

Knee braces from crotch of tree

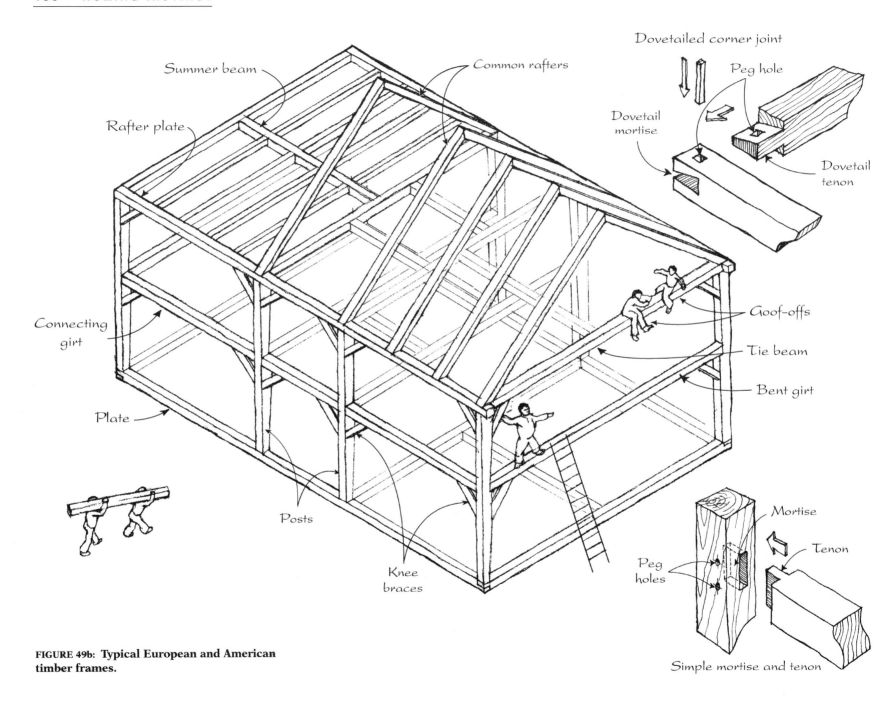

Dovetailed corner joint

Peg hole

Dovetail mortise

Dovetail tenon

Summer beam

Common rafters

Rafter plate

Goof-offs

Tie beam

Connecting girt

Bent girt

Plate

Posts

Knee braces

Mortise

Tenon

Peg holes

Simple mortise and tenon

FIGURE 49b: Typical European and American timber frames.

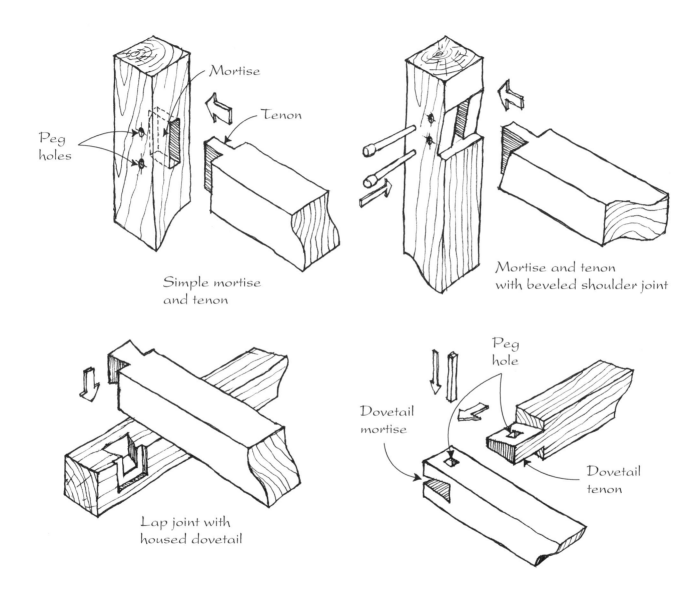

Mortise

Tenon

Peg holes

Simple mortise and tenon

Mortise and tenon with beveled shoulder joint

Lap joint with housed dovetail

Peg hole

Dovetail mortise

Dovetail tenon

FIGURE 50: **Timber frame joinery is just as elaborate and beautiful as furniture joinery.**

THE SHORT SHORT COURSE ON FRAMING YOUR HOUSE

In a 1923 publication by H. Vandervoort Walsh, *Construction of the Small House,* there is the following reference to an article in the January 18, 1855, issue of the New York *Tribune,* covering a meeting of the American Institute Farmers' Club:

Mr. Robinson said: . . . I would saw all my timbers for a frame house, or ordinary frame outbuilding, of the following dimensions: 2 × 8 inches; 2 × 4; 2 × 1. I have, however, built them, when I lived on the Grand Prairie of Indiana, many miles from sawmills, nearly all of split and hewed stuff, making use of rails or round poles, reduced to straight lines and even thickness on two sides, for studs and rafters. But sawed stuff is much the easiest, though in a timber country the other is far the cheapest. First, level your foundation, and lay down two of the 2 × 8 pieces, flatwise, for side-walls. Upon these set the floor-sleepers, on edge, 32 inches apart. Fasten one at each end, and perhaps one or two in the middle, if the building is large, with a wooden pin. These end-sleepers are the end-sills. Now lay the floor, unless you design to have one that would be likely to be injured by the weather before you get to the roof. It is a great saving, though, of labor to begin at the bottom of a house and build up. In laying the floor first, you have no studs to cut and fit around, and can let your boards run out over the ends, just as it happens, and afterward saw them off smooth by the sill. Now set up a corner post, which is nothing but one of the 2 × 4 studs, fastening the bottom by four nails; make it plumb, and stay it each way. Set another at the other corner, and then mark off your door and window places and set up the side-studs and put in the frames. Fill up the studs between, 16 inches apart, supporting the top by a line or strip of board from corner to corner, or stayed studs between. Now cover that side with rough sheeting boards, unless you intend to side-up with clapboards on the studs, which I never would do, except for a small, common building. . . .

The rafters, if supported so as not to be over 10 feet long, will be strong enough of the 2 × 4 stuff. Bevel the ends and nail fast to the joist. Then there is no strain upon the sides by the weight of the roof, which may be covered with shingles or other materials—the cheapest being composition or cement

roofs. To make one of this kind, take soft, spongy, thick paper, and tack it upon the boards in courses like shingles. Commence at the top with hot tar and saturate the paper, upon which sift evenly fine gravel, pressing it in while hot—that is while tar and gravel are both hot. One coat will make a tight roof; two coats will make it more durable. Put up your protistans of stiff 1 × 4, with strips to support the upper joist—then use stiff 2 × 4, with strips nailed on top, for the joist to rest upon, fastening all together by nails, wherever timbers touch. Thus you will have a frame without a tenon or mortise, or brace, and yet it is far cheaper, and incalculably stronger when finished, than though it were composed of timbers 10 inches square, with a thousand auger holes and a hundred days' work with the chisel and adze, making holes and pins to fill them.

To lay out and [timber] frame a building so that all its parts will come together requires the skill of a master mechanic, and a host of men and a deal of hard work to lift the great sticks of timber into position. To erect a balloon building requires about as much mechanical skill as it does to build a board fence. Any farmer who is handy with the saw, iron square, and hammer, with one of his boys or a common laborer to assist him, can go to work and put up a frame for an outbuilding, and finish it off with his own labor, just as well as to hire a carpenter to score and hew great oak sticks and fill them full of mortises, all by the science of the 'square rule.' It is a waste of labor that we should all lend our aid to put a stop to. Besides, it will enable many a farmer to improve his place with new buildings, who, though he has long needed them has shuddered at the thought of cutting down half of the best trees in his wood-lot, and then giving half a year's work to hauling it home and paying for what I do know is the wholly useless labor of framing. If it had not been for the knowledge of balloon frames, Chicago and San Francisco could never have arisen, as they did, from little villages to great cities in a single year. It is not alone city buildings, which are supported by one another, that may be thus erected, but those upon the open prairie, where the wind has a sweep from Mackinaw to the Mississippi, for there they are built, and stand as firm as any of the old frames of New England, with post and beams 16 inches square.

If your architectural tastes run toward simple shapes, and you want the free open spaces of a barn, the timber frame is a building technology you should consider. As we will discuss later, the choice of a timber frame will influence many other aspects of the project. For example, stress-skin sheathing for the walls, heavy plank flooring, centralized utilities, even certain bathroom fixtures are particularly suited to the architecture of the timber frame.

STICK FRAMES

Compared to the massive posts and beams found in timber frames, dimensional lumber does indeed seem like just so many sticks: $2'' \times 4''$, $2'' \times 6''$, $2'' \times 12''$. These rough-sawn dimensions are further reduced by about $\frac{1}{4}''$ to $\frac{1}{2}''$ in each dimension after drying and dressing. The sticks can be assembled a number of different ways. The first stick buildings were balloon frames; the studs ran uninterrupted from floor to roof. Today, most houses are platform frames; studs are interrupted at each floor. The accomplished builder uses both, sometimes in the same building, for the appropriate situation.

Structurally, stick frames are much less exacting than the timber frame. Where the timber frame concentrates all vertical loads on a few posts, the stick frame spreads the loads over several bearing walls consisting of dozens of studs. With all the perimeter and some interior walls taking the load, any one stud or rafter becomes less critical. Joints are less critical as well. Because of the number of pieces, the sticks are usually overlapped and fastened with nails; no intricate geometries to be notched out with chisel and mallet. In short, the stick frames use many small pieces connected in simple ways, whereas the timber frame uses fewer, larger pieces connected by elaborate joinery (Figure 51).

Architecturally, this is a trade-off. The stick frames will seldom have the massive, structural feeling of an exposed timber frame. Nevertheless, the stick frame is a good choice for complicated buildings with elaborate geometries. Curved walls, towers, complex roof shapes, multiple dormers, and most stepped shapes will usually be easier to build from sticks. Stick frames also use less of our precious timber resources.

Stick frames are usually categorized as systems of rules: the balloon frame, the platform frame, or the "value"-engineered frame. As builders and then developers adopted the stick frame, they proclaimed the benefits of "their system." It is true that fast, efficient construction with un-skilled labor is one of the big reasons stick framing eclipsed timber framing. And yet the real architectural benefits of stick framing are largely unrealized until "the system" is somewhat undone. Only by breaking out of the system can one be really expressive with it.

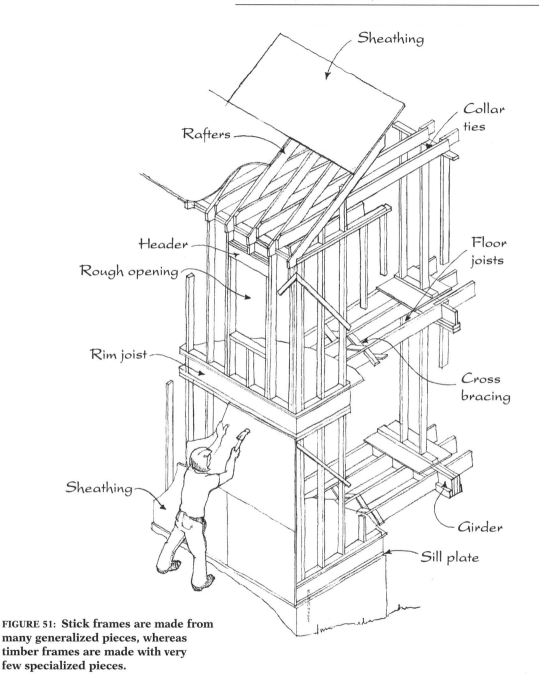

FIGURE 51: Stick frames are made from many generalized pieces, whereas timber frames are made with very few specialized pieces.

To abandon the 16″ or 24″ spacings at the center of the system requires a bit of money and knowledge. Dimensional lumber, it turns out, is also modular. Most of what you purchase at a lumberyard has been dimensioned to be even multiples, or fractions of, the 16″ or 24″ module. Lengths of framing lumber come in 2′ (24″) increments. Plywood and other sheet goods come in 4′ × 8′, 4′ × 10′, or 4′ × 12′ sheets. Even concrete blocks come in 16″ × 8″ × 8″ and lay up to form even 24″ lengths. Building exclusively within the modular system will minimize waste but may also minimize creativity.

To reduce cost and waste, commercial home builders have found ways to remove any stick or plank not absolutely required for structural integrity. The result was originally called "value-engineered," but when improperly implemented it resulted in less-durable buildings. As Yale engineer Martin Gehner concluded, these economy techniques will eventually demonstrate the "high cost of cheap construction." Nevertheless, it is important to reduce the flagrant consumption of our timber resources in mindlessly overbuilt frames. So says Steven Loken of the Center for Resourceful Building Technology (CRBT, P.O. Box 100, Missoula, Montana 59806). To help with this important objective, The Center's Director of Research, Tracy Mumma, compiled *The Guide to Resource Efficient Building Elements*. This is a list of materials and products that can reliably be used to reduce the use of timber in your house construction. Additionally, I suggest a look at *Cost Effective Home Building– A Design and Construction Handbook*, published by the National Association of Home Builders (NAHB). As you might imagine, the commercial home builders are more interested in their bottom line than saving our forested ecologies. Keep this in mind as you research "value-engineered" framing systems. While I applaud the good work done by Loken and Mumma, I remain skeptical of any system that claims to be an appropriate design solution, independent of site and bio region. Durable and sound construction will necessarily mean different things in seismic zones, hurricane regions, the snow belt, or the desert. That being said, a few illuminating pictures and a good bibliography are all we offer of value-engineered framing systems (Figures 52, 53, and 54). Draw your own conclusions, carefully.

Stick framing, in one form or another, is far and away the most widely used framing approach in use today. It's popularity is largely the result of its flexibility and, in most cases, its economy. This popularity is supported by a wood products industry that is just as broad. The choice of products available to finish off the stick frame is staggering. From fasteners to finishes, there are always half a dozen ways to skin the cat. Because of these endless choices, the work of the designer is all the more important. You must be aware of what you want. Every subcontractor and supplier will be happy to suggest that you do it this way or that way. These suggestions will often reflect what is on their shelves or in their truck, but they may not serve your architectural goals. Therefore, remember a few simple things:

1. There is no wrong or right way to design frames, there is only what you want (provided it will stand up and you can pay for it).
2. Regardless of what you want, it can probably be built with less lumber than most people use.
3. The more personal or unique your expression, the more likely a nontraditional or hybrid framing method will suit your needs. (See "Geometric Flexibility," later in this chapter.)

POLE BUILDINGS

Pole construction is an excellent and affordable framing choice for certain situations. Here the frame and the foundation are one. In pole construction the vertical, load-bearing members are poles: buried in the ground, continuous, and long enough to reach and support the roof. The diameter of the poles is usually about 6″ at the top. Because of their size, the poles are spaced quite far apart. Large-scale excavation and disruption of the site can be minimized (Figure 55).

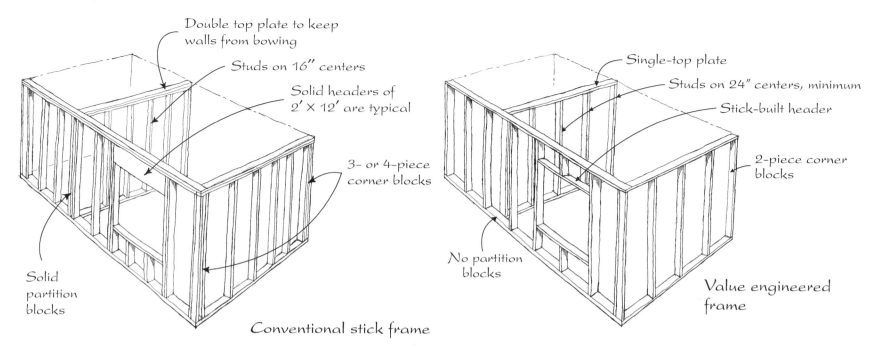

Double top plate to keep walls from bowing

Studs on 16" centers

Solid headers of 2' X 12' are typical

3- or 4-piece corner blocks

Solid partition blocks

Conventional stick frame

Single-top plate

Studs on 24" centers, minimum

Stick-built header

2-piece corner blocks

No partition blocks

Value engineered frame

FIGURE 52a: Value engineered framing only works if your lumber is very straight and clear. Sadly, this is increasingly not available.

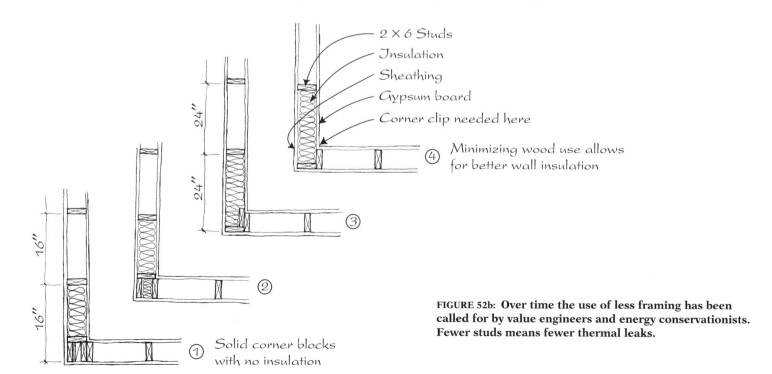

2 X 6 Studs

Insulation

Sheathing

Gypsum board

Corner clip needed here

④ Minimizing wood use allows for better wall insulation

24"

24"

③

16"

16"

16"

②

① Solid corner blocks with no insulation

FIGURE 52b: Over time the use of less framing has been called for by value engineers and energy conservationists. Fewer studs means fewer thermal leaks.

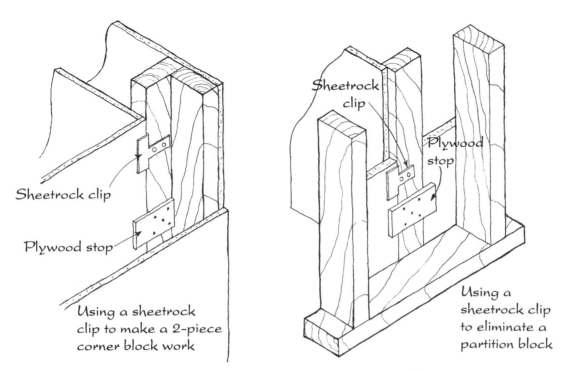

Sheetrock clip

Plywood stop

Using a sheetrock clip to make a 2-piece corner block work

Sheetrock clip

Plywood stop

Using a sheetrock clip to eliminate a partition block

FIGURE 53: Value-engineered framing uses clips and stops to eliminate lumber.

Finally, pole construction lends itself to steep sites. This can translate into fabulous views and lower land costs. Because the frame is also the foundation, the concrete subcontractor is eliminated from your budget and schedule.

Except for the way the frame touches the ground, it could be said that a pole frame is sort of a combination of timber framing and stick framing. The vertical members are few and large. This usually means the roof framing is also built of larger members. Rather than mortise and tenon joinery, the connectors are manufactured plates and bolts. Moreover, the walls and floors are built of smaller sticks. Pole frame construction is flexible. The knowledgeable designer may create the intricate massings of a stick frame or the robust proportions of a timber frame.

Perhaps the pole frame will come to be thought of as a truly vernacular American building type. With its utilitarian origins on the farm, it remains for the designer to detail and finish off the pole frame so that it becomes residential architecture. The structure must be understood and expressed. The large members allow for dramatic spaces at low cost. The poles have a strong vertical effect on the design, quite appropriate for hilly rural and suburban sites. But remember, there are problems of thermal and moisture protection that must be solved more rigorously than in farm buildings. Poles that run uninterrupted from outside into heated interior

Labor, time, and materials are all saved with the pole frame. Originally developed as an efficient method of construction for farm buildings, it has developed into a contemporary substitute for the more expensive timber frame. In its most utilitarian form, lateral girts replace the conventional wall studs, siding is vertical, and construction time is reduced.

Pole construction has advantages other than economy. Structurally, a round column is 18 percent stronger in resisting buckling than a rectangular one of the same cross-sectional area. In fact, for any

given species, a round timber will possess most of the bending strength of a smaller milled board graded "clear."

Another advantage of pole construction is resistance to high winds and/or flooding. It is a code-mandated framing choice along many shorelines. Because the poles are firmly anchored in the ground and because they run up through the entire frame, winds and other overturning forces are resisted throughout the building. High tides and flooding may damage the grade-level walls, but the entire structure remains sound.

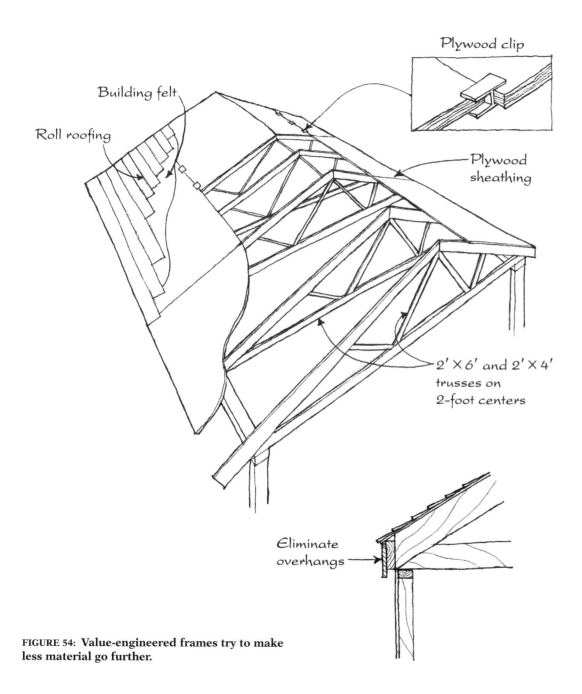

Plywood clip

Building felt

Roll roofing

Plywood sheathing

2' × 6' and 2' × 4' trusses on 2-foot centers

Eliminate overhangs

FIGURE 54: Value-engineered frames try to make less material go further.

spaces amount to a "thermal short circuit" when building in a cold climate. The same was true of the large post-and-beam frames before the advent of stressed-skin panels.

Building technologies that originate on the farm are often efficient and inexpensive. Making them habitable and aesthetically expressive, however, requires further design and engineering. On the bright side, in the hands of a creative designer/builder, pole construction holds great promise, which can be seen in the many fine pole-built homes already built (see Bibliography).

DOMES AND ZOMES

Not since the balloon frame has a framing system won the instant popularity that surrounded the geodesic dome in the sixties and seventies. With the famous Buckminster Fuller carrying the banner, the dome became more than a system. It became the symbol of technology's promise to offer the common individual a fully democratic lifestyle. It was to be a building type so efficient to assemble and service that its widespread use would single-handedly eliminate any housing shortages. "Efficiency" was the war cry. Approximating a sphere, the most efficient surface-to-volume container, the dome was proposed as an environmentally appropriate design solution. It also caught the spiritual momentum of the time with its large span-

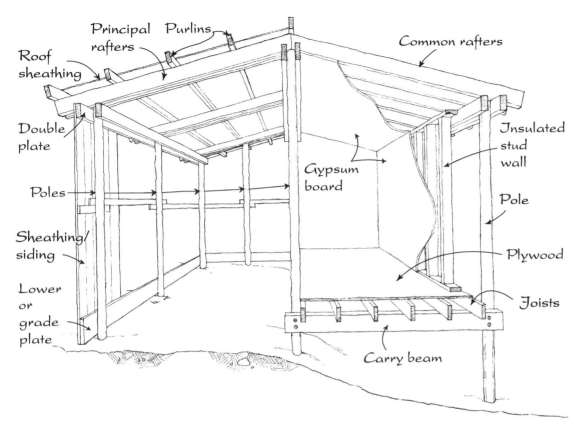

FIGURE 55: The basic parts of a pole barn, and how they may be finished off as living space.

Labels on figure: Roof sheathing, Principal rafters, Purlins, Common rafters, Double plate, Insulated stud wall, Poles, Gypsum board, Pole, Sheathing/siding, Plywood, Lower or grade plate, Joists, Carry beam

ning spaces so reminiscent of cathedrals and mosques. Even the beautiful mathematics seemed cosmic. This was clearly a framing system for the New Age!

Unfortunately, recent dome history is a story of this "music of the spheres" going flat. Fuller's brilliant ideas were inspired and motivated by his compassion for people's needs. However, in the hands of less capable or less caring fabricators, the results were often underinspired. It probably should have been expected. No building system could meet all those lofty expectations. Some of the failures were technical, some were political, and others, many others, were architectural. The way people live is not that uniform, not that round or that perfect (Figure 56).

A geodesic dome is sort of a three-dimensional truss. It is comprised of tri-angles, pentangles, and tetrahedra. More important to the builder, these shapes are all comprised of struts that are pretty much identical (in geometry, not loading). This fact allows the builder to easily pre-cut an entire dome frame with a little math and a radial arm saw. The big issue becomes the joint. Anywhere from three to six struts must be connected at a joint in a way that allows all the forces to be transmitted in a balanced fashion. This simple but demanding problem has attracted some of the most inventive minds in the building community. Joints were developed with plywood hubs, bolt-through tubes, steel plates, and a variety of less elegant configurations. These joint designs have enjoyed varying degrees of success. Also developed were the panel domes. Instead of building a framework to which sheathing would be affixed, panel domes consisted of precut and assembled panels. These were connected along their common edges. This involved more beveled carpentry than the frame approach, but at least the hub problem was minimized. In the end, there are probably as many variations on the dome as there are innovative builders.

The problems were leaks (as always) and the difficulty in building and then living in such an uncompromising shape. In 1989, thirteen years after building his first dome, the publisher of the famous dome books, Lloyd Kahn, came out with the pamphlet "Refried Domes." It was a trea-

FIGURE 56: Even a dome can "fit in" after it has been there long enough for the plants to grow.

tise on what didn't work about domes. The following is an excerpt from an article by George Oakes in that publication.

> In brief, here are the chief technical drawbacks:
>
> 1. The only kind of insulation you can legally use in a dome kit is superexpensive, flammable, and poisonous. (*Sprayed-on cellulose has overcome this problem.*)
> 2. The very shape of the house makes it difficult to conform to code requirements for placement of sewer vents and chimneys. (*Unless you place them at the center, which often works well.*)
> 3. Domes are difficult to roof. And if not roofed exceptionally well, they will leak like a sieve (*as with all buildings*).
> 4. All building materials come in rectangular shapes off the shelf. They have to be cut to fit triangular and other nonstandard shapes. Scrap from cutting—i.e., waste—ranges from about 10–20 percent, depending on the type of material.
> 5. Domes require about twice as much electricians' tape and electrical cable as conventional houses of similar size.
> 6. Foundations are critical. You can get away with a lot in conventional homes, but not in a dome.
> 7. Fire escapes are problematical, they're required, and they're expensive. Windows conforming to code can cost anywhere from 5 to 15 times as much as windows in conventional houses.

O.K., while all that may be, much of it is correctable (see the following section on zomes).

Nevertheless, domes are efficient, modular, and very easy to mass-produce. A vast clear-spanning space can be assembled from about a dozen identical parts. Today one can purchase a great variety of domes from different manufacturers. Each has developed a slightly different construction approach. Each claims to have all the problems licked. I will leave this up to you, as the shopper. Remember, it's not all insulation and leak prevention.

We're talking about a home here. What will it be like to live in a geodesic dome? Of all the framing systems above, this is the only one that insists on one and only one floor plan—a circle. This needs consideration. You may have to pack several together or build a very large dome in order to allow your desired room layout. Acoustics will be excellent (though perhaps a bit surprising). I've heard it compared to living in two band shells glued face to face. With no vertical walls, you may find hanging art or even a wall clock to be difficult (but nothing's impossible). Placing furniture will also require some imagination. Tables, chairs, and rugs all tend to be rectangular. Of course all of these things can be accommodated or adjusted. The real question is whether *you want* to shoehorn your life into this predetermined shape. But then maybe a shoehorn isn't needed.

Let's be honest. I like geodesic domes; really. But I've been giving a slightly critical spin to their presentation. This is because I've seen many students default to the ready-made designs provided by the precut dome manufacturers. Whether it's a precut dome, a precut log home, or a precut ranch—I'm always going to be a little critical. What are the chances that these prepackaged designs will accommodate *your* unique life-style and site perfectly? What are the chances that a home designed from demographic and marketing studies will be the house of your dreams? The chances are small. And yet, as unlikely as it may seem, there are still those who would go through the entire design process only to come up with a standard precut plan. Your program may live perfectly under the arched ceiling of a dome, but just remember, the shape of a house is supposed to conform to your life-style, not the other way around.

Zomes

That must have been what Steve Baer was thinking when he developed Zomes. This is another dome-like structural system, but the panels or faces are all zonohedra. Zonohedra? Ahh, yes of course, zonohedra! Zonohedra are polygons with equal and parallel edges (Figure 57). This is quite different from the geodesic triangles and pentagons. The parallel edges form "zones" and they allow you to stretch the shapes that can be formed (Zome = dome + zone). Zones are bands of parallel edges that run around the solid. These zones can be stretched, shrunk, or omitted completely to make the various zomes different shapes and sizes. Zomes can cluster

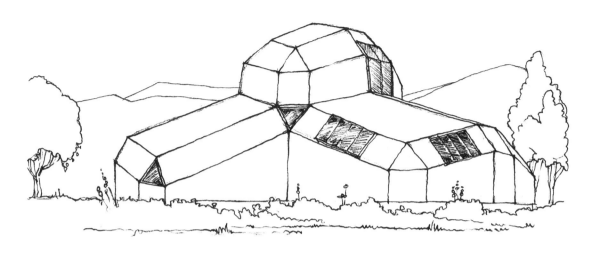

together like soap bubbles. Zomes can also pack several layers deep. There is very little published about zomes, but the book *Zome Primer* by Baer is the obvious starting point.

Zomes, though less structurally stable than domes, have many of their virtues without the constricting drawbacks. Material waste and building inspectors may still be a problem. Joints and leaks will always require attention. But if you're going to embrace a high-tech twenty-first-century framing system, this may just be the one. Its inherent flexibility allows you to design for the requirements of your site and your life-style. Always remember that site, program, and then building make up the Design Helix. If you can't flexibly respond to all three, you can't end up with a sensitively designed home.

Geometric Flexibility

Architects call the overall shape and proportions of a building its "massing." Windows, doors, finishes, etc., are not involved. The massing of a building is simply what the term implies.

In selecting a framing system for your design it is important to assess the system's ability to accommodate the massing of your design's geometry. For example, a geodesic dome is very inflexible in this regard. No matter what you do, it will always end up looking more or less the same. This isn't necessarily bad, it's just

FIGURE 57: **Examples of zome homes. Zomes are polygons with equal and parallel sides.**

not very flexible. Stick framing, in contrast, is extremely flexible. I think you can build just about any shape you want with enough little sticks. Timber framing lies somewhere in between.

It should be stressed that geometric flexibility is not a goal to be pursued for itself. However, if you *knew* you would be renovating in the future, wouldn't you choose a flexible construction technology? Generally, you don't choose a structural system until you have been around the design helix once or twice. Some designs may call for domes, some may call for pole frames, others will call for timber frames, and still others will require something not framed at all, like masonry or logs. Many designs use a combination of systems. The choice of technology should support the site and program considerations, as well.

If a design is straightforward and rectangular, a timber frame might be suggested. Also, when certain historic associations are desired, the timber frame is often an appropriate choice. When the design becomes unusual or curvilinear, however, I always think about stick framing or masonry; flexibility makes these good choices for contemporary designs. I've had little experience with domes or A-frames. To my mind, these systems make the geometry of the frame more important than the geometries of the site or the client's life-style. Still, I'm sure that someday I will run into someone whose life and site fit perfectly into and around a dome.

The closest I've come so far was a paramedic from Illinois. Kaya arrived at Yestermorrow bound and determined that she would design, build, and live in a dome. For two weeks, we encouraged her to take a fresh look at who she was, where she would be living, what her spouse and children might want and even the reasons for her love of domes. She wouldn't be swayed. She resolutely crammed her life into that dome. Organizing a circular floor plan is not easy. The dome is so structurally efficient it needs no interior walls and the exterior ones are all sloped. Kaya had to contrive interior walls just to house her mechanicals. But she insisted that everything was perfect.

Well, everything wasn't perfect. We could see this from the way she was approaching her floor plan. Kaya was trying to fit a conventional Midwestern floor plan into a circle. A circle doesn't have a front and back. So there is no obvious place for a front or back door, a front or back yard; indeed, there was no natural place for most of the basic elements in a conventional home. Kaya determinedly packed them in, awkward and forced. The Yestermorrow staff was almost ready to concede defeat.

The night before the final review, Kaya worked on her dome straight through until morning. At the final review, she announced a revelation. She didn't really like the dome for its structural efficiency. She wasn't happy with the circular floor plan.

She doubted whether a dome would complement her site. Plus, there seemed to be no end to the problems she had just trying to build a model.

"Still, I love this dome because it's difficult and unconventional. I realized last night that it is my own difficult and unconventional character that draws me to it."

"Do you think your family will be happy in it?" asked one of the reviewers.

"Possibly not, but it has taught me how a structure must reflect the lifestyles of the people living in it. For that, they should be grateful."

Kaya went back to Illinois and enrolled in architecture school. The next summer she returned to Yestermorrow with her husband and child. They spent two weeks designing a house that reflected the way they wanted to live together. I don't think she ever built a dome, but last winter Kaya sent me a photo of her first commission as an architect. She used a steel frame with a brick veneer.

Remember that every structural system has a degree of flexibility and that you can further increase the variations by mixing methods. For instance, large timber-framed roof systems can be used with stick-framed walls; a space-frame roof could float over log walls, masonry walls—*any* walls for that matter. Generally, anything can be built in several different ways. Some ways will just be easier, and only one will look the way you want it to.

CURVES

Since nature is curved and fluid, it should hardly be surprising that curvilinear form is found in vernacular architecture across every continent.

The stick-built curved walls and roof forms illustrated here all work and have all been used by the author (Figure 58 and 59). There are a few different approaches to the curved plates required for a curved wall. Although popular, the double-lapped ¾″ plywood is not my favorite. Edge grain and short pieces make for weak plates. I find solid wood, even if you use a layer of ply to connect it, is always better.

The key thing to remember with curved walls is that the upper and lower plates must be exactly the same. The plates are the horizontal boards at the floor and the ceiling of a stud wall between which we place the studs. If the plates are cut sloppily, you will be building a warped curve, not a cylinder. Clamp the plate stock together and cut both top and bottom plates at the same time. To "square" a curved wall (which is to verify that opposite sides are parallel and all corners are 90°) you can't simply measure diagonals as we do with flat walls. Instead, all studs and both sets of plates must be laid out and cut on the open deck, where a large set of trammel points (compass) (see Figure 59) can be employed. Then the wall must be built in place. As each stud is installed it should be plumbed and temporarily secured until all the studs are up and the top plates can be installed. If the identical plates are level and all studs are plumb, the curved wall will be "square" (plumb and level). Before the sheathing is attached, the open ends must be collared or secured by some other part of the framing. Otherwise, the flex of the sheathing will flatten the curve at the top of the wall where it is unrestrained.

If there is a door or window in a curved

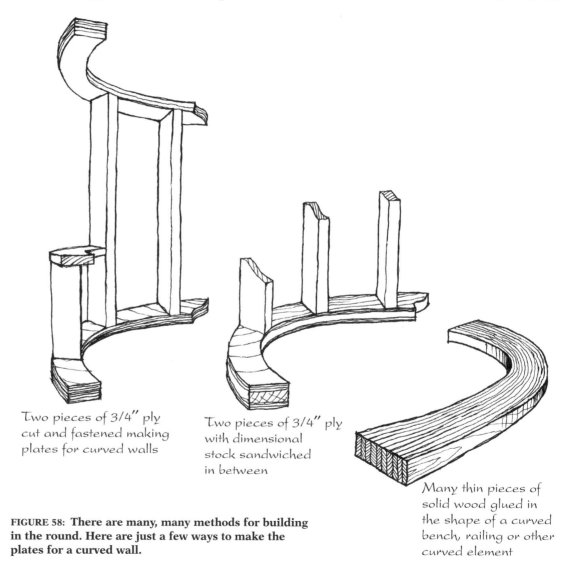

Two pieces of 3/4″ ply cut and fastened making plates for curved walls

Two pieces of 3/4″ ply with dimensional stock sandwiched in between

Many thin pieces of solid wood glued in the shape of a curved bench, railing or other curved element

FIGURE 58: There are many, many methods for building in the round. Here are just a few ways to make the plates for a curved wall.

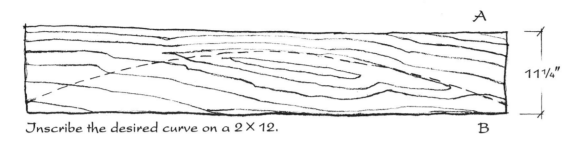

Inscribe the desired curve on a 2 X 12.

A

B

11¼"

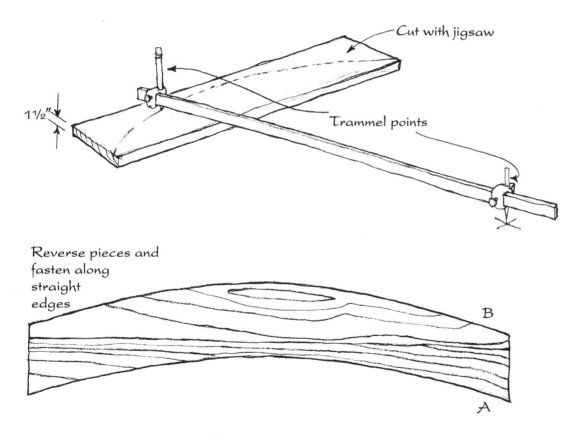

Cut with jigsaw

Trammel points

1½"

Reverse pieces and fasten along straight edges

B

A

FIGURE 59: One method for making a curved rafter.

wall, it will require a curved header at the top of the framed opening (called the Rough Opening, or RO). Any of several techniques may be employed. A header can be created with a curved box beam, which is nothing more than a short curved wall. Or, if insulation isn't critical, simply kerf a 2 × 10 and apply plywood to both sides. Kerfing a 2 × 10 means cutting many parallel saw kerfs about ½" deep along either side of the board. These kerfs, placed about 1" apart, allow the 2 × 10 to be bent. When the plywood is glued and screwed to either side, the curved board becomes rigid once again. Regardless of how you frame the RO, windows and doors in curved walls require a bit of extra consideration. Remember that the radial layout of your studs will make the inside dimension of the RO smaller than the outside. This will usually have an impact on the way you apply trim to that opening (see Figure 60).

Curved roofs *may* be framed with common rafters cut from 2′ × 12's or main rafters and purlins. The main rafters can be built-up on-site, or they can be manufactured off-site. The use of lenticular or bowstring trusses is a fine method for spanning a large distance with a curved roof. When choosing a roofing material, remember that a curved roof changes pitch from eave to ridge. At the eave the pitch will be steepest and gradually decrease until, at the top, it will be perfectly flat (see Figure 61).

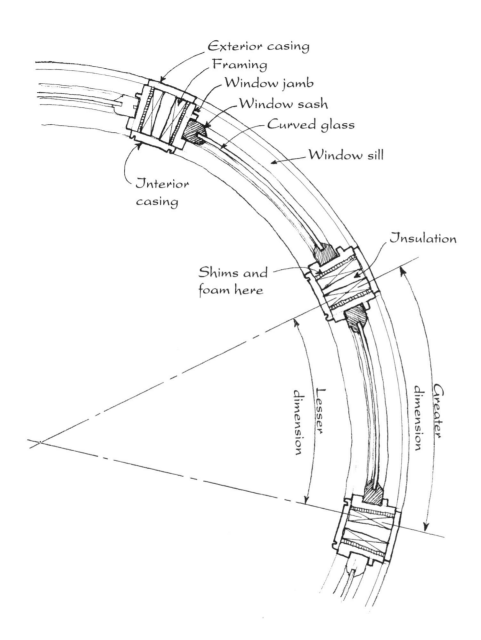

Exterior casing
Framing
Window jamb
Window sash
Curved glass
Window sill
Interior casing
Insulation
Shims and foam here
Lesser dimension
Greater dimension

FIGURE 60: Curved walls require special care when installing windows. Straight glass is cheaper but more awkward to install and less satisfying to the eye.

With all curved surfaces, it is important to use your eyes. Plumb and level will help a great deal, but the final test will be your eye. If there is a flat spot in the curve, the eye will pick it up before the string or level. I consider curved surfaces easier to build for just this reason. If it looks correct, it usually is. Just remember to inspect it from the direction that it will most frequently be seen.

CANTILEVERS

There is a good rule of thumb for cantilevers. Assuming the loads are uniform, not concentrated: *if "x" feet are to be cantilevered, then twice or three times "x" feet must be secured back into the building.* This won't cover all situations, but it's a good conservative starting point. Let's look at some of the implications (Figure 62). If the floor framing is to cantilever 6' out (*x*) then it must have 12' (2*x*) tied back into the building. Framing lumber longer than 20' is very costly. Sometimes the cantilever distance plus twice the cantilevered distance (a total of 3*x*) requires very long floor joists. Thus, in some cases you will be using one of the alternate framing variations shown. Just remember that the doubled or tripled joists must be checked with an engineer or architect if you don't want a bow in your floor (Figure 63).

Naturally, there are further options. If the architecture suggests it, the deck and roof loads can be supported by canti-

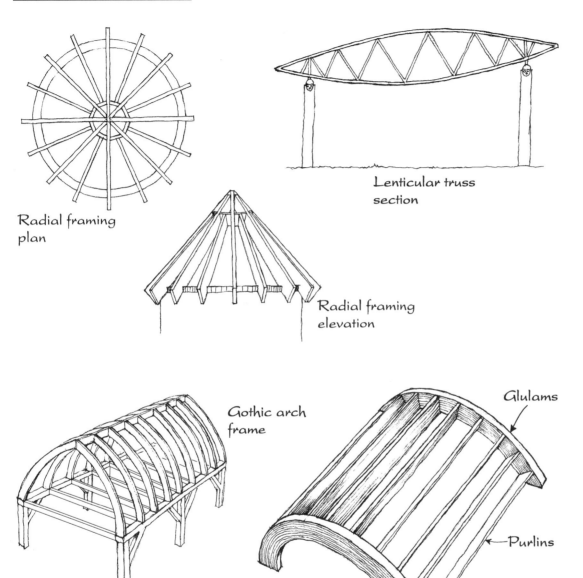

FIGURE 61: Framing systems for a few curved roof forms.

Radial framing plan

Lenticular truss section

Radial framing elevation

Gothic arch frame

Glulams

Purlins

Main Arches

levered walls. The framing in these walls should be as free of joints as possible and the top and bottom plates must be continuous. Any penetrations must be in the middle of the walls, *which must be sheathed with plywood on both sides*. This makes the whole wall into an 8′-deep box beam. When a beam is this deep, with window and door penetrations, it doesn't follow the x/2x rule. Here you must chase the loads and forces down and resolve them in the framing. This is another time to bring in the engineers. As usual, it is the design that determines your options (Figure 64).

BUILT-UP BEAMS

How does one design around the limited sizes and shapes available at the lumberyard? Having milled the tree into many small pieces, it now seems we may need to build it back up. This is common practice in stick framing, and the resulting member is sometimes stronger than the sum of the parts. This is because the checks, knots, and other imperfections are spread out evenly, rather than concentrated in one or two places.

There are a variety of methods for building up beams. The easiest approach is to simply nail several boards together. Stagger the joints by at least 4 feet to avoid weak spots. Also, alternate the direction of the bow, or crown, in each board so the beam comes out straight. This is the most

FIGURE 62: Typical cantilever using x/2x rule of thumb.

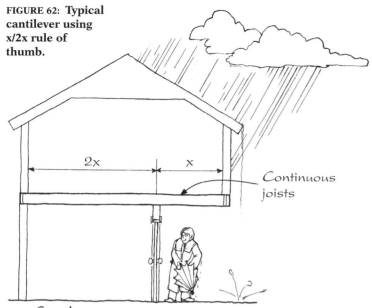

Cantilever over entry section

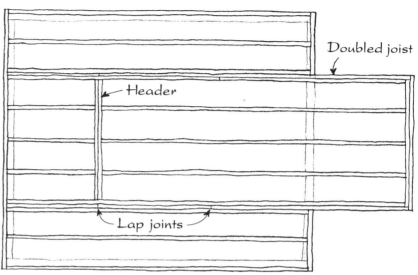

The header allows the use of shorter sticks for the floor joists

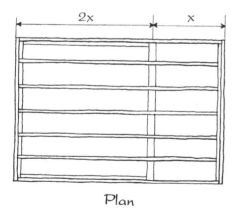

Plan

FIGURE 63: By configuring the framing with care, shorter and less costly lumber may be used to accomplish the same cantilever.

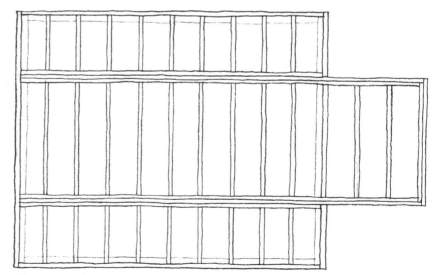

Changing the direction of the joists reduces the number of long sticks.

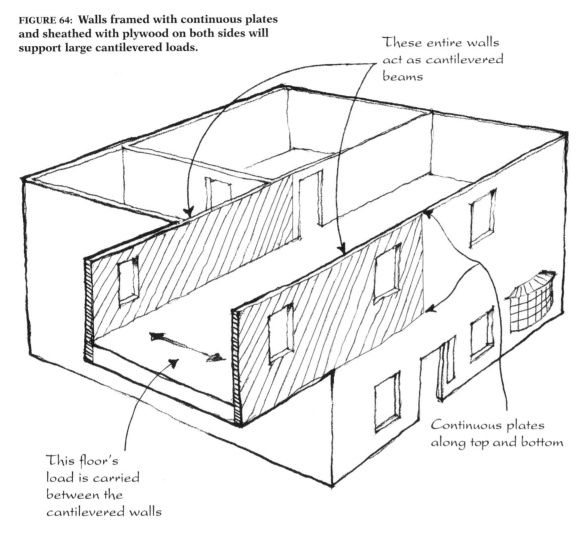

FIGURE 64: **Walls framed with continuous plates and sheathed with plywood on both sides will support large cantilevered loads.**

These entire walls act as cantilevered beams

Continuous plates along top and bottom

This floor's load is carried between the cantilevered walls

commonly used approach, and you can find examples in the basement of any sizeable stick-framed building.

Garage doors, however, require a slightly different approach. As garages have grown over the last few decades, the door headers have become impossibly long. If you attempt to span 20' with 2' × 12's nailed together, the number of 2' × 12's is such that the beam is thicker than the wall in which it is to be incorporated (Figure 65). A different approach is re-

quired. On site one can build a small stud wall with continuous doubled up sills and plates. This is then covered with plywood on both sides. Such a wall acts like an inside-out I-beam. Most of the structural material is placed in the tension and compression zones—the sill and plate. The plywood serves to hold them together, just like the web in an I-beam. And like that I-beam web, it carries shear forces generated between the compression and the tension zones. For this reason, all plywood joints should be kept away from the beam ends where the shear forces are highest. This is a very useful approach for long spans. It can easily be built to be the same width as the wall in which it's housed. As a result, its depth, and thus its ability to span, is limited only by windows or other penetrations in the wall. For this reason, some design/builders have expanded the use of the concept to whole walls. Designer/builder David Sellers uses walls, half-walls, and railings to span large spaces in his buildings (Figure 66).

Sheathed on both sides of the studs, these walls will span such great distances that the building can be assembled like a full-size version of the architect's cardboard model.

The engineering of built-up beams continues to evolve. Assembling small pieces of wood into larger beams is a natural for the manufacturing folks. Glulams, micro lams, and truss joists are all wood products designed to span long distances. Each

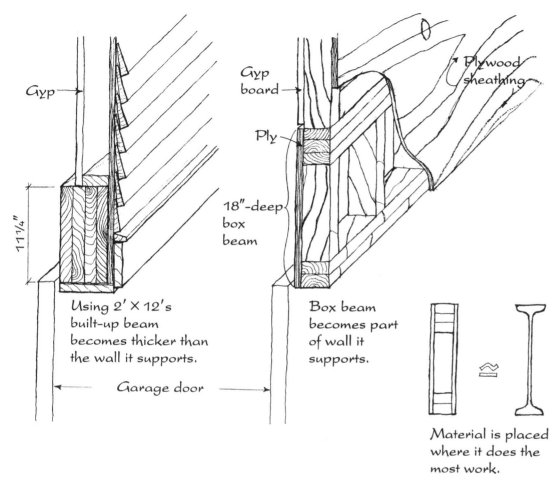

Gyp

11 1/4"

Using 2' X 12's built-up beam becomes thicker than the wall it supports.

Garage door

Gyp board

Ply

18"-deep box beam

Plywood sheathing

Box beam becomes part of wall it supports.

Material is placed where it does the most work.

FIGURE 65: Box beams span great distance without becoming bulky.

angles (Figure 68 gives a few examples). In residential construction, trusses are most frequently used in the roofs and floors. A little imagination reveals that many more creative uses might be made.

The roof truss, like so many construction products, comes in standard and custom sizes. Your local lumberyard will likely be able to supply you with roof trusses. They may even build them on location. This is handy for the designer who often has need of a nonstandard truss shape. After the trusses are ordered, the manufacturer will supply you with a "shop drawing." You must inspect this carefully for errors; this is the drawing from which they will build your trusses. After you have signed off on the drawing, any mistakes will be yours to keep. The trusses will be delivered to your site and, where possible, right onto the building. Ideally, you want to have the wall up and ready for their arrival. Make sure to ask for a delivery truck with a crane attached to it. The delivery truck can place the trusses right up on top of your wall plates. Then you will simply move and nail them into position. They're too big to play dominos with, so remember to brace them laterally until you have the roof sheathing in place, or they will fall over. It is all very fast and simple. The only drawback is the loss of attic space (Figure 69).

Floor trusses, or truss joists, come in far fewer shapes. Standard cross sections will carry loads and have limits for shear,

product is many small pieces of wood glued and joined into one larger member. Since they are manufactured from small pieces of wood, these products preserve our old-growth forests. They also tend to be more consistent, lighter weight, and easier to build with. Nevertheless, they

cannot be site-fabricated and this can often make a big difference (Figure 67).

TRUSSES

By definition, a truss is any spanning geometry of elements configured from tri-

FIGURE 66: **Innovative use of box beams and stress skin panels characterize David Sellers's early work.**

the manufacturer's instructions for installation and blocking.

☛ Architecturally, trusses may often be used to do double duty. The site-built truss, 3′ or 4′ deep, can span a generous living room and carry a large floor load. At the same time it might double as a railing. A pair of such trusses with a small floor deck between, constitutes an affordable bridge! Trusses don't have to be rough-hewn; they can be as delicate as lacework. There is nothing to keep you from choosing details and materials that make the truss into a fine architectural feature (Figure 70).

The key here, once again, is design. You, the design/builder, must design your truss. You can get a handle on the engineering from the books listed at the end of the chapter. Then, when you've settled on a truss that you like, have an engineer or professional check it out. Trusses are an efficient way to carry large loads or span long distances. The fun part is to also make them into expressive parts of the building's architecture.

bending, and deflection just like any dimensional wood joist. These trusses are meant simply to span; they can be used as joists or rafters. They are easily sized from the manufacturer's span charts. While more expensive than standard dimensional joists, they have several advantages: They can be installed very quickly. They can span longer distances. They provide more in-between space for insulation, ducts, and utilities. Like most manufactured products, they are very straight and consistent. Floor trusses may be easily picked out of a catalogue for almost any application. They are available through your lumberyard, but some manufactures will sell them directly. When using floor trusses, it is important to pay attention to

▥ Thinking about Frames

Have we exhausted the framing options? Hardly. We've just covered the basics. Moreover, we've not wandered too far from home. Many of the framing systems found in this country were originally developed in different and interesting ways by other cultures.

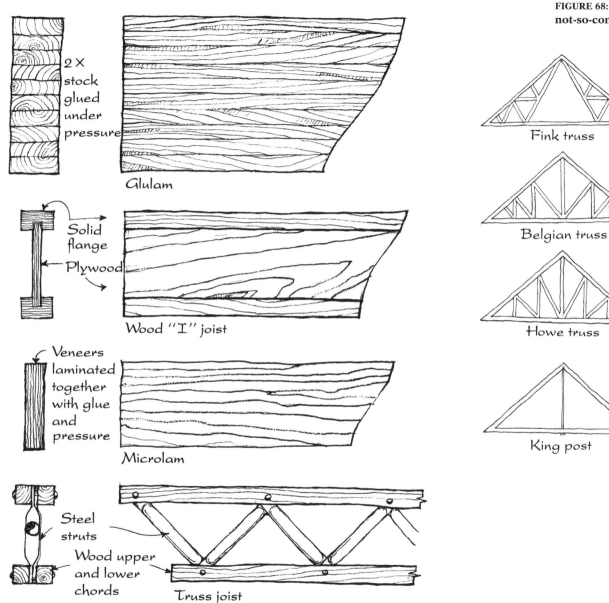

2 × stock glued under pressure

Glulam

Solid flange
Plywood

Wood "I" joist

Veneers laminated together with glue and pressure

Microlam

Steel struts
Wood upper and lower chords

Truss joist

FIGURE 67: Manufactured wood products for longer spans.

FIGURE 68: Some common, and some not-so-common, trusses.

Fink truss

Scissor truss

Belgian truss

Clerestory truss

Howe truss

Pratt truss

King post

Low-pitch Howe truss

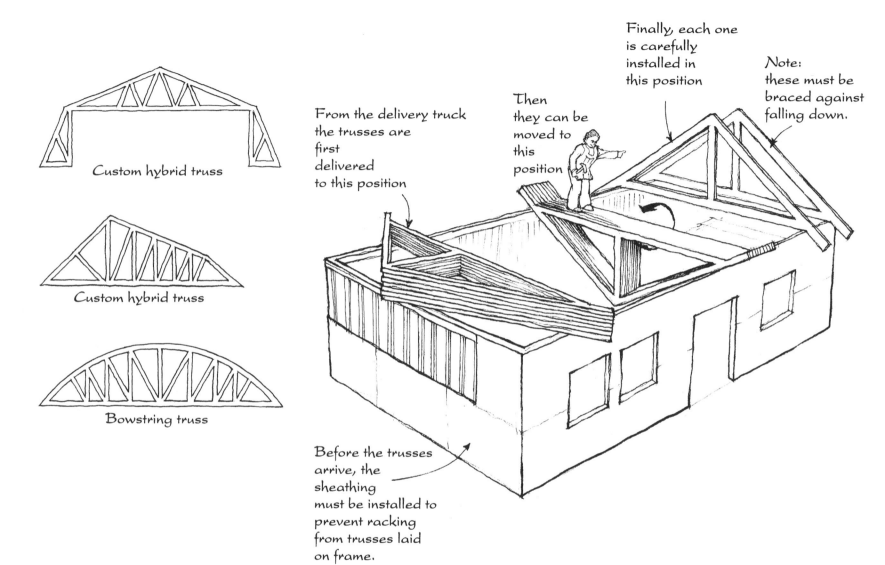

Custom hybrid truss

Custom hybrid truss

Bowstring truss

From the delivery truck the trusses are first delivered to this position

Then they can be moved to this position

Finally, each one is carefully installed in this position

Note: these must be braced against falling down.

Before the trusses arrive, the sheathing must be installed to prevent racking from trusses laid on frame.

FIGURE 69: **The whole reason for using trusses is to reduce labor costs by speeding erection.**

Our notion of the timber frame originated in England as the cruk frame. This was sort of a medieval A-frame. It developed into the timber frame and the Tudor half timber long before traveling to America (Figure 71). Beautiful variations can also be found in Japan, Scandinavia, Russia, and other countries with forests. Sweden's famous stave churches are timber frames with plank infill. Japan's temples are some of the most elaborately joined timber structures in the world. The Alps are dotted with small log and timber-frame shelters over three hundred years old. Africa and South America have equally varied and beautiful interpretations of the wood frame. Even in the comparatively short history of America, there have been many interpretations of the frame.

Frames need not be large or necessarily permanent. One of the best examples of a frame is found in the tent frame. Nomadic peoples have developed different tenting techniques in just about every climate and culture around the globe. One of my favorites is the yurt (Figure 72). This collapsible tent frame resembles a huge replica of the playpens in which I was held captive as a baby. They have been reinterpreted in many cultures and materials. We once built a twelve-sided yurt from dimensional lumber! Tent frames are endless in their shapes, materials, and architecture (Figures 73 and 74).

Equally light and impressive are the bamboo frames and scaffolding found

FIGURE 70: **"Stone Flower," a residence designed by architect Fay Jones.**

Early cruk

English box frame

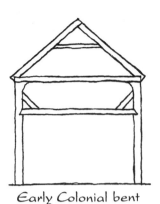

Early Colonial bent

FIGURE 71: Development of the timber frame.

Normally these are found in commercial construction, but some architects deftly use heavy steel or concrete in residential design (see Figure 75). Although such strong frames are seldom needed to bear the relatively small loads found in houses, light steel framing is an excellent and popular alternative to wood-stick construction. Just as flexible as dimensional wood framing, steel is affordable, fireproof, and reduces the impact on our forest resources. In many cities, it is required by code.

These are such strong materials that they are seldom chosen to bear the relatively light loads in houses.

Using a frame is an architectural decision and only one approach to making a building. The idea is to put up a skeleton and then hang systems and materials

throughout Asia and South America. In Hong Kong, a tornado once hit two buildings, both protected by scaffolding. One was protected by a bamboo scaffold and held fine, the other was surrounded by a conventional steel scaffold and it collapsed. Bamboo scaffolding has been lashed together as high as thirty stories, all without a nail! It is a miraculous material, growing as much as 4' in one day. In Asia, almost two million tons of bamboo are used annually in housing alone.

At the other end of the scale exists what I call "heavy" frames: steel and concrete.

FIGURE 72: Ancient Mongolian yurt used by nomadic shepherds.

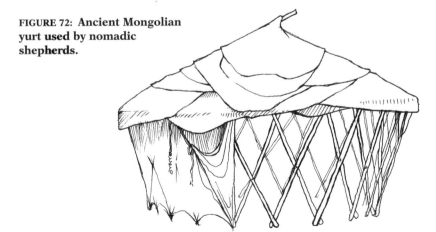

FIGURE 73: The modern "pup" tent is totally self-supporting.

FIGURE 74: Nomadic tents of the middle and far east have always provided an example of a building type that fits the culture and the climate perfectly.

within the members and attach other materials to the interior and exterior surfaces. It's not surprising that this approach should come naturally to us: Our bodies are configured this way. It is a very sophisticated approach allowing a great deal of variety and expression. But, as we shall see in the next section, it is but one of many alternatives.

What might lead a design/builder to embrace a framing system for the project at hand? Well, firstly, a look at the available materials. If the local materials lend themselves to a framing system, it is likely that this system should be considered. If, however, the local materials are sand and dirt, perhaps something else is suggested—maybe adobe. But that isn't the

FIGURE 75: **"The Hoagie House," residence by design/builders Jersey Devil, using a steel frame and wooden truss joists.**

whole story. Just because wood is a local resource, must it be configured into a frame? What about stacking the trees into a log home? Or using it like a masonry unit in a cordwood house? A quick survey of indigenous architectures will reveal that there are many ways of putting wood, or any material, together.

How you structure your building reflects what you want to make, how you want it to look, feel, and work. It may depend on the size of the rooms or the height of the ceilings. It may depend on your roof shape, heating system, windows, or finishes. These and many other things will be affected by your structural system and the choices that any system allows you to consider. In the end, it becomes a design decision. As always, the building becomes an expression of where it's built (the site) and how you live (the program).

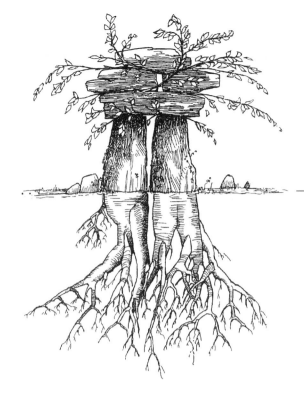

What Works and What Doesn't:
Looking at The Interconnected Effects of Gravity, Temperature, Moisture, and Ethics

It used to be that different building systems would be found in different regions of the country. This was the result of many influences, including the temperature and moisture conditions in a given location. Gravity has also played a large part in the shaping of our homes, but gravity is pretty much the same everywhere. However, the materials with which we overcome gravity differ in their abundance from place to place. Unfortunately, the characteristic use of materials and building systems is not nearly so connected to location in today's homogenous media culture. On

"This Old House," Bob Vila demonstrated how to renovate a colonial in New England, and it is used as a model for doing it "right" by viewers from coast to coast. Why? History, materials, and climate are not homogeneous from coast to coast. The way to do things "right" will usually be discovered much closer to home: Yea, regionalism! Hooray, vernacular architecture!

The first question in making your house is not whether it should be post and beam, balloon, or platform frame. The first question is whether it should

be frame at all. There are areas where masonry or adobe make better sense than the ubiquitous wood frame. Just as likely, you may be considering log, brick, stone, or even sod (earth-sheltered). What makes sense in one climate or region may be ridiculous in another. This applies to many other aspects of the building besides the structure. Foundations, roofs, windows, etc., all have regional traditions that make good common sense. I'm not saying you should mindlessly ape these traditions, but you should certainly study them. The underlying principles and problems addressed will be the same as those you must face.

IIIII Wood

More than half of the North American continent is, or was, heavily forested. Therefore, the odds are good that some form of appropriate wood structure evolved in your area. Since wood is still the most prevalent home-building material, it will be useful to have a better understanding of its properties.

Wood, you must understand, comes from trees (for now at least), living trees, which are just big plants, and we all know that the most important requirement for a healthy plant is—water. If you want to understand wood, you must remember that it always consists of between 5 and 50 percent water. The moisture content, or MC, is primarily what determines how a piece of wood behaves. And yet, one mustn't think that all wood is identical except for the amount of moisture it contains. Nothing is ever *that* simple.

Wood comes in a wonderful variety of species, shapes, and sizes. Each has unique characteristics, including strength, flexibility, stiffness, color, figure, and grain. Woods also vary in their ability to resist fungi, rot, and weather. Some, like those being taken from the rain forests, even have political and ethical characteristics. At Yestermorrow we no longer suggest using mahogany, teak, redwood, certain cedars, or old growth Douglas fir.

Walker's book *The Encyclopedia of Wood* has an excellent and current treatment of the different issues affecting many of the species being harvested today. Equally impressive is the CD produced by the Forest Partnership in Burlington, Vermont, called *Woods of the World Pro*. This database allows you to search all the wood species of the world based on any combination of properties you desire (color, grain, strength, cost, stability, etc.). Of course, there are dozens of rain forest trees that are still undocumented, but more are becoming available every day. This is a fabulous and up-to-date information resource. It is pretty easy to get confused, even confounded, when talking about wood. Hundreds of colors and figures are available from around the world.

A common misconception defines wood as "what you buy at the lumberyard" and if it's not there, it doesn't exist. This is like suggesting that fruits or vegetables not found in your local grocery don't exist! If we don't ask for better wood products, they won't become available.

Woods are classified as either hard or soft (see Table 3), deciduous or conifers, new or old growth, and by their botanical taxonomy (species). For the builder, however, what's most important is the physical behavior of the board in hand. Each board is different. Each must be sized up, like a new personality on the site. A board's personality starts with the tree, but it is greatly affected by the method of milling and drying.

There are two common ways of cutting boards (Figure 76). They are called *plane sawn* and *quarter-sawn* for hardwoods and *flat-grained* and *edge-grained* for soft woods. When using plane-sawn or flat-grained milling, the log is squared and then boards are cut tangent to the annual growth rings. When quarter-sawn or edge-grain milling is employed, the log is sliced into four quarters and boards are cut at right angles to the growth rings. The less expensive plane-sawed lumber dries faster and produces greater widths. However, it offers less strength and has a high tendency to shrink, warp, and twist. Where flat-grained lumber is used structurally, for its bending strength, the maximum slope of the grain (the angle the grain makes with an edge of the board) should not exceed one in twelve. In contrast to plane-sawn, quarter-sawn lumber is more stable, wears better, and holds paints and finishes better. Consequently, quarter-sawn wood is always costlier than plane-sawn wood.

When a tree is cut down, it may contain 30 to 300 percent more moisture than it will after drying. After it is milled, wood is stacked to dry with little pieces of wood—stickers—between each board. The rate at which drying proceeds depends

TABLE 3: GENERAL SUITABILITY OF DIFFERENT WOODS FOR VARIOUS APPLICATIONS

CLASSIFICATIONS

MAJOR USES	proportion of heartwood	size of knots	number of knots	toughness	strength as a post	stiffness	bending strength	decay resistance of heartwood	nail holding	ease of working	paint holding	freedom from warping	weight (dry)	freedom from shrinkage	hardness	WOOD NAMES	OTHER COMMON WOOD NAMES
																DECIDUOUS (hardwood)	
Flooring, veneer	B	B	B	A	B	A	A	C	A	C	-	C	A	C	A	Beech	
Veneer, paneling	B	B	C	B	A	A	A	-	-	C	-	A	B	B	A	Cherry	
Flooring, veneer, paneling, millwork	C	C	B	A	A	A	A	C	A	C	-	B	A	C	A	Maple	
Flooring, millwork	B	A	C	A	B	A	A	B	A	C	-	B	A	C	A	Oak	
																EVERGREEN (softwood)	
Shingles, paneling, construction	A	C	A	C	C	C	C	A	C	A	A	A	C	A	C	Cedar aromatic	-
Flooring, millwork	B	C	A	B	A	C	B	A	-	B	-	A	A	A	A	Cedar, eastern red	-Eastern red cedar, southern red cedar
Shingles, siding, sash, millwork	A	A	C	C	B	C	C	A	C	A	A	A	C	A	C	Cedar, western red	-Western red cedar
Construction, sash, millwork, flooring	A	B	B	B	A	A	A	B	B	C	C	B	B	B	B	Fir, douglas	-
Light construction, siding, sheathing	C	B	B	C	B	B	B	C	C	B	B	B	C	B	C	Fir, white	-Subalpine, California red fir, grand fir,
Construction, sheathing, siding, flooring	B	B	B	B	B	B	B	C	B	B	B	B	B	B	B	Hemlock	noble fir, Pacific silver, white fir
Construction, paneling, flooring, sash	A	C	A	B	A	A	A	B	A	C	C	B	A	B	A	Larch, western	-
Millwork, siding	B	C	A	C	C	C	C	B	B	A	A	A	C	A	C	Pine, north white	-Eastern white pine
Construction, sheathing	C	A	C	B	A	A	A	B	A	C	C	B	A	B	A	Pine, south yellow	-Loblolly pine, longleaf pine, pitch pine,
Sash, millwork, light construction	C	B	B	C	C	C	C	B	B	A	B	A	B	B	C	Pine, ponderosa	shortleaf pine, slash pine, Virginia pine
Sash, millwork, light construction	B	B	A	C	C	C	C	B	-	A	A	A	C	A	C	Pine, sugar	-
Sash, siding, paneling, millwork	A	A	C	B	A	B	B	A	B	B	A	A	B	A	B	Redwood	-
Construction, millwork	C	C	A	B	B	B	B	C	B	B	B	A	B	B	C	Spruce, eastern	black spruce, red spruce, white spruce

A - Among the woods.
    High in the particular class.
B - Intermediate
C - Low

Sources: Adopted from: U.S. Dept. of Agriculture Yearbook, 1949;
Hornbostal: *Materials for Architecture; Farmers Bulletin:* 1756;
Kern: *The Owner-Built Home.*

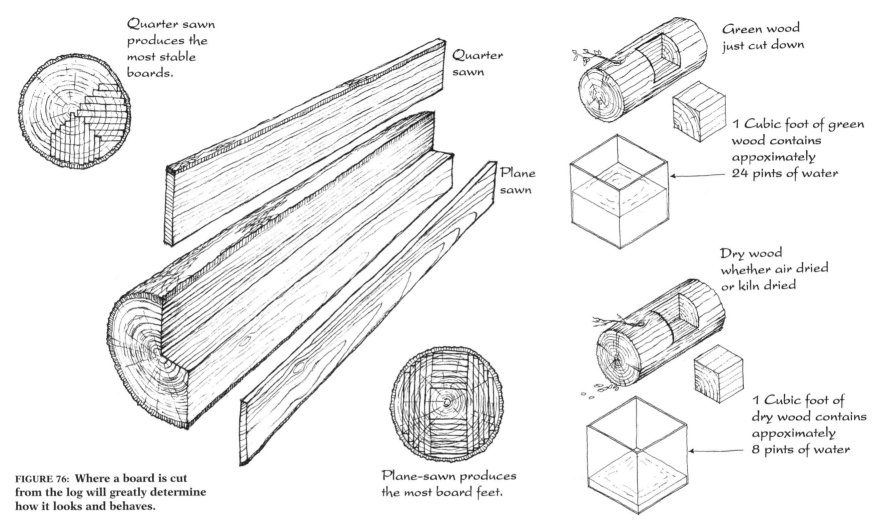

Quarter sawn produces the most stable boards.

Quarter sawn

Plane sawn

FIGURE 76: Where a board is cut from the log will greatly determine how it looks and behaves.

Plane-sawn produces the most board feet.

Green wood just cut down

1 Cubic foot of green wood contains appoximately 24 pints of water

Dry wood whether air dried or kiln dried

1 Cubic foot of dry wood contains appoximately 8 pints of water

FIGURE 77: Newly cut "green" wood will contain up to three times more moisture than dry wood. Wood for construction contains 6%–15% moisture.

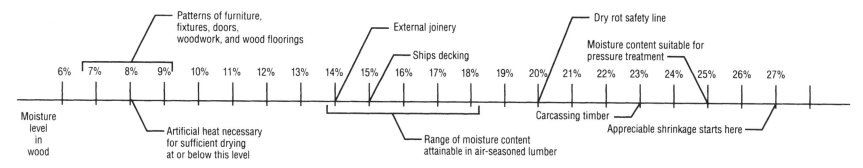

FIGURE 78: **Various uses of wood at different levels of dryness.**

on the wood species, the milling, the size of the boards, the ambient air conditions, and of course, the method of drying. It can be air dried or kiln dried. When wood is stacked and stickered in a warm dry spot it will eventually give up all but about 14 percent of its moisture (Figure 77). To reduce it further requires the use of additional energy, i.e., a kiln or a vacuum pump. Using these methods the moisture content can be reduced to 6 percent or even lower. In the drying process wood will shrink, both in width and length. However, shrinkage in length is normally too small to be considered. If the moisture content is higher than 19 percent the wood is called *green* or *unseasoned*. If it's lower, it is called *dry* or *seasoned* (Figure 78).

Building with green lumber can save money. It is a traditional and perfectly legitimate practice. Nevertheless, certain precautions must be observed. The holding power of a nail decreases by 75 percent in green lumber. Moreover, as the

wood dries, the shrinkage will back the nails out. This "nail popping" is directly proportional to both lumber shrinkage and to the depth of nail-shank penetration. By using the shortest nail that will do the job and only ring shank or annular nails, these effects can be minimized. To fully appreciate what is required to build with green lumber successfully, I suggest reading *Low Cost Green Lumber Construction* by Leigh Seldon, as well as consulting your local code requirements for using ungraded lumber.

You can determine the moisture content of your lumber by using a variety of methods. For the engineer, drying a sample in a specially calibrated oven gives the only acceptable results, but this is pretty cumbersome for the home builder. A moisture meter, available for about one hundred dollars, is more handy. Simply poke it into the sides of a couple of boards before your lumberyard shipment is unloaded (Figure 79).

Reject any seasoned wood that is over

19 percent MC. (Personally, I'd have trouble accepting anything above 14 percent.)

After wood is cut and dried, it is *dressed*, or *planed*. Dressed lumber has smaller and supposedly more consistent dimensions (see Table 4). In reality, this

TABLE 4: STANDARD DIMENSION OF COMMON SOFTWOOD LUMBER

Thickness	Minimum dressed	
	Dry	Green
1"	3/4"	25/32"
1 1/4"	1"	1 1/32"
1 1/2"	1 1/4"	1 9/32"
2"	1 1/2"	1 9/16"
2 1/2"	2"	2 1/16"
3"	2 1/2"	2 9/16"
3 1/2"	2"	3 1/16"
4"	3 1/2"	3 9/16"
5"	4 1/2"	4 5/8"
6"	5 1/2"	5 5/8"
7"	6 1/2"	6 5/8"
8"	7 1/4"	7 1/2"

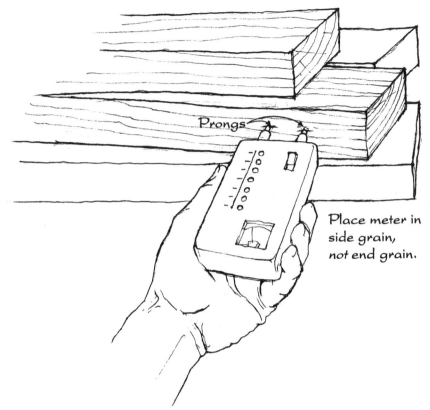

Prongs

Place meter in side grain, not end grain.

FIGURE 79: A hand-held moisture meter is handy when purchasing or drying wood.

lumber may still vary as much as $\frac{1}{16}''$ or even $\frac{1}{8}''$. Nevertheless, the intention is to supply the design/builder with a reliably consistent product and, for that reason, dressed lumber is often called *dimensional lumber*.

You should develop the practice of assessing the quality of a board quickly, as soon as you pick it up. Looking along the sides and edges, you will determine small (or not so small) variations.

If wood isn't dressed, it is referred to as *rough sawn*. Rough-sawn lumber can be green or dry. It is dimensionally less consistent but still fine for rough framing. It is also a great value. Since the lumber mills haven't spent the money to dress it, you get more wood for less cost.

Planks and boards have a vocabulary all their own. Tables 5 and 6 are like a basic inventory of what can be found in every lumberyard. Wood comes in a dizzy-ing array of sizes and shapes. It's helpful to be able to ask for it by name.

Loads and Structures

What?! Math? Engineering? Hey! Where is everyone going? C'mon, don't panic. If you can balance your checkbook, you can figure out the engineering for your house. It's all rule-of-thumb and charts. (Well, mostly . . .)

Regardless of the framing system you decide to use, its first order of business will be to hold up the house and every-thing in it. Happily, most framing meth-ods are more than up to the task. An MIT professor once claimed, "You can't say today's homes are overengineered, be-cause they aren't engineered at all!" He was talking about the overbuilt structures traditionally constructed by generation after generation of vernacular builders. Remember that house building, until very recently, was a regional practice, and most wood resources hadn't yet become scarce. History's design/builders rarely sought engineered efficiency. They sought dura-bility and soundness. If one stud is suffi-cient, then two will be better. The original builders weren't wasteful, they just "built to last."

At any rate, forest products have now become a precious resource. Affordable housing has become an embarrassing national agenda, and waste, as always, is still repugnant. Everyone must now design

TABLE 5: LUMBER ABBREVIATIONS

AD	Air-Dried		J&P	Jointed
ALS	Marican Lumber Standards		KD	Kiln Dried
BD	Board		LBR	Lumber
BD FT	Board Feet		LGTH	Length
BH	Boxed Heart		LIN	Lineal
BM	Board Measure		M	Thousand
BSND	Board Sapwood—No Defect		M.BM	Thousand (feet) Board Measure
BTR	Better		MC	Moisture Content
CV	Center V		RC	Red Cedar
DF	Douglas Fir		REG	Regular
DF-L	Douglas Fir—Larch		RGH	Rough
DIM	Dimension		R/L, RL	Random Lengths
DKG	Decking		R/S	Resawn
D&M	Dressed and Matched		R/W, RW	Random Width
EB1S	Edge Bead—One Side		S1E	Surfaced—One Edge
EB2S	Edge Bead—Two Sides		S2E	Surfaced—Two Edges
E&CBV2S	Edge and Center Bead		S2S	Surfaced—Two Sides
EV1S	Edge Vee—One Side		S4S	Surfaced—Four Sides
EV2S	Edge Vee—Two Sides		S1S&CM	Surfaced One Side and Center Matched
E&CV1S	Edge and Center Vee		S2S&CM	Surfaced Two Sides and Center Matched
E&CV2S	Edge and Center Vee		S4S&CM	Surfaced Four Sides and Center Matched
EM	End Matched		S1S1E	Surfaced—One Side—One Edge
FG	Flat or slash grain		S1S2E	Surfaced—One Side—Two Edges
FLG	Flooring		S2S1E	Surfaced—Two Sides—One Edge
FOHC	Free of Heart Center		T&G	Tongued and Grooved
FT. BM	Feet Board Measure (also FBM)		WRC	Western Red Cedar
H&M	Hit and Miss		WWPA	Western Wood Product Association
IND	Industrial			

TABLE 6: DIMENSIONS OF STANDARD LUMBER STOCKED AT LUMBERYARDS

Nominal	Actual	Max. Length	Nominal	Actual	Max. Length	Nominal	Actual	Max. Length
1 × 4	¾″ × 3½″	16′	5/4 × 4	1″ × 3½″	16′	2 × 4	1½″ × 3½″	16′
1 × 6	¾″ × 5½″	16′	5/4 × 6	1″ × 5½″	16′	2 × 6	1½″ × 5½″	22′
1 × 8	¾″ × 7¼″	16′	5/4 × 8	1″ × 7¼″	16′	2 × 8	1½″ × 7¼″	22′
1 × 10	¾″ × 9¼″	16′	5/4 × 10	1″ × 9¼″	16′	2 × 10	1½″ × 9¼″	22′
1 × 12	¾″ × 11¼″	16′	5/4 × 12	1″ × 11¼″	16′	2 × 12	1½″ × 11¼″	22′

and build as efficiently as possible. The trick is to build soundly but not wastefully. Figuring out how to structure your frame is one easy way to control waste in your house. More important, it provides exciting design possibilities.

The first thing to determine when structuring a building is what kind of forces must be dealt with. These are called "loads," and they can be described as follows:

Dead loads are the weights of the materials used in the structure. For example, a dead roof load includes the rafters, or trusses, and all of the roofing materials (see Appendix 7 for a listing of common building material weights).

Live loads refer to the changing weights or forces applied to the house. Live loads may be further categorized. Static live loads are those that are applied slowly and remain constant over periods of time, like the books in your library. Repetitive or fatigue loads occur numerous times per day, like the occupants walking across the room. Impact loads are just what they sound like: a tree falling on the house or a lot of snow and ice falling from an upper roof to a lower one.

Seismic loads are specified by the local codes, which are based on empirical records. They depend on which part of our ever-changing world you live in.

Snow loads are also regional and are specified in the code books.

Wind loads occur everywhere, but more predictably along the shore and in certain mountainous regions. Wind loads are often figured into the local snow-load requirements.

In Figure 80 you can see the variety of loads, live and dead, that affect the house frame. These figures may vary some for your area. Check with your local building office.

CALCULATING THE STRUCTURE FOR A TYPICAL FLOOR

Let's go through the very simple arithmetic involved in sizing the joists or rafters for a given span (refer to Figure 81). This is a simple square deck supported on either side by a load-bearing wall and a girder down the center.

A load-bearing wall is one that stands on or over a foundation condition designed to distribute loads to the ground. For the purposes of this discussion we will assume that the bearing capacity of the soil can handle anything we throw at it. This is actually true in the majority of cases. (See the discussion of unstable soils requiring special footings.) If the width of the house is too great to be spanned with one joist, another load-bearing wall must be located in the middle, perhaps more than one. This produces a series of bays

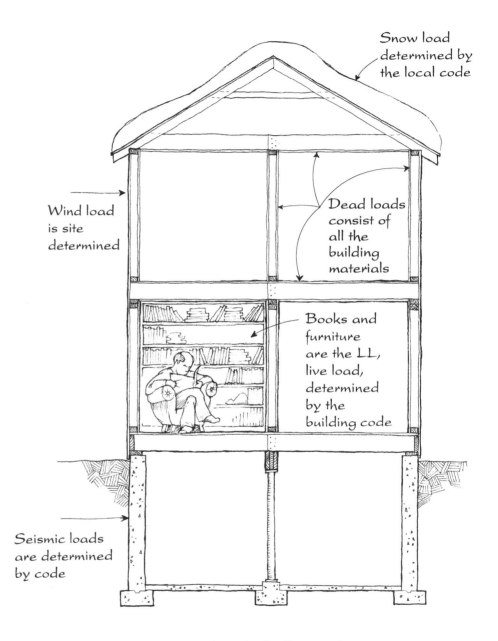

Snow load determined by the local code

Wind load is site determined

Dead loads consist of all the building materials

Books and furniture are the LL, live load, determined by the building code

Seismic loads are determined by code

FIGURE 80: Some typical "live" and "dead" loads affecting a house.

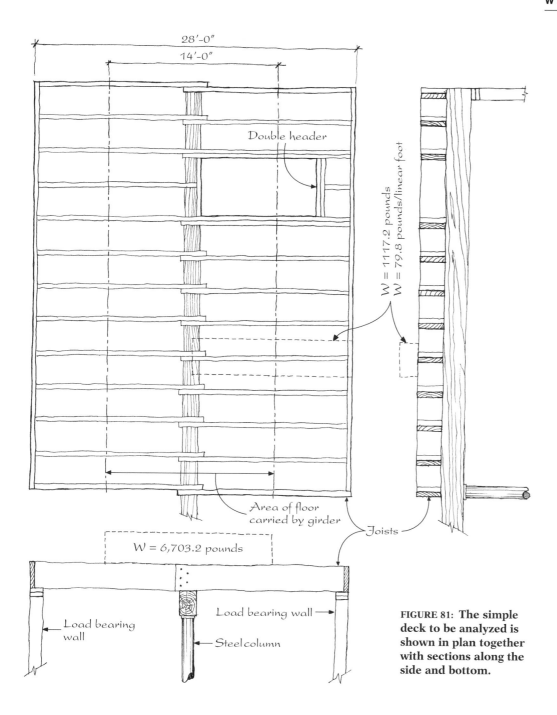

28'-0"

14'-0"

Double header

W = 1117.2 pounds
W = 79.8 pounds/linear foot

Area of floor
carried by girder

Joists

W = 6,703.2 pounds

Load bearing
wall

Load bearing wall

Steel column

FIGURE 81: The simple deck to be analyzed is shown in plan together with sections along the side and bottom.

that the floor joists can comfortably span. Unfortunately, it also produces a series of walls and separations that can break up the rooms in ways that don't work with your design. To get around this, we can use a heavy girder supported on two posts in lieu of the bearing wall. The girder might be a built-up beam, a glulam, or anything else properly calculated to carry the necessary load. This post and girder arrangement will be useful any time you want to get the loads down to the ground without putting a bearing wall right in the middle of a room.

This intermediate wall or girder configuration allows the joists to be smaller. This results in a thinner floor thickness, fewer steps between floors, and a less expensive structure. However, it also means less space in which to run mechanicals and more sound transmission. Therefore, in areas where forced-air heating is popular, traditional joists are giving way to the use of deep floor trusses to span the entire building width. These manufactured trusses can be up to 2' deep, which provides a generous space to run the duct work. The extra cost of the trusses is offset by the labor saved in the erection and easier installation of mechanicals.

O.K., now back to our simple deck. If this is an interior floor deck, it must carry a code-specified live load of 40 pounds per square foot (lbs. per sq. ft.). The structure to accomplish this will add a dead load of between 10 and 20 lbs. per sq. ft. The dead load is not code specified; it is the actual weight of beams, joists, girders, and flooring. (I am guesstimating here, but you can calculate it exactly from the material weights given in Appendix 7.) The combined live and dead loads can be estimated conservatively at 60 lbs. per sq. ft. Happily, these loads are considered to be "uniform," which means they are evenly distributed over the floor. By contrast, a "nonuniform" load might be drifting snow on a flat roof. Anything like a waterbed or piano would be considered a "point" or "concentrated" load. (See Appendices 7 and 8 for additional methods to calculate different load types.)

In our sample deck the floor joists are on 16" centers and spanning 14'. This means each joist will support 8" of floor along either side of it, with the other 8" being picked up by the adjacent joists (see Figure 82). We see that this amounts to an area of loading 16" (or 1.33') wide running the entire length of each joist. The joists in our example are 14' long, which translates into a load-carrying area of:

1.33 ft. × 14 linear ft. = 18.62 sq. ft.

for each joist. Since our combined (live plus dead) load per square foot is 60 pounds, the total load on each joist is:

18.62 sq. ft. × 60 lbs./sq. ft. = 1117.20 lbs.

This is called the *total* load and is designated with a capital "W." Don't confuse it with the *uniform* load, which is designated

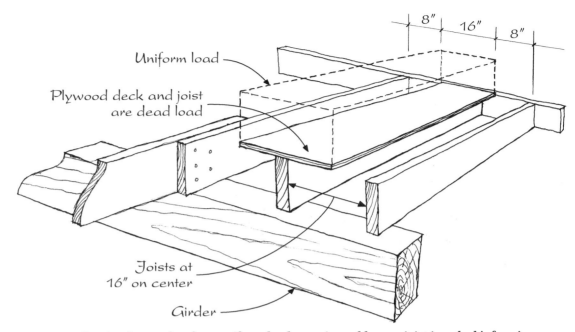

FIGURE 82: The visual metaphor for a uniform load experienced by one joist in a deck's framing system.

with a small "w." The uniform load is the load *per running foot* of beam or joist. We can find the uniform load, w, by dividing the total load, W, by the length of the joist. So, in our example, we would have:

$$w = W/14 \text{ ft.}$$
$$= 1117.20 \text{ lbs.}/14 \text{ ft.}$$
$$= 79.80 \text{ lbs. per linear ft.}$$

Why do we care what "w" and "W" are? We use them to pick our joist size from the charts (see Appendix 7) and we use them to determine the loads that are transferred to the bearing conditions at either end of the joist.

First let's decide what size joists we would like to use. Turn to Table 37 in Appendix 7 (or any other span chart available) and find the conditions that best describe our joist. We know what the "w" and "W" are, but we need to decide what kind of wood we are framing with. If it's kiln-dried, Douglas fir it will be stronger and stiffer than "green" spruce, white pine, or hem-fir. The chart of wood properties, Table 36, lists F_b, which is the bending strength of the wood, and E, which is a measure of its stiffness. Douglas fir has an F_b = 1,450 psi (pounds per square inch), and an E = 1,700,000 psi. This species of lumber will do the job with a 2 × 10 while, for comparison, pine (F_b = 1,000 psi, E = 1,300,000 psi) will require a 2 × 12. Now it's time to ask some questions:

How deep do you want your floor deck? How much shrinkage is tolerable? (Don't forget that shrinkage is maximum perpendicular to the grain.) How much depth do you need for drainpipe slopes or duct chases? (Soil pipes require a ⅛″ to ¼″ drop per running foot. See Chapter 17.) Will there be enough head height at the top of the stairs? What are the costs involved and which wood is locally available? Perhaps the joists should be on different centers: 24″? 12″? 6″? These issues may not need to be resolved immediately. However, they should be kept in mind as you go through the sizing of your frame. After you've done a few joists and girders, you will start to get an idea of what you're working with.

Few procedures illustrate the cyclical nature of design as clearly as frame design. Your structural members can always be deeper, wider, or reconfigured to give you the same structural results with a different architectural shape.

Assuming you have chosen to use 2 × 12 pine on 16″ centers for the joists, let's now move to sizing the girder. You should be aware that the "W" (total) carried by any joist will be evenly divided between the two supports it spans. This is true of uniform loads and all other load configurations that are symmetrical about the

center point of the beam. In our case, this means that each end of every joist will deliver 558.6 pounds in a concentrated load to the wall on one side and to the girder on the other. (See Figure 83b.) This simple arithmetic does not apply for nonuniform loading. Therefore, Appendix 7 has a procedure for converting all other loading configurations into *equivalent uniform loads*. This method of approximation is for ease of calculation and should be used with joists only. Major beams and

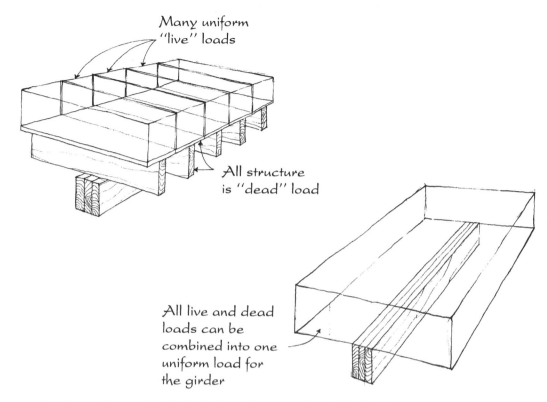

FIGURE 83a: **The loading on the girder is just a larger version of the loading on each joist.**

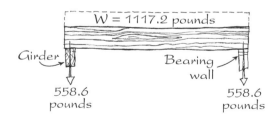

FIGURE 83b: **Uniform loads are distributed evenly to the supports at each end of the beam.**

girders should always be calculated using appropriate engineering or proper span tables (see Appendix 7).

The girder is 16′ or 192″ long. There is a joist every 16″, so 192″/16″ = 12 joists. But our girder has 12 joists on *each* side, so it is actually supporting 24 joist ends, each representing 558.6 pounds. Therefore, the total load, W, the girder must bear is equivalent to 24 joists × 558.6 lbs./joist = 13,406.4 lbs. Looking this up in the charts, we see that the following sizes could be used: 6 × 20 (@14,523 lbs.) or 12 × 14 (@14,554 lbs) in pine (@F_b = 1000 psi).

Yikes! These girders are way too big. This tells me we should shorten our span (or switch to steel). If we put a post in the middle of our span, the numbers will be reduced by half. Now our total load will be 6,703.2 pounds. Using pine, the span chart indicates an 8 × 12 or 6 × 14. These are still pretty chunky. If I don't want to put in another post, perhaps I must consider a glulam, a truss joist, or light steel. For now, however, I will go with the pine.

So, if the total load, W, equals 6,703.2 pounds, then dividing this by two will produce a concentrated load of 3,351.6 pounds at each end. This means at each end of the girder we need a supporting condition, or "equal reaction" as engineers call it, of the total load divided in half: 6,703.2 lbs./2 = 3,351.6 lbs. In our example, the girder sits on a load-bearing wall at one end and a properly sized post at the other. (See Appendix 8 for an expla-nation of how to design and size a wood column.) In the load-bearing wall, we place double studs under the girder to pick up the extra load; for the post, we can probably use a lolly column or a 4 × 4 wooden post.

At this point you can start to see the whole picture. The rafters pick up snow loads and transfer them, along with the dead loads, to exterior and interior bearing walls. The bearing walls are lined up over each other so they provide a continuous path for the loads all the way down through the building. Each level or floor also picks up live and dead loads, which are similarly transferred to these bearing walls. At the foundation, all the upper loads are concentrated over foundation walls or posts in the basement. These sit on footings designed to distribute the loads to the soil on which the building stands.

Girders, beams, and headers are used where spans are too great or penetrations must be made. If a stairwell penetrates a deck frame, the joists must be interrupted with a header built to take the loads around the opening. A header is usually a doubled or tripled joist. It is actually just a small girder running perpendicular to the other joists. Headers must be sized using the same method outlined above. Loads are totaled, resultant end loads are calcu-lated, and then the joists on either side of the opening must be doubled or tripled to safely transfer these loads to the bearing walls.

The structure of a building influences every other aspect of the design. Indeed, it's what allows your design to be built. If you want to design your own house, you *must* understand how it overcomes gravity.

Although the arithmetic must be re-spected, there are always several ways to frame a building. Whether timber frame, platform frame, pole barn, or A-frame, they all rely on the same basic principles outlined above. There's really nothing dif-ficult about this math. So give it a try before calling up the structural engineer or submitting to your builder's pro-nouncement: "It *must* be done *this* way."

Yestermorrow graduates are entitled to consulting or design review as part of their alumni privileges. Kim, a women who became a contractor after finishing the course, calls us about once a year. Kim started out tentatively with a simple ga-rage. We had to walk her through every joist. After once installing what the num-bers called for, she started to acquire an intuitive feeling for what was needed in a given situation. She doesn't rely exclu-sively on this intuition, but it serves as a guide. It also alerts her to any situation that might require some special engineer-ing. Such a situation came up when she built her greenhouse. She realized that any sagging or deflection in the main car-rying beam would crack the glass.

"Deflection" is the word engineers use for sagging. It's not so much dependent on a beam's strength as it is on stiffness. Stiffness is a function of the type of material from which the beam is made and the shape of its cross section. The measure of a material's stiffness is indicated by its modulus of elasticity, or E. For most woods E is in the neighborhood of 1,000,000 to 1,200,000 psi (see Appendices 7 and 8). For comparison, steel is usually 36,000,000 psi. To get a measure of the other factor—shape—one must calculate the moment of inertia, or "I" of the beam in question. (See Appendix 8 for further details.)

Once deflection has been calculated, there is an easy rule of thumb for deciding if it is excessive. Divide the length of the span in inches by the number 240. The result is the acceptable deflection in inches. If the ceiling will be plastered, divide the span by 360 to avoid any cracking. For example, Kim's greenhouse span was 14′. Converted to inches we get 168″. Divided by 240 this gives us about 0.7″ of deflection in the middle of the beam. If we divide by 360 we get about 0.47″. Since Kim was worried about glass, we decided to use the more conservative value. This means that the beam had to be designed to have less than 0.47″ of deflection at the mid span, less than ½″. Now 14′ isn't much of a span, but 0.47″ is a demanding deflection to design for. The resulting beam was far stronger than needed just to carry the loads. When a beam is overdesigned for most considerations in order to meet one particularly demanding criteria,

one says that criteria "controls." In Kim's case, the design of her beam was controlled by deflection (not bending, shear, or carrying capacity).

Each year Kim's framing gets just a bit more "gymnastic," and about halfway through the winter we expect a call. "I know about deflection, but what I was wondering this time . . ." I can only guess what she'll have for us next year. Cantilevers, structural ridge beams, stress-skin panels, box beams, trusses—there is really no limit to the many elegant ways to suspend a load between two points.

Thermal Considerations

It must be understood from the beginning that your choice of framing system will have a great impact on the thermal performance of the building. It will determine where and how much insulation you can place in the exterior walls. It will suggest a strategy for insulating the roof or attic. Moreover, there will be a host of connection details that must be resolved to prevent the slow leaking of heat through the building's shell. Malcolm Wells, the well-known architect and author, calls these leaks "thermal nosebleeds."

Chapter 15, on building envelopes, presents the detailed calculations used for quantifying the heat flow in and out of your house. These calculations are necessary for design and specification of interior climate control equipment: HVAC

(heating, ventilating, and air conditioning). For right now, however, we won't concern ourselves with the numbers. At this point I just want you to understand the basic principles of heat and moisture movement. In particular, I want you to see how the decisions you make about your frame lead to a particular insulation strategy and these, in turn, will determine the thermal performance of your house and ultimately your choice of HVAC equipment, and maybe even some of your final finishes. As I've said before, everything is connected.

The wall sections in Figure 84 illustrate a variety of different framing/insulation configurations. The thermal behavior of an insulated wall is quite different *between* the studs than *at* the studs. Wood isn't much of an insulator. Heat leaks out through the studs faster than through the insulation. The more studs in your wall, the lower its insulating value. This makes a good case for studs being at wider centers, say 24″ o.c. (on center). But if wide is good, isn't wider better? Not necessarily. If you are using plywood or waferboard sheathing, you must space your studs so one occurs at least every 4′ on center. This permits you to nail off the staggered seams between the 4′ × 8′ sheets of sheathing. This criteria is hardly restrictive; it allows spacings of 6″, 12″, 16″, 24″, and 48″. Unfortunately, fiberglass insulation doesn't come in all those widths. Also, the

Single-Stud wall— 16" o.c.

Single-stud wall— 24" o.c.

Single walls	R Values	
	Between framing	At framing
1. Outside surface (15 MPH wind)	0.17	0.17
2. Siding, clapboard	0.81	0.81
3. Sheathing, ½" CDX	1.32	1.32
4. Blanket insulation	**11.00**	—
5. 2 × 4 stud	—	**4.38**
6. Gypsum wallboard	0.45	0.45
7. Inside surface (still air)	0.68	0.68
Totals	14.43	7.81

Note that the low insulative value at the framing (7.81) can be minimized by using fewer studs (24" o.c. versus 16" o.c.)

Double stud wall staggered 16" o.c.

Double wall	R Values	
	Between framing	At framing
1. Outside surface (15 MPH wind)	0.17	0.17
2. Siding, clapboard	0.81	0.81
3. Sheathing, ½" CDX	1.32	1.32
4. Blanket insulation	**22.00**	**11.00**
5. 2 × 4 stud	—	**4.38**
6. Gypsum wallboard	0.45	0.45
7. Inside surface (still air)	0.68	0.68
Totals	25.43	18.81

FIGURE 84: The effects of framing on heat transmission.

wider the space between studs, the more difficult it is to frame doors and windows and to hang cabinets, towel bars, and other interior finishes.

When superinsulated houses came into fashion, builders tried to find ways of beating the thermal nosebleeds with double walls and staggered studs (Figure 85). This worked, but at the cost of building two houses, one inside the other. This is not just a figure of speech.

In the 1970s a fellow named Lee Porter Butler promoted the Thermal Envelope™ House. This was a house built with an unincorporated air space on all sides. This, he claimed, would wrap the entire living space in a thermal blanket that would keep it warm through the coldest winter. But his design didn't really work the way he thought. Today we realize that this design was the unintentional beginning of the "superinsulated" house concept. Let's face it, nothing insulates like *two* thermal envelopes, one inside the other (see Figure 86).

It soon became evident that reducing infiltration by building a tight house did far more for energy savings than building thick walls to slow conductive losses. What followed was years of creative but frustrating attempts to wrap the inside of a stick-built frame with polyethylene plastic film. Indeed, vapor barriers are now required by most building codes. Unfortunately, polyethylene sheet is very difficult to make truly airtight. So Joe Lstiburek

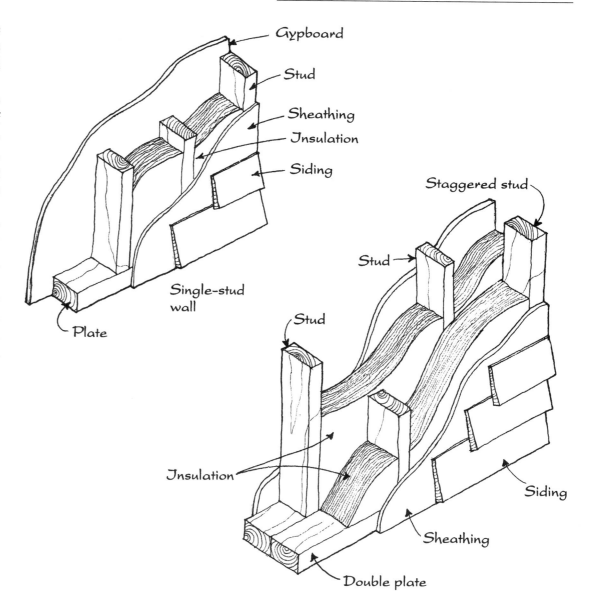

FIGURE 85: Superinsulated walls use staggered studs to prevent thermal bridging or "thermal nosebleeds."

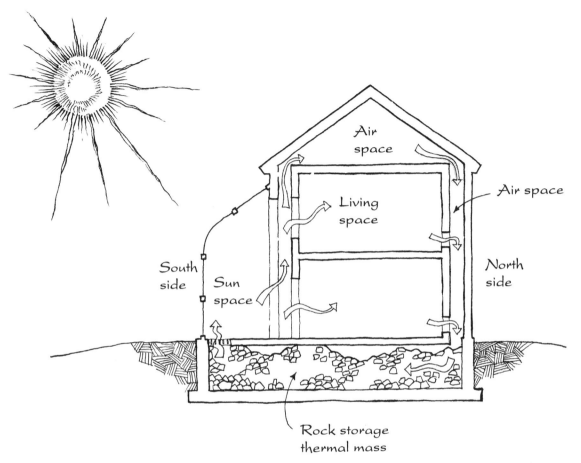

Air space

Living space

Air space

South side

Sun space

North side

Rock storage thermal mass

FIGURE 86: Perhaps the first superinsulated house was the original *envelope house*. Although the designers thought it was a circulating envelope of warm air that kept energy costs down, it was later learned that the tightness created by *two* thermal envelopes was the cause.

and some other Canadian engineers developed a more effective way of controlling moisture using the drywall. The Airtight Drywall Approach (ADA) uses gaskets between some of the critical framing members and the drywall to create an effective air barrier throughout the house.

This technique saves time and money by eliminating the polyethylene installation, but it requires a special approach to the framing. Again we see how framing details are intimately involved with thermal aspects of the house design.

While the stick builders may place a

stud every 24″, the timber framers have a bigger problem. Spans of 8′, 10′, even 12′ are perfectly reasonable spacings for the posts in a timber frame. Modern, energy-conscious joiners are constantly debating the most resource efficient method for hanging walls on their frames. Originally, necessary framing was placed between the posts, essentially building two frames: a timber frame with a stick frame between the posts. Besides being wasteful and expensive, this configuration was a very poor energy performer. The evolution of the modern timber frame has been a quest for the perfect blend of structural efficiency and thermal performance. In Figure 87 we have illustrated a few of the solutions developed over the years. The present consensus is that stressed-skin panels solve the widest spectrum of problems—except those concerning sustainability and the environment. As we will see again and again, there are certain ethical and political questions raised by our choice of materials and building methods. This is discussed further at the end of this chapter.

Now let's look at the ramifications of different framing solutions for the roof. Traditional wisdom states, whether cold climate or hot, a roof needs to be vented and insulated. The insulation keeps the heat in, or out, and the venting provides an escape path for any that leaks through. Failure to properly configure your roof assembly will lead to high energy use,

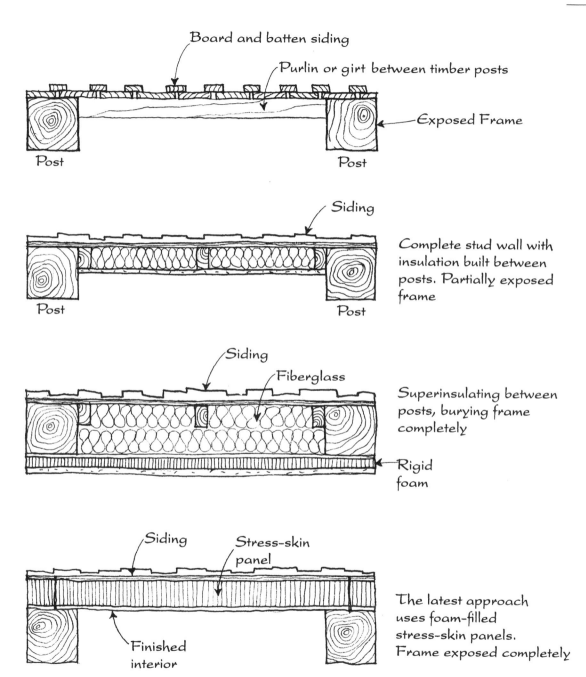

Board and batten siding

Purlin or girt between timber posts

Exposed Frame

Post

Post

Siding

Complete stud wall with insulation built between posts. Partially exposed frame

Post

Post

Siding

Fiberglass

Superinsulating between posts, burying frame completely

Rigid foam

Siding

Stress-skin panel

The latest approach uses foam-filled stress-skin panels. Frame exposed completely

Finished interior

uncomfortable rooms, and moisture problems, even rot (Figure 88).

The cold attic approach shows the traditional thinking for a stick-built attic in a cold climate. The insulation is placed in the ceiling/floor joists and the attic is vented through louvers at either end. This provides cold storage as well as positive control of heat and moisture. But as people started to renovate their attics, it became necessary to confine the venting to the same space as the roof framing. The second illustration (Figure 89) shows an idealized version of soffit/ridge venting. I say idealized because it often doesn't work as advertised. Here's the theory.

The warm air in your heated living space carries moisture in proportion to how warm it is. Leaking through the polyethylene vapor barrier, it finds cold external sheathing and exposed roofing nails. On these it condenses from a vapor to a liquid, or in very cold regions, to ice. Spring comes and the ice, melting into water, starts to flow. It flows into the roof insulation, reducing the R-value, and into the framing, where it promotes rot. If the roof is vented, it is hoped that the flow of air over the damp insulation will dry it out before the next season. During the winter,

FIGURE 87: **Timberframers have shown great creativity in dealing with the thermal leaks associated with most frames. Stressed skin panels solve most problems even though they sometimes incorporate environmentally dubious foam products.**

Two Traditional Ways to Vent a Roof

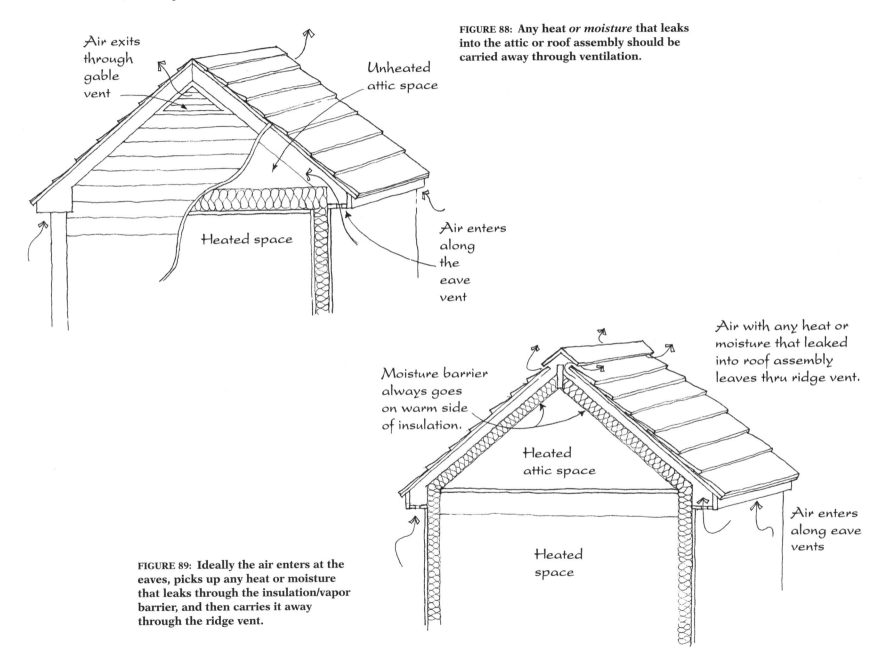

Air exits through gable vent

Unheated attic space

Heated space

Air enters along the eave vent

FIGURE 88: **Any heat *or moisture* that leaks into the attic or roof assembly should be carried away through ventilation.**

Air with any heat or moisture that leaked into roof assembly leaves thru ridge vent.

Moisture barrier always goes on warm side of insulation.

Heated attic space

Heated space

Air enters along eave vents

FIGURE 89: **Ideally the air enters at the eaves, picks up any heat or moisture that leaks through the insulation/vapor barrier, and then carries it away through the ridge vent.**

this venting has a further function: It helps reduce ice dams. To prevent ice dams it is important to carry off any heat that leaks through the roof from the living space below. Otherwise, this escaping heat will melt the snow on the roof, which will then follow gravity down to the overhanging eaves. Since the eaves have no source of heat below them, the water will quickly refreeze and eventually build up into a classic ice dam. When spring thaw arrives, the melting snow will produce an increase of flow that will back up behind the dam and leak through the shingles into the house.

In addressing this situation, design/builders must be clear on the different components making up the problem. Control must be exerted over:

1. the heat leaking through the insulation;
2. the moisture that is carried in heated air;
3. any cold surface that will allow condensation;
4. proper drainage paths for water resulting from this condensation or melting.

Let's look at the framing implications of each in a bit of detail:

1. To address heat loss, most designers look for a way to pack more insulation into the roof structure (see Figure 90). I've seen 2 × 12s used instead of 2 × 8s just so thicker batts of insulation could be installed. I've seen builders strap out the outer surface of the roof framing with rigid insulation board to reduce thermal bridging through the rafters themselves. Timber framers brought this approach to its logical conclusion with the use of stress-skin panels.

2. Controlling moisture movement through the building's exterior assemblies can be tricky. Fastidious barriers, gaskets, special paint, and even a slight negative pressure provided by the HVAC system have all been used with some success to deal with this problem. Even so, one can understand the simple wisdom in the old "cold attic" approach. With huge volumes of air between the roof and the living spaces, there is ample room for generous air changes and massive blankets of insulation. Another contemporary strategy

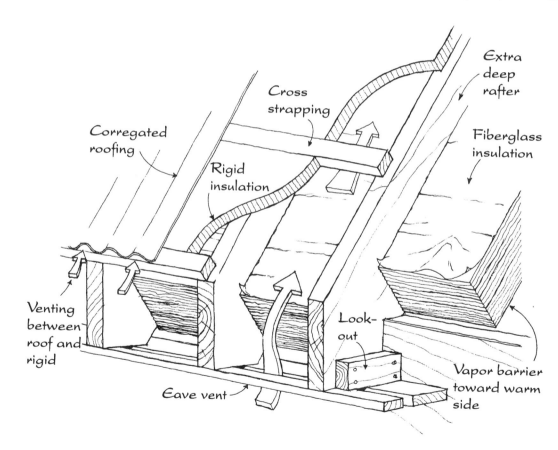

FIGURE 90: **Cross strapping minimizes thermal bridging through the roof framing.**

simply eliminates the path through which moisture-laden air might leak. By completely filling the spaces between framing members with insulation, moisture-laden air can't find a void in which to condense. On this basis many argue for stress-skin panels or rafter spaces completely filled with foam or blown in cellulose. But this approach means that there can be no conventional venting, as it would surely introduce moisture to the roof assembly. So, if you have designed a roof or framing system that is difficult to vent, this approach might be appropriate. But first check with your building inspector for vent requirements. Venting is going to be tricky for a geodesic dome, a yurt, or even for a clerestory shed roof, if you want the inside volume to look like the outside shape.

3. Without the cold surface for moisture to condense on, we wouldn't need to be so concerned if a little air found its way into the stud or rafter spaces. When designing and detailing a wall or roof section, it is important to be mindful of any elements, connectors or appliances that could provide cold, condensing surfaces for moisture. This problem is prevalent in plank & beam designs where the framing members penetrate through the walls to the outside. In pole built structures the same consideration must be given to protruding poles. These are not only thermal nosebleeds, they're opportunities for condensation and rot.

4. Providing for *penetrating water* or moisture may seem like a premature admission of defeat. Nevertheless, many builders use pressure treated wood for plates. Knowing that gravity will deliver the water to the lowest point, framing members at these locations are given an added degree of protection. I really can't embrace this solution, but I support the thinking that has led to it. Experience teaches that it is better to understand and accommodate water's nature than try to obstruct it.

Every aspect of a building contributes to its comfort and overall thermal performance. Here we have introduced a few basic issues linked to your framing design. It may seem tricky at first, but the nature of design means juggling as many balls as you can at the outset. You will see that design decisions affect structure which affects HVAC choices, which affects room size, which affects further design decisions. Start with a first run at your design and then after you're done, use the calculations in Chapter 10 to figure out what your design will require structurally. Need I say cycle back and do it again?

Thinking about Walls

COLD HUMID CLIMATE

If I'm building along a northern coast, I will be dealing with driving storms, brutal cold, and corrosive salt air. How do I think about a wall? What can I learn from the local builders?

To start with I know that insulation is always good and this seems like an opportunity for using plenty. A thick wall, properly framed, seems indicated. I decide to place shingles on the outside. This seems to be the local preference. It has worked for centuries, and I like the look of shingles. Anticipating the constant on-shore breeze, I better make this house as tight as possible. Two wall sections suggest themselves.

If the building is fairly simple, I might timber frame it and use stress-skin insulating panels for my walls. This choice allows me excellent insulation (up to R = 42), a minimum of cracks (one every 8' to 12') and I can still hang my shingles. Incidently, I would never place the shingles directly on the sheathing (nail base) of the panel. Shingles and clapboard are meant to "breathe." So I will cover my walls with Tyvek™ or some similar infiltration barrier, then strap the entire exterior (nail on 1 × 3s every 6" or so). I can nail my shingles to the strapping and then they can breathe from both sides. Because of the high winds, I may double strap the wall, one series of strapping vertical, one horizontal (Figure 91).

With an improperly built shingle wall the gusts of wind, even more than the steady blow, will actually pump the rain and weather into the wall. By adequately strapping and venting the wall, the shingles become what's called a "rain screen" (Figure 91). The gusts of wind will pres-

Timberframe
Stress-skin panel
Vertical strapping
Horizontal strapping

Shingles

FIGURE 91: Rain-screen construction prevents water from being forced into the wall assembly during high wind rainstorms.

surize the back and front of the shingles equally. The result is, less water gets into the wall.

Inside, on the warm side of the wall, we must consider moisture penetration. Since the entire wall cavity is filled with foam, there are no voids for the moisture to enter. Even if the air were to get through the gyp board, the interior foam is never cold enough to provide a surface for condensation. Clearly the stress-skin panel is a fine choice for cold climates.

On the other hand, foam panels don't meet *my* environmental standards and I rarely design "fairly simple" buildings. So I might just as likely consider a 2 × 6 stick-framed wall for its flexibility and try to make it as environmentally friendly as possible. I will place the studs on 24" centers to minimize the amount of heat lost through the framing (up to 20 percent in conventional framing). A stud wall will inevitably have more cracks than the stress-skin panel. I must take precautions against infiltration, so I spray 2" of adhesive-bonded cellulose into each cavity. On top of this I place 3.5" batts of unfaced fiberglass insulation. This starts my wall off at about R = 18. From there I can strap out the exterior and add rigid fiberglass for another couple of points. By putting it on the outside I further reduce the heat loss through framing members. I'm usually happy with anything over R = 20 in a wall. Rather than spend my money on more insulation, I will invest it on reducing infiltration (weather stripping, tightly caulked windows, sealed chimney and flue penetrations, etc.). Before strapping I must wrap the building with an air barrier (i.e., Tyvek™ or Typar™). The shingles will be installed just as on the previous wall. With fiberglass batts there are always voids and air spaces in the wall. Therefore, I must install a vapor barrier on the inside before installing the gyp board. This must be done carefully with special attention at the windows, doors, and other penetrations to control infiltration.

In comparison, the thermal performance of the stud wall may not be quite as good as that of the stress-skin panel wall. They are about the same at moisture and weather control. The stud wall is slightly less expensive, particularly if there are many corners or angles in the building. Of course, these are only generalizations until I run more precise calculations. All the same, I hope this gives you a general feel for some of the issues to be considered when thinking about a wall section for cold, windy locations.

HOT DRY CLIMATE

Now let's imagine we're building in a hot, dry region with a frequent but light breeze. It rains rarely except during the rainy season; and then, for three months, it's a deluge. It is very hot in the day and quite cool at night. The biggest problem seems to be the sun. Again, I imagine two wall sections.

The local vernacular has been adobe for centuries. There must be something to it. I can build a wall of traditional adobe or I can use the new manufactured adobe. The former has more mass, the latter is dimensionally more consistent. Either way, the idea is to create a massive wall that will delay heat penetration for at least twelve hours. The underlying principle of the traditional wall requires that it be thick enough to absorb heat all day and then give up the stored heat all night. Traditional adobe must be stuccoed or whitewashed regularly to prevent the periodic rains from turning it back to mud. There is little moisture vapor to worry about in this climate. Instead I might expect the occupant to run a humidifier occasionally. While the walls may absorb a bit of this moisture, it doesn't harm them. This is a simple, inexpensive wall that is perfectly appropriate for the climate.

On the other hand, perhaps my client

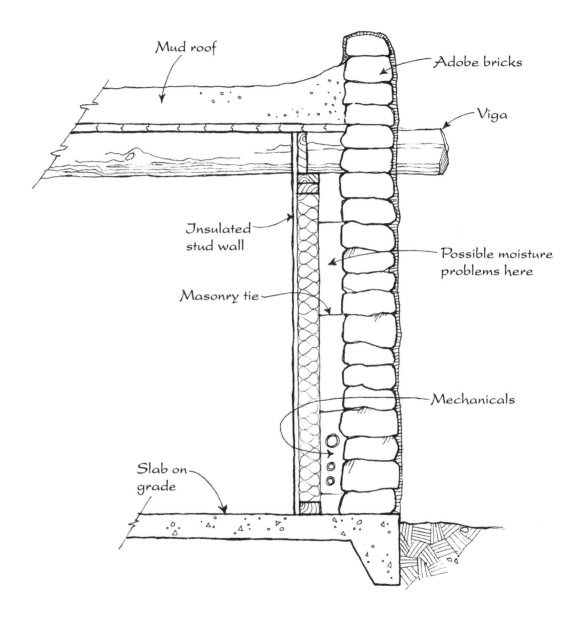

FIGURE 92: **Decoupling a masonry or adobe wall from the interior space makes it easier to engineer the HVAC system, but it's an expensive choice in the long run.**

wants the reliable comfort of an engineered indoor climate. If the sun were to go in for a few days, the former wall system might produce chilly nights. If the days were unusually hot, the heat would penetrate too quickly, making the interior uncomfortable. To guard against these rare occurrences we could design a wall similar to the stud wall described above. Instead of shingles, however, we will affix masonry ties to the outside and attach a thick adobe veneer as a finish (Figure 92).

This will give us the look of an adobe wall on the outside, but it will not behave like one. With an insulated stud wall in place, the adobe's thermal storage ability will be decoupled from the interior of the house. The adobe will absorb and release the heat of the day, but the insulation in the stud wall will not allow these cycles to be fully felt inside the house. Here we start to understand what engineers mean when they refer to "climate control." Such a wall allows us to calculate the worst case scenario and then size the air conditioning (or heater) accordingly. Of course there are a few complications, as always. With insulation we now have voids in the wall. These spaces could be sites for condensation and a vapor barrier must be installed on the warm side of the wall. But which side is that? The outside will be warmest during the day, the inside at night. In an arid climate, we can assume the moisture will arrive from the lived-in side, so the vapor barrier goes on the inside.

In comparing these two walls, we find the traditional adobe wall to be simple, affordable, and durable. We find that the composite wall is much more complicated, more expensive, and requires more energy. The design is the result of engineering habits carried over from other climates. In its defense, it provides a place for wiring, ducts, and other mechanicals. Also, if the numbers are rigorously crunched and it's built to spec, an engineered wall system *will* work. The interior finish of the walls can be consistent throughout the house. Perhaps most important, the composite wall allows structures to be built much higher than with conventional adobe.

The point here is that walls can and must be designed to fit the needs of the client and the climate. If you understand how moisture, heat, and insulation work, you can design an appropriate wall for any situation and within any architectural vocabulary.

What the Skeleton Supports

Whatever your choice of frame, it must support itself and everything else. You will hang insulation, siding, mechanicals, finishes—everything—from the frame. Each of these systems requires appropriate connectors: staples, glue, nails, brads, straps, etc. How all these connections are orchestrated will vary for different framing systems. Many of the choices made easily on

the basis of structure or thermal performance will have to be considered anew from the perspective of assembly. This is often an area of contention between the architect and the builder. Drawing a frame with insulation, sheathing, mechanicals, etc., is pretty easy; building it can sometimes be impossible. This aspect of making houses is dramatically streamlined and improved when a design/build approach is taken.

For example, the stress-skin panel is often the timber framers' choice of insulation. It nicely solves the structural problem of spanning between the posts and the thermal problem of minimizing thermal nosebleeds. But how do you hang a door or window; where do you locate mechanicals; and what do you nail your siding to?

One good solution deserves another, and stress-skin panel techniques have steadily evolved (Figure 93). By removing the foam and replacing it with framing, rough openings for doors and windows can be made in the panels (see Figure 94). By grooving (or pregrooving) the panels, one can create pathways for the electrical system. Plumbing and ducts, however, must be exposed or boxed into interior walls. For some, these requirements may have too great an impact on the design and the feeling of the interior. For these owner/builders stick frames, masonry, or something else may be a better choice.

The stick frame has plenty of structural voids in which you can hide mechanicals,

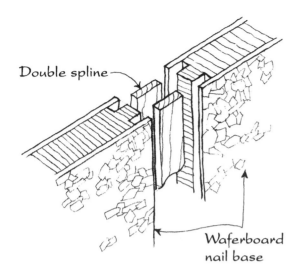

Double spline

Waferboard
nail base

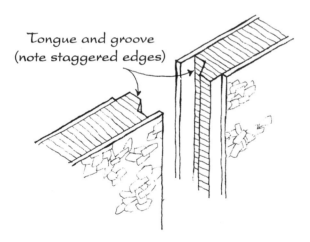

Tongue and groove
(note staggered edges)

FIGURE 93: A few of the many ways to join
stress-skin panels so as to minimize infiltration.

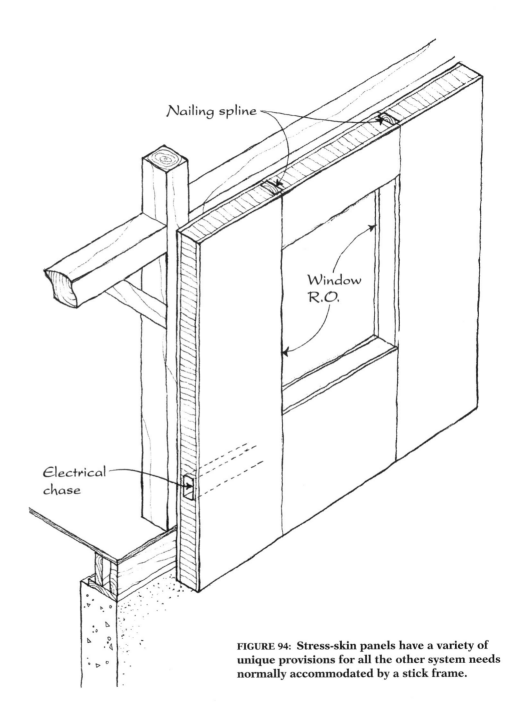

Nailing spline

Window
R.O.

Electrical
chase

FIGURE 94: Stress-skin panels have a variety of
unique provisions for all the other system needs
normally accommodated by a stick frame.

insulation, and even additional structure. Door and window openings can be reinforced easily. But thermal nosebleeds are cumbersome to deal with. Joints at the sills and floors are difficult to insulate. Some design/builders have covered the entire frame with 1″ to 2″ of rigid foam. Then the sheathing is applied over the foam with extra long nails that can go through the sheathing, through the foam, and into the studs.

This brings us to the question of different nail bases for siding (and roofing). The sheathing plays a structural, thermal, and logistical ($!) role in your design. It reinforces the frame against racking (shear); it plays a big role in infiltration control; and it greatly impacts most other construction procedures. Regardless of frame type, most sidings count on a plywood or "flakeboard" sheathing to provide an anchor for the nails. While this may be currently acceptable practice, I still get nervous about anchoring things to a mere ½″ of sheathing. I feel better if a certain percentage of the nails go into framing. This is no problem with stick framing; I just space my nailing pattern so that the siding nails go into the studs. But this can only work with horizontal sidings. For vertical sidings, shingles, or where stress-skin panels are involved, I have to add strapping. As discussed above, strapping is additional 1× material installed over the framing or sheathing, just to provide an air space between two materials.

One must also consider interior finishes when designing the building's frame. Gypsum board is today's most prevalent interior wall surface. If you are stick framing with studs on 24″ centers, the ½″ gyp board may deflect slightly between the studs, causing the seams to crack. This can be remedied by installing blocking, or using ⅝″ gypsum board. Either way you will be embracing a bit more cost. The blocking should be configured as shown in Figure 95. Formerly, when balloon framing created chimneylike voids between the studs from basement to attic, this blocking was called "fire blocking" and its primary purpose was to eliminate these paths for spreading fire. If you install true fire blocking, however, you will nullify the energy savings won by spacing the studs on 24″ centers to begin with.

Where stress-skin panels are used the considerations are different. Since the wall is solid foam, there are no fire pathways to be blocked. Panels can be pur-

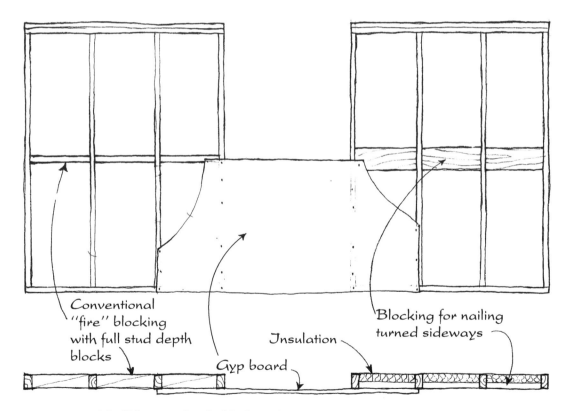

Conventional "fire" blocking with full stud depth blocks

Gyp board

Insulation

Blocking for nailing turned sideways

FIGURE 95: **As with all framing details, blocking should be configured to minimize heat loss.**

chased with gypsum board or nail base adhered to both sides. Finishing is simplified (if you can keep the gypsum surface from being damaged during construction). Some flexibility, however, is lost. Panels come in certain modular sizes. Window and door placement, even overall design will be somewhat affected by the dimensions of the module. Panels are now available with several different interior finishes, including some woods, gypsum, and Homasote.™ Because of the risk of damage during construction, I suggest that the panels be installed with nail base on both sides. This allows the widest flexibility in choosing your finishes and scheduling their installation.

The Truth about the Hard Choices in Design

In a sense, this entire book is about choices. The choices you make when you design and build your home convey who you are, your preferences, and what you believe in.

Normally not a topic found in "How To" books, the ethics of design/building are becoming extremely important in our resource-limited world. Increasingly, we are realizing that all communities are tied together through air, water, and commerce. What we mine in Ohio and manufacture in Pennsylvania can have a huge impact in Maine or Nova Scotia.

Before we can use them, all materials must be removed from the environment, processed (manufactured, assembled), packaged, and shipped. So, when we choose materials for our homes, the consequences go well beyond aesthetic and budgetary:

- The work conditions associated with collecting raw materials and manufacturing products
- The energy involved in fabrication, assembly, and shipping
- The health risks during collection, manufacture, installation, and even afterward (to you!)
- The creation and disposal of scraps, waste, and by-products

We now know that our dwelling and building practices determine the well-being of our global ecology more than any other human activity.

Some materials are so toxic that builders find using them unconscionable. For example, the production of extruded polystyrene insulation results in gases that endanger the ozone layer. Pressure-treated wood is legally considered "toxic waste" and must be disposed of in a special way. (Always use of a dust mask and safety goggles when cutting it.) Oil base and spray paints use highly volatile vehicles which are known carcinogens. With such materials the question always arises, "What shall we do with the scraps?" If we

burn them, the toxins are released into the air. If buried, the toxins leach into the water table. The best compromise for now is to take them to a *lined* landfill . . . but our landfills are running out of room. The only real solution is to find alternatives and discontinue the use of toxic materials altogether.

Additional questions are raised when we consider energy conservation. Many plastics, foams, glues, paints, and even plywood require enormous amounts of energy during manufacture. Moreover, any material not local to the building site requires packing and shipping, and thus additional energy. These associated energy costs are called the "embodied energy" of the material. Local and natural materials tend to have lower embodied energies than synthetic or imported materials.

In any domain, ethical choices are always among the most difficult. Everyone has rationalizations, excuses, and special explanations. But at least we can all agree that it is wrong to make beautiful homes in one part of the world at the expense and degradation of those in another. (Or did someone say, "Out of sight, out of mind"?)

Among the owner/builders I've taught, I note that when the choices are difficult, students blame the budget.

"I have absolutely no choice. The only thing I can even afford is this toxic, energy-wasting product, brand X. I know the manufacturer is raping the land and killing off endangered species but I simply don't have the money to be thinking about ethics."

But the issues are always more complex than the bottom line. I can remember several discussions like the following where students from different parts of the country discuss building strategies.

A student might declare, "I'm going to build the first straw-bale house in the state of Maine. It will be cheap and environmentally friendly."

"Don't be too sure," responds a student from Vermont. "We were going to build with straw bales and found that we had to buy the straw from Canada! The freight killed the project. Plus, who do you know in Maine experienced in stuccoing a straw bale wall? Anyone good will cost you dearly. We also want to have an environmentally friendly home, but we've decided to do it with wood."

"Wood? Environmentally friendly?" Now a student from Washington state joins the conversation. "The use of wood in our homes is what's responsible for the cutting of our last old-growth forests. In fact, whole areas of the northern forests are being clear-cut to meet the wood demand generated by the housing industry. That means erosion, loss of topsoil, loss of animal habitat, and loss of biodiversity."

"Hold on," responds the Vermonter,

"I'm cutting the wood from my own land. I'll be able to get the framing and the sheathing right off my backyard."

"Hmmm, aren't you worried about the wood shrinking? If I were going to frame with green lumber, I would want to use plywood for sheathing. Plywood is so straight and stable."

"But," worries one student, "isn't plywood a lot more expensive than using wood boards for sheathing?"

"Well, it all depends on the design complexity. The material costs will be higher using plywood, but the labor cost will be higher using boards. Depending on the shape of the house, either one might be more costly. You see, when you use boards, you must install diagonal bracing at all the corners to prevent racking. This is no big deal, but if you have a lot of corners it can start to take some serious time. I don't think most builders would sheath with plywood if it weren't significantly cheaper."

"But what about the toxicity? Plywood uses formaldehyde glues that give off fumes. The same is true of waferboard."

"Good point. We will use boards cut from on-site trees and let in diagonal bracing. The extra work will be worth the lower toxicity in our house."

"Not me," announces the another student. "I don't have enough money to be 'politically correct.' Once I start with that nontoxic stuff, I won't be able to use inex-

pensive foam insulation, standard paints and polyurethanes, or most synthetics. Why I won't even be able to put down a carpet using standard glues. They all give off fumes. But have you ever priced out the alternatives. Those organic paints, finishes, or carpets cost a mint!"

"So who has a suggestion?" As the instructor, I endeavor to keep these important debates going. "How can we have our cake and eat it too?"

Every class has at least one student that can't resist a rhetorical question. "Well, what about a compromise. If I couldn't afford to go nontoxic everywhere, I would do it where it had the greatest impact. Probably the interior finishes. After all, I hope to build a tight house, so I want fumes to be minimized on the inside first."

"Or," another student comes to life, "maybe it would make sense to use nontoxic wherever you can't easily come back and upgrade it. So that would mean anything buried in a wall or underground should have first preference."

"So are you saying that the finishes and floor glues would lose out to plywood and foundation insulation?"

"Weeell, I guess so. Hmmm, that would mean I live in all the interior fumes while saving up enough money to upgrade. This is a tougher decision than I thought."

"Exactly!" injects the shortsighted student. "And that's why I say that I'm just going to have to use the same old conventional way of doing things. They were developed to be affordable, and they still are. What's the matter with tradition? If it ain't broke don't fix it. My budget is small and I can't afford to be politically correct."

"But now we're creating the tradition," counters another student. "Why must we build stupidly just because others have? If vernacular architecture means houses designed in response to the culture and surroundings of the occupants, then maybe we need to update our current ver-

nacular. I would rather build a small, well-made home than a big stupid one. When we're gone, which do you think will get torn down first?"

"Yeah, well who cares?"

Phew! The ethics and politics of materials put a new spin on the vernacular traditions of building. It seems we can no longer endorse a building method just because "that's the way we've always done it." Regionalism must increasingly be bal-

anced with a perspective of our global village. In the end, this may turn out to be the most important incentive for industrialized nations to revitalize their vernacular dwelling traditions. Today's practice of purchasing homes as if they were products continues to propel us in an unhealthy and nonsustainable direction. Only when people reinvolve themselves in the *making* of their homes can the act of dwelling reflect a new and ethically sound global awareness.

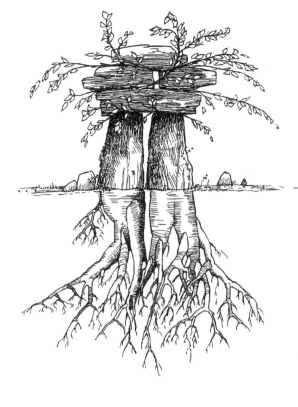

Masonry: Piling Things Up

Masonry may well be the single oldest means of building shelter. It is easily the simplest and most universal. The stacking up of some sort of masonry unit (stone, block, adobe, brick, tire, bottle, etc.) is traditional in every culture around the world. Because of the materials normally used, masonry also tends to be one of the most durable building technologies. (For instance, we all know it's the preferred construction technology of the three little pigs.)

Masonry receives a separate chapter in this book because it is such a great design/ build approach for making a wall. Regardless of whether you're stacking stones, bricks, or bales, the design of a masonry wall lies primarily in the hands of the mason assembling it. Most conventional architects agree that masonry is the one part of any project that needs personal supervision. This is particularly the case with stonework. Every stone is different and there are innumerable ways to assemble the puzzle. Without the designer's eye on site, the odds are small that a stone wall will be built the way it was drawn. Fortunately, the pace of masonry work is slow and there is a natural inclination to reflect on and adjust the composition as it grows.

Once I had a student who was clearly not interested in studio work. Though he had a very sensitive eye, he just couldn't make himself sit at the drafting table.

"What else is there to do? I want to *make* something," he said.

I led him to a pile of stones on one of our sites and explained, "We need a small retaining wall right along here. It must look like it was done by the same mason who did that one over there. You must also figure out how to rearrange the backfill so it will work with the site. Think you can handle it?"

He protested, "But that other guy must have had a stone saw; look how smooth that wall is."

"Nope, he just used his eyes."

I left him to his task but visited at the end of each day. By the end of the first day he had taken about a ton of stones and spread them all over the yard. He looked like he was setting out a huge jigsaw puzzle. In his mind he was inventorying every flat face in that pile of stone. By the end of the second day he had built a "practice" wall. It looked pretty good, but it didn't look much like the "smooth" one. At the end of the third day he had rebuilt it. I would have sworn that there had only been one mason on that job.

Each time I visited, he told me of the things he had learned about the stones. How they fit, which ones were more important than others, what the essential rules were; it was design/build at its best. It was *making*.

Though brick and block have a uniformity that reduces the impact of the mason's design decisions, there are still choices in color, joint thickness, pointing, and craft. There's no denying that the visual success of a masonry wall will usually depend on the mason more than the designer. Therefore, it is my suggestion that they be one and the same person whenever possible.

A masonry wall has many advantages for the design/builder of limited means. It's a simple method always made from units that a single builder can handle. Part of the richness and appeal of the brick wall comes from the fact that a brick is sized to fit the human hand. This gives any brick wall a wonderful texture and a human scale. Even though some masonry units require two hands, even fieldstones, concrete block, adobe, and tiles are easily handled by one person. Also, the tools of the trade are few and inexpensive. Besides a cold chisel and masons' hammer, all you need is a shovel, wheelbarrow, level, trowel, and a tape measure. Oh, and also some string. The first two advantages lead to a third—mobility. Since the units are small and the tools few, a mason can easily move onto a remote site. Certainly no one wants to carry each and every brick to a construction site, but some difficult sites make truck delivery just about impossible. If you have your heart set on such a site, masonry may be the best way to build.

Up until the late 1800s the vast majority of all large-scale construction was built from masonry. As our buildings grew taller, however, the thickness at the base of unreinforced masonry walls soon became fantastic. The famous Monadnock building in Chicago was only sixteen stories tall, but its walls were over 6' thick at the base! (See Figure 96.)

Fortunately, the side effect of this situation on residential-scale masonry has been all for the good. As the buildings grew taller, innovative minds set to extending and expanding the capacity of masonry walls. As a result of these efforts we have hollow-concrete block, high-strength mortars, efficient reinforcing techniques, and numerous new masonry units from which to choose. Design/builders rarely need most of these really high-tech materials or methods, but by keeping the technology

FIGURE 96: The walls of the Monadnock Building were over six feet thick at the base.

current, it remains as viable a choice for today's owner/builder as ever it was in the past.

▨ Mortar

While the choice of different masonry units may be endless, any that aren't "dry laid" will have one thing in common—mortar. Mortar is what goes between the masonry units and is every bit as important as the units themselves. The mortar serves a number of functions. Structurally it cushions the units, keeps them apart and bonds them together. Mortar accommodates the irregularities found in all masonry units. It supplies a location for metal ties or reinforcing to be integrated into the wall. Plus, of course, it has adhesive properties that bond the units together and keep out the weather.

There are many types of mortar, but they all consist of a cement, aggregate, and water. The cement is the bonding agent in mortar. It is likely to be Portland cement, hydrated lime, or a combination of the two. The aggregate is almost always a clean, fine sand. When color is important, the aggregate may be a ground marble, granite, or some other stone of color. Early mortars used lime, the only available cementitious agent that was easily worked, but it tended to harden slowly and have low compressive strength. If Portland cement is substituted for the lime, the mortar will have higher strength,

it will set faster, but it will be less workable. Today, to get the best of both worlds, mortar manufacturers combine both Portland and lime cements in their products. This gives good workability, strength, freeze/thaw durability, and reasonable hardening times. See Table 7.

While the structural importance of mortar is obvious, the aesthetic impact is sometimes overlooked. Since about 20 percent of an average brick wall's surface will be the mortar joints, this can be disastrous. Color choice and joint tooling will have a dramatic effect on the appearance of the masonry units and the overall wall. Manufactured mortar usually comes in two humble colors—light gray and dark gray. Other colors can be created with the use of colored aggregate or pigments.

Aggregates are preferred because they are less likely to affect the strength of the mortar. Tinting your mortar has to be done by trial and error in order to find the perfect color. Nevertheless, the following guidelines will help you get started:

- White sand, ground granite, marble, or stone dust give natural colors, but care must be taken to insure consistency from one batch to another.
- White sand, ground limestone, or ground marble with white Portland cement will give a white mortar.
- Suitable pigments include iron, manganese, and chromium oxides.
- Carbon black can be used for darkening, but it is difficult to get a true black since it should not make up

TABLE 7: MORTAR PROPORTIONS BY VOLUME

Type	Portland Cement	Hydrated Lime or Lime Putty	Masonry Cement	Maximum Damp Loose Aggregate	Minimum Compressive Strength (psi) after 28 Days
M High-Strength	1	¼	—	3	2500
	1	—	1	6	2500
S Medium-High-Strength	1	½	—	4½	1800
	½	—	1	4½	1800
N Medium-Strength	1	1	—	6	750
	—	—	1	3	750
O Low-Strength	1	2	—	9	350
K Very-Low-Strength	1	4	—	15	75

more than 2 to 5 percent of the cement.

- All pigments should be added sparingly and never in excess of 10 to 15 percent of the cement in weight.

Where appearance is important (and where isn't it?) I suggest you build a small sample wall using the masonry units and mortar you have decided on. Experience taught me the hard way that this is the only true test of what your finished wall will look like.

Stone

I have not recently heard of anyone using dry-laid stone for the walls of their house. That doesn't mean someone isn't doing it. But with the cost of heating and air conditioning moving ever upward, who can afford a house that is mostly cracks? Even so, there are still a few applications for this oldest of masonry technologies, even in snowbound Vermont.

I learned about dry-laid stone walls in my basement. I live in a house that was built around 1830. Like most of New England's vernacular of that vintage, the cellars have dirt floors and beautiful stone foundation walls. Most impressive is the fact that they are usually still intact after almost two hundred years! The way this works is remarkable. In Vermont we have frosts that normally go down 3' and frequently 6'. Naturally the frozen ground

can move a stone wall. The walls that have lasted did so through an interesting alliance of consequences. To begin with, the stone wall is usually surrounded by well-drained soil; this means there is very little water in the ground to freeze. Also, since the walls lack mortar, the heat of the house can easily find its way through the cracks. That keeps the ground from forming a frozen interlock with the stone. Finally, the lack of mortar means that there is nothing to crack or bind if the foundation moves a little. Naturally, it does. However, when spring rolls around, everything settles back exactly where it was. If the wall is properly constructed, it can go through hundreds of these freeze/thaw cycles without bulging or buckling.

If you ever renovate an older house, you may discover that these walls are not the same thickness all the way down. The general rule of thumb requires that the base be as wide as the wall is high. For that reason they are sometimes called "pyramid foundations." (See Figure 97a and b.)

Dry-laid retaining walls are built the same way, only they have no internal heat source to keep the frozen ground from bonding to them. For this reason it is doubly important that there be no moisture in the ground behind a retaining wall. The design of a stone retaining wall must include proper drainage to prevent hydrostatic pressure from pushing it over.

While dry-laid stone walls are still use-

ful and beautiful for some foundation work, they are poor choice for enclosing living space. Here the cracks must be filled with mortar. More than that, there must be provision for insulation and ventilation. The following illustrations show a sampling of different stone wall sections. Each addresses thermal comfort, moisture control, and infiltration. What they don't address is ease of construction and required craftsmanship. To build a stone wall freehand, even with mortar, is a demanding task. Design/builders must become accomplished at choosing stone to fit into an interlocking pattern that is both structural and aesthetically pleasing. This pattern must be kept consistent, but it must also allow for the special demands at the corners. Layout and scaffolding are additional considerations. Owner/builders considering this approach might well practice on a garden wall or a barbecue grill (Figures 98a and b).

Slip-Form Stone Walls

If you don't feel like tackling a trade that takes years to master, or if time is more important to you than craft, you can still have a house of stone. The use of *slip forms* turns the whole process upside down. Rather than repeatedly laying out some mortar and then fitting stone, slip forms allow you to place all the stones first, and then pour the mortar in between (Figure 99).

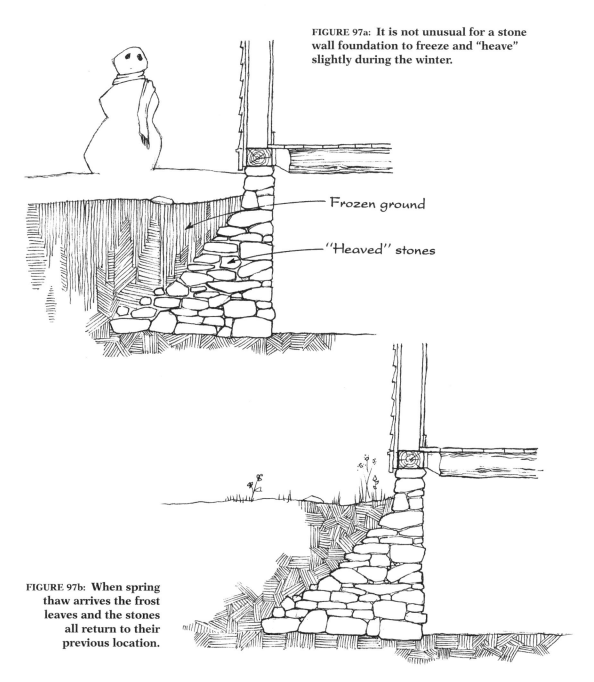

FIGURE 97a: **It is not unusual for a stone wall foundation to freeze and "heave" slightly during the winter.**

Frozen ground

"Heaved" stones

FIGURE 97b: **When spring thaw arrives the frost leaves and the stones all return to their previous location.**

The use of forms means you won't be working to a string or level. Once the forms are in place, you simply fill them with stone, pour in the mortar, wait between six and twelve hours, and strip. When the forms are removed the mortar will be soft and "green." This allows you time to remove excess mortar and work the joints. Walls of this type can be made extremely strong by using reinforcing steel or simply by making them very thick. Because you generally don't pour more than 24″ lifts (layers) at a time, even wide walls exert very little lateral pressure on the forms. Extra width also provides space for placing insulation and mechanicals within the wall.

An architect named Ernest Flagg is credited with developing this technique back in 1921. In his book *Small Homes, Their Economic Design and Construction* he outlined seven basic steps, which I have summarized below.

1. For a foundation, dig a trench well below the frost line and fill with crushed stone or rock to within 24″ of the surface. From there up use concrete or mortar.
2. At grade, place 4 × 4 sleepers horizontally across the wall with 8″ to 12″ sticking out on each side. Wrap them in 6 ml polyethylene so they may be easily removed later. These will form the base for your uprights.
3. Locate 4 × 4 uprights on each sleeper a few inches off the outside face of the wall on each side. These should be drilled every 6″ to accept pins for hold-

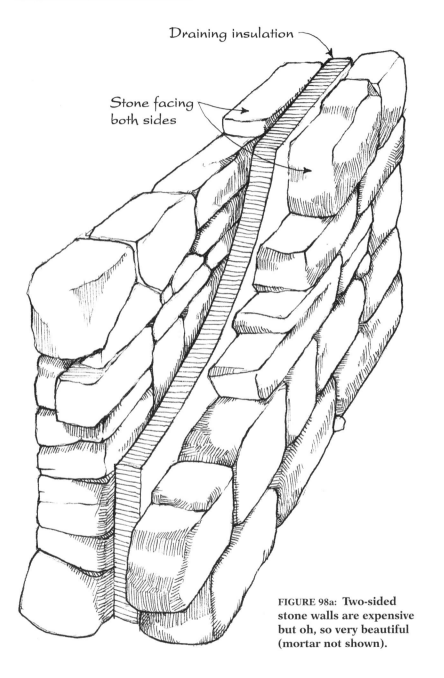

Draining insulation

Stone facing both sides

FIGURE 98a: Two-sided stone walls are expensive but oh, so very beautiful (mortar not shown).

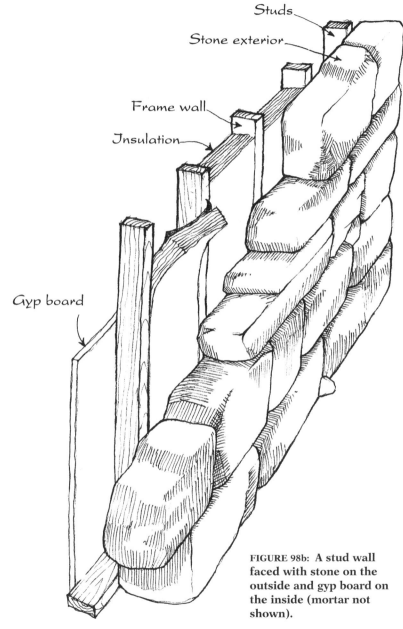

Studs

Stone exterior

Frame wall

Insulation

Gyp board

FIGURE 98b: A stud wall faced with stone on the outside and gyp board on the inside (mortar not shown).

FIGURE 99: Yestermorrow's version of Ernest Flagg's famous slip-form stone wall system.

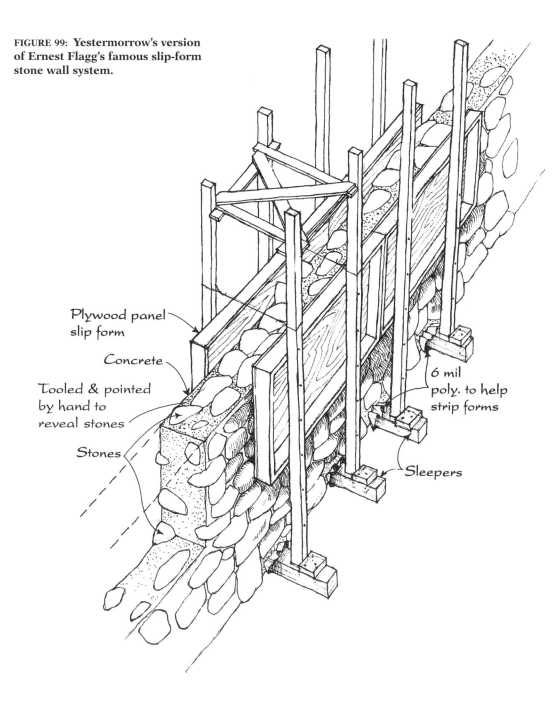

Plywood panel slip form

Concrete

Tooled & pointed by hand to reveal stones

Stones

6 mil poly. to help strip forms

Sleepers

ing the form boards as you work up the wall.

4. Plumb, brace, and attach all uprights to one another with a truss that will prevent the ongoing work from deforming the wall or throwing it off plumb.

5. Use three 2 × 10s (each side) to make movable forms. When in place, use spreaders to keep them open and shim against the uprights to insure they don't bulge or deform.

6. Hand place face stones against each side of the form. Fill the middle with rubble. Pour a wet mix of concrete (6″ to 8″ slump) with small aggregate in.

7. Release the forms the next day by removing the shims between the uprights and the outside of the 2 × 10s. Clean and point the joints. Move the forms up to the next set of pins.

Since Flagg first published this idea, it has been reworked by many innovative design/builders and applied by a hoard of energetic owner/builders. Helen and Scott Nearing wrote about it in *Living the Good Life*. Ken Kern, a legendary design/builder, touches on it in his book *Owner/Builder* and covers it more thoroughly in *Stone Masonry*. Mike McClintock gives it an entire chapter in his *Alternative House-building*.

Of course we had to try this at Yestermorrow. Since our courses are short, there was little time to get the students warmed up (our students arrive with no previous experience). We devised our own slip-form system using ¾″ plywood and 2 × 4s (because that's what our client happened to have around). This approach allowed the students to learn some basic carpentry while also learning about concrete, foundations, and masonry. Our first lift was below grade, and that turned out to be fortunate. After that, the wall proceeded more or less smoothly. There were long debates over which stone should go where. A sense of ownership developed between each student and the stones they placed. I can only imagine what we might have achieved given more time. I am convinced that this method can produce a wall just as striking and expressive as any other.

▥ Brick

I guess there is no other building material that better exemplifies the concept of "modularity" than brick. It takes thousands of bricks to make even a modest-size home. Thus, every aspect of the building becomes a multiple of this small handheld module. There appears to be no limitation to the use of this modular system. Brick has been laid into curves, corbeled into arches, and arranged into interlocking patterns limited only by the design/builder's imagination.

The use of brick predates the birth of our country by centuries. In Europe masonry buildings far outnumbered those built from wood. So visitors are often amazed when they discover that in America, the situation is reversed. Even today, only a small percentage of the homes in our country are built from brick. Much more than the Northerners, the colonists in the South imported the full spectrum of brick techniques found in France, England, and Holland. The abundant clay deposits close to the surface enabled the establishment of numerous small brick kilns. Even then, brick was more expensive than other building techniques and so the early houses were not always simple vernacular. Instead, they were the homes of the architecturally sophisticated and we find mostly Georgian- and Adams-style homes dating from that period.

Brick is a truly vernacular building material. Made from local clays and too heavy to ship affordably, brick tends to be found within a limited radius from the kiln. This makes it a natural choice for the vernacular design/builder. Originally brick was molded or formed of wet clay and then fired in big piles called "clamps." This wasn't a very controllable method, and there was a lot of variation in the bricks. Today's sophisticated methods offer control, reliability, and strength. Ironically, the most sought after of modern bricks are those that look like the old molded ones. As more of our built surroundings become mass-produced, we are increasingly starved for the imprint of craft. Brick walls are handmade.

A general understanding of how modern bricks are made will be a great help if you choose to navigate the numerous choices offered by today's brick manufacturers. The clays and shales are taken from the ground, crushed, screened, and sifted. Then the moisture content is adjusted. The three common methods for making bricks are largely a function of how much water is in the raw material. If there is a lot of water (20 percent to 30 percent), the clay is placed into molds, sometimes by hand. To keep it from sticking, the molds are lubricated with either water or sand. The resulting bricks are called *sand struck* or *water struck* bricks.

This technique, called the soft mud process, has been in use since early colonial times. An alternate method, called the dry press process, is used on clays that shrink excessively during curing. This method uses mechanized presses to place clay with less than 10 percent moisture into the molds. Lastly, the most modern and widely used technology is called the stiff mud process. Clay with about 12 percent to 15 percent moisture is extruded through a machine in long bars. As the clay leaves the extruder, it can be treated with dyes, glazes, and finishes. Then the treated bar of extruded clay is cut into single bricks. After the bricks are formed, regardless of method, they are dried and then fired. There are two types of kiln: the periodic kiln or the continuous-tunnel kiln. The former is like a modern-day version of the old clamp. The latter is a continuously moving conveyor of bricks that are fired as they travel through the long tunnel-shaped oven.

TABLE 8: MODULAR BRICK SIZES

Unit Designation	Joint Thickness	Manufactured dimensions			Modular Coursing
		Thickness	Height	Length	
Standard modular	⅜"	3⅝"	2¼"	7⅝"	3C = 8"
Engineer	⅜"	3⅝"	2¹³⁄₁₆"	7⅝"	5C = 16"
Jumbo brick	⅜"	3⅝"	2⅝"	7⅝"	1C = 4"
Double	⅜"	3⅝"	4¹⁵⁄₁₆"	7⅝"	3C = 16"
Roman	⅜"	3⅝"	1⅝"	11⅝"	2C = 4"
Norman	⅜"	3⅝"	2¼"	11⅝"	3C = 8"
Economy Norman	⅜"	3⅝"	3⅝"	11⅝"	1C = 4"
Handmade	⅜"	3⅝"	2¼"	7⅝"	3C = 8"
Triple	⅜"	3⅝"	4¹⁵⁄₁₆"	11⅝"	3C = 16"
SCR brick	⅜"	5⅝"	2¼"	11⅝"	3C = 8"
6-in. Jumbo	⅜"	5⅝"	3⅝"	11⅝"	1C = 4"
8-in. Jumbo	⅜"	7⅝"	3⅝"	11⅝"	1C = 4"

often proportional to the distance they must be shipped. But even the local products will vary in price depending on the finishes and how many you plan to purchase.

After you have chosen your bricks and decided on the mortar, there are still two major decisions before you can start building a brick wall. First, you must design the wall section, and second, you must decide on the bond pattern. There are many ways to build a brick wall: solid brick walls, cavity brick walls, reinforced brick, veneer over wood frame, veneer over block, or even veneer over poured-cast concrete. Different climates and ap-

In spite of the widespread use of this traditional building material, no standard brick sizes have evolved. Most bricks are roughly similar, but no two are exactly the same. Table 8 summarizes most of what is currently available. This list is not complete, and I have no doubt that it will change with time. Personally I find this lack of standardization comforting. After all, it is the local handmade quality of a brick that appeals to us and this would only be diminished if all bricks were the same (Figure 100).

Now that you know a little about the manufacture of bricks, there is only one thing left for you to do. Visit a brick vendor. Bricks come in as many finishes and colors as you can imagine. Their cost is

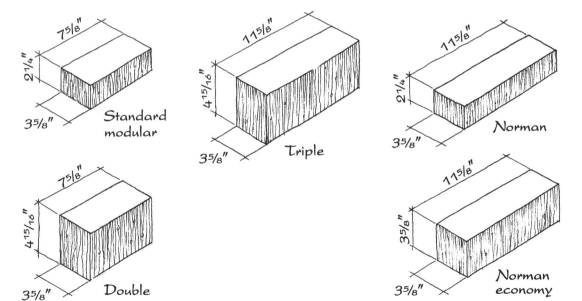

FIGURE 100: **Although there is no universal module among brick manufacturers, here are a few of the more common sizes.**

plications will call for different wall sections. Heavy loads found in multistory buildings will require solid walls. In cold climates, cavity walls allow the use of insulation, and a brick veneer over insulated wood frame will give even better thermal performance. Most residential applications use a veneer type wall (Figure 101).

Always of concern in masonry construction is moisture. It condenses easily on the inside of the brick surfaces and the resulting water can destroy the wall. Cavity-wall construction allows condensate, or other water that leaks into the wall, to drain to the bottom where it can exit through *weeps*. These are small holes or cotton wicks built into the wall to provide a path for the moisture to get out. When building a cavity wall it is important to prevent rubble and waste mortar from falling into the cavity and blocking it up. Such a blockage can force the water to pass through the bricks or mortar at random points in the face of the wall. This will promote efflorescence, the white chalky stain seen on the surface of some brick walls, which results from salts leaching out of the mortar. Usually it can be removed with a brush or one of the mildly acidic masonry cleaners. Nevertheless, it will come back repeatedly if it is caused by a blockage forcing the water through the mortar (Figure 102).

While the principles of sound masonry construction are few and straightforward,

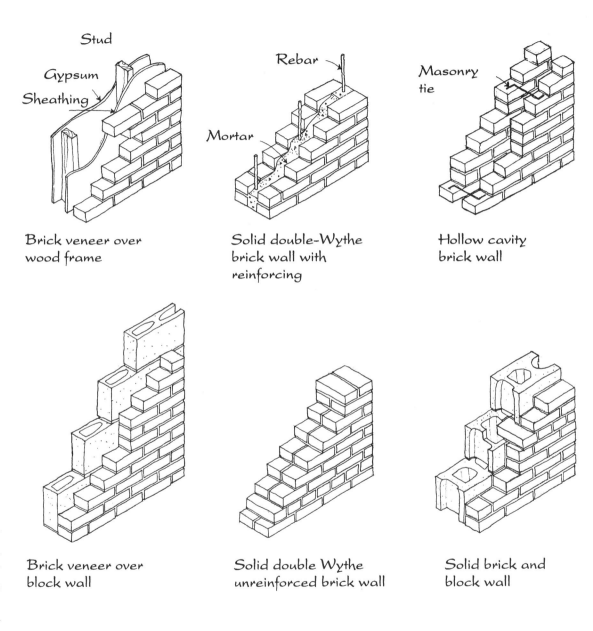

FIGURE 101: Various types of composite brick walls.

Stud

Gypsum

Sheathing

Brick veneer over wood frame

Rebar

Mortar

Solid double-Wythe brick wall with reinforcing

Masonry tie

Hollow cavity brick wall

Brick veneer over block wall

Solid double Wythe unreinforced brick wall

Solid brick and block wall

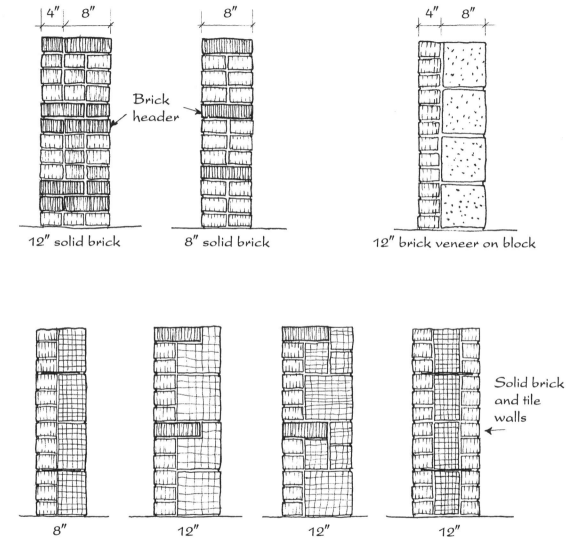

4″ 8″

8″

4″ 8″

Brick header

12″ solid brick   8″ solid brick   12″ brick veneer on block

Solid brick and tile walls

8″   12″   12″   12″

FIGURE 102a: **There are two schools of thought on masonry walls: solid or cavity. The cavity walls are more "modern" but solid walls are making a comeback. Here are some examples of the solid masonry wall.**

the options for expressive architectural effect are almost without limit. For example, let's imagine you have decided to use a brick veneer over a 2 × 6 wood frame with fiberglass insulation. You are now ready to make a major design decision—the layout pattern, or *bond*. The following illustrations should give you an idea of the many patterns available, but this presentation is hardly exhaustive. I urge you to take some time with this decision. Brick work is slow and labor intensive. It costs more and it lasts almost forever. You shouldn't just settle for a common running bond unless you are truly a "common running bond" sort of person. This same thinking should be applied when choosing the color and surface of your bricks, the mortar, and the detailing at doors and windows (Figures 103 and 104).

Now, having chosen your wall type, brick color, bond pattern, and type of joint there is little more to do but *finish* the design. I say "finish" because the choices mentioned above should not be made *a priori*. These are design decisions that present themselves in the cyclical course of designing your house. You may start with preconceived notions of brick color and wall type. As the design process evolves, however, you may discover that the cost of a brick cavity wall is prohibitive. You're presented with the choice of going to a less expensive brick or a different wall section. The final *look* of your house depends on the latter; the final *feel*

Cavity masonry walls

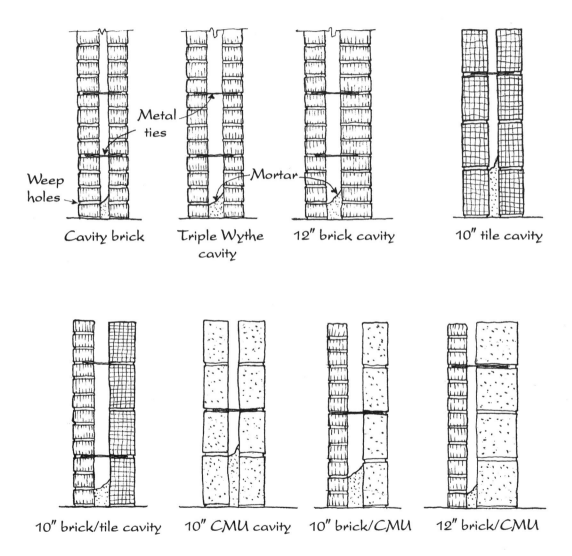

FIGURE 102b: Typical examples of modern cavity-type masonry walls.

depends on the former. Or perhaps the overall shape of your house goes from being tall to long. You may want to change your bond pattern to work better with the new massing. Or maybe you start with the windows. Proper detailing of a window requires an adequate lintel or arch. It must also have a draining sill. These can be designed in a number of ways. The particular design you select may well determine the bond and wall type for the rest of the wall.

At the outset there may seem to be a dizzying spectrum of options. Do not despair. I suggest that if you are in a cold climate you start with a brick veneer over a framed wall. If you are in a hot climate start with a brick veneer over a block wall. Consider insulation, moisture, ventilation, and cost. Look for further design direction from your massing, your windows, your soffit, and your local vernacular. This is a building technology that will require some thought if you are to keep your budget reasonable. It will also require a commitment to building a home, not just a product.

Concrete Block

This is the modern masonry equivalent of brick. The units are larger, cast from concrete, more uniform, and less costly. CMUs (cementious masonry units) have only been around a short time compared to most masonry materials. While the

Running bond

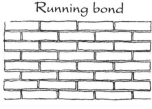

Stock bond

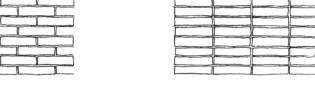

Common bond

English bond

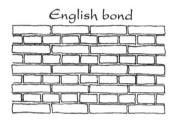

Flemish bond

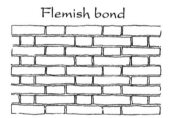

Flemish cross bond

Garden wall bond

Garden wall cross

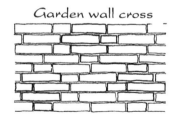

Spiral stretcher

Flemish spiral

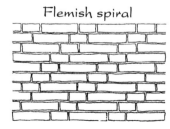

**FIGURE 103:
Brick bonds or
surface patterns.**

technology has developed quickly and impressively, it is still an adolescent when compared to brick, stone, or adobe. This is exciting for the design/builder. While much has been done, there is still plenty of room for innovation.

Concrete masonry is another technology well suited for the owner/builder. The blocks are far more economical than clay brick. They are cheaper per cubic foot of wall, plus they lay up faster. Even though a CMU requires two hands to install while a common brick takes only one, each CMU contains the equivalent of twelve common bricks.

Like bricks, CMUs come in endless shapes and sizes. But unlike brick, the industry has standardized around one basic module. A common block is nominally $8'' \times 8'' \times 16''$. Its actual size is $7\frac{5}{8}'' \times 7\frac{5}{8}'' \times 15\frac{5}{8}''$. This allows for a standard $\frac{3}{8}''$ mortar joint. There are many benefits to this module. The double-cube shape of the CMU allows for easy construction of corners, stretchers, and headers. Additionally, it is an even fraction of the 24″ framing module used in standard dimensional framing; 8″ divides evenly into 16″, 24″, 48″, and 96″. Concrete block also comes in a variety of fractional sizes, 4″, 6″, 10″, and 12″, to name but a few. Special solid, header, and bond-beam units are also available.

For foundations in hard to reach locations or where ready-mix concrete is very expensive, the CMU wall offers an afford-

FIGURE 104: The specific names for each orientation of a brick in the wall.

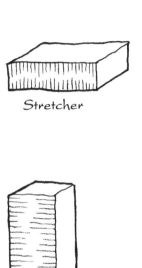

Stretcher

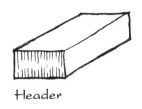

Header

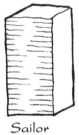

Sailor

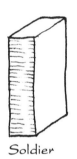

Soldier

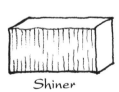

Shiner

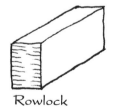

Rowlock

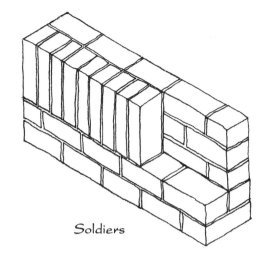

Soldiers

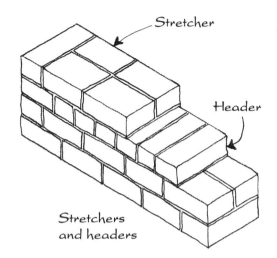

Stretcher

Header

Stretchers
and headers

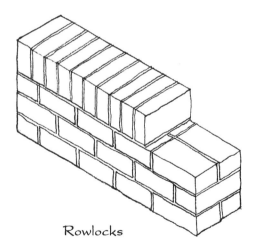

Rowlocks

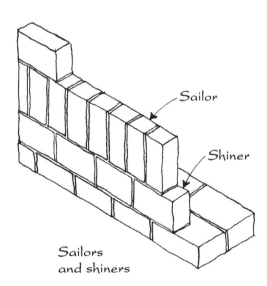

Sailor

Shiner

Sailors
and shiners

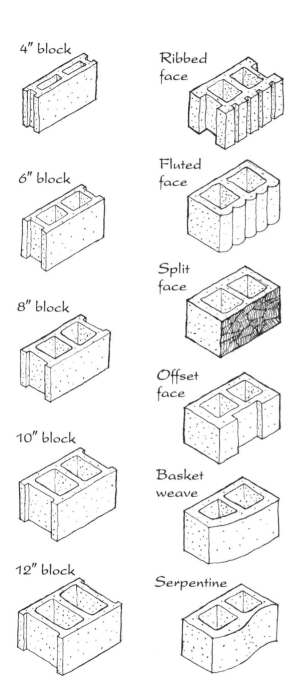

4" block

Ribbed face

6" block

Fluted face

8" block

Split face

10" block

Offset face

Basket weave

12" block

Serpentine

FIGURE 105: **Various common CMUs, or concrete masonry units.**

able alternative. In seismic regions, the voids in the block are filled with rebar and concrete. In cold climates, the cores are filled with any number of insulating products.

Once you are above grade, CMUs offer an endless array of finishes and textured faces (Figure 105).

The actual process of laying a block wall is as basic as masonry gets. Indeed, I have summarized the steps below because I feel it provides a starting point for thinking about all masonry construction. Brick, stone, or adobe will be different in detail, but the basic steps remain the same.

BUILDING A BLOCK WALL

Step 1

First construct a proper footing. (Refer to Chapter 8 for the fundamental procedure for laying out, pulling lines, forming, and pouring a footing.) It does not matter whether you use a perimeter footing or a floating slab, the block work is essentially the same (Figure 106).

Step 2

Using all available techniques (transit, level, string, geometry), lay out the outer face of the block wall on the footing. Take special care to square all corners and

double-check dimensions. Once this is done, I usually chalk the location of the inside face as well. This is also a good time to locate control joints. This is a general term for any juncture or seam designed to accommodate movement between the assemblies. As a block wall cures it will go through shrinkage that will cause cracks. Horizontal reinforcing can help reduce cracks, but control joints are the only guarantee (Figures 107 and 108).

Step 3

Before mixing any mortar, it is prudent to lay out the first course of block dry—without mortar. This reveals if any blocks must be cut. It is important to simulate the mortar joints accurately during this process. I usually use $3/8$" plywood as a shim or guide while placing the blocks. Don't cut any blocks at this point. If you're like me, your joints won't be as consistent as the plywood (though they should be).

Step 4

Any significant amount of block work will go more easily if you have a helper and an electric mixer for the mortar. Mix up enough mortar to lay a generous bed of mortar between at least two corners. It is a good idea to wet the footing or slab before laying out the initial bed of mortar along the chalk lines. The corner blocks should be laid first and with the utmost care. Mortar can still be tempered for about ninety minutes after it is initially mixed

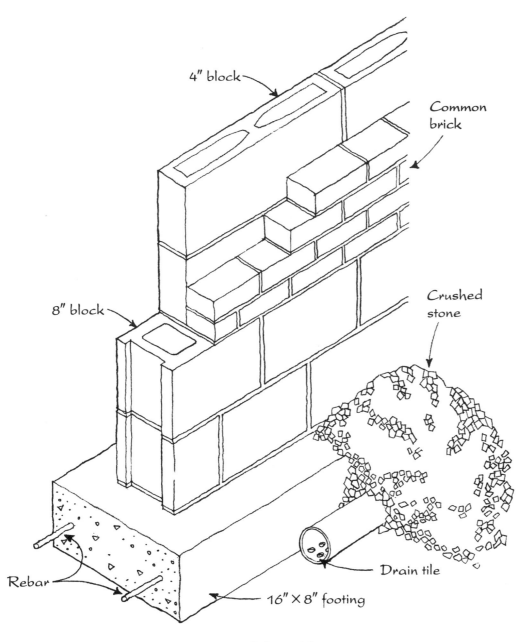

FIGURE 106: All masonry walls require a solid, well-drained footing.

(this means adding more water to improve workability). However, mortar should be discarded altogether if it hasn't been used within two hours of mixing.

Step 5

After the corner blocks are in place, "butter" the outer and inner edges, called the face shells, of each succeeding block and place them firmly in place. This is done with a downward and lateral motion to insure that the vertical joints are well filled with mortar. Placement is made somewhat easier if you hold the block with both hands and tip it slightly toward yourself. This gives you the best view of the wall below as you position it. The blocks should be placed so that the wider edge of the face shell is up. This will become the surface for the next layer of mortar.

Step 6

After three or four blocks are in place, use a four-foot level to align the front face and adjust the tops to a level line. The blocks can be moved by tapping them with the butt of your trowel. For some unknown reason, this particular action always makes me feel like a "pro."

Step 7

The final closure block is placed in the middle between two other blocks. It may have to be cut if the wall isn't a perfect multiple of 16″. Using a masonry saw, cut

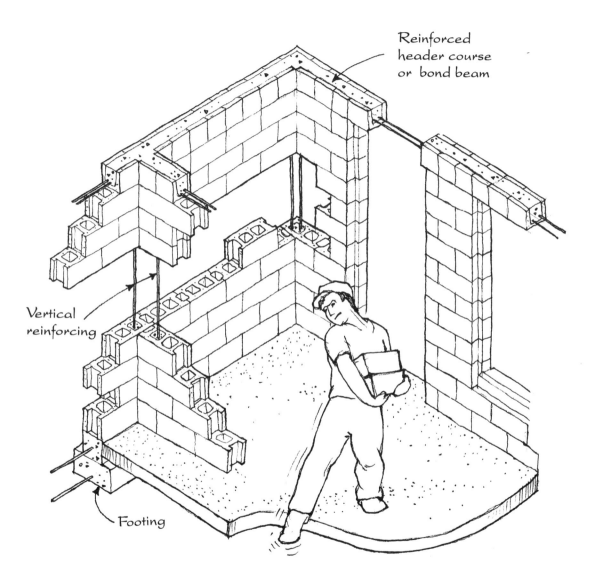

Reinforced
header course
or bond beam

Vertical
reinforcing

Footing

FIGURE 107: In seismic areas, fully reinforced cavities are required by code. Otherwise, every other void and one or two bond beams will be adequate.

the block to allow for a ⅜" vertical joint on each side. Butter both ends of both face shells and also all surfaces of the hole into which it must go. Carefully place the block and tap it into alignment. It is normal for excess mortar to squeeze out. If, however, mortar separates such that part of the bond is lost, the entire procedure should be redone.

After every possible attention has been paid to the laying of the first course, it is time to build the corners, or "leads." It is a wonderful quality of masonry that if you build straight and plumb corners, the walls between them will likely be the same (Figure 109).

Step 8

Each block is buttered with mortar on the face shells and one end. The other surfaces, including the webs, are not normally buttered.

Step 9

With each new course, the block is offset 8" or one-half of a block. At the same time, the design/builder should take careful measurements of height. If the wall becomes too high too quickly, the weight of the wall can actually squeeze the mortar out from between the lower joints. To insure that each course takes up only its allotted 8", some masons will use a story pole with the joint lines marked out on it. Then they need only hold the pole to the wall at different spots and it becomes

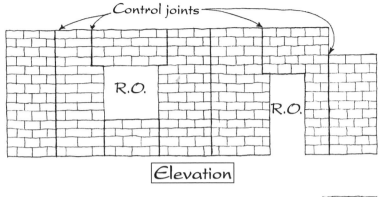

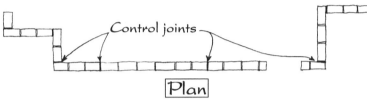

FIGURE 108: **Control joints keep a block wall from random cracking during thermal expansion or contraction.**

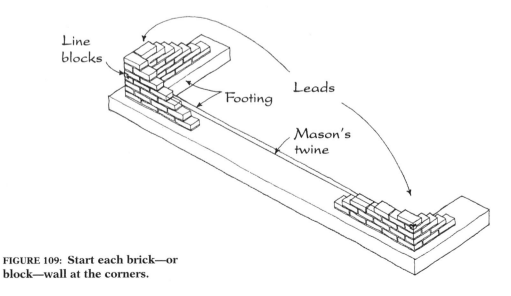

FIGURE 109: **Start each brick—or block—wall at the corners.**

clear if they are gaining or losing (Figure 110).

Step 10

Once the leads are in place it is time to pull the string lines for which mason's twine got its name. Using small offset blocks called "line blocks," pull a line between two corners. The line blocks suspend the string about ¾″ from the surface of the wall to prevent it from being distorted by any irregularities or blobs of mortar along the wall. Using this string as a guide, the next course of blocks can be filled in. Depending on the reinforcing schedule, you may be placing horizontal "railroad tracks" or other steel between the courses. (Railroad track is the colloquial term for a light reinforcing consisting of two parallel outer bars with many perpendicular bars connecting them—like a railroad track.)

Step 11

As you move up the wall, it is important to tool or "point" the joints between the blocks. This is done when the mortar is "thumb-print stiff" using a metal tool designed for the joint of your choice (Figure 111). The conventional concave joint serves to compact the mortar and force it tightly against the blockwork. It also has a significant visual impact. A nicely crafted wall is always distinguished by well-tooled joints.

Now, wasn't that fun? All of the forego-

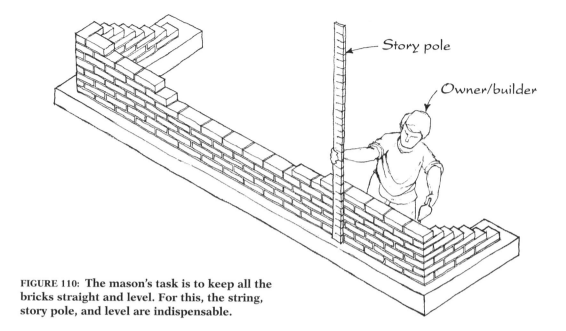

FIGURE 110: The mason's task is to keep all the bricks straight and level. For this, the string, story pole, and level are indispensable.

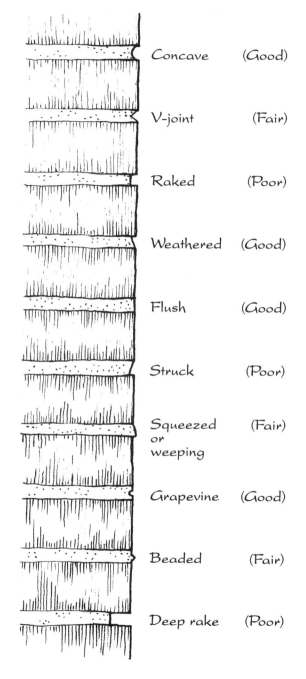

Concave	(Good)
V-joint	(Fair)
Raked	(Poor)
Weathered	(Good)
Flush	(Good)
Struck	(Poor)
Squeezed or weeping	(Fair)
Grapevine	(Good)
Beaded	(Fair)
Deep rake	(Poor)

**FIGURE 111:
Several common
pointing profiles.**

ing procedures are easily executed after a little practice and should be considered part of any designer/builder's palette of options. Additional procedures are required for adding special reinforcing, ties, lintels, pilasters, or architectural effects. As a backing for other masonry veneer, the block wall allows structure, veneer, and insulation to be built up simultaneously. In seismic areas, when the cores must be filled with concrete, we are lucky to have a new generation of small concrete pumps. The larger boom trucks are too expensive and very awkward. The small rental pumps that can be towed behind your truck have a smaller hose and a more sensitive volume control.

Special block shapes are available for lintels, beams, pilasters, and chimney flues. As a backing for other masonry veneer, the block wall allows structure, veneer, and insulation to be built up simultaneously.

The design possibilities for CMUs are more varied than precedents might suggest. This new chapter in the story of masonry is still unfolding. To date, most of it has been written by the large commercial sector of the building industry. Since commercial developers are primarily interested in the bottom line, block has usually been inspired by its affordability. Nevertheless, this is a material that has fabulous design potential and at a fraction of the cost normally associated with masonry.

Adobe

Adobe is as ancient as CMUs are contemporary. Adobe is simply mud. Its use is found around the globe in arid regions. Throughout history, adobe construction has been embraced by all types of people, from the simple farmer to the powerful elite. Though widely used in simple vernacular homes, it is also found in multi-story churches and municipal buildings. It is typically associated with owner/builders of moderate means, but it has recently enjoyed a resurgence among affluent preservationists and those interested in historic architectural styles.

There are churches, stores, and many other building types surviving today that reflect the incredible beauty and sophistication achieved with adobe long before modern materials became available.

Adobe is a vernacular technology with much to offer the first-time builder. It gives you a chance to learn without extracting a high price. Mistakes are easily fixed. If you need to add, remove, or reposition a wall, it is quite easy to disassemble it and adjust. While the adobe bricks may become damaged during the learning curve, repair is a simple process. Even fractured adobes will find a use later in the construction. And, of course, adobe is cheap. If you have lots of time and energy but little hard cash, adobe may well be the technology for you, provided your site has the right soil and climate.

Regardless of affluence, sophistication, age, or experience the Yestermorrow students interested in adobe seem to understand that the adobe's labor-intensive process is all that's required to imbue this simple mud with all the highest qualities of Vernacular Architecture. This is true. Not through unlimited budget or the finest hired craftsmen can you better embrace the special feeling obtainable by building your own. Because adobe has such a long tradition of being an owner/builder technology, those who choose it seem to better understand what's in the bargain. But remember, just because it has a tradition doesn't mean you must be constrained by historical styles. An *owner/*builder is also a *design/*builder.

One woman in her sixties arrived at Yestermorrow with a desire to build from adobe. Donna and her husband owned land, but the soils weren't ideal. Still, she intended to proceed with the plan, even if they ended up buying a different piece of land. Her husband was confined to a wheelchair. It was her feeling that an adobe dome would be the healthiest kind of residence. Donna was not a New Age flower child. Rather, she reminded me of a quintessential grandmother. She arrived at her design through the same helical process described in the foregoing chapters. Unintentionally, her floor plan looked like a Jungian mandala! This is not atypical of the behavior I have come to expect from students interested in adobe.

The soils necessary for adobe manufacture exist about everywhere. The four necessary ingredients are: clay (15 percent); silt (30 percent); sand (30 percent); aggregate (25 percent). It should be stressed that soil is an imprecise chemistry; these percentages represent rough averages. Adobes can be made successfully from soils varying in composition or even missing certain ingredients altogether. Your best bet is to make a few test bricks. If your local soil isn't adequate, you can temper it with material brought in from off site. Some design/builders will add "stabilizers" to the mix in order to improve erosion resistance. Portland cement, lime, and asphalt are the most commonly used stabilizers. Other structural additives include straw, manure, and proprietary products. Thus, soil type by itself does not determine whether or not you can build with adobe. In the end, Donna kept her land and worked with the soils on site.

Besides the right soils, making adobe does require periods of uninterrupted sun lasting long enough to bake the bricks. These minimal requirements explain why adobe construction has been found in so many areas other than the arid regions normally associated with it. And in those regions where the sun is insufficient, related mud technologies like rammed earth and cob have been successfully used. As early as 1839 we find a treatise published in Washington, D.C., on the use of rammed earth, and there is evidence of its use throughout the eastern seaboard.

The actual making of adobe bricks could not be easier. First, the thickness of the wall must be decided. Then a wooden form is built to dimensions that accommodate the wall design. With nothing more than this form and a shovel, you are in business! But this is hardly efficient. By using gang forms and a tractor with a loader, the rate of brick making can be increased exponentially. Even with just a wheelbarrow, a crew of two or three can make over four hundred bricks per day using a gang form (Figure 112).

While adobe brick sizes may vary, the proportions should approximate those of a CMU—twice as long as they are wide. The actual size of your module can be whatever your design calls for. Of course, weight will be an important factor. If the brick weighs more than 35 pounds it will be very hard work laying up the wall. Also, heavy-duty scaffolding will be required and breakage is likely to increase. Smaller adobes are easier to handle and work into arches and domes better than larger ones.

The actual wall design will be a function of your climate, architecture, soil, and ingenuity. As with other masonry, you

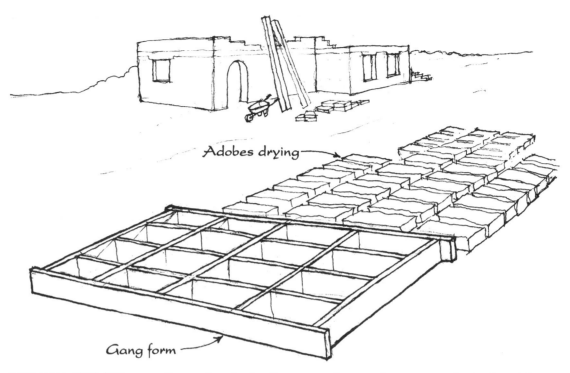

FIGURE 112: **With little more than a shovel, wheelbarrow, and a gang form you can be in the adobe business.**

can build walls of single width, multiple width, cavity construction, and with a variety of reinforcing. The choice will be yours. Cavity construction allows for insulation and moisture control in some climates, while a thick, solid wall will perform better in others. Studies of walls in the Southwest show that, on average, a 12″ wall functions well.

Reinforcing for adobe is primarily horizontal; the solid bricks make vertical reinforcing impractical. If a cavity wall is used, the vertical reinforcing may be placed between the walls. The most common form of reinforcing is the "bond beam," which caps the adobe wall and serves two purposes: It resists horizontal shear, or movement, and it distributes the roof or floor loads more evenly over the wall below. Bond beams are made of reinforced concrete or with heavy timber. In seismic areas, bond beams are often located at several heights in the wall. Besides strengthening the wall, this offers the design/builder opportunities for architectural expression (Figure 113). Also, the

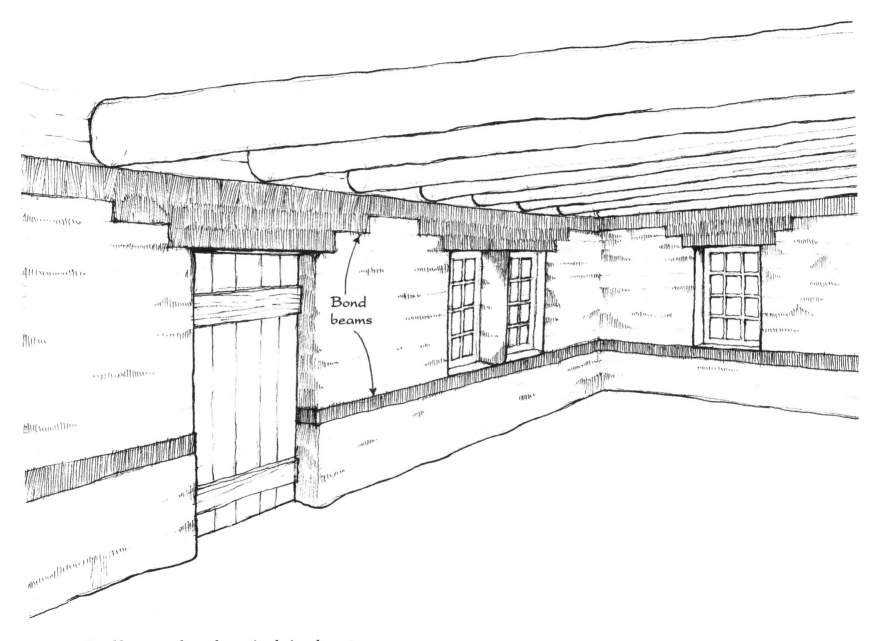

Bond
beams

FIGURE 113: Bond beams used as a decorative design element.

use of railroad track, the same reinforcing used with CMUs, can be placed between alternate rows of bricks. The mortar options for adobe include all the usual cementious mixes. In addition, the same mud used to make the bricks can be used as a mortar. Stone in the mortar must not exceed ⅜" in size.

The final consideration for any adobe wall is the exterior finish. Particularly if the adobe hasn't been stabilized, the exterior stucco or whitewash will be all important. A natural mud plaster will be the least expensive and very adequate to control erosion. However, it requires regular maintenance. Modern stuccos and plasters will protect the wall longer and without constant maintenance. But these finishes will cost more and have certain drawbacks of their own. The interior finish can be whatever the owner/builder desires. Conventional plaster or the more affordable whitewash are common choices. As with any other masonry wall, the interior can be strapped out to receive conventional gypsum board, wood paneling, insulation, and mechanicals.

As one of the oldest building technologies, it is hardly surprising that adobe comes with many undertones and associations. It's clearly a regional vernacular with a variety of cultural affiliations. In addition, I urge you to consider it as an affordable, easily learned approach to building a contemporary home expressive of you and your lifestyle. It is one of the most sculptural of all building methods and, thus, it is perfect for the creative designer/builder.

Other Masonry

If masonry is the act of stacking up masonry units, then we haven't covered the half of it. I've seen or heard of houses built from just about everything. A few common items that have often been stacked and mortared include bottles, cans, cordwood, and tires. Why even a log home falls under this definition, though I wouldn't really call it masonry.

One of my favorite examples comes from the early career of a gifted design/builder in my area. He was interested in earth-shelter construction and most of the books urged the use of concrete. He had no money, so that was out of the question. Then one day he happened by the local IBM plant while they were disposing of that week's used computer paper. (I guess this was before "recycling" had arrived in corporate America.) The wastepaper was bundled into 3' cubes. A deal was struck by which he could have all he wanted if he provided the means to remove it. So a month or two later he had stockpiled enough old printouts to build himself a home. Each cube was carefully wrapped in 6 mil. polyethylene. They were stacked, mortared, and caulked. Admittedly, this wasn't a hundred-year design solution but the price was more than appropriate.

You don't have to be broke to be interested in building with trash. Recycling and reuse hold obvious and natural advantages for the creative mason. For his recently completed home, actor Dennis Weaver hired Michael Reynolds, a design/builder who specializes in the use of recycled tires, cans, and rammed earth. Everything in Reynolds' architectural creations are made from recycled or organic material. This is a benefit to our planet, but it is also sound economics for the design/builder. If you have more time than money, or are interested in truly innovative construction, pick up one of Michael Reynolds's books.

While log homes aren't really masonry, cordwood construction certainly is. This is a system of masonry where tree pieces the size and shape of cordwood are laid up in mortar with the cut ends on the surface. Examples of this innovative building technology date back to the Great Depression when it was called "stackwall" construction. Lest you think this means it's a technology suitable only for the unexpectedly impoverished, I note that many examples from that era could sell for hundreds of thousands of dollars today. A study of cordwood history reveals simple capes, barnlike gambrels, utility sheds, and even large colonial homes. For the owner/builder it has all the right features. It's affordable, easy, and forgiving to work, has good insulation properties, and can accommodate other supporting technologies. Best of all, it allows the design/builder to explore design ideas that more traditional technologies might disallow. Since cordwood has never been adopted by the large-scale building industry, it is still a purely vernacular building method. There has been no standardization of parts or procedures. Mortar is still mortar, and gravity, of course, is still gravity. Your only constraints are the physics of the material and your own imagination. (See Figures 114 and 115).

The Code Thing

Here a word must be said about codes and zoning ordinances. (There are further words in Appendix 11.) Any of the older vernacular building methods will likely draw a bit more attention from code officials, especially if you are building it yourself. It is only natural for them to regard things "not from the book" with a bit of skepticism. Until very recently even adobe and log homes had trouble gaining acceptance. These two ancient building methods were brought into the twentieth century only when bigger builders hired the engineers necessary to verify their structural capabilities. As this book goes to press, straw-bale construction is being conditionally permitted for the first time in a few selected locations across the country. Even though a technology may be centuries old, if there has been no modern

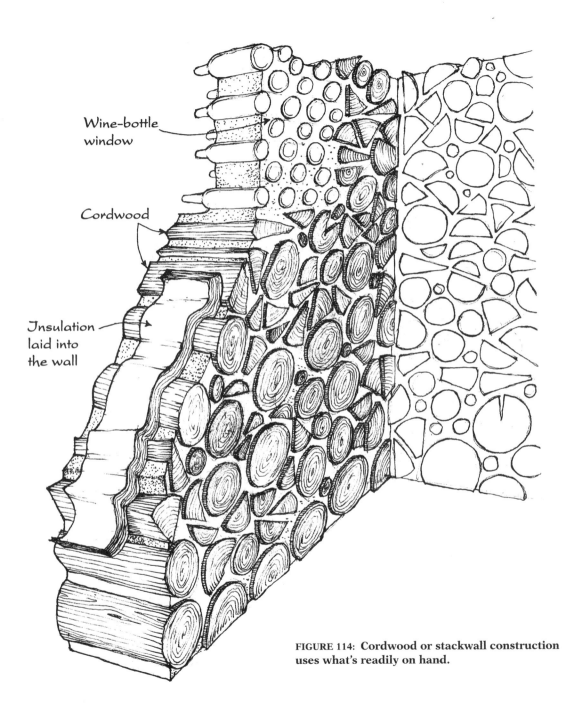

Wine-bottle window

Cordwood

Insulation laid into the wall

FIGURE 114: Cordwood or stackwall construction uses what's readily on hand.

engineering to evaluate it, you may have to do a little extra work to get your building permit. No problem.

Remember first that the code and the inspectors are there for your own good; they are trying to keep you from building something unsafe. Just as the building official is assumed to be an unbending stickler for the rules, the owner/builder is seen by him as an accident looking for a place to happen. Both stereotypes are not necessarily correct. If you want the inspector to be on your team, confer with him about your project as soon as possible. If he feels like he has been involved from the beginning, he will have an interest in seeing the building come to fruition. It will be a source of pride for him to show that distinctive buildings can be built under his guidance. On the other hand, if you just show up in his office with a set of strange-looking plans, he is more likely to give them, and you, the "treatment." And don't forget that you are asking him to do more work by looking at something new or different. Unusual building technologies, even if they used to be the conservative norm, will tend to get a different treatment than the cookie-cutter standards.

This is one of the more interesting issues to be addressed by the design/building community. The codes tend to promote safe, uniform, but often nonexpressive buildings. Clearly a market for these homes has been created. But what of the burgeoning number of people choosing to express themselves and their values through the building of a custom home? Values focused on community involvement, energy conservation, and environmental awareness frequently lead owner/builders to the early vernacular practices. These technologies often predate the codes. Modern issues and individual expression require that these traditional technologies be reinterpreted and updated. For example, Ben Brunberger at Benson Frames acquired a Ph.D. in the structural mechanics of timber-frame construction. Using computers and modern engineering, he and Benson are now creating completely new joinery to extend the age-old tradition of timber framing. Likewise, the solar builders of the

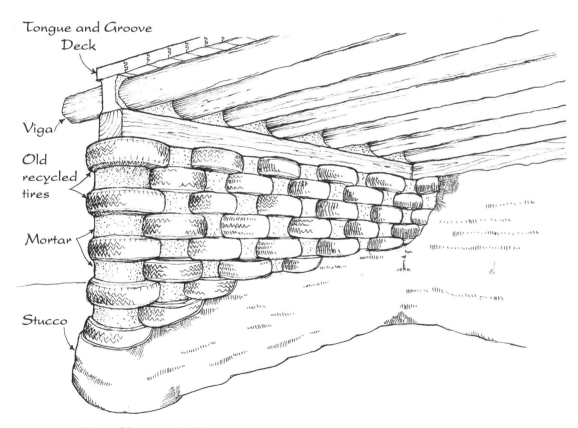

Tongue and Groove Deck

Viga

Old recycled tires

Mortar

Stucco

FIGURE 115: Using old tires to build a masonry wall makes your house into a benefit to the environment as well as your pocketbook.

sixties were often innovative visionaries, but they couldn't get financing from a bank. Those that insisted on updating the historic principles of building with the sun found themselves putting on a nail apron. This led eventually to more than just the revitalization of solar design and construction. It demonstrated that building was a natural way for anyone to express their convictions and lifestyle.

At the Yestermorrow School we see the national groundswell of owner/builders as an indication that we are again at a point in history when people wish to be involved with the making of their homes. Meaningless cookie-cutter designs are no longer sufficient. With this new involvement, owner/builders must update the building codes, zoning ordinances, and town plans that currently prescribe how we live.

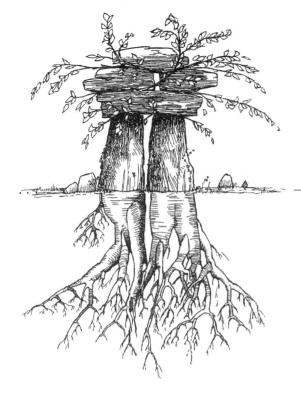

The Roof and the Sky

It's Friday morning at the end of a typical Yestermorrow design/build course. The students are rushing to complete the roof they have been working on for two weeks. It's an unusual roof, shaped like a scorpion. A wide hip roof at one end decreases in size along the long axis of the roof toward the "tail." At the tail, the roof curls up upon itself looking very much like a scorpion poised to strike. The effect is electric. And well it should be, since this roof protects a tiny pavilion specifically constructed for the power drop at Yestermorrow's gravel pit renovation project.

The power line will attach to the scorpion's tail. This is: The Power Pavilion (Figure 116).

Students can be seen working on strangely angled cuts for the framing, the sheathing, and the asphalt shingles. Nothing is simple. The instructors constantly assure the students that this roof is intentionally challenging and that their own may be much simpler. The students seem less concerned than the staff. But the most interesting thing about this roof is not the shape. It's not even the multicolored shingle design or the fancy detail at

the very tip of the tail. The thing that strikes most visitors is that the roof is not attached to a building. The entire roof—framing, sheathing, shingles, and all—is supported a few feet off the ground by a few sturdy sawhorses. All the students are working on it while standing in the Yestermorrow parking lot. Cars slow down as they pass.

The next day a logging truck helps us move the completed roof to the gravel pit. The rest of the pavilion had already been completed. Logging trucks are pretty common sights around here, and they are

FIGURE 116: **The Power Pavilion: Designed and built by John Connell and the Yestermorrow students.**

equipped with booms for moving logs much heavier than our little roof. Paul, the logger, simply scoops up our roof and places it on his truck. When we arrive at the site he scoops it up again and lowers it onto the waiting supports. Everything goes perfectly and I, for one, will never forget the vision of that logging truck being attacked by a giant scorpion as it motored down Route 100!

Rarely, of course, is the roof the first phase of construction, but it is arguably the most important. Indeed, it is the roof that provides the real sense of shelter in architecture. The walls of a house could be optional, even the foundation in some cases. But the roof is essential. It's the roof that really provides protection from the weather. Without a roof, we have merely a garden. (Merely!?) And yet, the roof is much more than a simple umbrella for your bubble diagram.

Think of the roof as that part of the building that touches the sky. This implies more than simply dealing with the weather. A roof is usually the highest part of any house and reads as a graphic silhouette against the sky. Like our heads, the sky belongs to that group of important things that are "on top." The attic, housed under the roof, is a realm of spirits and memories. It seems connected with those ethereal aspects of life that we all know exist but are rarely included on our list of "What I Want in My House." The roof

peak points to the heavens, and when we look at the roof we automatically do likewise. The roof is our connection with the cosmic sky. Even the flat roofs of the desert and the low-pitched roofs of the prairie result from this relationship. When the land is flat, the sky is big. The most important feature of big sky is where it meets the earth—the horizon. So the roofs in these regions align with the sky at its boundaries.

Paul Grillo, in *Form, Function & Design*, suggests that roof shape is a function of climate and natural resources (Figure 117).

The seacoast climate along New England shores has produced roof designs pretty much the same as those found in Norway. The *flat* roofs found in the American Southwest are also found in Tibet, Morocco, Saudi Arabia, and Iran. Wherever such indigenous homes are found, an environmentally friendly connection between climate and building form is still evident. Because these designs rely on the local weather to reduce energy consumption, the roof shapes must be appropriate. Consequently, there are generally more solar buildings in the West and Southwest than in the Northeast. Similarly, there are more earth-sheltered buildings in the snowbelt than in the south.

When thinking about your roof, therefore, you must not think simply about its construction. Remember that the roof

connects your house, and thus you, to climate and sky. Consider what kind of relationship you want to have with the sky. There are many expressive design opportunities in your roof. The shape, pitch, overhang, materials, and color must be carefully chosen if the final result is to harmonize with your site.

If you're like most people, roof jargon quickly becomes confusing. What's a gable or an eave? How is a gambrel different from a mansard? Where is the soffit on the overhang, and what about all the vents we hear about? Framing terms are even more confusing. What is the difference between a jack rafter, a common rafter, and a purlin? What are "look outs," cornices, frieze moldings, and the like? Can I wear a "collar tie"? The drawings that follow will help you understand the jargon. I find that architects and academics seem to be more concerned with labels and vocabulary than those who actually build these roofs. After all, it's wood that holds up the ridge whether you call it a rafter, a purlin, or a viga. Nevertheless, it's fun to use words that have been around since the beginning of building. And if you're going to design a distinctive roof that relates to your site and situation, it helps to know the lingo (Figure 118).

I don't expect you to just pick a roof from the pictures included here. This isn't a menu, it's more like a list of ingredients. Design/builders become adept at *combin-*

FIGURE 117: To some degree, roof shape is a function of climate and local resources.

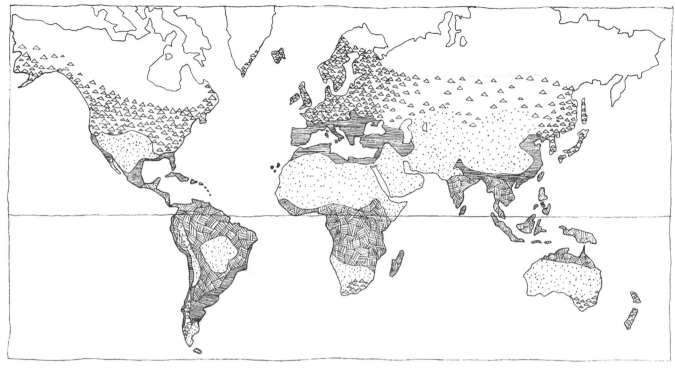

Steep roofs with shingles, slate, or flat tile

Slightly sloped roofs covered with Roman tiles

Flat terraced adobe roofs

Steep roofs covered with palmetto or other organic material

ing different roof types so that they can cover any configuration of walls. In addition to all the roof shapes, there are also many dormer possibilities (Figure 119).

In the initial phase of making a roof you consider your climate, your site, your cultural context, and yourself. Looking at all the options, you may develop some idea of what kind of roof you want. At this point you may not even have a floor plan, but certainly you have worked out a diagram. While most people lay out the walls right after they draw their bubble diagrams, the experienced design/builder may actually *start* with the roof. At the very least the walls and roof should be considered simultaneously. Do it any other way and you will have the cart before the horse. You can always place walls *under* a roof, but the opposite isn't so easy. I've seen many student projects that work beautifully in plan but over which no reasonable roof could ever be built.

The roof is the most important element

in the exterior architecture of your house. Try to keep the roof in mind from the moment you begin developing your bubble diagram.

⦀ Theory . . .

To help you design a roof, and certainly to build one, you must have an idea of how they work. The roof keeps sun, rain, and snow out of your house while keeping heat or conditioned air in. That seems simple enough. But what about the moisture in the roof assembly itself? What about ice dams? What about the concentrated water that comes pouring off your roof during a rainstorm? Also worth considering is the effect your roof has on the rest of the building. Wide overhangs will protect the walls and shade the windows. Really wide overhangs provide a protected zone for pedestrians or, when they become a porte cochere, for automobiles.

Happily, the underlying principles are about the same in all roofs regardless of shape or climate. The temperature/moisture basics were presented in Chapter 11, so let's apply them to a roof in a little more detail (Figure 120).

Inside the house we usually find 65° air at about 50 percent relative humidity. If the temperature is higher, the moisture content is usually higher (but the *relative* humidity may be lower). Outside the house we could find anything: heat, cold, rain, snow, wind—anything! (Well, maybe

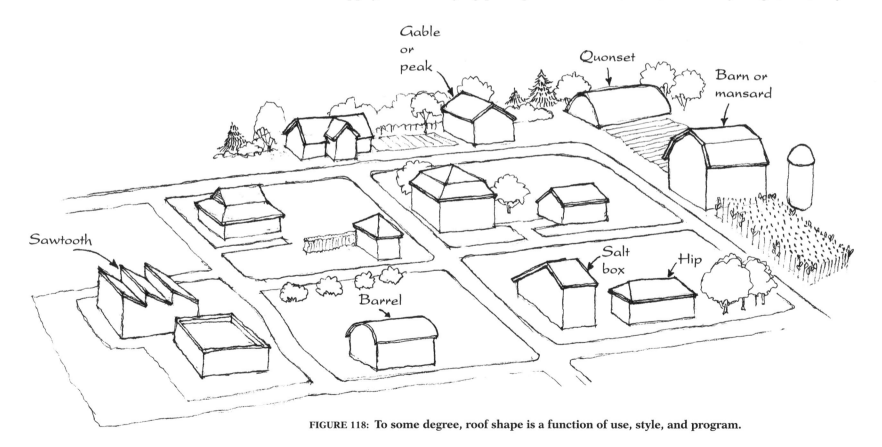

FIGURE 118: **To some degree, roof shape is a function of use, style, and program.**

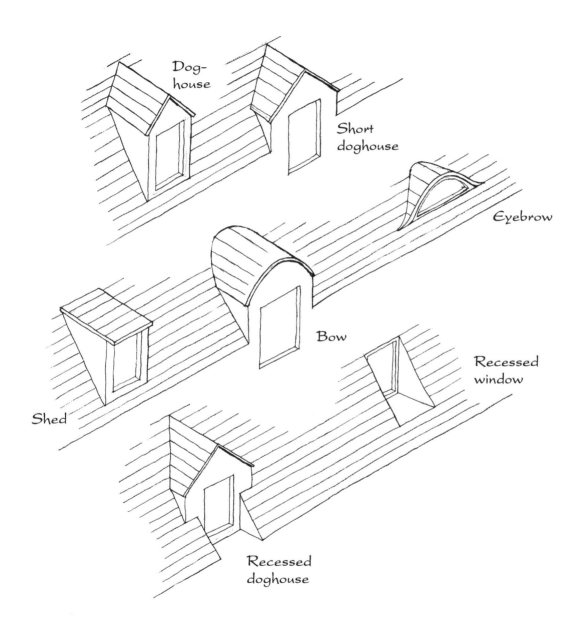

Dog-house

Short doghouse

Eyebrow

Bow

Shed

Recessed window

Recessed doghouse

FIGURE 119: For every roof there may be a whole range of dormers.

not "oobleck."*) Our question is: "What's going on inside the roof assembly?"

The second law of thermodynamics says heat always flows from the warm side to the cool side. If the roof is in Vermont, the inside air is going to be giving up its heat to the outside. If we are in Florida, the external heat will be making its way into the air-conditioned interior. In neither case are we happy about the situation. In both cases the transmission takes place *through* the roof and other assemblies.

The second thing to remember is that air holds moisture in proportion to how warm it is. Warm air holds more moisture than cold air. For every combination of temperature and moisture there is a thing called the "dew point." The dew point is that temperature at which the moisture in the air will condense into water, i.e., rain.

One situation any roof design should prevent is moisture-laden air condensing on a surface at dew-point temperature—especially if that surface is a rafter or other framing within the roof. Moisture vapor in a building can be damaging, but *liquid* water can bring disaster. The easiest way to avoid this situation is by placing enough insulation in your roof. In addition, it is a good idea to install a very good vapor barrier between the insulation and the interior of the building.

* from Dr. Seuss's *Bartholomew Cubbins and the Oobleck*

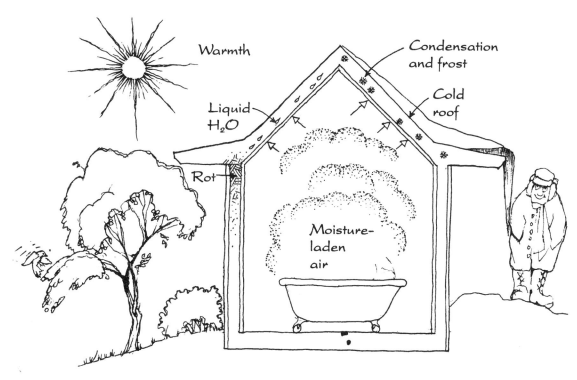

Warmth

Condensation and frost

Liquid H₂O

Cold roof

Rot

Moisture-laden air

FIGURE 120: **The moisture that leaks into a roof may stay frozen for the winter, but spring temperatures will produce water and then the rot will begin.**

Clever and straightforward as these measures may seem, experience shows that neither has very good odds of being well implemented. For a variety of reasons, a low-skilled member of the crew is often given the task of insulating and putting up the vapor barrier. Then it is all covered up with gypboard. As a result, many people live in homes with insufficient insulation and a moisture barrier having dozens if not hundreds of penetrations. The common exception is usually a house constructed by the owner. Even though unseen, owner/builders tend to be fastidious about what goes into their walls and roof assemblies.

Since owner/builders are still the exception rather than the rule, conventional practice ventilates the interior of the roof assembly. This is done for the same reason we ventilate basements and crawl spaces. If we assume we can't keep the water out, we had better provide openings for it to evaporate away at some future time. In a roof it is hoped that the moisture that has condensed into water during the winter will evaporate and be carried away by the summer's warm ventilating breezes. And this works—usually. The truth is, however, that we don't have a perfect understanding of exactly when it will work and when it won't. The best we can say is—usually! I guess this is good enough for the building officials of our land, because venting your roof is a code requirement in most states.

Since Vermont is one of the few states where code enforcement is still evolving (and since I love stretching the rules), I have taken the opportunity to experiment with different types and levels of venting. I have built roofs without venting that show no signs of moisture damage after twelve years. I have also built roofs that are so well vented that we can't keep the bedrooms warm. One good rule of thumb suggests:

Venting aperture ≥ attic floor area/150

The total vent area must equal or exceed the attic floor area, divided by 150.

This may serve as a starting place, but I wouldn't expect to find any hard and fast rules on this matter. Why? Because successful venting depends on *local climate* and prevailing winds. What works in one region may be too much or not enough in another. If you want to know what works in your area, study the older buildings. (But study them *well*. A loosely constructed soffit with no vent grills is not the same as an unvented roof!) Also talk with some of the builders who have been in the area the longest, particularly those who do renovation. Venting is less mysterious to those who have built and rebuilt enough roofs in an area.

Today's ventilation strategies are aimed primarily at venting the rafters and insulating the roof assembly itself. It wasn't always thus. Before housing costs became so horrific, the roof simply covered the attic, which was unused, unheated, and easily vented at the gables. This meant there was a large volume of slow-moving air between the outside weather and the interior living space. Although this is an unpopular solution for today, there is much to be learned from this historic configuration. It worked well in both cold and hot climates.

Remember that the **heat** is always trying to move to the cold **side** of an assembly. In the snowbelt **this** means the snow on your roof is constantly melting ever so slightly, and dribbling down to the eave. Eventually it dribbles out onto the overhang, where there is no heat escaping from the inside. Here it freezes into the annoying ice dam. In a hot climate the heat penetrates the roofing and heats up the interior of the roof assembly, which, in turn, heats up the interior of the building. Now, if we had the old-fashioned attic with gable vents, the heat would never get out to the snow or into the ceilings. Today's economic replacement is the "cold" or double roof (Figure 121).

As seen in the illustration, the double-roof assembly incorporates a ventilation space that traps the heat as it moves through the roof. A chimney effect is produced that brings cooler air in from the eaves and sends the hot air out at the ridge. In a cold climate, this means the outer surface that the snow is sitting on stays cooler, which reduces melting run off that would freeze over the eaves. In a hot climate, the chimney effect is turbo-charged in the double roof. The powerful ventilation that develops prevents the heat from building up in the roof assembly. The interior air conditioning needn't keep pace with ever escalating heat levels. Clearly the double roof can save money and energy in most climates.

⦚ . . . and Practice

Theory is important, but only as it informs practice. The experienced design/builder

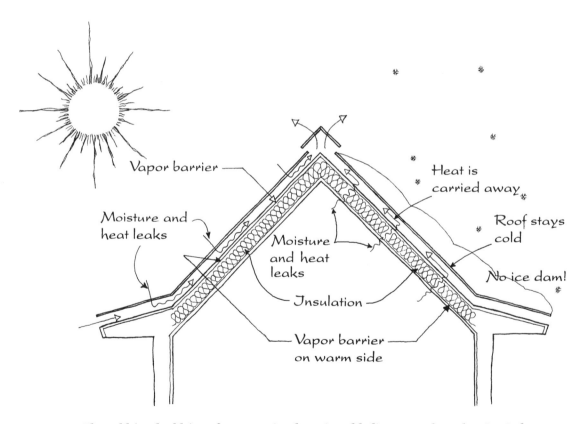

FIGURE 121: **The cold (or double) roof prevents ice dams in cold climates and overheating in hot climates. The vapor barrier is always installed on the warm side of the assembly.**

knows that choosing a particular roof design commits him/her to an extensive series of assembly requirements. The design/builder thinks of every phase in the making of a roof and evaluates which is the best configuration, material, and method for the situation.

An example of this process may be useful. Let's imagine we're making a house in Ohio. This isn't a big snowbelt area, but the winters can get plenty cold, and one or two big "dumps" are to be expected each season. Likewise, the summers aren't much compared to Texas or the Midwestern plains, but they can be very humid and make anyone uncomfortable for a week or so. Let's suppose we are building a frame house with a brick veneer (as this is a favorite of many Yestermorrow students).

A brick house means a substantial house, so the roof will want to be likewise. A generous overhang, say 3' to 4', produces a substantial and protective-looking roof. Additionally, this will help keep the weather off the brick joints. With a brick house the general shape is often simple. In such situations I might consider using trusses in the roof assembly. If the massing is more complicated, with ells, angles, or wings, I tend to use rafter framing, as it is more flexible. I will also use rafters if there are a lot of dormers. This is really a case-by-case issue. If the pitch of the roof is steep enough, rafters will give you usable space under the roof. For the

lower-pitched roofs where the attic will just be a utility space, a truss system can often mean a big savings in labor. In this example I will assume that there are places for both approaches. Trusses and rafter framing are often combined.

I've already designed the basic roof shape, so the first thing I will consider is the design opportunities at the soffit. This is where the walls and roof meet. It is one of the two most important junctures in the entire house (the other is where the walls meet the foundation). I want to incorporate vents, overhang, and appropriate visual interest at this location. I also want the assembly to be reasonably straightforward. In the simplest arrangement, a notch called the "birdsmouth" is cut so that the rafter sits squarely on top of the upper wall. The location of the birdsmouth determines how much of the rafter hangs over the wall. The geometry of this notch is a function of the roof's pitch (Figure 122).

Generally, I oversize my rafters. This means they are deeper (wider) than is actually necessary to carry the roof loads. There are several reasons for this. The venting of a thick roof assembly is easier to build and more likely to work. Also, the birdsmouth will be more easily accommodated if the board is wide. The deeper the rafters, the more insulation I can fit in. And finally, deeper rafters can be located farther apart. This means there will be fewer thermal shortcuts through the framing (Figure 123).

Back at the overhang, I am reconsidering the rafter tails, that portion of the rafter that extends beyond the birdsmouth. Let's say my rafter needs to be 18' long to span from ridge to wall, and it needs to be 22'6" to make it all the way to the eave. Whenever framing lumber is ordered in lengths that exceed 20' there is a premium cost per foot. (See Table 6 in Chapter 11.) So I decide to build the overhang and soffit separately, with smaller boards. This is very common. Moreover, as soon as that decision is made, it occurs to me that I may want to change the pitch of the overhang. This gives an attractive appearance frequently found on barns and railroad stations. It is also a way of getting more protective overhang.

So far, I have been assuming this roof will have a heated (or cooled) living space directly below it. Otherwise I might have been thinking more about trusses. Since trusses can be ordered in any shape or size, I would have them delivered with the overhang already built (Figure 66).

Also, trusses exert no lateral (outward) thrust at the top of the walls. In general a roof must handle snow loads and dead loads, i.e., the weight of the building materials making up the roof itself. These loads exert a downward force that tends to flatten a roof. As the ridge sinks down, the rafter ends push out. This is the lateral thrust referred to above. If the lateral thrust is contained, the ridge can't sink and the roof stays straight. When using trusses, the lateral thrust is taken care of by the triangulation in the trusses. But when building with simple rafters this thrust must be contained by other framing: collar ties, collar beams, or a structural ridge, etc. (Figure 124a).

Collar ties are the most common solution for containing the lateral thrust created by a roof. Essentially, the collar ties make the roof into a truss (remember, a truss is any configuration of triangles). In the simple cape, the attic floor serves as the collaring assembly. In buildings with knee walls the collar ties must be above the floor, usually forming the ceiling joists. A rule of thumb for locating collar ties dictates that they be at least one-third the vertical distance from the peak to the

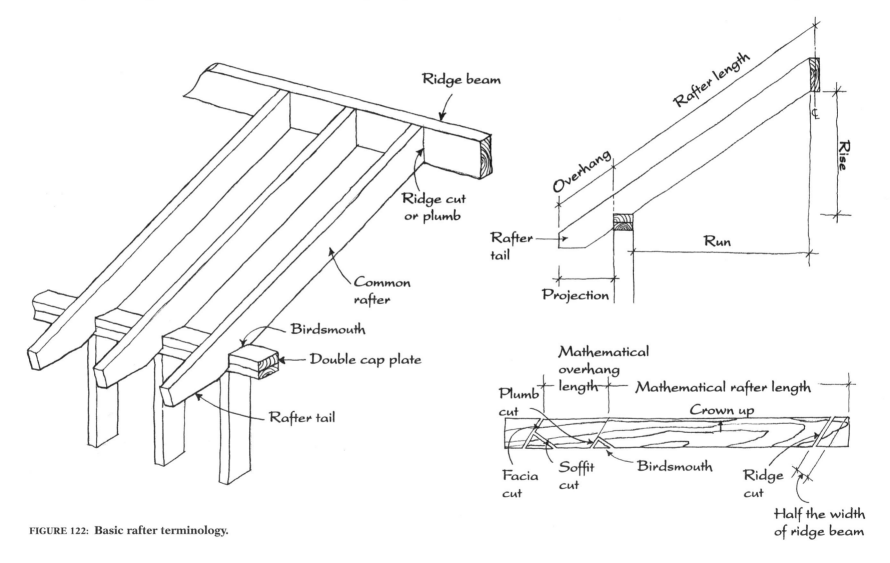

FIGURE 122: **Basic rafter terminology.**

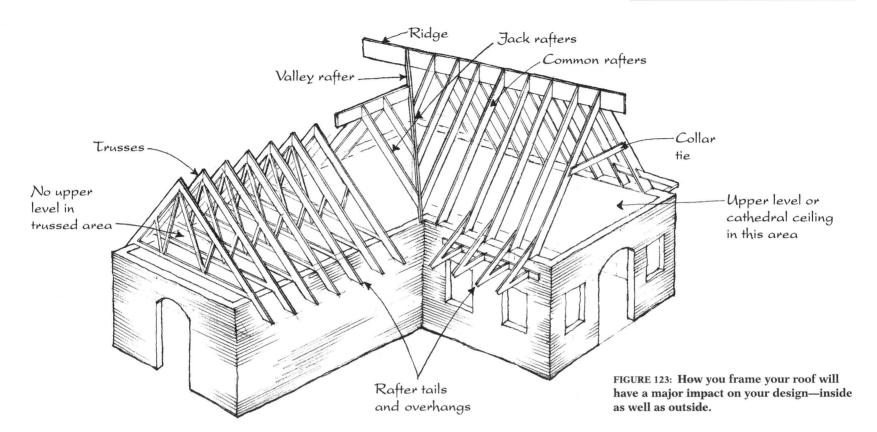

Ridge

Jack rafters

Common rafters

Valley rafter

Collar tie

Trusses

No upper level in trussed area

Upper level or cathedral ceiling in this area

Rafter tails and overhangs

FIGURE 123: How you frame your roof will have a major impact on your design—inside as well as outside.

level on which the rafters rest (Figure 124b).

Unfortunately, this can sometimes mean they are too low to allow headroom. Never fear, solutions exist.

The *structural ridge beam* eliminates the need for collar ties. If the ridge beam is sized adequately to carry half the roof load (calculations required) then the ridge will not be able to sag. If the ridge can't sag, then there can be no thrust or movement at the eaves. Problem solved! Just make certain that the ends of the ridge

beam sit on a load-bearing member or wall that transfers the loads all the way to the foundation (Figure 125).

Another clever solution carries the lateral thrust with a *lateral collaring beam*. If the world were upturned 90°, the sideways thrust from the roof would look the same as a typical uniform vertical load on any simple beam. Therefore, why not design a beam that will carry that load and build it on its side (Figure 126).

I have used this approach more than once with great results. The depth of the

collaring beam is such that it may be incorporated into a shelf or closet space.

Getting back to my example, I have decided that I want the ceiling under the roof to continue past the collar ties all the way up to the ridge. Although I know from experience that the upper peak may collect the occasional cobweb, I can't resist. There is something so clear and honest about seeing the peak from the inside. It gives the interior space some of the sheltered feeling that the roof communicates from the outside. The only problem is

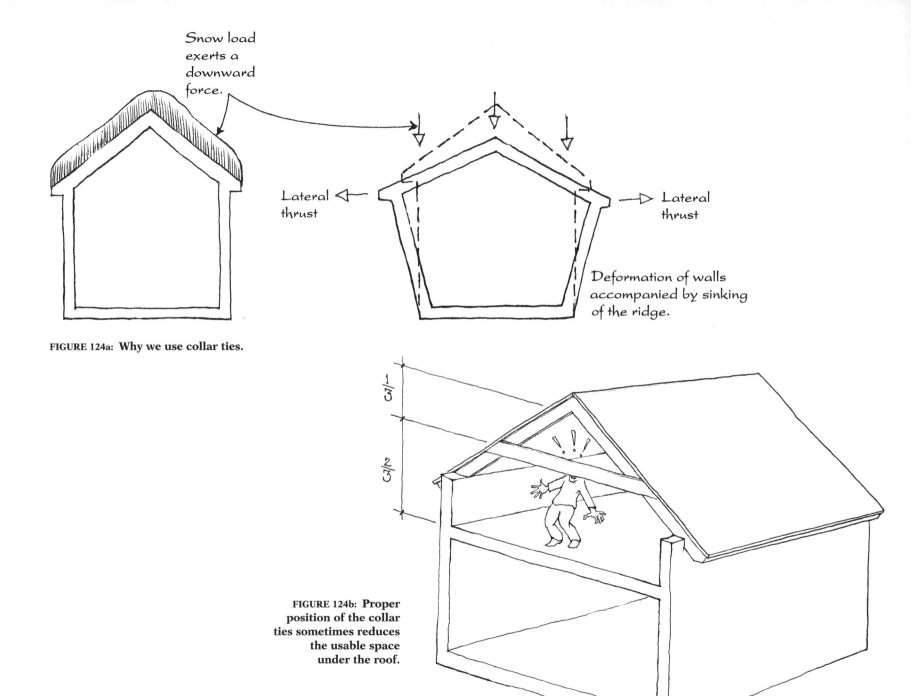

Snow load exerts a downward force.

Lateral thrust

Lateral thrust

Deformation of walls accompanied by sinking of the ridge.

FIGURE 124a: Why we use collar ties.

FIGURE 124b: Proper position of the collar ties sometimes reduces the usable space under the roof.

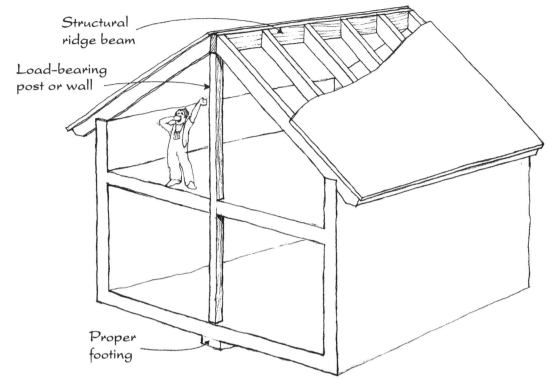

Structural
ridge beam

Load-bearing
post or wall

Proper
footing

FIGURE 125: Using a structural ridge beam is one way to get better headroom and still have a stable roof.

what to do with all those collar ties. Hmmm. An idea bubbles up from early times. When timber framing first came to this country, the roofs were built with just a few large timbers called "principal rafters." In between the principal rafters there were smaller lateral members called purlins. If I use this strategy I will reduce my rafter pairs, and thus my collar ties, from several dozen to just a few. This will give the space an open feeling that the collar ties will only heighten.

Cycle, cycle, cycle. I'm not out of the woods yet. The orientation of the lateral purlins blocks the vertical venting from eaves to ridge. This framing system comes from a time when the attic wasn't heated! Hmmm. But, as is often the case, the solution comes with a dividend. If I insulate and vent above the rafter/purlin layer, I can use very light lumber to inexpensively house the insulation and support the roof sheathing. Moreover, the beautiful rafters and purlins can now be exposed to the interior of my house (Figure 127).

This isn't the cheapest way to build, mind you, but neither is it outrageously expensive. Moreover, the added energy performance will have a long-term payback. Also, the heavy timber-framing and the thicker roof assembly seem to go perfectly with the substantial appearance of the brick walls.

The purlin construction also has an effect on the way I build my overhangs. With common rafters I could have attached my overhang framing to a rafter every 16" to 24". Now rafters only occur once every six feet so I must fasten my overhang in a different manner. Perhaps I should consider supporting from below rather than hanging on from above. This opens possibilities for ornamental brackets, knee braces, or even posts.

The point here is to explore all the possibilities presented by every necessity. I can figure out several ways to build the overhang, or the whole roof, for that matter. The idea is to find that particular way that best expresses what I'm trying to do with the rest of the building. I usually try to make my architecture look like it resulted from some agenda peculiar to the human condition. In short, I think design is about people and what they try to make of life. So in this example, I want the architecture to express the act of building. Beyond how the parts are assembled, this means that the actual drama of the construction process should be legible in the final design solution. Thus I will tend to favor exposed brackets with mortise

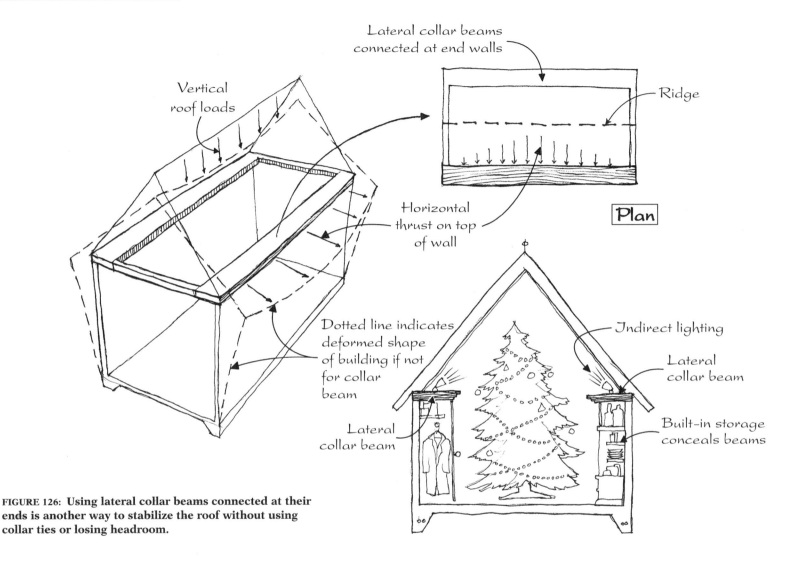

Vertical roof loads

Lateral collar beams connected at end walls

Ridge

Horizontal thrust on top of wall

Plan

Dotted line indicates deformed shape of building if not for collar beam

Indirect lighting

Lateral collar beam

Lateral collar beam

Built-in storage conceals beams

FIGURE 126: Using lateral collar beams connected at their ends is another way to stabilize the roof without using collar ties or losing headroom.

and tenon joints over hidden trusses with manufactured connector plates.

Just to summarize, we started with a decision to take the ceiling to the peak. Then there were too many collar ties and they were in the way. This led us to choose a different way of framing the roof. In turn, the framing required that we reconfigure the insulation and venting. This resulted in a beautiful ceiling treatment and an improved roof-to-wall proportion. All of this has created some new opportunities at the soffit. Still to be decided is the roofing material and final detailing.

Cycle, cycle, cycle. Design is the result of looking and relooking at the opportunities. The process of building always points to new opportunities and alternatives. By inspecting all the different ways to build the same basic roof, we come upon many different architectural solutions. Because

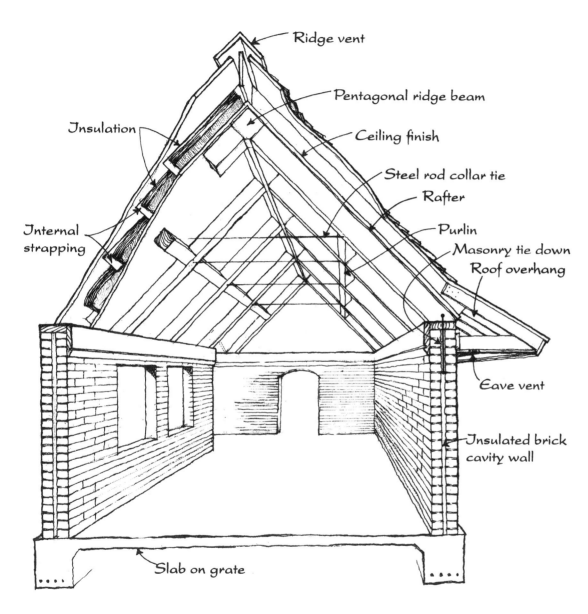

Ridge vent

Pentagonal ridge beam

Insulation

Ceiling finish

Steel rod collar tie

Rafter

Internal strapping

Purlin

Masonry tie down

Roof overhang

Eave vent

Insulated brick cavity wall

Slab on grate

FIGURE 127: One possible roof design for a simple masonry house.

they evolve from the central act of making the building, they avoid the applied look that has come to characterize so much of today's contemporary architecture.

▥ Roofing

After the roof framing and the roof sheathing have been decided, there remain the questions of what to put on the very outside. This is the *roofing*. The available options can be organized by roof slope or pitch. As the pitch gets steeper, there are more options. This is fortunate, since a steeper roof also becomes more of a visual element. Flatter roofs primarily exhibit their soffits or overhangs.

It is useful to think of different roofing choices according to their size and the material they are made from. The four basic material categories are: organic; mineral; metal; hydrocarbon. The different approaches within each group can be divided into systems with lots of little pieces (and cracks) or very few large pieces with only a few seams. Shingles or tiles are examples of the former; metal sheets or roll roofing are examples of the latter.

Organic roofing includes wooden shingles, shakes, boards, or thatch. Though not used in America, thatch is by far the oldest and most universal roofing. Even today it is found around the globe. In the well-forested areas of the world, wood is equally popular. The basic wood shingle is a miracle of natural fitness. The cellular structure of wood is awash in sap, resins, and other organic hydrocarbons. When wood is exposed to the weather, the sun's heat draws these fluids to the surface. The lighter alcohols and ethers are evaporated away, while the heavier ones are distilled into thicker protective tars. After several seasons of the sun and the cold, the wood weathers into a stable, rot-proof material impregnated with its own natural creosote. The resins of woods like cedar, redwood, cypress, or mahogany contain additional substances that act as natural pesticides. Properly installed, we find wood can last hundreds of years in the weather, even without paint!

Where timber isn't plentiful, other roofings have developed. For instance, if clay is abundant, tiles are fabricated. When clay is scarce, then simple earth and even concrete can be used. Reinforced with straw, earth tiles can be laid as a flat roof supported by logs called "vigas." Another example, and perhaps the most striking of mineral roofings, is the slate shingle. Easily surviving centuries of weather, slate roofs normally fail only when their fasteners corrode or the underlying structure collapses. Slate shingles are still available in a variety of colors, and the methods for hanging them have improved. While not a cheap roof, it is one of the few that will never deteriorate from sun, wind, or rain—not even from acid rain.

Metal roofing systems used to make a similar claim. The corrosives in the rain, however, have changed all that. I put a copper roof on just a few years ago. The whole job took a little over four weeks. By the time the last pan was installed, the first pan was already black with oxidation! Nevertheless, it is still a good roofing material. Metal roofing usually comes in sheets. These are either folded together or interlocked. The former method, called *standing seam*, makes a very high quality roof and can be fabricated from galvanized steel, aluminum alloy, copper, lead-coated copper, stainless steel, or an alloy called "tern" metal. The interlocking sheets of metal are less expensive and found frequently on farms and in the country. Sheet-metal roofing is made by a variety of manufacturers. Although stereotyped as a "budget" or utility roofing, it now comes in several colors and shapes, has a full spectrum of accessories, and is increasingly used by design/builders in the construction of double (cold) roofs. The biggest advantage of metal is the large sheets in which it is available. Fewer joints means fewer leaks and faster installation. Metal shingles are also on the market. These are highly ornate interlocking shingles that are stamped from a variety of metals. They are used primarily in historic restoration.

Finally we come to the petroleum-based products offered (at least until the oil runs out) by the industrialized building industry. These range in style from the familiar asphalt shingle to the many high-tech membrane roofings. Asphalt, in combination with different minerals, has been made into a variety of roofings, including asphalt shingles, roll roofing, fiberglass-reinforced shingles, asbestos shingles, and even reinforced corrugated sheets in a variety of colors. Reflecting our cultural bias, these manufactured petroleum products are far and away the most commonly used roofings in America today. While they are cheaper at first, they only last fifteen to twenty years before they must be replaced. Of course, for anyone thinking of a house as a product, this is plenty long enough. For an owner/builder, however, the life cycle cost-savings of a metal, slate, or even sod roof may prove more desirable.

Just a Suggestion

With anything as complex as the making of a house there have to be priorities; they give us a starting point and help us navigate the Design Helix. Perhaps the kitchen is the most important room, perhaps wood is the favorite material, maybe wood heat is imperative, etc. In the end this is all up to the personal discretion of the owner/builder. I would like to humbly suggest that the roof become the most important part of your building's envelope. It is the essence of shelter, it is the highest and most prominent shape, and it is "on top." It is the anthropomorphic equivalent to your head, to your mind and to your psyche. Like your mind, it is central to your survival and our success as a species (phew, heavy!).

ROOF ORIENTATION IN THE SNOW BELT

In the snowbelt one must always keep in mind where the roof will shed its load. Since designs are done in the comfort of a studio, and the construction usually takes place in the warmth of the summer, it is not unusual for first-time designers to orient the roof without adequate consideration for snow. But if the foot of snow that collected on your roof overnight is deposited on your front steps, you may have to leave the house through a window.

This situation seems to occur even more frequently in garage design. I don't know why. Maybe it's because the garage is usually designed after the main house and so the designer is attempting to fit it into the overall design. The roof is often oriented for composition rather than function.

If your roof eave runs along a wall with doors, you can expect to have trouble. The snow from that roof will shed onto the ground in front of the doors. Naturally, there are a few standard remedies. The addition of an appropriate-size dormer may help by deflecting the snow to either side of the door. The best, of course, is to simply reorient the roof so that the door is in the gable end.

There are three types of doors commonly used in garages: the barn door, the hinged door, and the roll-away door. The hinged door is the most demanding in that it requires that all snow be removed before it can be opened. Even if it's in a gable end with no snow from the roof to contend with, the driveway must be shoveled before you can open the hinged door.

The sliding barn door is a bit more manageable. If the snowfall is light, the barn door will often slice through the snow with no additional effort. Even if it requires some shoveling, it's never very much. That is, unless the door is under an eave. In that case there may be quite a bit of shoveling.

A dormer will help deflect snow, but door design must still be considered.

Finally, there is the contemporary garage door that rolls away like a rolltop desk. This clever door has neither to swing nor slice through the snow. Regardless of how much snow falls during the night, you will be able to open your garage door with the flick of a button (or a slight grunt, if it's one of the manual units). But even this type of door doesn't solve the problem of snow deposited from the roof. After it opens, with button or grunt, you must still shovel the driveway before you can back out your car.

Well, Vermonters have solved this problem with characteristic efficiency. They just don't build garages. It's remarkable, in a climate where a garage would seem more needed than ever, that so few Vermonters have them. Nevertheless, what applies for garage doors also applies for *all* doors. And Vermonters know it. You'll rarely see a door placed under an eave without adequate protection against the snow that will build up on the roof. So take a page from the book of those clever Yankees and consider the snow when you're designing your roof.

FIGURE 128: Roof orientation determines where snow and rainwater will be concentrated. This is an important consideration when using hinged doors.

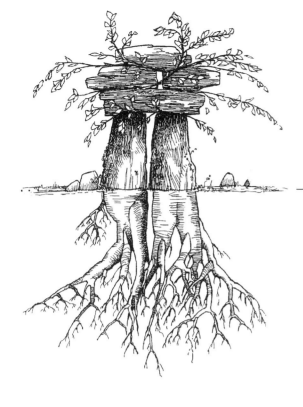

A Window For Your Spirit, A Door For the Dance

They say the best way to learn something is to teach it. I certainly agree. By far, my deepest educational experience with respect to doors and windows was the first summer I spent with a class of architecture students designing and building sections of an experimental house. The curriculum in this type of course is organized so the students build the house in roughly the same sequence they might draw it in the studio. This means they build all the walls first and then they come back to cut in the windows and doors. I hasten to point out that in normal practice this is *not* the way we advise design/builders to make buildings (unless their clients are very patient and very wealthy). In the magic world of education, however, this peculiar process isolates issues of massing, scale, proportion, and composition. More importantly, it demonstrates clearly how the building process "informs" the design process.

The task at hand this particular summer was to design and build fenestration (a big word meaning "windows") for the south-facing walls of the building.

Architecture students, an argumenta-

tive lot by nature, will often display a sort of prima donna attitude which they imagine to be a trait of famous architects. Surprisingly, many design schools tacitly encourage this. I call it the "Howard Roark Syndrome." One of Ayn Rand's fictional characters from her book *The Fountainhead*, Howard Roark blew up one of his buildings rather than allow another architect to change the design. And though I generally deplore and reject the stereotype of architects as prima donnas, my students that summer really were unable to agree on anything. Each student's proposal was immediately ripped apart by the others. There was no agreement on the big questions and even less on the smaller issues. What was a window? What did it want to be? What was a good window? How should they work? What was the difference between fenestration and windows? What was the essence of "windowness"?

They couldn't even agree on defining the problem. As the instructor, I felt I should offer a little guidance. So at this point I really had to reinspect my assumptions about windows. In conversation (and, of course, debate) with the students, we came up with the following program for fenestration:

A window, it can be said, is any penetration in a wall fulfilling the following five functions:

1. It must provide weather protection.
2. It must provide natural light.
3. It must provide view (usually).
4. It must allow ventilation.
5. It must be part of a composition that harmonizes with the overall architecture of the building.

As you might guess, the last criterion is fairly subjective and of disproportionate importance to the architect suffering from the Howard Roark Syndrome.

Composition and weather protection are considerations best understood from the exterior of the building. The others—view, light, and ventilation—are primarily related to the interior program. In general,

architecture students tend to consider buildings as objects or sculpture. Consequently, they usually have more energy for the exterior composition than the interior program. This bias allowed the prima donnas to torpedo each other's design proposals. Whenever one student would present their vision for the fenestration, the other students would point out how poorly it addressed the building's interior needs. This went on for over a week.

For my part, I wanted to clarify the problem without actually supplying the solution. I constantly brought the students back to the five requirements. Consider them all, I insisted, and present your proposals accordingly. After another week of full-scale mock-ups, debate, drawing, more debate, models, debate, and then more mock-ups and debate—finally everyone's efforts were rewarded. And the solution they devised was truly brilliant! (See Figure 129.)

Realizing that whatever worked for the outside program was usually not quite right for the inside (and vice versa), the students elected to separate the two agendas (Figure 130). The exterior composition was designed using a small curtain wall. This allowed the greatest flexibility of shape and required the fewest joints or mullions to leak. The innovation was that this huge expanse of glass was suspended 3″ in front of the structural wall of the building. This meant the actual wall could be penetrated in selected places to coordi-

nate with interior needs for view and light. Moreover, this could be accomplished without worrying about glazing details, weather, or exterior appearance. The ventilation was placed discretely at the sides as part of the exterior composition.

I realize that this may strike some as a "cop-out." I agree that it would have been amazing if we could have found a way to incorporate all interior and exterior requirements into one window design. Nevertheless, the students' final solution was innovative and compelling. More to the point, it addressed and forever clarified the five basic considerations that must be considered when designing fenestration—at least for me. Hopefully, the students learned something as well.

When most students, indeed most anyone, thinks about windows and doors they are often thinking of them as merely products. What do they cost, how easy are they to install, how long is the guarantee, what kind of glass and storm protection do they come with, and above all, *how are they rated??* These are the concerns of the prudent shopper. They are excellent concerns, as far as they go. But if they are the entirety of the owner/builder's interest, then priorities and values have become confused. Because a window is first and foremost a penetration in a wall. Walls, as discussed in Chapter 9, are about separation and enclosure. Windows and walls are opposites. When Buddha thinks of the

FIGURE 129: Students solved a complex fenestration problem with this innovative glazing design.

yin of "wallness" he can't help but think also of the yang of "windowness."

The Experience of a Window

A window allows mere eyesight to take the viewer beyond a wall. By this means, that which has been separated is partially brought back together. This is a daily but profound experience that we simply take for granted. The design/builder's placement of windows governs and filters what may be introduced into the experience of a room.

Every window should be carefully placed. A window facing east brings the sunrise into your bedroom or breakfast nook. A north-facing window may contrast the winter's fury with the warmth of your study or den. A kitchen window facing a garden brings the role of nature into that room for preparing the food. A window at the end of a hall might line up with a distant landmark, orienting occupants with the world at large, even as they pad along to the bathroom.

Windows are like picture frames. A small window suggests a specific purpose or focus. It becomes a peephole in the wall. Or, if the window becomes large, it can obliterate the wall. Separation is eliminated and everything comes inside, uncontrolled. A window's location makes us move our heads to align with what we want to see outside. Indeed, the overall placement of windows in a house per-

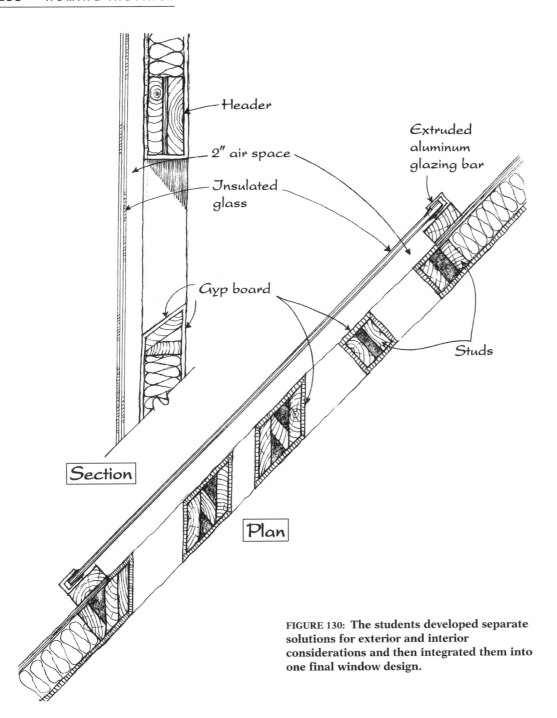

Header

2″ air space

Insulated glass

Gyp board

Section

Extruded aluminum glazing bar

Studs

Plan

FIGURE 130: The students developed separate solutions for exterior and interior considerations and then integrated them into one final window design.

suades us to circulate throughout the architecture. The child in us exclaims, "Look what you can see from here! Look out here! And here!"

More than just the vista, it is the configuration of the penetration itself that shapes our experience. Windows allow us to sense the substance of the walls. The thick walls of a masonry building are really perceived while looking through a window or entering a door. A window seat allows us to meditate with the plane of the wall. Half in and half out, the window seat allows us the ultimate in security and comfort. Some windows have mullions further filtering and framing the view. Or perhaps the glass is old and its liquidlike optics give everything a slow dance as you pass by. Windows in a dormer permit us to view and feel the roof. Half of our body is below the rafters and half stands above. This wonderful feeling of security while being in the treetops is normally experienced only by roofers.

Another aspect of the window experience comes from its use. Old double-hung windows, when they aren't painted shut, are a wonder of cleverness with their weights and interlocking sash. But they don't let you lean out like the casement. A well-built casement opens wide like a door. It also offers a snug feel when the crank brings the window tightly closed. Before crank mechanisms, the old bronze brackets with holes and a pin allowed you to adjust how far the window was open.

These are still available and may be something to consider installing the next time you strip the gears on one of those cheap handles and can't get the window to operate.

Beyond the hardware and operation there is also the quality of the wood, the paint or finish, the mullions, and the glass itself. Manufacturers are now offering a variety of woods, painting with epoxies and bonding muntins directly onto the glass. The glass may be double- or triple-paned; low-E; filled with argon gas; or just old-fashioned single panes with a storm window. These last considerations focus mostly on how well a window controls heat flow. Since windows are the "thinnest" points in your thermal envelope it pays to give their energy performance serious attention. A little extra spent up front may quickly be repaid in fuel savings over time. Unfortunately, comparing the thermal performance of windows has become a lot like picking stocks and bonds. Architects, builders, and home-building enthusiasts pore over magazine reviews and spec sheets while visiting home shows and sales rooms. If you're not interested in making window selection your next hobby, consider the Certified Products Directory published annually by the NFRC (National Fenestration Rating Council). Look up the windows commonly available in your area and compare them with those commonly reviewed as "the best" in all the magazines. Then consider

the cost difference and calculate your payback.

But above all, remember that a window is an experience far more than a product. While shopping for your units, visualize them in the context of the walls for which they're planned. Consider the material and craftsmanship. Although ease of installation, quick delivery, and low price are appealing features, they are soon forgotten. It is the quality of the window *experience* that will persist over the life of your house.

Before moving on to doors, I want to share a little more of what the architecture students debated that summer. The discussion didn't revolve around specifications or *Consumer Reports*. Rather it focused on *how to think about windows*. Although the facts and figures are important and must be studied, it is the underlying attitude with which you design your fenestration that concerns us first.

VIEW

The first thing any window provides is a view. Placing the window in a certain location gives the occupant access to a particular view. This view is further modified by the size of the window. Little windows focus a view and "cinematize" it. By that I mean that the view seen through a little window changes depending on your proximity and angle to it. If you walk past a

small window, what is seen changes like a little cinema. At any given distance you can only see so much, but if you move closer, the "screen" enlarges. You are the cameraman; you control the view. A larger window, say a picture window, operates differently. It allows everything into the room at all points. You can see more or less the same vista regardless of what your position is in the room. The view becomes like wallpaper in which the light and weather change. A large window can bring a delightful natural ambience into a space. It can also spill the room's energy and rob the occupants of feeling enclosed, snug, or secure. Happily, the design/builder is on site while the rough openings (RO) for the windows are being framed. He or she can reflect on the initial openings and adjust as needed (Figure 131).

Mullions and muntins (different words for the same thing) are another view modifier. When glass could only be made in small panes, muntins were required to assemble the panes into reasonably-sized windows. Today, of course, they are entirely optional. Nevertheless, there is a huge market for windows with "true" divided lites. This requires real muntins, not to be confused with the bogus "snap-in" muntins. Each will provide a very different experience, yet both will arrest your vision as it tries to focus on the view beyond.

Muntins announce and define the plane of the glass. Sometimes this is good. Some

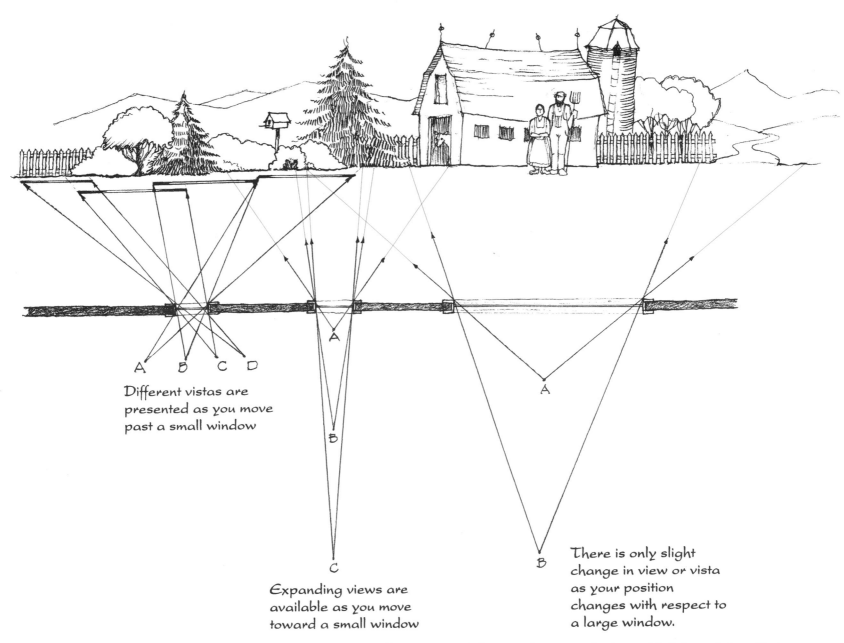

Different vistas are
presented as you move
past a small window

Expanding views are
available as you move
toward a small window

There is only slight
change in view or vista
as your position
changes with respect to
a large window.

FIGURE 131: **Smaller windows provide more dynamic light and view effects. Larger windows produce pervasive but stable light and view effects.**

windows are primarily for natural light and the view is not that amazing. In such an instance, a beautifully mullioned window may be a more attractive visual than the view. This is how leaded or beveled glass succeeds. Mullions also break down the scale of the window, both inside and outside. If the design calls for a large window, but you don't want to lose the feeling of enclosure, mullions may do the trick. Also, any window with large undivided glazing will necessarily look more modern. For preservationists, or even those preferring a more traditional appearance, the muntins will provide a welcome effect. At least a few of the bigger window vendors will allow you to design your own muntin patterns. This comes with some added cost, but it is often worth it. Nothing picks up and transmits the lines of a building's architecture the way the muntins do.

Several manufacturers offer a variety of true divided-lite windows in standard sizes. These can be had with a variety of different glazings (types of glass). The glazing determines heat and light transmission, discussed a little further on.

LIGHT

Along with view, every window will provide access to some natural light. Sunlight, whether direct or diffuse, is a powerful energy. It can brighten and even heat our homes. But it can also bleach color out of interior appointments and produce glare where we are trying to work. Diffused light, either from overcast sky or translucent glazing, will provide deeper penetration of sunlight into a room. Shadows will be softer and glare less annoying. Alternately, direct sunlight on a clear day will produce distinct shadows, and more glare. In hot regions the sun can easily overheat your home. There is a tremendous amount of solar heat even in diffuse daylight.

Design/builders must wrestle with conflicting goals when they consider the use of natural light. An energy-efficient window design will be different for hot climates than for cold, and they may both be different than a design to maximize natural *daylighting* (using sunlight in lieu of electric light to illuminate the interior spaces). How windows are positioned, how they are shuttered, and what glass they employ determines how sunlight enters our spaces.

For daylighting we want to bring the light as far into the building as possible. This suggests skylights, clerestory windows, light scoops, and light-colored floors to bounce the light beyond the windowed edge of the room. Daylighting can make a significant difference in the cost of illuminating your house (assuming you're in the fine habit of turning off the lights when you leave a room). These savings justify the construction of *light shelves*. (See section on *Daylighting*, Chapter 18, p. 340.) A light shelf is a horizontal surface built inside and out of a window which bounces the daylight off the ceiling of the room to be illuminated. Beyond saving money, light shelves reduce glare while producing soft even light that can't be beat. Light shelves are but one of many different ways to glean the benefits of daylighting without suffering from the sun's harsh, damaging rays. They can work beautifully with the formal architecture of your home, accenting the horizontals and giving depth to your walls. As you design your own light-controlling features, always remember the sun's path in the sky (Fig. 132). While overhangs and light shelves can control the high midday sun (south), they can do little to mitigate the low harsh rays of sunrise (east) or sunset (west). This low-angled sunlight is better controlled with vertical louvers, deep set windows, or interior blinds. (See Figure 146 on page 278.)

In cooler regions, we want to maximize heat gain. This means we want maximum direct sunlight penetration, even though it can cause glare and shadows. We want the heat. We want to provide a floor or wall that can take the brutal abuse of the sun's rays, and that usually means tile or other masonry. Also, these materials store the day's heat for even redistribution during the cooler times of the day. Nevertheless, such a sun-collecting window design will require careful programmatic consideration. Which activities, during what parts of the day, can comfortably be placed within such solar radiation? How much south-facing glass is enough, and what

Fenestration for
daylighting and
composition

FIGURE 132a: Fenestration for daylight or composition will often differ from that for solar heat gain.

FIGURE 132b: Fenestration for solar gain.

happens when the sun isn't out? Cycle, cycle, cycle. These and many other aspects of solar design have been worked out for many years. It remains for the design/builder to reapply these well-understood design principles to a particular site and climate.

In warmer regions, the sun becomes an adversary and shuttering devices must be installed to reduce its penetration into the building. To use natural daylight, we must place our windows on the north side of the building, using as few as possible. But even where cooling is the goal, the sun's power can help. Properly placed windows, high up on a building, will produce a chimney effect, or draft. In conjunction with vents and louvers, the house will be constantly ventilated. In some areas, air is brought into the building below grade, cooled by the earth. This amounts to free, solar powered air conditioning! (See illustration on page 292.)

We can see that any use of natural light will have a tremendous effect on the architecture. It will affect the building's orientation, the design of roof overhangs, the position and design of the windows, even the interior finishes. Window design is hardly a cut-and-paste process. Successful fenestration schemes must be custom-configured for each site and climate.

Windows currently on the market come with a number of features to modify or control the sunlight. Primary among them is the glass. Glass continues to evolve and provide us with new and stunning capabilities. We are all familiar with "single-strength" float glass. This is the simple glass found in most picture frames and it should never be used in windows (the exception being historic or leaded windows). The glass in most windows today is usually plate glass. Plate glass comes in a variety of colors and is usually configured into a double glazing called thermopane. The colors are the result of coatings or chemicals actually added to the glass. The coating you will hear the most about is that associated with low-E glass (low emissivity). This coating, when facing the warm side of the window, effectively reduces the heat radiation passing through the glass. This means that in a hot climate it reduces heat gain, and in a cold one, it reduces heat loss. Today we hear more and more about "miracle" coatings that allow the glazing to turn opaque when the temperature gets too high or when a thermostat applies a low current. These will undoubtedly be affordable and commonplace within the next few decades. For the present, our best glazing strategies rely on double or triple glazing, storm windows, and shades. Table 9 summarizes the insulating impact of adding additional panes of glass. (R-values are a measure of resistance to heat loss. They are further explained in the next chapter. The values in the chart are relatively accurate approximations. Exact values would depend upon window size, edge conditions, and other minutiae. The consequences of these values will be better understood when we use them in the heat gain/loss calculations presented in the next chapter.)

For special situations, the glazing industry supplies us with tempered glass, wire glass, laminated glass, pattern glass, tinted glass, and of course, the entire range of acrylic and polycarbonate plastics. Each has specific characteristics: R-value, strength, flexibility, coefficient of expansion, how much and what spectrum of light is transmitted, cost, life-span, etc. Fear not, these complexities will rarely affect your design process unless you are designing a greenhouse, a solar collector, or a public building. For the vast majority of residential situations, glass is usually: $\frac{3}{8}''$ to $\frac{3}{4}''$ thermopane with a low-E coating, maybe filled with argon.

I should mention that glass is only one way to control the light and energy that passes through a window. Movable shutters and blinds are usually cheaper and more effective. (See R. Argue, *The Super-Insulated Retrofit Book*, published in Canada in 1981 by Renewable Energy, page 94, for more details on insulating windows.)

VENTILATION

Windows are either operable or fixed. Operable windows allow ventilation when you want or need it. Operable windows of a certain size are required as emergency egress (exits) in bedrooms. On the down side, operable windows always have higher infiltration rates. Even with today's sophisticated weather seals, an operable window will let more air through. This may not be

TABLE 9: APPROXIMATE R VALUES FOR DIFFERENT GLAZING CONFIGURATIONS.

Window Type	R Value*
Single Glass	1.06
⅝" Double-Insulating Glass	2.17
⅝" Double-Insulating Glass w/Storm (Triple Glazing)	3.33
¾" Double-Insulating Glass	2.27
¾" Double-Insulating Glass w/Storm (Triple Glazing)	3.23
¾" Double-Insulating Glass Low-E w/Argon Gas	3.00
¾" Heat Mirror Triple-Insulating Glass	3.40
¾" Heat Mirror Triple-Insulating Glass w/Storm (Quadruple Glazing)	4.50
1" Double-Insulating Glass	2.31
1" Heat Mirror Triple-Insulating Glass	4.20
1" Double-Insulating Glass w/Mylar Film	8.00

*Approximate R-values based on center-of-glass measurements made by Hurd Inc.

an issue for you. But if it is, consider separating the ventilation from the window. A fixed window is just that; it doesn't open or move. This allows it to be much tighter against the weather. Yestermorrow students decided to get the benefits of a fixed window by moving the ventilation to a separate location in the building.

Not only does this sometimes make sense, it can often save money—oops! I shouldn't have mentioned the "M" word yet. Experience with clients and Yestermorrow students has taught me that the mere mention of *saving money* can end any further desire to deliberate over different window options. Be careful here. The money saved is not always great and the loss of a quality window experience can be severe. There is something truly wonderful about the simple act of opening a window, leaning out, and smelling the fresh air. Don't miss it just to save a few pennies.

WEATHER PROTECTION

While weather protection is important, I think it is often given a little too much emphasis. In truth, a window unit should not be required to give bullet-proof weather protection under all conditions. If the building is prudently sited, with generous overhangs and proper detailing, the window unit itself shouldn't need to meet NASA shuttle standards. Nevertheless, here are a few guidelines to keep in mind while shopping:

- Fewer joints, cracks, or mullions, means fewer leaks.
- A casement or awning window usually prevents infiltration better than other window configurations within a given manufacturer's line.
- A double hung unit usually has the worst infiltration rating in a given manufacturer's line.
- Thermopane prevents heat loss and condensation in a cold climate but shading and ventilation will save more money in a warm one.
- In order to keep the cold from being conducted right through the sash, all framing pieces are interrupted by a piece of insulating material called a *thermal break*. A window without thermal breaks in the sash and frame is a dinosaur.
- Wood windows are warmer, both in appearance and fact.
- Cheap vinyl- or aluminum-clad windows may rot. Quality ones won't.

Windows are one of the few design areas about which our students often know more than the instructors. They are aware of *all* the marketing claims, laboratory tests, and magazine reviews. It's really impressive. I don't want to sound cynical, but sometimes I fear too much is made of these technological claims. Almost any window will keep out the rain and snow. Few will completely keep out the wind. And none really offer significant insulation or control over heat flow. A single pane of glass has an R-value of approximately 1. An argon-filled piece of triple-pane with a storm unit might have an R-value as high as 8 Great, an 800 percent improvement! But it's still only 8. Compared to even a poorly insulated wall, this window is a thermal "hole." Let's accept it. If you want to keep the sun or heat on one side of the window, invest in shutters, sweaters, and sunglasses, not high-tech glazing.

ARCHITECTURAL COMPOSITION

Most builders simply position the windows so the tops are even with the tops of the interior doors: 6'8". Yikes! What a missed opportunity! Windows are what give any building life. Indeed, people couldn't live in a house without windows. Windows should be arranged to express outwardly the human activity and life within. If the inner life is ordered and organized, so may be the fenestration. But proper fenestration need not be orderly or straight any more than life is.

Even on a house where all the windows are aligned, we will often find a rogue window on the stairs or in the bathroom. Frequently it is this wayward penetration that creates the tension needed to energize the rest of the composition.

Of course, fenestration can be used to express more than human activity. It might also be used to expose the structure of the building, express the hierarchy of spaces or reflect the path of the sun (Figure 133).

Thinking About Windows

I always find fenestration to be among the most exciting and challenging aspects of architectural design. If you have never given it a try, here is the Yestermorrow step-by-step procedure for your first cycle.

Let's assume you have already drawn up a scale plan that reflects your bubble diagram.

Step 1

Place your design, drawn to scale, on the site plan. In your mind's eye, take a walk through the house. Don't rush it. Take your time and imagine several scenarios. Incidentally, this absolutely cannot be done without drawing in the furniture. If you don't know where it goes, cut out some paper furniture that can be moved about. Play house!

Step 2

As you imagine the activities of your day, place a window anywhere you think one might enhance the activity being imagined. This could include interior windows that connect one room to another. Where will you be looking when you awake? while you shower? during breakfast? answering the phone? the doorbell? meditating? Place a window, place a window, place a window . . . and don't forget that window seat in the stair landing!

Step 3

From your imagined location in the building, draw view lines. These establish a big "v" with the vertex at the viewer and the two legs passing through either jamb of the window. Adjust the window's width if necessary to see just what you want (Fig. 134a and b).

Step 4

Now go to the exterior elevations. (These are scale drawings of the outside facades.) Using your scale, locate all the windows and draw them in. As a starting point, align the head of each window at 6'8" above the finish floor level. Place the sill at whatever height makes common sense. Don't forget to leave room for beds, desks, bureaus, and other furniture along the

FIGURE 133: "Confetti Windows". Donoghue residence designed and built by John Connell of Y.B.G. Inc. The client wanted "happy" fenestration.

wall. Draw in 4″ to 6″ casing (trim) all around the window. Add muntins and shutters where appropriate.

Step 5

Congratulations. This is the simplest, most uninspired fenestration scheme con-ceivable. But it's a start. Now let's fix it up.

Step 6

Look at each elevation of the house as part of an overall composition. Remind your-self of everything you are trying to say or express with your design. Use "X-ray vision" to see what's happening behind the walls. Now, change the window configura-tion to better suit your design goals. For now, adjust window placement up and down only. Keep lateral movement to a minimum. Don't be afraid to eliminate windows. Remember the interior experi-

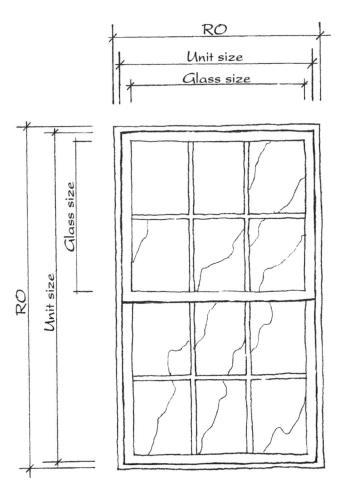

FIGURE 134a: The basic dimensions of every window can be found in the catalogue.

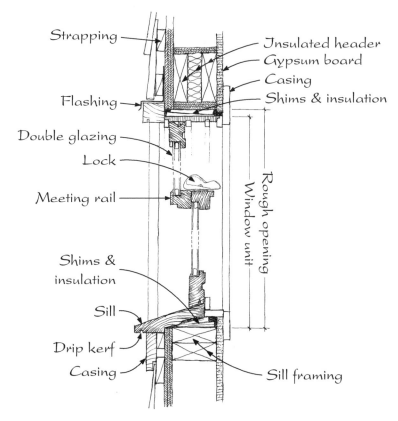

FIGURE 134b: A lot goes on at a window. Neither the R.O. nor the unit dimension will fully describe the whole visual experience.

ence that first suggested the window. An easy way to explore options is to photocopy the elevations and then use tracing paper to quickly generate different window schemes.

Step 7

Once you arrive at an inspired window composition, cycle back and check the location of the windows on the plan. Some may have become wider, some narrower, and some may have been eliminated. See if any movement is possible in others. Go back to the elevation. Then cycle to the plan. Cycle and recycle as many times as you must. Find an exterior composition that works with the interior program and also expresses your architectural agenda. No problem, right?

Step 8

So much for the easy part. Now look in your window catalogues for units with similar dimensions to those you have drawn. Don't feel bad if they don't exist; mine never do. You will have to compromise (tough luck all you Howard Roarks). Unless your budget allows for custom windows (and that's a *big* allowance) you will find that your fenestration is generally a compromise between an ideal composition and an affordable variation on the theme.

The process by which you arrive at the ideal tells you what you want from each window; why you place it there; what

you hope its effect will be. You want to understand the contribution each window makes. As you struggle to strike a balance between design and budget, you can prioritize your needs and desires. Some windows may get smaller; some may even disappear. The important ones will remain and, ideally, the overall design statement will survive.

Of course this isn't the only way to fenestrate a house and you may want to modify or carry it further to make it right for you. Still, it's vastly superior to the line-'em-up-until-your-$-runs-out approach. Plus, it's a good way to understand what you want from the windows in your design.

Windows are a costly item in any house. When you're ordering them, you'll want to get it right. Most manufacturers offer several options so a window can be specifically configured to fit into the particular wall you've designed. This suggests that you have developed your design sufficiently to know the overall thickness of the walls and from what they're made: wood or masonry? You must also know the finishes on both sides. You must know from which side of the wall you will be installing the unit and what the final trim details will be.

Let's do a little homework in the window catalogue of your choice. Most catalogues are pretty similar in that each window is shown with several dimensions associated with each side of it. To start,

you want to find the rough opening dimensions. (The rough opening is the unadorned hole in the framing or masonry into which you will place the unit.) It is usually ½″ to 1″ larger than the actual unit. This leaves space for adjusting the window to plumb and level. Shims (cedar shingles are best) are used to make these final adjustments. Insulation will fill any remaining space once the window is fastened in the wall. Most catalogues show the following dimensions for each side of a given window unit:

> RO: rough opening
> unit: overall dimension of frame or box
> sash: the framework holding the glass
> lite or glass: the actual panes of glass

This information is very important during the design process when you are trying to visualize what your fenestration will look like (Figure 134).

So now let's imagine you're on the phone with the vendor. This could be a lumberyard or a special window dealer, or even, as in my neighborhood, an outfit that sells garage doors. It's surprising who sells windows. Anyway, you have a list of units you want to order. After reciting your list of units, the conversation might proceed something like this:

"You want jamb extensions?" asks the vendor.

"Huh?" you parry.

"How thick's your wall? You want extensions?"

You see, most manufacturers will supply your windows in a variety of standard jamb widths. Normally, this will be the dimension from the outside face of your exterior sheathing to the inside face of the interior finish *plus* $1/16''$. The additional sixteenth of an inch allows for discrepancies in materials or assembly. For example, if you have a 2 × 6 stud wall with $1/2''$ flake board for exterior sheathing and $5/8''$ fire-rated gyp board on the interior, your jamb calculations will be the following:

2 × 6 framing	($5\frac{1}{2}''$ actual size)
$1/2''$ flakeboard	($7/16''$ actual size)
$5/8''$ gypboard	($5/8''$ actual size)
$1/16''$	(*unless there's a reason to make it different*)
$6\frac{5}{8}''$	total jamb dimension for window unit

You say confidently, "I'll need a $6\frac{5}{8}''$ jamb."

"Six and five-eighth inches, uh?" (Your particular jamb dimension may not be one that they offer as a standard.) "O.K., fine, will that be the same for all units?" (Or it may.)

If your wall requires nonstandard jamb dimensions (common in renovation), you will have to get the next larger size and plane it down. Alternately, you can get the unit without extensions and install your own when the windows arrive on site. I usually ask them how the jamb extensions are attached and from what wood they are made. Being rather picky, I like to make and attach my own. This means I have design options. I can choose any species of wood and perhaps mill it to a custom shape that works with a special casing design.

Nevertheless, it's always easier and cheaper to have them do it.

"How about the glass?" he asks. "Thermopane?"

"Yep."

"Low-E?"

"Uh, I guess. How much is it?" Low-emissivity glass is worth the extra 5 to 10 percent in most climates. It will pay for itself within five years. But if you go with it, you must get it on all windows. Low-E glass is a slightly different color than normal glass. Indeed, most glass has a distinctive color. Keep this in mind when doing renovations.

"How 'bout argon gas?" is usually the next question.

"Argon gas? What . . . from the planet Krypton?" you wonder to yourself. Argon gas is a way to improve the R-value (insulating value) of thermopane glazing. By filling the void between the two panes of glass with this inert gas it slows the flow of heat and reduces the likelihood of condensation.

"Uh, how much is it without the argon gas?"

"We're not done yet. You want brickmold casing?" The guy's questions seem endless.

(Brick mold is a standard exterior casing profile available on just about all windows; it's commonly found on tract homes and condos. If you are working on an historic building or even in an historic style, brick mold won't serve. Generally it is too small and makes the window look "undernourished." You have two choices. Ask for a square casing or no casing at all.)

"How about a $4/4''$ (four quarter) by $5\frac{1}{2}''$ square casing of clear pine?" you venture.

"Nope, we got $3/4''$ by $3\frac{1}{2}''$ or $3/4''$ by $5''$, what's your pleasure?" Standards are standards. Well, don't be intimidated.

"Well, how much can I save if I take them in the box?"

This phrase, "in the box," is another way of saying that you don't want any casings at all. (Plus it shows you either know what you're talking about, or attended Yestermorrow.)

The vendor will next ask you whether you want them primed.

"Sure." Seems reasonable, right? But what about the interior? Might you want to use a stain or polyurethane on the interior?

"Well, can I just get them primed on the outside?"

He should say yes, unless you're ordering clad or metal windows.

"Screens and storms?"

Depending on where you live, these are usually a great idea. I always get both. But find out if they are aluminum or wood, who makes them, and how they operate. There are many different formats.

"Are the screens inside or outside the storm panel?"

"Well, the storm panel is a thermopane sash that slides up in the summer. The screen doesn't move. But you can take it out for window washing."

"What? So I'm always looking through a screen? Hey fella, what are you trying to sell me here?"

"Sorry, I didn't know. Listen, for just a fifty percent price increase we have this other line . . ." And so it goes.

This should complete the list of basic questions in any window order, but there is still plenty to talk about. Do they come with hardware? Who makes them? What color are they? Can they be another color? Can you save money if this or that is omitted? How about the warranty? What if the thermopane fails or is cracked? Do they make the windows available in different woods? Last but not least, *How much?* and *When?* Standard units should be available within three weeks to two months, but don't be surprised if it's longer. Custom windows can often take up to three months!

⁞⁞⁞ Doors

If windows are about view, light, and ventilation, doors are just as surely about ceremony, circulation, and security. Like windows, doors present an interruption in the effect of the wall. A wall encloses or separates, but a window or door moder-

ates this effect. While a window allows access for vision or light, a door gives way to the entire human being, with all five senses. While a window represents a singular experience, a door can set up an entire choreography of experiences. So, of course, it's important where and how you place your doors.

Location, it should be clear by now, confers meaning. If you enter a room through the center of its longest wall, this will be quite different from entering off center or at the corner. Coming into a space along its main axis gives command and a certain formality to the entrance. Entering along a wall is less formal, but sometimes more comfortable. People generally feel more secure if they can be close to a wall or corner. Entering a large room at center stage, so to speak, can be intimidating. This is particularly true if that room is filled with people. Entering and leaving a bathroom, for example, is an action that is more comfortable if done discreetly.

When Yestermorrow students make their first attempts at laying out a floor plan, they often start by drawing a big rectangle. This they label the "great room" or the "country kitchen." Along the perimeter of this generalized space a number of smaller rooms are attached with connecting doors. Unintentionally, the room has been transformed into a large circulation space. At this point it should probably be relabeled "hall." (See Figure 135.)

This is one reason door placement is so important. The front door often comes straight into this main room with little or no ceremony. Similarly, a bathroom and perhaps the basement stairs may also empty into this room. The connection to the kitchen, in contrast, is sometimes very carefully considered. Sometimes it's a pass-through, a counter, a swinging door, or maybe a level change (Figure 136).

Let's consider the doors and their locations a little more carefully. Entry to and from a room is an everyday occurrence and so drama or ceremony is sometimes overlooked. This amounts to a substantial missed opportunity. For example, the front door is a formal, ceremonial portal into the public areas of our home. Welcoming guests and staving off intruders (like unwanted salesmen) should be considered in the design and layout. A foyer or air lock placed between the exterior and the interior serves this purpose. In this interstitial zone a more intimate and relaxed welcome can be accomplished *before* the guest is confronted with the full scope of the occasion. Conversely, a salesman or survey taker can be efficiently dispatched without giving them access to the inner sanctum of your home. A backdoor or side door may be far less ceremonial. These are utility entries and tend to be all business. They are designed for ease of delivery, efficient access, good circulation, etc.

On the inside of the house, bathroom doors always need a bit of consideration.

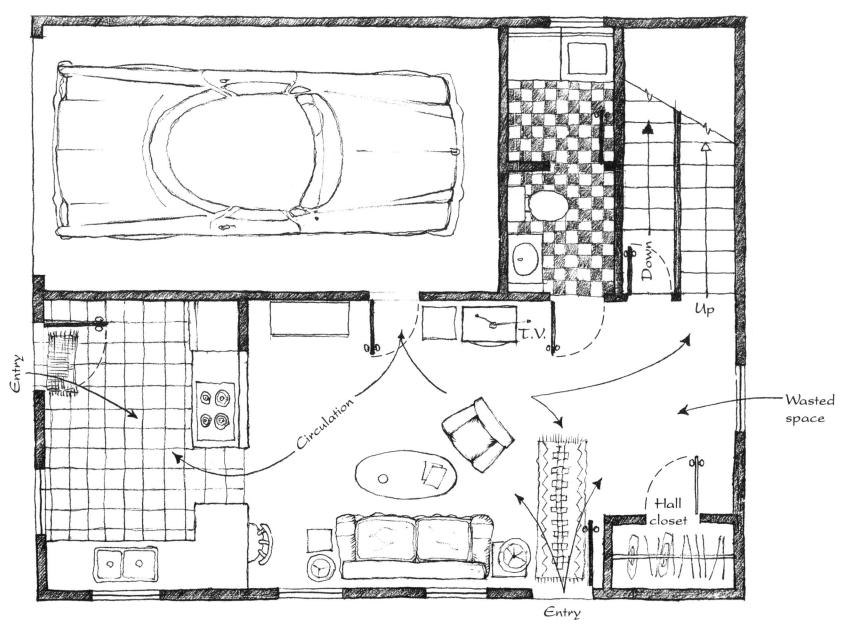

FIGURE 135: In this plan, circulation conflicts with room use because of door placement and room layout. In this case, the open plan provides no well-defined areas for quietly sitting or talking.

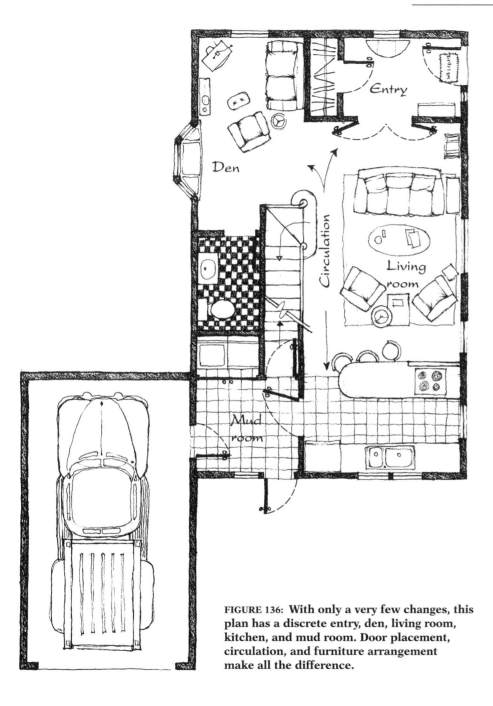

FIGURE 136: With only a very few changes, this plan has a discrete entry, den, living room, kitchen, and mud room. Door placement, circulation, and furniture arrangement make all the difference.

People usually prefer not to make a major production out of a visit to the lavatory. Additionally, people sitting in the living or dining room hardly need to be entertained with the sound of a flushing toilet as the guest rejoins the group. Location of doors is very important. As you place doors in your design, consider the human behavior they will engender. Door location also affects circulation and furniture placement. Door swings must be allowed for.

Finally, remember how the door placement will affect the perception of architectural space in your home. A door requires us to position our bodies in a very particular way. This means we will be taking in a fairly predetermined arc of vision. Work with this. Arrange doorways so they become "presentation" experiences. Perhaps passing through a doorway sets one up to look out a window at the end of a hallway. Or perhaps you come into a bedroom and the bed is directly on axis—or off axis. Whenever I draw any doorway, I always include the arc of the door swing. Then I imagine what it would be like to pass through the door. What will be seen? Should I imagine a window, another door, a piece of furniture, etc.? Is there a better place for the door?

The design/builder understands that a doorway is more than just an interruption in the wall. It is a swinging door with hinges and a doorknob and casings on three sides. It sometimes has a threshold, weather-stripping, locks, and a screen/

storm accessory. All of this must be considered when placing the door. If it is too close to a corner of the room, there may be insufficient room for the casing or the doorknob. Perhaps the door swing can work from one side only. If it's a pocket door, it needs adequate wall space for the pocket. Exterior doors in the snowbelt need to open inward. Otherwise, a big snowstorm could block your door. In windy or rainy regions, the threshold seals better if the door opens out.

Glass in any door must be acrylic, polycarbonate, or tempered safety glass. Every exterior door should have a window associated with it. Few things are as universally felt as the sense of rejection generated by a door without a window. A small window to either side not only suggests warmth and life within, it allows the occupant to visually identify who's at the door. Security is very much a part of any portal. What a door must keep out depends on the situation. A bedroom door must simply maintain acoustical and visual privacy. No window needed. An entry door accessible from the street should have adequate locks and hardware to deal with the neighborhood it opens on. It also needs a window. Be aware that when a door is closed, it "heals" the wall. Enclosure and separation are reinstated.

A door must also maintain thermal security. In this regard, exterior doors are to be respected and admired, particularly wooden ones. Where I live the climate sometimes offers up winter temperatures of −20°F and almost no humidity. That's on the outside of the door. On the inside the owner is maintaining a climate of about 65° with 50 percent humidity. This means a difference of 85° or more through a mere 2″ of wood! Plus, there is moisture involved. This explains why exterior doors must be built to accommodate movement and finished to seal out the weather. Raised panel doors are more than just a stylish tradition. They are one of the best time-tested solutions to the exterior door problem. They allow for the inevitable movement in the wood. The newer metal doors don't have this problem, but they have others. If you are considering a metal door, make sure it is constructed with thermal breaks.

As a matter of convention, exterior doors are 1¾″ thick and interior ones are 1⅜″ thick. I should quickly add that this is hardly cast in stone. If you build a door of a different thickness, however, keep the hardware in mind. Most hardware is designed to accommodate these standards.

IT DON'T MEAN A THING IF IT AIN'T GOT THAT SWING

When you're specifying or buying a door you will need to know whether it's a "right-hand" or "left-hand" door. Since doors are normally approached equally from both sides this can be rather confusing. There are three conventions for establishing the swing of a door. They all lead to the same label for a given door, but the methods of determination are significantly different. Around our office each convention has die-hard proponents. Thus, every time we must list a door order, the chronic door swing debate is rekindled:

Method 1. *Watch the hinges, or inswing/ outswing*
Face the door from the outside of the building or room. Whichever side the hinges are on determines whether it's a right-hand or left-hand door. Then, if it opens toward you it's a reverse or inswing; if it opens away from you it's a standard or outswing. This leads to designations like: left-hand reverse, right-hand inswing, etc. This can become confusing, since a right-hand reverse is the same as a left-hand outswing viewed from the other side.

"Too complicated," insist the others. "Always remember the KISS principle! You'll never remember it." O.K., that may be, so then we have:

Method 2. *Watch the knob*
With the door opening toward you, the knob indicates the handing of door. If the knob is on the left it's a left-hand door; if it's on the right it's a right-hand door. It doesn't matter which side you're on as long as the door is opening toward you. Very simple.

"No way. It's only simple until you get to a door with a storm door and you forget to view each door from opposite sides. You'll end up ordering a storm door that won't work. I've seen it happen."

DISCRETE ROOMS OR OPEN PLAN?

Among the most common attributes of contemporary design is the so-called open plan, or rooms without walls. Rather than use walls, this approach to spatial definition depends on ceiling heights, floor finishes, furniture layout, half walls, and lighting to make "room spaces." Functions are associated with areas rather than actual enclosed spaces. This permits a flow of space that works very well with today's less formal life-styles. Even students interested in traditional designs usually insist on the "country kitchen" where everything happens in one big room. The kitchen is open to the eating area, which is contiguous to the living room and the den. Visual contact is maintained throughout even if people are doing different things in different spaces.

This is all very different from the discrete rooms with four full walls that make up most traditional designs. A room usually contains a specific function or programmatic requirement. In a way, a room is a miniature building design. It has an entry condition (maybe two), a main space, secondary attributes, maybe a window or two, and it is configured to serve a particular purpose. I often think of rooms as generalized stage sets on which many different variations of the same theme will be enacted. Walls, windows, doors, finishes, and furniture are all chosen and configured to support the action. It's very specific, almost formal, compared to the flexible ebb and flow in an open plan layout.

Let's consider the differences in what one experiences as they arrive and circulate through the two plans illustrated below. The air lock entries are identical, but as you come into the main house with the open plan, everything spreads out before you. In one sweeping glance you can see the dining area, kitchen, sitting area, and even the door to the back deck. The stairs are immediately to the right, but with everything else they seem to be a rather small event. Essentially the open plan allows a visitor to take in everything at once. After that, they are free to go where they wish in whatever order suits them.

By contrast, in the plan with walls, as you leave the air lock you enter a small foyer in which the stairs are the main event. This little room seems to be a greeting area. There are no chairs or closets. The idea seems to be that visitors may be met, interviewed, and welcomed—if they're expected. Or, if they don't pass muster, perhaps they may be shown the door (the traveling

(Continued)

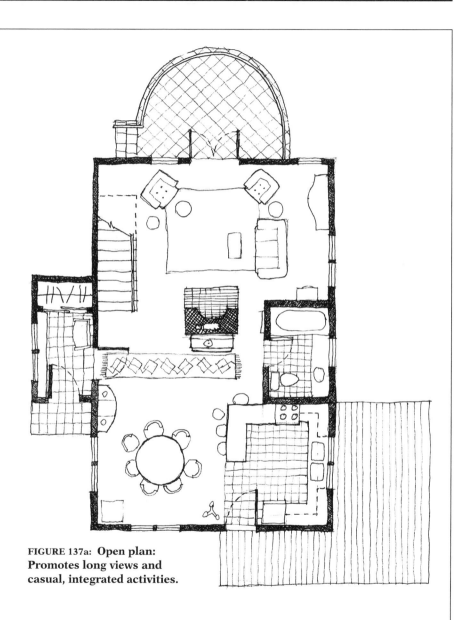

FIGURE 137a: Open plan: Promotes long views and casual, integrated activities.

salesman, rogue boyfriend, or meddlesome neighbor). Nothing is revealed about what's going on in the house. This little room shares doorways with the dining room, the living room, and the more private utilitarian spaces. Depending on which door the host opens, you are treated to a meal, engaged in conversation, or allowed to hang up your coat on the way to the bathroom.

It's pretty easy to see that walls and rooms will bring order, even formality, to one's life. A visitor doesn't just come in and wander about. They are guided through a sequence of doors by their host or hostess. Things aren't apparent all at once, but are revealed in a distinct order. Each room or space is self-contained. When you are in the dining room, that's the only place you are. You can't see the people in the kitchen or living room. You're just dining. When you leave the dining room to go to the bathroom, you will make a rather explicit, even ceremonial, exit, and then later you will make an equally ceremonial reentry. Rooms bring focus and order to human activity.

As you consider and assess the differences between open plan and fully divided rooms, try not to make them mutually exclusive. You might use both approaches in the same building. You may be formal about dining but casual about cooking. The kitchen may open to a family room and/or porch, but dining may take place in a discrete room of its own. Of course, bedrooms are usually self-contained and private. Nevertheless, open planning is often used to arrange the master bedroom/bathroom suite. Some activities require the acoustical privacy only walls can provide. Even a strong devotee of open plans will see the wisdom of putting reading, study, or critical music appreciation in a separate room.

Placement of walls has a lot of effect on which rooms and spaces work together. The relationship between the back deck and the interior is quite different in the two plans. With walls, the deck and the kitchen are seen as one configuration. They go together. Without walls, the deck is connected equally to the dining area and the kitchen.

When laying out your rooms, consider the entries, exits, and stairways with particular care. These are focusing situations. When you pass through a doorway or move along a stair, your vision is temporarily focused in one direction. Your visual experience is narrowed and so it often carries more

(Continued)

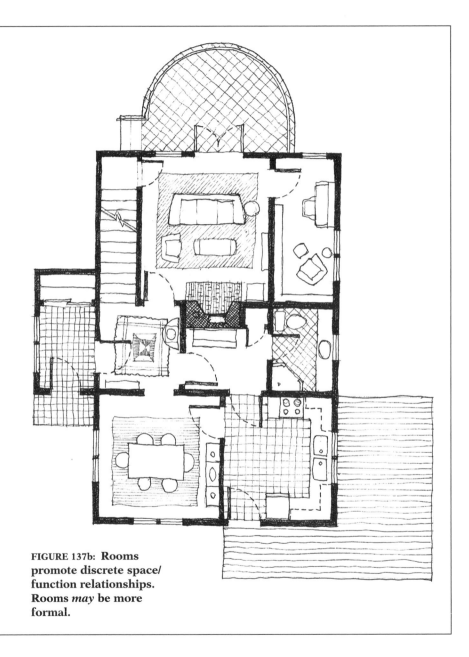

FIGURE 137b: Rooms promote discrete space/ function relationships. Rooms *may* be more formal.

impact. I like to set up a spatial or visual experience with these focusing conditions. For instance, when you get to the top of the stairs there might be a beautiful window or a striking piece of artwork or some other architectural experience right in front of you. Or, you enter a room through a door that is on axis with the fireplace or another door or some other key aspect of the room. Alternately, a door in the corner that brings you into a room along the wall can give a very secure entry experience. A doorway can set up all sorts of subtle and not so subtle effects.

When you leave the bathroom in the walled plan, you are in another little space; a sort of decompression room. You can plan your next move. In the open plan, when you leave the bathroom you will immediately be at the kitchen island, in the dining room, and facing the front door—all at once. Successful open plans require adroit use of sight lines. This means arranging things so that they afford some of the visual separation of walls. For instance, if the bathroom door were lined up with the chimney mass it would give a slightly more discrete feeling to entering and leaving the bathroom.

To wall or not to wall—is that really the question? No, it really isn't. There are endless opportunities to use both approaches. What is important is that you are aware of your options and the effects of your choices. A door in one wall of a room is not the same as the same door in another wall of the room. Moreover, no wall at all is not the same as a half wall or a transparent wall or a ceiling change, floor change, etc.

As with so much of vernacular architecture, the deciding factor is you and how you live.

O.K., so finally we have the bullet-proof method:

Method 3. *Watch your butt* (hinges are properly called "butts")

This method is usually called "butt to butt." Place *your* butt against the doorjamb on the side where the hinges (or butts) will be attached. From this vantage point, a right-hand door will open to your right, a left-hand door to your left. This is the exact same nomenclature as Method 2, only there is less opportunity for confusion.

HARDWARE

Other than the furniture, doors and windows are usually the only parts of your house that move. They are wonderful gadgets. And for a gadget to have appeal, it must do its trick smoothly and consistently. Remember the potter who insisted on fine-quality hardware? For her, the feel and action of a door was as important as its looks. Don't overlook the importance of hinges, knobs, knockers, and catches. I frequently order pre-hung doors without the latch hardware so I can install my own favorite brand. It doesn't have to be expensive to be satisfying. When dealing with bathrooms, there is often a desire to have the hinges and knobs match the metal finishes on the plumbing fixtures. This is easy to do if you think ahead.

ONE DOOR'S STORY

This doorway was designed and built by Yestermorrow students (Figure 138). It is the only entry to a very symmetrical piece of architecture. The students wanted to informalize the entry just a bit by throwing off the proportions of the two doors. The rest of the composition was then designed to reestablish the balance of the

FIGURE 138: A door made from cedar, Douglas fir, mahogany, glass, and lead-coated copper by Yestermorrow students.

composition. It was further decided that the doors should say something about the house. Therefore, the window, with some additional inlay, was fashioned in the exact shape of the building's footprint on the site. Note how the window and door handle are worked into the design. The bottom of the door was clad in lead-coated copper. This symbolizes the banks of the nearby Mad River and refers to the present corrosive state of the hydrological cycle in our watershed. The little square window allows the family pet to be part of greeting anyone at the door.

This door is special. It tells a story and gives the visitor something to ponder while waiting to be admitted. More than just a reminder of the house, it attempts to locate the building in the landscape. This helps everyone who experiences this door to connect better with the site and the building. This level of architecture content would be inappropriate for every door in your home. And yet, as an example of what five architecture students design/built for a front door, it should give you an idea of what's possible. Why not make entering your home as exciting and thoughtful as you can?

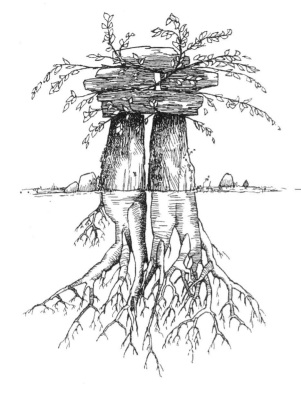

Understanding the Thermal Comfort of Your Building's Envelope

By this point in the book, I hope you're starting to think about the building as a whole rather than a sum of parts. Unavoidably, the format of a book is linear: a chapter on foundation, a chapter on walls, a chapter on doors, a chapter on windows, etc., etc. But the Design Helix wraps that linear presentation back on itself. Site, program, building, site, program, building . . .

Now you are at the chapter on thermal comfort. This is a function of the entire envelope. You must think about the building as an integrated whole, or as they say south of the border: the whole enchilada!

Your *foundation* sits in the ancient earth, connected with history's vibrations, chumming it up with the local ecology. It must support your home forever.

Your *roof* faces the heavens and must fend off the weather. The attic space within will house the mind and spirit of your home.

Your *walls* take the great weights (visual as well as actual) of the roof and transmit them to the foundation. More than that, they enclose what is yours. Inside is defined from outside; meaning is carved from chaos. The personal order of spaces becomes a stage on which your life will unfold.

Taken all together these three systems form the *building envelope.* More importantly, they encompass a universe with an independent climate designed and controlled by the owner. Ultimately the building envelope provides both survival and comfort.

Indeed, basic survival and some comfort is provided by almost any home. A tract house, a trailer home, even a camper provides these basic amenities. But our goal is to accomplish more than the basics. Architectural design, when sucessful, takes the same resources and satisfies the same basic goals, but with expressive personal gestures. The whole idea is to survive eloquently, expressing something of what your life is about. Exuberance, tradition, delight, politics, sentiment, family, what-you-will; there are no restraints on what one expresses while surviving. Every aspect of your design, even the radiators and the insulation, contributes to the success (or failure) of your grand design. Architecture raises survival to an art form just as the culinary profession transforms basic eating into gourmet dining.

▥ Heat Flow

There are a few common facts that never cease to amaze me, even though I have known them for years.

1. Chemically speaking, the salinity of human blood is essentially the same as the water in the ocean.
2. The Empire State Building was built under budget and in less than twelve months.
3. People will become sick if their body temperature changes by more than 2°C.

The first two facts don't concern us here. However, the last one really gets me thinking. If two little degrees can make us sick, think what would happen to most of

the people of the world if we hadn't figured out how to build homes and control the temperature. Buildings allow our species to survive. Heat is necessary not only for comfort, but for survival. At the same time, if we don't improve the design of our homes, the energy we waste and the CO_2 we produce are more likely to spell our extinction!

It's the building envelope that allows us to sequester a corner of the universe and keep it comfortable. To do this we must know a little about the thermodynamic rules that govern heat and energy movement. The central rule is that heat and energy always flow toward the cold. This is the famous Second Law of Thermodynamics, and could be restated as "Heat never stays where you want it." It means your house will lose heat in Vermont and it will gain heat in Texas. How fast this happens depends on how you design and build. It also depends on the time of year and the time of day.

As everyone knows, there are many strategies for maintaining a comfortable environment. We will discuss them in the next chapter. For now, let's get an understanding of how to calculate and deal with the gain or loss from our house (Figure 139).

HEAT LOSS

Whenever it is hotter inside than outside, heat starts to leak out of a house. This

happens in four different ways simultaneously: *conduction* through the envelope's assemblies; *infiltration* through cracks in the envelope; and, finally, *radiation* from different parts of the envelope.

Conduction

Much depends on what materials the building envelope is made from and the ability of these materials to arrest the heat flow. Every material has a known thermal conductivity. This property is symbolized by the letter "k" and is measured by the inch. Heat flow is inversely proportional to thickness, so the more inches the slower the heat flow. The resistance to heat flow, r, is simply the inverse of the conductance; r = 1/k. Total resistance, R, for any given building assembly (wall, roof, etc.) will be the sum of all the r's making it up:

$$R = r + r + r + r + \ldots$$

These little r's may be additional inches of the same material or all the different materials in the wall; that is, the sheathing "r," plus the fiberglass "r" plus the gypsum board "r," etc. (adding up all of the wall-component "r" values will give you your total R). Even though R is the value used by advertisers to sell this window or that insulation, engineers use the inverse of R, which is U, for the total thermal *conductance* of an assembly:

$$U = 1/R$$

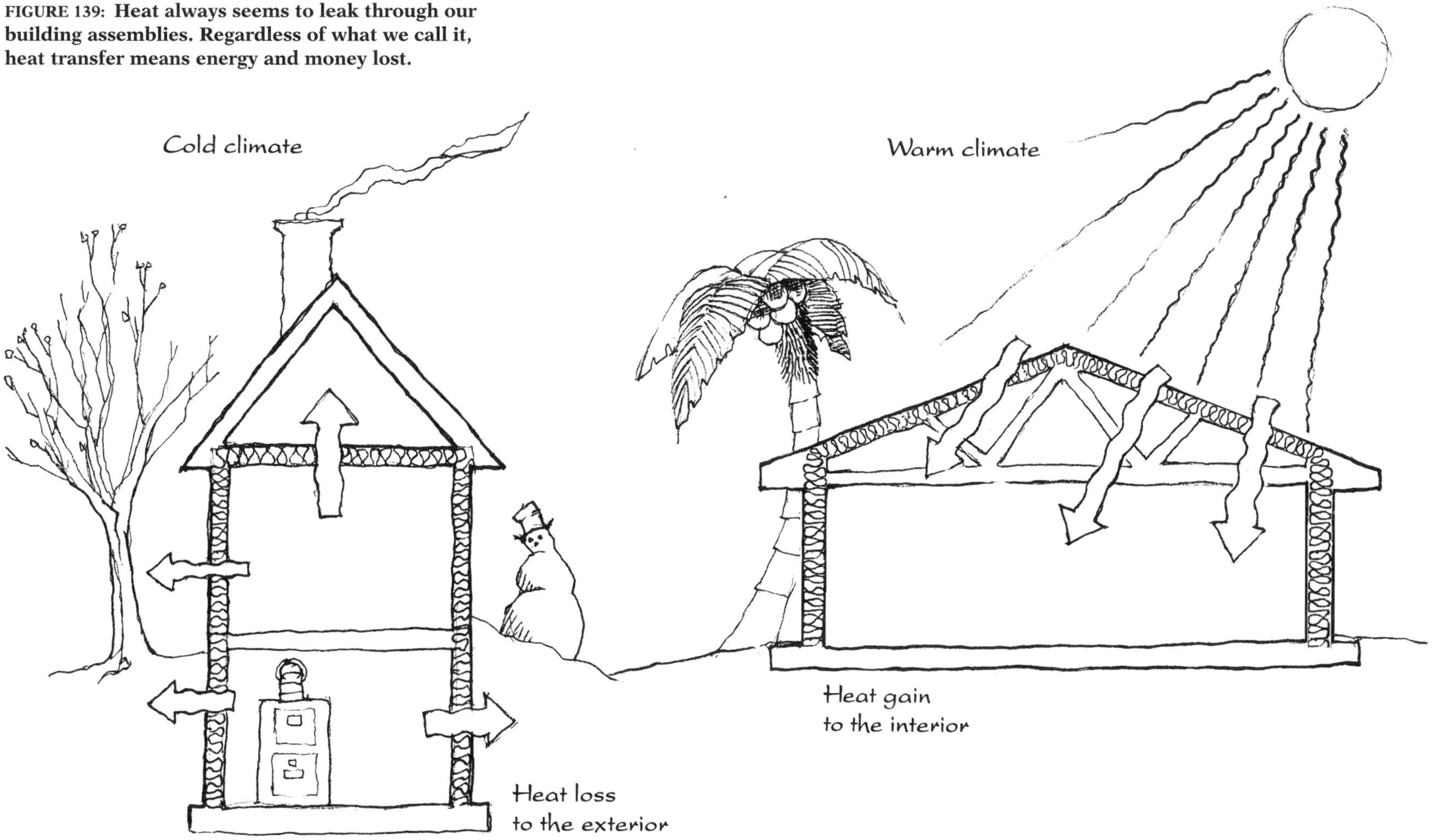

FIGURE 139: **Heat always seems to leak through our building assemblies. Regardless of what we call it, heat transfer means energy and money lost.**

Cold climate

Warm climate

Heat loss
to the exterior

Heat gain
to the interior

The U of any assembly is measured per square foot. Therefore, the more exposed square feet in an assembly, the more heat moving through it. This makes good intuitive sense, right? The final condition affecting conductive heat flow is *delta T* or $(T_i - T_o)$. This is the difference between the inside and outside temperatures. Of course, delta T will be changing constantly as the day runs its course and the seasons come and go. Heat loss will always proceed at a greater rate when there is a greater delta T; i.e., when it's the dead of winter or the middle of the night.

We can see that conductive heat flow is a function of: material properties; material thickness; total area exposed; and delta T. The general design equation that brings all these factors together is:

$$Q_{conduction} = (T_i - T_o)UA$$

Where:

Q: conductive heat loss in BTUs per hour (BTU = British Thermal Units, BTUH = British Thermal Units per Hour)

T_i: temperature indoors in °F

T_o: temperature outside in °F

U: thermal conductivity of total wall assembly, BTUs/hr. – ft.² – F. (hr. = hour; ft.² = square foot; F = degrees fahrenheit)

A: area of assembly in square feet

Exchanging 1/R for U we get the equivalent equation:

$$Q_{conduction} = (T_i - T_o)A/R$$

Either will work. And this equation will quantify heat *gain* in hot climates as well.

Before moving on to other forms of heat loss, remember that conductive heat loss is best controlled by your choice of materials at design time. This is one reason the early New Englanders chose wood over stone to build their homes, even though both were plentiful. Today, it might lead you to use 2×6 framing instead of 2×4s. It might lead you to choose wooden doors and windows over metal ones. It might even lead you to consider an all-weather wood foundation over a conventional concrete one.

Speaking of foundations, heat loss to the earth is figured slightly differently. If you are building with a conventional concrete or block foundation, the calculation

is very simple. The ground temperature in your area must be known, just as the air temperature must be known when you figure the heat loss through above-grade walls. Happily, the ground temperature varies much less than the air. Plus, the deeper you go, the less affected it is by above-grade weather conditions. But ground temperatures aren't commonly listed. So instead we use the next closest thing—the local *groundwater temperature*. This is usually known by the local water utility or well driller. The section of a basement wall above grade is evaluated the same way as any other assembly, using the foregoing equation. For subsurface assemblies, however, all that's needed is the groundwater temperature and Table 10.

The equation is simply:

$$Q_{foundation} = U_{fdn} \times A$$

where:

Q_{fdn}:   heat loss through foundation assemblies in BTU/hr.

U_{fdn}:   special heat-flow value based on groundwater temperature from Table 10 expressed in BTU/hr.-ft.²

A: the area of the subsurface assembly, wall or floor, in square feet

The heat flow through the basement walls is assumed to be twice that of the floor and the actual U value for concrete basement floors is assumed to be 0.10. If

TABLE 10: HEAT LOSS FOR BASEMENT WALLS AND FLOORS BELOW GRADE

Ground Water Temperature °F	Basement Floor Loss BTUH/Sq. Ft.	Below Grade Loss BTUH/Sq. Ft.
40	3.0	6.0
50	2.0	4.0
60	1.0	2.0

Source: Reprinted with permission of the American Society of Heating, Refrigerating, and Air-Conditioning Engineers from the 1972 ASHRAE Handbook—*Fundamentals*, p. 378.

you are designing a basementless house on a slab, the calculation is slightly different but no less simple. This method is included in the sample heat loss calculation found in Appendix 3.

Unlikely as it may seem, conductive thermal flow can be expressed architecturally. Thick walls, window seats, and heavily cased double glazed windows with thermal shutters will add a feeling of snugness. The new stucco systems (Dryvit, Sto, etc.) allow the covering of an entire building with rigid foam (1″ to 4″), which is then protected by a high-impact epoxy stucco. Depending on how it's detailed, these systems can make your home look almost like it's wearing a down jacket (Michelin Man?). Even if you don't choose to express this aspect of your house architecturally, it will still be responsible for a number of construction details. A few examples might include:

- Elimination of thermal leaks through the framing can be accomplished with double framing, foam sheathing, cross strapping, or some combination of these methods.

- Since it is nearly impossible to over-insulate, you may find that you build your walls from 2 × 6s, 2 × 8s, or even 1 × 10s.
- Overhanging your wall framing 2" at the rim joists allows you to insulate at the floor framing with 2" foam. The same trick works where the framing hits the foundation (Figure 140).
- Contemporary earth-bermed architecture takes advantage of the smaller conductive losses to the ground. Even a conventional house will benefit from insulated and bermed foundation walls.
- Insulated glass is used in all windows, including those in the doors.
- Wood or insulated windows and doors with thermal breaks and storm sash.
- Thermal breaks are installed wherever masonry comes out of the ground and between all exterior and interior assemblies (Figure 141).

Infiltration

Human beings, no less than any other living thing, need fresh air. In houses, we call this ventilation. When ventilation is unintentional or excessive, we call it infiltration. Every structure will suffer a certain amount of infiltration. The amount will

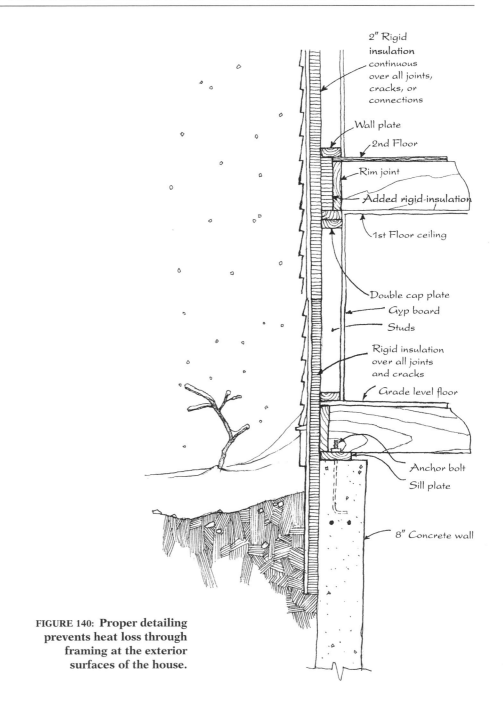

FIGURE 140: Proper detailing prevents heat loss through framing at the exterior surfaces of the house.

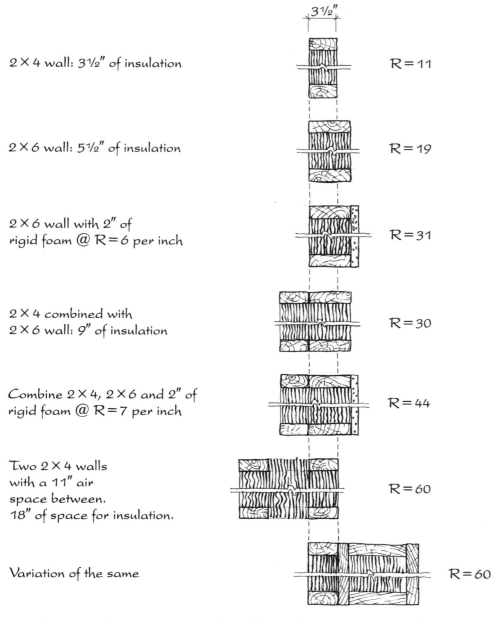

2 × 4 wall: 3½" of insulation   R = 11

2 × 6 wall: 5½" of insulation   R = 19

2 × 6 wall with 2" of
rigid foam @ R = 6 per inch   R = 31

2 × 4 combined with
2 × 6 wall: 9" of insulation   R = 30

Combine 2 × 4, 2 × 6 and 2" of
rigid foam @ R = 7 per inch   R = 44

Two 2 × 4 walls
with a 11" air
space between.
18" of space for insulation.   R = 60

Variation of the same   R = 60

3½"

FIGURE 141: Examples of R-factors developed by adding thickness to a wall assembly. Each example is drawn between two adjacent studs.

depend on the quality of construction and the care taken in design to control leaks like open doors, bathroom venting, kitchen venting, open chimneys, or flues.

There are two ways to calculate infiltration. The easiest, but least accurate, is called the *air exchange method*. It is based on an estimate of the total number of air changes in the space under consideration. This might be an entire house or just a room. The basic equation is:

$$Q_{infiltration} = nV(T_i - T_o)0.018$$

Where:

Q: total infiltration heat losses per hour in BTUH (BTU/hr.)

n   number of air changes per hour

V: total cubic feet of the space

T_i: temperature indoors in °F

T_o: temperature outside in °F

0.018:   a constant equivalent to the number of BTUs required to raise 1 ft.^{3} of air 1°F.

This equation is easy to use because there are few variables to calculate other than the volume and delta T (that's $T_i - T_o$). The big variable is "n," the number of air changes per hour. Since Q (total heat loss) is directly proportional to "n" the difference between 1 and 1.5 or 2 will be substantial.

To give you a feel for it, assume a lower limit to be 0.5 changes per hour and an upper limit to be 2.5 changes. The lower figure might be attained if the house is built with the utmost care and attention to infiltration reduction. This would include the use of high-quality doors and windows, a modern fireplace damper, caulk around all pipe and vent penetrations, check-dampers on all venting appliances, a fastidiously installed vapor barrier, plus about 50 pounds of caulk or foam used at all the joints. The design of the house would include air locks or mud rooms at all entries, an independent air supply for fireplaces, and a site plan that considers the prevailing winds. Such a house would be considered "tight," even *very* tight. While it might have as few as 0.5 air changes per hour, that air would be stale, dank, and filled with unhealthy fumes and odors.

I remember one house built by a friend of mine when superinsulated theory was just becoming popular. He had taken every precaution to insure that there were no air leaks. He had done his job well. But when it was time to tape the gypsum board, he discovered the joint compound wouldn't dry. There was so little fresh air that the moisture had no place to go. He even opened windows and doors, but it didn't help. Finally, he had to rent a dehumidifier.

When a house has so little infiltration, it becomes imperative to supply positive ventilation for reasons of health as well as comfort. In cold regions, an air-to-air heat recovery system is a positive ventilation device that preheats incoming fresh air with the heat captured from the exhausted stale air. In warm regions, cooled make-up air is supplied by air conditioning in the HVAC system.

Now let's look at the other end of the scale. A house over seventy-five years old with double-hung windows, open flues, leaky basement windows, or other construction shortcomings might easily have an exchange rate of around 2 or even 3 air changes per hour. (But if you have an older house, don't automatically assume you have this kind of infiltration.) When the infiltration rates get very high, a heat loss calculation will be meaningless. Because if the air changes are over 2 or 3 per hour, the situation qualifies for what my grandmother used to call "Heating the all of outdoors!"—my apparent intention when I left the door open as a child.

For initial guesstimates, if you want to use an average, start with 1.75 air changes per hour. For older homes you could use 2; for newer, well-built homes, use something more like 1. If you are estimating the infiltration losses in just one room, there is a rule of thumb: the air changes will equal the number of walls exposed to the outside, but never more than 2.

If you just don't feel good about guesstimating the number of air changes, use the more accurate method of calculation called the *crack method*. This method is based on the rate at which air leaks through cracks around windows and doors. It is still just an estimate, but it is more accurate because it is based on actual losses at different temperatures, pressures, and wind speeds. Typical rates of infiltration for different situations are summarized in Table 11.

Of the several formulae for calculating crack-length heat loss, I prefer the following:

$$Q_{infiltration} = (LI/2)(T_i - T_o)0.018$$

Where:

Q:	total infiltration heat losses per hour in BTUH
I:	infiltration rate in cubic feet of air per hour-foot of crack (Table 11)
L:	total number of feet of crack around all penetrations
V:	total cubic feet of the space
T_i:	temperature indoors in °F
T_o:	temperature outside in °F
0.018:	a constant equal to the number of BTUs required to raise 1 ft.^{3} of air 1°F

Although this is only an approximation, it is a good one for residential design.

If you're starting to get the idea that calculating infiltration losses can be complex, while the need for elaborate precision is wanting, you're on the right track. I'm not saying it's unimportant, mind you.

One air change per hour means you are replacing *all* the air in your house with unheated air, *every hour!* This means you

TABLE 11: ESTIMATED INFILTRATION (I) THROUGH CRACKS OF WINDOWS AND DOORS (CUBIC FEET OF AIR/HOUR-FOOT OF CRACK)

Type of Window and Door	Wind Velocity Miles per hour					
	5	10	15	20	25	30
DOUBLE-HUNG, WOOD SASH WINDOWS						
Around frame in masonry wall—not caulked	3	8	14	20	27	35
Around frame in masonry wall—caulked	1	2	3	4	5	6
Around frame in wood frame construction	2	6	11	17	23	30
Total for average window, non-weatherstripped, 1/16" crack and 3/64" clearance. Include wood-frame leakage	7	21	39	59	80	104
Total for average window, weatherstripped, 1/16" crack and 3/64" clearance. Include wood-frame leakage	4	13	24	36	49	63
Total for poorly fitted window, non-weatherstripped, 3/32" crack and 3/32" clearance. Include wood-frame leakage	27	69	111	154	199	249
Total for poorly fitted window, non-weatherstripped, 3/32" crack and 3/32" clearance. Include wood-frame leakage	6	19	34	51	71	92
DOUBLE-HUNG METAL WINDOWS						
Non-weatherstripped, locked	20	45	70	96	125	154
Non-weatherstripped, unlocked	20	47	74	104	137	170
Weatherstripped, locked	6	19	32	46	60	76
ROLLED SECTION STEEL SASH WINDOWS						
Industrial pivoted, 1/16" crack.	52	108	176	244	304	372
Architectural projected, 1/32" crack.	15	36	62	86	112	139
Architectural projected, 3/64" crack.	20	52	88	116	152	182
Residential casement, 1/64" crack.	6	18	33	47	60	74
Residential casement, 1/32" crack.	14	32	52	76	100	128
Heavy casement section, projected, 1/64" crack.	3	10	18	26	36	48
Heavy casement section, projected, 1/32" crack.	8	24	38	54	72	92
OTHER WINDOW TYPES						
Hollow metal, vertically pivoted windows	30	88	145	186	221	242
DOORS						
Well fitted	27	69	110	154	199	—
Poorly fitted	54	138	220	308	398	—

Source: Adapted with permission of the American Society of Heating, Refrigerating, and Air-Conditioning Engineers from the 1981 ASHRAE Handbook—Fundamentals

must completely reheat (or cool) your house once every hour. Of course, things aren't really that bad. This is really just the average for which we design. Actual infiltration is a constantly changing function of wind pressure, temperature difference, construction quality, and patterns of user behavior. Unfortunately, we can only control the last two variables. Sound building practices linked with prudently designed layout will result in the best balance of a tight house and a healthy environment.

(The example we have provided in Appendix 3 uses the air change method *and* the crack method. First, the air change method is used to calculate the total heat loss for the building. This is needed to size the boiler or furnace. Then the crack method is used to calculate the proportional heat loss for each room. This is needed to size the individual radiators or duct registers.)

Good designers acknowledge the importance of infiltration in a number of ways. Streamlined building shape can reduce the impact of wind. The effects of wind can also be mitigated by carefully placed landscaping, trees, and hedges. Earth-bermed architecture can also eliminate infiltration. Porches, airlocks, foyers and entry halls all denote an understanding of the heat loss that results from people coming and going. Design/builders often arrange utility and storage spaces along the north side to buffer the main living areas from any cold air that might leak in. Even if there isn't an explicit design gesture, infiltration must be considered by the design/builder in many smaller construction procedures. A partial short list might include:

- All windows and doors will be weather stripped. The shim space between the jambs and the framing will be filled with foam or caulk.
- Vertical penetrations like chimneys, flues, vent stacks, etc., will be caulked or sealed where they penetrate the exterior wall or roof assemblies.
- Ducts and vents will have check dampers in them to reduce back flow of air.
- Building wraps (Typar™, Tyvek™, etc.) are replacing tar paper as exterior air barriers because they come in 20′ rolls, permitting fewer cracks than the 3′ rolls of building paper.
- Chimneys are fitted with airtight dampers, preferably at the top.
- Make-up air for ventilation systems is brought in through a heat exchanger.
- In some cases, gypsum board may be gasketed to the framing. This is a new method of moisture and infiltration control called the "airtight drywall approach." (A new and economical way to deal with heat loss—see Bibliography.)
- Outlets and switch boxes, when on

exterior walls, are gasketed or sealed to prevent infiltration.
- Storm doors and windows are fitted to all units.

The list could easily go on. Once you become aware of the importance of tight construction, you will find many other little improvements that you can implement as you build.

Convection

Convection is rarely calculated when heat loss is figured. Nevertheless, it's worth mentioning, as it has an appreciable effect. Convection is the transfer of heat by fluids in free contact with solid surfaces. In a house, this happens when the cold air drops off a large window or patio door. The heat in the air is absorbed by the cooler glass. As the air cools it becomes denser. This denser air falls, of course, and thus gives birth to a "draft." By placing a heat register or radiator under the window, we heat the glass and neutralize this phenomenon. The glass is heated so this condition is eliminated. This reduces the production of drafts on the inside. On the outside, however, the warm glass loses its heat to air moving by the building. Indeed, with even a small breeze, the convective heat lost at a window can be substantial. Convective losses, when calculated at all, are found by the formula:

$$Q_{convection} = Ah(T_i - T_o)$$

The usual meaning of the letters applies.

Q: total convection losses per hour in BTUH

h: coefficient of convection in BTU/hr-ft-°F (1-10 depending on wind: 1 = still air, 10 = windy)

A: total area being considered in sq. ft.

T_i: temperature indoors in °F

T_o: temperature outside in °F

The coefficient of convection is a bit of a moving target; it depends on how fast the wind is moving. This is an estimate that the design/builder must make just as we must estimate air changes, or delta T. How wonderfully like a cookbook this engineering is! Everything seems to be an estimate, a rule of thumb, or an approximation.

Convection losses are usually assumed to be covered by the calculations for conductive losses. Nevertheless, let's take a detailed look. If we have a patio door 6′8″ × 5′, that amounts to about 33 square feet. Let's assume it's winter and estimate the temperature to be about 20°F with the wind up around 12 mph. Using a calculation (that no one really wants to see) we get h = 7 BTU/hr – ft² – F. If the indoor temperature is kept at 65°F our delta T = 45°F. The formula tells us how much heat we will be losing from that slider.

$$Q_{convection} = Ah(T_i - T_o)$$
$$= 33 \times 7 \times 45$$
$$= 8,000 \text{ BTUH}$$

While this is only a small fraction of the total heat loss for the house, it is a rather large amount of heat to be simply losing to the breeze! Depending on the efficiency of your heat maker, this amounts to the heat contained in 6 to 8 cubic feet of natural gas, or 2 kw-hours of electricity. Most importantly, this is a *perceivable* heat loss. When standing next to the patio door, you will actually be able to feel the loss of heat. Convective heat loss is controlled through design rather than engineering or radiator sizing. *Where* you place the heater is more important than *how big* it is.

Radiation

The final process by which heat flows from your house is heat radiation. Radiation is the transfer of heat by electromagnetic waves. Although usually not as evident as conduction and convection, radiation takes place all the time. Any heated body, including your own, will give off heat the same way the sun does—radiantly. This means that the heat is sent out like light waves. Heat waves can also be absorbed or reflected just like light waves. This is why some insulation comes with a foil backing. If the foil faces the warm side of the wall and if (and *only* if) there is an air space, the foil will reflect leaking radiant heat back toward the source (Figure 142).

Radiant heat, being an electromagnetic wave, is described by engineering calcula-

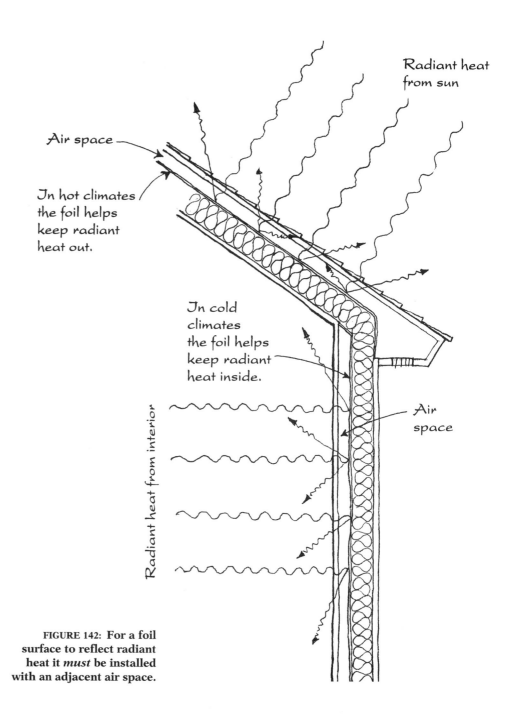

FIGURE 142: For a foil surface to reflect radiant heat it *must* be installed with an adjacent air space.

tions that can get pretty hairy. In the sophisticated solar engineering for energy demonstration projects, radiation losses are always considered. However, the owner/builder's more balanced architecture rarely if ever calls for these complex computations. It's simply not a big enough effect to pay for the engineering. Radiant heat becomes a much bigger issue in hot climates where it is often the primary cause of heat gain. Shading and choice of materials can reduce radiant gain dramatically.

Of the different modes of heat loss, radiant loss has produced the fewest expressive designs. I personally know of no buildings designed around a concern for radiant heat *loss*. On the other hand, radiant *gain* (and its reduction) have precipitated any number of architectural shapes and forms: Overhangs, shadow lines, shutters, etc., are all sculptural responses to radiant heat gain. Moreover, the wide use of low-E glass in our homes is a direct response to this form of heat movement. Generally, windows and glazings are the areas where we can expect impressive developments in radiant heat control. Also "miracle" insulation with foil backings are being used more. These produce real advantages in warm climates, but I've yet to be convinced of their effectiveness in cold ones.

You don't have to be a rocket scientist to understand the consequences of heat loss. Whether it's convection, conduction, radiation, or infiltration, heat loss translates into less comfort for more money. Through trial and experience the design/builder becomes aware of the thermal implications of different design decisions or different methods of construction. Yet for owner/builders, there won't be several projects. There probably will be only one. If this is your situation, you must rely on models and calculations to get a sense of the thermal behavior in your proposed design. The best way to do this is to run several heat loss calculations. Long and cumbersome as this process may appear, it is quick and cheap compared to the alternative.

In Appendix 3 we have run through one example from start to finish. Each formula is explained as it is used. These are not detailed analyses, but the approximate results produced will normally be adequate for sizing equipment. More importantly, the calculations are simple enough for you to run a few times under different weather conditions. This will give you an intuitive sense of what your design decisions mean in terms of energy use and comfort.

HEAT GAIN

You don't have to be living in the sunbelt to be curious about the heat gain in your house. You need only be interested in passive solar heating or figuring the payback on another few inches of insulation or a new air conditioner. Indeed, you might simply be interested in making a very comfortable room on the west side of your home. In these and other situations, you need some way of estimating how much heat will flow *into* the building.

Some situations call for reducing this flow, while others seek to harness it. If the heat is being used as free fuel, you will be calculating *heat gain*. If it's seen as a problem (in a cooling climate) you'll be calculating *cooling load*. Cooling load is the sum of heat gain from the sun plus that generated by equipment and people inside the building.

It shouldn't surprise you to learn that the theory, variables, and calculations for heat gain are basically the same as those for heat loss. Heat moves into the building the same way it moves out, primarily through air infiltration, conductive, and radiant transmission. To calculate cooling loads involves the addition of only a few more considerations:

- The design temperatures are usually 75°F inside and 100°F outside. This gives a delta T of only 25°F.
- Since the sun is the source, radiant heat transfer becomes much more of a factor. Shading and coefficients of emissivity must be figured into the calculations.
- A 30 percent latent heat gain results from keeping moisture and humid-

ity at comfortable levels. When moisture is condensed it gives off heat.

- Each occupant generates about 550 BTUH, depending on the activity they're involved in.
- Most houses have relatively small cooling loads, ranging from 20,000 to 60,000 BTUH. Equipment small enough to meet these demands usually lacks any ability to adjust capacity other than cycling the condenser on and off. Dehumidification takes place only when the unit is on.

The effect of these few additional considerations is substantial. Since heat gain and cooling load are largely the results of conditions outside the house, conditions that change constantly, only a very few days each season will approximate the conditions designed for. In spite of this, it is desirable to specify equipment that is the very smallest that adequately provides comfort and good performance. This aims to keep condenser cycling down while minimizing initial and distributed costs. From the foregoing it should be apparent that accurate cooling load calculation is even more critical in residential applications than in larger nonresidential situations.

Fortunately, the engineering criteria of most houses don't vary that much. Within a climatic region simplified calculations are available from your air conditioning supplier or your local power company.

These make the sizing of air conditioning equipment easy and accurate (enough for our purposes). Since they are designed to sell electricity and air conditioning, however, these sizing methods are somewhat limited. If you want to employ solar design principles, you will need to know a little more about the numbers.

Windows

Although glass represents a thermal hole when you're trying to keep costly heat inside, it is also the best place to collect free solar heat from outside. Any window not facing north constitutes what's called a "direct gain solar configuration" (Figure 143). This means it takes solar energy directly into the house, without the storage or delivery systems found in "active" solar strategies. If there are enough windows in the correct orientation it can add tremendously to the heating of your house during the winter. However, in the summer these same windows can create a furnace, as we shall see.

The main factors contributing to how much solar energy is captured by a window are:

orientation: compass direction, also called azimuth

angle of incidence: acute angle formed between the sun's rays and the plane of the glass

glass absorption: sunlight energy used to heat up the glass

shading coefficient of glass: a constant that accounts for glass thickness and number of panes

transmissivity of the glass: total amount of solar energy that gets through the glass in any form

There are a few other things such as the content of iron oxide in the glass, the ground reflectivity, and the thickness of the glass that also have an effect, though somewhat less. The new glazing films and coatings add yet another level of complexity. You can see that the calculation of heat gain through a window might well be seen as the engineering equivalent of an IRS return! Happily, the American Society of Heating, Refrigeration, and Air-conditioning Engineers (ASHRAE) has combined the ground reflectance and glass type into one term called the *solar heat gain factor*, or SHGF. A partial listing of SHGF values for different orientations of single-paned vertical glazing follows (Table 12).

The units for SHG factors are BTUH/ sq. ft. This turns the heat gain calculations into child's play. The SHGF is simply multiplied by the shading coefficient (SC) to get the heat gain per square foot of glazing. The SC accounts for glass thickness and number of panes (Table 13).

So now, the formula for heat gain through any window can be found with the equation:

$$Q_{sg} = A \times SHGF \times SC$$

Where:

Q_{sg}:	solar gain in BTUs per hour
A:	area of glazing in square feet
SHGF:	the solar heat gain factor in BTUH/sq. ft.
SC:	the shading coefficient, which has no dimensions

To get anything this complex reduced to such simplicity always requires a few assumptions. In this case the assumptions are mostly embodied in the SHGFs provided by the ASHRAE engineers. These values assume a cloud-free clear sky and a ground reflectance of 0.2. The SC assumes there are no coatings on the glass. These are reasonable assumptions and any differences in your particular case are unlikely to be significant.

The real excitement in this exercise occurs when you calculate the heat gained from a window and then subtract that which is lost. Remember at the outset we used the following equation to arrive at the heat loss through any assembly:

$$Q_{conduction} = (T_i - T_o)UA$$

Where:

Q:	conductive heat loss in BTUs per hour (BTUH)
T_i:	temperature indoors in °F
T_o:	temperature outside in °F

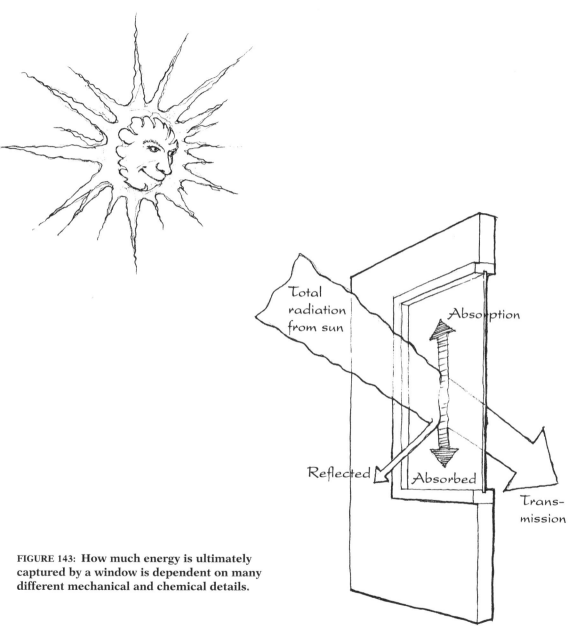

FIGURE 143: **How much energy is ultimately captured by a window is dependent on many different mechanical and chemical details.**

TABLE 12: SOLAR POSITION AND INTENSITY; SOLAR HEAT GAIN FACTORS* FOR 40 DEGREES NORTH LATITUDE

Date	Solar Time A.M.	Solar Position Alt.	Solar Position Azimuth	Direct Normal Irradiation, Btuh/sq ft	N	NE	E	SE	S	SW	W	NW	Hor.	Solar Time P.M.
Jan 21	8	8.1	55.3	141	5	17	111	133	75	5	5	5	13	4
	9	16.8	44.0	238	11	12	154	224	160	13	11	11	54	3
	10	23.8	30.9	274	16	16	123	241	213	51	16	16	96	2
	11	28.4	16.0	289	18	18	61	222	244	118	18	18	123	1
	12	30.0	0.0	293	19	19	20	179	254	179	20	19	133	12
			Half Day Totals		59	68	449	903	815	271	59	59	353	
Feb 21	7	4.3	72.1	55	1	22	50	47	13	1	1	1	3	5
	8	14.8	61.6	219	10	50	183	199	94	10	10	10	43	4
	9	24.3	49.7	271	16	22	186	245	157	17	16	16	98	3
	10	32.1	35.4	293	20	21	142	247	203	38	20	20	143	2
	11	37.3	18.6	303	23	23	71	219	231	103	23	23	171	1
	12	39.2	0.0	306	24	24	25	170	241	170	25	24	180	12
			Half Day Totals		81	144	634	1035	813	250	81	81	546	
Mar 21	7	11.4	80.2	171	8	93	163	135	21	8	8	8	26	5
	8	22.5	69.6	250	15	91	218	211	73	15	15	15	85	4
	9	32.8	57.3	281	21	46	203	236	128	21	21	21	143	3
	10	41.6	41.9	297	25	26	153	229	171	28	25	25	186	2
	11	47.7	22.6	304	28	28	78	198	197	77	28	28	213	1
	12	50.0	0.0	306	28	28	30	145	206	145	30	28	223	12
			Half Day Totals		112	310	849	1100	692	218	112	112	764	
Apr 21	6	7.4	98.9	89	11	72	88	52	5	4	4	4	11	6
	7	18.9	89.5	207	16	141	201	143	16	14	14	14	61	5
	8	30.3	79.3	253	22	128	225	189	41	21	21	21	124	4
	9	41.3	67.2	275	26	80	203	204	83	26	26	26	177	3
	10	51.2	51.4	286	30	37	153	194	121	32	30	30	218	2
	11	58.7	29.2	292	33	34	81	161	146	52	33	33	244	1
	12	61.6	0.0	294	33	33	36	108	155	108	36	33	253	12
			Half Day Totals		153	509	969	1003	489	196	146	145	962	
May 21	5	1.9	114.7	1	0	0	0	0	0	0	0	0	0	7
	6	12.7	105.6	143	35	128	141	71	10	10	10	10	30	6
	7	24.0	96.6	216	28	165	209	131	20	18	18	18	87	5
	8	35.4	87.2	249	27	149	220	164	29	25	25	25	146	4
	9	46.8	76.0	267	31	105	197	175	53	30	30	30	196	3
	10	57.5	60.9	277	34	54	148	163	83	35	34	34	234	2
	11	66.2	37.1	282	36	38	81	130	105	42	36	36	258	1
	12	70.0	0.0	284	37	37	40	82	112	82	40	37	265	12
			Half Day Totals		203	643	1002	874	356	194	171	170	1083	

(Continued) ⑴⑴⑴►

June 21	5	4.2	117.3	21	10	21	20	6	1	1	1	1	2	7
	6	14.8	108.4	154	47	142	151	70	12	12	12	12	39	6
	7	26.0	99.7	215	37	172	207	122	21	20	20	20	97	5
	8	37.4	90.7	246	29	156	215	152	29	26	26	26	153	4
	9	48.8	80.2	262	33	113	192	161	45	31	31	31	201	3
	10	59.8	65.8	272	35	62	145	148	69	36	35	35	237	2
	11	69.2	41.9	276	37	40	80	116	88	41	37	37	260	1
	12	73.5	0.0	278	38	38	41	71	95	71	41	38	267	12
Half Day Totals				242	714	1019	810	311	197	181	180	1121		
July 21	5	2.3	115.2	2	0	2	1	0	0	0	0	0	0	7
	6	13.1	106.1	137	37	125	137	68	10	10	10	10	31	6
	7	24.3	97.2	208	30	163	204	127	20	19	19	19	88	5
	8	35.8	87.8	241	28	148	216	160	29	26	26	26	145	4
	9	47.2	76.7	259	32	106	194	170	52	31	31	31	194	3
	10	57.9	61.7	269	35	56	146	159	80	36	35	35	231	2
	11	66.7	37.9	274	37	39	81	127	102	42	37	37	255	1
	12	70.6	0.0	276	38	38	41	80	109	80	41	38	262	12
Half Day Totals				211	645	986	850	347	197	177	176	1074		
Aug 21	6	7.9	99.5	80	12	67	82	48	5	5	5	5	11	6
	7	19.3	90.0	191	17	135	191	135	17	15	15	15	62	5
	8	30.7	79.9	236	23	126	216	180	40	22	22	22	122	4
	9	41.8	67.9	259	28	82	197	196	79	28	28	28	174	3
	10	51.7	52.1	271	32	40	149	187	116	34	32	32	213	2
	11	59.3	29.7	277	34	35	81	156	140	52	34	34	238	1
	12	62.3	0.0	279	35	35	38	105	149	105	38	35	247	12
Half Day Totals				161	503	936	961	471	202	154	153	945		
Sep 21	7	11.4	80.2	149	8	84	146	121	21	8	8	8	25	5
	8	22.5	69.6	230	16	87	205	199	71	16	16	16	82	4
	9	32.8	57.3	263	22	47	195	226	124	23	22	22	138	3
	10	41.6	41.9	279	26	28	148	221	165	30	26	26	180	2
	11	47.7	22.6	287	29	29	77	192	191	77	29	29	206	1
	12	50.0	0.0	290	30	30	32	141	200	141	32	30	215	12
Half Day Totals				116	300	803	1045	672	221	117	116	738		
Oct 21	7	4.5	72.3	48	1	20	45	41	12	1	1	1	3	5
	8	15.0	61.9	203	10	49	173	187	88	10	10	10	43	4
	9	24.5	49.8	257	17	23	180	235	151	18	17	17	96	3
	10	32.4	35.6	280	21	22	139	238	196	38	21	21	140	2
	11	37.6	18.7	290	23	23	70	212	224	100	23	23	167	1
	12	39.5	0.0	293	24	24	26	165	234	165	26	24	177	12
Half Day Totals				83	143	610	989	783	245	84	83	535		

(*Continued*) ⅢⅢ➡

					N	NW	W	SW	S	SE	E	NE	HOR.	←P.M.
Nov. 21	8	8.2	55.4	136	5	17	107	128	72	5	5	5	14	4
	9	17.0	44.1	232	12	13	151	219	156	13	12	12	54	3
	10	24.0	31.0	267	16	16	122	237	209	50	16	16	96	2
	11	28.6	16.1	283	19	19	61	218	240	116	19	19	123	1
	12	30.2	0.0	287	19	19	21	176	250	176	21	19	132	12
	Half Day Totals				61	71	442	884	798	267	62	61	353	
Dec 21	8	5.5	53.0	88	2	7	67	83	49	3	2	2	6	4
	9	14.0	41.9	217	9	10	135	205	151	12	9	9	39	3
	10	20.7	29.4	261	14	14	113	232	210	55	14	14	77	2
	11	25.0	15.2	279	16	16	56	217	242	120	16	16	103	1
	12	26.6	0.0	284	17	17	18	177	253	177	18	17	113	12
	Half Day Totals				49	54	380	831	781	273	50	49	282	
					N	NW	W	SW	S	SE	E	NE	HOR.	←P.M.

ᵃTotal solar heat gains for DS (⅛ in.) sheet glass. Based on a ground reflectance of 0.20 and values in Tables 1 and 9.
Source: Reprinted with permission of the American Society of Heating, Refrigerating, and Air-Conditioning Engineers. From the 1985 ASHRAE Handbook—*Fundamentals*, 390.

TABLE 13: SHADING COEFFICIENT FOR SINGLE GLASS AND INSULATING GLASS

Type of Glass	Nominal Thickness	Solar Transmittance	Shading Coefficient
Single Glass			
Regular Sheet	⅛ inch	0.87	1.00
Regular Plate/Float	¼ inch	0.80	0.96
	⅜ inch	0.75	0.91
	½ inch	0.71	0.89
Insulating (Double) Glass*			
Regular Sheet	⅛ inch	0.87	0.90
Regular Plate/Float	¼ inch	0.80	0.83

*Factory fabricated units with 3⁄16, ¼ or ½ in air space.

Source: Reprinted with permission of the American Society of Heating, Refrigerating, and Air-Conditioning Engineers. From the 1985 ASHRAE Handbook—*Fundamentals*.

U: thermal conductivity of total wall assembly, BTUH/ft.^{2}–°F (1/R)

A: area of assembly in square feet

And if we combine the equations for gain and loss together we can determine the net heat flow per hour for any given window.

Net Heat

Flow = Heat Gain − Heat Loss

$$Q_{net} = (A \times SHGF \times SC) - (T_i - T_o)UA$$

While this may seem like an unwieldy equation, a few examples will demonstrate how very simple it is to use. Moreover, I think you will be fascinated enough by the results to repeat the exercise for your own designs.

Example

Imagine all the windows in your house are the same size (boring, yes, but it serves the point). You want to figure out how many to place on each side of your house. Let's figure out what the consequences will be on heat and comfort.

Your window's size is 3′ × 4′ (12 sq. ft.) and it's glazed with ½″ Thermopane (this has a ¼″ air space between two ⅛″ panes of glass). The four sides of the house face northeast, southwest, northwest, and southeast. It's at 45° to the cardinal points. You're building on the 40°N latitude and you want to know the situation in February, the coldest month of the year. It's 10 A.M. on February 21, as you start your calculations.

From Table 12 we find the SHGFs to be:

NE 21
NW 20
SW 38
SE 247

and don't forget that these are the total numbers of BTUH per square foot, *if the sky is clear*. Note the difference from one orientation to another. The shading coefficient for your window is .83 or .90 depending on the type of glass. Let's use .90 and call it regular sheet glass. This takes care of the heat gain variables; now let's consider the heat loss.

If the outdoor temperature averages around 0°F during February our delta T will be 65°F. Let's use 70°F as a round number. Finally, the U for your window will be 0.58 (from Table 14), which also means the R value will be R = 1/U = 1.72. If we fill in all the values for the northwest window our equation gives us the bad news:

$$Q_{net} = (A \times SHGF \times SC) - (T_i - T_o)UA$$
$$= (12 \times 20 \times .90) - (70 \times .58 \times 12)$$
$$= 216 - 487.2$$
$$= -271.2 \text{ BTUs!}$$

This is the amount of heat lost through this window in that particular hour on that particular day. Naturally, different results can be expected for different times on different days. Remember also that we are at 40° north latitude. A very different set of results will be found using a chart for 30° north latitude (i.e., New Orleans).

TABLE 14: COEFFICIENT OF TRANSMISSION (U) OF VERTICAL GLASS

Description	$U = \dfrac{BTUH}{FT\,SQ\,°F}$
Single Glass	1.09
Insulating Glass—Double	
¼ inch Air Space	0.63
½ inch Air Space	0.58
Insulating Glass—Triple	
¼ inch Air Space	0.46
½ inch Air Space	0.35
Storm Windows	
¼ inch Air Space	0.55
Glass Block	
6 × 6 × 4 inches Thick	0.58
12 × 12 × 4 inches Thick	0.51

Source: Reprinted with permission of the American Society of Heating, Regrigerating, and Air-Conditioning Engineers.
From the 1985 ASHRAE Handbook—*Fundamentals*.

Well, this is not great but it shouldn't be surprising. After all, the north side of a building never gets direct sunlight in February. The really bad news is that this is as good as it gets. If it clouds up, gets colder, or when night falls, the losses will become even greater. However, put in perspective, this is only about half of the heat generated by one warm body. Insulating shutters could reduce this loss dramatically.

Having looked at the worst case, let's look at the best: a southeast window boasts the highest SHGF. At the same time in February the calculation for this orientation yields the good news:

$$Q_{net} = 2667.6 - 487.20$$
$$= 2180.4 \text{ BTUs (gained during the same}$$
$$\text{hour but on the other side of the house)}$$

Remember that this is absolutely free heat and you'll understand why people are so enthusiastic about passive solar.

The rest of the windows will be left as an exercise for the reader. (Sorry, but I've wanted to do that ever since I was a high school student. I wish I could leave more things as "exercises" for others, don't you?)

This example should make it obvious that the number and placement of windows will have a huge effect on the amount of heat captured by your house. The house in the example was located at N40 latitude (meaning cold) and the south-facing windows, even when they were 45° from true south, contributed measurably to the heating of the house. In less severe climates the contribution is even larger.

It's not hard to imagine calculating the total heat loss for a dwelling and then adding enough windows to supply the needed heat. This thinking is essentially sound, but there are two major complications. First, the heat doesn't arrive in even hourly bundles. So the issue of storage and distribution becomes very important. Second, if your glazing scheme can heat the house in the dead of winter, what will life in those rooms be like during the height of summer? Shading and sun angles can save the day here while also making significant contributions to the architecture.

The issue of storage is usually dealt with in one of two ways. Either there is a special provision for the heat to be stored in nearby mass such as concrete, stone, water, etc., or it is left to the interior structure of the house to absorb, i.e., the walls, floors, and furniture. The following chart can give you a rough idea of what ratio of floor space and glazing area you should keep in different locations (Figure 144).

The chart in Figure 144 results from plotting the following equation for many different values. While you probably won't ever have to use it, it's presented to give you an idea of what affects the heat flow in your house:

$$Adg/Afs = (24Uo(T_i - T_o))/(SHGF \times SC)$$

The different variables represent the following:

Adg: the direct gain area of glass in sq. ft.

Afs: the necessary floor area in sq. ft.

T_i: temperature indoors in °F

T_o: temperature outside in °F

SHGF: the solar heat gain factor in BTUs/day-sq. ft. This is slightly different than the *hourly* SHGF used in the previous example. Here we have averaged all the different SHGF values for the entire day in January.

SC: the shading coefficient, which has no dimensions (Table 13).

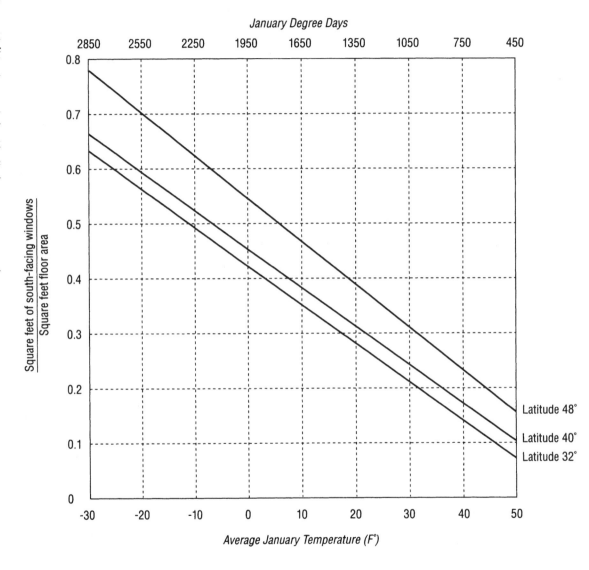

FIGURE 144: **Ratio of direct heat gain in window area to floor area required to heat a residence on a clear day in January.**

24Uo: overall daily building loss per sq. ft. of floor per degree day. This averages out to be around 8 BTU/sq. ft.-degree day for a conventionally built and insulated home.

So how do you use this magic chart? It's actually more of a check against the worst case conditions. Figure out the ratio of glazing to floor area in your design. If it falls on or close to the line for your latitude, you may expect the house to perform well, other things aside. If, however, it falls nowhere close to the line, you should expect to install either a pretty big heater, a lot of air conditioning, or both.

Keep in mind that despite all the numbers we're still working in approximate terms, developing rules of thumb to be used during the initial design phase. These will indicate configurations that should capture enough energy on a clear day to maintain an average interior temperature of 65° during a cold day in January. Internal loads like appliances and human activity could raise this average to 70°F. High winds, excessive infiltration, or poor design might lower it to 60°F or less.

In any case, temperature swings depend on the amount of thermal mass involved. The more mass, the more stable will be the internal temperature. This throws some light on the traditional use of thick adobe walls in the south and the heavy radiators or radiant slab floors in the north.

Other heat-gain considerations that will impact your architecture include sun angles and shading. Whether you are utilizing solar design principles or just designing an air conditioning system, these are major issues. Sun angle and shading should be considered during preliminary design and all the way through design development. Few aspects of house design will bear more fruit for less effort.

Consider our local star (the Sun). It rises low in the east and sets low in the west. Over the course of a day its path takes it high over our house. At noon it reaches its highest point in the sky. This high point changes from month to month. The sun at high noon in the winter is always lower than at high noon in the summer. (See discussion of solar site selection in Chapter 4.) Indeed, nothing is totally identical about the sun's path from day to day or place to place. It's a moving target and it presents itself differently to every location on earth. Still, we can make a few generalizations for everyone:

- The sun's rays will be long and low at sunup and sunset. Windows facing east and west will allow the sun to penetrate deep into the building.
- The sun's rays will be closest to perpendicular, though rarely exactly perpendicular, at noon each day.
- The sun's path will be lower in the sky during the winter, with its lowest course being on the *winter solstice*, December 22.
- The sun's path will be higher in the sky during the summer, with its highest course being on the *summer solstice*, June 22. Indeed, the sun is so high during summer that it rises in the *north*east and sets in the *north*west (see Figure 145).

To be sure, there is much more math and jargon that may be learned if you choose to really study the sun's behavior. If you want a house designed to make fullest use of the sun's energy, a mastery of this math and theory is inevitable (and, happily, pretty simple). Nevertheless, the foregoing basics are all the technical material on sun angles we're going to cover here. It's more than adequate for preliminary design. For final design and fine-tuning I refer you to any of the books in the Bibliography (especially, Don Watson's *Climatic Building Design*).

Each year there are a number of Yestermorrow students who bristle at the idea of designing a 'solar' home:

"Ugly! I don't care how much they save, they are *ugly*. You're not getting me to live in one."

"Yeah," adds another, "they look like huge wedges of cheese!"

"O.K.," I agree, "but we don't have to design them ugly just because others have. Solar homes *can* be well designed." (See illustration on page 277.)

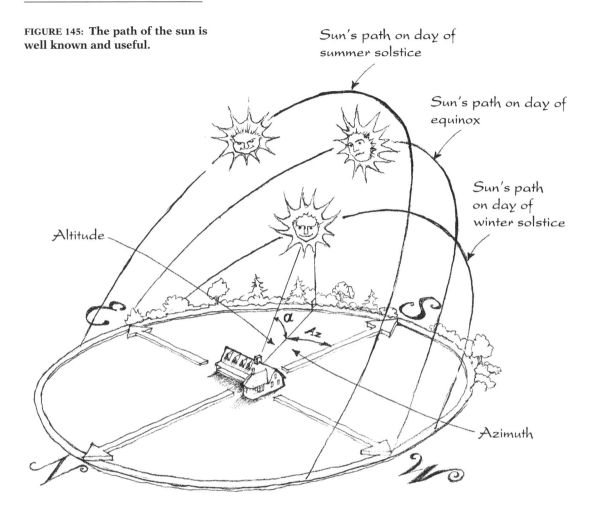

FIGURE 145: **The path of the sun is well known and useful.**

Sun's path on day of summer solstice

Sun's path on day of equinox

Sun's path on day of winter solstice

Altitude

Azimuth

excess heat build up during a summer day. Without a knowledge of sun angles, however, the overhang may be too large, so that the windows end up shaded in the winter as well (Figure 146).

Now, let's consider the rooms to the east and west. There might be a kitchen or breakfast nook on the east, a den or living room to the west. No matter how invigorating sun is in the morning, generally harsh glare is just harsh glare. No matter how unspeakably beautiful a sunset may be, no one will be watching if the room that views it has been turned into an oven during the last few hours of the day. Overhead shading, so effective on the south, is useless against east or west light. It can never project far enough from the building to control the low eastern or western sun. Designers have long known that *vertical* shading works best for low sun. Along with vertical grillwork or appropriate shades deeply set windows can also help control low-angle sun.

The play of daylight across your home is all-important. The patterns of light and shadow are essential to the sculptural qualities of architecture. Unfortunately, the ultraviolet rays that accompany sunlight are unhealthy and destructive. Too much sun will fade the colors in fabrics, prints, and artwork. It is equally damaging to antiques and furniture finishes. Fortunately, technology seems to have addressed this problem. Special films like Heat Mirror, found in Hurd windows, reduces ultraviolet rays by over 99 percent.

Perhaps you don't see yourself living in a solar home, with large planes of sloped glazing and radical angles all about. Fair enough, but even a traditionalist of unwavering resolve has good reason to comprehend sun angles and shading.

Sunlight is a natural element just as helpful and destructive as water. These two have been shaping our vernacular homes since the beginning of time. Understanding sunlight will not only save money and effort, it will provide you with a much, much more *comfortable* home.

For example, consider any room with a view to the south. In northern states, this room is likely to have its share of windows. With proper overhangs, these windows can easily be shaded to prevent

"Kids Brook Residence." This solar greenhouse adds heat, filters gray water, and supports orchids. It was added to an 1830s cape.

Although at the time of this writing, Heat Mirror adds about 30 percent to the cost of a window, if we continue to destroy the ozone layer, this may seem like a pretty good deal.

▦ **Thinking About the Envelope**

Thinking about the building envelope begs some questions. It is an imprecise topic. The envelope of an historic saltbox on the New England coast cannot be considered in the same way as an earth-sheltered home in Minnesota. The envelope issues are location-specific: different in every climate, every region, and with every building technology. It reminds me of the conundrum I face when traveling by plane to a distant city. Which clothes should I pack? I hate being overheated, but being cold is just as bad. I must pack a flexible, adjustable wardrobe.

Envelope design mediates our relationship with the "all of outdoors" as my grandma would say. At the same time, it is a very regional consideration. The envelope must respond to the weather, the geography (did I mention seismic design?), the local materials, and traditional methods. That's in addition to expressing your personal program and architectural tastes.

In summary then:

- Consider "sustainability":
  Conservation of energy is our most
    efficient use of resources.
  Reduce greenhouse gas genera-
    tion.
  Use local building materials.
  Make provisions for flexible heat-
    ing, ventilating, and cooling.
  Adjust thermal mass for comfort.
- Study the technologies that have been in your area the longest. Don't just ape them, *understand* them. Bring them up-to-date. If local tradition uses masonry, figure out why; if it uses wood or some other technology, discover the thinking behind that tradition. Use the underlying principle of traditional building practices to choose from the best envelope strategies currently available.
- Choose materials and methods that serve your needs and your program.
- Consider what the materials suggest

in terms of foundation, wall, and roof design.

- Choose a massing and roof shape that responds to local weather conditions.
- Fenestrate it intelligently with windows that promote human comfort—psychological and physical.

While you're taking all the steps and advice given above, be careful not to let the engineering overpower your design intentions. Of course you want to build a solid, intelligent building that will last hundreds of years, but that doesn't mean you can't express yourself and have a little fun at the same time. Within yesterday's building traditions and tomorrow's technologies, there is still plenty of room for a brand-new building that is yours alone. Keep your eye on your goals. I realize this may be sounding like a golf lesson: *keep your eye on the ball, straighten your elbow, head down, feet aligned, firm grip, etc., etc.—now uncoil smoothly and hit it!* And of course the ball goes about 10′ along with a huge glob of turf. But if all this seems like a lot to consider, just remember, it is no more than what owner/builders have been doing for centuries. We have a little catching up to do, yes, but there's plenty of time.

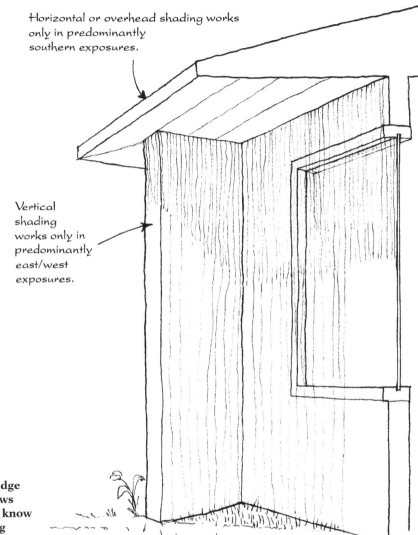

Horizontal or overhead shading works only in predominantly southern exposures.

Vertical shading works only in predominantly east/west exposures.

FIGURE 146: A knowledge of the sun's path allows the design/builder to know which type of shading device to install for each orientation.

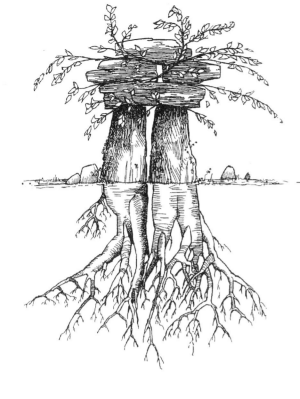

Energy, Choices, and Heating Systems

Two Yestermorrow students from very different backgrounds, Bob and Margaret, are debating different heating fuel choices for their future homes.

"All I know is that I will never consider using gas. I just don't feel safe with it," says Margaret, a Yestermorrow student of late middle age.

"Yes, my wife and I have decided gas *and* oil are out," declares Bob emphatically. "All fossil fuels produce carbon dioxide, which produces global warming."

"So what will you use, electricity? The cost of that is prohibitive. And anyway, they use coal and oil to generate it."

"No, not electricity. I think it's between wood and solar." Young Bob, newly married with no children, is clearly making his decision based on principle. "If there's enough sun in my area, I'll use it. Otherwise, I'll have to use wood."

"Oh, I could never be carrying all that wood around. Imagine the dirt and clutter." Margaret, sixty-two and widowed, is going to choose her fuel based on comfort, first and last. "I've always had oil and I've always liked it. The truck comes and fills up my tank without even asking. They just bill me. I've never run out and I don't have to think about anything but the thermostat."

"Well," Bob ventures cautiously, "maybe thinking about just a bit more might be good."

People can be funny in their attitudes about thermal comfort and the technology that furnishes it. Students arrive at Yestermorrow with all sorts of preconceived notions. Some of these notions come from the media, some from power company marketing, and some from environmental PR. But the most inflexible attitudes often come from years of experience. Like so much of residential design, there is no universal answer. The heating, ventilation, and air conditioning (HVAC) of a house reflects the designer's personality.

In this chapter I hope to show you a designer's approach to the HVAC equipment in your home. It's really not that technical, though numbers and quantities are considered. As with so much of design, the broadest scope of considerations produces the best final solutions.

Consider the envelope. (Chapter 15). How is it fabricated, and of what? Which will be easier to install, ducts or pipes? What's in the walls? How well insulated are they, and with what? Is there a lot of direct solar gain? How will the interior configuration affect air flow?

Consider the heat flow analysis. (Appendix 3). How much heat is lost from each room? How much is gained? What is the total heat loss for the house? And the gain? What will the current cost of heating/cooling the house be? Will it go up or down in the future?

Consider your environmental values. Consider the environmental impact of your HVAC system. Is the fuel renewable? Is manufacturing of the technology environmentally responsible? Would you call your thinking "farsighted" or "short-sighted"? Is there a toxic waste or pollutant associated with your preferred technology? Will it make the world better for your kids? Does it affect the ozone layer, global warming, air quality?

If you are design/building a "solar" house, the considerations listed here will go beyond merely choosing an HVAC system. They will affect and give form to your overall design. They may even be explicitly expressed in your architecture. Your envelope, heat flow analysis, and distribution system are likely to be more highly considered from the outset. Building your solar design will beg many of the same ethical questions associated with a conventional design. For instance, rigid foam insulation conserves energy, but the manufacture of certain types destroys the ozone layer. Most wood-burning stoves pollute, even though wood is a renewable fuel. Ethical conflicts and issues still remain to be solved, even for enlightened designers. "Green," or "sustainable" design is among the fastest-changing areas of today's architecture.

Consider your fuel choice. Any fuel can provide heating and/or cooling (with the possible exception of using wood to run your air conditioner). Is your fuel choice locally available? Who provides it and how dependable are they? Is the price likely to go up or down predictably? What are the regional side effects of bringing this fuel to market? What is the impact of storing this fuel on your premises? Can you and your family feel safe with this fuel; are there safety precautions?

Consider the distribution system. As we discussed in the previous chapter, there are several ways of moving heat: conduction, convection, and radiation. How you move heat into or out of a space depends on the distribution system. Is it a forced-air system? baseboard hot water? radiant floor? radiant ceiling? a fan-coil unit? Is there a noise associated with the delivery? How fast does it respond to the thermostat? Can it handle heating, cooling, filtering, and humidity control? Along with cost (always a criteria), style and performance should be primary concerns. Your choice of distribution system will determine how your HVAC looks as well as how it works.

These five considerations may fall in a different order of importance for each reader. That's fine. Moreover, there may be special factors like health or family tradition that play a role. Nevertheless, this handful of concerns is a solid basis for evaluating any HVAC strategy. Since we have already considered the envelope and the heat flow analysis in a previous chapter, let's start with a discussion of environmental ethics and fuel choice.

Some Heavy Questions

As the world gets smaller, environmental concerns are bound to infuse every aspect of our lives. Questions concerning the use of certain building materials revolve around the issue of "sustainability." Questions concerning fuels and energy also revolve around the issue of "renewability." Renewable fuels are those that replenish themselves regularly and may be considered inexhaustible. The influx of solar energy and the continual growth of trees are two common examples of renewable fuels. Technically, all fuels are indirectly "solar" fuels, and thus renewable. The sun's energy produces the wind (windmills), the hydrocycle (hydroelectric), photosynthesis (biomass), and the very light itself (photovoltaic). Even oil, coal, and natural gas are the products of an ancient geological chemistry that was initiated with sunlight. But coal, oil, and gas are not considered renewable fuels, as the accompanying chart should make clear (Figure 147).

Anything that dwindles in supply becomes more expensive as it does so.

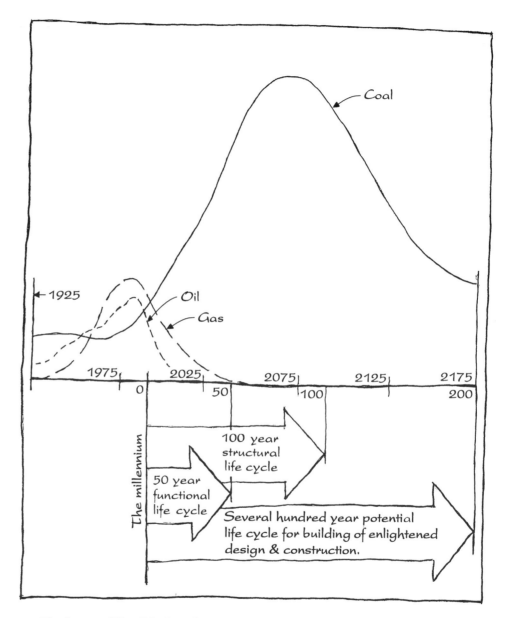

FIGURE 147: **The future of fossil fuels is dim and getting dimmer. Buildings constructed today will outlast the fossil fuels we use to operate them. Many design decisions that look good today will prove foolish over the long life of a well-built house.**

Hence, even a simple bottom line calculation reveals the stupidity of using nonrenewable fuels. But the ethical questions do not arise from the bottom line. It is the environmental destruction, irreversible and global, that every design/builder using fossil fuels must address. As we struggle to extend our conventional fuel supplies our drilling and mining is systematically trashing the environment: the oceans, the Arctic, the mountains, etc. Moreover, when we *burn* any fuel, even at 100 percent efficiency, we produce "greenhouse" gases (CO, CO_2) that are dramatically changing our global atmosphere.

"But certainly one boiler isn't going to end the world." (Margaret is getting nervous.)

"My furnace is already installed. You can't expect me to actually take out a perfectly good furnace?" (Ralph is incredulous.)

Every time an oil, gas, or coal heating unit is installed, it adds one more vote in favor of environmental pillage. Inconsequential as one little furnace may seem, put together with all the rest they constitute a huge "installed market." The bigger the installed market, the more reason to look in Alaska, the Grand Canyon, or the Antarctic for oil. I never present these unsettling facts without observing some discomfort on the faces of a certain portion of the students.

"I don't want to be a bad guy," says a yuppie from Washington, D.C., "but the cost of heating and cooling a home with alternative fuels is still not really justifiable, is it?"

"And anyway, there's really not enough sun in my part of the country," says another.

"Burning wood causes just as much pollution as fossil fuels, maybe more now that they have high-efficiency boilers," rationalizes a third.

This is a tough issue and a full discussion of global ethics is beyond the scope of this book. Still, I'll gladly admit to some personal opinions and preferences. Indeed, as the writer I am tempted to take this opportunity to press them on you. But don't panic; I won't. Ethics are too important to treat as a trendy debate. Moreover, it involves far more than personal likes and dislikes. Ethics is the study of right and wrong. Environmental ethics, therefore, is the study of what is right or wrong for life on our planet. This is a complex subject and the right path is not always clear. Even if we don't have all the answers, we must at least be aware of the issues. As an owner/builder, you and your children will live with the decisions you make.

Energy Sources

Not all energy is used for heating or cooling, as the illustration shows (Figure 148): Although heating and cooling account for the majority of energy use, there are other areas of significant consumption.

The materials and methods used in the construction of a house represent a hefty amount of energy already spent, called *embodied energy*. We've already mentioned the energy necessary to transport materials. It takes energy to extract a material from the environment. Then it takes energy to refine the material and put it in a usable form. Materials such as aluminum take vast amounts of electricity to manufacture and bring to service. Wood, on the other hand, has a relatively low embodied energy. Materials must be cut, shaped, and tooled with different energy-consuming methods. Lastly, there is the energy needed to place the materials in the building. All of these "hidden" energy requirements must be met whenever you specify a material or product. Imagine how things would change if people were mindful of *all* the energy used to build a house (Table 15).

Not all fuels are created equal. Some fuels have more energy content and some fuels release their energy more easily. The efficiency of boilers, furnaces, stoves, and air conditioners vary widely. The following table gives a rough idea of simple heating potential for different fuels (Table 16).

Unavoidably, this is an "apples and oranges" comparison, but I think it's a good starting point. Apparently electricity is the most costly and the most efficient. But this, in actual fact, is not so!

ELECTRIC POWER (NOT REALLY A FUEL)

The electricity that arrives at your home is normally generated at about *30 percent*

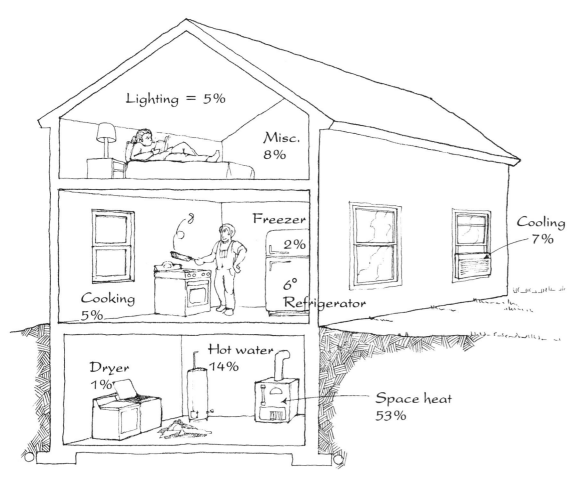

Lighting = 5%

Misc. 8%

Freezer 2%

Cooling 7%

Cooking 5%

6° Refrigerator

Dryer 1%

Hot water 14%

Space heat 53%

FIGURE 148: Approximate energy use breakdown for a typical single family home.

over a grid by centralized utility companies. The initial cost of installing electric heat or air-conditioning (AC) is usually quite low. For that reason, developers often specify it. Within a year, however, the high operation costs will make electric heat or AC far more expensive than any other fuel choice. This goes on for the life of the system and at the ever increasing cost charged by the utility.

Electricity is typically used to generate "resistance heat." This is exactly the same as what takes place in your toaster or hair dryer. Electricity is forced through high resistance tungsten wires, which turn red hot. There is, however, a better way. (Not for making toast, maybe, but for heating your house.) Heat pump technology, which has been around for years, really became popular when energy costs began to climb. The heat pump is just what the name implies. Using compressor technology like that in your refrigerator or air conditioner, the device "pumps" heat into or out of your home, depending on the season. Thus a heat pump cools in the summer (by pumping heat outdoors) and heats in the winter (by pumping heat indoors). It is most efficient in moderate climates and not useful at all in extreme climates. At 40°N latitude (i.e., Reno, Denver, Philadelphia) it is about twice as efficient as straight resistance heating.

Pollution and cleanup are costs associated with any fuel used to generate electricity in a centralized plant. These costs are usually ignored in order to give a more

efficiency and it loses another 3 percent in distribution. This clean, easy fuel, once the promise of our most futuristic American Dream, has revealed itself to be the most expensive and possibly the most environmentally taxing. Electricity can be generated with fossil fuels, nuclear fuels, hydrogenerators, wind generators, photovoltaic cells, or trash-fueled steam genera-

tors. Each of these sources has different economic and environmental impacts. For example, photovoltaic cells and wind generators are localized sources of electricity. They have a relatively high initial cost and then operate almost for free. However, the vast majority of electricity is generated by coal or oil-fired and hydroelectric generators. This power is sold

TABLE 15: TOTAL ENERGY EMBODIMENT IN SELECTED BUILDING MATERIALS (SHOWN IN BTU PER UNIT OF MATERIAL, AT JOB SITE)

Material	Unit	Total Embodied Energy (BTU per unit, at job site)
Wood products:		
Lumber	Board foot	7,600–9,800
Shingles		7,300
Flooring		10,300–14,300
Mouldings		17,900
Glulam		16,700
⅜″ plywood (softwood)	Square foot	5,000–5,800
Paints	Gallon	437,000–508,500
Asphalt roofing:		
Rolls	Square foot	7,800–11,000
Shingles		25,600–29,700
Mineral-surfaced insulating board siding		67,500
Glass:		
Flat glass: double strength	Square foot	15,430
Flat glass: tempered		72,600
Plate and float glass, ⅛″ to ¼″ thick		48,000
Laminated plate glass, ¼″ and over		212,500
Stone and clay products:		
Common brick	Per brick	14,300
Ceramic-glazed brick		33,413
Quarry tile	Square foot	51,000
Ceramic mosaic tile and accessories, glazed		63,600–68,700
Concrete block	Per block	31,800
Ready-mix concrete	Cubic yard	2,594,300
⅜″ gypsum board	Square foot	5,300
Mineral wool insulation, 4½″ thick	Square foot	8,300

Source: Reprinted by permission of John Wiley and Sons. From McGuinness and Stein, *Mechanical and Electrical Equipment for Buildings*, 6th ed., p. 18.

rosy picture of the technology and of the plant. Even with a heat pump, the efficiency of electricity as a fuel only approaches 60 percent of the original fuel capacity used to generate it; worse if the electricity is generated by a nuclear power plant. Nuclear power generation has so many inherent and related problems that the cost to produce one kilowatt is really hard to assess.

It must be said that electricity, once generated, is without peer as the cleanest and most refined energy. It is capable of things that no other fuel can offer. Try running your stereo with coal or operating a garage door with cordwood! Electricity accomplishes some really wonderful things in today's home. It can power a television set with somewhat less than 30 watts; it can run your computer with about 200 watts; and it enables a telephone conversation on barely 15 watts. As a fuel for heating, however, I am always reminded of one Vermont engineer's assessment:

TABLE 16: ENERGY CONTENT OF DIFFERENT FUELS

Fuel Source	Unit Cost	Energy Value per Unit	% Efficiency	Quantity of Fuel Necessary to Provide One Million BTUs of Usable Heat	Cost to Provide One Million BTUs of Usable Heat
anthracite coal	$0.08 per lb.	12,000 BTU/lb	65–75%	111–128 lbs.	$8.33–$9.62
natural gas	$0.008697 per cu. ft.	1,000 BTU/cu. ft.	70–80%	1,250–1,428 cu. ft.	$10.87–$12.42
wood pellets	$0.07 per lb.	8,000 BTU/lb.	80%	156 lbs.	$10.55
heating oil	$0.699 per gallon	140,000 BTU/gal.	70–80%	8.9–10.2 gals.	$6.24–$7.13
mixed hardwood	$110 per cord	21,400,000 BTU/cord	50%[a]	.0934 cords	$10.28
white oak	$170 per cord	30,800,000 BTU/cord	50%[a]	.065 cords	$11.04
softwood	$95 per cord	15,800,000 BTU/cord	50%[a]	.1266 cords	$12.03
electricity	$0.09–$0.10 per kwh[c]	3,414 BTU/kwh	95–100%[b]	292.9–308.3 kwh	$29.06–$30.59

[a]Based on air tight "smolder" burning stoves < 900°   [b]Does not include off-sight production efficiencies.   [c]Depends on volume and peak/off-peak season.   Source: Author.

"Crimminy, heatin' with electricity is like cuttin' butter with a chain saw!"

COAL (NONRENEWABLE); GREENHOUSE GASES

Although coal has been a "modern" fuel since before we settled the New World, it doesn't enjoy much current popularity. There was a time, about a century ago, when coal was *the* fuel of choice. It was purchased and delivered by the ton. Coal stoves can still be found in some Victorian homes, but they are rarely used.

Coal is dirty. This is the main reason coal fell from favor. It is dirty before it is burned and it's dirty afterward. Though coal has a high energy content per pound, it is still bulky. Movement and storage invariably produce great quantities of dust and dirt. Moreover, it is hard to light. You have to make a wood fire first, just to get the coals started. Thus, in addition to being dirty, coal can also be difficult.

All the same, coal is enjoying a comeback. For one thing, there are more coal resources remaining than any of the other nonrenewable fossil fuels. By our former reasoning, this means that coal ought to be the least expensive of the fossil fuels. Unfortunately, it is still bulky to handle and difficult to ignite. To address these shortcomings, the coal industry has devised ways of distilling liquid fuels from solid coal. These liquid derivatives are as easy to handle and burn as natural gas and oil. Unfortunately, the cost of the refining makes the distillates just as expensive as these other fuels. Where coal really shows some promise is when it is compared to wood. Pound for pound coal has much more energy than wood. Moreover, wood is perhaps the only other fuel that is even more awkward to handle.

So if you're living in an area where there is coal available—Ohio, Pennsylvania, West Virginia—it might be worth considering. Call up the suppliers and get the cost per ton. Ask for the price history, i.e., how frequently has the price gone up in the last five years? ten years? fifteen years? You can probably learn who sells the latest coal burning heaters from these same folks. This technology has evolved considerably. Today you can purchase coal burners of different sizes, with automatic loaders, reburning chambers, draft inducers, etc. All these innovations combine to make the burning of coal a much more convenient and economical enterprise than it used to be. Spurred by these developments, and the 1973 oil embargo, many suppliers of conventional fuels have added coal to their offerings.

OIL (NONRENEWABLE); GREENHOUSE GASES

Oil is still the heating fuel of preference for most Americans. Combining ease of handling, high energy content, clean-burning characteristics, and competitive pricing (subsidized by your tax dollars), this fuel is hard for most users to give up. People hate to hear that drilling will soon commence in the fishing grounds, the national parks, and the nature preserves; still they shake their heads as if to say:

"What else can we do? Burning oil is the only way of life for us."

Though the majority of oil is used in transportation and industry, the third largest use is space heating. Is this the best use for this nonrenewable resource? I think not. We should be confining the use of nonrenewables to those situations for which we have developed no substitute. Eventually we must understand that oil will run out. It will become an exotic substance. This is not the distant future I'm talking about. Oil will probably cease to be available within the lifetime of every properly built home currently on the drawing table.

The oil industry has made efforts to put off their day of reckoning. Oil furnaces and boilers have recently been developed that burn at over 90 percent efficiency. This will prolong the usefulness of the technology at least as a backup source of heat. However, even at these efficiencies, any oil system installed today is guaranteed to be a growing expense within the next twenty-five years.

GAS (NONRENEWABLE)

Gas comes in several forms: natural gas, propane, liquid petroleum (LP gas), and methane. Only the methane is renewable. While the heat content of these gases may differ, the basic virtues of using these fuels are the same: They are clean and highly efficient. In large cities one can often buy gas from centralized utilities with supply lines under the roadways, just like water and sewage. In rural areas, LP gas or propane is delivered in tanks. Like oil, these tanks are kept full with regular deliveries from your supplier.

Gas-heating technology has become so advanced that the combustion efficiencies are starting to compete with electricity. When electricity's off-site costs are considered, gas is far more efficient. Today's high-efficiency boilers and furnaces don't actually burn the gas at all, they explode it the way a car's engine does. Some of these so called "pulse" units have efficiencies above 95 percent. Gas is also a fuel that enjoys several applications besides heating. Many people prefer gas cookstoves. Also available are gas clothes dryers, air conditioners, refrigerators, and even air conditioners. While electric models are also available, none of these appliances come in models powered by oil, wood, or coal. For many people this can be a deciding factor. Doing many things with one fuel is often more attractive than running supply lines or getting deliveries for each different use.

If there is a favored child in the gaseous family of fuels, it has to be methane. This gas is generated whenever organic material composts. Current research is exploring ways to collect it from beneath our landfills. It has been generated and used by resourceful farmers for years. In its liquid form, methanol, it makes a fine substitute for gasoline. It is the primary fuel in Brazil. In America, however, it is hardly available. Most likely this will continue to be the case until the oil industry figures out how to control its production. Nevertheless, since it comes from organic matter, it is renewable. That means its wider use will be good for everyone, no matter who's controlling the business.

WOOD (RENEWABLE)

Because of recent developments, wood is now one of our nation's most viable heating fuels. Of course, burning cordwood in a fireplace or stove is nothing new. These are traditional and even somewhat romantic approaches toward heating. While wood-burning stoves are more popular than ever, they are often considered as backup heat only. Somehow wood is still not widely embraced as a central heat source. Why? Probably because it doesn't respond to one of the basic promises of our Great American Dream: the promise of *convenience*. Our expectations of a house do not include too much "effort." We see our dream homes as large appliances that take care of our every need. The idea of cutting, storing, and loading wood into a stove is not part of this image. So wood heat is relegated to backup status. "Designer" wood-burning stoves with nickel-chrome details, glass doors, and clever draft controls have become very popular. Unfortunately, they have done little to advance the understanding of how to use wood as a primary fuel.

Airtight stoves merely smolder the wood. At best they burn at about 800°F. This is a very inefficient way to burn wood. It is a practice held over from early days when wood was almost the only heat source. Back then it was important (meaning convenient) to have hot coals when you awoke each morning. Coals made it easy and fast to rekindle the fire each morning. But the price paid for this convenience was poor efficiency, pollution, lots of ash, creosote, and chimney fires. Today we know that the best way to burn wood is at about 2,000°F using a draft inducer (electric fan or bellows). By this means there is almost no ash or creosote, no pollution, and over 80 percent of the available BTUs are extracted from the fuel. I heat my office with this technology and I can say that it is a joy every time the chimney sweep comes by.

"Want me to look at your main flue?" he always inquires. "No charge if it doesn't need cleaning. Can't be too careful with creosote, y'know."

"Sure, sure," I respond. "And check the fireplace chimney as well." At the end of the day he always shows up with his final bill and a perplexed look.

"You sure you didn't have someone else clean out that main flue recently? It's mighty clean for this late in the heating season."

While there is no question that I get the most heat from my wood, not everyone would call it convenient. They say wood is the one fuel that will warm you three times: Once while you're splitting it, once while you're stacking it, and a third time when it's burned. If you heat with wood, it must be incorporated into your life-style. The handling of the wood becomes an annual ceremony, like raking leaves in the fall. Stoking the furnace becomes a welcome break in the day's routine, like getting a glass of water or answering the telephone. Wood heat can also be made more convenient through appropriate design. Wood storage, stove access, clean outs, ash heaps, etc., etc., all need to be considered when designing a wood-fueled heating system.

I placed my wood-fired boiler in a utility room just off the back porch, by the backdoor. I can get to it from inside or outside. The wood is stored on the porch so it's accessible and easy to throw in whenever I'm on the way in or out.

In very cold regions, wood heat usually requires a backup system. Otherwise, you must draft a neighbor to keep the fires banked anytime you wish to be gone for more than a day. Most serious wood boilers or furnaces are equipped with a gas or oil backup burner.

These days you needn't be Paul Bunyan to heat with wood. The awkward storage and handling of cordwood has been overcome with wood pellets. "Pelletized" wood can be stored and stoked the same way coal has been for years, with automatic feeders. Pelletized wood is the result of new harvesting and industrialized burning techniques. Rather than cut into cordwood, timber is chipped at the time of harvest. Chipping has the advantage of allowing recycled paper, inferior tree species and damaged timber to be utilized as fuel. These raw materials are ground into sawdust, mixed with binders, and pressed into pea-sized pellets. In effect, the wood has been made granular, like a seed. Also, the energy content per volume is more uniform. This form of wood can be loaded into a burning chamber using an adjustable auger just like those used to feed coal burners (Figure 149).

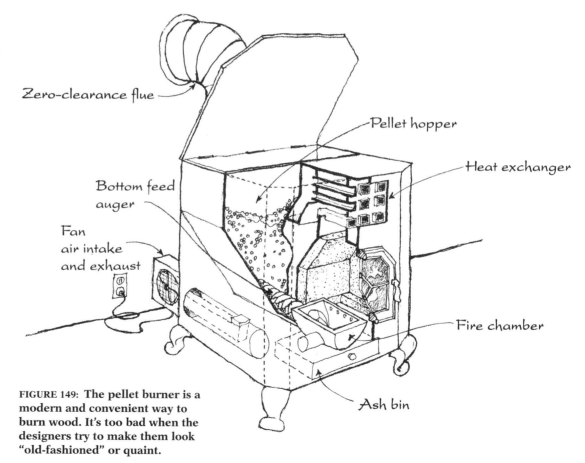

Zero-clearance flue

Bottom feed auger

Fan air intake and exhaust

Pellet hopper

Heat exchanger

Fire chamber

Ash bin

FIGURE 149: **The pellet burner is a modern and convenient way to burn wood. It's too bad when the designers try to make them look "old-fashioned" or quaint.**

Fabulous! We now have a renewable resource, wood, that is convenient, automatic, and uses recycled content. The American Dream goes sustainable! Unfortunately, the cost of pelletizing still makes it almost as expensive as oil. Moreover, all the stoves designed for pelletized fuel are ugly (to my eye). It shouldn't be long, however, before the economics and technology mature. The *new* American Dream is now mandating something convenient, clean, and *renewable*. Although wood continues to be the only fuel that heats three times, we now have the option of letting it heat once and for all.

FIREPLACES

There was a time, before the wood-burning stove, when most wood was burned in fireplaces. Long before they invaded the wooded shores of this country, Europeans were heating their masonry mansions with nothing more than a small bonfire burning in the center of the room. Smoke was a big problem (Figure 150).

Eventually, fireplace design evolved, and, along with a properly constructed flue, campfire technology became highly sophisticated. Fireplaces have long been built with special care and knowledge of proportions and angles. These fireplaces not only drew well, they radiated a smoke-less heat well into the room rather than taking it all up the chimney. By the late sixties, however, the development of mod-

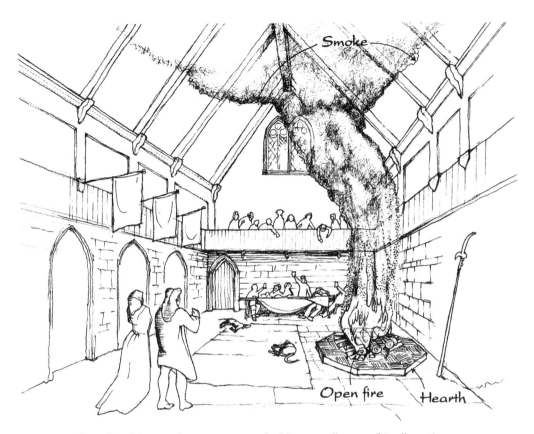

FIGURE 150: Before the chimney there was no such thing as a "no smoking" section.

ern heating alternatives had pushed the art of building a proper fireplace into obscurity. Responding to this situation, Vrest Orton wrote his much needed little book, *The Forgotten Art of Building a Good Fireplace* (Appendix 10). This book, along with the following diagram, should be all anybody needs to build a proper functioning fireplace (Figure 151).

Such a fireplace, besides being a romantic and comforting hearth in your home, will also add a perceptible warmth and reduce your heating bills in fall and early spring. The fireplace will never be the most efficient use of wood, but it will always be the most pleasant.

SOLAR (RENEWABLE)

Heating and cooling with the sun's energy is not new. Indeed, it is the single oldest means of making our homes comfortable.

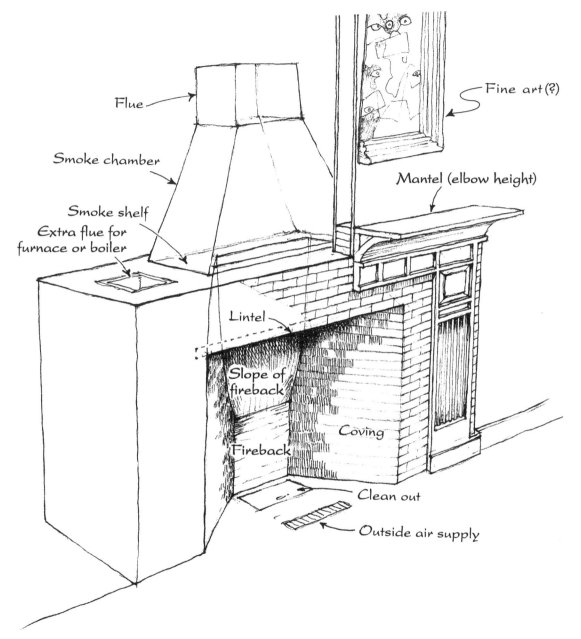

Flue

Smoke chamber

Smoke shelf
Extra flue for
furnace or boiler

Fine art (?)

Mantel (elbow height)

Lintel

Slope of
fireback

Coving

Fireback

Clean out

Outside air supply

FIGURE 151: The basic components of the modern, well-proportioned fireplace and flue.

Nevertheless, in our short industrialized history it has become so totally eclipsed by the use of fossil fuels that many now think of it as "alternative." Happily, this misconception is being corrected.

Like the heat pump, solar performance is dependent on the local weather. It works best where there is plenty of insolation (sunlight), and it works most dramatically where cold temperatures and snow accompany clear sunny skies. Thus we find solar heating has become very "normal" in the high-altitude communities around the Rocky Mountains. California has outlawed the use of anything but solar for heating swimming pools. Florida has been using collectors to heat their domestic hot water since before the turn of the century. In areas where there is ample sun, solar is used regularly on large commercial buildings as well as residences.

The solar renaissance is good for all of us. Its success in the sunny regions of our country has made it a conventional fuel once again. Design/builders can look for a solar installer in the yellow pages the same way they might look for a plumber. Today's solar technicians "know their stuff," and the technology of their trade continues to advance remarkably. The number crunching needed to determine how many collectors you will need or your mass-to-glass ratio is now all very well worked out. Accurate rules of thumb have demystified the sizing procedures. All this means solar heat, whether it's "active" or "passive," can be embraced reliably and at a reasonable price.

Passive solar heat is the energy captured with just windows and building configuration. For example, a greenhouse, south-facing windows, or a long east/west massing are all passive solar features. The engineering now exists to predict exactly how many BTUs a given shape or glazing scheme will contribute toward your heating needs. In Appendix 3 we present simple calculations for finding the heat gain/loss through any window. For a more comprehensive explanation of the full-scale calculations (all simple math), relevant books are included in the Bibliography. There are also some fairly sophisticated programs available for those with a personal computer.

Active solar refers to any of a variety of devices used to capture the sun's energy and store it for later use. The descriptor, "active," refers to the fans, pumps, and other mechanical devices used to control the flow and storage of heat. The most common active systems employ solar collectors for heating domestic hot water or swimming pools. Less common but still "active" arrangements include fan-driven Trombe walls and double-envelope designs. Also, tracking reflectors and photovoltaic arrays are active systems. Generally, active systems *use* energy (in fans, motors, and pumps) to *collect* energy (with collectors, reflectors, and trackers).

Some of the more interesting systems are "hybrids," using a combination of technologies. For example, some of our instructors built a south-facing structure where the domestic water was heated by the sun and the living space was heated by wood. They used home-built collectors and a power-drafted boiler like the one discussed above. All the pumps and fans were powered by electricity produced by a wind generator. One of our students was inspired. He designed and built a house that uses solar heat with gas backup. His pumps run off a wind generator that is backed up by batteries and the grid. Another is using photovoltaics for everything, including the actual construction of the building. He has a large battery bank that is backed up by a Honda generator. His utility bill for six months is about the same as what it costs me to fill up the gas tank in my truck! All three of these systems belong to "tinkerers," so they are perhaps a touch more complex. A good hybrid system for most people should subscribe to the KISS principle (see Glossary). This means primarily *passive* design with a few *active* devices to increase human comfort.

Active solar is really an engineer's delight and a tinkerer's dream. There is much to calculate and plenty to "rig up" and monitor. Numbers predict expectations and graphs give everything a visual effect; thermostats, dials, pumps, and fans can be added to your heart's delight. I should know; I am a sucker for active systems. When they are working it is pure magic. Think of it: *free energy!* But I warn you, things can turn messy in a minute. Pumps can fail, collectors can overheat, dampers may jam, etc. No active system is ever as simple and elegant as a well-designed window. Though I'm attracted by the excitement that surrounds innovation, today's solar collectors are so reliable that they hardly *seem* innovative. They just seem smart. I now specify them routinely, without any fuss. In contrast, photovoltaics are still an emerging technology. I would give anything for a P.V. array on my roof—even though I live in the cloudiest area east of the Rockies! I could tinker to my heart's content. I mention all this for the benefit of readers similarly afflicted. So if you find hybrid solar romantic or adventuresome, remember what it will take to follow it through.

Mainstream solar technology is no longer an "alternative." It is just like gas or oil technology: well understood and available from a variety of vendors and installers. The equipment is reliable and the performance can be assured. Guarantees and warranties are normal. Repair and maintenance can usually be had from the installer. For anyone building in the sunny regions of this country, this clean, renewable, and affordable energy resource is the only way to go. (Books in the Bibliography will equip you with the information needed to install your own or become an informed buyer.)

ALTERNATIVE ENERGY (RENEWABLE)

Alternative energy sources include photovoltaic, hydroelectric, wind, methane, and some forms of active solar. However, *alternative* is a misleading term. It suggests that energy from these technologies is somehow different from that supplied by the conventional fossil fuels. Not so! A BTU is a BTU, even if the ones gleaned from the sun or wind seem warmer than those metered out by the utilities. Perhaps it would be better to call these technologies *low-polluting*, since compared to more "conventional" modern technologies, these sources of energy have a reduced impact on our environment. However, since these sources are often decentralized, they cannot supply energy instantly or constantly the way centralized utilities can. You cannot always flip a switch and count on wind, water, or sun.

Because of their dependence on the whims of weather, low-polluting energy systems require storage. If we are heating or cooling, the storage is called "thermal mass," and typical examples include water, stone, concrete, or tile. If we're talking about generating electricity using systems such as wind generators, small hydro generators, or photovoltaics, the storage will likely be batteries or the grid. (Provisions exist in some areas that allow homeowners to sell their low-pollution-generated energy back to the utilities!) In any event, the larger the storage capacity, the more reliable the low-polluting energy system becomes. If the wind stops blowing or the sun is clouded over, it is the storage or backup that must carry the dwelling until things improve. If the storage is inadequate, the homeowner must go without.

For almost any reasonably sized storage, there is the rare weather sequence that outlasts its capacity. However, if the dwelling is within reach of centralized energy sources, it is easy to design in backup power. Many people with wind generators or photovoltaics use the "grid" as a backup and as storage (instead of batteries). Those relying on solar collectors often use a gas or oil burner when the sun disappears.

Low-polluting energy sources are an excellent investment. Although they are sometimes more costly at installation, they rely on a free source of fuel. Typically, they pay for themselves in under five years. When hidden and lifetime costs of other fuels are compared to the "alternatives," it is clear that even the most efficient conventional fuel technology is wasteful and expensive.

SOLAR COOLING

Maybe it's because the sun delivers only heat that so many students are surprised by the opportunities for using solar and low-polluting energy systems for *cooling*. Because of its prominence in hot regions, the sun should be understood and harnessed even more readily than in cold regions. What a resource! Here are a few examples:

- *Ventilation:* Ventilation is central to any cooling strategy. Happily, much basic air movement can be accomplished using active or passive techniques. Actively, photovoltaics can supply electricity to operate fans, pumps, and air-conditioning. Passively, airflow can be created by properly designed solar chimneys, monitors, or cupolas. These generate gravity, or "chimney," effect that pulls cool air in at the bottom to replace the hot air being ejected above (see illustration on page 292).
- *Earth Tubes:* Earth tubes use gravity-induced airflow to pull air through long, terra-cotta channels buried in the earth. As air travels through these channels, it is cooled, while humidity is absorbed by the material.
- *Evaporative Cooling:* An ancient form of air-conditioning was accomplished by passing hot air over a body of water or even a moist cloth. The "heat transpiration" required for the moisture to evaporate would actually result in a lowering of the temperature in the air. Since, in this technique, the air picks up moisture, it is particularly favored in hot, *dry* regions.

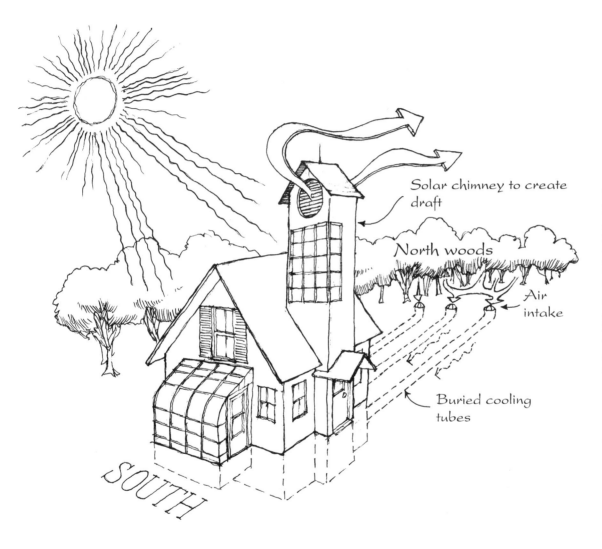

Solar chimney to create draft

North woods

Air intake

Buried cooling tubes

SOUTH

The solar chimney creates a draft that pulls air through the buried tubes. This air will be cooled, but not dehumidified.

- *Landscaping and Massing:* In conjunction with a passive ventilation system, shade trees can be planted densely and close to the building. As heated air is ejected from solar chimneys, makeup air can be brought into the building through doors or windows facing the shaded exterior. This incoming air will then be as cool and pleasant as sitting in a shady grove.

Hopefully this quick survey of fuels and energy resources will give you some bearings as you make one of the more important determinations about your future home. Your choice of fuels will reflect who you are no less than your choice of paint color. When friends ask, "How did you decide to heat it?" or when you tally your year-end utility bill, the decision you make here will stare back at you. It will be either a source of personal expression or an unavoidable embarrassment.

Distribution Systems

Regardless of which fuel(s) you finally select, there will be more than one way to distribute the warmth or cooling to the spaces in your house. A complete control of indoor climate involves heat, humidity, ventilation, and air conditioning. Many regions will not need all aspects of the indoor climate artificially maintained. We don't use air-conditioning in Vermont and you won't find much central heating in

Florida. Ventilation and humidity control, however, are beneficial everywhere.

The distribution system moves and removes the heat, cooling, and humidity from the different spaces of a house. The two most common transport media used in this connection are water (or antifreeze) and air. Steam is still used in larger installations but rarely in residences. Systems with water as the media are called "hydronic" systems. Those using air are often referred to as central air or, sometimes, forced air. Hydronic systems carry more heat in less space, pipes being smaller than ducts. Central air has a faster reaction time and can carry humidity and cooling as well as heat. Debates over which provides better comfort have always been a part of this subject and I believe they will continue beyond the end of time. There is, in fact, no one type of system that is better than another. But engineered systems are generally better than seat-of-the-pants designs provided by the installer. The truly comfortable system is the one properly designed for the climate, fuel, architecture, and *your life-style*.

Yestermorrow students sometimes tire of all the different choices at every level of design. Sometimes they just want a formula.

"Just tell me the one that's best: What do you use? Just tell me what to put down." Betsy has already finished her floor plan. She just wants to specify a HVAC system and be done.

"C'mon, Betsy," I chide, "are we not a nation of shoppers? Let's look at the options. Let's look at the latest thing!"

"Do we have to?"

In truth, it would be folly to attempt an exhaustive coverage of all the latest products. Instead, we can discuss the traditional options, giving their primary strengths and weaknesses. This will be an overview, just to get you started. There will always be a "new and better" version and each is available with a variety of bells and whistles. By understanding the basics, you will be better prepared to do local research when the time comes for you to specify your own system.

AIR SYSTEMS (USING DUCTS AND FANS)

"One Zone" Convection

This is a natural place to begin, since it has been around the longest. A fire pit at the center of a tepee; a fireplace in the middle of a log cabin; or a wood-burning stove on the first floor of a row house: These are all one-zone hot air systems. They have no duct work, but simply distribute the heat by convection and radiation. This is still a very viable and economical way to heat your home *if* the design accommodates it.

Many of today's homes with open plan or large common room layouts are well heated by an adequately-sized wood (or coal) stove. Penetrations in the ceilings can extend this comfort to the upstairs.

Convection is a tricky thing, however, and more than one design/builder has been unsatisfied with the results of simply placing a stove in the geometric middle of the floor plan. It is not uncommon to have heat stratification, hot spots, cold spots, and drafts. These can often be corrected with the use of vents, wall fans, and floor registers. Sometimes the heat can be coaxed around by maintaining a certain pattern of open and closed doors (don't rely on this if you have kids or pets). People using convection to distribute the heat develop a very good understanding of how heat works in their house. It is also an approach with very low initial cost. It uses renewable fuel and the heat it delivers is said to be some of the most comfortable. On the down side, it can somewhat constrain the room layout and it can dehumidify a house to the point of discomfort. Air conditioning, including humidification, must be added separately. This strategy is best used in homes or additions of simple geometries, few rooms, and less than 1200 square feet.

Common bells and whistles: heat exchanger to supply hot water; catalytic converter (not really optional); warming or cooking surface; pelletized fuel; fancy water pot to serve as old-fashioned humidifier.

Multi-Zone Central Air

Since hot air rises, the obvious evolution for convective heat systems locates the heat maker in the basement and delivers the treated air through ducts to the separate rooms. This was done long before there were fans or dampers. The air moved by convection only. Some of the wood-fired units can still be found in the basements of older homes. Their massive size and simplicity are endearing. A friend of mine who still keeps his running has named it the "Throbulator"! Today's fossil-fueled version of the Throbulator is about as big as a small filing cabinet.

Central air has an advantage in that heating, cooling, humidity control, and air cleaning can all be accomplished through the same unit. The ducts can easily be configured to service several zones, or rooms, independently. Moreover, the engineering is all worked out so there are few if any surprises after installation. "Tuning" the system and daily control of comfort is easy, if not wholly automatic. (No special configuration of doors.)

Like so many advanced technologies, one must be aware of installers who cut corners to appear cheaper. Get references and visit installed systems. Air ducts not only carry noise, but when improperly sized they can generate it. Long duct runs can lose more heat than they deliver. Poorly balanced systems will cycle frequently and even cause drafts. These are the standard faults found by critics of the central air system. But none of them need pertain if the system is properly designed and installed. I have had the pleasure of working with good, energy-conscious engineers in my use of central air systems. I winced when they told me how much space I must devote to duct runs. But I later praised them when the system ran smoothly and delivered consistent comfort in all weather conditions. An episode that proved the rule occurred when I once let the installer talk the client into a redesign. This redesign, he claimed, would provide exactly the same comfort for half the cost. (Beware! There is no free lunch!) The resulting system left some rooms cold and others noisy. When I complained about the noise, he reduced the airflow until the room was quiet—but cold. Many return ducts had been eliminated so the system was impossible to balance. The furnace cycled constantly.

Now normally, I listen to the mechanic's advice as much as the engineer's (and certainly more than the architect's). But I must say, it will be a long time before an installer convinces me that they have a better design at half the price than an engineer who has taken the time to design it properly. The engineering is so thoroughly worked out for a central air system that one can truly predict the performance. Noise and draft can be reduced to any desirable level. Sure, an engineer costs more, but they're worth it. After all the repairs and adjustments necessitated by the installer's inexpensive alternative, I learned a lesson in the high cost of cheap construction.

A fully engineered central air system will always be more expensive. Remember, however, that this is the only format that does it all: heating, air-conditioning, humidity control, ventilation, and even air filtration.

Radiant Floor—Hot Air

The first radiant floors (the Romans had them) were forced air and this technology still exists today. (Hydronic radiant slabs, using embedded water pipes rather than air, are discussed below.) Aluminum forms are placed on a concrete subfloor. More concrete is then poured over the forms. This produces a matrix of air spaces that maximize the surface area between hot air and concrete. A less expensive (and less efficient) version can be made with an array of hollow concrete masonry units. In any event, you can see that the floor becomes very thick, 8″ to 10″, and very heavy. This is probably not a great distribution system for the second floor (Figure 152)!

This approach was adopted by a doctor who came to Yestermorrow in pursuit of his long postponed dream of becoming an architect. He reasoned that the use of this system allowed the superior comfort of a radiant slab without forfeiting the flexibility of central air. He was design/building for his retirement on the shore. There was a heating season and a cooling season where he lived, plus the need for considerable dehumidification. His design allowed him to take preheated air from his green-house, dehumidify it as it went through his furnace, then heat the radiant slab and return it to the greenhouse. The system worked well, but he doesn't claim it was a money saver.

Although probably not the only approach, the doctor used a system developed by: Air Control Systems; 14625 Carmenita Road, Suite 220; Norwalk, CA 90650.

The hydronic version (discussed later) requires less space, is slightly less expensive, and can be installed easily in bathrooms and the second floor. Nevertheless, it can't humidify, clean, or cool the air. Also, it should be noted that radiant floors somewhat constrain your choice of finishes. Because of their insulating properties, rugs, carpet, and rubber sheet goods must be used sparingly. Tile, slate, hardwood, and stone are better choices.

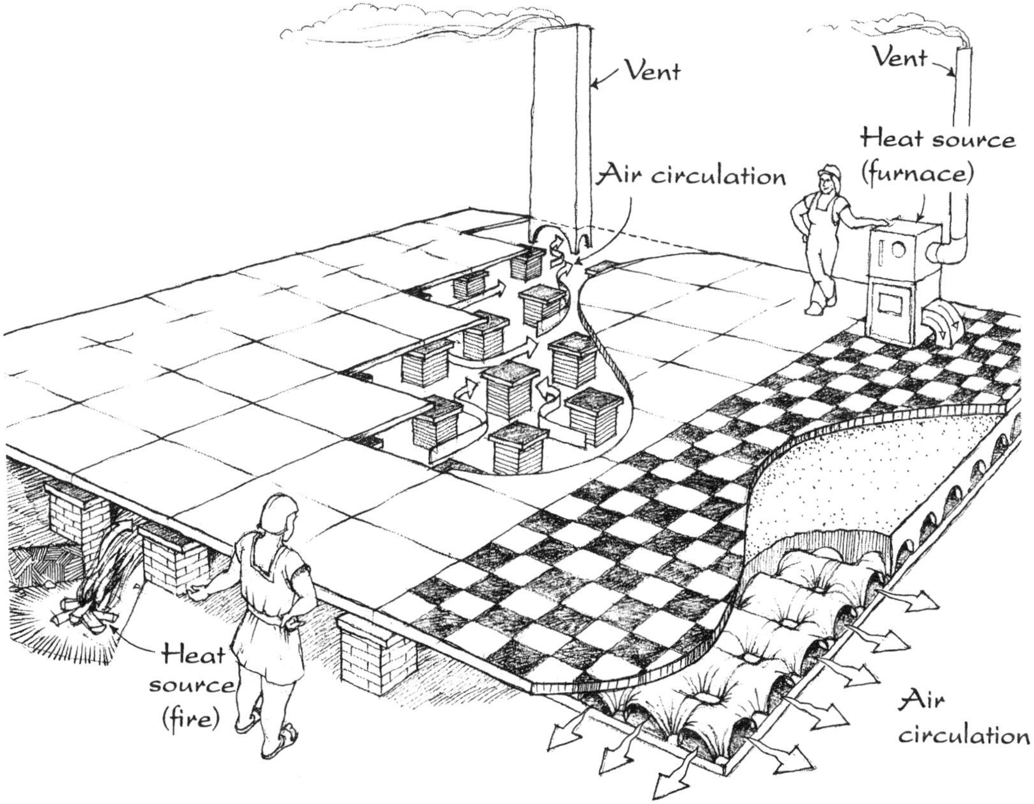

Electric Baseboard

I wouldn't be honest if I pretended I liked this form of heating. Inefficient, difficult to control, draft producing, and ugly, the only reason for using electric baseboard is because it's cheap to install. But that's the *only* time it will be cheap. It is just about the most expensive (and dumbest) way to heat space. There, I've got that out of my system.

Electric baseboard heat is an approach that uses convection to induce air past the heated elements. The units are placed under windows and along exterior walls to blanket the room in a layer of warm air. One of its few attractions is the speed with which it reacts. The thermostat can turn it on and off like a light. This allows it to be installed independently in each room: infinite zoning! Its supporters say this makes it more efficient. (Bah!) Many people complain that it dries out the air. Humidification and air conditioning must be installed separately.

The first winter we moved to Vermont I lived with all electric baseboard heat. The next summer I replaced it all with a four-zone, state-of-the-art, wood-fired hydronic system.

"Pretty classy," said my friends and neighbors. "Aren't ya overdoin' it a bit?"

FIGURE 152: The contemporary hot air floor works on the same basic principles as those used by the Romans.

Well I guess not. The electric bill savings paid for the entire system in just two years!

Hydronic Systems (using pipes and pumps)

BASEBOARD HOT WATER:

Hydronic baseboard heating is the most widely installed distribution system, by far. Of the choices that perform well, they are the least expensive to install. Consequently, they are used by responsible developers far and wide. This has produced a great market demand and it has been answered by manufacturers of every caliber.

There are a few very well designed baseboard units. The Swedes came up with a product that, when installed, looks just like a regular 1 × 6 wooden baseboard. Since it is installed instead of the usual baseboard, one doesn't even recognize it as a heating unit. It evenly blankets the walls with warm air. As with most things Swedish and attractive, these are not cheap.

Among more traditional baseboard units there are also levels of quality. The cast-iron variety is durable and looks like it. They have been around for years so they also look a little traditional. While not glamorous, if properly detailed, these units can look fine. The next choice, top-of-the-line "fin-tubes," are a good compromise. They are slightly better built and deliver more BTUs per foot than the residential-grade fin-tubes. This means you need to look at fewer units in each room and those will be more attractive. The last choice, residential-grade units, are not very well built and deliver less heat per foot. Installed at floor level, it isn't long before they are dented and scratched. Once the cowling is deformed, the convection action over the fins becomes retarded. In short, cheap baseboard units look ugly, are built poorly, and perform badly. But they're cheap (Figure 153)!

As a design/builder I have experimented with building custom enclosures for fin-tubes normally housed in commercial grade units (Figure 154).

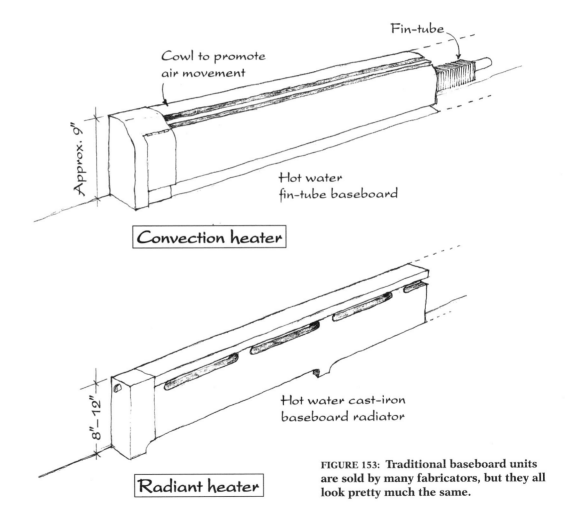

Cowl to promote air movement

Fin-tube

Approx. 9"

Hot water fin-tube baseboard

Convection heater

8" – 12"

Hot water cast-iron baseboard radiator

Radiant heater

FIGURE 153: **Traditional baseboard units are sold by many fabricators, but they all look pretty much the same.**

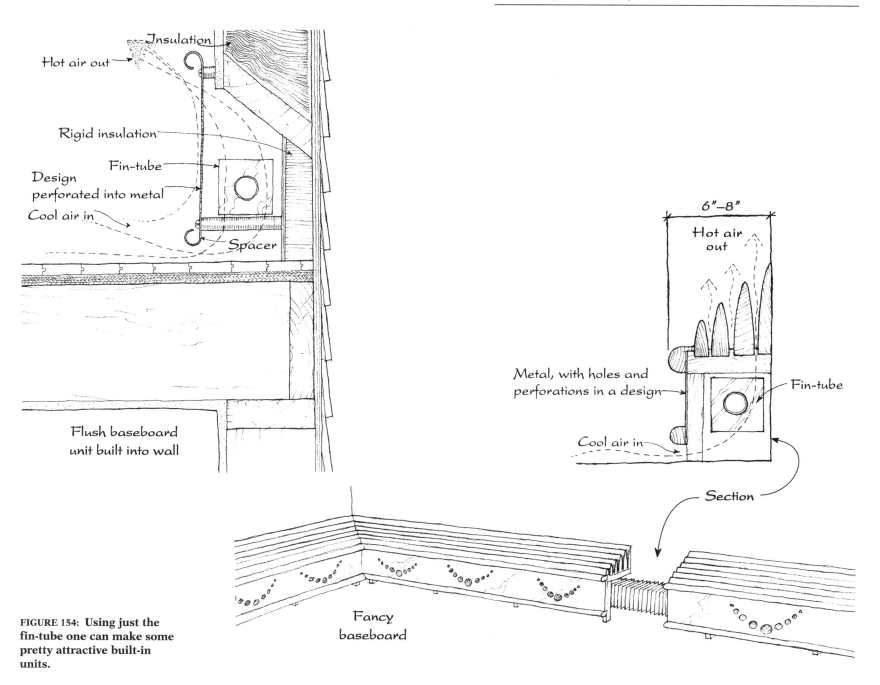

Insulation

Hot air out

Rigid insulation

Fin-tube

Design perforated into metal

Cool air in

Spacer

Flush baseboard unit built into wall

6"–8"

Hot air out

Metal, with holes and perforations in a design

Fin-tube

Cool air in

Section

Fancy baseboard

FIGURE 154: **Using just the fin-tube one can make some pretty attractive built-in units.**

This certainly has more aesthetic appeal, but I'm not sure it produces the most air flow over the fins. Nevertheless, I recommend this approach to economize on radiation without having it look too bad. Fin-tubes can be built into parts of your house that you must build anyway. For example, they can be built into the stair risers, the kick space, even the interior walls. A small fan pumping air over a fin-tube increases the distribution of heat greatly (Figure 155a and b).

As custom housings for fin-tubes become more elaborate, it's only natural to start thinking of them as radiators.

RADIATORS

The classic radiator is a cast-iron assembly comprised of several hollow sections bolted together. The hot water or steam passes through them, but not as quickly as through a fin-tube. When full, they hold several gallons of hot water. The heat is distributed by radiation and convection. A radiator is cast with airways running through it that promote convection currents. Air is constantly passing through and over the radiator. This mode of distribution is the same as that used by fin-tubes, only at a larger scale. However, being large metal objects, radiators actually deliver quite a bit of heat as electromagnetic radiation.

Radiators have been refined over the years, especially in Europe; they are rarely made from cast iron anymore. Now they

are stamped and welded steel with durable enamel finishes. The enamel is a better surface for radiating heat, and the lighter stamped steel has a faster reaction time. The modern radiators are often hung on the wall, allowing easy cleaning of the floor below them (Figure 156).

Radiators are positioned using the same game plan as baseboards. That is,

under windows and along exterior walls. Of course, radiators are much more compact than baseboard units, so they can be specified to be the same width as the window, leaving the rest of the wall open for furniture. While modern radiators are not as ornate or distinctive as the old cast-iron models, contemporary manufacturers do make an effort. The European designs are

FIGURE 155a: There are many opportunities to build in heating elements. The trick is to insure adequate air movement.

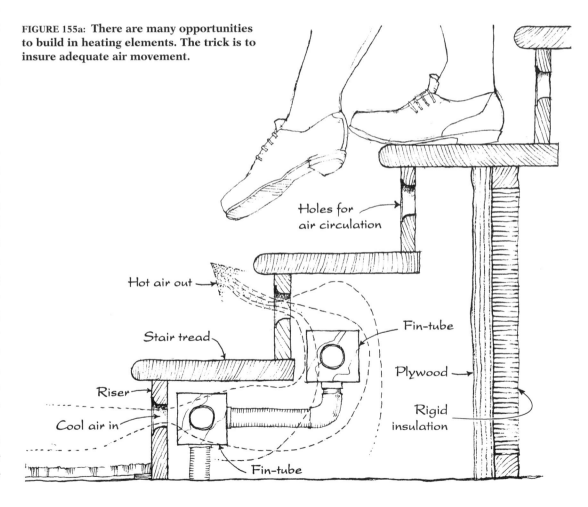

Holes for air circulation

Hot air out

Fin-tube

Stair tread

Plywood

Riser

Rigid insulation

Cool air in

Fin-tube

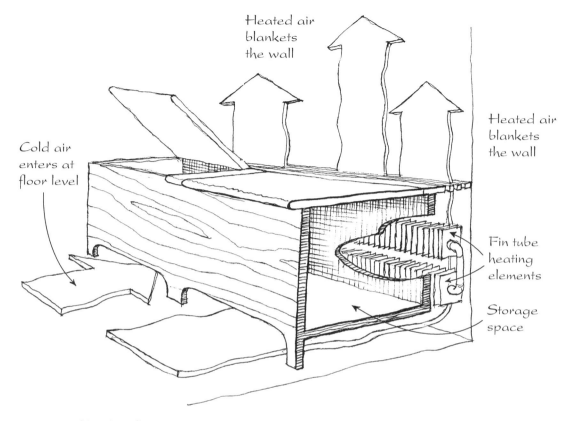

Cold air enters at floor level

Heated air blankets the wall

Heated air blankets the wall

Fin tube heating elements

Storage space

FIGURE 155b: (*Continued*).

simple and sometimes even elegant. Also, because they are compact and don't run along the baseboards, furniture layout is much easier.

RADIANT FLOOR—HYDRONIC
This is the latest advance in hydronic distribution. I shouldn't make it sound new, because it isn't. Still, radiant floor technology has really come into its own. This is largely owing to the more reliable plastic

pipes now available and the new light-weight gypsum floor material. It's also a matter of cost. Even though it is still more expensive than most distribution systems, radiant installations are becoming more affordable all the time.

Radiant floors transfer heat through conduction and radiation. Convection also plays a slight role. The entire floor is warmed by small pipes running within or directly below it. Today's systems can be

engineered to work with concrete, tile, wood, slate, stone, and a few special carpets.

Naturally, the harder and heavier surfaces work the best. Radiant heat is emitted more efficiently from hard surfaces such as tile, slate, or stone (Figure 157). (A rug, on the other hand, is too much of an insulator to be a good choice for radiant heat transfer.)

The most intriguing claim of radiant floor advocates (read "salesmen") is that lower temperatures are required from this type of heating due to its application directly to the feet. This is sensible heat applied directly to the part of our bodies responsible for registering when we are cold. If our feet are warm, the logic goes, then the rest of our body will be comfortable at a slightly lower temperature. This may be true. I've lived with radiant heat and quite like it. However, I give the credit to the evenness of the heat. Since the warmth is the same everywhere, there are almost no drafts. If the house is tight and well insulated, the heat will not stratify. Taken together, the overall evenness of the heat allows us to be comfortable at a slightly lower temperature.

In a less technical vein, radiant heat is the hands-down winner for furniture placement. There are no radiators or baseboards by the windows. There are no grills or registers to be blocked. The only thing to be avoided is large thick rugs. If you install a radiant floor and then "insulate"

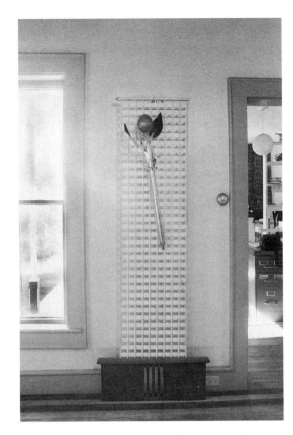

FIGURE 156: An innovative radiator made by Runtel Inc.

it with a rug, the obvious result will be a cold room.

At Yestermorrow we renovated an old farmhouse. The interior was opened up dramatically from basement to ridge. When we were finished, there were over nine levels where formerly there had been but two. It was a superinsulated house, so we didn't worry about heat stratification. But most of the levels opened onto each other, so we did worry about drafts spilling from level to level. The natural selection for this house was, of course, a radiant floor. As with all hydronic systems, there is no air conditioning or humidity control. Nevertheless, we were able to zone the house and even make the bathroom floors extra warm. It's a very impressive system.

CONSERVATION

Most students are surprised when they learn that the really big savings—the biggest of all—will always come from conservation. Building a tight, well-insulated house is the best strategy for reducing energy costs. For every extra dollar spent on insulation, weather-stripping, air barriers, or gasketing, your house will use less fuel than if you spent double the amount on a more efficient heating or cooling system. Saving energy is less glamorous but always more cost effective than using energy in the latest high-efficiency equipment.

▥ Conclusion

Creating an indoor climate isn't simple. Neither is it something to be left entirely in the hands of a "professional" with formulae and rules of thumb. What may be comfortable for one can be disastrous for another. I often wear only a T-shirt while my wife has on a sweater. Thermal comfort is a personal thing.

So are ethics. The fuel you choose and the efficiency with which you use it will say much about your values. Indeed. "values" is the right word, here. For many people their preferred ethical choice is not one they can afford easily. How can I burn wood if my job prevents me from stoking the fire? The cost of a solar collector means I won't be able to afford the fuel-efficient car I've got my eye on? Who ever heard of ethics in a book about building? What's the point? Well . . .

Design and construction is a constellation of decisions and choices. Some are no-brainers. Others seem intractable. Our personal ethics are the logic that guide us as we try to make the best decisions *possible.*

"Yes, well the best I can afford will be baseboard electric," Jason declares. "What am I to do?" I've watched this student hate his project more with every passing day. He is working on such a tight budget that he sees the whole procedure as an exercise in denial.

"What's the total cost budgeted for baseboard electric in your house?" challenges Bob. "And what do you figure your yearly power bill will be?"

"I can get them installed for $1,200 and if the winters are mild, it won't cost me more than $1,200 per year. Maybe less if I wear sweaters."

"Aha!" Bob thinks he has it solved. "That adds up to $2,400. Quite a budget. If you take just $2,000 of that and add it to what you already have budgeted for insulation and weather stripping, I'll bet you can reduce your annual heating requirements to almost nothing. With the leftover $400 you can shop for a used wood-burning stove."

"You think so?" Jason brightens visibly.

"Let's do the numbers." Bob and Jason retire to a quiet area in the studio. "Now how about this air conditioner, do you really need it?"

Several years later the frustrated Jason sent us a photo of his newly completed home. It had small, economical massing with well-considered proportions and details. In his letter he revealed how it only uses one cord of wood per winter. In the summer it stays cooler than any other house he knows. His friends now consult him on all matters concerning energy conservation. His letter concludes ". . . so it's been quite an adventure. People come all the time and marvel at how little energy it uses. My friends kid me about being a conservation nerd! Can you believe it? Me, talking up superinsulation as a way to save money. The funny thing is, I think I really am a conservation nerd. It really makes me feel good to come home to a house that stays comfortable in all seasons *without* adding to the world's woes."

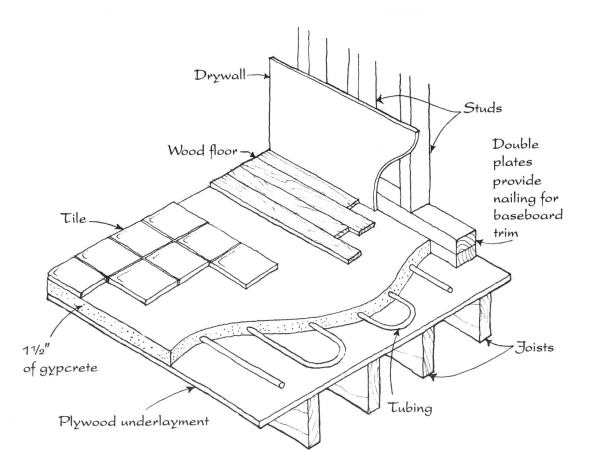

FIGURE 157: **The conventional hot water-type radiant floor will accommodate a wide variety of floor finishes.**

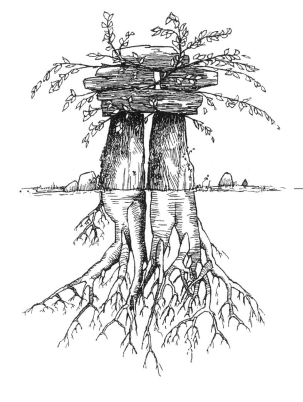

Plumbing and DWV (Drainage, Waste, and Venting)

I have often heard it said that people in the building trades today are better educated than ever before. With that in mind, here's one of the few plumber jokes that can be printed:

Once there was a lawyer who hired a plumber to install a bathroom in his office. When the lawyer learned how much the job would cost, he was aghast.

"How could it cost so much for just a sink and a toilet?" he whined. "How much could the materials cost?"

"It's not the materials, it's the labor," said the plumber.

"I see. And just what do you make an hour?" asked the lawyer in a prosecuting tone.

The plumber unabashedly informed the lawyer of his hourly wage.

"What!? That's outrageous!" cried the lawyer. "Why, I don't make that much an hour and I'm a *lawyer*."

"Of course," responded the plumber. "I didn't make that much either when *I was a lawyer*."

Saving money is only one reason to understand the principles and theory behind your mechanical systems.

Theory!?! What theory?

Ah yes, and this is the point in most Yestermorrow classes where the non-techies suddenly have business elsewhere. If this is your inclination, please relax. This chapter (and the following one on electricity) will be presented in an easy, conversational mode. The arcane code issues and highly technical fixture calculations (although fun) will be left to the books in the Bibliography. For now, I merely want you to understand enough about your mechanicals to form an attitude about them. Like every other aspect of your house, the mechanicals hold potential for architectural design.

It is unfortunate that plumbing is rarely seen as a hands-on opportunity by most owner/builders. Though I say "rarely," I won't say "never." Many have wired and plumbed their own homes. It gives great satisfaction and suggests numerous and unexpected design opportunities. Also, you never have to wait for the plumber if something needs service. Still, these trades are heavily delineated with codes and procedures. Safety is a constant concern. (If you feel that you may want to install these systems yourself, more than one chapter of instruction will be needed. There are several books listed in the Bibliography that will get you started.) While local laws vary, most states at least permit you to plumb your own home. Nevertheless, you must submit to all the usual inspections, which are often more rigorous for owner/builders. The friendship of a licensed professional, if you know one, will be invaluable.

Even if you don't cut every pipe or sweat every joint, you must still be the *designer* of your plumbing system. It can be as functional or as expressive as you choose. A great quantity of gleaming copper and shiny chrome are used in most plumbing systems. If it weren't hidden in the walls, you might think a "plumbing tree" a rather nice sculpture. The pipes, tanks, and valves would serve as a constant reminder of your membership in the water cycle. We humans use and abuse a lot of water.

▦ Expose the Plumbing?!?

You may wonder what there is to express through the design of your plumbing system. Well, you might articulate your attitude or philosophy concerning water and waste. You might express your priorities or ethics (there they are again!). Or you might wish to have the visual benefit of all that copper you're paying for. You will be paying about the same for your plumbing system regardless of how it's done. Shouldn't you consider it an opportunity? Why can't this aspect of your home reflect you and your personal values?

If you think our plumbing doesn't already send a message, perhaps you're just too close to the situation. Most readers have only experienced one type of plumbing system and it's largely been hidden. To take a fresh look let's pretend an extraterrestrial scout has been sent to study planet Earth. Imagine how the report might read:

> Over 75 percent of the planet is covered with water. Moreover, the main inhabitants—humans—are themselves made up of 95 percent water. *Water*, the report continues, is the single most crucial substance in the planet's entire ecosystem. It is absolutely central to the survival of humans, as well as everything else on the planet.
>
> The ecology is easy to understand, but the human species are truly bizarre, possibly dangerous to themselves and the rest of the planet. What makes them so odd is their relationship to this precious water. Whenever they eliminate bodily waste, they mix the waste with the largest amount of water feasible. A few ounces of waste is normally diluted in several gallons of fresh water. Huge pipes and elaborate systems have been constructed to carry the tainted water long distances so that it can be added to a great network of rivers and oceans on the planet. Beyond just human waste, every waste of any kind is dissolved in massive volumes of water! With this as the evidence, the alien's report concludes:
>
> *There appears to be no* intelligent *life on this planet.*

This may seem like a comical presentation of our water usage, but it's tragically accurate. Furthermore, we persist in this wholesale attitude of waste every time we install a conventional DWV system (drainage, waste, and venting). "Out of sight, out of mind" is the basis for most plumbing systems. The water comes from a far-off place, presumed safe and clean. Since the pipes are hidden underground and in the walls, the average person is unaware of water until they turn on a faucet. Surprise? Magic? No, we just assume the water will always be there when we need it. From the toilet tank, shower head, or spigot it passes a tiny distance to the drain. In that small journey it is transformed from our most valuable natural resource to liquid waste. The waste lines, no less than the supply pipes, are carefully hidden in the walls. Where that waste goes becomes someone else's concern—out of sight, out of mind.

A Quick Overview

Let's get the big picture. Water comes and goes and comes again. Where does it come from? Where does it go? How do we fit in?

WATER ARRIVES

Water comes from the sky. When it arrives it is relatively clean, but not entirely. It percolates into the earth, where it is filtered through different mixes of organic and mineral soils. This process can produce varying effects.

The varied porosity of the soil separates the water into *groundwater* and *surface water*. Where the earth is impervious, or the grade is steep, the water stays on top, running downhill to form rivers, streams, and ponds. This surface water tends to be innoculated with the organic materials commonly found composting on the ground. This can make it risky to drink, even in the country. Groundwater, on the other hand, percolates deep into the earth, where it collects in underground streams called aquifers. The upper face of the aquifer closest to the surface is referred to as the "water table." This was discussed previously in the section on foundations.

Water from the deep aquifers holds the best promise for drinkable water, though it is rarely absolutely pure. It can be retrieved through several different types of wells. *Dug wells* are used when the water table is close to the surface. As the name implies, these are hand (or backhoe) dug holes usually lined with a spring box to keep the sides from caving in. *Driven wells* are constructed by driving a perforated pipe into a gravel aquifer. They are rarely driven beyond a depth of 50'. *Drilled wells* are the most common and versatile. Using heavy equipment, a 6" to 10" hole is drilled down to bedrock. A steel casing is placed into this hole and sealed to the bedrock. Once bedrock is reached no casing is required. These wells may be drilled to almost any depth. In our area they rarely go beyond a few hundred feet, but in other regions they often go deeper—and shallower. Check with your local driller to get an average. The cost is usually about fourteen to twenty dollars per foot until you reach bedrock, and then half that cost from there on. A deep well may be expensive, but it will also hold reserves of water in storage. A healthy flow of water, over five gallons per minute, reduces the need for storage. But I know of people who get along fine with wells that are very deep and produce only a half gallon per minute. Because it will always increase storage and usually increase flow, I advise that you keep drilling beyond the first seams of water (Figure 158).

If you get your water from a municipal

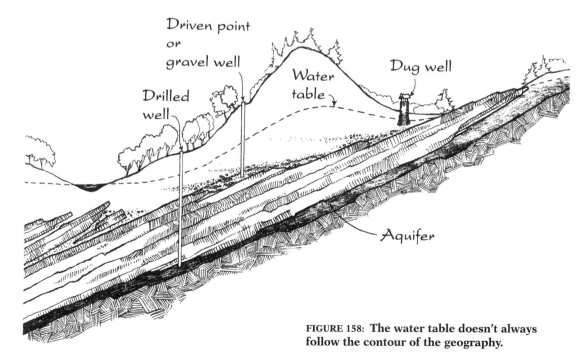

FIGURE 158: The water table doesn't always follow the contour of the geography.

water system, it is probably collected from many drilled wells, springs, and reservoirs. The laws of the land require that the water be treated for color, hardness, mineral content, and bacterial impurities. Additionally, it is usually chlorinated or fluorinated. All this reduces the water to a pretty distasteful substance. Nevertheless, it is safe to drink.

If you get your water from a deep well, it will likely have minerals, salts, and possibly sulfur or manganese in it. I *always* have the water tested, just to see what I've got. The state will often test your water without charge. (See your town clerk for a form and details.) I have water tested for bacteria, hardness, and iron. These are the only things I consider problems. The bacteria will make you sick. The iron will stain and clog your fixtures. The hardness blocks up your pipes and makes it difficult to clean your clothes. Beyond these few impurities, any additional mineral deposits will only improve the taste of most well water. (It's also said to be better for making beer.)

WATER IS USED

Water, once in the house, has its own little hydrocycle. It arrives under pressure (usually around 40 to 60 psi) from a pipe in the foundation wall. Upon entering the house, or after the pressure tank if you have a well and pump, the water line divides to supply the hot-water heater. Now we have

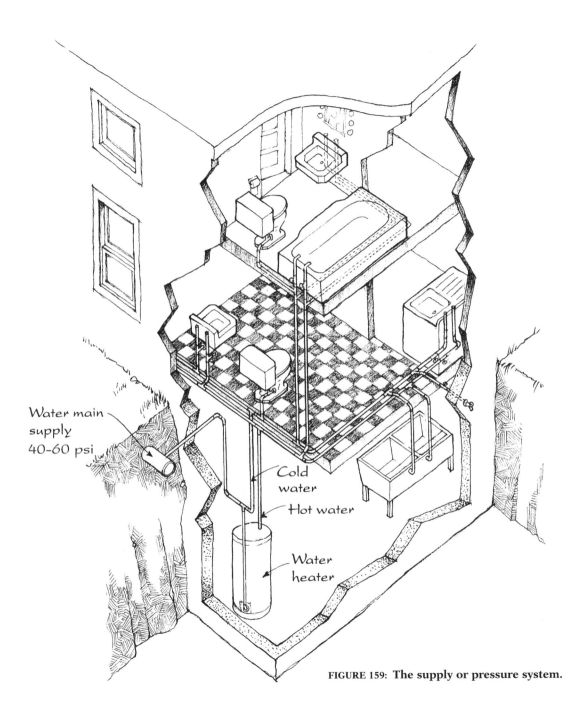

Water main supply 40–60 psi

Cold water

Hot water

Water heater

FIGURE 159: **The supply or pressure system.**

a hot main (coming from the water heater) and a cold main (coming directly through the wall). Hot and/or cold supply lines are run to every fixture in your house (only cold water to the toilets, please). This even includes the refrigerator, if you have an automatic ice maker or drinking water dispenser. Once the water is used, it is gathered together through a series of drains and waste pipes. At the lowest point in the house, all the water used has been rejoined as wastewater. It now makes its way back through the foundation wall.

Naturally this indoor hydrocycle is a gross oversimplification. The typical residential water system also includes a vent system, boiler supply, water treatment, fixtures, appliances, traps, valves, and gauges. We'll touch on these in more detail shortly. For now I just want you to understand that within the house the water is separated into many uses, both hot and cold, then recombined into one waste stream that passes out to sewage treatment (Figures 159 and 160).

WATER IS DISPOSED

Of course, we don't really "dispose" of water. Having contaminated it with a variety of waste, the final task is to clean it up and return it to Nature's big hydrological cycle.

In a rural situation this is normally done with an on-site septic system. When properly designed, such a system is a mar-

vel of nature. It relies on microbes and bacteria to actually break down and digest the wastes in the sewage. The main waste pipe leaving the house travels 15′ to 25′ before emptying into a septic tank. This concrete tank, about 750 to 1,500 gallons, is configured so the solids will settle out to the bottom of the tank. Although some *anaerobic* digestion takes place at the bottom of the tank, it is not complete, so

sludge must be pumped out every few years. Anaerobic digestion is a microbic process that requires no oxygen. Nevertheless, it is still a living process. If you pour powerful toxins (Drano, paint thinner, etc.) down your sink drain, they will kill this process and you will have to pump your tank more frequently (Figure 160).

After leaving the tank, the liquid effluent is introduced to a leaching field. This

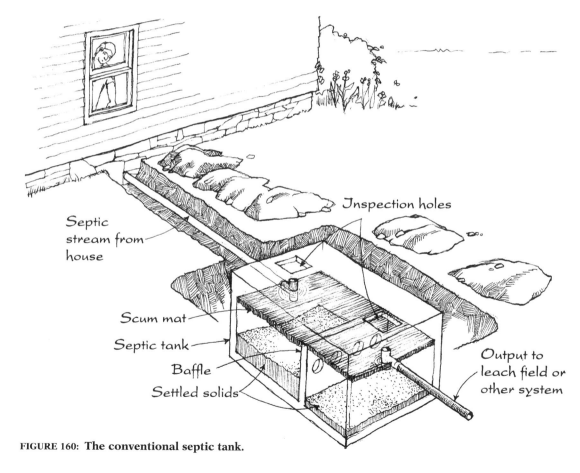

FIGURE 160: The conventional septic tank.

is a series of perforated pipes about 12" to 18" underground, bedded in sand. Here the *aerobic* digestion takes place. This process requires oxygen, and it is for that reason that the pipes are close to the surface. The effluent is distributed over a large area as it leaves the pipes and filters through the sand. Here the aerobic microbes and bacteria will break it down into harmless (indeed beneficial) substances. As the water filters through this leaching field, it is cleansed. Since the lowest elevation of the leaching field matrix must be at least 4' above any clay or ledge and 3' above the highest point of the water table, the water is filtered through an additional 3' of earth before rejoining the water supply.

If you live in the city you will miss out on all this drama. Municipal sewer systems collect everyones' waste at a big central treatment plant located well away from the center of activity. Out of sight, out of mind. More on this later.

▥ **Some Design Decisions**

Let's walk through the plumbing system as a design/builder. Many things have to be decided and, as always, there will be aesthetic as well as life-style consequences. Any code issues will be covered by one of the two national plumbing codes: the National Standard Plumbing Code or the Unified Plumbing Code.

The first design issue connected with your plumbing system concerns the well. Many factors constrain its placement. The heavy drilling equipment must be able to reach the site and set up. Usually the well must be located at least 50' from any leaching field, 25' from the septic tank, and 10' from any sewer. Some municipalities will increase these minimums. After the well is dug you must decide if the top of the well casing will be buried or remain above grade. It is easier to reach and service above grade, but it may not be in a location that looks great. This often calls for some landscaping or creative stonework. One Yestermorrow instructor buried his well head because it attracted lightning.

The great majority of pumps used today are submersible. They go right into the well casing and pump from the bottom of the well. Underground wiring and waterline must be planned between the well and house.

Once inside the building, the water is stored in a pressure tank. When the pressure gets to a preset level, a controller on the tank turns off the pump. The compressed air in the tank now pushes the water to any point in the house, upon demand. The controller monitors the tank and turns the submersible pump on whenever the pressure gets below the set level.

After the pressure tank, but before anything else, the water should be treated, if required. This is where you remove the iron, sulfur, manganese, and other impurities that constitute "hard" water. There are quite a few technologies on the market, even ones for killing bacteria. Ask for the ones that don't use chemicals or electricity.

Now that your water is clean, some of it should be heated. There are several technologies here as well. The traditional hot-water heater can be leased from your gas company. Alternately, there may be a hot-water "leg" on your boiler (a loop inside the firing chamber) or you may be interested in the "instantaneous" heaters that have gained popularity. Let's look at each of these in a bit more detail (Table 17).

The traditional hot-water heater is just a large, moderately insulated storage tank with a heating element in it. While they're made in both gas and electric models, I prefer the gas models for all the reasons given in the section on heating. If you buy or rent this technology, the first thing to do is increase the insulation. Otherwise, this tank will just sit in your basement losing heat. When it loses enough heat, the *aquastat* (a thermostat for water) will reignite the fuel. It takes considerable energy to keep 40 to 80 gallons of water hot at all times. You will reduce that energy considerably if you insulate the tank. Also, the size of your tank will effect your energy bill. Larger tanks allow longer showers, but they also consume more energy.

For those with a hydronic heating system, the boiler usually has the capacity to heat the domestic hot water with a sepa-

TABLE 17: SIZING YOUR WATER HEATER USING HUD-FHA* MINIMUM STANDARDS

No. of Bathrooms	1 to 1½			2 to 2½			
No. of Bedrooms	1	2	3	2	3	4	5
Gas							
Size in Gals.	20	30	30	30	40	40	50
Recovery (gal./hr.)	23	30	30	30	30	32	40
Electric							
Size in Gals.	20	30	40	40	50	50	65
Recovery (gal./hr.)	10	14	18	18	22	22	22
Oil							
Size in Gals.	30	30	30	30	30	30	30
Recovery (gal./hr.)	59	59	59	59	59	59	59
Tankless							
Supply (gal./hr.) (No Storage!)	180	180	180	300	300	420	420

*Department of Housing and Urban Development (HUD)
Federal Housing Authority (FHA)

rate heat exchanger called the *hot-water leg.* This is an economical way of making your boiler do double duty . . . in the winter. The trouble with this arrangement becomes apparent in the summer. Who wants to keep their boiler cranked up all summer just for hot water.

This led those clever Europeans to develop an instantaneous heater, sometimes called a "tankless," or "supply-on-demand," water heater. Powered by gas (or wasteful electricity), these tiny units only heat the water upon demand; there is no storage. Whenever you turn on a fixture, the pressure change within the pipe is sensed and a series of burners are automatically ignited. These burners are trained on a heat exchanger in such a manner that water flowing through the unit is fully heated in a matter of seconds! When the water is turned off, the flames are extinguished. No hot water is stored and, therefore, no heat is wasted. Moreover, as long as the hot water is called for, it never runs out. These units are great for ski or beach houses where large groups of occupants all shower within a short space of time. The down side of tankless heaters is their dependence on flow rates to determine water temperature. Sometimes it's hard to get every possible temperature of water at every flow rate.

These remarkable devices began showing up in this country in the late sixties. They can be had in a variety of sizes and are now also available as "instantaneous"

boilers. When the thermostat calls for heat, it turns on a circulator as well as the tankless heater. Hot water mixed with antifreeze arrives in the distribution system within seconds. This arrangement combines the convenience of electric heat with the better energy efficiency of gas.

At this point we have hot and cold water. Before we leave the mechanical space, let's look at the layout. We must have room for a boiler (or furnace), a pressure tank, possibly some treatment tanks, a hot-water heater, and all the necessary piping. Just as you would draw furniture into the living room, draw this equipment into your mechanical space. If you don't know the exact size of each device, presume each has at least a 3′ × 3′ footprint and requires access on three of its four sides. Beside allowing for proper fit, this exercise should give you an idea of what it will be like to install and service these units. Do you need a floor drain? Is it located properly in the foundation drawings? Where will the power come from? Imagine a dire situation. The power goes out and the basement floods! You want to empty it with a gas-powered pump. Where will it be placed? Is there a window access for the hoses? Can you reach the controls of all equipment easily? OK, that's enough drama.

Now the water must be delivered to the different rooms in the house. Primarily this means the kitchen, bathrooms, and laundry. Normally this is done with ¾″ or

1″ pipes, depending on the number of fixtures being supplied. The main lines to a given room should always be larger than the branch lines feeding each fixture. This is how we avoid scalding our spouse when we flush the toilet. This is how we are able to run the dishwasher and the washing machine at the same time. Proper pipe sizing is the secret to all those pressure problems that plague older plumbing systems.

Running these lines is rarely a problem. Finding ¾″ in a wall or floor assembly is pretty easy. But remember, when drilling holes in floor joists, you want to keep them toward the centerline of the board and away from the middle third of the span (Figure 161).

When running them close to the surface of a wall, protection plates will prevent puncture from the random sheetrock nail or picture hook. You think this never happens? The stories are endless!

In cold climates water lines should never be housed in an exterior wall. Sooner or later the conditions will be right and they will freeze (and burst!). There are few things more demoralizing—not to say costly—than having a water line explode inside a wall. Is this the voice of experience? Of course. Have I placed pipes in exterior walls? Of course. Every rule and guideline needs to be tested. As with many design/builders, I consider my home to be 50 percent domicile, 50 percent research and development. But that's a different issue. And I don't place pipes in exterior

walls anymore, even when they're super-insulated. Take my word for it.

Waste and venting lines are larger and much more difficult to house within a 3½″ wall. We will discuss them shortly, but I mention them in advance because they often determine layout of fixtures and supply lines.

I am not rigorous about stacking bathrooms or making the plumbing tree as tight as possible. I have found that there is very little additional cost between plumbing that serves plumbers and plumbing that serves the occupants' life-style. Nevertheless, it is important to consider where the pipes will be located. Some may need

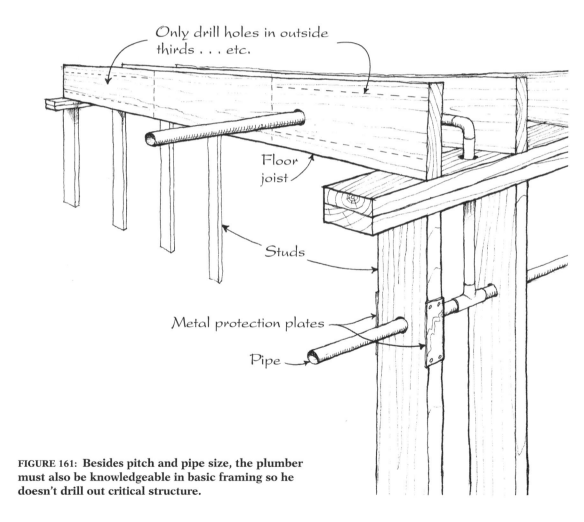

FIGURE 161: **Besides pitch and pipe size, the plumber must also be knowledgeable in basic framing so he doesn't drill out critical structure.**

to be serviced or occasionally turned off. Waste lines need clean outs. Every fixture should have isolation valves, since you may want to isolate different branches for service and maintenance. Where space permits, pipes are usually housed in the walls. On occasion a special chase or mechanical space must be provided.

So don't just assume the plumber will figure everything out for you. By addressing the needs of your mechanical system, you're more likely to be pleased with how they are interwoven into the fabric of your house. For instance, a mechanical chase might double as a laundry chute or an acoustical barrier. It is prudent to consider the mechanical locations early in the design of a home (Figure 162).

So far, we have been discussing the supply, or *pressure system*. Now we will describe the *drainage, waste, and venting* (DWV) system. The supply system brings the water in and distributes it; the DWV system recollects it and takes it back out.

Having arrived at the various fixtures, clean, potable water is now transformed into one of two types of waste water: gray water or black water. *Black water* is the sewage containing feces and other bodily elimination. Essentially, it is water from toilets and it can be dangerously toxic. *Gray water* is the water stream containing all the other household waste. Gray water comes from sinks, showers, baths, washing machines, and dishwashers. The toxicity of gray water depends on what you

FIGURE 162: **This ancient stone building (1080 A.D.) was updated with modern plumbing. While destroying the beauty of this fine old building, the external installation provides us with a fabulous full-scale demonstration of drainage, waste, and venting.**

Source: Reproduced with permission from John Wiley and Sons from McGuinness, Stein, & Reynolds, *Mechanical and Electrical Equipment for Buildings*, 6th ed.

throw down your drain. Traditional DWV systems don't separate these waters (which amazed our alien researcher). They are collected into the same pipes and the leaching field is sized for their combined volume (Table 18).

The example in the following section shows how to design and size the septic system for a conventional home. Note the size of the leaching field and how much it may be reduced when gray water is separated. This is important because the leaching area may not be used for any other function. It may not be used for a vegetable garden or as a parking area. It may not support a driveway, a patio, or be

TABLE 18: WASTEWATER GENERATED BY A FAMILY OF FOUR

Water Events	Number per Day	H₂O Gallons per use	Total H₂O Used
Toilet	16	5–7	100
Bath/shower	2	25	50
Laundry	1	40	40
Dishwashing	2	7	14
Garbage Disposal	3	2	6
Total			210 or 53* gal./Person

*To allow for overages and unusual events, waste-handling systems are sized using 75 gal./person as a design criteria for interior use. But this does not include watering lawns, washing cars, etc.

paved in any way. It must be kept free and clear. Moreover, all this assumes you have soil that percolates properly. For those with poor soils or a high (perched) water table, this conventional leaching field will not even be permitted. In these cases an engineered system must be constructed at considerable expense. Whoa! We started out discussing DWV and suddenly we're in the backyard with an engineered leaching field! What gives?

Cycle, cycle, cycle. Your site design seems to be connected with your waste-plumbing considerations. If you want to save money and real estate on leach field design, you may have to spend a bit more on waste plumbing. Separating gray and black water means two separate DWV systems. This needn't mean twice the cost, however, because the only duplication is at the main waste stack, where everything gets thrown together. Now we need two stacks instead of one. The individual fix-tures are still drained and vented in the normal fashion.

What's "normal" venting? (See Figure 163a, b, c, d.) The best teaching aid for demonstrating the principle of venting is a beer can (or any canned liquid). If you punch only one hole in the top and try to pour or drink from it, you will meet with difficulty. The liquid starts to drain but that quickly produces a vacuum inside the can. So after a bit of liquid has exited, a bit of air must enter. This give and take produces the characteristic "glug, glug, glug" associated with pouring from a narrow aperture. Now, if we place another hole in the can, the flow accelerates and becomes smoother. This is because the beer can flow from one hole while the resulting vacuum is normalized through the other. For the very same reason, all drains must have vents (Figure 163b). And because they have vents, they must also have traps. Why?

The vents allow the toilet, sink, or shower to drain properly. Unfortunately they also create a chimney effect. The methane and other gases produced in the septic tank are naturally drawn right up through the drainpipes and into the bathrooms and kitchens. Stinko! This is prevented by using a trap, or liquid blockage, that prevents the gases from entering the house (Figure 163c). Therefore, *every fixture* must be vented and have a trap. The size and type of trap depends on the fixture. Toilets have the trap built into their porcelain bases, but all other fixtures must be trapped at installation (Figure 163d).

Venting can become a bit confusing. This is because there are so many ways of venting different fixtures in different situations. The venting for a sink in a kitchen island is different than that for a simple lavatory. We have direct venting, reventing, wet venting, circuit venting, loop venting—there is a special venting configuration for just about any situation. They're all designed to relieve the vacuum caused by a plug of water traveling down the drain-pipe. Vent sizing is determined by *fixture units*. A fixture unit is an engineering term referring to 7.5 gallons per minute. The plumbing code assigns to every fixture a specific number of fixture units for supply and a different number for drainage.

This is where the plumbing can really

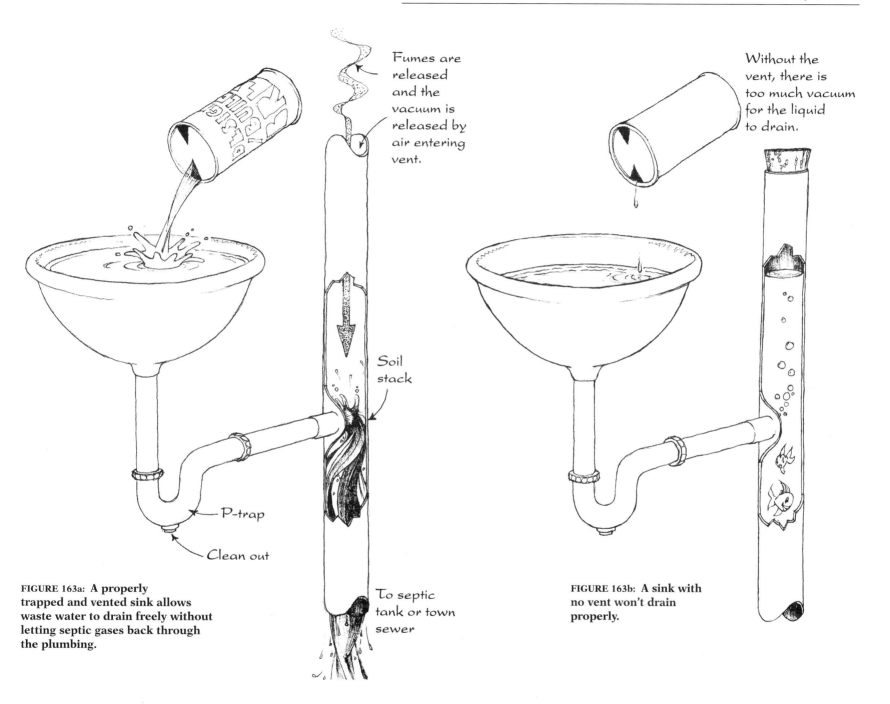

Fumes are released and the vacuum is released by air entering vent.

Soil stack

P-trap

Clean out

To septic tank or town sewer

FIGURE 163a: A properly trapped and vented sink allows waste water to drain freely without letting septic gases back through the plumbing.

Without the vent, there is too much vacuum for the liquid to drain.

FIGURE 163b: A sink with no vent won't drain properly.

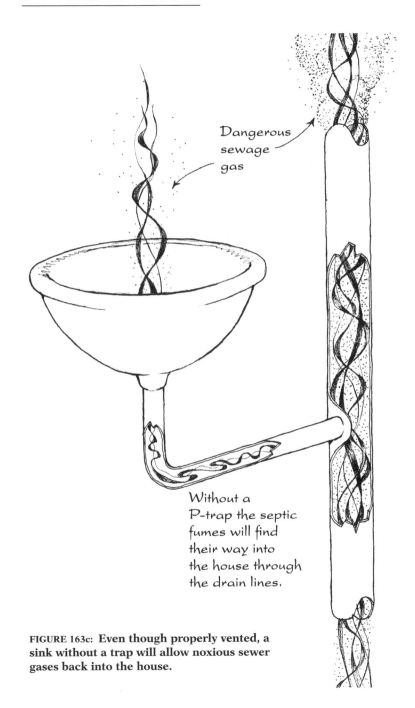

Dangerous sewage gas

Without a P-trap the septic fumes will find their way into the house through the drain lines.

FIGURE 163c: Even though properly vented, a sink without a trap will allow noxious sewer gases back into the house.

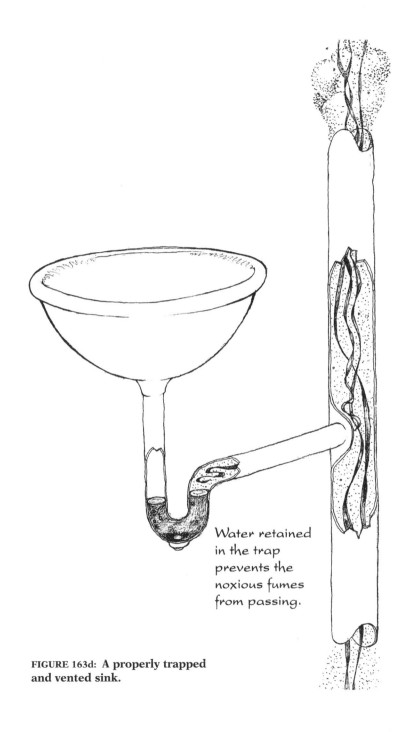

Water retained in the trap prevents the noxious fumes from passing.

FIGURE 163d: A properly trapped and vented sink.

affect design and room layout. The length and size of vent pipes is determined by the number of fixture units being vented and the size of the main waste stack. The following charts give an idea of how freely different fixtures can be placed and still fall within vent restrictions (Tables 19, 20, and 21).

In my experience, a good plumber can find a way to vent almost anything by making a few last-minute design changes. So, take some time to consider where the main stack will go. Work it into the plan, but also consider where it will come through the roof. Also remember that sewage passing through waste lines can make noise. Batt insulation makes inexpensive soundproofing.

If you choose to segregate the gray and black water, you will have two main stacks. The black water must be disposed of in a conventional leaching field or municipal sewer; the gray water may be filtered and used in your garden. The Clivus Corporation makes a filter specifically for this purpose, but there are many alternatives that may cost less. Books in the bibliography explain several methods for constructing filtration systems with readily available parts (Figures 164a and b).

Since you're now thinking about recycling your gray water (I hope), perhaps it may also be possible to interest you in a *composting toilet.*

Composting toilets use little or no water. They are not connected to the plumbing

TABLE 19: SIZE AND DRAINAGE FIXTURE UNIT VALUES OF NONINTEGRAL TRAPS FOR VARIOUS PLUMBING FIXTURES

Type of Fixture	Normal Trap Size (in inches)	Drainage Fixture Unit (dfu)
automatic clothes washer standpipe	2	3
bathtub	1½	2
bidet	1¼	1
dishwasher	1½	2
drinking fountain	1¼	½
floor drains	2	2
kitchen sink	1½	2
lavatory	1¼	1
shower head	2	2
sink	1½	2

Source: The Building Officials and Code Administrators *BOCA National Plumbing Code*, 1990.

TABLE 20: MAXIMUM LENGTH OF INDIVIDUAL, BRANCH, CIRCUIT, AND LOOP VENTS FOR HORIZONTAL DRAINAGE BRANCHES

Diameter of Horizontal Drainage Branches (inches)	Slope of Horizontal Drainage Branch (inches per foot)	Diameter of Vent (inches)			
		1¼	1½	2	2½
		Maximum Length of Vent (feet)			
1¼	⅛	NL*			
	¼	NL			
	½	NL			
1½	⅛	NL	NL		
	¼	NL	NL		
	½	NL	NL		
2	⅛	NL	NL	NL	
	¼	290	NL	NL	
	½	150	380	NL	
2½	⅛	180	450	NL	NL
	¼	96	240	NL	NL
	½	49	130	NL	NL

*NL means No Limit

Source: The Building Officials and Code Administrators (BOCA) National Plumbing Code, 1990.

TABLE 21: SIZE AND LENGTH OF VENT STACKS AND STACK VENTS

Diameter of Soil or Waste Stack (inches)	Total Fixture Units Connected to Stack (dfu)	Diameter of Vent (inches)						
		1¼	1½	2	2½	3	4	5
		Maximum Length of Vent (feet)[a]						
1¼	2	30						
1½	8	50	150					
1½	10	30	100					
2	12	30	75	200				
2	20	26	50	150				
2½	42		30	100	300			
3	10		42	150	360	1040		
3	21		32	110	270	810		
3	53		27	94	230	680		
3	102		25	86	210	620		
4	43			35	85	250	980	
4	140			27	65	200	750	
4	320			23	55	170	640	
4	540			21	50	150	580	
5	190				28	82	320	990
5	490				21	63	250	760
5	940				18	53	210	670
5	1400				16	49	190	590

[a]Length measured from vent to open air

Source: The Building Officials and Code Administrators (BOCA) National Plumbing Code, 1990.

system and require no waste lines. Nonetheless, they must be vented. There are numerous composting toilets on the market, of which the Clivus Multrum, developed in Sweden, has enjoyed the most popularity. All composting systems rely on the same basic principles. Solids from the toilets and the kitchen are collected in a manner that allows the water to evaporate through a vent. The remaining solids will support the aerobic microbes and bacteria that turn the sewage into safe, stable compost. This compost, less than 10 percent of the original volume of waste, is nutrient rich and may be safely used as a fertilizer. In some composting toilets additional heat is used to accelerate the composting action. Others rely on proper air circulation and the heat generated by the actual composting processes. These toilets, and the accompanying technology, will have a definite impact on your house design. Study them in the plan and in sections to understand how they will be incorporated best (Figure 165).

In communities that aren't unequivocally rural (or at least in Sweden), composting toilets and gray water systems are probably going to raise an eyebrow. These are clearly alternatives to the status quo. For this reason, should you choose this route, you can anticipate a deeper acquaintance with your plumbing inspector and health officials. I've never met one yet who has a composting toilet. My advice is to be well versed in your subject prior to the initial meeting. Besides a knowledge of the basic principles, you will need a clear set of drawings, sizing calculations, and a list of other approved installations. Don't lose heart and don't be reluctant. These may be new ideas for the code-approved communities of our urban centers, but they have been successfully employed for decades in rural and suburban areas all over the world.

The key question is, how can we hope to better recycle our resources if the very design of a conventional septic system works so hard to keep us unconscious? It's the "out of sight, out of mind" phenomena. In the end, the water becomes waste-

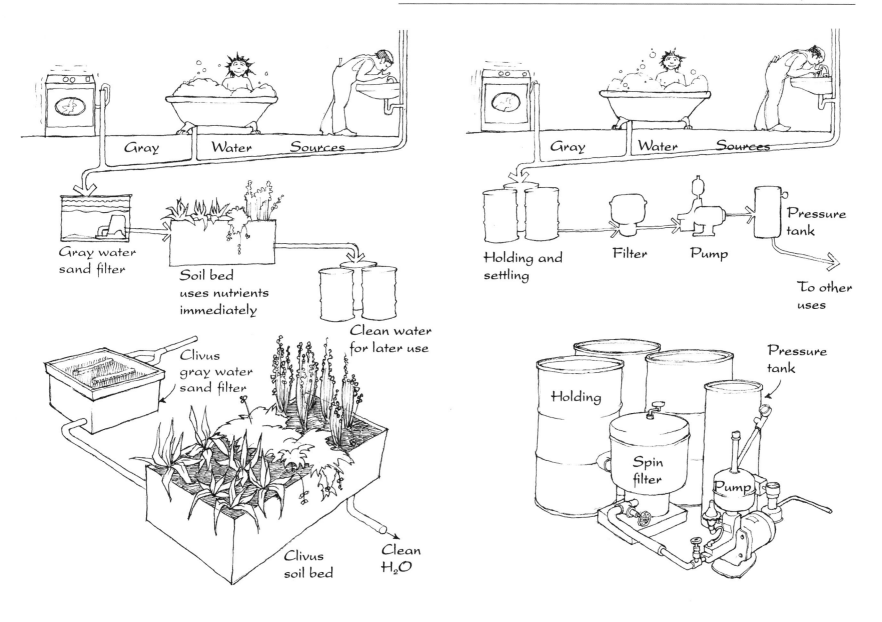

FIGURE 164a: Some gray water systems filter the water, while others seek to *use* the nutrients that would be filtered out.

FIGURE 164b: One possible system with all the basic components required to collect, filter, and reuse gray water.

water, whether gray or black, and must be offered back to the land for purification. If you live in a city with municipal treatment, you can offer it only to the city sewer. In your stead, the municipal sanitation folks will return it to the hydro cycle via central treatment. There is an economy in treating wastewater this way, but there is also something lost. If the waste that Los Angeles pumps into the Pacific Ocean in one day were to be properly composted it would amount to over 200 tons of fertilizer (7 percent nitrogen, 14 percent phosphorus, 12 percent potassium). That's enough to produce over 5,000 tons of vegetables! In a country where top soil is being lost at an alarming rate and farmers are paying ever higher prices for chemical soil amendments, it seems like a huge mistake to waste valuable compost material.

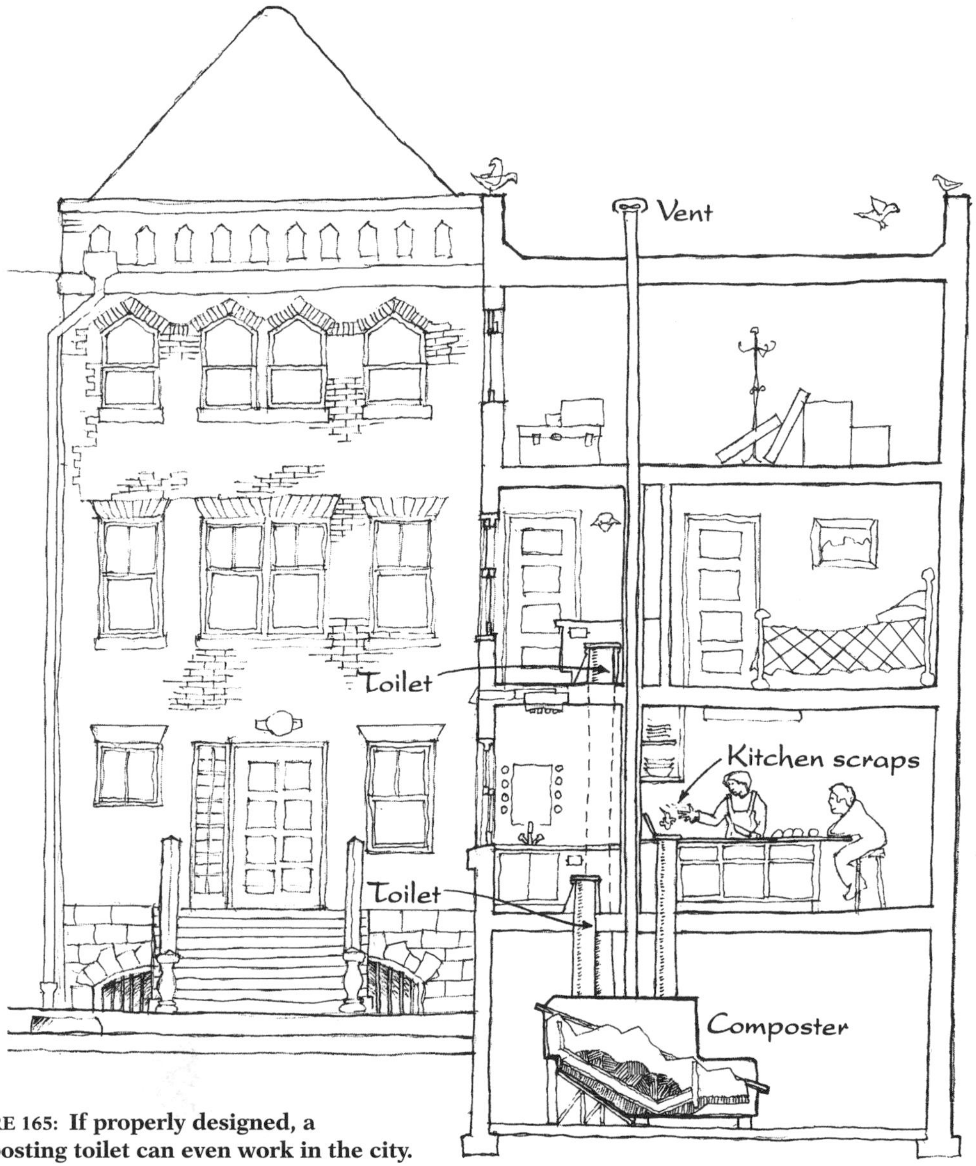

WATER IS SAVED!

Gray water systems and composting toilets are the beginning of a whole new way of thinking about wastewater. Today, most people understand that potable water is precious and must be conserved. Moreover, what previously was considered to be sewage is now understood to be a valuable biological nutrient.

We can make a good start at saving water by using "low-flow" showerheads and toilets. Such devices have reduced water consumption dramatically in dry regions where they are mandated by code. Even greater reductions can be accomplished by using gray water systems to filter and recycle all non-toilet-related water.

Finally, the biggest payoff comes from considering the way we deal with black water, or sewage. Whether collected by the municipality or treated at each individual site, sewage must be treated as a *resource*.

FIGURE 165: **If properly designed, a composting toilet can even work in the city.**

Understanding this biological nutrient means we can beneficially apply it to local marshlands or, in colder climates, use it to support a greenhouse. We now know that certain plants and microbes commonly found in wetlands are perfectly suited for the digestion (purification) of black water. What we think of as biological waste is actually a rich food source for these marshy ecosystems.

Besides conserving water, a biological approach to wastewater purification means we reserve less prime land for leaching fields and build fewer chemically based treatment facilities. It also means we become conscious of our place in natural biological cycles.

If that doesn't float your boat, how about the fact that this approach to wastewater also saves a lot of money? I (like most) often find this more compelling than high ideals. Conserving water, and using biological wastewater treatment, means we can affordably develop "problem" sites; those marginal lots with poor soils or steep grades usually cost less. Money is saved on real estate, on water, and on fertilizer. Best of all, instead of being subdivided, our prime farmland can now be used for agriculture!

Percolation Tests and Real Estate Values

If you would like to consider on-site treatment, you will need to discover what kind of soils you have. This doesn't require elaborate analysis. We just want to know how fast the effluent will percolate into the ground. If it drains too quickly, there won't be adequate time for the aerobic digestion. If it drains too slowly, the field may have to be immense. To establish the percolation rate you must conduct the following test (Figure 166):

Step 1. Dig a hole no smaller than 12″ × 12″ and about 12″ deeper than the bottom

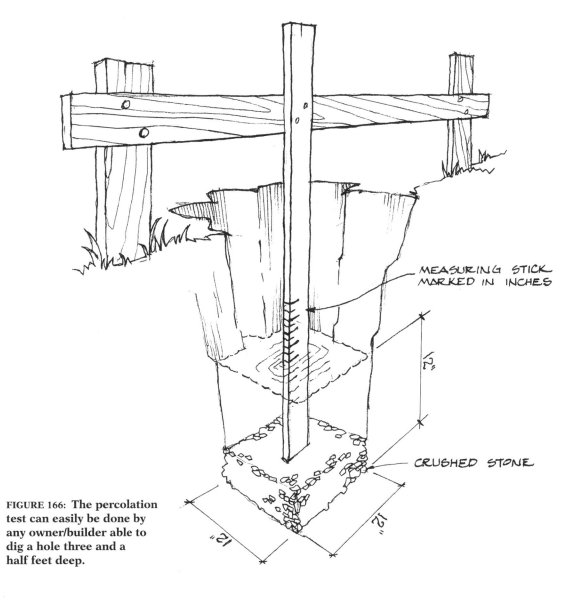

FIGURE 166: The percolation test can easily be done by any owner/builder able to dig a hole three and a half feet deep.

MEASURING STICK MARKED IN INCHES

CRUSHED STONE

12″

12″

of the proposed leaching field—say 3'6". The bottom of the hole should be covered with about 2" to 3" of gravel and the sides should be free from tooling or smeared mud that might effect absorption.

Step 2. Fill the hole and keep it full for twenty-four hours. This saturates the surrounding soil and simulates conditions under actual use.

Step 3. Position a measuring device similar to that shown in the illustration. Keep about 12" of water in the hole for another twelve hours.

Step 4. Finally, adjust the water level to be 6" above the top of the gravel. Take readings at thirty-minute intervals for the next four hours. Use the drop found in the last thirty-minute interval to calculate percolation. If it all drains out before the time is up, start over and use ten-minute intervals for one hour. Again, use the final interval to calculate your percolation rate.

Step 5. Use the following charts to calculate the size of your septic tank and how many feet of drain tile will be required for your home (Tables 22 and 23).

Now that you know your soil characteristics you can determine the size of your septic tank and overall leaching-bed area. This calculation assumes a flow of 75 gallons(!) per day per person (frightening, no?). See Figure 167.

The following two examples give an idea of how a gray-water system, and greenhouses, might reduce leaching field size.

TABLE 22: SEPTIC TANK CAPACITY FOR ONE- AND TWO-FAMILY DWELLINGS

Number of Bedrooms	Septic Tank (Gallons)
1	750
2	750
3	1,000
4	1,200
5	1,425
6	1,650
7	1,875
8	2,100

Source: *The BOCA National Private Sewage Disposal Code*, 1984, p. 48.

Example One

You're designing a large but conventional house for eight occupants. It will have six bedrooms and three and one half baths. But these are unenlightened folks and they have a dishwasher, a garbage disposal, and no water-saving devices. Having conducted the perc test, you know that

the soil is only fair. It took eleven minutes for the water to fall 1" (step 4, above).

First we will size the septic tank. From Table 22 we can see that six bedrooms will require a tank with at least 1,650 gallons of capacity. If you round up to the next largest size, you will have a little more time between pumpings. (Septic tanks should have the sludge pumped out every three to five years.)

Now let's figure out how much area we need to absorb the effluent. From Table 23 we learn that 250 square feet of area at the bottom of the leaching trenches is required *for each bedroom*. Since we have six bedrooms we will need 6 × 250 = 1,500 square feet of combined area at the bottom of all our leaching lines. A 2'-wide trench will have 2 *square feet* within every running, or lineal, foot of trench. So if we divide 1,500 square feet by 2 it tells us that we need 750 lineal feet of trench. The

TABLE 23: MINIMUM ABSORPTION AREA FOR A RESIDENCE

Percolation Class	Percolation Rate (minutes required for water to fall 1")	Seepage Trenchesᶜ or Pitsᵇ (sq. ft. per bedroom)	Seepage Bedsª (sq. ft. per bedroom)
Class 1	0 to less than 10	165	205
Class 2	10 to less than 30	250	315
Class 3	30 to less than 45	300	375
Class 4	45 to 60	350	415

[a] Seepage Bed: an excavated area larger than 5' in width that contains a bedding of aggregate and has more than one distribution line
[b] Seepage Pit: an underground receptacle so constructed as to permit disposal of effluent or clear wastes by soil absorption through its floor and walls
[c] Seepage Trench: an area excavated 1' to 5' in width that contains a bedding of aggregate and a single distribution line
Source: The BOCA *National Private Sewage Disposal Code*, 1984, p. 36.

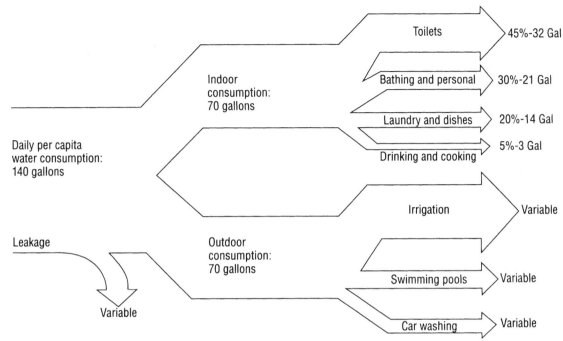

Source: Murray Milne, *Residential Water Reuse*, by California Water Resources Center Report No. 46, University of California/Davis, September 1979, p. 9.

FIGURE 167: Residential water consumption.

Example Two

In this example, the former occupants move away and eight enlightened Yestermorrow graduates move in. Right off, they put low-flow devices on all the showers and faucets. The toilets are easily modified to reduce water use dramatically. Being "greenies," they have endless plans for the yards surrounding the house: a fruit orchard, nut trees, a stand-alone greenhouse, lots of flower gardens, and one huge vegetable garden. Also, they want a regulation volleyball net close to the pool (after all these *are* Yestermorrow graduates). But wait! It turns out there isn't enough room for a proper volleyball court because the best level area is all used up with leaching fields. What to do? See photograph on page 324.

They decide to separate, filter, and recycle the gray water. It can be used to wash the car, irrigate the gardens, even top off the pool. The black water, after settling, will be treated in the greenhouse.

trenches are 2′ wide and they are separated by 2′, so the total area needed will be 4′ wide and 750′ long, or 3,000 square feet. This is a square approximately 55′ on a side, plus it must have a 10′ setback on all sides (Table 24).

To give the fullest picture, don't forget that most municipalities now require that the property have adequate room for a second full-sized replacement field as well (Figure 168a and b).

TABLE 24: SET-BACK REQUIREMENTS

Element	Building	Cistern	Foundation Wall	Lake, High-Water Mark	Lot Line	Pond	Reservoir	Spring	Stream or Watercourse	Swimming Pool	Water Service	Well
Type of System						Separation (distance in feet)						
Absorption Field	25	50	25	50	5	50	50	100	50	15	10	50
Treatment Tank	5	25	5	25	2	25	25	50	25	15	5	25

Source: The BOCA *National Private Sewage Disposal Code*, 1984.

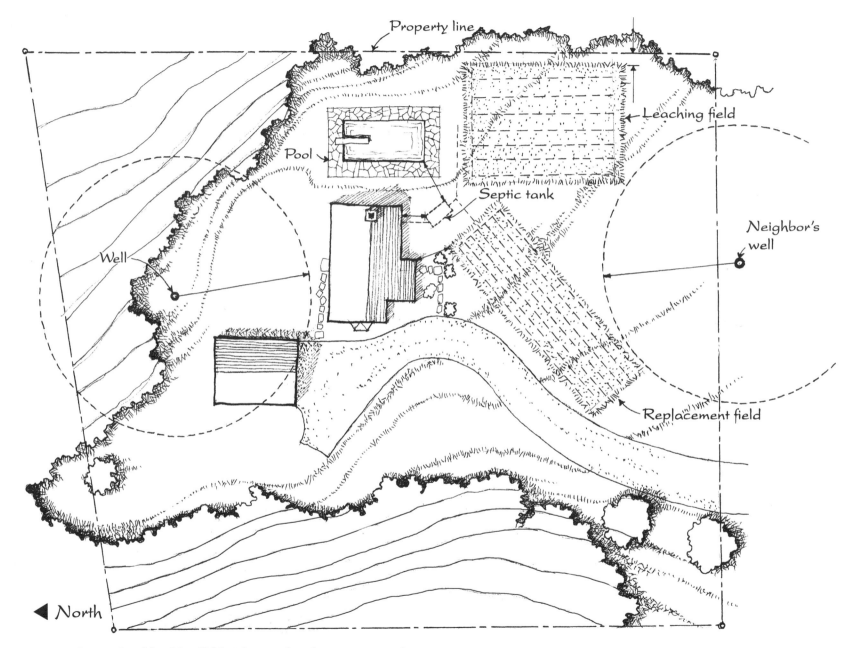

Property line

Leaching field

Pool

Septic tank

Neighbor's well

Well

Replacement field

◀ North

FIGURE 168a: Conventional leaching fields take up a lot of space on your site.

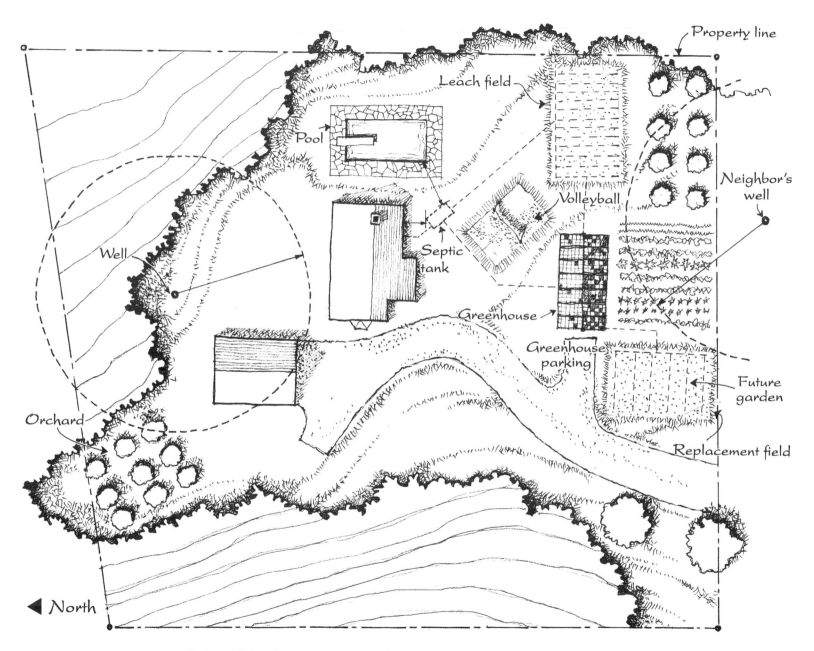

Property line

Leach field

Pool

Volleyball

Neighbor's well

Well

Septic tank

Greenhouse

Greenhouse parking

Orchard

Future garden

Replacement field

◀ North

FIGURE 168b: A gray water system will allow full leaching to be accomplished in less space, plus help reduce water usage.

Only a small part of this greenhouse is used to treat the waste from three 3-bedroom homes. The remaining space is shared by the homeowners for recreational use.

Some of this biologically purified water will also be used for irrigation, but the great majority will be sent to the leaching field. So how big will this leaching field have to be?

Even though the low-flow toilets barely use 2 gallons per flush, the Yestermorrow folks use the extravagant rate of 7 gallons in their calculations. Moreover, they assume each occupant will produce a total of 35 gallons of black water per day. (This is *very* conservative, but it is still small compared

to conventional calculations.) If each person represents 75 gallons of total water use each day, they are assuming 40 gallons will be gray and 35 will be black.

The black water, after passing through a 2000-gallon settling tank (see Table 22) will pass through an engineered marsh in the greenhouse (see illustration above) where it will support a variety of grasses, flowers, and even some small trees. After that it will pass through a sand filter and an ultraviolet sterilizer (or equivalent).

These electrical sterilizers are not required if all the purified black water will eventually be sent to a leaching field. However, since the Yestermorrow folks want to use some of this purified water on their gardens and in the pool, it must be totally clean and nontoxic—in short, potable.

The gray water will pass through a smaller settling tank (500 gallons) and then through a sand filter. This will render it clean enough for a variety of outdoor uses. (If they want to use it in the pool, it still has to be run through an ultraviolet sterilizer.)

Now, suppose it's winter and there are no gardens to water, cars to wash, or pools to top off. How big must the leaching field be to take all the black wastewater, filtered or not? Let's see, there will be eight occupants producing 35 gallons of black water each day—280 total (8 people × 35 gallons/day = 280 gallons daily). This compares well to the 600 gallons produced by the previous household (8 people × 75 gallons/day = 600 gallons daily). I should mention, however, that the 75-gallon/day rate doesn't include washing cars, watering the lawn, or topping off the pool. These are additional uses for clean water that may be supplemented by our treatment efforts. Moreover, this setup means we are reducing the wastewater volume by over half, so we can downsize the leaching field accordingly.

Hooray! The new occupants save money, increase water supply, *and* get their volleyball court. In fact, since the effluents from the greenhouse and the sand filter are so clean, even this smaller leaching field will probably never become "plugged." This means the land designated for the replacement leaching field can also be used for gardens, games, orchards, etc.

About now you should be wondering, "Is this all just business as usual down at the local building and health departments?" And of course, the most likely response has to be "No." Code officials like status quo, which means you can do anything you like to your wastewater, but in the end it all has to go into a municipal sewer or a code-approved on-site septic system. The majority of our bureaucracies are still in the age of "out of sight, out of mind."

Not to despair, there is a light on the horizon. In the water-starved western states, gray water conservation is beginning to look better. In Los Angeles, gray water management is being studied as a potential billion-dollar-a-year savings. In the South, outdoor marshlands are being used increasingly to augment municipal sewage treatment and protect the water table. Even in the Northeast there are signs of curiosity in areas where the soils are poor for traditional leaching methods. Indeed, even conservative old Vermont has passed legislation to conditionally permit systems like the one described above. So just give your local health department or septic engineer a call. Chances are you can now treat your "wastewater" as a valuable resource, and

maybe even get a volleyball court or garden in the bargain.

Plumbing and Glossy Design

A peek into most living rooms of the past reveals a stage set for the show: "This Is How We Live Our Life." Of course, very little living actually occurred there. Like the front door, the living room was intended only for certain occasions. It was meant to send a message, usually about material comfort.

Now we know that *every* aspect of our homes results from design decisions implemented or forfeited. Thus, it is impossible for our homes *not* to express who we are and what's important for us. The plumbing and bathrooms, no less than the front door and living room, are the results of our personal preferences and values. In today's fast-paced world of shrinking resources and casual society, the "This Is How We Live Our Life" show is currently featuring kitchens and bathrooms. These rooms, with their gleaming plumbing and shining surfaces are equally capable of sending a message. What will that message be? As always, the Yestermorrow students hold forth. . . .

"Hey, I'm putting my money where it will do the most good every day. I don't need a living room for weekend socializing. I need a big den or a *great room* that I can come home to every single night."

". . . So? What's wrong with a big bedroom? It's the *master* bedroom." One stu-

dent became defensive when I pointed out that the bedroom was actually larger than the living room.

"Well, I need the space for my exercycle, a little sitting area, and the television. I don't want to feel cramped. The walk-in closets are essential. Both my wife and I work in offices and we use a lot of clothes."

The bathroom? "Well, the master bathroom should be an extension of the bedroom, in my opinion. I want two sinks, two showers, a steam bath, and a whirlpool spa instead of just a bathtub. Those things can even be *in* the bedroom, but I want the toilet and the bidet to be in separate rooms. Oh, and lots of tile. We love tile. . . ."

"Hey, if we're going to build a custom home, I want it to be the way we've always dreamed about. When we come home at the end of the day, we want to relaaax. We work hard; we deserve a little indulgence, a few toys."

I ask people to describe how they use their kitchens. One woman's response is both revealing and typical: "In our house, everyone is always in the kitchen. Even though we have a den with nice chairs, everyone is always sitting around in the kitchen. So I figure, let's use a little of our budget on the room where we spend all our time. I want slate countertops, a commercial stove, lots of cabinets with glass doors, and I want one of those pot racks hanging from the ceiling with loads of gleaming copper pots. Also, I need one of those silent dishwashers and probably two sinks. What do you think makes a good kitchen floor . . . ? Wood? Cork? Carpet? . . . I think I want imported Italian marble."

The point is that the bathroom and the kitchen have become the perfect replacement for the living room. They clearly express how we want to live today. Of course we rarely live the lifestyle suggested by our bathrooms and kitchen, any more than former generations had time to live the lifestyles implied by their living rooms. Still, that's where we put our big moves . . . and spend the big bucks!

To keep you thinking, I want to suggest that you reconsider your first list of desires for the kitchen and bathrooms.

Generally, first-time designers gravitate toward the most precious materials, resources, and artisans. Imported marble, exotic woods, *Corian* counters, and tiled floors all look very good in the magazines, but not so great on your bank statement. The reason they are so expensive is because they have high embodied energy. They come from far away, or they require special fabrication and installation.

Why not design a kitchen that is just as stunning, maybe even more comfortable, from local, natural materials? I try to use the locally available stones, woods, craftspeople, and artisans. Also, I try to avoid manufactured products that embody a lot of energy—laminates, composites, and plastics. I find the natural materials wear much better. An old soapstone sink or slate floor develops patina and character, while old laminate counters or plastic accessories just look dingy and dog-eared.

Express yourself! That's what I do. For me, water is the most important aspect of these rooms, so I put my money there. High-design plumbing fixtures look great with old stone sinks. Bathroom basins can be made from hammered brass or locally crafted ceramic. The opportunity for architectural expression is as vast and varied as all the different personalities in the world.

David Sellers, a design/builder of great renown, designed an affordable shower that inflates to take up most of the living room. This gives him an enormous

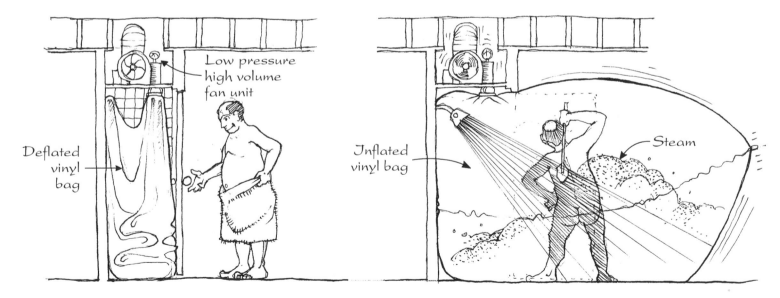

FIGURE 169: Sellers's shower bag before and after inflation.

FIGURE 170: Sanford's kitchen sink with pressure meters that dance while you clean the dishes.

shower that can be stored in a closet when not in use (Figure 169). Jim Sanford, another design/builder at Yestermorrow, places large brass gauges on all his fixtures. Washing the dishes is like visiting Casey Jones in his locomotive! (See Figure 170.) Kathy Meyer uses antique fixtures and brass in her design/built home. What have I done? Well (promise you won't tell), I own the state's first unlicensed gray water system, and it helps keep the plants in my greenhouse healthy (Figure 171).

What will you do?

FIGURE 171: Deep-bed planter used to filter gray water. The plants are fed by the nutrients that are filtered out.

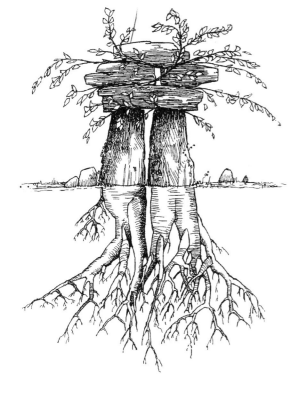

Power and Lights

Isn't it strange? Nothing suggests modern convenience and futuristic life-style so much as electricity. Electricity, we are told, will allow the most fantastic things to become commonplace in the "near future." And yet, scientists don't really know what electricity is! Oh, they know how to generate it and how to use it, they know how it behaves and misbehaves, but at the most fundamental level, science is still in the dark as to the essential nature of electricity. As lightning its awesome power becomes frightening. Gigantic surges of electrons pour down from the sky, splitting trees and boiling the very air. At the other end of the spectrum, in a computer or the brain, electricity flows in equally minuscule amounts. Almost immeasurable, these small voltage drops account for all neural and synaptic communication. Amazing, yes; but we still don't know what it *is*.

In your house, electricity will provide convenience and lighting. Even without waiting for the future, it is easy to be impressed with the gifts of electric power. Arriving in wires less than an ⅛" in diameter, this stuff allows us to keep our food cold, our beds warm, and raise the garage door without getting out of the car! On a more serious level, electric lights have really transformed our entire world, allowing us to continue our activities 24 hours a day. The lighting of an area will dramatically transform the behavior of those in it. Whether it's "mood" lighting in your dining room or mercury-vapor lamps in a crime-ridden neighborhood, electric lighting has a striking effect on human behavior.

Careful here, for electricity is a double-edged sword. Even as it gives us great freedoms, it extracts a price. Like an addict, modern society seeks ever greater supplies of cheap electricity. In this pursuit we rationalize the damming or rivers, the burning of nonrenewable fuels, and the construction of ill-designed nuclear power plants. We are becoming more aware of these consequences, but we've still got a long way to go. When designing for the use of electricity in a house, I try to keep in mind the source of this magic stuff. If it's coming from the grid, I know its generation has huge hidden costs, both environmental and fiscal. I resolve not to waste it.

A Basic Overview

Electricity comes in two flavors: 110 volts, used for lighting and most appliances; and 220 volts, used for heavy appliances and some HVAC equipment. These are both *alternating current,* or AC. Alternating current is not to be confused with the steady variety found in flashlights or car batteries. That's *direct* current or DC.) Depending on the situation, electricity is distributed about your home through a variety of code-approved conductors. The most common of these are plastic-sheathed cable, flexible metal cable, and rigid plastic or metal conduit. Regardless of the outer appearances, inside all of these conductors you will find either three wires (black, white, and copper for 110 volts) or four wires (black, red, white, and copper for 220 volts). If you find anything else, be cautious.

These wire colors follow strict conventions . . . and so should you. The "juice"— your basic 110 volt, 60-cycle, alternating current arrives in a black wire, sometimes called the "hot" wire. It returns "to ground" (0 volts) in the white wire, sometimes called the "common" wire. The appliance or light is connected between these wires, completing the circuit. There is also an uninsulated third wire (sometimes green) called the ground wire. This is a safety backup and doesn't normally carry any electricity. Its purpose is to offer an additional path to ground for stray or shortcircuited electricity. Remember, electricity always wants to get "back to ground," and it always chooses the path of least resistance. Without the ground wire, the path might be *you.*

The 220 volt flavor also arrives in two wires, one red and one black, each carrying 120 volts. These two currents are said to be out of phase. This means that when one is 120 volts *above* ground (0 volts), the other is 120 volts *below* ground. Consequently, any device connected between them will experience the combined difference, or 220 volts. Special motors and appliances are designed to complete the circuit. The 220 volt AC is more efficient and produces less wear on the machines designed to use it.

The classic explanation of electricity relies on an analogy with water. *Volts* are equivalent to electrical pressure, while *amperes* (amps) are electrical volume. When you multiply the volts times the amperes the result is *watts,* which is equivalent to the total electrical rate of flow. Every electrical fixture or appliance carries a watts rating, which indicates how much electricity will flow through it. If your toaster is rated 1,000 watts, that's how much power will flow through it. If you keep your toaster on for an hour, you will consume 1,000 watt-hours (and your toast will be vaporized). The power company charges you for the number of watts-hours, or kilowatts-hours (1 kilowatt equals 1,000 watts), you use each month.

The wires and equipment that bring your electricity are sized to handle between 100 and 400 amps. (Amperes, remember, are the "volume".) At the panel box (where all the circuit breakers are located), this electrical volume is subdivided into smaller 15- or 20-amp circuits that are safer and protected by individual circuit breakers. Typically, you might expect to have the outlets in one room on a 20-ampere circuit. Assuming 110 volts, this will allow a power use of:

$$\text{110 volts} \times \text{20 amperes} = \text{2,200 watts, or 2.2 kilowatts}$$

If your son plugs a 3,000-watt amplifier for his rock and roll band into this outlet, it will throw the circuit breaker. This is just one typical example of why design/builders must understand the electrical system.

Design

Like every aspect of your house, if *you* don't design your electrical system, it will end up designed by default. Electrical wiring is one of the areas least frequently embraced by the owner/builder. Accordingly, it is an area commonly designed by the electrician. Electricians are trained professionals, but they are not designers. It is not part of their procedure to ask:

"Where should I put the bathroom light switch?"

"Do you want lighting under your kitchen cabinets?"

"Should some of the outlets be operated by a wall switch?"

"How much power do you think you will need?"

"Where do you want the electric power to enter your house?"

"Do you prefer incandescent or fluorescent lighting?"

"Do you want a switched outlet by your bed? Where will the bed be located?"

How about your cable? Your phones? Your stereo speakers? Even your computers!?! The electrical profession is largely shaped by electrical, fire and safety codes. So expect electricians to make decisions that are safe (which is great!) and easy to install (not so great). This can mean you buy too much power, switches end up in the wrong place, lighting is inadequate, overpowering or left out altogether. To avoid all that, let's go through the basic issues involved in designing the electrical system for your house. This is design, not installation, and does *not* require a license or any knowledge of engineering.

THE SERVICE ENTRY

The first decision must be your source. Will it come from the grid or will you generate your own? Most people still get their power from a centralized utility. Assuming that's the case, you will want to find the pole nearest your property. This represents your own little piece of the grid. If there isn't a pole close by, you will have to have the power brought in. Every power company has a formula for the cost of installing additional poles. So you will make an appointment with someone from your utility company to come out and look at your site. They will tell you how everything "must be done." Since there are always options and alternatives, it's best to be ready with how *you* want it to be done.

Do you want your power to come in overhead or underground? Most people prefer underground. "Oh those unsightly overhead wires!" At the risk of sounding like a nut, I would like to defend the much maligned overhead wire approach. It's less expensive to install and easier to maintain. For me, it also has more visual appeal. There is something lyrical about the power lines loping down a country road. In the winter they become interesting snow sculpture and in the summer they make a bandstand perch for birds. In the city, the congestion of wires at a corner pole can often be sculptural, making me ponder where they all go. In contrast, underground service is just more of that "out of sight, out of mind" approach. When it breaks or needs service, the ground has to be dug up. This isn't so easy if it's frozen rock solid. OK, so you may think I'm a nut, but how the power gets to your house is a basic design decision. You have your opinion, I have mine.

Whether above or below grade, the main cable that carries wire from the grid to your house is called a service drop. It ends up at the meter. Consider this. The meter will be a significant visual element on your house. You must keep it in mind while drawing up the elevations. Like the vent stacks and the basement door, you must make it fit in. And since the circuit breaker box and main disconnect are usually located on the other side of the wall from the meter, it is important to consider the interior design as well. It is expensive and ill-advised to have the breaker box too far from where the power enters the house. The breaker box should be easily accessible and well lit.

THE WIRING

From the breaker box electricity is carried to all receptacles and fixtures through conductors—wires. This is the distribution system. It too has a visual aspect whenever it's not hidden in the walls. There are several types of conductor:

- Romex™: a plastic-shielded flexible cable that can be snaked through the walls and framing. (Romex is a product name; the proper general term would be "2NMB," standing for two conductors contained in a non-metallic binding.
- EMT: stands for electro-mechanical tubing or conduit; available in metal or plastic. This is "plumbing for power" and can be very attractive if installed with care and creativity. The wires must be placed in the conduit after it is installed.
- Greenfield: a flexible metal conduit or raceway. This is just the insulator, not the wires. (Greenfield™ is also a product name.)
- BX Cable: a metal armored, flexible cable similar to Greenfield, but with the wires already inside.
- Wiremold™: a shaped raceway that runs on the wall surface or along the moldings carrying several wires within. (Wiremold was the first to come out with this product, but there are now several manufacturers of metal and plastic raceway systems in designer colors, profiles, and finishes.)
- knob and tube: insulated wires held away from the wall by white porcelain fittings (quaint but obsolete).

Romex™ is by far the most commonly used conductor. Like Kleenex or Xerox, this product's name has become synonymous with the generic item. Of all the options, it is the least expensive.

And at the Ends of the Wires . . .

All connections must be made within accessible metal or plastic junction boxes; no exceptions. This includes connections, splices, fixtures, and switches: if the wire is bare, it must be in a box. There is a logic here. Electrical fires normally start where there is sparking. The risk of sparking is highest at the connections. If all connections are housed in metal or plastic containers, chance of fire is much reduced. Moreover, this allows future inspection and modification of the wiring. This is a necessary compromise to the "out of sight" approach in modern design. The modern aesthetic doesn't include seeing *how things work.*

Yet that is exactly what the surface-mounted conductors have in their favor. Generally, Greenfield™ and EMT are found in commercial applications because they meet the most rigorous safety requirements. Alternately, Wiremold™ is a surface-mounted conductor designed to be retrofitted into existing interiors. For this reason it is used in a lot of renovation work.

In addition to being easy to install, surface-mounted conductors have a visual,

and therefore *architectural,* quality. The eye follows the alignment of the conduit and, at some basic level, understands the whole system. (This was part of the appeal of the Knob & Tube also). Finally, surface-mounted conductors reduce penetrations into exterior walls, thus preserving the envelope's tightness. I've experimented with the use of surface-mounted conductors with great success (Figure 172).

THE LAYOUT

Before drilling any holes or running the wire, you must figure out where things go. This is the most important part of designing your electrical system. No one can do this for you. The method I employ starts in the studio, but the final design is field-tested before installation.

The following symbols are used to designate the different fixtures and lamps normally found in a home (Figure 173).

Start with a copy of your floor plans and draw in the symbol for each fixture. Just make up symbols for anything unusual, i.e., a built-in popcorn popper, overhead fan, etc. Also locate where you want the switch for each item. Draw a dotted line between the fixture and its switch. Voila! You're designing the electrical system.

Continue by locating all the receptacles. A receptacle, or outlet, is the slotted location where you place the plug. When two receptacles are placed together, it's called a *duplex.* Code requires an outlet within 6' of any location along a wall. This

FIGURE 172: **Surface-mounted EMT can easily become a design element if installed thoughtfully.**

means your outlets can't be farther than 12′ apart. Doors, windows, and any section of wall over 2′ long must be included in the calculation. Sometimes you may find it convenient to have one of the receptacles in a duplex operated by a wall switch. That way you can enter a room and turn on a table lamp with a switch by the door. If you choose to do this, don't forget to indicate it on your electrical plan with a switch and a dotted line (Figure 174, dining room).

Take some time as you plan your electrical layout. This is a real exercise in visualizing your future. How will you live in this house? Where will the furniture be?

Consider bedside lamps, desk lamps, vacuum cleaner outlets, and other special needs. What about floor outlets under the dining room table? Use a storyboard to imagine the sequence of going to bed at night. Can you turn off all the lights easily as you retreat to your bedroom? What sequence of lights will you turn on if awakened in the middle of the night?

This whole process is only the beginning. You have located the fixtures, switches, and outlets *in the plan only.* How high off the floor would you like your outlets? your switches? your wall sconces? your counter conveniences? You have to look at all your interior elevations

and draw in the electrical components. This serves two purposes: You discover whether there is any conflict with other aspects of the wall, say a heating register; and you get to preview what the wall will look like when built. (What do you mean, you weren't going to bother drawing all the interior elevations?!? Now you know just one reason why they are important.)

To give you a sense of the level of detail required, here is a preliminary checklist of electrical considerations. It's just a starting point, not a substitute for going through the design in your mind and imagining the details of how you will set up and live in your new home:

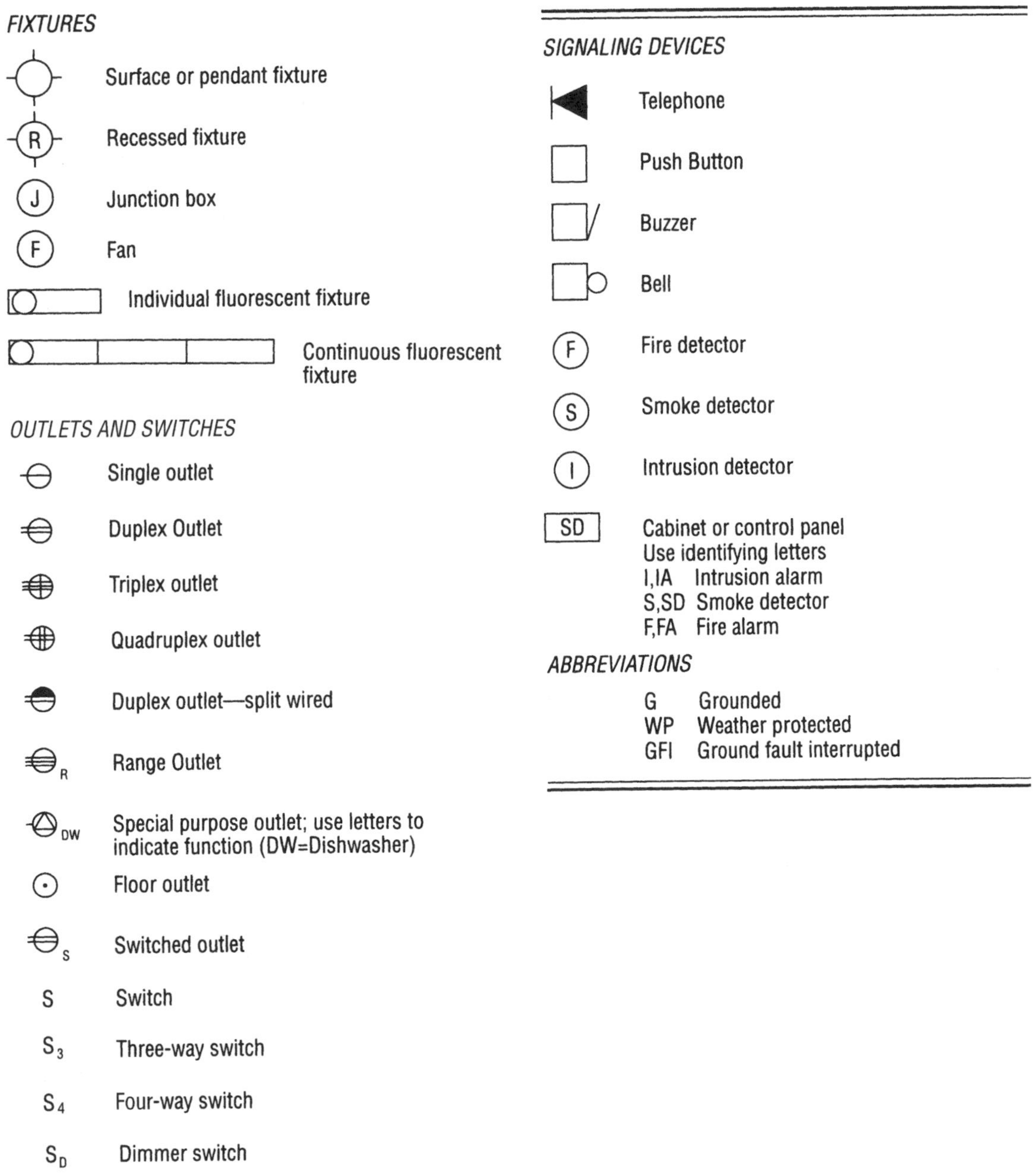

FIXTURES

◯ Surface or pendant fixture

Ⓡ Recessed fixture

Ⓙ Junction box

Ⓕ Fan

▭ Individual fluorescent fixture

▭ Continuous fluorescent fixture

OUTLETS AND SWITCHES

⊖ Single outlet

⊖ Duplex Outlet

⊕ Triplex outlet

⊕ Quadruplex outlet

⊖ Duplex outlet—split wired

⊖ᵣ Range Outlet

⬠ DW Special purpose outlet; use letters to indicate function (DW=Dishwasher)

⊙ Floor outlet

⊖ₛ Switched outlet

S Switch

S₃ Three-way switch

S₄ Four-way switch

S_D Dimmer switch

FIGURE 173: **A short list of frequently used electrical symbols.**

SIGNALING DEVICES

◀ Telephone

▫ Push Button

▱ Buzzer

▭ Bell

Ⓕ Fire detector

Ⓢ Smoke detector

Ⓘ Intrusion detector

▭ SD Cabinet or control panel
Use identifying letters
I,IA Intrusion alarm
S,SD Smoke detector
F,FA Fire alarm

ABBREVIATIONS

G   Grounded
WP Weather protected
GFI Ground fault interrupted

EXTERIOR AND LANDSCAPE LIGHTING:
- Over doors and entries
- Illuminating garage entry
- Walkways, garden paths, and at all steps
- Patios, decks, barbecue areas
- Security
- Weatherproof outlets, at least one on each side of the house

VESTIBULES AND MUD ROOMS:
- Good general lighting
- Closet lights
- Outlets
- Security control

KITCHEN:
- Good general lighting, probably on a dimmer
- Task lighting directed on all counter surfaces
- Outlets every 3' to 4' along the work areas
- Decorative mood lighting for any eating areas, on a dimmer
- Special circuits for ice box, stove, dishwasher, trash compactor, and microwave; all location heights to be determined by manufacturer's instructions
- Special circuit for electric range, if you must use one (I think it's a bad idea.)
- Special circuit for hood ventilation and integrated lighting
- In warm climates you may have overhead fans and air conditioners.

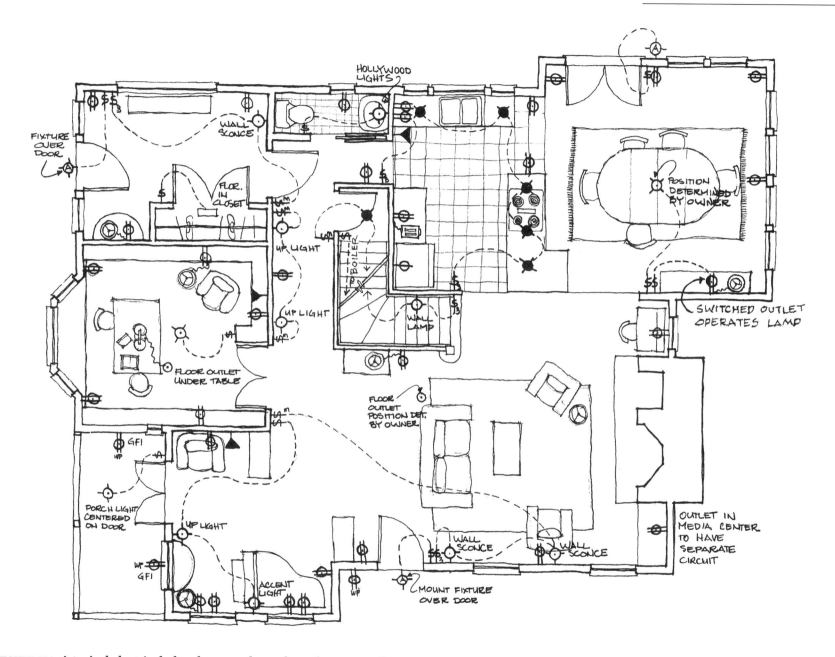

HOLLYWOOD LIGHTS

FIXTURE OVER DOOR

WALL SCONCE

FLOR. IN CLOSET

UP LIGHT

UP LIGHT

TO BOILER

FLOOR OUTLET UNDER TABLE

WALL LAMP

POSITION DETERMINED BY OWNER

SWITCHED OUTLET OPERATES LAMP

FLOOR OUTLET POSITION DET. BY OWNER

GFI

PORCH LIGHT CENTERED ON DOOR

UP LIGHT

WP GFI

ACCENT LIGHT

WALL SCONCE

WALL SCONCE

MOUNT FIXTURE OVER DOOR

OUTLET IN MEDIA CENTER TO HAVE SEPARATE CIRCUIT

FIGURE 174: A typical electrical plan does not show where the wires will actually be placed. That's left for the poor electrician to figure out.

DINING AREA:

- Decorative mood lighting on a dimmer
- Floor outlet under the table for the occasional use of an electric warmer, carving knife, or toaster
- Wall sconces on separate switch from overhead lights
- Outlets convenient to any hutch or sideboard
- In warm climates you may have overhead fans.

LIVING AREAS:

- Good general lighting on a dimmer
- Outlets for every table lamp, TV, stereo center, desk, couch, or other special use
- Floor outlets for floor lamps and sitting areas not against walls
- Special "framing" lamps to illuminate any art or wall events
- Focused or task lighting as required
- One outlet on the mantle
- Switched outlets as required for any of the above items
- In warm climates you may have overhead fans.

HALLWAYS AND CIRCULATION:

- One duplex every 10′ or 12′ along the wall
- Good general lighting
- Low wattage decorative lighting for navigation at night
- Special lighting for art or other wall events

BEDROOMS:

- Task lighting and outlet at each side of the bed
- General lighting for the room
- Nightlight
- Security system control box or keypad
- Outlet at every bureau, table, or chest
- Special lighting for art or other wall events
- Outlet for every exercise contraption with electronic readout
- In warm climates you may have overhead fans.
- Be mindful of EMFs (electromagnetic frequencies) in the bedroom

BATHROOMS:

- Good general lighting
- Light in shower
- Lighting at sink and mirror that minimizes shadows on face
- Duplex at sink for electric razor, hair dryer, toothbrush, etc.
- At least one outlet on each wall
- Good light for reading on the toilet(!)
- Ceiling ventilator with light

STUDY:

- Good general lighting
- Special task lighting designed for each work surface or desk
- Two duplex (four outlets) minimum at any desk; computers, printers, calculators, pencil sharpeners, special desk lamps, etc.
- Floor outlet at any reading location for floor lamp
- Outlet for every table lamp, TV, stereo center, desk, couch, or other special use
- In warm climates you may have overhead fans.

DEDICATED CIRCUITS (HOMERUNS!):

- Computers
- Freezers, refrigerators, appliances, air conditioning
- Table saw, other 220-V applications

A Few Generalizations

- All outlets in the kitchen, bathroom, outside, or in any other damp location must be *ground fault protected* with GFI (Ground Fault Interrupt) components. These devices automatically shut themselves down if the protective grounding wire becomes loose or disconnected. They also react more quickly in the event of a short circuit (like a TV set falling into the bathtub).
- Switches should be located and chosen with human behavior in mind. Three-way switches allow a fixture to be operated from two different locations, say the top and bottom of a flight of stairs. Four-way switches are available if you wish to power them from more than two locations.

Dimmers allow you to adjust the intensity of a lamp fixture. These are useful when the area to be lit is adjacent to windows or serves several different functions. A dining room table needs brighter light if it's also being used as a study hall for the kids. Special dimmers and ballasts must be used if the fixture is a fluorescent or halogen. Timers are useful for automatically turning off lights. I have my exterior lights on timers. With my two teenagers, I am presently considering replacing all our light switches with timers. There are also special switches that will turn on/off upon detecting sound, motion, or temperature. These may be useful for security lighting and special conveniences. Finally, door-operated switches are handy for turning on lights when you open a closet.

Check It Out

The best way to test drive your electrical design is with a Magic Marker. Once the house is framed and a roof is on, get your family and spend some time there. Using different-colored markers, mark the locations of every switch and outlet—right on the framing. On the floor, indicate how the doors will swing, just like you did in the drawings. When that's all done, play house! Pretend you're coming home on a rainy night and have to fumble for your door keys. . . . Where's the light? Imagine cooking breakfast or dinner. Pretend you're using every appliance in the kitchen. Act out a typical evening: put out the cat, brush your teeth, get into bed, read a book, and then arm the security and turn out the lights . . . without getting out of bed!

It's important to remember the choreography as you go through this exercise. Are all the light switches at the right height? Which way do the doors swing? Are there switches behind the doors? Can you plug in every appliance and light without using an extension cord? What about the vacuum cleaner?

This is a fun exercise and invariably turns up a lot of information. Most families can't stay on task. Discussion of lamp locations invariably leads to furniture layout. This leads to discussions (did I say debates?) over how shared spaces will be utilized. Soon the family members are excitedly talking about all aspects of their new home. The information is good. Part of lighting design, part of *all* design, accepts flexibility and change. You and your family are not static. Everyone is growing and changing. Your needs will do likewise. As you think about your lighting layout, consider several different storyboards. This is a good time to reconsider programmatic aspects of your design because it is normally not too late to make adjustments. Some of us say it's never too late.

Lighting

Lighting design is a whole study by itself. It really determines much more than whether you can see adequately. The comfort, utility, mood, and ambience of a room will all be determined by the lighting. This is an area you should consider carefully. There is no reason why you can't produce wonderful lighting effects if you use common sense and follow a few guidelines.

First, analyze the space to be lit. What activities or functions will take place? What are the specific lighting needs for reading, eating, watching TV, playing pool, or just lounging? Are there any special objects or locations that need to be lit? Sculpture, art, plants, or a photo gallery? Where will people sit and what will they be doing? Will there be any natural light from windows? What is the mood or quality of light you seek? How can windows, clerestories, monitors, or skylights help bring natural light into the deep interior rooms? How will your lighting effect or emphasize your architectural design?

Keep in mind that indirect lighting is usually more comfortable than direct, point source illumination. On the other hand, nothing is more aggravating than having insufficient light. Ambient or indirect lighting sets the mood in a room. Accent lighting focuses on a special aspect of the room. Task lighting is designed specifically for a work surface.

Indirect lighting is provided by concealing the source of light. The illumination comes from light bounced off of walls, ceiling, or floor. This produces a pleasant, even level of light. When the light is reflected from the ceiling it tends to be cooler, and a bit calmer. Alternately, illumination of surfaces in the lower part of the room will add warmth. These effects can be adjusted by using special lamps and placing the circuit on a dimmer. See also *Daylighting*, below.

Accent lighting can give a sense of depth to a room by drawing the eye toward a specific area or visual event in the room. Generating a "pool" of light will also create drama. This can be used for artwork, display, or to anchor an arrangement of furniture.

Task lighting has its greatest application in the kitchen, bathroom, and study. Wherever there is a work surface with a specific activity, task lighting should be considered. Desk work and reading is best served with generous amounts of diffuse light coming over the shoulder or from the side. Kitchen counters are often illuminated with special fluorescent fixtures mounted under the upper cabinets. The bathroom mirror needs even lighting on all sides to avoid shadows. A billiard table requires a very specific task light. It must be hung to maximize illumination of the playing surface but not interfere with play. Tradition dictates that it also not spill over the table edge or become general lighting. Very dramatic.

For the first-time design/builder there is often a tendency to simply lace the ceiling with a grid of track lighting. This allows lots of adjustment later on. I've tried this myself. It's O.K. as a compromise, but it never produces an effect equal to that of a well-thought-out lighting scheme. The sensitive use of wall sconces, floor lamps, task lighting, indirect valence lighting, recessed lights, and a few specialty fixtures will answer just about all your lighting needs. Even though flexibil-

ity is a virtue (which we'll discuss shortly), don't just throw in track lighting because you don't want to bother visualizing the behavior in the rooms (Figures 175a–d).

LAMPS AND LIGHTS

As you shop for your different light fixtures, you will quickly discover that there is a baffling selection of lamps to choose from. The term "lamp," when used by a lighting designer, refers to the bulb. Your

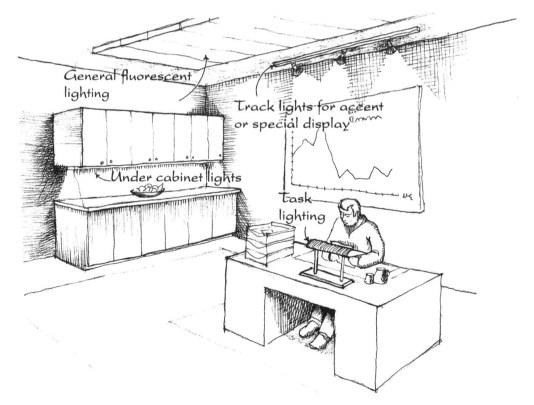

FIGURE 175a: Typical lighting for an office or workplace.

Track lights illuminate wall of art

Downlights wash stone fireplace

FIGURE 175b: **The use of contemporary light fixtures in a traditional-style home.**

pulse, increase skin response, and excite brain wave activity. Cool or blue lighting will reduce the pulse, skin response, and brain wave activity.

Generally, incandescent lamps give off warm color light and fluorescent lamps give off a cool bluish illumination. However, both types of bulbs may now be found in just about any color spectrum you desire. You can purchase fluorescent tubes that radiate a perfect replica of the daylight spectrum (ask for 5000 Kelvin). Incandescent bulbs are available that radiate bright white, blue, pink, or any other color. It's simply a matter of knowing where these lamps are sold. They don't

Wall sconce for low level light

FIGURE 175c: **Mood lighting at an entry door.**

basic selection includes incandescent, fluorescent, mercury, tungsten, sodium, halogen, metal halide, and neon. And of course there's a low-voltage version for many of them (which requires a transformer and different wiring). It's enough to make us long for the days of candles and kerosene lamps.

Different lamp formats can generally be judged by two basic qualities: color and/or energy efficiency. The color of different lamps is very, very important. Research has revealed varied but significant physiological effects from different colors. Warm or red lighting tends to quicken the

Accent light for plant or sculpture.

FIGURE 175d: **Accent lighting with a recessed pin spot.**

normally stock them at your grocery store; you must go to a lighting store.

Incandescent lamps produce light by forcing electricity through a tungsten filament, which glows from the resistance. Fluorescent lamps produce light by exciting a gas, which activates a special coating on the inside of the tube. The color is determined by the gas mixture and the frequency at which it is excited. Most of the other lamps burn filaments suspended in an inert gas bulb. These produce intense light that is difficult to control and tricky to use in residential applications.

In general, the fluorescent and low-voltage lamps will save you electricity. The new compact fluorescent bulbs supply remarkable testimony to this fact. When a normal 60-watt incandescent is replaced with a 14-watt compact fluorescent, the estimated savings is about fifty dollars over its nine-thousand-hour life. The level of illumination is the same.

Daylighting

Believe it or not, a major fraction of our lighting program occurs while the sun is still up. Any room or space without a window will need some general lighting pretty much all day, and especially toward the late afternoon. Even rooms with windows may need a bit of additional lighting on the far side of the room. In larger buildings like schools and office towers it has been shown that these interior lighting

requirements can cost plenty. Moreover, the usual solution of fluorescent fixtures with cheap ballasts and narrow color spectrums leaves much to be desired. Indeed, they are a proven health hazard for some folks.

Even on a cloudy day, there is so much illumination available from the sky that it seems a waste not to take advantage of it. Fortunately, it's easy and inexpensive to do so. The trick is to bounce the available daylight off of light-colored surfaces (walls, ceilings, panels, etc.) in such a way that it penetrates deep into the building. (See illustration below.) Properly placed light-shelves, skylights, clerestories, or light "scoops" can all but eliminate the need for general electrical lighting in many situations. Besides providing free

illumination, daylighting design reduces glare and controls solar gain.

Finally, the use of natural daylight "activates" your architecture. As the sun moves from extreme east to extreme west it will gradually shift the illumination on and within your home. This subtle indication of the time passing makes a room more comfortable and healthy.

Off the Grid!

Not everyone is living within affordable reach of a central utility. Vacation homes and camps are often sited specifically to avoid any contact with the crush of civilization. Island homes and some farm buildings may also be without centralized power. Even many who could, choose not

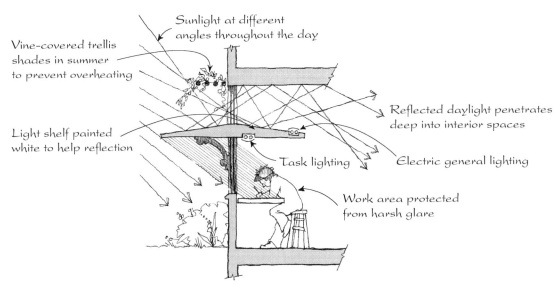

Sunlight at different angles throughout the day

Vine-covered trellis shades in summer to prevent overheating

Light shelf painted white to help reflection

Reflected daylight penetrates deep into interior spaces

Task lighting

Electric general lighting

Work area protected from harsh glare

Light shelves and properly positioned windows can save you money while controlling glare.

to tie into the grid. We've already discussed the hidden, and not so hidden, environmental costs underlying "cheap" conventional electricity (see Chapter 16, page 282). By disconnecting from the grid you will repay more of that environmental debt than a lifetime of tax-deductible donations to your favorite nonprofit. Moreover, the expense of generating your own has been greatly reduced over the last decade or so.

Whether ethical or practical, if you decide to generate your own power, you can choose from several technologies:

- *hydroelectric generation:* There are a variety of residential-scale turbines currently on the market (Real Goods Supply or Sunny Side Solar in Brattleboro, VT). Even a small brook with a cross section of no more than a few square feet (about 30 to 40 gallons per minute) can provide much of the power your house will need (150 watts continuous power with a Burkhart-Harris or similar impulse turbine). There are a variety of different turbines. There are also batteries, inverters, rectifiers, etc., that are part of a complete system. With so many design choices, you should plan on doing some research and study before installing your first system.
- *wind generation:* Farmers have been harnessing the wind for decades. If you have adequate wind on your site it can be turned into electricity or used to pump water. Wind generators are available in sizes from 1 kilowatt up. They require a tower and occasional maintenance. Those with a fear of heights might do better with a different soft path.
- *photovoltaic electricity (PV):* A solar cell is a silicon device that turns sunlight directly into electricity. These days they are most frequently seen on solar-powered calculators. Behind the scenes, however, are over forty thousand Americans who currently provide for their electrical needs solely with PV-generated power. A one-time payment for a proven technology with no moving parts starts to sound like a pretty good deal, especially since the cost of the technology is shrinking faster than any of the other soft technologies (thanks to Texas Instruments and NASA).
- *fuel-powered generator:* This option will get you off the grid, but you will still be hostage to the oil vendors. Generators run on gasoline, diesel, or LP gas. They are a proven technology and a great source of *backup* power. But the eventual cost of the fuel could easily make them more costly than the alternatives—including the grid.

If you elect to use any of these technologies you will undoubtedly be digesting a few more books on the matter. There is a lot of technical stuff to assimilate before you're off the grid; we certainly haven't room here to present all the nuts and bolts in a comprehensive way. Nevertheless, we'll get you through the first step and then suggest some additional reading. The first step is to assess whether there is enough wind, water, or sun on your site to make the project viable.

HYDRO POTENTIAL

The amount of power available from a stream is a function of the volume or quantity of water flowing and how far it falls, or the *head*. If you know these things, you can determine the number of available watts by either of the following formulae:

$$P = QHe/11.8 = AvHe/11.8$$

where:

P = power in kilowatts (kw)
Q = water flow in cubic feet per second (cfs)
H = head in feet
A = average cross section of stream in square feet
v = velocity of the water in feet per second (fps)
e = efficiency of the technology being used, see below (no units)
11.8 = This is a constant that accounts for the density of water and also converts the ft.-lbs./sec. into kw

There are a variety of traditional turbine and waterwheel designs. Each has a slightly different efficiency. The following chart gives approximate efficiencies, e, for the most common configurations.

WATERWHEELS:

undershot	25%–45%
breast	35%–65%
poncelot	40%–60%
overshot	60%–75%

TURBINES:

reaction	80%
impulse	80%–85%
crossflow	60%–80%

Figure 176a–d: Examples of the above waterwheels.

The average velocity of the water, v, is easy to determine. Simply measure the time it takes a piece of wood to float over a measured distance. This velocity along the surface will be higher than that for water moving along a stream bed, where there is more drag. Therefore, multiply your measured speed by .8 to get the average velocity.

The average cross-sectional area of a stream is found through a calculation like those annoying word problems we all struggled with in high school (Figure 177).

The depth of the stream is measured at regular intervals and then averaged. The width of the stream is easily measured directly. The product of these two numbers will yield the average cross-sectional area of the stream.

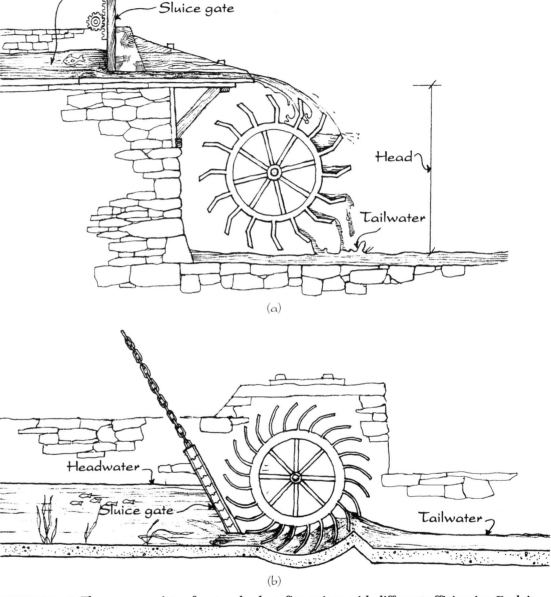

(a)

(b)

FIGURE 176a–d: There are a variety of waterwheel configurations with different efficiencies. Each is suited for a particular type of hydro site. (*a*) An overshot wheel. (*b*) A poncelet wheel.

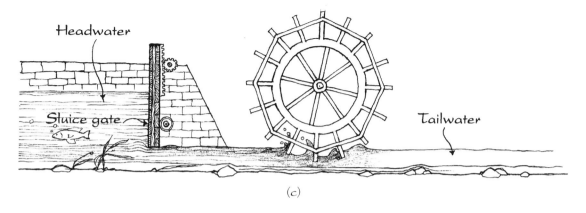

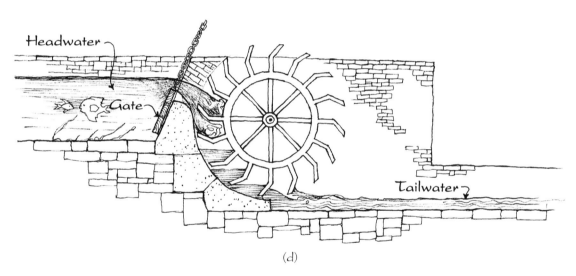

FIGURE 176a–d: (*Continued*) (*c*) **An undershot wheel.** (*d*) **A breast wheel.**

Like anything else, the scale of your operation will affect how easy it is to set up and maintain. Tiny hydro (less than 500 watts per day) is easy, affordable, and unlikely to be your only source of power. As your hydroelectric aspirations get larger and your dependence on it becomes more exclusive, you can expect to wrestle with a few more problems. Some of these might include:

- As the dams, conduits, and penstocks get larger, so does their engineering, construction, and, of course, expense.

- Dams and intakes must be maintained constantly. Dams must be adjusted for seasonal variations in the water level. Intakes and protective grates must have flotsam and debris removed regularly.

- Larger installations require federal and state permits that can be costly and time-consuming to obtain. Often the hydro rights for a site are owned by someone other than the property owner.

- Primary dependence on a hydro installation requires a more thorough analysis of what will be generated. One must determine the flow rates at different times of the day and different times of the year, and allow for anomalies like floods and droughts.

After completing these calculations you may be at the beginning of an exciting and rewarding project. Even if your results indicate a mere 200 watts, keep in mind that 200 watts will be generated twenty-four hours a day (if the stream flow is constant). With adequate battery storage you could easily have 1800 (1.8 kw) watts available for the few hours each day when you need lights.

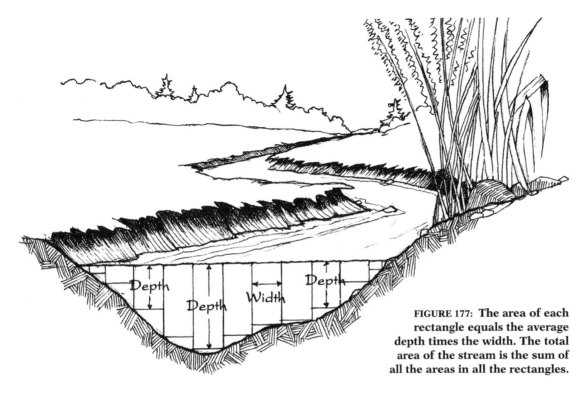

FIGURE 177: The area of each rectangle equals the average depth times the width. The total area of the stream is the sum of all the areas in all the rectangles.

WIND POTENTIAL

The wind, and the potential power in it, is characterized by wide fluctuations. Measuring it at any given time is no problem, but estimating the overall average will take some doing. You can generate this data yourself over twelve or more months or contact a local weather station (the National Climatic Center, the National Oceanic and Atmospheric Administration [N.O.A.A.], U.S. Weather Service, airports, etc.) Though fairly easy, the problem with the latter approach is that it is rarely accurate. The wind speed at your particular site is likely to be slightly different than that at the airport, weather station, etc. As we will see, the available power relates to the cube of the wind speed (v^3). This means a difference of just a few mph could have a dramatic effect. With this in mind, the best approach is a compromise. Take readings for a few months in each season so you can establish a relationship between your site and theirs. Measure the speed and direction. Suppose you find that your readings are generally about 10 percent higher than theirs and the winter direction is out of the north. This means that you can use their twelve-month historic data adjusted 10 percent for your site. It isn't quite as accurate as taking the data directly from your site, but it's good enough.

The device for measuring wind speed is called an anemometer and they are not too expensive. However, the anemometer measures only *instantaneous* speed. To get *averages* you would have to stand there all day, taking recordings every few minutes. Devices that do this for you are called wind odometers or wind data accumulators and they cost between one hundred and two hundred dollars. One excellent source for these is NRG Systems, 110 Commerce St., P.O. Box 509, Hinesburg, Vermont 05461. They make them for every budget, and their cheap ones are worth the money. Also, in their book, *More Other Homes and Garbage*, Leckie describes how to build one with an inexpensive calculator for about thirty dollars (Figure 178).

Once you have the necessary data for your site, you are ready to determine how much power you might generate with it. The formula is:

$$P_{gen} = .005e \, (K_a)(K_t)Av^3$$

Where:

P_{gen} = power in watts (W)
.005 = a coefficient that accounts for the different units and the density of air
e = the conversion efficiency of the equipment being used, .2–.25 for

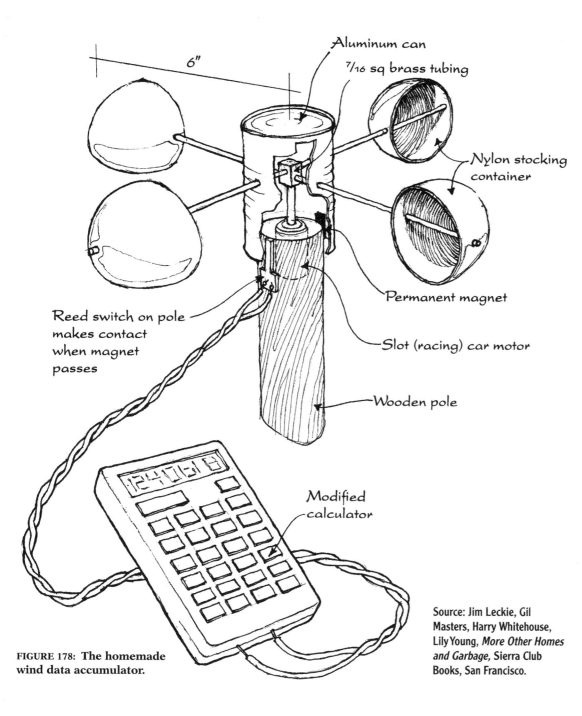

6"

Aluminum can

7/16 sq brass tubing

Nylon stocking container

Permanent magnet

Slot (racing) car motor

Wooden pole

Reed switch on pole makes contact when magnet passes

Modified calculator

FIGURE 178: The homemade wind data accumulator.

Source: Jim Leckie, Gil Masters, Harry Whitehouse, Lily Young, *More Other Homes and Garbage*, Sierra Club Books, San Francisco.

typical equipment used in residential applications

K_a = a corrective multiplier for altitude; the air density decreases as the altitude increases

K_t = a corrective multiplier for temperature; the air density decreases as the temperature increases

A = the cross-sectional area of the windmill (square feet).

v^3 = the estimated monthly velocity of the wind (mph) cubed

It is very important to understand that the amount of power in the wind is related to the velocity *cubed*. This means that a doubling of wind speed results in an eight-fold increase in power generated. Now you can see why a little difference between the wind on your site and that at the weather station could have a big effect.

If the cross-sectional area of the windmill is assumed to be that met by a horizontal-axis wind machine with propeller diameter D (in feet) our equation above can be written:

$$P_{gen} = .004e(K_a)(K_t)(\pi r^2)(v^3)$$

Here we can see an important relationship: The power generated is directly proportional to the square of the prop radius. This means that if you double the diameter of your windmill prop you will get four times more power from a given wind condition.

TABLE 25: ALTITUDE CORRECTION FACTOR

Altitude (feet)	K_a
0	1.000
2,500	0.912
5,000	0.832
7,500	0.756
10,000	0.687

The following tables gives you the different correction multipliers for air density (Tables 25 and 26).

As you conduct these calculations, remember that power and energy are not the same thing. Power is measured in *watts* and energy is measured in *watt-hours*. Energy is power over a given time period. We buy energy, not power, from our utility. Your electric meter measures kwh, or kilowatt-hours.

When you shop for a wind generator, you will find that they are rated according to certain wind speeds. A wind generator's design determines how much of the available wind power can be converted into

TABLE 26: TEMPERATURE CORRECTION FACTOR

Temperature (°F)	K_t
0	1.130
20	1.083
40	1.040
60	1.000
80	0.963
100	0.929

electrical energy. The P_{gen} in the foregoing equations represents the number of watts (KW) generated at any given instant for a particular wind speed. But you buy electricity in KW *hours*, not KW, so wind generators are rated by how much energy they will produce in a standardized wind condition over a set period of time—usually 25 mph for twelve hours.

After you have an idea of the wind potential on your site, the next step is to figure out your daily electrical consumption. Unless you have a superior site, you shouldn't expect to meet all your needs all the time. I asked Jito Coleman, wind guru and alternative energy engineer, how to tell a good wind site.

"Well, if there's so much wind that it's generally annoying to visit the site, then it *might* be a viable wind site. But if it's *always* annoying, so annoying that people wouldn't want to live there, then it's probably a good wind site."

Jito has been designing and installing wind generators all over the world for more than twenty years. When it comes to residential installations he cautions: "Wind isn't for everyone. Your site must have unusually good winds. It can be improved or defeated by microconditions like trees, ridges, and other tall buildings. Even a good site rarely has adequate wind twelve months out of the year."

Not to make it too daunting, Jito encourages the following resources for those who are serious about wind power:

Wind Energy Resource Atlas of the United States
Pacific Northwest Laboratory
Richland, WA 99352

The Wind Power Book
by Jack Park
Cheshire Books
514 Bryant Street
Palo Alto, CA 94301

Wind Power Monthly
Vrinners Hoved
8420 Knebel, Denmark
or
P.O. Box 496007 Suite 217
Redding, CA 96099-6007

PHOTOVOLTAICS

Like wind power, photovoltaic generation of electricity is subject to the whims of weather. While we have data for average annual insolation (sunlight), even the weatherman can't tell us exactly when and how much we will get on any given day. All we can really depend on is that all available sunlight will arrive during the day. Therefore, photovoltaics are normally used to charge battery banks. These then become the source of power at night.

Photovoltaic arrays are rated in watts. A 35-watt array will generate 35 watts when it is exposed to full sunlight. It will generate less if it's overcast or late in the day. Most PV installations support 12- or 24-volt lighting and appliances. This means that a 35-watt array will produce just about 3 amps of current when fully illuminated (Figure 179).

$$3 \text{ amperes} \times 12 \text{ volts} = 36 \text{ watts}$$

or

$$36 \text{ watts} / 12 \text{ volts} = 3 \text{ amps}$$

Unfortunately, just because you install 1000 watts of equipment doesn't mean you will always get that much power. So you can see that the first step in assessing the viability of photovoltaics is to find out how

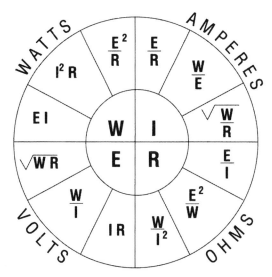

I = current in *amps*, named for French physicist A. W. Ampere

E = electromagnetic force in *volts*, named for Italian physicist A. Volta

R = resistance in *ohms*, named for German physicist G. S. Ohm

W = power in *watts*, named for English physicist James Watt

FIGURE 179: The Ohm's law mandala. This chart shows the relationship between watts, ohms, amps, and volts.

PV SYSTEM SIZING WORKSHEET

Step 1:
Calculate total daily load

Device	Quantity	Watts (E × I)	Hours per day used	Days per week used	Average watt hours per day
————	————	× ————	× ————	× ————	/7 = ————
————	————	× ————	× ————	× ————	/7 = ————
————	————	× ————	× ————	× ————	/7 = ————
————	————	× ————	× ————	× ————	/7 = ————
————	————	× ————	× ————	× ————	/7 = ————

Maximum AC Surge ———— Watt hours ————

Step 2:
Allow for 2% wire loss (1.02) or actual loss
80% battery efficiency (1.25) or actual efficiency
90% inverter efficiency (1.11) or actual efficiency
Or skip inverter step for DC loads

Watt hours × 1.02 × 1.25 × 1.11 = Daily Watt hours
———— × 1.02 × 1.25 (× 1.11) = ———— Watt hours

Step 3:
Calculate the required array peak watts using yearly average or worst-month peak sun hours

Daily Watt Hours / Peak Sun Hours = Array Peak Watts
———— / ———— = ———— Peak Watts

Step 4:
Calculate the number of solar modules required. For 24-volt DC systems, round up to the next even number (i.e., 11 = 12)

Array Peak Watts / Module Wattage Rating = Number of Modules
———— / ———— = ———— Modules

Step 5:
Calculate the battery bank size.

Daily Watt Hours × Multiplier (Fig. 202g)
× 2.5 (for 40% depth of discharge)
× Temperature Correction Factor (Fig. 205) =
———— × ———— × 2.5 × ———— = ————

Source: Joel Davidson, *The New Solar Electric Home*, p. 338.

much sun will hit your site. The accompanying charts are from J. Davidson's book *The New Solar Electric Home* (Figures 180a–g and Table 27).

Davidson provides us with a very concise worksheet (see page 347) that will help even the mathematically fearful through the exercise of calculating their photovoltaic requirements.

As an example let's consider what it would take to power a typical-size home in Warren, Vermont:

1. At 900 watts used for about six hours each day, our daily use would be 5,400 watt-hours, or 5.4 kwh. This equals 37.8 kwh per week.

2. Assuming we're off the grid (no inverter) we will incur two percent wire losses and hope for 75 percent to 85 percent battery efficiency. So our real weekly demand will be:

**37.8 kwh × 1.02 (wire losses) ×
1.25 (battery efficiencies) =
48.2 kilowatt-hours per week**

3. The number of peak sun hours per day in the winter is 2.5 and it runs up to a bit over 4 in the summer. As an average we will use 3 hours of peak sun per day. Thus, if we divide our daily requirement into the available solar resource we get:

**5400 watt-hours/3 hours of peak sun
= 1800 watts**

One way or another, we need a photovoltaic array that will generate 1800 watts each instant of the three hours of peak sun arriving on average each day. That will give us our daily requirement of 5400 watt-hours.

4. If we use modules rated at 55 watts, we will need:

**1800 watts/55 watts per module =
32 modules(!!)**

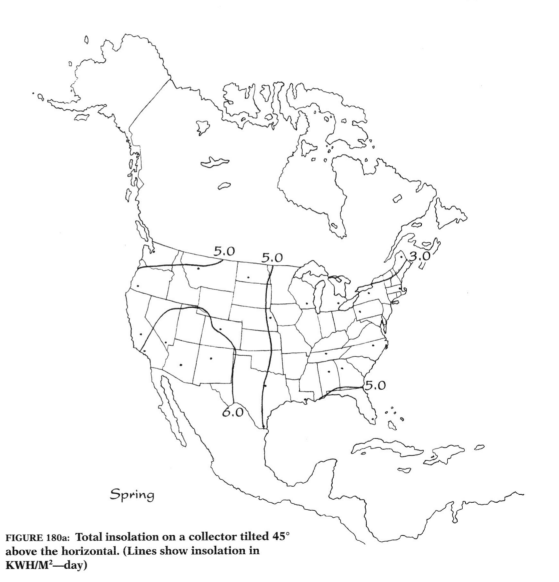

FIGURE 180a: Total insolation on a collector tilted 45° above the horizontal. (Lines show insolation in KWH/M²—day)

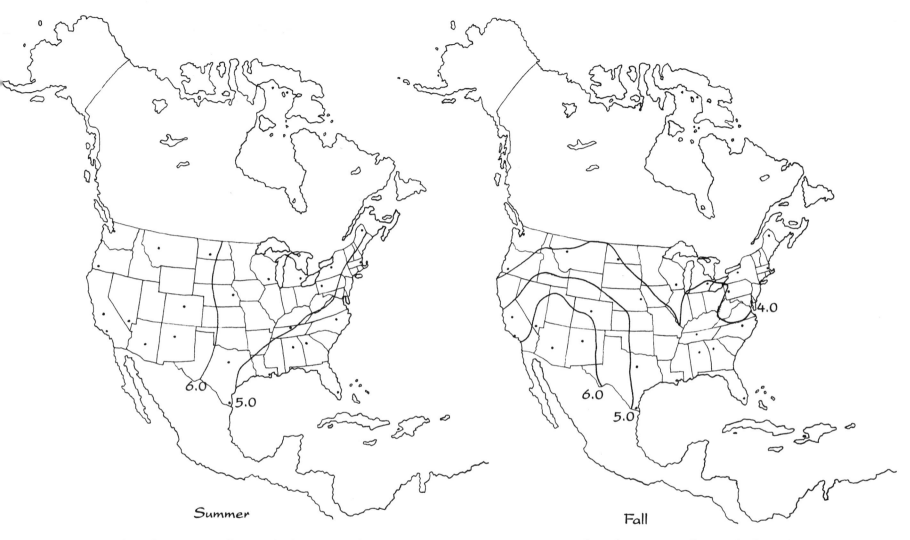

Summer

Fall

FIGURE 180b: Total insolation on a collector tilted 45° above the horizontal. (Lines show insolation in KWH/M²—day)

FIGURE 180c: Total insolation on a collector tilted 45° above the horizontal. (Lines show insolation in KWH/M²—day)

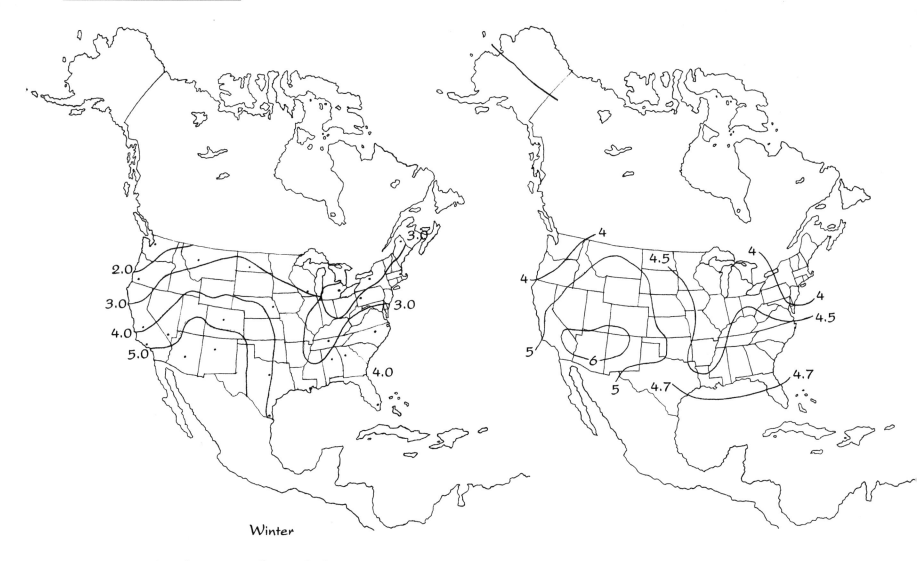

FIGURE 180d: Total insolation on a collector tilted 45° above the horizontal. (Lines show insolation in KWH/M²—day)

FIGURE 180e: Peak sun hours per day (yearly average). (Lines show insolation in KWH/M²—day)

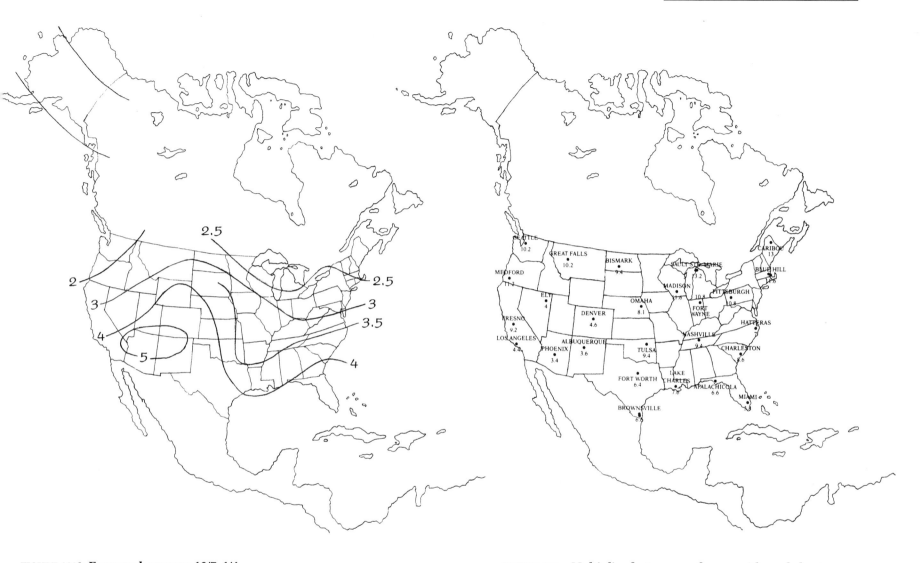

FIGURE 180f: Four-week average 12/7–1/4.

FIGURE 180g: Multiplier factors map for use with worksheet.

TABLE 27: PEAK SUN HOURS

Average Daily Insolation Availability for a South-facing Surface Tilted at Latitude + 15° (kwh/m²)

	Winter	Spring	Summer	Fall	Annual
Albuquerque	6.14	7.18	6.72	7.12	6.79
Atlanta	3.78	5.20	5.03	4.91	4.73
Birmingham	3.70	5.05	4.84	4.91	4.63
Bismarck	3.57	5.09	5.73	4.43	4.71
Boston	2.83	4.24	4.66	3.89	3.91
Brownsville	4.18	5.42	5.64	5.15	5.10
Caribou	2.92	4.88	4.62	3.20	3.91
Dallas–Fort Worth	4.31	5.21	5.75	5.45	5.18
Denver	5.60	6.37	6.01	6.35	6.09
Detroit	2.53	4.42	4.91	3.82	3.93
Fresno	3.76	6.64	6.90	6.44	5.95
Great Falls	3.23	5.22	5.95	4.64	4.77
Las Vegas	6.21	7.49	6.78	7.02	6.88
Madison	3.20	4.84	5.12	4.04	4.31
Medford	2.30	5.25	6.40	4.54	4.64
Miami	5.01	5.47	4.67	5.07	5.05
Nashville	3.12	4.77	5.24	4.44	4.40
New Orleans	4.11	5.26	4.88	5.16	4.85
Omaha	4.19	5.16	5.58	4.80	4.94
Phoenix	5.91	7.36	6.65	6.99	6.73
Pittsburgh	2.23	4.09	4.68	3.66	3.68
Raleigh-Durham	3.57	4.97	4.88	4.55	4.49
Seattle	1.59	4.24	5.13	3.05	3.52
Syracuse	2.00	4.08	4.70	3.24	3.51

TABLE 28: TEMPERATURE CORRECTION FACTORS

Temperature °C	Correction Factor	Temperature °F
−10	1.10	+14
−15	1.55	+5
−20	2.05	−4
−25	2.75	−13
−30	3.50	−22
−35	4.25	−31

And it could actually require even more panels depending on local temperature (Table 28).

It is easy to see that Vermont is a difficult place to live a life powered solely by photovoltaics. Today the average cost for installed PV electricity is a little over $10/watt. At that price, this system would cost over $18,000! If the life of the system was twenty-five years the annual cost would be about $720 per year (not counting interest or inflation). At today's prices for utility-supplied electricity, this doesn't seem to make much sense. No house using 37.8 kwh each week ever runs up an electrical bill of this magnitude.

So this explains why few people in the North are leaving the grid for photovoltaics.

But what if you aren't on the grid? Perhaps you are building a house on a remote hillside, say ½ mile from the closest power pole. It's normal for the electric company to charge $6 to $9 per foot for running in the primary power. Of course, that's for overhead power; underground might cost 30 percent or so more.

.5 miles × 5280 ft./mile × $6.50/ft. = $17,160

Now this is a different ball game. If we deduct the access cost from the PV installation cost, everything looks a lot better.

($18,000 − $17,160)/25 years = $33.60 per year

I would be thrilled with this electric bill!

If you know the cost of bringing in commercial power, and you know the amount of available sunshine in your area, you can easily calculate how far into the boonies it pays to bring the grid. Generally, you can see that the further you go, the more attractive PV alternatives become.

What if it were a break-even situation? The grid is pretty reliable but it's an "out of mind" solution and has hidden costs. The PVs are environmentally friendly, but require that you understand how your power works. A lot depends on the extent of cloudy periods in your area. The nights and overcast days are overcome with batteries and generators. These are the parts that will need the most care and maintenance over the life of your system.

GENERATORS

Design/builders have made use of gas, diesel, and LP-powered generators for a long time. They are hardly an "alternative" technology and the fuel they consume is nonrenewable. Nevertheless, they have a place in this discussion. Portable generators have energized many a construction crew building in the wilderness. Even around town, if the power company can't keep up with the contractor's schedule, the foundation forms are often built with portable power.

Generators are a good backup power source for any home. Storms and other unforeseeables can black out whole communities for several hours, sometimes days. In that time refrigerated food can be lost, water can't be pumped, furnaces and boilers become inoperable. Such inconvenience can be avoided by the installation of a backup generator. For the house powered by wind, hydro, or photovoltaics the generator is doubly useful. It provides power during times of repair and maintenance. Plus, it can keep batteries charged and healthy.

If you are considering a permanent installation, I suggest you look into generators that can be fueled with LP gas. This is efficient, clean-burning, and reduces wear on the engine. It can be delivered by truck or brought to remote sites in small portable tanks.

APPLIANCES

Another important component of energy independence is reducing how much you need. We can reduce the size of our PV array, our wind or hydro generator, and, above all, our battery banks if we *reduce our electricity consumption*. For instance, besides excellent gas stoves you can now find incredibly efficient gas refrigerators (Amana, SunFrost, etc.), gas operated clothes dryers (White Westinghouse), superefficient washing machines (Bosch), and a full spectrum of gas-powered light fixtures.

Wind, water, and sun—what fabulous ways to generate electricity! These are the truly futuristic modes of powering our communities. Happily, they are no longer "experimental" or fringe. Sure, the big commercial utilities will continue to be the norm for most people buying power, but even they are now investing in these clean methods of natural generation. And small-scale power generation is becoming more and more popular in every region of the country. If this sounds like something that would fit your lifestyle, you can get more information from the following publication:

Home Power Monthly
"Hands On Journal of Homemade Power"
P.O. Box 520
Ashland, OR 97520
www.homepower.com

Whether you choose to buy electricity or generate your own, it is clear that it should be considered carefully in the design of your home.

Phone, Fun, and Security

When thinking about your electrical system don't forget the phone, the sound system, intercom, cable TV, thermostat wire, possibly a security system, a computer network, and—and the doorbell. These wiring subsystems are installed at the same time as the basic power. They can be immensely helpful in fleshing out your design intentions. While "playing house," visualize where you listen to music, watch

TV, or use the phone. And imagine where you and your family will be accessing the web or other computer services. These will become a bigger part of our lives in the near future. Place the security system controls where you can activate and deactivate them conveniently. In addition to controls by the doors, I suggest a station at the bedside. It's mighty comforting when you awake to something going bump in the night.

The Attitude (One More Time, with Feeling)

If *you* don't design your electrical system, it will be designed by your electrician and his code book. No less than any other part of your house, the electricity can give form and meaning to your architecture, if you choose to let it. It can bring light, sound, and feeling to every room in your house. Your interpretation of this modern magic—the cables, the fixtures, switches, sound, light, etc.—will be seen on almost every surface of your home. Alternately, you may decide it should be hidden away, "out of sight and mind." Either way, this is the nervous system for the modern home. It's the sense of sight, hearing, and control that you have from a magically removed location. It really is magic. Don't pass by this great opportunity to illuminate and energize your design.

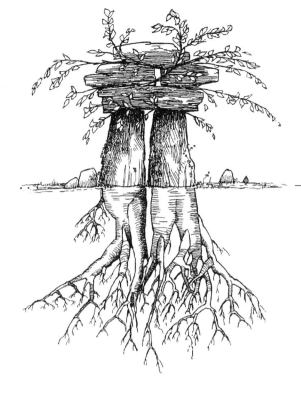

Finishes, Finishing, and Punchlist

And now for the exciting conclusion . . .

Conclusion!?! Already? But we can't be finished. What about the kitchen design, the bathroom design, the floors, the counters, the paint . . . ? How is a hardwood floor installed? How are vinyl and ceramic tile laid? How are fireplaces and chimneys constructed? The stairs!! We didn't cover the stairs. How are stringers cut, treads installed, and balusters built? Isn't there something we should know about carpets? How do the baseboards work? Which is better, plaster or gypsum board? Yikes, we just *can't* be finished.

No, actually, it's very hard to be "finished" in the sense of "all done." Let's face it, people are a moving target. Houses that truly fit the lives and life-styles of their occupants are destined to change. A design that's perfect for a single occupant seldom suits a couple. Likewise, the newlywed couple will have one sort of program, the family with children will have another. And as the children grow, the program will grow and change again. Finally, the children will go out on their own and the house may seem too big. The constant changes that take place in peo-

ple's lives are the most frequently cited reason for selling, renovating, or moving.

Among the design/builders I know, few have totally finished homes. They are always finishing one room while ripping another apart. Speaking from experience, this is not necessarily the best approach for everyone. Still, it's interesting to note what design/builders say when asked how they can live like that, always in flux.

"Actually," says John, one of our instructors, "I think I'll always be tweaking the design a bit. It's pretty easy work if you let the roof and foundation stay put, though even those have to be reconsidered now and then. It's all pretty normal once you look at home design as a central part of living your life. I really don't think of it as something to be finished up. I enjoy it, and what's even more important . . . so does my wife."

"Yes, but don't you ever just want to be done? Wouldn't it be nice to call it finished so you could just live in it?" One of the students, Ed, is doubtful.

"Maybe someday." John teaches studio as well as site courses. "But I keep seeing new things that I want to try. I find it fascinating that the things I designed and built just a decade ago are no longer working. Not big things, mind you. For instance, look at this island in the kitchen. When I originally renovated the kitchen, all my kids were young. We could all fit around the counter with room to spare. Now, ten years later, they are teenagers with friends. It's no longer possible for everyone to have a seat. But, if I redesign the counter on an angle and move the stove to the left, there will again be plenty of room for everyone. I think I will rip this thing out next fall."

"Really? Just for your kids?"

"Sure. I'm happy to change my place however I must to live the life I want to live. If I want my kids and their friends to keep hanging out around our place, and I do, I'd better consider them in the program."

"Sheesh." Ed shakes his head. "I want my place finished completely before I move in, and I'm not sure I could change it afterward. I think I'd rather just buy another place and move."

"Well, that's a pretty normal approach," admits John. "But if you don't want to move, then it's the house that must do the changing. I like it here and I have a lot of friends in this community. Have you ever heard of the old saying 'The only reason to finish a house is to sell it or to die.'?"

John is being a little dramatic, but you get the point. Design/building your own home is one of life's central adventures. It will surely take more time than just having the professionals "do you up." There will be switchbacks and change orders; there will be cash flow crises and technical difficulties; there will be conflicting requests from different family members, and the term *finished* will become relative, as in, "Well, everything is finally finished . . . in *this* room, anyway."

But you wouldn't be reading this book if there weren't a part of you that understood this adventure for what it is.

IIII Punch List

No chapter on finishing would be complete without some mention of the punch list. This is a list of all the little things left to do before the project is complete. You will be carrying one around for months. Almost everyone sets their sights on the finish line far too soon. But things keep cropping up and the end always stays just

a few more days into the future. This can be demoralizing if you aren't prepared for it. Instead, try to define your own finish line and make it something attainable. Like any other aspect of the project, it will reflect who you are and how you live. Some will need every detail "punched out" immediately, while others will live with exposed insulation for a year. Most will fall somewhere in between.

IIII Finishes

Just as you should be thinking about the roof while laying out your foundation, it's important to have your finishes in mind while you're doing the framing. Except for paint, most finishes have certain dimensions that must be accommodated. They also may require special fasteners or adhesives. Finally, some finishes demand specific substrates. For instance, ceramic tile should be installed on cement backer board; linoleum looks best over a smooth pressboard subfloor; skim coat plaster needs a special gypsum lath, sometimes called "blueboard." These requirements are best considered in advance.

Flooring is particularly critical. Assume that the tile in your kitchen is a quarry tile; it will likely be ½" or more thick when installed. Now imagine linoleum or rubber sheet on the floor in the downstairs bathroom; this may be a mere ⅛" thick. If the two floors meet at the doorway, you have a problem. Height changes in floor surfaces are potential hazards for tripping. The answer is to install the subfloors at different heights. This may mean framing the floor slightly differently.

The point is that decisions about final finishes can have important impacts on the very earliest phases of construction. Once again we must remember the cyclical nature of design and construction. A well-designed home will be coherent. This coherence results from considering the end at the beginning and the beginning at the end.

This leads to an apparent conflict. If a building must be totally resolved before starting construction, how can the design/builder make changes and modifications as the building process unfolds?

Not to worry. If you originally designed with ¾″ hardwood floors in mind, that hardly constrains you. Most floor finishes will accommodate that ¾″ dimension. Those that are thinner will require another layer of ⅛″ or ¼″ plywood to take up the slack. Those that are thicker may need a little more fussing, but remember (and this is important), *there's always a solution for every problem.*

A more ambitious change could involve moving walls, windows, or doors. In such instances, every part is being moved so the overall design will remain coherent. If the change is in the exterior walls, however, you will be making changes to your roof and foundation also. This may be costly.

"See," says Ed, "every time you turn around there's a costly problem. If my house isn't figured out and finished before I move in, there are sure to be *big* problems."

"So?" John seems unruffled. "Problems can be solved. There are a zillion different finishes and surfaces that you can employ in your house. Each one has specific installation requirements. Can you expect to be an expert on every one? No, you can't. So I do the best research I can, and then jump in. If the game changes (or *I* change it), I'll figure it out as I go. I rather like the challenge of figuring out new materials and solving the problems associated with their installation."

▥ Problem Solving

It's time to discuss the secret weapon of all accomplished design/builders. This is not a generalization. Every single design/builder of any ability possesses this one essential capacity. I'm talking about the ability to *solve problems on the fly.* In fact, it's not too much to say that problem solving *is* design/building.

I often tell the students that I really don't know how to build. Because every house is different and every project has unforeseeable problems. The only house I really know how to build is the one I've just built. If I were to rebuild that house over and over again, we would call them tract homes, cookie-cutter designs, or developers' dreams. The whole point of

building dozens of identical "units" is to reduce problems and increase assembly-line efficiency. But I don't build "units." I build custom homes, and each one is a unique portrait of the people for whom it was designed. Unavoidably, each one will also be unique in the problems it presents.

Ask any builder and they will tell you that it is simply not possible to chase every problem out of a building before starting construction. So why get involved? Who in their right mind would embrace a process that was sure to present problems? Design/builders (of sound body and mind) are perfectly comfortable in this context because of their ability to solve problems on the fly. This is a hard-won talent based on experience.

It starts in the studio. The design process is certainly about solving problems: How will the load-bearing walls be lined up without crowding the rooms? Where will the mechanicals go if the design is all "open plan"? Is it possible to vent a sink in an island counter? What can be changed to allow the necessary headroom above the stairs? How can we minimize space wasted on hallways?

These are pretty standard problems. They are routinely solved in the studio. Many hours are spent and much paper is lost. In the end, the design/builder decides, the documents are finished, and it's time to break ground. At that point, they know that *all* the problems are not solved, but those that haven't been will

EVALUATING YOUR ELEVATIONS

Elevations can be tough. In architecture school we used to work on our plans until the last week before presentation. Then, in a seven-day superhuman push, we would develop the fenestration, siding, trim, and general proportions of the rest of the building. Perhaps this practice is responsible for some of the ugly architecture we see today.

At any rate, although a whole other book could be devoted to elevations alone, there are a few tricks that I find myself repeating at the desk of almost every Yester-morrow student. I summarize them below using the accompanying illustration.

Roof Pitch

Not all roofs are perfectly symmetrical. Even if you're not designing a classic colonial saltbox, it's pretty common to have roof planes of uneven lengths on either side of the ridge.

Rule of Thumb: Keep the same pitch for all the roof planes even if they are different sizes.

There is seldom anything attractive or clever about having random roof pitches. Nor is there anything special about having a right angle (90°) at the ridge. Anyone undertaking the construction of a house must learn to cut angles. If you're really in love with the *look* of a right angle at the ridge, use a 12/12 pitch (45°). Use this pitch on *both* sides of the ridge.

General Trim

The trim on a house has the distinction of making more impact for less money than almost any other part of the building. This is a generalization, yes. But I'm not talking about dentil moldings and elaborately built-up classical friezes. I'm talking about the option of having trim *at all* versus the option of omitting it. Certainly, if you eliminate trim you will save some money. But not much. And you'll save even less by reducing your trim to miserly dimensions. Any kind of trim will take a certain amount of labor to install. As with most things these days, the labor is more costly than the materials. So if you're paying for the labor, you might as well have them put in properly proportioned material. It costs the same to install.

For instance, I always use ⁵⁄₄″ stock at my corners or any other place where the siding touches the trim work. Most "product" home builders use 1 × for trim. This is actually only ³⁄₄″ thick. Clapboard or shingles will stick out beyond (be "proud" of) this dimension when they abut at the corners, windows, doors, etc. Another exam-

(Continued)

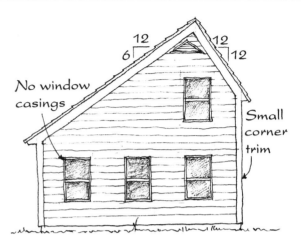

FIGURE 181a: Before: Uneven roof pitch is awkward. Window layout is uninspired. Trim is too narrow and weak.

FIGURE 181b: After: Substantial corner and rake trim give the building a look of substance and proportion. Equal roof pitches give a feeling of stability. Window layout is more generous and balanced.

ple involves the quality of wood used. Many builders will use number 2 pine for their trim. I suggest number 1 select. You will certainly pay more for this material, but you will more than get it back in savings on labor. You won't have to work around knots, cups, splits, and warps. Also, the paint will adhere better and your trim will move less over the long run.

Rule of Thumb: If you have any questions or uncertainties about which size board to use for a particular piece of trim, use the larger.

While you're thinking about trim, remember to "back prime" it. This means paint the side that will be placed against the building.

"What? Paint the side you can't see??" is the common reaction. Yes, of course. If you don't, it will absorb moisture. If you paint the outside and not the underside, the board will absorb moisture unevenly. This will cause warping and joints that open up as the seasons change.

See also shadow lines and built-up trim in the next section.

Roof Trim

Usually you are standing on the ground when you look at the trim along the rake of a roof or under the soffit. In other words, you are looking up. When designing the trim for any part of a roof, remember that the viewer will be looking up. They will need clear definition to see form and volume against the brightness of the sky.

Form and shape are best articulated with shadows, shadow lines, and highlights. To get shadows you may need more than one piece of wood. Typically you will do better if you have one lapped over another, casting a shadow line. You can get further definition and highlights by using a router to put a profile along the edge of these pieces of wood. If that seems too involved, use your circular saw to run a saw kerf parallel to the board's edge, like a pinstripe.

Rule of Thumb: Remember that generous trim effects come from the play of light and shadow. This is one reason moldings have traditionally been built up from many pieces of wood. The more pieces, the more shadow lines.

Naturally, proportion plays a role with roof trim just as it does with all trim. The wider your boards, the more massive will be the visual effect of the trim. The more shadow lines or highlights, the lighter the visual effect.

Points of transition, say from the rake to the corner boards, will be enhanced if you give them some special attention. Have some fun with your trim. Let it become expressive. Trim doesn't have to exist merely to cover the cracks between the different pieces of the building.

Window (and Door) Trim

Never (even though they say "never say 'never.' "), never omit the casing trim around your windows. Regardless of how modern you may think trimless windows appear, it is very, very rare that windows without trim look like anything so much as they look like you ran out of money.

Rule of Thumb: Always trim out your windows with casings that are at least $3\frac{1}{2}$" wide and at least $\frac{5}{4}$" thick. Even beefier trim may be appropriate in certain cases. Do not use the "brick molding" that most window manufacturers supply with their windows.

Of, course, it's always dangerous to venture a rule or formula in matters of visual proportion. Nevertheless, I am so distressed by the number of houses that I see without window trim that I am willing to offer such a rule. Certainly, you will do better if you use your eye and your visual intelligence to decide what proportions work best. And remember that whatever you specify can probably be installed by the window fabricator before your units are shipped.

---

probably be easier to solve during the construction process.

On site, problem solving continues from the first footings to the final finishes. Discrepancies in materials, dimensions, schedules, and cost will all present a daily menu of little problems. The design/builder takes them in stride. Everything can be corrected. Everything can be adjusted. The grand design will prevail! It may look a little different or take a little longer, but its essence will survive. This is because the design/builder deals with all contingencies from a fully informed position. He is aware of the design goals as well as the construction requirements. All problems are solved both architecturally *and* technically.

Final Finishing

This brings us to the end of your first book on design and construction. Certainly there will be many more. You must learn about contracting, estimating, scheduling, and financing. It would be handy for you to learn about making doors, casework, cabinets, stairs, and all the general shop procedures. Eventually, there will be all those finishes to choose. Also light fixtures, plumbing fixtures, and kitchen appliances. I wish I had the time and space to cover all those areas, but they will wait. (In the Epilogue, there are some suggestions for using the Yestermorrow School and other building professionals.)

The goal for this book was to get you familiar with the *overall process;* to present all the pieces. Hopefully, you now have an armature onto which you can add the subspecialties of design/building. In the language of this book, you have a framework on which to hang additional information. Some of that information will come from reading and studying. Most of it will come from action.

There is only so much that can be learned from reading and talking. In this field, hands-on action is the shortest road to knowledge. You don't have to start with an entire house. Build a deck, a garage, or a gazebo. Add a screen porch or renovate your basement. Try to find a project that has a little of everything: a small foundation, some framing, roofing, a couple of windows, maybe a door, plumbing, a little electrical, and, of course, finishes. This might be a mud room entry with a hose spigot outside. Alternately, this could be a garage or a gazebo with a bar! Maybe your kids need a clubhouse. Whatever it is, expect to learn a lot. Design and draft it up in detail. Take your drawings to the lumberyard, the hardware store, the plumber, and the electrician. Each will give you advice. *This* is learning.

Your first step is to build some confidence (read this book). Your second step is to decide who you are and who you want to be (you're on your own here). The rest of the steps will take you along the broad, cyclical path of the Design Helix.

Stay alert and enjoy the adventure. It's your life and your home.

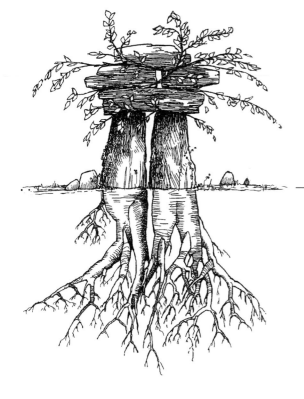

Epilogue: You and Yestermorrow

Making a home takes a lot of blood, sweat, and tears. By the time we've seen it through, we will have some new and dear friends. Likely as not, we will also have involved some old friends and members of our family. It will take significant time, maybe over a year. A special thing happens when one spends a lot of time on site with friends and family—we *bond*. We see the weather and the seasons come and go. We learn about the habits of our neighbors and the metabolism of our neighborhood. And we *commit*. Putting thousands of dollars and years of our lives into a project is a huge commitment. It makes us part of the scene, for better or worse.

When people go to the incredible effort of making their own place, they like to think that it will be there for a while. Maybe a great while. I often justify the effort or expense of some renovation by setting it in a long-term context: "OK, maybe this took some extra elbow grease (time or money), but at least it will still be here when my grandchildren move in."

Grandchildren?!

This is the first consequence of a vernacular building tradition. We cherish our homes. We value our neighborhood and our whole situation. We have returned to the real meaning of "to settle." When we put down roots like this it's normal to imagine that the house will be in the family for more than one generation. Of course it's unfair to assume that the kids will want to live there when they grow up, but we do it anyway. And the whole family invests in that home by living the best years of their lives there. This is where the memories will remain, etched into the walls and floors and landscape of the family homestead. Nobody wants to lose that.

Whether things will work out that way or not doesn't really matter. That's simply the natural way we think once we've committed to a place. This leads directly to the next big consequence of a vernacular building tradition. We embrace *quality*. Even though we live in a disposable society, we don't want to think of our homes falling apart or being torn down because they're not worth the upkeep. So we look for the best materials and methods we can afford. We not only build a home solid in the beginning, we repair it (rather than patch it). Let's face it, we build better when we think we're building for several generations . . . or even for the remainder of our own years. We build to last.

A vernacular building tradition is also likely to produce healthier homes. Owner/builders are the first to spurn hazardous building materials—toxic glues and paints, insulation or carpets that trap dirt or give off toxic gases, anything containing asbestos or lead. Because we're doing our own construction, even products that are dangerous primarily during installation are likely to get passed over—treated lumber, insulating foams, products containing VOCs (volatile organic compounds), creosote, roofing tars, and many toxic glues.

Another beneficial consequence comes from owner/builders' concerns that go beyond their property. When we settle with a long-term vision, we want to know that the water supply will be clean, the streets will be safe, the schools will be good, and that our neighbors will share these concerns. Once we've committed to a place and joined a community, it's usually not long before we're volunteering for civic duties like the town planning commission, the zoning board, or even (gasp!) the school board! This can lead to a better awareness of land use. Besides the macro issues like where the landfill is located, keeping water reservoirs clean, and preserving animal habitat, this also includes micro issues like your septic system and your composting and recycling practices.

This brings us back to our own property where landscaping and building size will have a big impact on energy consumption. Owner/builders know better than most what energy is expended to heat or cool a house. When we install our own mechanical systems, we become hyperaware of how much they cost in both energy and dollars (which are ultimately the same thing).

You can see where I'm going with this. In addition to being good citizens, owner/builders tend to become environmentalists. I'm not talking about the preachy political types that are always telling us what we should and shouldn't do. I'm talking about common sense, don't soil your own nest, protect your family—*human nature*. When we build our own homes, we commit to a place. Once we've done that, it's only natural to take care of it. To take care of it we have to understand it.

In many different ways, helping us understand how to better make our homes is the shared vision of everyone at the Yestermorrow School.

Your Way

Whether you choose to attend the Yestermorrow School or simply to read this book you are undertaking a process that will eventually lead you to the making of your own home. As I have repeatedly mentioned, there is no single correct way to go about doing this. And though the variations are endless, I want to mention a few examples of past students' methods, just to get you thinking creatively about your own approach.

- *Design but don't build:* Of all the challenges presented by making our own homes, design is the one most widely embraced. I applaud this, of course. Nevertheless, as we all know, design is much more than just drafting, and it doesn't stop until after the construction is finished. If your only involvement will be with the design, you owe it to yourself to do a thorough job.

  Try to find an architect or designer/builder from your area who will work with you. Interview several. Ask them if they will review and comment on your design work. Pay them by the hour. When you are certain that the design is what you want, ask them to give you a bid on preparing the construction documents. It's normal to find willing designers at the local college, university, or technical school. Alternatively, if you can't find a suitable design professional in your area, call up Yestermorrow, where you can chat with dozens of them.

The idea here is to get into a dialogue with an architect or designer without having them take over the entire process. What you want is a coach.

- *General contracting:* This is a very popular format. Many students wish to have control of the design and construction but cannot afford the time to be on-site for several months. After these students attend the Yestermorrow School, they complete the design and then hire, organize, and supervise the builder and subs. This really keeps you on top of what's being done on-site. While there is money to be saved this way, it is usually less than imagined. To realize these savings, expect to allocate at least 40 percent of your workweek and some of your weekends to the effort. General contracting is not something that fits neatly into evenings and spare time.
- *Be the gopher (go-for) on your own site:* Beyond the savings, some stu-

dents want access to the construction process simply to ensure compliance with their design intentions. These people will often hire a builder and arrange to work on his or her crew. This is a good strategy. If you are always on-site, the builder can always get your input. Since you are also the designer, it's like having the architect and client always on call.

If you go this route, don't do so just to realize "huge" savings. You won't. Remember that you are replacing only forty hours per week from the builder's payroll, and those are likely to be the least costly hours (since you're just a gofer). Nevertheless, this arrangement does save some money, and more important, you will have an intimate understanding of everything that goes into your house.

- *Plumbers, electricians, masons, and specialists:* In most municipalities certain aspects of the house must be installed by licensed professionals. This is for various reasons, but mainly safety. If you are excited about doing your own plumbing, electrical, or other specialty work, do not lose hope. Ask if there is a local ordinance that forbids you from doing the work. Even if there isn't, your next step should be to befriend a professional. Frequently

they will oversee or inspect your work for a nominal fee. This is how I wired and plumbed my house, and it was money well spent.

I've learned a lot of things this way. For instance, I asked my roofer if he would teach me how to install a standing-seam metal roof.

"Why sure," he said. "I'll teach you and even sell you the materials and lend you the tools. Your roof designs are always funky shapes, and the more you do the less I have to!" This works just fine for both of us.

- *Build but don't design:* For those who wish to build their homes but want to leave the design to others, well . . . I can only have pity. Nevertheless, if that's your choice, it will still be necessary to read plans and specifications. More important, you will need to be a good on-site problem solver. Even those predrawn plans and prefabricated kits will present plenty of unforeseen problems. (I speak from experience here.) The important thing is to keep your eye on the big picture and not let daily surprises push you off course.

As the builder, you will have effective control over the budget, but you still may not be able to know what everything will cost before you start. How much will the well cost? What will the chimney cost? What type of light fixtures will you decide on? How about the landscaping? Because of these and other unknowns, it is prudent to affiliate with a seasoned building professional *from your local area*. They can give you good estimates and suggest appropriate allowances. Ideally, you should look for someone who can solve problems and has broad contacts in the trades. One of the biggest problems for the first-time builder is finding and retaining quality subcontractors.

These are only a few suggestions. There are as many ways to organize the design and construction of a house as there are people with the determination to do it. Obviously, the more involvement the better. But don't be discouraged if logistics, money, or schedule seem to be obstacles. There is always a way, and the one that works for you is the right way . . .

Aghhhhh! The possibilities are endless!

Hurray! What a wonderful world of opportunities!

Some readers will be distressed and others elated to learn that the design/ building of their dream house cannot be attained by following a universal, step-by-step formula. Instead, this is a cat that can be skinned a zillion different ways, depending on your budget, schedule, program, and personality. The best way for you will likely be just slightly different than that for anyone else.

It's important to decide which parts of the project you should embrace and which should be delegated. It is also important to have some backup.

Assembling your team of professionals, nonprofessionals, family, and friends is very important to the outcome of the whole project. If you do it right, you will end up with much more than just a home. If you do it wrong, you risk costly mistakes and bad feelings about the final outcome. Make you nervous? Then consider attending Yestermorrow! In this wonderful (frightening?) sea (morass!) of alternatives (decisions?) and rewards (consequences!), the Yestermorrow Design/Build School stands always ready to help. And by now, you might just be wondering how?

▥ Yestermorrow (the soft sell . . .)

Here is an organization where professionals shed the intimidating veil of their profession to become teachers. Clients gather in small groups and are treated as students. In this way, architectural design, often costly and elitist, becomes affordable and accessible to everybody. Hopefully, more people will become involved with the design and construction of their homes so these homes will more truly reflect who they are and what values they hold. (That's what the subtitle of this book means.) Throughout history, this process has produced what we cherish today as "vernacular architecture."

Founded in 1980, the Yestermorrow Design/Build School offers courses year round for both do-it-yourselfers and career track students. Originally known for its two-week hands-on intensives, the school now presents courses in a range of formats, from one-day tutorials to eight-week college-accredited programs. Admission to most of these courses is "open" and based on matching students' needs with course content. Also, organizations like Stanley Tools USA, MacDonalds Foods, Real Goods Inc., and the Oglala Tribe of the Lakotas have contacted Yestermorrow to teach complex problem solving to their employees.

Yestermorrow attempts to configure classes so that people can fit them into contemporary work schedules. Part of the school's effort to rejuvenate a residential vernacular includes offering the information so that it accommodates today's lifestyles. Students attend from all over the country, which means they usually don't have much more than a two-week vacation from their work . . . sometimes less. Nevertheless, making a house is a serious undertaking which requires solid preparation. Many students will attend several short courses while they are saving money, looking at land, or otherwise getting ready to build.

The core curriculum consists of residential design, drafting, model building, construction, mechanical systems, and a variety of woodworking courses. Additional shorter classes offered include:

landscape design
stone masonry
architectural crafts
ornament
kitchen and bathroom design
estimating and scheduling
solar energy and design
electrical wiring
plumbing
restoration and reuse
power and shop tool use
metal work
architectural trim and finishes
"sustainable" or "green" design and
     construction

It should be noted that in addition to the specific solar and "sustainable" offerings, *all* courses must conform to the school's commitment to an environmentally sustainable vernacular architecture. *Build to last*.

The school retains only teachers who "practice what they preach." There is little use for "textbook teachers" in such a hands-on school. Hailing from all over the United States, Mexico, and Canada, the teaching staff consists of over forty professionals from the architectural, construction, and allied fields. Licensed architects work alongside professional builders in the studio as well as on the site. The woodworking instructors are all practicing cabinet or furniture makers. Because of the emphasis on design/build integration, most of the architects have building experience and, likewise, the site and shop instructors have extensive knowledge of design.

At Yestermorrow, the students convene in very small classes. There are a couple of reasons for this. First is safety. Many of the programs at Yestermorrow involve hands-on instruction in the use of power tools and shop equipment. Experience has shown that a teacher-student ratio of about 1 to 4 is best. Just as exacting as safety on the site is personal attention in the studio. Students come to Yestermorrow with a variety of projects: new homes, renovations, rural sites, urban sites, log homes, timber frames, solar homes, superinsulated homes, straw-bale homes, geodesic domes—the list is endless. It is essential that each student receive the specialized instruction needed for his or her particular situation. Yestermorrow doesn't have a standardized curriculum. It can't. Each student is different, each site is different and so, each project is different.

▥ The Future of Vernacular, or Owner-Built, Architecture

The essential measure of any school is really the people who comprise it and their shared values. The people who work at Yestermorrow, different as they are in many ways, share a common hope that regular folks can once again be actively involved in the making of their own homes. Naturally, this is a dream that stretches far into the future and has many consequences. Just imagine . . .

The Yestermorrow School can be contacted at:

Yestermorrow Design/Build School
RR1, Box 97-5
Warren, VT 05674
(802) 496-5545

APPENDICES

Program Questionnaire

Many programs are distilled from the answers to questionnaires like the two that follow. There is nothing definitive or all-encompassing about these questionnaires. I organized these questions for this book but no one questionnaire is right for all people. There are other excellent alternatives in Charles Moore's *The Place of Houses* or Christopher Alexander's *A Pattern Language*. In any event, these are just starters—something to get you thinking. You will likely ignore some issues while adding others that are unique to your project.

Thinking About the Site:

These questions will be easier to answer after you have spent some time exploring and analyzing your site. Take the list with you while visiting the site. Have these questions bouncing around in your head while you're bouncing around the site.

1. What's the single best thing about your site? Water? View? Privacy?
2. What's the worst? Noise? Soils? Access?
3. What could easily be improved?
4. What's best left alone?
5. How do you get onto your site? How do you move about? What kind of drive is possible?
6. Are there any easements or covenants? Are your neighbors friendly? What are the boundary conditions?
7. What do you need from your site? Is there septic capability in the soils? Is there a good garden spot? Are there rocks or trees that might become building materials?
8. Where will you dig your well, if you need one? Where will the municipal water, power, and sewer come from (city sites)?
9. What are the most valuable things that your site offers? Views? Privacy? Proximity?
10. Are there seismic, hurricane, or other special considerations in your region?
11. What does your site need from you? Is there any danger of erosion? Flooding? Loss of habitat?

12. What kind of plants, shrubs, or trees might be supported by the soils?
13. What can you see from your site? Remember also that your activities are visible to any place you can see from your site.
14. What can you smell on your site? What can you hear?
15. How far into the future can you visualize your site? Imagine the flow of water and the passing of seasons. Imagine the maturing of trees and shrubs. Imagine the eventual build-out of your dream house.
16. Where does the prevailing wind come from?
17. Locate all the compass points. Where does the sun rise? Set? Where is high noon (south)?
18. Where does the water drain or collect on your site? Where will the snow collect and drift?
19. When the driveway is plowed, where will the snow go?
20. Is there any natural shade on your site?
21. What's the biggest expense represented by your site? (This could be maintenance or development or a specific purchase.)
22. How long will you own your site?
23. What is the least expensive thing you can do to improve your site?
24. List all the other animals or plants that you suspect may live on your site, or even visit it. Indicate how welcome or unwelcome each is.
25. Where will the garden go? The pool? The tennis court?
26. Where will the compost go? The trash cans?
27. Where is the best place to picnic? Barbecue? Sunbathe?
28. Where does the most noise come from? On site or off?

Thinking About the People:

Each member of the family should consider these questions separately and then the whole family should do it as a group. Dialogue is the most important ingredient. It's no good having one person answer all the questions for everyone. I've seen it happen: total anarchy, possibly bloodshed! It is a well-known fact that designing a home can be stressful. Things you always thought were agreed on turn out to be pet peeves. Husbands may develop opinions about kitchens. Wives sometimes reveal new bathroom requirements. Children speak out for teenagers' rights! Nevertheless, the discourse is an essential part of the design process. Everything can be resolved with enough discussion and a bit of compromise. It's when issues are passed over or ignored that they later erupt in disastrous proportion.

I have made two lists here; one for bubble diagrams and one for storyboards.

Questions for Bubble Diagrams:

1. Regardless of importance, list every human activity that you can think of, even ones like sleeping or waiting for the shower. Include your current activities and also the new ones for which you hope to provide. Think into the future. This will likely take weeks. Everyone needs a pad and tape measure.
2. Now try to put the list in order of importance. What are the most important things? Which would you give up or wait for?
3. That was too quick. Do it again and this time don't worry about erasing or using arrows.
4. Now write a sentence or paragraph about each of the first ten activities. Better yet, draw a little cartoon with lots of detail.
5. Group or arrange the activities according to how many family members and/or friends will be involved and how frequently.
6. Now group them again, in a different way. Your choice.
7. Characterize each behavior or activity as one of the following: quiet, loud, private, public, cozy, social (add or replace with your own criteria).
8. For each activity, list the activities that are most likely to precede them and/or follow them (e.g., cooking, then dining, then socializing; returning from work, then swimming, then cooking; awakening, then breakfast, then getting to the car).
9. List ten important ceremonies or celebrations that will take place at your house. Use a few sentences to describe the essence of each one. Front-door greetings, birthdays, New Year's, Halloween, etc.
10. Order them by importance to you and your family.
11. Order them by frequency (or any other way that makes more sense to you).

Questions for Storyboard Diagrams:

1. How will you wake up? What's in the room? What can you see? smell? hear? Picture your bed. Is anyone else in it?
2. Picture your way to the bathroom. How many sinks are there? Is there a tub or a shower? Who is with you? What are they doing?
3. Where do you keep your clothes? Is it a work day? What are you doing today? Picture the journey from the bedroom to the kitchen. Are there stairs? What are they like? Describe the experience of coming down the stairs.
4. Do you eat breakfast? Do you make a lunch? Who is at the breakfast table? What can you see from the kitchen? Where is the paper? Where is the *coffee!?* (Ahem.)
5. Picture the entire layout of your kitchen, where everything is: the location of the stove, the refrigerator, the sink, etc. Try to imagine every move it takes to prepare your morning meal.
6. What else must be done before starting the day? Will you be at home today or at work? What about other times?
7. How do you get to the car? Is there a garage? What's the weather like? Is the car comfortable to get into? Are there doors to open? Snow to shovel? What's the driveway experience like? Will there be rain? Wind?
8. What happens after breakfast? Is there a project? Do you work at home? Will there be visitors? children?
9. Where will your visitors enter the house? Where will they hang their coats? How much space will be needed for the activity? What kind of lighting will be required? Will they be here for lunch?
10. Will the lunch be eaten indoors or out? Where?
11. Describe the preparation of your lunch, where everything is, and where everyone is sitting. Who is in the kitchen?
12. Don't forget clean up. Where is the dishwasher (if there is one)? How do the dishes get from the table to the sink? to the dishwasher? Where do they go when they come out of the dishwasher?
13. What happens after lunch? Do you have a different project or more visitors? Do children come home from school? What will be needed for the afternoon's activities? Are they indoors or outside? If inside, what kind of space and lighting will be needed?
14. When you go outside for activities, what will you need? Is there storage for equipment or clothing? Try to think about all the things that happen when you make the transition from inside to outside and vice versa.
15. What happens at the end of the afternoon? Do the "hunters" and "gatherers" return? Do they arrive by foot or automobile? What are they bringing back? Tools? Bags? Supplies? Where do all the different things go?
16. Is there a ceremony or tradition for when people return to the house?
17. Do the children eat separately or does the entire family have dinner together? When? Where?
18. Who is involved with dinner preparation? Describe the "choreography" in as much detail as you can imagine. Where does everyone sit or stand?
19. What happens when you have a formal dining occasion? Is there a separate room or table? Where are the special utensils stored? What is the lighting like? What else is this room or table used for?
20. What happens after dinner? Where do the members of the family go? What do they do? Are there chores?

21. Who goes to bed first? What is the sequence of retiring for the night? Are there ceremonies or traditions?
22. Picture the journey to your bedroom. Do you turn off lights? Let out animals? Are there stairs or doors to deal with? Describe what it's like to climb the stairs and be on the second floor after dark. Which lights are on? What can you see or hear?
23. Who is in the bathroom? What will you do in the bathroom? What is the lighting like? the floor? the walls?
24. What do you do before falling asleep? Do you read in bed? Do you cuddle? What can you see? hear? smell?
25. Where is the light switch?

Now simply repeat the previous questions for every special day of the year. No problem, right?

Thinking About the Building:

Everyone has more feelings about buildings than they realize. The following questions are meant to get them on the table at the outset.

1. List every conceivable part or room or assembly found in a house. (Don't be stingy or picky. The winner has the longest list. Give yourself ten points for each one.) For instance: baseboard, molding, raised panel door, track lights, floor joists, exposed beams, low-flush toilets, heat pump, ceiling fan, storm door, thermopane, Low-E glass, Styrofoam, plywood, oil paint, bricks, concrete, steel beams, laminate, ceramic tile, vinyl tile, weather strip, dehumidifier, true divided lites, security system, window seat, inglenook, foyer, back stairs, wall sconce, porte cochere, attached garage, etc., etc.
2. Circle only those that might occur in a house designed specifically for you.
3. What things do you like to find in a house?
4. What things do you *insist* on finding in a house?
5. What things do you dislike in a house?
6. In general, what sorts of materials do you like to find in a house?
7. What are your preferences, if you have any, in the following areas:
   - the foundation: block, concrete, brick, posts, etc.
   - the structure: brick, timberframe, log, geodesics, straw bale, etc.
   - windows and doors: wood, metal, divided lites, style, size, etc.
   - siding: shingles, clapboard, tiles, board and batten, stucco, brick, stone, metal, glass(!), etc.
   - roofing: shingles, metal, tile, rubber, slate, etc.
   - heating or cooling systems: hot water, forced air, radiant, baseboard, fireplace, stove, etc.
   - fuel: wood, oil, gas, solar, electric, photovoltaic, wind, etc.
   - lighting: natural, fluorescent, incandescent, track, indirect, etc.
   - interior finishes: omigod, where do we start?
   You shouldn't worry if you don't have a strong opinion in each area.
8. Do you prefer houses seen from the road or hidden at the end of a driveway?
9. Do you appreciate a formal front door? Or will one door serve all occasions?
10. Do you want specific rooms for specific functions: dining room, living room, kitchen, etc.?
11. Do you enjoy open planning and contemporary layouts?
12. Do you want/need a one-story house or a multileveled structure?
13. How much do you want a fireplace and where?
14. Do you think you need a full basement? What will happen there?
15. What is your favorite house? What is the cleverest thing you've ever seen?
16. What architectural styles do you like, if any? Cottage, shingle, colonial, federal, modern, prairie, mission, Spanish colonial, Greek revival, Tyrolian, log, Shaker, international, etc.
17. Do you like wide overhanging roofs?
18. Do you like picture windows?
19. Do you like sliding glass doors? French doors?
20. What kind of window do you prefer: casement, double hung, awning, hopper, jalousie, slider, etc.
21. What do you think about screen porches versus patios? How about decks? second-floor decks? What about balconies?
22. Have you ever considered a widow's walk or lookout tower?

This is really just a preliminary inventory. Things you have strong feelings about should be considered from the start. Areas where you don't will be new terrain for you to explore. Even long-standing biases may be challenged by new materials or methods. Eventually you will learn about the many different options you have in each area. I think of them as colors on a palette. You needn't use them all on each painting. Moreover, it's not their individual qualities but rather their combination that's most important.

Remember that this is only one questionnaire organized around the site, people, and building that will make up your home. Don't forget to blend in your answers to the endless questions, Chapter 6. All together your desk should be littered with information about who you are and how you want to live. Taken together, these responses and notions describe the design "problem" to be solved. Since that sounds so negative, we usually call it the Program.

National Weather Information: Degree Days

TABLE 29: AVERAGE MONTHLY AND YEARLY DEGREE DAYS FOR THE UNITED STATES

State	Station	Avg. Winter Temp	July	Aug.	Sept.	Oct.	Nov.	Dec.	Jan.	Feb.	Mar.	Apr.	May	June	Yearly Total
Ala.	Birmingham ....A	54.2	0	0	6	93	363	555	592	462	363	108	9	0	2551
	Huntsville ....A	51.3	0	0	12	127	426	663	694	557	434	138	19	0	3070
	Mobile ....A	59.9	0	0	0	22	213	357	415	300	211	42	0	0	1560
	Montgomery ....A	55.4	0	0	0	68	330	527	543	417	316	90	0	0	2291
Alaska	Anchorage ....A	23.0	245	291	516	930	1284	1572	1631	1316	1293	879	592	315	10864
	Fairbanks ....A	6.7	171	332	642	1203	1833	2254	2359	1901	1739	1068	555	222	14279
	Juneau ....A	32.1	301	338	483	725	921	1135	1237	1070	1073	810	601	381	9075
	Nome ....A	13.1	481	496	693	1094	1455	1820	1879	1666	1770	1314	930	573	14171
Ariz.	Flagstaff ....A	35.6	46	68	201	558	867	1073	1169	991	911	651	437	180	7152
	Phoenix ....A	58.5	0	0	0	22	234	415	474	328	217	75	0	0	1765
	Tucson ....A	58.1	0	0	0	25	231	406	471	344	242	75	6	0	1800
	Winslow ....A	43.0	0	0	6	245	711	1008	1054	770	601	291	96	0	4782
	Yuma ....A	64.2	0	0	0	0	108	264	307	190	90	15	0	0	974
Ark.	Fort Smith ....A	50.3	0	0	12	127	450	704	781	596	456	144	22	0	3292
	Little Rock ....A	50.5	0	0	9	127	465	716	756	577	434	126	9	0	3219
	Texarkana ....A	54.2	0	0	0	78	345	561	626	468	350	105	0	0	2533
Calif.	Bakersfield ....A	55.4	0	0	0	37	282	502	546	364	267	105	19	0	2122
	Bishop ....A	46.0	0	0	48	260	576	797	874	680	555	306	143	36	4275
	Blue Canyon ....A	42.2	28	37	108	347	594	781	896	795	806	597	412	195	5596
	Burbank ....A	58.6	0	0	6	43	177	301	366	277	239	138	81	18	1646
	Eureka C	49.9	270	257	258	329	414	499	546	470	505	438	372	285	4643
	Fresno ....A	53.3	0	0	0	84	354	577	605	426	335	162	62	6	2611
	Long Beach ....A	57.8	0	0	9	47	171	316	397	311	264	171	93	24	1803
	Los Angeles ....A	57.4	28	28	42	78	180	291	372	302	288	219	158	81	2061
	Los Angeles C	60.3	0	0	6	31	132	229	310	230	202	123	68	18	1349
	Mt. Shasta C	41.2	25	34	123	406	696	902	983	784	738	525	347	159	5722
	Oakland ....A	53.5	53	50	45	127	309	481	527	400	353	255	180	90	2870
	Red Bluff ....A	53.8	0	0	0	53	318	555	605	428	341	168	47	0	2515
	Sacramento ....A	53.9	0	0	0	56	321	546	583	414	332	178	72	0	2502
	Sacramento C	54.4	0	0	0	62	312	533	561	392	310	173	76	0	2419
	Sandberg C	46.8	0	0	30	202	480	691	778	661	620	426	264	57	4209

State	Station	Avg. Winter Temp	July	Aug.	Sept.	Oct.	Nov.	Dec.	Jan.	Feb.	Mar.	Apr.	May	June	Yearly Total
	San Diego ....A	59.5	9	0	21	43	135	236	298	235	214	135	90	42	1458
	San Francisco ....A	53.4	81	78	60	143	306	462	508	395	363	279	214	126	3015
	San Francisco C	55.1	192	174	102	118	231	388	443	336	319	279	239	180	3001
	Santa Maria ....A	54.3	99	93	96	146	270	391	459	370	363	282	233	165	2967
Colo.	Alamosa ....A	29.7	65	99	279	639	1065	1420	1476	1162	1020	696	440	168	8529
	Colorado Springs ....A	37.3	9	25	132	456	825	1032	1128	938	893	582	319	84	6423
	Denver ....A	37.6	6	9	117	428	819	1035	1132	938	887	558	288	66	6283
	Denver C	40.8	0	0	90	366	714	905	1004	851	800	492	254	48	5524
	Grand Junction ....A	39.3	0	0	30	313	786	1113	1209	907	729	387	146	21	5641
	Pueblo ....A	40.4	0	0	54	326	750	986	1085	871	772	429	174	15	5462
Conn.	Bridgeport ....A	39.9	0	0	66	307	615	986	1079	966	853	510	208	27	5617
	Hartford ....A	37.3	0	12	117	394	714	1101	1190	1042	908	519	205	33	6235
	New Haven ....A	39.0	0	12	87	347	648	1011	1097	991	871	543	245	45	5897
Del.	Wilmington ....A	42.5	0	0	51	270	588	927	980	874	735	387	112	6	4930
D.C.	Washington ....A	45.7	0	0	33	217	519	834	871	762	626	288	74	0	4224
Fla.	Apalachicola C	61.2	0	0	0	16	153	319	347	260	180	33	0	0	1308
	Daytona Beach ....A	61.5	0	0	0	0	75	211	248	190	140	15	0	0	879
	Fort Myers ....A	68.6	0	0	0	0	24	109	146	101	62	0	0	0	442
	Jacksonville ....A	61.9	0	0	0	12	144	310	332	246	174	21	0	0	1239
	Key West ....A	73.1	0	0	0	0	0	28	40	31	9	0	0	0	108
	Lakeland C	66.7	0	0	0	0	57	164	195	146	99	0	0	0	661
	Miami ....A	71.1	0	0	0	0	0	65	74	56	19	0	0	0	214
	Miami Beach C	72.5	0	0	0	0	0	40	56	36	9	0	0	0	141
	Orlando ....A	65.7	0	0	0	0	72	198	220	165	105	6	0	0	766
	Pensacola ....A	60.4	0	0	0	19	195	353	400	277	183	36	0	0	1463
	Tallahassee ....A	60.1	0	0	0	28	198	360	375	286	202	36	0	0	1485
	Tampa ....A	66.4	0	0	0	0	60	171	202	148	102	0	0	0	683
	West Palm Beach ....A	68.4	0	0	0	0	6	65	87	64	31	0	0	0	253
Ga.	Athens ....A	51.8	0	0	12	115	405	632	642	529	431	141	22	0	2929
	Atlanta ....A	51.7	0	0	18	124	417	648	636	518	428	147	25	0	2961
	Augusta ....A	54.5	0	0	0	78	333	552	549	445	350	90	0	0	2397
	Columbus ....A	54.8	0	0	0	87	333	543	552	434	338	96	0	0	2383
	Macon ....A	56.2	0	0	0	71	297	502	505	403	295	63	0	0	2136
	Rome ....A	49.9	0	0	24	161	474	701	710	577	468	177	34	0	3326
	Savannah ....A	57.8	0	0	0	47	246	437	437	353	254	45	0	0	1819
	Thomasville C	60.0	0	0	0	25	198	366	394	305	208	33	0	0	1529

State	Station	Avg. Winter Temp	July	Aug.	Sept.	Oct.	Nov.	Dec.	Jan.	Feb.	Mar.	Apr.	May	June	Yearly Total
Hawaii	Lihue ....A	72.7	0	0	0	0	0	0	0	0	0	0	0	0	0
	Honolulu ....A	74.2	0	0	0	0	0	0	0	0	0	0	0	0	0
	Hilo ....A	71.9	0	0	0	0	0	0	0	0	0	0	0	0	0
Idaho	Boise ....A	39.7	0	0	132	415	792	1017	1113	854	722	438	245	81	5809
	Lewiston ....A	41.0	0	0	123	403	756	933	1063	815	694	426	239	90	5542
	Pocatello ....A	34.8	0	0	172	493	900	1166	1324	1058	905	555	319	141	7033
Ill.	Cairo C	47.9	0	0	36	164	513	791	856	680	539	195	47	0	3821
	Chicago (O'Hare) ....A	35.8	0	12	117	381	807	1166	1265	1086	939	534	260	72	6639
	Chicago (Midway) ....A	37.5	0	0	81	326	753	1113	1209	1044	890	480	211	48	6155
	Chicago C	38.9	0	0	66	279	705	1051	1150	1000	868	489	226	48	5882
	Moline ....A	36.4	0	9	99	335	774	1181	1314	1100	918	450	189	39	6408
	Peoria ....A	38.1	0	6	87	326	759	1113	1218	1025	849	426	183	33	6025
	Rockford ....A	34.8	6	9	114	400	837	1221	1333	1137	961	516	236	60	6830
	Springfield ....A	40.6	0	0	72	291	696	1023	1135	935	769	354	136	18	5429
Ind.	Evansville ....A	45.0	0	0	66	220	606	896	955	767	620	237	68	0	4435
	Fort Wayne ....A	37.3	0	9	105	378	783	1135	1178	1028	890	471	189	39	6205
	Indianapolis ....A	39.6	0	0	90	316	723	1051	1113	949	809	432	177	39	5699
	South Bend ....A	36.6	0	6	111	372	777	1125	1221	1070	933	525	239	60	6439
Iowa	Burlington ....A	37.6	0	0	93	322	768	1135	1259	1042	859	426	177	33	6114
	Des Moines ....A	35.5	0	6	96	363	828	1225	1370	1137	915	438	180	30	6588
	Dubuque ....A	32.7	12	31	156	450	906	1287	1420	1204	1026	546	260	78	7376
	Sioux City ....A	34.0	0	9	108	369	867	1240	1435	1198	989	483	214	39	6951
	Waterloo ....A	32.6	12	19	138	428	909	1296	1460	1221	1023	531	229	54	7320
Kans.	Concordia ....A	40.4	0	0	57	276	705	1023	1163	935	781	372	149	18	5479
	Dodge City ....A	42.5	0	0	33	251	666	939	1051	840	719	354	124	9	4986
	Goodland ....A	37.8	0	6	81	381	810	1073	1166	955	884	507	236	42	6141
	Topeka ....A	41.7	0	0	57	270	672	980	1122	893	722	330	124	12	5182
	Wichita ....A	44.2	0	0	33	229	618	905	1023	804	645	270	87	6	4620
Ky.	Covington ....A	41.4	0	0	75	291	669	983	1035	893	756	390	149	24	5265
	Lexington ....A	43.8	0	0	54	239	609	902	945	818	685	325	105	0	4683
	Louisville ....A	44.0	0	0	54	248	609	890	930	818	682	315	105	9	4660
La.	Alexandria ....A	57.5	0	0	0	56	273	431	471	361	260	69	0	0	1921
	Baton Rouge ....A	59.8	0	0	0	31	216	369	409	294	208	33	0	0	1560
	Lake Charles ....A	60.5	0	0	0	19	210	341	381	274	195	39	0	0	1459
	New Orleans ....A	61.0	0	0	0	19	192	322	363	258	192	39	0	0	1385
	New Orleans C	61.8	0	0	0	12	165	291	344	241	177	24	0	0	1254
	Shreveport ....A	56.2	0	0	0	47	297	477	552	426	304	81	0	0	2184

State	Station	Avg. Winter Temp	July	Aug.	Sept.	Oct.	Nov.	Dec.	Jan.	Feb.	Mar.	Apr.	May	June	Yearly Total
Me.	Caribou ....A	24.4	78	115	336	682	1044	1535	1690	1470	1308	858	468	183	9767
	Portland ....A	33.0	12	53	195	508	807	1215	1339	1182	1042	675	372	111	7511
Md.	Baltimore ....A	43.7	0	0	48	264	585	905	936	820	679	327	90	0	4654
	Baltimore C	46.2	0	0	27	189	486	806	859	762	629	288	65	0	4111
	Frederick ....A	42.0	0	0	66	307	624	955	995	876	741	384	127	12	5087
Mass.	Boston ....A	40.0	0	9	60	316	603	983	1088	972	846	513	208	36	5634
	Nantucket ....A	40.2	12	22	93	332	573	896	992	941	896	621	384	129	5891
	Pittsfield ....A	32.6	25	59	219	524	831	1231	1339	1196	1063	660	326	105	7578
	Worcester ....A	34.7	6	34	147	450	774	1172	1271	1123	998	612	304	78	6969
Mich.	Alpena ....A	29.7	68	105	273	580	912	1268	1404	1299	1218	777	446	156	8506
	Detroit (City) ....A	37.2	0	0	87	360	738	1088	1181	1058	936	522	220	42	6232
	Detroit (Wayne) ....A	37.1	0	0	96	353	738	1088	1194	1061	933	534	239	57	6293
	Detroit (Willow Run) .....A	37.2	0	0	90	357	750	1104	1190	1053	921	519	229	45	6258
	Escanaba C	29.6	59	87	243	539	924	1203	1445	1206	1203	777	456	159	8481
	Flint ....A	33.1	16	40	159	465	843	1212	1330	1198	1066	639	319	90	7377
	Grand Rapids ....A	34.9	9	28	135	434	804	1147	1259	1134	1101	579	279	75	6894
	Lansing ....A	34.8	6	22	138	431	813	1163	1262	1142	1011	579	273	69	6909
	Marquette C	30.2	59	81	240	527	936	1268	1411	1268	1187	771	468	177	8393
	Muskegon ....A	36.0	12	28	120	400	762	1088	1209	1100	995	594	310	78	6696
	Sault Ste. Marie ....A	27.7	96	105	279	580	951	1367	1525	1380	1277	810	477	201	9048
Minn.	Duluth ....A	23.4	71	109	330	632	1131	1581	1745	1518	1355	840	490	198	10000
	Minneapolis ....A	28.3	22	31	189	505	1014	1454	1631	1380	1166	621	288	81	8382
	Rochester ....A	28.8	25	34	186	474	1005	1438	1593	1366	1150	630	301	93	8295
Miss.	Jackson ....A	55.7	0	0	0	65	315	502	546	414	310	87	0	0	2239
	Meridian ....A	55.4	0	0	0	81	339	518	543	417	310	81	0	0	2289
	Vicksburg C	56.9	0	0	0	53	279	462	512	384	282	69	0	0	2041
Mo.	Columbia ....A	42.3	0	0	54	251	651	967	1076	874	716	324	121	12	5046
	Kansas City ....A	43.9	0	0	39	220	612	905	1032	818	682	294	109	0	4711
	St. Joseph ....A	40.3	0	6	60	285	708	1039	1172	949	769	348	133	15	5484
	St. Louis ....A	43.1	0	0	60	251	627	936	1026	848	704	312	121	15	4900
	St. Louis C	44.8	0	0	36	202	576	884	977	801	651	270	87	0	4484
	Springfield ....A	44.5	0	0	45	223	600	877	973	781	660	291	105	6	4900
Mont.	Billings ....A	34.5	6	15	186	487	897	1135	1296	1100	970	570	285	102	7049
	Glasgow ....A	26.4	31	47	270	608	1104	1466	1711	1439	1187	648	335	150	8996
	Great Falls ....A	32.8	281	53	258	543	921	1169	1349	1154	1063	642	384	186	7750
	Havre ....A	28.1	28	53	306	595	1065	1367	1584	1364	1181	657	338	162	8700
	Havre C	29.8	19	37	252	539	1014	1321	1528	1305	1116	612	304	135	8182

State	Station	Avg. Winter Temp	July	Aug.	Sept.	Oct.	Nov.	Dec.	Jan.	Feb.	Mar.	Apr.	May	June	Yearly Total
	Helena ....A	31.1	31	59	294	601	1002	1265	1438	1170	1042	651	381	195	8129
	Kalispell ....A	31.4	50	99	321	654	1020	1240	1401	1134	1029	639	397	207	8191
	Miles City ....A	31.2	6	6	174	502	972	1296	1504	1252	1057	579	276	99	7723
	Missoula ....A	31.5	34	74	303	651	1035	1287	1420	1120	970	621	391	219	8125
Neb.	Grand Island ....A	36.0	0	6	108	381	834	1172	1314	1089	908	462	211	45	6530
	Lincoln C	38.8	0	6	75	301	726	1066	1237	1016	834	402	171	30	5864
	Norfolk ....A	34.0	9	0	111	397	873	1234	1414	1179	983	498	233	48	6979
	North Platte ....A	35.5	0	6	123	440	885	1166	1271	1039	930	519	248	57	6684
	Omaha ....A	35.6	0	12	105	357	828	1175	1355	1126	939	465	208	42	6612
	Scotts Bluff ....A	35.9	0	0	138	459	876	1128	1231	1008	921	552	285	75	6673
	Valentine ....A	32.6	9	12	165	493	942	1237	1395	1176	1045	579	288	84	7425
Nev.	Elko ....A	34.0	9	34	225	561	924	1197	1314	1036	911	621	409	192	7433
	Ely ....A	33.1	28	43	234	592	930	1184	1308	1075	977	672	456	225	7733
	Las Vegas ....A	53.5	0	0	0	78	387	617	688	487	335	111	6	0	2709
	Reno ....A	39.3	43	87	204	490	801	1026	1073	823	729	510	357	189	6332
	Winnemucca ....A	36.7	0	34	210	536	876	1091	1172	916	837	573	363	153	6761
N. H.	Concord ....A	33.0	6	50	177	505	822	1240	1358	1184	1032	636	298	75	7383
	Mt. Washington Obsv.	15.2	493	536	720	1057	1341	1742	1820	1663	1652	1260	930	603	13817
N. J.	Atlantic City ....A	43.2	0	0	39	251	549	880	936	848	741	420	133	15	4812
	Newark ....A	42.8	0	0	30	248	573	921	983	876	729	381	118	0	4589
	Trenton C	42.4	0	0	57	264	576	924	989	885	753	399	121	12	4980
N. M.	Albuquerque ....A	45.0	0	0	12	229	642	868	930	703	595	288	81	0	4348
	Clayton ....A	42.0	0	6	66	310	699	899	986	812	747	429	183	21	5158
	Raton ....A	38.1	9	28	126	431	825	1048	1116	904	834	543	301	63	6228
	Roswell ....A	47.5	0	0	18	202	573	806	810	641	481	201	31	0	3793
	Silver City ....A	48.0	0	0	6	183	525	729	791	605	518	261	87	0	3705
N. Y.	Albany ....A	34.6	0	19	138	440	777	1194	1311	1156	992	564	239	45	6875
	Albany C	37.2	0	9	102	375	699	1104	1218	1072	908	498	186	30	6201
	Binghamton ....A	33.9	22	65	201	471	810	1184	1277	1154	1045	645	313	99	7286
	Binghamton C	36.6	0	28	141	406	732	1107	1190	1081	949	543	229	45	6451
	Buffalo ....A	34.5	19	37	141	440	777	1156	1256	1145	1039	645	329	78	7062
	New York (Cent. Park) C	42.8	0	0	30	233	540	902	986	885	760	408	118	9	4871
	New York (La Guardia) ......A	43.1	0	0	27	223	528	887	973	879	750	414	124	6	4811
	New York (Kennedy) ....A	41.4	0	0	36	248	564	933	1029	935	815	480	167	12	5219
	Rochester ....A	35.4	9	31	126	415	747	1125	1234	1123	1014	597	279	48	6748
	Schenectady C	35.4	0	22	123	422	756	1159	1283	1131	970	543	211	30	6650
	Syracuse ....A	35.2	6	28	132	415	744	1153	1271	1140	1004	570	248	45	6756

State	Station	Avg. Winter Temp	July	Aug.	Sept.	Oct.	Nov.	Dec.	Jan.	Feb.	Mar.	Apr.	May	June	Yearly Total
N. C.	Asheville C	46.7	0	0	48	245	555	775	784	683	592	273	87	0	4042
	Cape Hatteras C	53.3	0	0	0	78	273	521	580	518	440	177	25	0	2612
	Charlotte . . . . .A	50.4	0	0	6	124	438	691	691	582	481	156	22	0	3191
	Greensboro . . . . .A	47.5	0	0	33	192	513	778	784	672	552	234	47	0	3805
	Raleigh . . . . .A	49.4	0	0	21	164	450	716	725	616	487	180	34	0	3393
	Wilmington . . . . .A	54.6	0	0	0	74	291	521	546	462	357	96	0	0	2347
	Winston-Salem . . . . .A	48.4	0	0	21	171	483	747	753	652	524	207	37	0	3595
N. D.	Bismarck . . . . .A	26.6	34	28	222	577	1083	1463	1708	1442	1203	645	329	117	8851
	Devils Lake C	22.4	40	53	273	642	1191	1634	1872	1579	1345	753	381	138	9901
	Fargo . . . . .A	24.8	28	37	219	574	1107	1569	1789	1520	1262	690	332	99	9226
	Williston . . . . .A	25.2	31	43	261	601	1122	1513	1758	1473	1262	681	357	141	9243
Ohio	Akron-Canton . . . . .A	38.1	0	9	96	381	726	1070	1138	1016	871	489	202	39	6037
	Cincinnati C	45.1	0	0	39	208	558	862	915	790	642	294	96	6	4410
	Cleveland . . . . .A	37.2	9	25	105	384	738	1088	1159	1047	918	552	260	66	6351
	Columbus . . . . .A	39.7	0	6	84	347	714	1039	1088	949	809	426	171	27	5660
	Columbus C	41.5	0	0	57	285	651	977	1032	902	760	396	136	15	5211
	Dayton . . . . .A	39.8	0	6	78	310	696	1045	1097	955	809	429	167	30	5622
	Mansfield . . . . .A	36.9	9	22	114	397	768	1110	1169	1042	924	543	245	60	6403
	Sandusky C	39.1	0	6	66	313	684	1032	1107	991	868	495	198	36	5796
	Toledo . . . . .A	36.4	0	16	117	406	792	1138	1200	1056	924	543	242	60	6494
	Youngstown . . . . .A	36.8	6	19	120	412	771	1104	1169	1047	921	540	248	60	6417
Okla.	Oklahoma City . . . . .A	48.3	0	0	15	164	498	766	868	664	527	189	34	0	3725
	Tulsa . . . . .A	47.7	0	0	18	158	522	787	893	683	539	213	47	0	3860
Ore.	Astoria . . . . .A	45.6	146	130	210	375	561	679	753	622	636	480	363	231	5186
	Burns C	35.9	12	37	210	515	867	1113	1246	988	856	570	366	177	6957
	Eugene . . . . .A	45.6	34	34	129	366	585	719	803	627	589	426	279	135	4726
	Meacham . . . . .A	34.2	84	124	288	580	918	1091	1209	1005	983	726	527	339	7874
	Medford . . . . .A	43.2	0	0	78	372	678	871	918	697	642	432	242	78	5008
	Pendleton . . . . .A	42.6	0	0	111	350	711	884	1017	773	617	396	205	63	5127
	Portland . . . . .A	45.6	25	28	114	335	597	735	825	644	586	396	245	105	4635
	Portland C	47.4	12	16	75	267	534	679	769	594	536	351	198	78	4109
	Roseburg . . . . .A	46.3	22	16	105	329	567	713	766	608	570	405	267	123	4491
	Salem . . . . .A	45.4	37	31	111	338	594	729	822	647	611	417	273	144	4754
Pa.	Allentown . . . . .A	38.9	0	0	90	353	693	1045	1116	1002	849	471	167	24	5810
	Erie . . . . .A	36.8	0	25	102	391	714	1063	1169	1081	973	585	288	60	6451
	Harrisburg . . . . .A	41.2	0	0	63	298	648	992	1045	907	766	396	124	12	5251
	Philadelphia . . . . .A	41.8	0	0	60	297	620	965	1016	889	747	392	118	40	5144
	Philadelphia C	44.5	0	0	30	205	513	856	924	823	691	351	93	0	4486

State	Station	Avg. Winter Temp	July	Aug.	Sept.	Oct.	Nov.	Dec.	Jan.	Feb.	Mar.	Apr.	May	June	Yearly Total
	Pittsburgh ....A	38.4	0	9	105	375	726	1063	1119	1002	874	480	195	39	5987
	Pittsburgh C	42.2	0	0	60	291	615	930	983	885	763	390	124	12	5053
	Reading C	42.4	0	0	54	257	597	939	1001	885	735	372	105	0	4945
	Scranton ....A	37.2	0	19	132	434	762	1104	1156	1028	893	498	195	33	6254
	Williamsport ....A	38.5	0	9	111	375	717	1073	1122	1002	856	468	177	24	5934
R. I.	Block Island ....A	40.1	0	16	78	307	594	902	1020	955	877	612	344	99	5804
	Providence ....A	38.8	0	16	96	372	660	1023	1110	988	868	534	236	51	5954
S. C.	Charleston ....A	56.4	0	0	0	59	282	471	487	389	291	54	0	0	2033
	Charleston C	57.9	0	0	0	34	210	425	443	367	273	42	0	0	1794
	Columbia ....A	54.0	0	0	0	84	345	577	570	470	357	81	0	0	2484
	Florence ....A	54.5	0	0	0	78	315	552	552	459	347	84	0	0	2387
	Greenville-Spartanburg ....A	51.6	0	0	6	121	399	651	660	546	446	132	19	0	2980
S. D.	Huron ....A	28.8	9	12	165	508	1014	1432	1628	1355	1125	600	288	87	8223
	Rapid City ....A	33.4	22	12	165	481	897	1172	1333	1145	1051	615	326	126	7345
	Sioux Falls ....A	30.6	19	25	168	462	972	1361	1544	1285	1082	573	270	78	7839
Tenn.	Bristol ....A	46.2	0	0	51	236	573	828	828	700	598	261	68	0	4143
	Chattanooga ....A	50.3	0	0	18	143	468	698	722	577	453	150	25	0	3254
	Knoxville ....A	49.2	0	0	30	171	489	725	732	613	493	198	43	0	3494
	Memphis ....A	50.5	0	0	18	130	447	698	729	585	456	147	22	0	3232
	Memphis C	51.6	0	0	12	102	396	648	710	568	434	129	16	0	3015
	Nashville ....A	48.9	0	0	30	158	495	732	778	644	512	189	40	0	3578
	Oak Ridge C	47.7	0	0	39	192	531	772	778	669	552	228	56	0	3817
Tex.	Abilene ....A	53.9	0	0	0	99	366	586	642	470	347	114	0	0	2624
	Amarillo ....A	47.0	0	0	18	205	570	797	877	664	546	252	56	0	3985
	Austin ....A	59.1	0	0	0	31	225	388	468	325	223	51	0	0	1711
	Brownsville ....A	67.7	0	0	0	0	66	149	205	106	74	0	0	0	600
	Corpus Christi ....A	64.6	0	0	0	0	120	220	291	174	109	0	0	0	914
	Dallas ....A	55.3	0	0	0	62	321	524	601	440	319	90	6	0	2363
	El Paso ....A	52.9	0	0	0	84	414	648	685	445	319	105	0	0	2700
	Fort Worth ....A	55.1	0	0	0	65	324	536	614	448	319	99	0	0	2405
	Galveston ....A	62.2	0	0	0	6	147	276	360	263	189	33	0	0	1274
	Galveston C	62.0	0	0	0	0	138	270	350	258	189	30	0	0	1235
	Houston ....A	61.0	0	0	0	6	183	307	384	288	192	36	0	0	1396
	Houston C	62.0	0	0	0	0	165	288	363	258	174	30	0	0	1278
	Laredo ....A	66.0	0	0	0	0	105	217	267	134	74	0	0	0	797
	Lubbock ....A	48.8	0	0	18	174	513	744	800	613	484	201	31	0	3578
	Midland ....A	53.8	0	0	0	87	381	592	651	468	322	90	0	0	2591
	Port Arthur ....A	60.5	0	0	0	22	207	329	384	274	192	39	0	0	1447

State	Station	Avg. Winter Temp	July	Aug.	Sept.	Oct.	Nov.	Dec.	Jan.	Feb.	Mar.	Apr.	May	June	Yearly Total
	San Angelo ....A	56.0	0	0	0	68	318	536	567	412	288	66	0	0	2255
	San Antonio ....A	60.1	0	0	0	31	204	363	428	286	195	39	0	0	1546
	Victoria ....A	62.7	0	0	0	6	150	270	344	230	152	21	0	0	1173
	Waco ....A	57.2	0	0	0	43	270	456	536	389	270	66	0	0	2030
	Wichita Falls ....A	53.0	0	0	0	99	381	632	698	518	378	120	6	0	2832
Utah	Milford ....A	36.5	0	0	99	443	867	1141	1252	988	822	519	279	87	6497
	Salt Lake City ....A	38.4	0	0	81	419	849	1082	1172	910	763	459	233	84	6052
	Wendover ....A	39.1	0	0	48	372	822	1091	1178	902	729	408	177	51	5778
Vt.	Burlington ....A	29.4	28	65	207	539	891	1349	1513	1333	1187	714	353	90	8269
Va.	Cape Henry C	50.0	0	0	0	112	360	645	694	633	536	246	53	0	3279
	Lynchburg ....A	46.0	0	0	51	223	540	822	849	731	605	267	78	0	4166
	Norfolk ....A	49.2	0	0	0	136	408	698	738	655	533	216	37	0	3421
	Richmond ....A	47.3	0	0	36	214	495	784	815	703	546	219	53	0	3865
	Roanoke ....A	46.1	0	0	51	229	549	825	834	722	614	261	65	0	4150
Wash.	Olympia ....A	44.2	68	71	198	422	636	753	834	675	645	450	307	177	5236
	Seattle-Tacoma ....A	44.2	56	62	162	391	633	750	828	678	657	474	295	159	5145
	Seattle C	46.9	50	47	129	329	543	657	738	599	577	396	242	117	4424
	Spokane ....A	36.5	9	25	168	493	879	1082	1231	980	834	531	288	135	6655
	Walla Walla C	43.8	0	0	87	310	681	843	986	745	589	342	177	45	4805
	Yakima ....A	39.1	0	12	144	450	828	1039	1163	868	713	435	220	69	5941
W. Va.	Charleston ....A	44.8	0	0	63	254	591	865	880	770	648	300	96	9	4476
	Elkins ....A	40.1	9	25	135	400	729	992	1008	896	791	444	198	48	5675
	Huntington ....A	45.0	0	0	63	257	585	856	880	764	636	294	99	12	4446
	Parkersburg C	43.5	0	0	60	264	606	905	942	826	691	339	115	6	4754
Wisc.	Green Bay ....A	30.3	28	50	174	484	924	1333	1494	1313	1141	654	335	99	8029
	La Crosse ....A	31.5	12	19	153	437	924	1339	1504	1277	1070	540	245	69	7589
	Madison ....A	30.9	25	40	174	474	930	1330	1473	1274	1113	618	310	102	7863
	Milwaukee ....A	32.6	43	47	174	471	876	1252	1376	1193	1054	642	372	135	7635
Wyo.	Casper ....A	33.4	6	16	192	524	942	1169	1290	1084	1020	657	381	129	7410
	Cheyenne ....A	34.2	28	37	219	543	909	1085	1212	1042	1026	702	428	150	7381
	Lander ....A	31.4	6	19	204	555	1020	1299	1417	1145	1017	654	381	153	7870
	Sheridan ....A	32.5	25	31	219	539	948	1200	1355	1154	1051	642	366	150	7680

Notes: a From ASHRAE *Guide and Data Book,* base temperature 65°F
     b A indicates airport, C indicates city
     c Average winter temperatures for October through April, inclusive
Source: Reprinted with permission of the American Society of Heating, Refrigeration, and Air-Conditioning Engineers, *The 1989 ASHRAE Fundamentals—Handbook.*

Heat Loss Calculation Example

Let's say that our sample house is a single-story house with a slab on grade and 10 ft ceilings (see illustration on page 381). In order for us to purchase the appropriate furnace, we need to know what the heat loss of our house is going to be under severe conditions. The climate we are in has cold winters during which the average temperature is 20°F. We would like our ambient inside temperature to be 68°F. To begin, we must subtract the outside temperature from the inside temperature, which gives us a "delta t" of 48°F.

$$\Delta t = (t_i - t_0)$$
$$\Delta t = (68°F - 20°F)$$
$$\Delta t = (48°F)$$

We will use the Δt of 48°F and the following formulae to calculate the heat loss of our house through glass (glazing), walls, ceilings, and floors. Heat loss through these assemblies takes place in several different ways: conduction, infiltration, and radiation. Radiation is so slight that it isn't worth calculating. We will only consider the heat losses caused by conduction and infiltration. Let's begin by calculating the heat loss resulting from conduction, which is the transfer of energy (heat) through a medium by direct molecular interaction.

Heat Loss by Conduction (Through Glass, Walls, Ceiling, and Floors)

The formula for heat loss calculation by conduction is:

$$Q_{conduction} = \Delta t \times A / R$$

Q = heat loss (by conduction), in BTU/hr
Δt = temperature difference between inside and outside: $(t_i - t_0)$, degrees Fahrenheit
A = area exposed, in square feet
R = R-value of the assembly (i.e., roof, wall, window, etc.)

- **Heat loss through glazing:**

R-value of glass (from Table 9 on page 243):
We are using a standard double pane window $R_{glass} = 1.75$

Area of glazing:

Dining rm:	(3) 1'8" × 4'0" window units (glazing ≅ 1'6" × 3'8" ≅ 5.5 sf)	= 16.5 sf
Living rm:	(1) 2'4" × 4'0" window unit (glazing ≅ 2'0" × 3'8" ≅ 7.3 sf)	= 7.3 sf
Living rm:	(1) 2'6" × 4'0" window unit (glazing ≅ 2'2" × 3'8" ≅ 8 sf)	= 8.0 sf
Kitchen area:	(2) 2'6" × 4'0" window units (glazing ≅ 2'2" × 3'8")	= 16.0 sf
Bedroom:	(2) 2'0" × 4'0" window units (glazing ≅ 1'8" × 3'8" ≅ 6 sf)	= 12.0 sf
Bathroom:	(1) 2'0" × 4'0" window unit (glazing ≅ 1'8" × 3'8")	= 6.0 sf
Bathroom:	(2) 1'0" × 1'0" window units (glazing ≅ 2'0" × 3'8")	= 14.6 sf
Air lock:	(2) 2'6" × 6'8" doors (glazing ≅ 2'0" × 6'0" ≅ 12 sf)	= 24 sf
Living rm:	(2) 1'8" × 3'0" doors (glazing ≅ 1'6" × 2'10" ≅ 4.3 sf)	= <u>8.5</u> sf

$$A_{glass} = 113 \text{ sf}$$

Heat loss through glazing:

$$Q_{glass} = A_{glass} \times \Delta t / R_{glass}$$
$$Q_{glass} = 113 \times 48/1.75$$
$$\boxed{Q_{glass} = 3,100 \text{ BTU/hr}}$$

- **Heat loss through walls:**

R-value of wall: (See Figure 183 on page 383)
Our walls are made of a ⅝" layer of gypsum board, 2 × 6 studs (Douglas fir), filled with 5½" of fiberglass insulation, ½" plywood, a vapor barrier, and shingle siding.

From ASHRAE 1985 Fundamentals, page 23.6, Tables 3A and B (see bibliography page 433, Chapter 15), we get the following R-values (1/U) = R:

⅝" gypsum board	R = 00.56
Fiber glass insulation 5½"	R = 19.00

Vapor barrier single ply	R = 00.06
½″ plywood	R = 00.62
Wood shingles	+ R = 00.87
Total wall R-value per wall section:	R = 21.11

Typically we round off to a slightly lower R_{wall} value. This will somewhat account for the thermal bridging through studs and other through-wall framing. Therefore we assume:

$$R_{wall} = 20.00$$

To determine the area of the wall, we must subtract the area of the windows:

$$A_{wall} = 10' \times 122' - A_{glass}$$
$$A_{wall} = 1,220 \text{ sf} - 113 \text{ sf} = 1,107 \text{ sf}$$

Heat loss through the walls is therefore:

$$Q_{wall} = A_{wall} \times \Delta t / R_{wall}$$
$$Q_{wall} = 1,107 \times 48 / 20.00$$
$$\boxed{Q_{wall} = 2,657 \text{ BTU/hr}}$$

• **Heat loss through ceilings:**

Since our attic space is unheated, the heat loss through the ceiling will be the same as if it were exposed to the outside temperature.

R-value of ceiling:

Ceiling joists are 2 × 12, giving approximately 12″ of fiberglass insulation. Again referring to Table 3A, ASHRAE, p. 23.6 for R-values of individual materials.

$$R_{ceiling} = 0.56 \text{ (gypsum board)} + 0.06 \text{ (vapor barrier)} + 38.00 \text{ (fiberglass insulation)}$$
$$R_{ceiling} = 38.62$$

Rounding down to R = 37 will take into account the effects of thermal bridging through the framing.

Given the overall dimensions of the ceiling, we can calculate the area:

$$A_{ceiling} = (21'6'' \times 27'0'') + (12'6'' \times 19'6'')$$
$$A_{ceiling} = 824.25 \text{ sf}$$

The heat loss through ceiling:

$$Q_{ceiling} = A_{ceiling} \times \Delta t / R_{ceiling}$$
$$Q_{ceiling} = 824.25 \times 48 / 37$$
$$\boxed{Q_{ceiling} = 1,069 \text{ BTU/hr}}$$

• **Heat loss through slab: (See Figures 184a and b)**

The perimeter loss calculation for concrete slabs is:

$$Q_{slab} = f \times P_{slab} \times \Delta t$$

where:

f = Slab heat loss factor in BTU/hr – ft – °F
P_{slab} = Perimeter of slab in feet
Δt = Temperature difference between inside and outside in degrees Fahrenheit

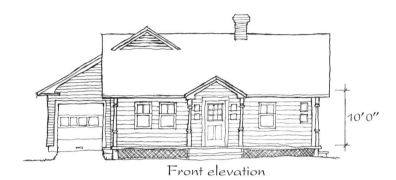

Front elevation

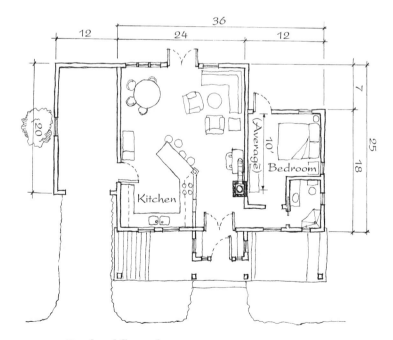

FIGURE 182a: Roof and floor plans.

Garage side elevation

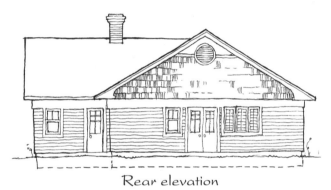

Rear elevation

Bedroom side elevation

FIGURE 182b: Elevations.

The easiest way to calculate heat loss through slabs simply uses a factor (f) from Table 30. This factor depends on how much insulation is installed along the slab perimeter. To get your slab heat loss, simply multiply the Δt by the appropriate factor (f) and the result by the perimeter of your building. Note: Where the garage adjoins the house is a tricky situation. Since the garage is not a heated area, we assume that this edge is exposed to the outside.

Therefore, assuming our slab perimeter is covered with $1\frac{1}{2}''$ thick rigid insulation (R = 3.33) that goes down 2 ft below grade, we can find our slab heat losses as follows:

$$Q_{slab} = 0.50 \ (f\text{ factor}) \times 122 \text{ (slab perimeter)} \times 48 \ (\Delta t)$$

$$\boxed{Q_{slab} = 2{,}928 \text{ BTU/hr}}$$

If we add up the conductive heat losses through all assemblies, we arrive at the total:

$$Q_{conduction} = Q_{glazing} + Q_{wall} + Q_{ceiling} + Q_{slab}$$
$$Q_{conduction} = 3{,}100 + 2{,}657 + 1{,}069 + 2{,}928$$

$$\boxed{Q_{total\ conduction} = 9{,}754 \text{ BTU/hr}}$$

Heat Loss by Infiltration through Walls (air-change method)

The other way that our house can lose heat is through infiltration, which takes place when air leaves a heated space and takes thermal energy with it. The warm air is replaced by cold air, which must be heated in order to maintain a comfortable temperature. Infiltration can be defined as the unintentional air exchange that occurs because of various leaks in the house. There are two ways to calculate infiltration losses: the crack method and the air-exchange method. The air-exchange method is based on the total number air changes per hour for a dwelling of a given volume and is much the easier of the two methods. We will calculate the heat loss of our house due to infiltration using the air-exchange method:

Heat loss by infiltration formula (air exchange method):

$$Q_{infiltration} = n \times V \times \Delta t \times 0.018$$

where:

0.018 = a constant
n = number of air changes per hour
V = volume of the house in cubic feet
Δt = temperature difference between inside and outside in degrees Fahrenheit

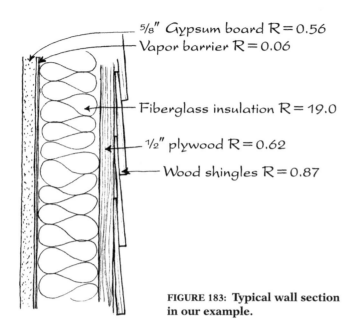

FIGURE 183: **Typical wall section in our example.**

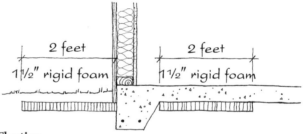

SLAB HEAT LOSS FACTOR

f (BTU/Hr-ft-°F)	Total width of insulation (vertical and/or horizontal)		
Insulation R-value	1 ft	1.5 ft	2 ft
6.76	0.29	0.26	0.25
5.00	0.38	0.35	0.33
4.00	0.49	0.44	0.42
3.33	0.58	0.52	0.50
2.85	0.67	0.61	0.59
2.5	0.77	0.70	0.67
0		0.81	

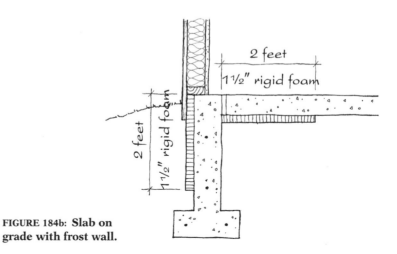

FIGURE 184a: **Floating or Alaskan slab.**

FIGURE 184b: **Slab on grade with frost wall.**

NUMBER OF AIR CHANGES:

For new construction, with air locks at every exterior door, dampers in the chimney, and other such heat-saving precautions, it is not unreasonable to have an air change per hour factor (n) of about 1.25.

$$n = 1.25$$

Volume of the building:

$$V = \text{foot print} \times \text{room height}$$
$$V = 824.25 \text{ sf} \times 10 \text{ ft}$$
$$V = 8,242.5 \text{ ft}^3$$

Heat loss due to infiltration:

$$Q_{\text{infiltration}} = 1.25 \times 8,242.5 \times 48 \times 0.018$$
$$Q_{\text{infiltration}} = 8,902 \text{ BTU/hr}$$

Total building heat loss:

$$Q_{\text{TOTAL}} = Q_{\text{infiltration}} + Q_{\text{conduction}}$$
$$Q_{\text{TOTAL}} = 8,902 + 9,754$$
$$\boxed{Q_{\text{TOTAL}} = 18,656 \text{ BTU/hr}}$$

Now that we have calculated the total heat loss for our house (18,656 BTU/hr), we can size the furnace.

Equipment sizing

- **Furnace size (in btu):**

To be conservative, the output of the furnace should be 20 percent above our calculated Q_{TOTAL}:

$$\text{Furnace Capacity} = 1.2 \times Q_{TOTAL} \text{ (18,656 BTUH)}$$
$$\text{Furnace Capacity} = 22,387 \text{ BTU/hr}$$

- **Radiator size (in btu):**

Let's calculate, in a more detailed way, the heating requirements of the bedroom and bathroom. In addition to the heat loss by conduction through the windows, doors, walls, ceiling, and floor we will also calculate the amount of infiltration that takes place along the edges of doors and windows. Here we use the crack method to calculate heat loss by infiltration around windows and doors.

HEAT LOSS THROUGH BEDROOM GLAZING:

R-value of glass (from ASHRAE 1985 Fundamentals, p. 27.10, Table 13):
We have standard double-pane windows

$$R_{glass} = 1.75$$

Area of glazing:

Bedroom: (2) 2'0" × 4'0" ea. (glazing: 1'8" × 3'8" $\cong$ 6 sf) = 12.0 sf

$$A_{glass} = 12 \text{ sf}$$

Heat loss through glazing:

$$Q_{glass} = A_{glass} \times \Delta t / R_{glass}$$
$$Q_{glass} = 12 \times 48 / 1.75$$
$$Q_{glass} = 329 \text{ BTU/hr}$$

HEAT LOSS THROUGH BEDROOM WALLS:

R-value of wall:

$$R_{wall} = 20.00$$

The area of the wall:

$$A_{wall} = (10' \times 10') + (12' \times 10') - A_{glass}$$
$$A_{wall} = 208 \text{ sf}$$

So the heat loss through the exterior walls is:

$$Q_{wall} = A_{wall} \times \Delta t / R_{wall}$$
$$Q_{wall} = 208 \times 48 / 20.00$$
$$Q_{wall} = 499 \text{ BTU/hr}$$

HEAT LOSS THROUGH BEDROOM CEILING:

R-value of ceiling:

$$R_{ceiling} = 37$$

Area of ceiling:

$$A_{ceiling} = 150 \text{ sf}$$

The heat loss through ceiling:

$$Q_{ceiling} = A_{ceiling} \times \Delta t / R_{ceiling}$$
$$Q_{ceiling} = 150 \times 48 / 37$$
$$Q_{ceiling} = 195 \text{ BTU/hr}$$

HEAT LOSS THROUGH BEDROOM SLAB:

$$Q_{slab} = f \times \text{(perimeter length)} \times \Delta t$$
$$Q_{slab} = 0.81 \times (12' + 10') \times 48$$
$$Q_{slab} = 855 \text{ BTU/hr}$$

TOTAL heat loss by CONDUCTION for the bedroom: (thru all assemblies)

$$Q_{conduction} = Q_{glazing} + Q_{wall} + Q_{ceiling} + Q_{slab}$$
$$Q_{conduction} = 329 + 499 + 195 + 885$$
$$\boxed{Q_{conduction} = 1,908 \text{ BTU/hr}}$$

HEAT LOSS BY INFILTRATION THROUGH BEDROOM WALLS:

Heat loss due to infiltration (crack method):

$$Q_{infiltration} = \tfrac{1}{2}(L \times I) \times \Delta t \times 0.018$$

$(L \times I)$ = rate of infiltration in cubic feet per hour
  L = length of crack in feet around perimeter of door or window
  I = infiltration factor (see Table 11, Chapter 15) cubic feet/hour-foot of crack
  Δt = temperature difference between inside and outside: $(t_i - t_o)$

As in the total building heat loss calculation, we will assume $\Delta t = 48°F$. In looking at the floor plan and the elevations, the bedroom has two walls exposed to the exterior, one with two 2' × 4' windows and the other with one 2' × 4' window and a 3'0" × 6'8" door.

Note: We do not need to take into consideration the walls that are not exposed to the outside since the temperature difference (Δt) on either side of the wall is zero ($\Delta t = 0°F$).

(2) Double-hung windows, weather stripped of dimension $2'0'' \times 4'0''$ ea. Length of crack (perimeter):

$$L = 24' \quad (12' \text{ for ea. window})$$

Using Table 11 (Chapter 15), we assume a wind velocity of about 10 mph, the infiltration factor is:

$$I = 26 \quad (13 \text{ for ea. window})$$

For the windows, the heat loss will be:

$$Q_{windows} = \tfrac{1}{2}(L \times I) \times \Delta t \times 0.018$$
$$Q_{windows} = \tfrac{1}{2}(24 \times 26) \times 48 \times 0.018$$
$$Q_{windows} = 269.6 \text{ BTU/hr}$$

(1) Door, under the same type of conditions. We assume this is new construction, therefore the doors will be well-fitted.

Door dimension of $3'0'' \times 6'8''$

Length of crack (perimeter):

$$L = 19'4''$$

Infiltration factor (again using Table 11):

$$I = 69$$
$$Q_{door} = \tfrac{1}{2}(L \times I) \times \Delta t \times 0.018$$
$$Q_{door} = 19.3 \times 69 \times 48 \times 0.018$$

$$Q_{door} = 575.3 \text{ BTU/hr}$$
$$Q_{infiltration} = Q_{door} + Q_{windows}$$

$$\boxed{Q_{infiltration} = 575.3 \text{ BTUH} + 269.6 \text{ BTUH} = 844.9 \text{ BTU/hr}}$$

Total Heat Loss for the bedroom:

$$Q_{Bedroom} = Q_{infiltration} + Q_{conduction}$$
$$Q_{Bedroom} = 844.9 \text{ BTU/hr} + 1,908 \text{ BTU/hr}$$

$$\boxed{Q_{Bedroom} = 2,752.9 \text{ BTU/hr}}$$

Once again we can size the heating equipment, in this case the radiator, using the total heat loss for the bedroom (2,752.9 BTU/hr).

- **Radiator size (in feet):**

Baseboard hydronic radiators give out about 500 to 700 BTU/hr for every foot of length. So, for this room we need

$$\text{Good radiator length} = Q_{Bedroom}/700$$
$$= 4 \text{ feet of high quality radiator}$$

$$\text{Average radiator length} = Q_{Bedroom}/500$$
$$= 6 \text{ feet of radiator}$$

As you can see, radiator quality can determine how much of your room must be given over to baseboard radiators. This is a big design consideration in every room.

APPENDIX 4
Drafting Conventions

Drafting is the art of accurately depicting your design in such a way that it can be built as you intend. At its core, drafting is a language. We use it to communicate with builders, plumbers, roofers, code officials, and, of course, bankers. You need not take a year of training at your local technical school to successfully draft up your design. As with any language, drafting comes in many dialects, the two most common being traditional *orthographic drafting* and the more recent *computer aided drafting* (CAD). For starters, I suggest you stay away from the many computer programs currently on the market. They are costly, have a long learning curve, and suffer from a tendency to "design" your house for you.

Conventional drafting requires only a few inexpensive drawing tools and about a morning of instruction (and practice, practice, practice!). At Yestermorrow, we teach all new students how to draft within the first day, and they are proficient within a week. Of the tools shown in Figure 185, the most important ones include a scale, an adjustable triangle, and a drafting board with T-square or parallel rule.

A scale is nothing more than a three-sided ruler with a different scale of measurement on each face of the triangle. One side will have ¼" and ⅛" scales on it, which are the most commonly used. The parallel rule or T square slides up and down your drafting board, allowing you to make multiple horizontal lines that are all perfectly parallel. The adjustable triangle, which rides and slides along the upper edge of your T square, allows you to make multiple parallel lines at any angle with the horizontal lines. Thus, you can make a very nice box by drawing two parallel horizontal lines with your T square and then two vertical lines with your triangle. (But a box is a silly place to start any design . . . try drawing an octahedron.)

Additional (optional) drafting tools that can make life easier and your drawings a little sharper include a compass or a circle template, a bathroom template, an erasing shield, and maybe different-size triangles.

In addition to these basic tools you will, of course, need tracing paper, drafting tape (to hold your trace onto your board), pencils (of different weights—F, HB, and 3H), a sharpener, and an eraser. You can purchase the technical version of these everyday items or use the ones we all learned about in kindergarten. If a four-year-old can work 'em, I'm sure the rest of us can. Don't be worried if you erase a lot; indeed, you should plan on it. A drafting brush is used to sweep the offending erasure filings onto the floor. If you're like me, you will have to vacuum after every design session.

With very little invested in time or money, you are now ready to start making lines. There are loads of different line types in drafting, each meaning something different. These are the "words" in the language of drafting. Although technical drafting has an extensive syntax of line types and their meaning, we have provided just the few that you will need to get started (Figure 186).

Drafting is like any other kind of drawing in that you will use a continuum of line weights and thicknesses to represent a variety of different things. The trick is to have a system and stay consistent. The lightest lines are used to indicate measurements, material finishes, windows, doors, etc.

DOOR AND WINDOW SCHEDULE

Windows	Rough Opening	Unit Dimension	Sill Height	Head Height	Notes:
Ⓐ	2'11" x 3'9"	2'10" x 3'8"	3'0"	6'8"	Double-Hung
Ⓑ	2'11" x 4'9"	2'10" x 4'8"	2'0"	6'8"	Double-Hung
Ⓒ	1'6" x 3'0"	1'5" x 2'11"	3'0"	6'0"	Casement
Ⓓ	2'0" x 4'9"	1'11" x 4'8"	2'0"	6'8"	Fixed
Doors					
①	3'0" x 6'8"	2'10 x 6'7½"		6'8"	Provided By Owner
②	5'6" x 6'8"	2@ 2'8" x 6'7½"		6'8"	Bifold Doors
③	2'10" x 6'8"	2'8" x 6'7½"		6'8"	Solid Core Door
④	5'0" x 6'10"	2@ 2'5" x 6'9½"		6'10"	Glass Door
⑤	2'8" x 6'8"	2'6" x 6'7½"		6'8"	Solid Core Door

Information found in a typical door or window schedule.

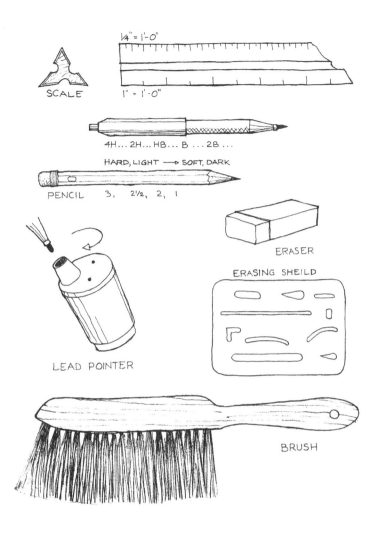

FIGURE 185: Drafting tools.

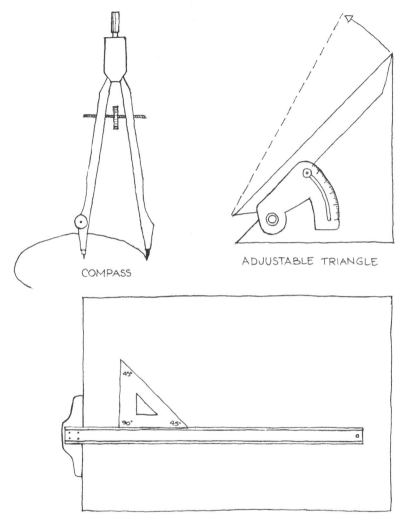

T-SQUARE, TRIANGLE AND DRAWING BOARD

The heaviest lines are used wherever you cut through some part of the building. That includes all walls in a *plan* (assumed by convention to be cut at about 4′0″ above the floor) and all wall, floor, and roof assemblies in a *section*. You can see these darker lines used in plan (Figure 187) and section (Figure 188). Different dotted lines are used to indicate things above or below the plan at hand. These might include a balcony or skylight (above) or a beam or mechanical chase (below).

Stair runs are always cut at the 4′0″ level when they are going up, but they are drawn in their entirety when going down (Figure 189). Sometimes people will dot in the stairs that exist above the 4′0″ cut-line.

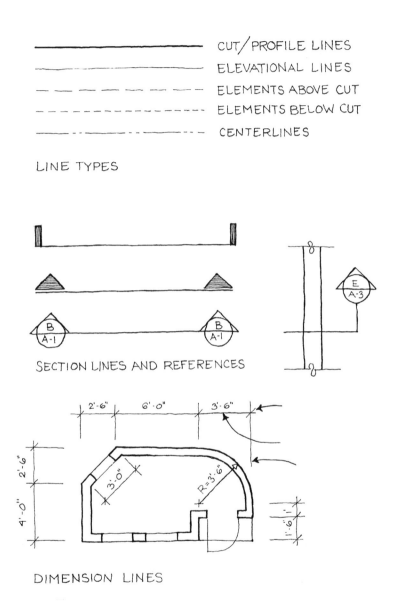

——————————— CUT/PROFILE LINES

——————————— ELEVATIONAL LINES

— — — — — — ELEMENTS ABOVE CUT

- - - - - - - - ELEMENTS BELOW CUT

—— — —— — —— CENTERLINES

LINE TYPES

SECTION LINES AND REFERENCES

B
A-1

B
A-1

E
A-3

2'-6"   6'-0"   3'-6"

2'-6"

4'-0"

3'-0"

R=3'-6"

1'-6"

DIMENSION LINES

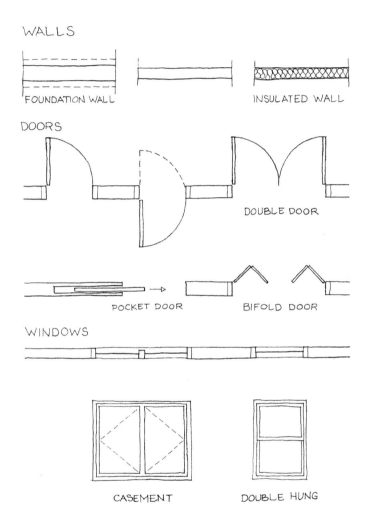

WALLS

FOUNDATION WALL   INSULATED WALL

DOORS

DOUBLE DOOR

POCKET DOOR   BIFOLD DOOR

WINDOWS

CASEMENT   DOUBLE HUNG

FIGURE 186: Lines.

PLAN

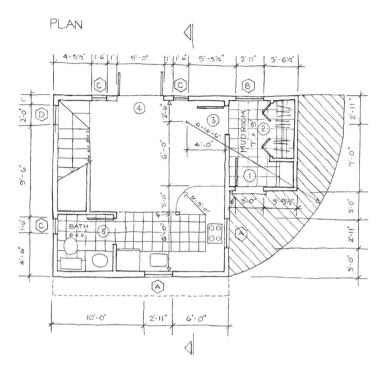

FIGURE 187: Typical floor plan.

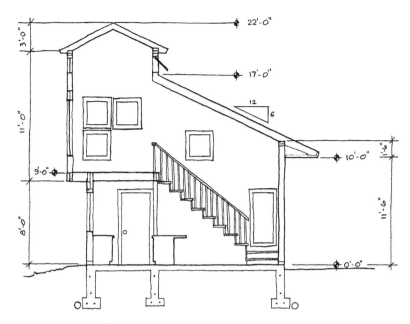

FIGURE 188: Typical building section.

Architecture can be accurately described wtihin three basic drawing types: *plan*, *section*, and *elevation*. These drawings are parallel cutaways at various points thorughout the building. The plan is a horizontal cutaway, while the sections and elevations are vertical cutaways. In order to make the measurements accurate, we always make our section and elevation cuts *parallel* to the walls being depicted (thus the name *orthographic* drafting). We could draw sections and elevations that were skewed to the geometry of the building, but then they would be warped and not to scale. These drawings are sometimes undertaken to get the aesthetic feel of an elevation, but they are very confusing to the builders and bankers. Remember, drawings are a vehicle for communication. If people are getting confused, you are missing the whole purpose. Always choose a drawing type that best shows the information you are trying to communicate. A freehand perspective would be better for showing architectural aesthetics, while an elevation should be used to show finishes and window placement. Sections are ideal for showing the structure and how the stairs work.

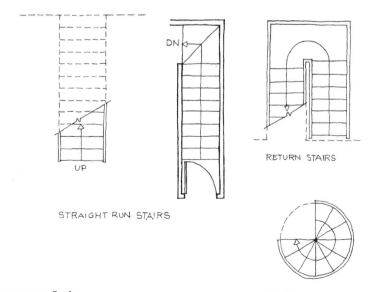

FIGURE 189: Stairs.

Naturally, there is a whole lot more to drafting than what is presented here. But for now, while you are developing your preliminary design, this is all the drafting sophistication you need. *Design* drafting must show only how the rooms and spaces will be arranged in three-dimensional space. Also, they must show the proportions and the materials. You want to draw your design accurately and to scale. You want the drawings to be clear enough so others can discuss your design with you. You want to use your drawings to build a scale model.

After many cycles around the Design Helix, when you think you are ready to prepare construction documents, that's when you'll need to get more involved in *technical* drafting. We have listed a few good books in the bibliography for those interested in mastering this wonderful language.

Foundation Design Guide

Introduction:

Every design/builder keeps a notebook of their favorite charts, rules of thumb, and frequently used facts. This appendix contains most of the important data I refer to when designing foundations, retaining walls, or anything involving concrete.

General Facts Concerning Concrete:

1. The Mix

The strength of concrete is determined largely by the proportions of the mix and the cement/water ratio. The following chart will help you mix or purchase different strengths of concrete.

When you order the garden variety concrete from your neighborhood ready-mix plant, it is usually what they call a five- or six-bag mix with a 2,500 to 3,000 psi compressive strength. Although you can't count on it, this mix is usually made with added strength to cover unforeseen site conditions. These "conditions" might be the use of admixtures or water to ease handling. Admixtures are chemicals that increase workability, freeze protection, or curing time. The strength is often reduced by admixtures, so it is best to specify your concrete by the required strength. Too much water also weakens the concrete. If you take care with the amount of water added, the placement, and the curing, a 2,500 psi concrete may well have 3,500 psi strength.

1 bag = 94 lbs of Portland cement

Rule of Thumb: Since today's modern concrete is specified by its compressive strength rather than the less precise practice of calling out the number of bags, use a 3,000 psi strength (a six-bag mix) concrete as a minimum. Although a 2,500 psi concrete used to be the same as a five-bag mix, the modern material frequently contains dyes and admixtures so that a five-bag mix might not actually contain five full bags of Portland Cement.

2. The Aggregate

Concrete needs to have a range of aggregates, from fine sand up through ¾″ stone, sometimes larger. The maximum size of aggregate can be specified when you order as follows:

fine aggregate:	sand thru ⅜″ max.
standard aggregate:	⅜″ thru ⅝″ max.
coarse aggregate:	⅝″ thru 1½″ max

Rule of Thumb: For small members—beams, slabs, walls, and columns—use ¾″ maximum for coarse aggregate. For larger members, thick footings and retaining walls, use up to 1½″ max.

3. The Steel

Steel reinforcing bars take all the tensile forces exerted within a concrete member. However, steel also rusts. If the rust is allowed to continue into the member, it will destroy the indispensable bond between the steel and the concrete. Therefore all reinforcing, snap ties, and other steel must be fully embedded in the concrete. Use good-quality mortar to parge all snap ties after they have been broken off.

Reinforcing bars (rebar) come in different sizes designated by the number of eighths of an inch in the diameter. For instance, if the diameter is ⅜″ it's a number 3 bar; if the diameter is ¾″ it's a number 6 bar.

Size	Diameter	Area	Perimeter	Weight
#3	⅜″ = 0.375	0.11 in.²	1.18 in.	0.38 lb/ft
4	½″ = 0.5	0.20	1.57	0.67
5	⅝″ = 0.625	0.31	1.96	1.04
6	¾″ = 0.75	0.44	2.36	1.50
7	⅞″ = 0.875	0.60	2.75	2.04
8	1″ = 1.00	0.79	3.14	2.67
9	1⅛″ = 1.12	1.00	3.54	3.40
10	1¼″ = 1.27	1.27	3.99	4.30
11	1⅜″ = 1.41	1.56	4.43	5.31
14	1¾″ = 1.69	2.25	5.32	7.65
18	2¼″ = 2.25	4.00	7.09	13.60

Rule of Thumb: All reinforcing must be covered by no less than 1½″ of concrete, or 3″ if the building element will be in direct contact with the ground (i.e., a footing).

The concrete cover is measured from the edge of the bar to the nearest exposed edge of concrete. It is also important that the rebars not be placed, or displaced, too close to one another. All rebars should be tied and fastened securely, since the concrete exerts a powerful force when it is poured into the forms.

Rule of Thumb: The minimum clear distance between adjacent bars should be equal to the bar diameter or 1½ times the maximum aggregate diameter, whichever is greater.

Rule of Thumb: In a typical full foundation, place two number 4 bars in the footing and two more on each snap tie in the wall.

Rule of Thumb: Place the rebar along the side of the member where the tensile stresses must be carried (usually away from where the load is coming from).

TEMPERATURE STEEL:

This is the term used for light steel reinforcing placed in slabs to withstand the forces created by temperature changes and shrinkage from curing.

In residential construction welded wire fabric is most frequently used to control surface cracking in slabs. Welded wire fabric is an orthogonal grid of wire or small bar welded at every joint. The conventional designation for welded wire fabric (WWF) is:

longitude × transverse—longitudinal diameter × transversal diameter

with a "w" or a "d" indicating wire type, for example,

4 × 8 − w10 × w16

refers to a welded wire fabric that has the following configuration:

spacing of longitudinal wire	4″
spacing of transverse wire	8″
area of longitudinal wire	0.10″²
area of transverse wire	0.16″²
w indicates a smooth wire	
(d indicates a deformed wire)	

The following chart summarizes properties for wire sizes used in WWF:

W or D Number	Cross Sectional Area (sq. inches)	Diameter (inches)
W18 or D18	0.18	0.48
W14 or D14	0.14	0.42
W12 or D12	0.12	0.39
W10 or D10	0.10	0.36
W8 or D8	0.08	0.32
W6 or D6	0.06	0.28
W4 or D4	0.04	0.22
W2.9 or D2.9	0.029	0.192

Rule of Thumb: To determine the amount of temperature steel (WWF) for a given slab, assume a 6″ × 6″ array and use the following formula to determine the cross-sectional area required per foot of slab in each direction. Then look up the proper wire size in the table above:

Area of Temperature Steel (assuming yield strength Fy = 60,000 psi) =

.0216 (inches) × slab thickness (inches)

Area of Temperature Steel (assuming yield strength Fy = 40,000 psi) =

.024 (inches) × slab thickness (inches)

4. Placing and Curing:

Concrete weighs about 150 pounds per cubic foot, so you have to take some care when placing it in the forms, or anywhere, for that matter. A wheelbarrow full of concrete requires a substantial board to bridge a ditch or ramp up to the top of the forms. When concrete is poured into a deep form, it should not be allowed to fall more than 8 feet. Otherwise the aggregate will separate from the cement. Once poured, separation will also occur if the concrete is overvibrated.

Rule of Thumb: Configure excavation and formwork to allow the concrete truck to reach all forms with its chute. Minimize use of wheelbarrows.

The period of drying and hardening concrete is called *curing*. Proper curing is necessary to produce quality concrete. The requirements for proper curing are favorable temperature and abundant moisture. The ideal temperature is 70°F.

TABLE 30: CONCRETE MIXES

KIND OF CONCRETE WORK*	Mix by Volume Job Damp Materials			Workability or Consistency	Water Added at Mixer Per Bag. Gallons	A One Bag Batch Makes This Volume of Concrete Cu. Ft.	Materials for One Cubic Yard of Concrete			Water Added at Mixer Gallons
	Cement Bags	Sand Cu. Ft.	Stone, Gravel Cu. Ft.				Cement Bags	Sand Cu. Ft.	Stone, Gravel Cu. Ft.	
Footings Heavy Foundations	1	3.75	5	stiff	6.4	6.2	4.3	16.3	21.7	27.6
Watertight Concrete for Cellar Walls and Walls Above Ground	1	2.5	3.5	medium	4.9	4.5	6.0	15.0	21.0	29.5
Driveways Floors Walks } One course	1	2.5	3	stiff	4.4	4.1	6.5	16.3	19.5	28.7
Driveways Floors Walks } Two course	1	Top 2	0	stiff	3.6	2.14	12.6	25.2		45.3
	1	Base 2.5	4	stiff	4.9	4.8	5.7	14.2	22.8	27.8
Pavements	1	2.2	3.5	stiff	4.3	4.2	6.4	14.1	22.4	27.5
Watertight Concrete for Tanks, Cisterns and Precast Units (piles, posts, thin reinforced slabs, etc.)	1	2	3	medium	4.1	3.8	7.1	14.2	21.3	29.3
				wet	4.9	3.9	6.9	13.8	20.7	33.7
Heavy Duty Floors	1	1.25	2	stiff	3.4	2.8	9.8	12.3	19.6	33.9
Mortar for Laying Concrete Building Units	1	6 plaster sand	1 sack 50 lbs. Hydrated Lime	medium	12.5	5.5	4.9	29.4	4.9 sacks of lime	61.2

*Many specifications require proportioning and measuring by weight with accurate control of a specified maximum allowable water content.

Source: Reprinted with permission of Van Nostrand Reinhold from *Don Graf's Basic Building Data*, 1949.

Rule of Thumb: Mist all slabs with clean water for the first twenty-four hours after finishing. Cover forms with plastic sheet to keep the moisture contained.

Rule of Thumb: While concrete sets up in twenty-four hours, it gains most of its final strength after seven days of curing.

Heating the water in the mixture is sufficient precaution if the weather is moderately cold. Curing concrete must never be allowed to freeze. If conditions require that the concrete be placed in very hot or very cold weather, ask the supplier for suggested admixtures. There are chemicals that allow concrete to be poured in the dead of winter or at high noon in the desert. There are also admixtures to reduce the water used in the mix, increase fluidity, increase air content, etc., etc. These admixtures reduce the "bag mix" ratio and usually reduce strength somewhat. Check with your engineer or supplier.

Rule of Thumb: Always have reliable access to water, power, and plastic when pouring and curing concrete.

Rule of Thumb: Forms should be stripped after twenty-four hours. Never strip the forms in less than twelve hours. Green concrete is soft and can be shifted out of plumb by premature stripping. It is best to protect and cure concrete for at least seven days.

Rule of Thumb: Never backfill a foundation wall until the floor deck has been built to support the upper edge of the wall against overturning.

Try to avoid loading concrete excessively during its first seven days of curing. Nevertheless, it is normal for the floor deck to be built immediately after the forms are removed. This is not considered an excessive load.

Rule of Thumb: If you must cut, alter, or drill concrete, it should be done in the first few days after the forms are stripped, while it is still "green."

Foundation Parts and Retaining Walls:

Footings:

The footings must be formed and poured on undisturbed soil that is well drained and will not freeze.

Rule of Thumb: In areas where there is frost, locate the footings 12″ below the code-mandated frost line.

Footings need to be reinforced for loads from above as well as any frost movement from below. This means that residential concrete installers often place the rebar in the middle of the footing. However, if you use a commercial concrete contractor and place the footings well below the frost line, there should be no reason to worry about frost heaving. In this case, it is best to place the rebar three inches from the bottom of the footing, as it will only be receiving loads from above.

Rule of Thumb: The minimum *width* of a footing should be twice the thickness of the foundation wall.
The minimum *depth* of a footing should be equal to the thickness of the foundation wall.

Footings can be more precisely sized using the following formula. If the building exceeds two stories in height, additional engineering may be required (reinforcing, concrete mix, etc.).

$$A = P/s$$

Where,

A = the minimum horizontal bearing surface required, usually the width of the footing multiplied by the perimeter of the building; in square feet.

P = the total load of the building; in pounds

s = bearing capacity of the soil; in pounds per square foot

Estimating the weight of an entire house may seem like a strange and difficult exercise, but Buckminster Fuller was doing it all the time. He was always demonstrating how a geodesic dome supplied more shelter, pound for pound, than any other approach. For your purposes, it will suffice to add the roof loads, the floor loads, and then 10 pounds per square foot for the materials in any assembly: floors, ceiling, walls, etc. To get the best results, you should do the calculation for each wall and interior support separately. Some sections of wall may carry more load than others; interior supports will likely carry a bit less than perimeter supports.

Slabs:

Concrete slabs are either poured on grade or supported on columns and walls as floor slabs in a concrete building. One rarely deals with the second type in residential construction. Therefore, we will use the term to mean only slabs poured on grade.

Slab construction is one of the least expensive foundation options. A slab can be poured to just about any size and reinforced to handle almost any loading. A large slab must accommodate expansion and differential movement. By providing expansion joints or cutting in control joints, unsightly cracking may be kept to a minimum.

Rule of Thumb: Slabs should not exceed 20′ in any dimension without a control joint to confine cracking.
Slabs should not exceed 30′ in any dimension without an expansion joint to allow movement.
No continuous slab should be L-shaped in plan. It should consist of several rectangular slabs with control joints.

Expansion joints need to allow a little movement. One proven detail allows the rebar in each slab to extend a foot or two into a pipe cast in the neighboring slabs. This allows adequate alignment as well as some room for movement. Expansion joints of this type must be thoroughly caulked, top and bottom, to prevent ground moisture from rusting out the steel. This assumes that each slab has adequate structural integrity and proper soil conditions below.

To avoid the use of steel, a tongue and groove-type joint might be used to allow controlled movement. This joint looks and operates pretty much the same as the wooden joint of the same name.

Rule of Thumb: Standard residential slabs need only be 4″ of 2,500 psi concrete with continuous WWF submerged 1″ from the upper surface.
Heavy-duty or light commercial slabs need to be 6″ of 2,500 psi mix with number 3 bar at 18″ on center, in both directions. If the soil is questionable, use a *floating* slab, with thicker edges and additional reinforcing.

Retaining Walls:

Retaining walls are freestanding walls that resist the thrust of a bank of earth on one side. There are three basic types of retaining walls: the "L" type, the "T" type (also known as the cantilever type), and the mass, or gravity, type.

The **L** type uses the weight of the earth on the heel of the wall to resist lateral slippage and overturning. Note that the wall is effective regardless of the orientation of the **L** toward or away from the bank.

The **T** type, or cantilever, wall has both a heel and a toe and, like the **L** type, the weight of the earth on the heel prevents overturning.

The *counterfort* wall is similar to the cantilever wall except that the vertical wall is tied to the base at regular intervals by triangular-shaped brackets.

The *mass*, or *gravity*, type wall uses its mass to resist overturning. Because of their sheer mass, gravity type walls require very little reinforcing.

Rule of Thumb: Gravity walls are usually used up to 8′ in height. L or cantilever walls are typically used from 8′ to 25′. Counterfort walls are most economical above 25′.

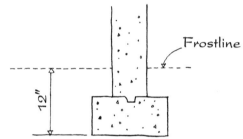

1. The bottom of the footing should be at least 1′0″ below the depth of local frost

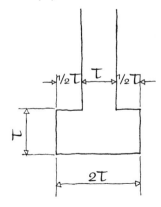

2. The footing should be as deep as the wall thickness being supported (T) and twice as wide ($2T$)

FIGURE 190: Rules of thumb for footing.

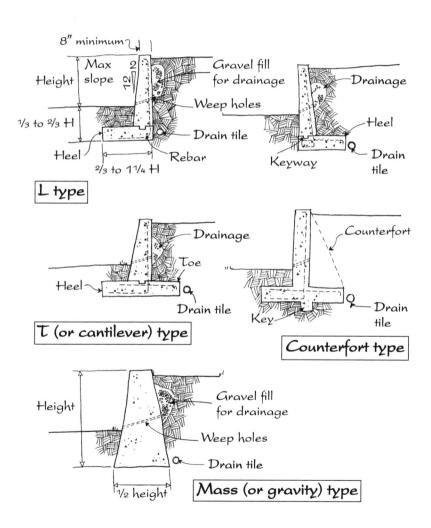

FIGURE 191: There are four types of retaining walls: "L" type, "T" type, counterfort, and mass.

Two methods that seem to go hand in hand are the gravel footing and the wood foundation. The gravel footing is better known as the trench foundation. It is based on the theory that adequately drained fill can't freeze or heave because it has no moisture content. The wood foundation uses pressure-treated wood instead of masonry for the foundation walls, based on the premise that adequately poisoned wood won't support the little bugs that are essential to rot. Let's look at each of these two methods in a little more detail.

The Trench Foundation:

There are many variations of this age-old foundation method. What follows is but one, yet they are all based on the same underlying principles.

A trench must be dug to a depth of at least 1' below the *known* frost line (as opposed to the code-indicated frost line). The bottom of the trench should be compacted. It is then filled with crushed stone between ½" and ¾" in size. This structural fill is placed in 12" lifts and compacted between lifts. At the depth of the known frost line a foundation drain is installed that must drain to daylight. The gravel is leveled off and compacted at 8" to 12" below the elevation of finish grade. The final stem wall that will support the first-floor deck is constructed at this point. The top of the trench should be protected from surface water either by plastic membrane or a layer of impervious soil (clay). Final grading should be sloped to shed water away from the building.

This foundation system is based on the following principles:

1. Structural fill, when compacted, will not settle appreciably.
2. Crushed stone will drain completely.
3. If there is absolutely no moisture in the subsurface support of a building it can not freeze and heave.
4. Adequate measures have been taken to prevent surface water from entering the trench from above (clay or membrane).
5. Adequate measures have been taken to prevent the invasion of the water table from below (foundation drain).
6. The soil surrounding the trench will support the lateral pressures generated by the load of the house on the gravel.
7. The stem wall under the first-floor deck is soundly built and designed to spread the house loads evenly over the gravel.

Any variation of a trench foundation that meets all these assumptions will supply good, long-lasting support for a moderately-sized house. It will also cost quite a bit less than a concrete foundation. But you won't have a full basement, which is why we now turn to the wood foundation.

The Wood Foundation:

Known either as the all weather wood foundation (AWWF) or the permanent wood foundation (PWF), this technology saves money by allowing the carpenters to build the foundation walls. Again, there are many variations.

This approach can be used to build full basements or crawl spaces. The footing may be wood, concrete, or stone.

The materials used must all be impervious to rust, rot, or corrosion. All the wood must have a proven natural resistance to rotting in soil, or be heavily pressure treated and marked with a specification stamp indicating that it can stand *direct contact with the earth;* for instance, AWPB-FDN. The wood should not have a moisture content above 18 percent (see Table 31 and 33). The nails and other fasteners must be either stainless steel or hot-dipped galvanized. Plywood is to be nailed at 4" to 6" along all edges and 8" to 12" in the field. All joint and seams must be caulked or glued using one of the following products:

Inmont Presstite Tape #579.6 Inmont Corporation 39th and Chouteau St. Louis, MO 63166	#5411 Acrylic Latex Caulk The Franklin Glue Company Columbus, OH 43207
Duribbon Sealant 4040-60 National Starch and Chemical Corp. (Bondmaster Division) 10 Finderne Avenue Bridgewater, NJ 08807	Silpruf Silicone Products Department General Electric Company Waterford, NY 12188
Inmont Presstite Caulk #579.64 Inmont Corporation 39th and Chouteau St. Louis, MO 63166	#5230 Wood Adhesive Adhesives, Coatings & Sealers Div. 3M Company 3M Center St. Paul, MN 55101

Everywhere it is important to lap or stagger joints. This includes the sills, the sheathing, and the cap plates. Glued, nailed, and lapped joints are your first line of defense against leaks.

So far, everything mentioned is generally accepted practice by anyone building wood foundations. What follows are the issues that depend on a builder's personal style. These include the footings, the slab or floor, and the final waterproofing of the wall. I admit to my biases and I'll give equal time to others.

One very commonly used footing scheme is a variation on the trench foundation mentioned above. A 4" to 6" lift of compacted crushed stone is placed over the entire footprint of the building. The walls arrive with 2 × 12s nailed to the bottom plate of each section. This is the footing. The walls are tilted up, leveled, and temporarily supported. When they are all in place, a cap plate is installed to tie them together. Finally, a 4" slab is poured using the walls as forms. This means that the slab is keyed into the walls, which keeps them from moving. It also prevents them from kicking in when they are back-filled. The slab and walls are all bearing on the lift of compacted stone.

TABLE 31: APPROPRIATE LUMBER SPECIES FOR WOOD FOUNDATIONS

Group	and Grade
A	Douglas Fir No. 1 Southern Pine No. 1 KD
B	Douglas Fir No. 2 Southern Pine No. 2 KD
C	Hem Fir No. 2
D	Lodgepole Pine No. 2 Northern Pine No. 2 Ponderosa Pine No. 2

The plywood most commonly used for the AWWF is APA RATED SHEATHING EXP 1 marked PS 1, usually referred to as CDX. APA RATED SHEATHING EXT can also be used and, if appearance is a factor, use A-C EXT, B-C EXT, C-C Plugged, or MDO. All should be Group 1 species. Ungrooved textured 303 plywood siding may also be treated for use in the AWWF to match or complement the siding on the upper stories.

The plywood should be at least ½ inch CDX, if the face grain is parallel to the studs. If the face grain is across studs, ⅜ inch may be used provided the difference in height of fill on opposite side of the foundation does not exceed three feet. If the difference exceeds three feet, use Table 11.

Some builders find this a little risky. The finished floor is just a few inches from the potential water in the crushed stone. Suppose there is a leak? Also, many builders can't feel comfortable with just a 2 × 12 and some gravel as the footing. This group of builders are fond of pouring a conventional footing with steel reinforcing and anchor bolts. Then the wood foundation can be erected on these. If a slab is to be poured, it can be leveled with the footings at a later time or poured monolithically at the same time as the footings. While this configuration is structurally more sound, it still does little to prevent water from leaking under the sill.

For the true "belt and suspenders" builder (me), I suggest the "T footer." This is a conventional footing poured monolithically with a 1′ stem wall. The wood wall sits on the stem wall in a manner that allows the plywood to extend down over the wall all the way to the footing (see illustration at right). This lapping of the joints produces excellent water protection and the T-shape is even stronger than a conventional footing. I still start with a compacted 4″ lift of crushed stone or sand and I still have the option of pouring a slab or, preferably, building a wood floor. The down side to this bullet-proof approach is, of course, cost. The footing is elaborate and takes considerable time to form up and pour. This is what wood foundations were developed to avoid.

The final water protection is also a hotly contested issue. The standard treatment consists of a 6 mil poly sheet intermittently bonded to the wall,

all joints lapped and taped, hanging uninterrupted from cap to sill plate. I guess this is O.K. if you're selling the building and moving to a distant state. But I wouldn't use it on *my* house. No, instead, I used bituthane. This is a roofing membrane usually placed under the flashing in valleys or along the eaves. It has adhesive on one side. It's easily three times the cost of the poly and ten times more reliable. Some builders go even further and use actual rubber membrane roofing. We used that method on the new foundation for the Yestermorrow offices. I have to say, it strikes me (even me) as a bit of "overkill." Still, it all depends on the particular application.

The final debate concerns the interior vapor barrier. Promoters of wood foundations are always extolling the warm habitable space so easily pro-

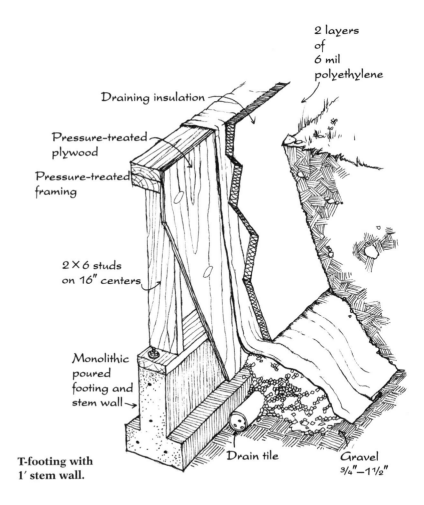

T-footing with 1′ stem wall.

vided by finishing off the inside. Skeptics point out that this produces the textbook formula for trapped moisture and rot within the wall. With a vapor barrier on the inside and another on the outside, the wall simply cannot "breathe." I must admit that this strikes me as a legitimate concern. Consequently, I caulk and seal the gypboard to the studs of the foundation wall. Then I use a plaster-based joint compound (Durabond 60) and fiberglass tape at all the joints. These are my best defense against water migrating into the wall. My oldest wood foundation is only fifteen years old at the time of this printing, but there is no sign of moisture within the walls.

So with all these pros and cons, does the wood foundation work? Yes, so far. Will it last one hundred years? I don't know, we aren't there yet. Ask me again in fifty.

Structural Requirements

Size of footing plates, framing members and thickness of the sheathing are determined in the same manner as those for crawl space foundation walls. The Footing Plate Selector Chart (Table 32) is at right.

TABLE 32: MINIMUM FOOTING PLATE SIZE[1,2]

For one- and two-story house construction only

	Roof—40 psf live; 10 psf dead Ceiling—10 psf 1st floor—50 psf live and dead 2nd floor—50 psf live and dead		*Roof—30 psf live; 10 psf dead Ceiling—10 psf 1st floor—50 psf live and dead 2nd floor—50 psf live and dead*	
House width (feet)	*2 stories*	*1 story*	*2 stories*	*1 story*
32	2×10	2×8	2×10[3]	2×8
28	2×10	2×8	2×8	2×6
24	2×8	2×6	2×8	2×6

[1]Footing plate shall be not less than species and grade combination "D" from Table 8.

[2]Where width of footing plate is 4 inches (nominal) or more wider than that of stud and bottom plate, use ¾ inch thick continuous treated plywood strips with face grain perpendicular to footing; minimum grade APA Rated Sheathing 48/24 EXP 1 marked PS 1. Use plywood of same width as footing and fasten to footing with two 6d galvanized nails spaced 16 inches.

[3]This combination of house width and height may have 2×8 footing plate when second floor design load is 40 psf live and dead load.

Source: *APA Design/Construction Guide*, (all-weather wood foundation, American Plywood Association).

TABLE 33: MINIMUM PLYWOOD GRADE AND THICKNESS FOR BASEMENT CONSTRUCTION

30 pcf equivalent-fluid density soil pressure

		Face grain across studs[2]			*Face grain parallel to studs*		
Height of fill (inches)	*Stud spacing (inches)*	*Grade[3]*	*Minimum thickness[1]*	*Span Rating*	*Grade[3]*	*Minimum thickness[1,5]*	*Span Rating*
24	12	B	½	32/16	B	½	32/16
	16	B	½	32/16	B	½ (4 ply or 5 layer)	32/16
48	12	B	½	32/16	B	½[6] (5 layer)	32/16
					A	½	32/16
	16	B	½	32/16	A	⅝	42/20
					B	¾	48/24
72	12	B	½	32/16	A	⅝[6] (5 layer)	42/20
	16	A[4]	½[6]	32/16	B	¾[6]	48/24
86	12	B	½[6]	32/16	A	⅝[6]	42/20
					B	¾[6]	48/24
	16	A	⅝	42/20	A	⅝[7]	42/20
		B	¾	48/24			

[1]Crawl space sheathing may be ⅜ inch for face grain across studs and maximum 3 foot depth of unequal fill.

[2]Minimum 2 inch blocking between studs required at all horizontal panel joints more than 4 feet below adjacent ground level (also where noted in details).

[3]Minimum plywood grades conforming to "U.S. Product Standard PS 1, Construction and Industrial Plywood" are:
A. Structural I Rated Sheathing Exposure 1
B. Rated Sheathing Exposure 1

If a major portion of the wall is exposed above ground, a better appearance may be desired. The following Exterior grades would be suitable:
A. Structural I A-C, Structural I B-C or Structural I C-C (Plugged)
B. A-C Exterior Group 1, B-C Exterior Group 1, C-C (Plugged) Exterior Group 1 or MDO Exterior Group 1 or Ungrooved Group 1 303 plywood siding.

[4]For this combination of fill height and panel grade, only Structural I A-C or Structural I Rated Sheathing Exterior may be substituted for improved appearance.

[5]When face grain is parallel to studs, plywood panels of the required thickness, grade and Span Rating may be any construction permitted except as noted in the table for minimum number of plies required.

[6]For this fill height, thickness and grade combination, panels which are continuous over less than three spans (across less than three stud spacings) require blocking 2 feet above bottom plate. Offset adjacent blocks and fasten through studs with two 16d corrosion resistant nails at each end.

[7]For this fill height, thickness and grade combination, panels require blocking 16 inches above bottom plate. Offset adjacent blocks and fasten through studs with two 16d corrosion resistant nails at each end.

TABLE 34: MINIMUM STRUCTURAL REQUIREMENTS FOR BASEMENT WALLS

Wall height—8 feet. Roof supported on exterior walls. Floors supported on interior and exterior bearing walls.[1,2] 30 lbs. per cu. ft. equivalent-fluid density soil pressure—2000 lbs. per sq. ft. allowable soil bearing pressure.

			Uniform load conditions					
			Roof—40 psf live; 10 psf dead / Ceiling—10 psf / 1st floor—50 psf live and dead / 2nd floor—50 psf live and dead			Roof—30 psf live; 10 psf dead / Ceiling—10 psf / 1st floor—50 psf live and dead / 2nd floor—50 psf live and dead		
Construction	House width (feet)	Height of fill (inches)	Lumber species and grade[3]	Stud and plate size (nominal)	Stud spacing (inches)	Lumber species and grade[3]	Stud and plate size (nominal)	Stud spacing (inches)
2 Stories		24	D	2 × 6	16	D	2 × 6	16
		48	D	2 × 6	16	D	2 × 6	16
	32 or less	72	A	2 × 6	16	A	2 × 6	16
			B	2 × 6	12	B	2 × 6	12
			C	2 × 8	16	D	2 × 8	16
			D	2 × 8	12			
		86	A*	2 × 6	12	A*	2 × 6	12
			B	2 × 8	16	B	2 × 8	16
			C	2 × 8	12	C	2 × 8	12
		24	D	2 × 6	16	D	2 × 6	16
		48	D	2 × 6	16	D	2 × 6	16
	24 or less	72	C	2 × 6	12			
			D	2 × 8	16	C	2 × 6	12
		86	A*	2 × 6	12			
			B	2 × 8	16			
			C	2 × 8	12	D	2 × 8	12
		24	B	2 × 4	16	C	2 × 4	16
			D	2 × 4	12	D	2 × 4	12
			D	2 × 6	16	D	2 × 6	16
	32 or less	48	D	2 × 6	16	D	2 × 6	16
		72	A	2 × 6	16	A	2 × 6	16
			B	2 × 6	12	C	2 × 6	12
			D	2 × 8	16	D	2 × 8	16
		86	A*	2 × 6	12	A*	2 × 6	12
			B	2 × 8	16	B	2 × 8	16
			C	2 × 8	12	D	2 × 8	12

Construction	House width (feet)	Height of fill (inches)	Uniform load conditions					
			Roof—40 psf live; 10 psf dead / Ceiling—10 psf / 1st floor—50 psf live and dead / 2nd floor—50 psf live and dead			Roof—30 psf live; 10 psf dead / Ceiling—10 psf / 1st floor—50 psf live and dead / 2nd floor—50 psf live and dead		
			Lumber species and grade[3]	Stud and plate size (nominal)	Stud spacing (inches)	Lumber species and grade[3]	Stud and plate size (nominal)	Stud spacing (inches)
1 Story								
		24	B	2 × 4	16			
			D	2 × 4	12	D	2 × 4	16
			D	2 × 6	16			
	28 or less	48	D	2 × 6	16	B	2 × 4	12
		72	C	2 × 6	12	C	2 × 6	12
		86				A*	2 × 6	12
						B	2 × 8	16
			D	2 × 8	12	D	2 × 8	12
		24	D	2 × 4	16	D	2 × 4	16
		48	B	2 × 4	12	B	2 × 4	12
	24 or less	72	C	2 × 6	12	C	2 × 6	12
		86				A*	2 × 6	12
						B	2 × 8	16
			D	2 × 8	12	D	2 × 8	12

[1]Studs and plates in interior bearing walls supporting floor loads only must be of lumber species and grade "D" or higher. Studs shall be 2 inches by 4 inches at 16 inches on center where supporting one floor and 2 inches by 6 inches at 16 inches on center where supporting 2 floors. Footing plate shall be 2 inches wider than studs.

[2]If brick veneer is used, see page 23 for knee wall requirements.

[3]Species, species groups and grades having the following minimum (surfaced dry or surfaced green) properties as provided in the National Design Specification:

		A	B	C	D
F_b (repetitive member) psi	2 × 6, 2 × 8	1,750	1,450	1,150	975
	2 × 4	2,050	1,650	1,350	1,150
F_c psi	2 × 6, 2 × 8	1,250	1,050	875	700
	2 × 4	1,250	1,000	825	675
F_{c1} psi		385	385	245	235
F_v psi		95	95	75	70
E psi		1,800,000	1,600,000	1,400,000	1,100,000
Typical lumber grades		Douglas fir No. 1 / Southern Pine No. 1 KD	Douglas fir No. 2 / Southern Pine No. 2 KD	Hem fir Nor. 2	Lodgepole Pine No. 2 / Northern Pine No. 2 / Ponderosa Pine No. 2

Where indicated (*), length of end splits or checks at lower end of studs not to exceed width of piece.

Earthquake Basics

Seismic activity varies over the different regions of the country. Although the map shown here appears orderly and precise, earthquakes are anything but predictable (Figure 192). They are always big news because, even with the best available science, we just don't know when or where they will occur. It is exactly this quality that brings out the gambler in so many home owners. After all, they reason, if one hasn't gotten me so far, why worry? The answer to this carefree question can be read in any of the news clippings about recent quakes along the San Andreas Fault or even worse disasters in Central and South America. Thousands of lives and millions of dollars are at risk whenever an earthquake strikes. Most of what is lost, both lives and property, will result from inadequate building design and construction.

Earthquakes are the result of tectonic plates, huge sections of the earth's crust, slipping and shifting by one another. Although the earth moves up and down as well as laterally, the vertical forces created by a quake are usually not considered; it is the horizontal movement that does the most damage. Imagine your house and the ground it sits in moving back and forth at 10 to 30 mph. Even though the distance may be less than a few inches, the ground motion comes to an abrupt halt or changes direction with such frequency that a brittle building is quickly shaken to pieces. This vibration is often likened to the feeling of a subway passing directly below you. (A former Costa Rican resident told me this metaphor lacked the essential feeling. Instead he offered, "Imagine your house being picked up in the mouth of a huge dog intent on breaking it up by viciously shaking it until it is limp and dead!") (Figures 193 and 194).

Earthquake resistance can be built into your home by keeping these horizontal forces in mind while you design. Because of the varied and unpredictable intensity of seismic activity it is probably impractical to hope for total earthquake protection. There will always be a bigger one. Consequently, the level of safety provided by code requirements is only aimed at reducing loss of life resulting from fire and falling debris. You may want to do more. In addition to minimum code requirements, there are several rules of thumb that should be kept in mind as you design and build.

Shape

In both plan and elevation a simple symmetrical shape is less likely to be shaken apart than one that is highly articulated. Setbacks, step backs, angles, and wings all concentrate the horizontal earthquake forces. Very slender or elongated configurations will suffer from the wave motion that can set up in such shapes.

Layout should be an even mix of walls at right angles to one another.

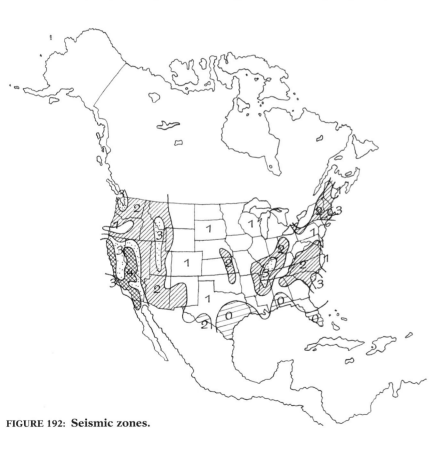

FIGURE 192: Seismic zones.

This gives the overall geometry a beneficial stiffness. Also, shorter walls are less likely to vibrate into pieces.

Openings

Too many windows or doors in a wall will greatly reduce its earthquake resistance. A totally glazed wall, or one that is so fully penetrated with openings as to be more opening than wall, may be rejected by the building inspector. The high torsional flexibility of a house with only three resisting walls makes them unsuitable in active seismic areas.

Openings are less of a liability when they are evenly spaced. If they are concentrated in one area they will concentrate forces during an earthquake.

Wherever possible, heavy lintel construction should be detailed to prevent falling during an earthquake.

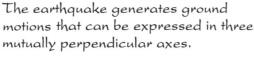 The earthquake generates ground motions that can be expressed in three mutually perpendicular axes.

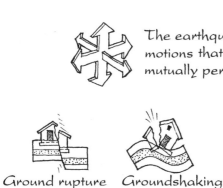

Ground rupture Groundshaking Differential subsidence Liquefaction

Main causes of foundation failures

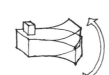

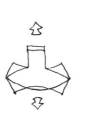   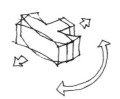

Motions of typical plan shapes

FIGURE 193: Ground shaking.

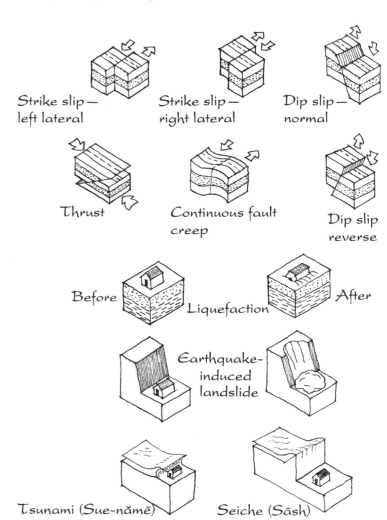

Strike slip — left lateral Strike slip — right lateral Dip slip — normal

Thrust Continuous fault creep Dip slip reverse

Before Liquefaction After

Earthquake-induced landslide

Tsunami (Sue-nămē) Seiche (Sāsh)

FIGURE 194: Fault terminology and types.

Wall Design

If appropriately designed and detailed, timber and reinforced concrete can survive an earthquake well. The idea is to have ductility at the joints while maintaining stiffness and continuity within the walls. The framed wall with plywood sheathing is a good choice. It has the necessary shear strength to resist horizontal forces during a quake. Diagonal bracing or diagonal sheathing are good alternatives if plywood is not used. In contrast, an unreinforced brick or brick-veneer wall is a poor choice. If you are building with block or adobe, use bond beams every 4' to provide continuity. (See Figure 113).

Your foundation wall is one of the more important areas to design for earthquake resistance. The clear choice is reinforced concrete. In the event of a quake the walls will be flexed back and forth. The concrete will crack readily and the steel will end up doing most of the support work. Therefore, a good design strategy calls for the steel to be heavy but the concrete to be relatively thin. Flexibility is the key. The steel should be placed on the outer faces, both sides, of the walls. This will provide tensile resistance to the bending from both directions. There should be plenty of vertical steel as well. What we want is a grid of number 4 or number 5 bars spaced at 12" on center. This will hold the cracked concrete together and, thus, support the building.

Whether you have a full basement or merely a crawl space, the foundation walls should be laid out with adequate horizontal shear resistance. The convention of using just perimeter walls and interior posts and girders to support the first floor deck leaves the building subject to considerable side sway damage during an earthquake. Shear walls at right angles to the perimeter walls will make the building less vulnerable.

Horizontal Planes

The floors and ceilings maintain important continuity throughout the building during an earthquake. A split level poses more of a risk than a single-level design. Again, this is the idea of minimizing setbacks and odd shapes.

The horizontal plane that represents the most danger is the roof. A heavy tile or earth roof can be very dangerous in an earthquake. To insure that it doesn't break up, the roof should be properly supported at regular intervals and the ceiling at the eave level should be designed to prevent spreading and collapse.

Connections

Remember the seismic rule of thumb: *flexibility is fine; brittleness is bad.* So that means connections should be able to endure bending and vibration without failing. The most vital areas to be concerned with are at the interfaces between the foundation and framing; the walls and the roof; and any setbacks or corner conditions. Metal strapping, brackets, and hangers should be used freely in wood construction. Foundation J-bolts are essential.

Chimneys and Masonry

Any component that is greatly stiffer than the rest of the building can cause considerable damage during an earthquake. A masonry chimney in a wood-frame house is particularly vulnerable. There are two possible solutions. In many cases the chimney or other stiff element can be made structurally independent from the rest of the building. The only difficulty involves the detailing of the movement gaps. Alternately, the two different elements can be fastened securely together. This is a bit riskier. When a timber structure is tied to such a stiff component, it becomes a horizontal shear-resisting element. This requires that the building and the chimney be designed accordingly and that the connection be stronger than is normally the practice.

Taken all together these guidelines may suggest a pretty dreary house: no setbacks, simple shapes, flat floor planes, few doors and windows. Yikes! Such a building might not be missed if it did fall victim to the Big One. But that's really the wrong way to think of this. These are not meant to be constraints, simply guidelines. Almost any house design can be detailed to survive an earthquake if proper care is taken. In areas of severe seismic activity (zones 3 and 4; see Figure 192) I suggest the use of an engineer. Don't ask the engineer what you may do first. Design your home first. Then ask the engineer how to make it resistant to earthquake damage.

APPENDIX 7

Structures for Everyone: Beams and Span Charts

The great majority of all structural calculations for residences are simply supported beams. These include joists, girders, beams, rafters, and headers. A simply supported beam is one that has only two supports, not three or more. Because this is such a prevalent configuration, this appendix has been included to give a better understanding of the numbers and equations involved.

In all simple beam calculations, it is easiest when the loads are uniformly distributed over the length of the span. Unfortunately, life isn't quite that simple. Loads tend to bunch up here and there into what engineers call "concentrated loads" or even "point loads." To avoid anxiety associated with the calculations for such loading, we have also included a procedure for changing all asymmetrical concentrated loads into nice uniformly distributed *equivalent* loads.

How, you may wonder, can we play so fast and loose with these calculations? Isn't engineering a precise practice? Well yes, but there are margins of safety built-in everywhere. The code includes a safety factor in the live loads. The span charts include safety factors and so do the allowable stresses published by the wood associations. Of course, we're not suggesting that you should be cavalier with structural calculations. Quite the contrary. Nevertheless, wood is a remarkably forgiving material and the following simple math will allow anyone with a basic math sense to get a feeling for joist and beam sizes.

Sizing Joists and Girders with Span Tables

Dead loads are comprised of the actual weight of materials (see Table 35) while live loads are determined by code. Both are in pounds per square foot (psf).

The following examples use two charts:

The Bending Characteristics of Some Common Woods (see Table 36) and The 14′ and 16′ Span Charts (see Table 37).

Sizing the Joists

Using Figure 195 (right), let's visualize the weights and calculations we are performing. In our example, the combined loads directly affecting

the floor joists are the dead load of 20 psf (DL) and the live load of 40 psf (LL):

$$DL + LL = 60 \text{ psf}$$

The uniform load (w) is the combined load per foot of joist in pounds per linear foot (plf):

$$w = 60 \text{ psf} \times (16''/12'') \text{ (see Figure 194)}$$
$$w = 80 \text{ plf}$$

The total load (W), in pounds, supported along the entire length of each joist (L) is therefore:

$$W = w \times L$$
$$W = 80 \text{ plf} \times 14 \text{ ft}$$
$$W = 1,120 \text{ lbs}$$

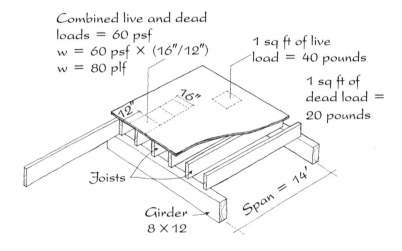

FIGURE 195: Live loads and dead loads.

404

From the chart on "Bending Characteristics of Some Common Woods," let's select spruce-pine-fir (SPF) with the following characteristics:

$$Fb = \text{Bending stress} = 1,000 \text{ psi (normal loading)}$$
$$E = \text{Modulus of elasticity} = 1,300,000 \text{ psi (maximum)}$$

With this information, refer to the appropriate span chart (Table 37: 14'0" span in our case) and, using the column with our bending stress value (Fb = 1,000), find a value for W that is as close as possible to 1,120 pounds or slightly greater. For our purpose, a 2 × 12 will be appropriate since the total load it is capable of carrying (W = 1,506) is greater than the actual load (W = 1,120) and the value for E (1,119,000) is less than the maximum allowable E (1,300,000).

Sizing the Girder

Each joist, from the preceding example, will transfer half of its total load to the girder, and the other half to the bearing wall:

Loading from each joist-1,120 lbs/2 = 560 lbs. Our girder spans 16'.

The joists bearing on it are spaced 16" on center, so the total number of joists can be found as:

$$\# \text{ joists} = 16'/16''$$
$$\# \text{ joists} = 12$$

TABLE 35: WEIGHTS OF STANDARD MATERIALS AND BUILDING ASSEMBLIES (IN POUNDS PER SQUARE FOOT OF MATERIAL)

Floors

Finishes:

Cement finish—1" topping	12
Ceramic tile—¾" quarry	10
Marble	13
Terrazzo—1" thick	16
Hardwood flooring—¾"	4
Softwood flooring—¾"	2.4
Wall-to-wall carpet	2

Assemblies:

2 × 10 wood deck (outdoors)	8–10
2 × 10 wood deck (interior) w/unfinished floor and ½" drywall ceiling	8–12
Concrete flat slab w/unfinished floor and suspended ceiling	80–90
Concrete on metal deck w/unfinished floor and suspended ceiling	65–70

Walls

Finishes:

Brick per 4" thickness	40
Granite per 4" thickness	59
Limestone per 6" thickness	55
Marble per 1"	13
Sandstone per 4"	49
Slate per 1"	14
Tile, ceramic	2–10
Plaster	8

Assemblies:

2 × 4 stud wall w/plates, 8'	1.6
	(½ lb. per lin. ft.)
2 × 6 stud wall w/plates, 8'	2.5
	(¾ lb. per lin. ft.)
2 × 4 stud wall w/½" drywall both sides	8
	(2.3 lb. per lin. ft.)
2 × 4 stud wall w/plaster both sides	19
	(5.5 lb. per lin. ft.)
2 × 4 exterior wall w/insulation and wood siding	11
	(3.2 lb. per lin. ft.)
2 × 4 exterior wall w/insulation and brick veneer	47
	(13.7 lb. per lin. ft.)
Glass block per 4"	18

Roofs

Finishes:

Concrete roof tile	9.5
4 ply built-up	5
5 ply built-up	6.5
Copper and other metals	1.5–2.5
Lead, ⅛"	6–8
Asphalt shingles	1.7–2.8
Wood shingles	2–3
Slate ³⁄₁₆"–¼"	7–9.5
Slate ⅜"–½"	14–18
Cement tile	13
Clay tile	8–16
Clay tile in setting bed	15–20

Assemblies:

Skylights	5
2 × 10 rafters, ½" sheathing, fiberglass insulation, ½" drywall	15

TABLE 36: BENDING CHARACTERISTICS OF SOME COMMON WOODS

(Note: All woods specified below are considered to be surfaced dry or surfaced green and of maximum moisture content less than 19%)

Wood Types (2 × 5 or wider)	Allowable bending stress (F_b)			Compressive stress parallel to the grain (F_c)	Modulus of Elasticity (E_{max})
	Normal loading	Snow load	7-day loading		
California Redwood	1400	1610	1750	1100	1,250,000
Douglas Fir—Larch	1450	1670	1810	1000	1,700,000
Eastern White Pine	950	1090	1190	675	1,100,000
Hem—Fir	1150	1320	1440	825	1,400,000
Hem—Fir (North)	1100	1260	1375	800	1,400,000
Lodgepole Pine	1050	1210	1310	700	1,200,000
Ponderosa pine—Sugar pine	975	1120	1220	670	1,100,000
Sitka Spruce	1050	1210	1310	700	1,300,000
Spruce—Pine—Fir	1000	1150	1250	675	1,300,000
Western Cedars	1050	1210	1310	750	1,000,000
Western Hemlock (north)	1250	1440	1560	890	1,400,000

F_b = allowable bending stress in psi (pounds per square inch)

F_c = compressive stress parallel to the grain in psi

E_{max} = maximum modulus of elasticity in pounds per square inch (psi)

Adapted from: various publications and pamphlets of the National Forest Products Association, 1619 Massachusetts Avenue N.W., Washington, D.C. 20036

Total load on girder:

W = # joists × end load per joist

W = 12 × 560 lbs.

W = 6,720 lbs

With this information, we refer to the appropriate span chart (Table 37: 16'0" span in this case) and under the appropriate bending stress value (Fb = 1,000), we find a value for W as close as possible to our 6,720 pounds or slightly greater. For our purpose, an 8 × 12 will be appropriate since the total load it is capable of carrying (W = 6,888) is greater than the actual load (W = 6,720) and the value for E (1,252,000) is less than the maximum allowable E (1,300,000).

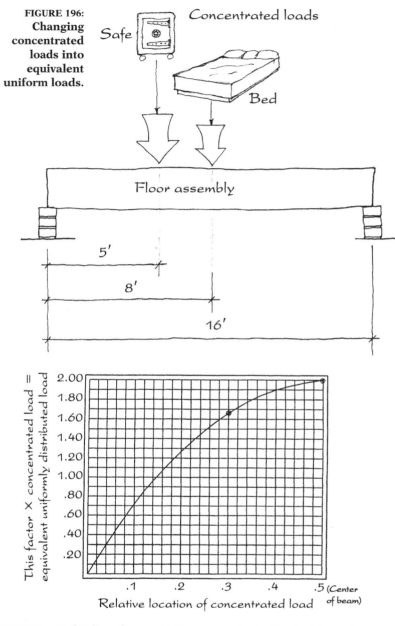

FIGURE 196: Changing concentrated loads into equivalent uniform loads.

FIGURE 197: Multipliers for converting concentrated loads into uniform loads.

TABLE 37: SPAN CHARTS

14'0" SPAN	Fb	900	1000	1100	1200	1300	1400	1500	1600	1700
SIZE OF BEAM										
2 × 10	W	916	1018	1120	1222	1324	1426	1527	1629	1833
	w	65	72	80	87	94	101	109	116	130
	E	1225	1362	1498	1634	1770	1907	2043	2179	2451
2 × 12	W	1356	1506	1657	1808	1958	2109	2260	2410	2712
	w	96	107	118	129	139	150	161	172	193
	E	1008	1119	1231	1343	1455	1567	1679	1791	2015
2 × 14	W	1881	2090	2299	2508	2717	2926	3135	3344	3762
	w	134	149	164	179	194	209	223	238	268
	E	855	950	1046	1141	1236	1331	1426	1521	1711
3 × 6	W	540	600	660	720	780	840	900	960	1080
	w	38	42	47	51	55	60	64	68	77
	E	2061	2290	2519	2749	2978	3207	3436	3665	4123
3 × 8	W	938	1042	1147	1251	1355	1460	1564	1668	1877
	w	67	74	81	89	96	104	111	119	134
	E	1564	1737	1911	2085	2259	2433	2606	2780	3128
3 × 10	W	1527	1697	1867	2037	2206	2376	2546	2716	3055
	w	109	121	133	145	157	169	181	194	218
	E	1225	1362	1362	1770	1770	1907	2043	2179	2451
3 × 12	W	2260	2511	2762	3013	3264	3515	3766	4017	4520
	w	161	179	197	215	233	251	269	286	322
	E	1007	1119	1231	1343	1455	1567	1679	1791	2015
4 × 6	W	756	840	924	1008	1092	1176	1260	1344	1512
	w	54	60	66	72	78	84	90	96	108
	E	2061	2290	2591	2749	2978	3207	3436	3665	4123
4 × 8	W	1314	1460	1606	1752	1898	2044	2190	2336	2920
	w	93	104	114	125	135	146	156	166	208
	E	1564	1737	1911	2085	2259	2433	2433	2780	3475

16'0" SPAN	Fb	900	1000	1100	1200	1300	1400	1500	1600	1700
SIZE OF BEAM										
4 × 14	W	3986	4429	4872	5315	5758	6201	6644	7087	7973
	w	249	276	304	332	359	387	415	441	498
	E	960	1066	1173	1279	1386	1493	1599	1706	1919
4 × 16	W	5255	5839	6423	7007	7591	8175	8759	9343	10510
	w	328	364	401	437	474	510	547	583	656
	E	836	929	1021	1114	1207	1300	1393	1486	1672
6 × 12	W	4546	5051	5556	6061	6566	7071	7576	8081	9092
	w	284	315	347	378	410	441	473	505	568
	E	1126	1252	1377	1502	1627	1753	2003	2003	2253
6 × 14	W	6264	6960	7657	8353	9049	9745	10441	11137	12529
	w	391	435	478	522	565	609	652	696	783
	E	960	1066	1173	1279	1386	1493	1599	1706	1919
8 × 10	W	4230	4700	5170	5640	6110	6580	7050	7520	8460
	w	264	293	323	352	381	411	440	470	528
	E	1126	1515	1667	1818	1970	2122	2273	2425	2728
8 × 12	W	6199	6888	7576	8265	8954	9643	10332	11020	12398
	w	387	430	437	516	559	602	645	688	774
	E	1126	1252	1377	1502	1627	1753	1878	2003	2253

Where: Fb = Ultimate bending strength in psi
W = Total load in pounds
w = Uniform load per length in pounds per linear feet—plf
E = Modulus of elasticity in $psi \times 1,000$

Source: National Forest Products Association
1619 Massachusetts Avenue, N.W.
Washington, D.C. 20036

Changing Concentrated Loads into Equivalent Uniform Loads (Figures 196 and 197)

(Because all span charts assume a uniform load, it is often useful to convert a concentrated or point load into a uniform load. In our example we show a safe and a waterbed producing concentrated loads.)

Location of the safe with respect to nearest support:

$$5' / 16' = .31$$

From the graph, the associated factor is about **1.70**

Location of the waterbed with respect to nearest support:

$$8' / 16' = .50$$

From the graph, the associated factor is **2.0**

Multiply each of the factors with their respective point loads and by adding them, you have the equivalent uniform load:

$$(2.0 \times 300 \text{ lbs}) + (1.7 \times 500 \text{ lbs})$$
$$= 1,450 \text{ lbs}$$

The total uniform load on the beam is now: W = 1450 lbs. If we divide by the span, we can find w, the equivalent unit uniform load.

$$1,450 \text{ lbs} \div 16 \text{ ft} = 90.6 \text{ lbs/ft} = w$$

Structures for the Brave: Deflection, Columns, Modulus of Elasticity, and Moment of Inertia

For those who don't blanch at the sight of an exponent or a square root, this appendix offers a simple introduction to some slightly more advanced concepts in the world of structures.

The moment of inertia, **I**, is a way of calculating the influence of shape on a beam's strength. Which will be stronger, a 2 × 8 or an 8 × 2? Even though they represent the same amount of wood, the shape and orientation make a big difference.

Also, there is the question of deflection. Whether it is a springy floor or a crack in the ceiling, excessive deflection is the culprit. The equation for deflection would have looked intimidating before the age of calculators. Today, anyone who can balance their checkbook should be comfortable figuring out deflection.

Finally, we present calculations for column sizing. In any house there are just as many posts, studs, and columns as there are joists, beams, and girders. So why do the columns rarely get engineered? Because generally houses are comfortably overbuilt in the vertical direction. Most stick-built houses would stand up with only one out of every five studs used. Timber framers, on the other hand, must always calculate their post sizes.

The calculations that follow should be an eye opener even for the seasoned builder.

Moment of Inertia (Shape)

(for simple uniformly loaded rectangular wood beams)

$$\text{I} = \textbf{moment of inertia in inches}^4$$
$$\text{I} = \textbf{bd}^3\textbf{/12}$$

The moment of inertia is a measure of strength for a particular shape.

There are a few things that need to be mentioned about the moment of inertia. First of all, don't let the units throw you. I once spent hours trying to visualize an inch to the fourth. There is no such thing and it really doesn't matter (or help). Far more interesting is the fact that **I** gets larger in proportion to **b**, the width of the beam. This makes pretty good intuitive sense. More wood, more strength. Even more important, however, is the fact that **I** becomes larger in proportion to the *cube* of **d**, the depth. What the equa-

tion is telling us, in its own way, is that the strength of a beam is increased dramatically when we make it deeper and only moderately when we make it wider. If you understand nothing else about the moment of inertia, this will still serve you well on the construction site.

Actual Maximum Deflection:

(for simple uniformly loaded rectangular wood beam)

$$\Delta_{actual} = \textbf{maximum deflection in inches}$$
$$\Delta_{actual} = \textbf{k} \times \textbf{(wl}^4\textbf{/EI)} \quad \textbf{or} \quad \textbf{5wl}^4\textbf{/384EI}$$

k = constant = 5/384
w = uniform load in pounds per linear inch (= plf/12)
l = length of beam in inches
E = modulus of elasticity (proportion of load to beam deflection) in psi
I = moment of inertia in inches^4

See bending stress and modulus chart.

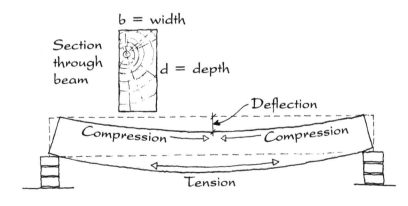

FIGURE 198: Typical simply supported beam.

Deflection is the amount of sag in a loaded beam (see Figure 198, page 408). It is determined by the material and the shape of the beam. If you look at the intimidating formula you will note that the deflection is inversely proportional to the **E** (modulus of elasticity) and the **I** (moment of inertia). This means that the material and the shape play a big role in how much a beam sags. Sounds right to me. The bigger the **E** and/or the **I**, the smaller the deflection. Conversely, the deflection gets larger in direct proportion to the load, **w**, and the span, **l**. This also seems to make good common sense. As mentioned above, this is the most important thing to assimilate from all these formulae. It is rare that you would need to actually calculate the precise deflection. And if you do, keep in mind that the equation above only works for simply supported uniformly loaded beams. There are other, even scarier, equations for asymmetrical loading or point loading. And then, if you do push through the fearful calculations, what do you do with the results? How do you know if ½″ is too much deflection? What about ⅜″ or ¾″? You need only compare your results with the following rule of thumb for allowable deflection. It is easy to calculate and gives you an idea of approximately what you're aiming for: If your calculated deflection is less than the allowable deflection, you shouldn't have any problems.

Maximum Allowable Deflection:

For gypsum board: $\Delta_{max} = l/240$
For plaster: $\Delta_{max} = l/360$
Necessary conditions: $\Delta_{actual} < \Delta_{max}$

The span, **l**, in the equation above should be entered in inches. The resulting fraction is the approximate allowable deflection in inches.

Just so you can see it done, what follows is an actual deflection calculation using the same example we started with back in the previous appendix, and in Chapter 10 before that. Let's see, as we left our hero . . .

Calculation of Joist Deflection

From our previous example on joist loads (see Appendix 7), we had a total load of **W** = 1,120 pounds for each joist and had also selected 2 × 12 spruce/pine/fir (spf) joists. Our first step will be to figure out the moment of inertia for each joist:

$$I = bd^3/12$$
$$I = 1.5 \times 11.25^3/12$$
$$I = 1.5 \times 1,423.82/12$$
$$I = 178 \text{ in}^4$$

Also we had a uniform load (w) of:

$$w = 80 \text{ plf}$$

For ease of calculation, we will convert all units from feet to inches. Our uniform load will become:

$$w = 80 \text{ plf}/12$$
$$w = 6.66 \text{ lbs per inch}$$

We used spruce joists for that 14′ span:

$$I = 14 \text{ ft}$$
$$I = 168 \text{ in.}$$

From the same chart where we got our bending stress (Fb) values, we get the modulus of elasticity for a spruce joist:

$$E = 1,300,000 \text{ psi}$$

All that remains to do is to "plug in" the values for:

w (uniform load in lbs. per inch);
l (length of joist in inches);
E (modulus of elasticity in psi);
I (moment of inertia in in⁴).

That gives us the following:

$$\Delta_{actual} = 5/384 \times wl^4/EI$$
$$\Delta_{actual} = 5/384 \times (6.66)(168)^4/(1,300,000)(178)$$

And we get the actual joist deflection in inches:

$$\Delta_{actual} = 0.298 \text{ in.}$$

Now we must make sure that this is not excessive by comparing it to Δ_{max}:

$$\Delta_{max} = l/360$$
$$\Delta_{max} = 168/360$$
$$\Delta_{max} = 0.466 \text{ in.}$$

Δ_{actual} is smaller than Δ_{max}. We are therefore well within our permissible deflection of 0.466 inches. After all, 0.298 inches is only about 5/16″, only a hair more than a quarter inch. Surely we can deflect that much.

Wood Column Design

Slenderness ratio: ratio of unbraced length (**l**) of column to its narrower side (**d**):

$$l/d$$

P (safe load that can be carried by a column:)

$$P = F'c \times A$$

A = Cross section area of the solid wood column.

F'c = Compressive strength parallel to grain
(Fc with adjustment factors)

Note: The adjustment factors must be used when appropriate.

Three categories of columns—short, intermediate, long—will determine which factor to use:

short columns: no adjustment factor needed

If   l/d < 11   Then   F'c = Fc

intermediate columns: using $k = .67\sqrt{E/Fc}$

If   11 < l/d < k   Then $F'c = Fc \times \left[1 - \frac{1}{3} \left(\frac{l/d}{k} \right)^4 \right]$

long columns: using $k = .67\sqrt{E/Fc}$

If   k < l/d   Then $F'c = \frac{.3E}{(l/d)^2}$

What's all this hoopla about short columns, long columns? Can't we just look at the cross sectional area of a column and see if there's enough material to support the loads? Well, no. Here again we find it's a combination of material *and* shape that determines structural performance. Columns, as they get longer and thinner, want to go noodly. They buckle out of a straight alignment and suddenly they are in a bending situation rather than a purely compressive situation. The answer to this problem is called lateral support. The more frequently a column is fastened along its length, the stronger it becomes. This isn't a change in material, it's a change in configuration or lateral support.

In residential construction, we rarely calculate posts because we seldom run into loading situations that exceed the capacity of a 6 × 6 post. Indeed, the common stud wall is usually overbuilt by a safety factor of 4 or 5 (to allow for all the checks, knots, defects, etc.). Nevertheless, the following calculation is worth following. You will be amazed at the staggering difference between the capacity of a 4 × 4 and a 6 × 6. So once again, with our reader on the edge of their seat, we pick up the story where we left off.

Sizing of Columns

If we had 6″ × 6″ columns supporting each end of the girder (which in the example of Appendix 7 had a total load, W, of 6,720 pounds), the transferred load to each column would be half of the total load, 3,360 pounds. The fibers of the wood will therefore be under compression along the grain of the wood. From the wood stress charts, the allowable compressive strength parallel to the grain (**Fc**) for a Douglas fir column is Fc = 1,000 psi and the modulus of elasticity is **E** = 1,700,000 psi. The floor to ceiling height (which will be our unbraced length) is 8′ (96″) and our column width is 5.5″. Our slenderness ratio is:

$$l/d = 96″/5.5″$$
$$l/d = 17.45$$

Since **l/d** > 11 the column is either an intermediate or a long column, we must find k in order to determine which:

$$k = .67\sqrt{E/Fc}$$
$$k = .67\sqrt{(1,700,000/1000)}$$
$$k = 27.6$$

The value for **l/d** (= 17.45) is greater than 11 but less than k (= 27.6), therefore the column will be considered an intermediate one since the following is true:

$$11 < l/d < k$$

The modified value of Fc, for intermediate columns is:

$$F'c = Fc \times \left[1 - \frac{1}{3} \left(\frac{l/d}{k} \right)^4 \right]$$

$$F'c = 1000 \times \left[1 - \frac{1}{3} \left(\frac{17.45}{27.6} \right)^4 \right]$$

$$F'c = 946.7 \text{ psi}$$

The maximum allowable load on our 6 × 6 column will be:

$$P = F'c \times A$$
$$P = 946.7 \times 5.5 \times 5.5$$
$$P = 28,639 \text{ lbs.}$$

The maximum allowable load (**P**) on an 8′-long, 6 × 6, Douglas fir column is 28,639 pounds, which is far greater than the actual load of 3,351.6 pounds. We could, without difficulty, use a 4 × 4 column; the new slenderness ratio (**l/d**) will be:

$$l/d = 96″/3.5″$$
$$l/d = 27.42$$

Since the value of **k** remains the same (k = 27.6), our new column is still considered an intermediate one and the new value for Fc is:

$$F'c = Fc \times \left[1 - \frac{1}{3} \left(\frac{l/d}{k} \right)^4 \right]$$

$$F'c = 1000 \times \left[1 - \frac{1}{3} \left(\frac{27.42}{27.6} \right)^4 \right]$$

$$F'c = 678.5 \text{ psi}$$

The maximum allowable load on our 4 × 4 column will be:

$$P = F'c \times A$$
$$P = 678.5 \times 3.5 \times 3.5$$
$$P = 8{,}311.6 \text{ lbs}$$

This is a lot closer to our actual load on the column. And yet, you can see that a 4 × 4 column is still significantly overdesigned. If we were to brace the post halfway up, calculation would show that the load could be supported by a 2″ × 4″! This, dear reader, is truly amazing, and so I leave the calculations as an exercise for you. Don't miss the exciting conclusion of this action-packed mystery. Get your calculator and start working on it today!

Framing Square Basics: Laying Out a Rafter

Among all the basic tools you will acquire in preparing to build your first house, none is so versatile and so overlooked as the square. This ancient tool brings Euclid's geometry and Pythagoras's theories to the construction site in the handy form of an L-shaped piece of steel. And even though Euclid and Pythagoras aren't the stars they were, now that the hand-held calculator has upstaged their act, the framing square continues to amaze and impress.

Framing squares are a great value and far more versatile than their simple shape suggests. For about twenty dollars they are available in steel or aluminum, with the aluminum being costlier and more likely to go "out of square." As Figure 198 shows, there is a long and a short blade. The longer one is called the "body" and the shorter, the "tongue." These two meet at a right angle that is called the "heel." The body is 24″ long; the tongue is 16″ long and 1½″ wide. These become really significant dimensions when you frame a building with rafters, joists, and studs on 16″ centers. (Also, all your dimensional lumber, 2 × 4s, 2 × 6s, 2 × 8s, etc., is actually 1½″ across the narrow dimension.) Anyway, the flat sides of the square are called the face and the back. On quality squares they are imprinted with edge scales and rafter tables. For twenty dollars you should insist on a square that comes with a booklet of instructions explaining these tables.

The utility of a framing square is based on the Pythagorean geometry of right triangles (triangles that have two sides meeting at 90°). Thus, a logical first use for the square is making, checking, and marking right angles. This is particularly the case when dealing with the large timbers used in post and beam construction. Moving to the more sophisticated tasks of laying out rafters or stair stringers requires a basic understanding of Pythagoras's theory.

There are only two important things to understand here:

Rule One: *The proportions of the sides and the angles in any triangle don't change, regardless of how much you enlarge or reduce it.*

Rule Two: *In any right triangle, the relationship between the hypotenuse and the two sides making the right angle is:*

$$a^2 + b^2 = c^2$$

where a and b are the sides, and c is the hypotenuse. (See illustration at right.)

Rafters:

The layout of a common rafter is an exercise that clearly demonstrates the use of a framing square. The sloping side or hypotenuse of the right triangle implied by the framing square can be seen as a miniature version of the sloping rafter itself. Thus, you will find that architects usually depict the pitch, or slope, of a roof as a little right triangle drawn above the roof on the elevation drawings. This triangle designates the unit rise, unit run, and slope of the roof all in one little symbol. The *run* is the distance measured horizontally under the rafter. The *rise* is the vertical distance that goes with the run. So far, everything makes pretty good sense. The *unit* rise is simply the distances covered in 12″ (one unit) of run. Since, according to rule one, the relationships of a triangle remain the same independent of size, this unit triangle will have the same slope and angles as our full-sized rafter. Moreover, the unit triangle can be re-created anywhere on site with your handy dandy framing square. Pretty convenient, no?

Now we are ready to take a piece of rafter stock from the pile of lumber and determine the length of the rafter. This is called "stepping off" the rafter and it eliminates the use of rafter tables or calculators. As seen in the illustration (Figure 199), place the square against the board such that the rise, 5″, aligns on the tongue and the unit run, 12″, aligns on the body. Now scribe lines on the outside of both the tongue and the body to mark the location of the square. The line scribed along the tongue is called the "plumb

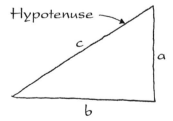

Pythagorean theorem $a^2 + b^2 = c^2$

FIGURE 199: Using a framing square to lay out a 5-pitch (5 in 12) rafter

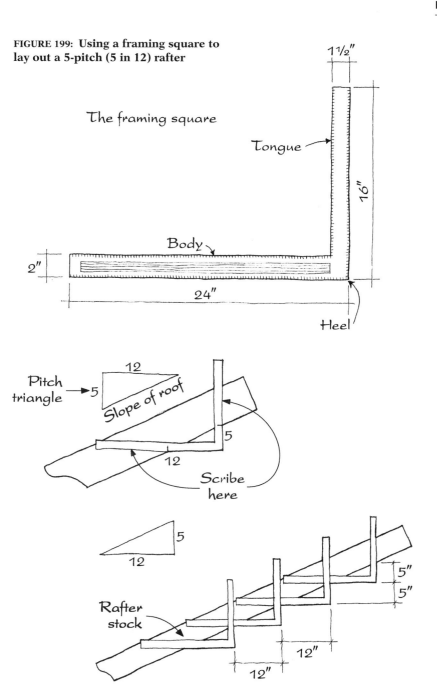

line"; the line scribed along the body is called the "level line." Next, slide the square along the rafter until the 5" mark on the *outside* of the tongue aligns with the previous level line scribed on the board. Make a new level line at the 12" point on the outside of the body. Repeat this process as many times as there are feet (units) in the running distance of the rafter. So if the rafter spans 13', the stepping-off process is repeated thirteen times. This distance is sometimes called the "half span" since it represents half the distance spanned by two rafters.

The stepping off can be facilitated by the use of "framing square nuts" or "stair gauges" (see Figure 200b). These are stop guides that can be attached and adjusted along the edge of the framing square. This allows you to set up a particular slope and know that it will be replicated exactly each time you move the square. In our example we would attach the nuts to the tongue and body at 5" and 12". Then, each time we moved the square, the realigning would be simple and accurate.

When stepping off is complete you will have the basic rafter laid out

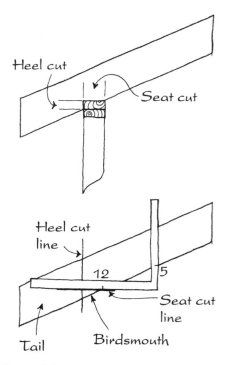

FIGURE 200a: Birdsmouth layout.

FIGURE 200b: Framing nuts permit easy alignment of the square at a preset rise and run

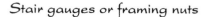
Stair gauges or framing nuts

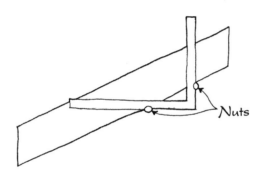
Nuts

FIGURE 200c: Framing configuration for rafters.

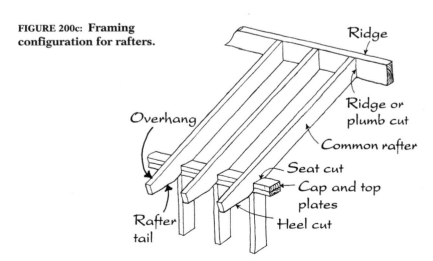

Ridge

Overhang

Ridge or plumb cut

Common rafter

Seat cut

Cap and top plates

Heel cut

Rafter tail

FIGURE 200d: Rafter terminology

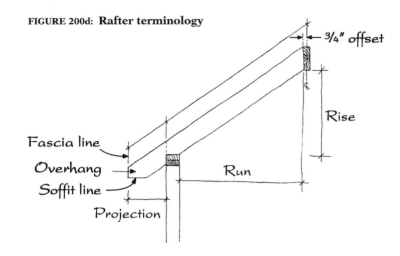

3/4" offset

Rise

Fascia line

Overhang

Soffit line

Run

Projection

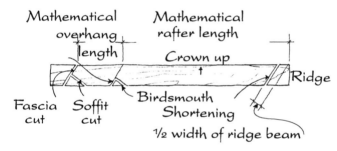

Mathematical overhang length

Mathematical rafter length

Crown up

Ridge

Fascia cut

Soffit cut

Birdsmouth

Shortening

½ width of ridge beam

with a plumb line at the top (ridge) and a seat cut line at the bottom (birdsmouth). The final treatment of the eave end will depend on the size and design of the overhang. Some overhangs have a plumb facia; others have angled ones. Some use a square soffit (Figure 200d). As you can see in the illustration, a rafter overhang is just like a miniature rafter where the projection is similar to the half span or run. Use the heel cut at the birdsmouth to begin layout.

In addition to common rafters, a framing square is really all you need to cut stair stringers, layout winders, build polygons, domes, yurts, lay out circles, even lay out and cut rafters with a curved edge. Indeed, there is little that stands in the way of the design/builder who has mastered the theory and use of the framing square. Calculators may be faster, roofing tables may seem more convenient, but for versatility and reliability there is no equal for the good old steel square.

APPENDIX 10

Count Rumford's Basic Relationships for Fireplace Design

1. The width of the fireplace ranges from two to three times the depth.
2. The height of the fireplace is three times the depth.
3. The back wall width is equal to the depth.
4. The vertical back wall height is the same as the back wall width.
5. The inclined back wall height (from the top of the vertical back wall to the throat) is the fireplace opening height plus the height from the lintel to throat (12″) minus the vertical back wall height.
6. The height from the lintel to the throat is 12″.
7. The depth of throat is no less than 3″ and no more than 4″.

TABLE 38: DIMENSIONS FOR A FIREPLACE (IN INCHES)

(Based on Count Rumford's relationship)

Depth	Width	Height	Back wall width	Vertical back wall height	Inclined back wall height
8	16–24	24	8	8	28
9	18–28	28	9	9	31
10	20–30	30	10	10	32
12	24–36	36	12	12	36
14	28–42	42	14	14	40
16	32–48	48	16	16	44
18	36–54	54	18	18	48
20	40–60	60	20	20	52

Source: Author

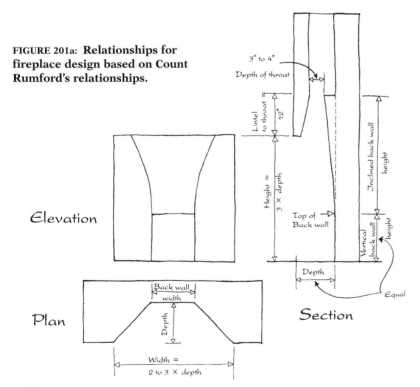

FIGURE 201a: Relationships for fireplace design based on Count Rumford's relationships.

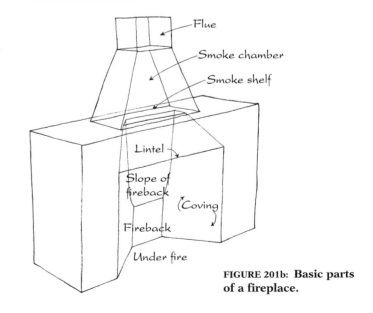

FIGURE 201b: Basic parts of a fireplace.

Building Codes and Your Friend the Inspector

At the Yestermorrow School, where we encourage our students to design *and build,* the questions always come up:

"What about the building inspector?"

"In my state the law requires that we use architects."

"Don't you have to be a licensed contractor?"

"Yeah, I think it's against the law to build if you're not a contractor, or at least a subcontractor. We can't build our own house."

"It's probably a felony."

We are conditioned to fear anything about which we are unfamiliar. That's why the humans always kill the extraterrestrials in the movies. That's also why we fear the building inspector. We just don't know what they want. Well, let's have a look.

First of all, remember that the codes and inspectors are there for *your safety.* There are plenty of ways to burn, electrocute, or maim yourself if you attempt to build with inadequate knowledge. Since we are a society of specialists and professionals, much of the common sense of building has been forgotten or lost to the general public. And so we have codes. The codes are written to provide guidelines and standards in the absence of a vernacular tradition. The nonindustrialized societies have no codes, not because they are primitive, but because they don't need them. Their traditions of building are as much a part of their culture as TV is part of ours. (Hey, maybe we should consider a TV code, with guidelines for watching and inspectors and standards!) Anyway, for the time being, we need codes and should learn how to use them.

On page 418 is a map indicating where each code is used. Happily there are only a handful for the whole continent. Your first job is to find the code that has jurisdiction in your area and purchase the latest copy. Many of these codes publish a special "residential version" that is less expensive and far less complicated. Ask for it.

If you are like most of us, when you look through your codebook you will be impressed and intimidated. Can any one person really be expected to know all this and remember it all while designing and building their first house? I admit, it's a bit more involved than getting your driving license. But happily there already is one person who has already learned and will remember all this while you're building your first home. . . . the building inspector.

After you have looked over your code, it's time to meet the inspector. This is a very important occasion. Make an appointment and take some time familiarizing the inspector with your intended project. Ask for suggestions and guidance. Don't try to sell, test, or argue. Besides being a wealth of knowledge, *building inspectors have the last word* on what is or isn't built. They are even more important than what is written in the code. They can choose to overlook a codebook guideline or they can require that you meet a higher standard. At all costs, you want these guys on your team.

In addition to the basic building code, you will discover the plumbing code, the electrical code; why there's even a sewage disposal code. Different communities use these codes to different extents. In low-density rural areas, the basic code may be all that's used. In high-density areas or cities, all the codes are followed rigorously. Your project will be inspected several times throughout the construction process; after the forms are up, after the framing is complete, after the mechanicals are in, before the walls are closed up, etc. etc. At each visit, the inspector must accept your work before you can proceed to the next phase of construction. So here again, you want a good relationship with your inspectors. If they like you and your project, they are likely to help you anticipate upcoming requirements. They may even help you solve problems, if they have the time.

Time, as usual, is the big constraint. Keep in mind that inspectors are overworked and chronically short of time. Prepare your documents thoroughly before visiting the building department. Make sure everything is ready before asking for an inspection. If the building inspectors are short-tempered or unfriendly, it is more likely to be the schedule they are keeping than anything you have done. As with so many things, if you place yourself in their shoes, it will be easier for you to reap the benefits of their knowledge.

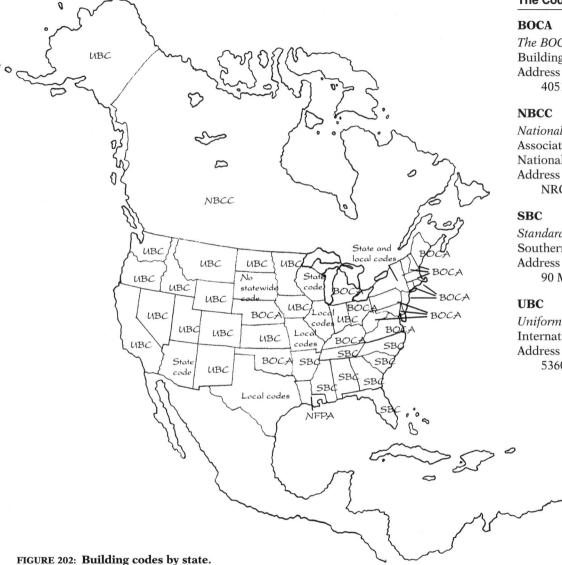

FIGURE 202: Building codes by state.

The Codes

BOCA

The BOCA National Building Code
Building Officials & Code Administrators International, Inc.
Address for ordering:
    4051 West Flossmoor Road, Country Club Hills, IL 60477

NBCC

National Building Code of Canada
Associate Committee on the National Building Code
National Research Council of Canada
Address for ordering:
    NRCC, Ottawa, Ontario K1A0R6

SBC

Standard Building Code
Southern Building Code Congress International Inc.
Address for ordering:
    90 Montclair Road, Birmingham, AL 35213-1206

UBC

Uniform Building Code
International Conference of Building Officials
Address for ordering:
    5360 South Workman Mill Road, Whittier, CA 90601

Glossary

1 × and 2 ×   pronounced "one by" and "two by," both are nominal designations for groups of lumber. 1 × is found at the lumberyard in a range of sizes from 1 × 4 to 1 × 12 and is typically used for trim and casings. 2 × also comes in a range of sizes, from 2 × 4 to 2 × 12; it is typically used for framing walls, floors, and roofs. The actual dimension of these pieces in inches is slightly smaller than the nominal designation. For example, a 1 × 4 measures ¾" × 3½".

AC/DC   Alternating Current and Direct Current are the two basic consumer forms of electricity. They are just what they say. Direct current flows in one direction continuously, directly. Alternating current changes the direction of its flow 60 times every second. This is the reason it is sometimes called 60-cycle current. For purposes of generation, safety, and transmission alternating current has become the standard sold by power companies across the nation. If you generate your own, however, you will likely be using direct current.

AWWF   all-weather wood foundation, a foundation made with specially treated wood to withstand weather and rot.

accent lighting   draws the eye to a special object or area, provides dramatic interest and adds excitement.

acrylic   a transparent plastic material in sheet form, used widely as glazing in windows and skylights. Although it is fragile, acrylic has a long life; it will not yellow or degrade, but it is expensive.

adobe   sun-dried brick or building block made of a mixture of clay and straw. Adobe is best used in arid or semiarid climates where clay is readily available and the insulating properties of the brick can be taken advantage of. (See Figure 112.)

aerobic digestion   the breaking down of human waste by microbes, this process requires oxygen. *See also* **anaerobic digestion.**

amps, or amperes   a unit of electrical current or flow. Amps tell us how much electricity is flowing, the rate. Amperage is quite different from voltage, which is a measure of intensity or energy. This difference becomes obvious when we consider that 12-volt car batteries are advertised as having 300–400 amps of starting current, while house current trips the fuse at a mere 20 amps. Amps are a measure of flow, DC or AC.

anaerobic digestion   the microbic breaking down of human waste that takes place in the bottom of a septic tank without oxygen. *See also* **aerobic digestion.**

anemometer   a gauge for determining the force or speed of the wind.

annular nails   a nail with a shank that has many sharp rings or ridges. The shaped shank provides increased holding power; the nails are used for underlayment, shingles, and paneling.

aquifers   veins of water found in ledge or gravel, below the earth's surface. (See Figure 5.)

argon   an inert gas that does not combine chemically with any other element. It glows with a purple light when an electric current passes through it. Argon is used with neon in "neon" lights and also in windows as an insulator between two sheets of glass; argon is denser than air and therefore provides better insulation.

ASHRAE (American Society of Heating, Refrigerating and Air-Conditioning Engineers)   the organization that publishes the bible of heating and air conditioning, the *Handbook of Fundamentals.*

auger feed   a corkscrew-shaped device which "feeds" wood pellets to the burning chamber in a wood pellet burning stove.

awning   a window that is fixed along the upper edge of the sash and opens out; the resulting configuration is like an awning.

BTU   *see* **British Thermal Unit.**

BTUH   BTUs per hour.

ballasts   the choke coil used in fluorescent lighting to prevent the 120 volt 60-cycle power from destroying the fluorescent tube.

balloon frame   an older system of stick frame construction in which uprights or studs extend the full height of the frame and horizontal structural members are nailed to them. This is different than platform framing, though they are both referred to as "stick" framing. *See also* **platform frame.**

banana   slang for a bow shaped warp in a piece of lumber.

bank run gravel   this is not really gravel at all, but a gravelly soil comprised of boney sand and a

419

small amount of clay. It takes its name from the fact that it is taken directly from the bank of the pit. There is no filtering or screening.

Baroque an architectural style prevalent from the late sixteenth century to the early eighteenth century, characterized by curved lines and ornate embellishment.

baseboard, hot water or electric heat distribution systems that run around the perimeter of a room at baseboard level. (See Figure 153.)

batterboards two stakes with a crossbar used by surveyors as an adjustable fastening point when laying out a foundation with strings. The term probably refers to the appearance of the assembly when complete. They are usually a mishmash of old boards and bad nailing. (See Figure 28.)

Bauhaus a school of architectural design founded by Walter Gropius and others in the early twentieth century at Dessau, Germany; noted for its philosophy, which embraces mass production and an industrial aesthetic.

beam any structural element that horizontally spans between two or more bearing points, such as walls, posts, etc.

bearing capacity the maximum amount of weight a soil can support without excessive settling. Usually expressed in pounds per square foot.

berm *see* **earth berm**

beveled glass patterned glass made from cut-glass pieces assembled with lead came. Sort of like a stained-glass composition with Baccarat crystal instead of Depression glass.

birdsmouth a triangular notch cut in the underside of a rafter that allows it to sit securely on the top plate of the wall. (See Figure 200a.)

black water all wastewater from toilets carrying human excrement. *See also* **gray water.**

blue board 1: rigid foam insulation; comes in various sizes—2′ × 8′ sheets are the most common—and thicknesses from ½″ to 2″. 2: plasterboard lath.

board and batten wood siding of alternating wide and thin boards; the thin boards are applied on top of the wide boards to cover the joints.

bond adhesion between mortar and masonry units; also, patterns formed by the exposed faces of masonry units, such as flemish bond, running bond, garden bond, etc.

bond beam in adobe construction, a steel-reinforced concrete beam poured in place along the top of a wall to consolidate and strengthen it against damage from earthquakes.

boney a slang term used to describe sand or soil with an abundance of oversized rocks in it. The rocks are the bones. "Why this fill is so boney, you could play hide 'n' seek between the boulders."

bow deviation *flatwise* from a straight line from end to end of a piece of wood. *See also* **crook.**

bowstring truss a type of truss shaped like a strung bow. The bottom cord is straight and the upper cords form an arch from one end to the other. Possibly this would be Robin Hood's preferred roof form.

box beam a long spanning built-up beam constructed like a stud wall with plywood on each side. Very useful for spanning large living rooms, garage doors, or other large distances. (See Figure 65.)

breaker box short for circuit-breaker box or panel box, a metal box where all circuit breakers are installed and labeled in pen (not pencil).

breast shot waterwheel a type of waterwheel that receives water halfway up its height. Breast wheels can be inefficient and hard to build. (See Figure 176d.)

brick molding the standard molding profile used for the casing with every factory-built window.

British Thermal Unit a measure of energy; it's the amount of energy required to raise the temperature of 1 pound of water by 1°F; 252 calories, or

about the same amount of heat as is given out by burning one kitchen match.

bubble diagram a schematic representation of spatial relationships and programmatic requirements.

builders level a telescope like tool used to determine a given elevation or height at different points of land, along a foundation wall, inside a building, etc. Looking through the level, anything seen in the cross hairs is known to be at exactly the same elevation. Thus, they are in the same level plane. *See also* **transit.**

building envelope the perimeter of the building, made up of the walls and roof, that separates the interior space of the building from exterior.

butt 1: a type of door hinge that attaches to the edge of a door; also, the side of the doorjamb where the hinges attach. 2: A butt joint is one made between any two square-edged pieces of wood.

Byzantine an architectural style evolved at Constantinople about the fifth century A.D. The round arch and the use of domes are characteristic.

capillary action adhesive force between water and another material that pulls water through a small opening or along fibrous material. This is what sucks water up a plant's stem and also into your untreated concrete foundation wall.

cartesian grid the orthogonal grid used by mathematicians to depict x-y relationships.

casement a window that pivots along the vertical edge of the sash.

casing the molding used to trim window and door openings, inside and out.

catalytic converter a ceramic filter in the flue of wood stoves that promotes complete burning of flue gases.

change order a document that confirms a modification in the construction documents among the builder, architect, and owner and, more to the point, the cost consequences. In general, change orders are feared by clients because they allow the builder to reprice the work when there are usually few alternatives. Owner/builders, of course, have none of these fears.

chase 1: (verb) to run after; to pursue. In construction, to chase means to allocate a pathway for services; for example: "In the timber frame house we had to chase the mechanicals up the very few interior walls"; 2: (noun) an open pathway, usually within walls, used to run electrical, plumbing, and other mechanical wires, cables, pipes, etc., throughout a building.

check 1: In wood, a lengthwise grain separation, usually occurring through the growth rings as a result of seasoning. 2: Also what you use to pay the truck driver when your lumber comes.

check damper usually used on a bathroom or laundry vent to prevent cold air from blowing in when the fan is not in use.

circuit venting, or loop venting in plumbing, a venting configuration where several fixtures drain into one soil pipe, which is then vented at the end.

clad windows window sashes covered with or made of extruded vinyl or aluminum; the weather-resistant nature of these materials makes these windows almost maintenance-free.

clamp 1: before there were modern kilns, bricks were fired by stacking them in a large pile, covering them with mud, and building a fire about the pile. This was called a clamp. 2: Today the term is much more likely to mean a portable vise that allows two or more boards to be held together; as in "he clamped the boards together while the glue dried."

clean out in plumbing, an accessible opening in the drainage system used to clear out debris and other obstructions.

clerestory an outside wall with windows that rises above the roof.

Cob construction an ancient vernacular approach to building that uses a mud, clay, straw mixture. The mixture is formed into small corn-cob-sized bricks, which are placed into the wall while still wet. This gives the building a very handmade, very sculptural look.

coefficient of expansion a measure of how much a material enlarges or shrinks due to temperature change. In glazing, glass has a low coefficient because that means it maintains its size through large temperature swings. Plexiglas™, on the other hand, has a high coefficient of expansion, which means it is not dimensionally stable. If used in a Siberian window, the outside would shrink and the inside would expand, resulting in the glazing bowing inward, possibly cracking. The difference from summer to winter would be dramatic. The size of the Plexiglas™ would change so radically that all seals and caulking would be disrupted, resulting in heat loss and leaks. Does it strike the reader that I seem to know a lot about what can go wrong with Plexiglas?

collar ties a horizontal framing member fastened between two opposite rafters such that a truss is formed with the collar tie being the lower cord. Collar ties must not be higher than two-thirds the distance from the height of the eaves to the ridge. Sometimes this means they are too low to allow headroom and other roof structuring strategies must be used. *See also* **structural ridge** and **truss.**

Colonial an early American architectural style still prevalent today, characterized by simple forms and clean details.

compacting machine used to compact layers of soil in preparation for a slab foundation.

composting toilet a toilet that processes human waste through natural biological action; this system does not require a leaching field.

compressive force a force that pushes (as distinct from those that pull). Weight under the effect of gravity is the everyday notion of compressive force. In building, compression always occurs in tandem with tension. *See* **tensile force.**

control joint in masonry construction, a continuous vertical joint designed to allow longitudinal movement while maintaining lateral stability.

corbel (noun) a projecting or spanning form made of successive courses of masonry units slightly cantilevered one over the other; also "corbeling."

cornice an exterior detail that occurs where the roof soffit meets the wall; or, an interior molding detail where the ceiling and wall meet.

counterfort retaining wall a T-shaped retaining wall reinforced on the back-filled side every few feet with a triangular tie; also known as a counterfort.

covenant a condition written into a real estate deed that remains attached to the land in the event of a sale.

crack method heat loss for a building can be calculated based on the number and overall length of cracks around windows and doors.

crook deviation *edgewise* from a straight line from end to end of a piece, measured of wood. *See also* **bow.**

crown slang for a crook.

cruk frame the original European post and beam frame using large, curved timber in opposing pairs, which served as both posts and rafters. Not found on the American continent.

cup deviation *flatwise* from a straight line across the width of a piece of wood.

curtain drain a trench filled with stone and perforated pipe that follows the perimeter of the building to intercept and redirect surface and subsurface water. Also called a 'french drain.'

curtain wall   an exterior wall of a building that is supported entirely by the building frame, rather than being self-supporting or load-bearing.

damp proofing   any procedure used with concrete or foundation construction to prevent the migration of water vapor into the foundation assemblies. Common systems use tar, cementious coatings, or polyethylene sheet.

damper   a flap to control or restrict the passage of gases; found in the throat of a chimney or in an air duct.

daylighting   a design strategy that configures the building assemblies so as to maximize the amount of natural light penetrating deep into the building. This approach significantly reduces costs associated with electric lighting.

dead load   the weight, expressed in pounds per square foot, of building elements that are part of the structure.

decay   disintegration of wood substance due to the action of wood-destroying fungi.

deciduous tree   a tree that loses its leaves in the winter. Its wood is dense and sometimes called "hardwood." *See also* **evergreen.**

ΔT = (T$_i$ – T$_0$)   the difference between the design temperature inside and the temperature outside. When calculating heat loss and designing your heating system, you must choose an interior temperature that you hope to maintain on one of the colder days of the year. You, the designer, choose the interior temperature and the day of the year, called the "design day."

demand water heater   *see* **instantaneous boiler.**

dew point   specific combination of humidity and temperature at which moisture in the air starts to condense out, or rain. Air holds more moisture at higher temperatures and less at lower temperatures. So moisture that stays in vapor form in a well-heated space may condense into liquid if it leaks into a chilly wall or roof assembly. If the temperature is always kept very high inside your wall or roof assemblies (or the moisture level very low), there should be little trouble with condensation and rot in them.

dimensional lumber   the framing lumber available in commercial lumberyards. Called nominally 1×, 2×, or 4×, this wood is always smaller to allow for drying and planing.

double framing   two stud walls side by side, designed to give maximum insulation and minimum air leakage through the studs. Because the studs are staggered, there are no continuous members from interior to exterior to allow the passage of air, or heat.

double hung   a window consisting of two sashes, one on top of the other; to open the window, the lower sash slides up past the upper sash.

dovetail   a traditional cabinetry joint with interlocking fingers that connects two pieces of wood at the corner.

downspout   a vertical pipe connected to the gutters for carrying water from the roof to a lower level or to the ground.

drainage fixture unit (dfu)   a measure of the probable discharge from various types of plumbing fixtures into the plumbing system, used to calculate pipe sizes.

drain tile   perforated pipe used in a curtain, foundation, or french drains.

dressed lumber   rough-sawn lumber becomes dressed lumber when it is run through a planner or planner molder. It is dressed on one or more sides. When dressed on all four sides it is called S4S. *See also* **dimensional lumber.**

drilled well   a conventional well, referred to as a drilled well to differentiate from a dug well or a driven-point well.

driven point well   a well most suited for porous soil, consisting of a perforated pipe driven into the earth.

drywall   *see* **gypsum board.**

duct   a hollow conduit, commonly of sheet metal, used to circulate air for heating and cooling.

dug well   a relatively wide and shallow well, dug into the earth and lined with masonry, steel, or timber.

duplex   1: a single structure that contains two complete living units, such as a two-family house; 2: electrical: two outlets grouped together in one fixture. The majority of all residential outlets exist in this format. 3: a nail used for temporary fastening.

DWV   Drainage, Waste, and Venting systems.

Dymaxion house   a house designed by Buckminster Fuller to make maximum efficient use of materials.

earth berm   a pile or wall of earth fill often placed against a house wall to provide insulation; or between a road and a house it cuts down the noise. Also used as a verb: "We bermed up the patio to keep neighbors from dropping in. Then we bermed the north side of the house foundation to protect against the winter wind. What did you berm today?"

earth-sheltered house   any building where the designer makes use of the earth by putting it next to or on top of the building for energy conservation.

easement   a legal permission to pass over or have utilities pass over land belonging to another party. *See also* **covenant.**

eave   the horizontal edge on the low side of a sloping roof.

edge grained   lumber sawn parallel to the pith or center of the log and approximately at right angles to the growth rings.

efflorescence   a fluffy powder or stain that can appear on brick, stone, or concrete walls. It is caused by water soluble salts that leach out when trapped water seeps through the masonry. And just for comparison, the bubbles in your soda pop or Alka Seltzer are effervescent, eporfescent, uh, phosflorescent, incandescent, wait a minute, I'll get it, uh . . . effervescent!

elevation   a two-dimensional scale representation of an exterior or interior wall surface.

ell   an extension or a wing of a building, usually at right angles to and smaller than the main structure.

embodied energy   an overall summation of the amount of energy put into the manufacture and distribution of a product, including mining, refinement, transportation, and shipping costs.

EMT   stands for Electro-Mechanical Tubing. This is what we commonly refer to as electrical conduit.

engineered septic system   usually refers to a mound system, but actually includes any situation in which the soil has been tested by a perc test and the septic system then designed by an engineer to meet local codes.

equinox   either of two days of the year when the day and night are approximately equal. These days occur halfway between the summer and winter solstices when the sun is at its furthest and closest proximities to the earth.

evergreen tree   a tree that keeps its needles or leaves throughout the year and is, thus, "forever green." The wood of most evergreens is less dense than deciduous trees and so they are sometimes called "softwood" trees. The evergreen species are very old compared to the deciduous and are among the first to repopulate a damaged site. *See also* **deciduous tree.**

face shells   the front and back top edges, but not the center webs, of a concrete block. The face shells are where the mortar goes when laying up a block wall.

fan coil unit   a hydronic heat exchanger with a fan; the transfer of heat is increased by the action of the fan blowing air over the coil.

fenestration   taken all together, the windows in a building. Also, the particular arrangement of the windows. One might say, "The fenestration for a building of this size is excessive," or, "We think the fenestration on the south elevation looks functional, while the fenestration on the east is more interesting."

fiberglass batts and blanket insulation   precut flexible sections of insulation designed to fit in-between framing members, batts are 4′ and 8′ long and 16″ to 24″ wide; rolls have the same width as batts but are up to 100′ long. Both types have a vapor barrier on one side and edge strips or flanges, which can be stapled to framing members.

filter fabric   industrial strength filter paper. Actually, it looks like carpet underlayment. It is used in the building of roads and to cover perforated pipe installed in foundation drains and curtain drains. In all cases its purpose is to keep the finer particles from clogging up the drainage.

fin-tube radiator   a heat distribution component consisting of a pipe or coil heating element surrounded by thin foil fins that dissipate the heat.

flat grained   lumber that has been sawn approximately parallel to the pith and growth rings of the log. In other words, the rings form an angle of less than 45° with the face of the board, giving a relatively parallel, or flat grain.

float glass   the most common type of glass found in windows today. It is manufactured by floating a ribbon of molten glass across a bath of molten tin, where it hardens before ever touching a solid surface.

floor plan   a map view or drawing of a horizontal slice through a building, generally about 4 ft above the floor.

floor register   a grill or set of louvers in the floor that allows and often regulates the passage of hot air from below.

fluorescent lamp   an electric discharge lamp, consisting of a cylindrical glass tube coated with a mixture of phosphorus and sealed at both ends; the tube contains inert gases, generally argon and low-pressure mercury vapor, that work with the phosphorus to radiate light. The particular mixture of phosphorus used governs the quality of light. Fluorescent lamps were once thought of as cold and harsh, but they now come in a full spectrum of colors and are inexpensive.

footing   wide base that spreads the load from the building and foundation out to the supporting earth.

forced hot air   a heat distribution system that supplies hot air to rooms via ducts and registers.

foundation drain   a perforated 4″ pipe embedded in crushed stone that runs around the foundation at the footing to carry ground water away from the building. Someimes called a *French drain.*

foyer   an entrance hall or vestibule.

french drain   *see* **foundation drain.**

frieze molding   found just below the cornice on the exterior of a building where the wall and roof overhang meet, or on the interior where the wall and ceiling meet.

frost heave   movement of the earth due to the freezing and expansion of moisture below the surface.

frost wall   a short concrete foundation wall that extends just below the frost line.

Fuller, Buckminster (1895–1983)   inventor/promoter of the geodesic dome.

gable   the triangular end of a roof.

galvanic action   corrosion caused by the electrical exchange of ions produced when dissimilar materials are brought into contact, especially under damp conditions.

galvanizing a means of preventing corrosion by applying a zinc coating to steel. This is not something you can do at home.

gambrel a roof comprised of four planes and two different pitches; the uppermost planes of the roof form a shallow pitch; the lower, more steeply pitched, planes join the upper roof to the walls.

gang forms connected forms of similar size; often a grid of wood or metal used to mass-produce adobe bricks.

geodetic survey a topographical map prepared by the United States Geological Survey (USGS).

GFI stands for Ground Fault Interrupter. A circuit breaker or duplex outlet used for wiring in wet locations, i.e., bathrooms, greenhouses, outdoors, etc. The GFI fixtures have much faster response in the event of a short circuit, such as a radio falling into the bathtub.

girt horizontal members connected to major posts at mid-height in a timber frame house. Typically for supporting wall cladding.

glazing 1: the act of installing glass or other transparent material in a window, door, skylight, etc. 2: As a noun for the transparent (usually glass), components of a building. One might say, "The glazing in this house cost enough to put a few kids through college." Or one might say, "I have been glazing and reglazing the windows in this school. Every time I fix one, another seems to break."

glulam beam a manufactured beam made of several pieces of wood glued together under pressure. These beams are stronger and more consistent than solid lumber. They can be purchased straight, curved, and in just about any length.

Gothic name given to medieval architecture in Europe from the mid-twelfth century to the Renaissance. The pointed arc, flying buttress, and ribbed vault are characteristic.

gray water all wastewater from nontoilet plumbing fixtures and appliances in the home, including baths, basins, clothes washers, dishwashers, showers, and the kitchen sink. Gray water and black water together make up all the wastewater in a household.

Greek Revival a style prevalent during the mid-1800s in both residential and civic architecture. Greek Revival is adapted from classic Greek architecture. The most popular features are the temple front, with its pediment and columns of either the Doric, Ionic, or Corinthian orders.

greenfield armadillo-like, metallic, cable sheathing.

grid short for utility or electrical grid, the interconnected network of centralized power companies used to buy, sell, and deliver electricity. If you buy electricity from a utility, you are said to be "on the grid." If you generate your own electricity, you are "off the grid."

Gropius, Walter (1883–1969) famous German architect and founder of the Bauhaus school of design.

ground an electrical term referring to deliberately connecting parts of a wiring installation to a grounding electrode held at 0 volts. The purpose of grounding is safety, to reduce the danger of electrical shocks.

gypsum board also known as gypboard, drywall, plasterboard, or sheetrock; an interior facing panel made of gypsum (hydrous calcium sulfate) sandwiched between two paper faces. People seem to be divided on this stuff. They either love it or they hate it.

halflap 1: a type of roll roofing that is applied just as the term indicates—with each piece lapping the other by half. 2: Much less common, this term is also sometimes used to describe a wood siding with a shaped edge that allows one board to overlap another.

-handed door a door is referred to as a right-handed door or a left-handed door based upon the side of the door that the handle appears on (right or left) and the direction of swing (in or out). The butt-to-butt rule is useful for identifying handed doors: With your butt against the butt of the doorjamb where the door hinges attach, if the door is on the right it is a right-handed door; if the door is on the left, it is a left-handed door.

head in hydroelectric power, the head is the vertical distance (in feet) that water falls. The amount of power obtainable from a stream is proportional to the size of the head.

header 1: in wood construction, any member that spans an opening in a wall, as a lintel or a joist that supports other joists; 2: in masonry construction, a masonry unit that ties together two wythes with its edge exposed in the face of the wall.

heat exchanger any device that transfers heat from one medium to another, water to air or air to air. One specific type of heat exchanger is a unit that transfers the heat from warm exhaust air to cooler intake air as it provides adequate fresh air.

heat pump a device that uses compressor technology similar to that used in refrigerators or air conditioners to "pump" heat from outside air or from groundwater into a house.

heat transfer factors product of the u-coefficient and the temperature difference between the inside and outside. Heat loss for a building can be established by multiplying the heat transfer factor by the area of the building surface.

helical having or displaying the qualities of a helix, or screw.

helix a spiral.

hollow core door a door made of two faces of wood veneer with an air space in between and solid wood spacers along the edges. This is a very inexpensive door with poor acoustical properties and usually associated with lower budget construction. In truth, however, there is such a thing as a good hollow core door. Also they make great drafting tables.

honeycombing   if the concrete is not mixed properly or if it is poorly vibrated the result will be honeycombing. This is the condition where the cement doesn't fully engulf the aggregate along the surface of the forms. When the forms are removed the resulting honeycomb is both cosmetically and structurally unsatisfactory.

hopper   a window that is hinged along the lower edge of the sash.

horizontal collaring beam   a beam or framing configuration that runs along the top plate of a wall on which a roof sits. When properly designed, the collaring beam transfers all the thrust loads to the end walls, thus preventing the wall from bowing out due to roof loads. It is a clever way to eliminate the clutter of collar ties in the space under the roof. (See Figure 126.)

humidity, absolute and relative   *absolute* humidity is the total amount of moisture held in the air at a given temperature; *relative* humidity is the amount of moisture that air can hold at a given temperature relative to the total amount.

HVAC system   refers to the mechanical systems of a building: **h**eating, **v**entilating, and **a**ir **c**onditioning.

hydroelectric   producing or relating to the production of electricity by water power.

hydrologic cycle   the path that water travels through the environment, characterized by evaporation, condensation, precipitation, and percolation. (See Figure 5.)

hydronic heating system   a system that circulates warm water through convectors to heat a building. Baseboard hot water is an example of a hydronic heating system. So is a radiant floor.

hydrostatic pressure   when water impinges on a foundation wall without adequate drainage, it builds up water pressure. Even though the water isn't moving, there is this pressure and it will eventually push water through any flaws or cracks in the wall.

ice dam   a layer of ice that forms on the unheated overhang of the roof. As the ice builds up it can actually contain water runoff and cause it to leak back into the roof. This can all be prevented by proper venting and insulation.

impulse turbine   a turbine that uses the kinetic energy of water squirting out of a nozzle at high speed to turn the turbine wheel. Impulse-type turbines are usually used in high head situations. *See also* **head.**

incandescent lamp   consists of a tungsten filament inside a gas-filled sealed-glass envelope. Current passing through the high-resistance filament heats it to incandescence, producing light.

indirect lighting   general lighting that provides illumination for an entire space. *See also* **accent lighting** and **task lighting.**

inglenook   a configuration of benches on either side of a fireplace; popularized by the architect Frank Lloyd Wright.

insolation   the amount of sunlight impinging on a surface at a given time.

instantaneous boiler   a tankless water heater that produces hot water only when needed. Because the instantaneous boiler, or *demand water heater*, as it is often called, heats only a small amount of water at a time, it is more efficient than the traditional water heater, which keeps a large volume of water hot continuously.

insulating glass   also called double or triple glazing; *see* **Thermopane.**

isolation valve   valves installed in the supply pipes of a fixture or appliance so that it may be isolated

and/or removed for service without draining the entire system.

Italianate   a residential style from the mid- to late 1800s. Characterized by a rectangular house of two or three stories, a low-pitch hipped roof with supporting brackets, and often a cupola.

jack rafter   a rafter that spans the distance from the wall plate to a hip or from a valley to the ridge.

jalousie   an adjustable window, shade, or door that is formed from horizontal slats of wood, metal, or glass.

jamb   the side and head surfaces of a door, window, or other opening.

joinery   the field and practice of designing, cutting, and assembling wooden connections, usually used in the context of furniture making.

joist   A horizontal framing member used in stick frame construction to make spanning assemblies. More specifically we refer to floor joists, ceiling joists, deck joists, etc.

joist hanger   a metal bracket used with nails to attach joists to a beam. This eliminates the need to notch the wood. Besides saving labor and time, this method of connection is stronger and better suited to construction in seismic areas.

k = conductivity   the BTUH rate of heat flow through 1 square foot of a homogeneous material 1″ thick for a 1°F temperature difference between its two surfaces.

kerf, sawkerf   a narrow slot or notch part way through a board, typically cut with a table or circular saw.

keyway   A slot formed in a concrete surface for the purpose of interlocking with a subsequent pour of concrete. The end result is a more stable joint between the two pieces of concrete.

KISS   standing for **K**eep **I**t **S**imple **S**tupid, this is a school of thought that some people adhere to. I can't really speak for it myself. Also a rock band.

The group is believed to be particularly popular with framing carpenters because of the complementary quality of the music to the sound of circular saws.

knee wall   a short vertical wall (2′ to 4′ high) commonly found on the second story of a cape between the floor and the bottom of the sloped ceiling. Building such a wall leads the builder to spend a lot of time on his knees.

knot   break or limb embedded in the tree and cut through in the process of milling; classified according to size, quality, and number.

laminated glass   a type of safety glass made by sandwiching transparent vinyl between two sheets of tempered glass. If and when it breaks, the vinyl holds the glass shards together and prevents pieces from falling from the frame.

leaching field   in a rural septic system, this expanse of ground receives effluent through perforated pipes. Effluent is aerobically decomposed by microbes and bacteria in the leaching field. Contrary to rumor, actual leeches are not involved in this process in any way.

leads   the end or corner sections of a brick wall, built up and stepped back on successive courses. These points determine the location of the wall; a line is attached to the leads as a guide for constructing the remainder of the wall between them. (See Figure 109.)

Le Corbusier (1887–1965)   A French artist whose interest in architecture ushered in a school of design that is still very much alive today. Among many other things he developed design ideas that addressed mass production of housing; he worked out a system of proportions, based on human anatomy, called the *modular;* and he pioneered the questionable notion of a house as "a machine for living."

ledge (or ledge rock)   immovable strata of stone, the tip of which is usually revealed in the last corner of your foundation hole to be excavated. (See Figure 30.)

lenticular truss   a lens-shaped truss with a curved upper and lower set of cords. Popularized by the Jersey Devil on their Hill House project, many design/builders now use this type of truss because it is easy to build on site and very strong. Yestermorrow students used it on a project in 1983. (See Figure 61.)

Levitt, William   a developer in the forties, responsible for the famous Levitt towns.

lift   a layer of soil, gravel, sand, or other fill. A lift of fill is usually between 6″ and 24″ deep. For instance one might say, "Fill and compact the excavation with 6″ lifts of bank run gravel."

lintel   in masonry construction, a beam or supporting member placed over an opening in a wall. A lintel is typically used above doors and windows.

lites   the individual panes of glass in a window or door.

live load (LL)   the weight, expressed in pounds per square foot, of items such as furniture, people, snow, etc., that are in addition to the weight of the structure itself. The live load is determined by code.

look outs   framing for a roof overhang at the gable end. Sometimes called the "ladder."

Low-E (emissivity) glass   is float, plate, or sheet glass that has a thin metallic coating that allows full-spectrum sunlight to pass through but reflects the ultraviolet and infrared wavelengths of the energy spectrum and reduces the radiant heat that escapes back out. Low-E glass is used to make single- or double-glazed windows, depending on the climate. The E side of glass should always face the cold side of the window, which means it faces out in the northern regions and faces in where air conditioning is used.

low-flow device   any plumbing fixture that reduces water use by reducing the flow. A low-flush toilet and a water-saver shower head are examples of such devices.

main disconnect   a single switch located between the panel box and the meter that shuts off all the flow of electricity from the grid to the house.

make-up air   the air that is introduced to a house to take the place of that which is exhausted either through ventilation or leakage.

mansard   a roof configuration consisting of a flat or shallow pitched roof on top with short, steeply sloped roofs on all sides that join the top to the walls. This roof form was widespread in the Victorian and Queen Anne styles. *See also* **gambrel.**

massing   the overall proportions of a structure; the general form or geometry without regard for detail.

mechanicals   a general term for plumbing, electrical, HVAC (heating, ventilating, and air conditioning), and DWV (drainage, waste, and venting), etc.

metes and bounds   a precise method of measuring and defining land that uses a single reference point.

miasma   a vapor from marshes; formerly supposed to poison the air.

microlam   short for microlaminated, this is a family of manufactured boards composed of many layers of veneer laminated together. Very strong.

moment of inertia $I = bd^3/8$; determines the role that shape plays in the strength of a beam.

mortise   a slot cut in a timber to receive the tenon of another timber to form a joint. (See Figure 49.)

mound system   an engineered alternative to a leaching field; when soils are poor, additional fill is brought in and piled up, hence the name, mound.

mullions   the strip of wood between neighboring lites that holds the glass; usually vertical.

muntins similar to mullions, these are strips of wood or metal that contain the panes of glass in a window or door.

NOAA National Oceanic and Atmospheric Administration—a national organization that keeps track of all weather records.

Norman name given to the Romanesque style in England.

OC *on center*. When framing, joists or studs are laid out by their centers; as in "The rafters will be two feet on center (OC)."

ohm a unit of electrical resistance. Resistance reduces current, so ohms are inversely proportional to amps. (See Figure 179.)

one-hundred-year floodplain the greatest area flooded by a river in any one-hundred-year period. There is also a five-hundred-year floodplain that covers a wider area.

outlet where the plug goes to get electricity; two outlets together are called a duplex.

overhang short for roof overhang; this is the portion of the roof that sticks out beyond the exterior wall. (See Figure 122.)

overshot waterwheel a type of waterwheel that accepts water at the top of its rotation; its downward moving side is overbalanced by the water and this keeps the wheel in slow rotation. (See Figure 176a.)

pace or **pacing** the length of one's stride used to approximate a distance on site. (Also an indication that an owner/builder is having a problem.) One might say, "She paced off the building site using her time-proven thirty-one-inch pace. A later survey revealed that she was a mere four inches off."

Palladio (1508–1580) Italian mason of the Renaissance era. In his buildings he combined Renaissance ideas with Roman forms and proportions. Author of the *Quattro libri dell' architet-*

tura, an illustrated treatise on architecture. He is probably thought by most to be a window designer for Marvin or Pella. A Palladian window has become the generic term for a round-top window flanked by two symmetrical casements.

parge to repair a surface with a thin layer of mortar.

pencil vibrator a particular type of concrete vibrator used in wall forms. It draws its name from the long flexible shaft that can be snaked into the thin forms. Actually it might be better called the Snake Vibrator . . . but it isn't.

phase change material any of a number of materials that store heat by going through a change in state from solid to liquid or liquid to gas, etc.

photovoltaic cells semiconductors that convert sunlight directly into electricity.

photovoltaic (pv) array a group of pv cells wired in series or parallel and mounted in a frame to make installation more efficient.

pier A vertical support, usually in the context of foundations, such as a pier foundation, wherein a building is supported from several individual points rather than on a continuous wall or slab. (*See also* **slab; frost wall**).

pilaster a portion of a wall acting as a vertical column and projecting from one or both wall faces.

pitch accumulation of resin in wood cells.

pitch-pocket an opening between growth rings that usually contains or has contained resin, bark, or both.

plane sawn a method of milling where the log is cut into boards parallel to one another and independent of the grain. *See also* **quarter sawn**. (See Figure 76.)

plasterboard *see* **blue board.**

plate glass developed in the seventeenth century and commonly used throughout the 1800s, this

type of glass is manufactured by placing molten glass in frames and spreading it into sheets with rollers. It is then cooled and polished.

plates in stick-frame construction, the horizontal framing elements at the top and bottom of a stud wall; also referred to as the top plate, cap plate, sill plate, shoe, sole, etc.

platform framing a wooden building frame made up of small closely spaced members where floor members rest on top of wall members. (See Figure 51.)

ply a layer, as in a layer of veener in plywood or a layer of felt in a built-up roof membrane.

pointing the process of tooling or finishing the masonry joints between brick or block after the wall is laid up. If the mortar erodes or falls out from between the bricks in an older structure, one hears of it being repointed. Pointing can leave the mortar in a number of different profiles for aesthetic or weathering effect. A slight concave joint is the most common pointing. (See Figure 111.)

polar geometry the geometry of relationships described by an angle and a distance from a point.

porte cochere a term derived from the French word for a covered entryway, originally for a horse-drawn cart called a *cochere*. Used today for cars and/or people; it's essentially a fancy term for an attached carport.

post an upright, vertical support that carries a load from a beam to a concentrated point below.

potable water water that is suitable for drinking.

power drop (no, it's not a weight-lifting term.) The meter, panel box, and main cable from the pole bringing power to the house. Think of it as where the electricity "drops" out of the grid to power your house.

program an overall plan or outline for the design and construction requirements of a house. The program includes space minimums, client needs, budget, schedule and material specifications.

P.T. heard at the lumberyard as "peetee" lumber, this label means the wood is *pressure treated*. P.T. wood comes in 0.2, 0.4, and 0.6 varieties, each referring to the pressure under which the preservative was applied. Only the 0.6 is suitable for foundations or continuous contact with the ground.

pulse heater any boiler or furnace that "explodes" rather than burns its fuel. This results in higher efficiency.

purlins a horizontal element in timber framing that runs perpendicular to the main rafters. (See Figure 49.)

quarter sawn a method of milling in which the log is cut along the radius so as to produce the most stable grain and figure in the resulting boards. *See also* **plane sawn.** (See Figure 76.)

R-value resistance to heat flow. Heat transmission coefficients are expressed as conductivities (k) through one inch of material. For a total thickness of (L) inches, the resistance to heat flow (R) = L/k. If this doesn't help, remember: the higher the R-value, the better!

raceway conductors a generic name for surface-mounted enclosures that carry electrical wire and conductors.

radient ceiling heating elements, usually electric, are embedded in the ceiling to radiate heat into a room. This method of heating is favored by bald people.

rafter table a chart of different-pitched roof rafters in terms of length, rise, and run.

rafter tail not to be confused with rooster tail, a rafter tail is the end portion of the rafter that extends beyond the outside wall.

railroad tracks slang for a lightweight reinforcing running between two rows of concrete block.

raised panel door a door consisting of a frame with fitted panels. The pieces of the frame are called "rails" and "stiles". The loose joints around the panels allow for expansion and contraction of the wood caused by seasonal changes.

rammed earth an old form of earth construction in which the earth is compacted into forms. Not unlike concrete construction, the walls are reinforced with steel. Not unlike adobe construction, the outside of the walls must be stuccoed or whitewashed to protect them from the elements.

rebar a shortened version of "reinforcing bar." Rebar is the steel used in concrete to resist tensile stresses. It is numbered according to the diameter divided by $\frac{1}{8}$". If it has a $\frac{3}{8}$" diameter it is a number 3 bar; if it has a $\frac{3}{4}$" diameter it is a number 6 bar.

rectifier an electronic device for transforming alternating current (AC) into intermittent direct current (DC).

release oil (or release agent) release oil is sprayed on concrete forms prior to placing the reinforcing steel, to ease their removal later. Used motor oil works just as well, but it will stain, so it should only be used on concrete that won't be seen.

replacement field a backup leaching field comparable in size to the primary leaching field. Required by code.

resistance heat heat produced by forcing electricity through a high-resistance wire. Very wasteful.

ridge beam beam at the junction of the top two edges of a peak roof, where the upper ends of the rafters are fastened. (See Figure 123.)

ring shank nails used for flooring or anywhere wood must be kept from working loose. These nails have raised rings or ribs around the shank of the nail.

rise vertical distance between the top plate of the wall and the ridge of the roof.

RO, rough opening the opening created in the framing to accommodate the subsequent installation of a door or window. The RO is always slightly larger than the unit to be installed. This allows for leveling and shims. Most windows and doors have ROs specified in their catalogues.

Romex™ like Kleenex, the Romex™ brand name has become the generic term for a type of plastic-sheathed electrical cable that is most commonly used in interior house wiring.

rowlock a brick laid so that its small end is visible in the wall face. (See Figure 104.)

run horizontal distance from the peak of the roof to the edge of the wall, this is the same as the half span.

sailor a masonry unit, set on end with its broad face parallel to the wall face. (See Figure 104.)

sand-struck brick a brick produced by molding wet clay; the molds are sanded to prevent sticking.

screed a strip of wood or metal used to place and level concrete in the forms or when pouring a slab. One might say, "I used a rough wooden screed on the footers, but I will use a fine metal one when it's time to screed the slab." (See Figure 35.)

scupper a protruding drain spout that is usually found in masonry construction; used to drain roof areas behind a parapet wall.

section a view or cutaway drawing through a building allowing one to see the inside. A section is the preferred drawing for depicting the structure of a building.

shake 1: a lengthwise grain separation between or through the growth rings. 2: wooden shingle produced by splitting cedar along the grain. *See also* **shingles.**

sheathing the rough, unfinished, outside covering applied to the framing of the floor, walls, and roof of a stick-frame structure. (See Figure 51.)

sheetrock *see* **gypsum board.**

shiner a masonry unit laid lengthwise with the face parallel to the wall face. (See Figure 104.)

shingles and shakes small, wooden units which are nailed in a lapped fashion on roofs and walls as a weatherproof exterior finish. Shingles are available in stock sizes with smooth sawn surfaces. They are also available in a variety of shapes used to make patterns in the siding. Shakes are hand split from a block of wood and are thick and rough in appearance. Besides size and texture, the difference between a shingle and a shake is that a shingle is sawn on both faces, a shake is split on one or both faces. Shingles are used on roofs and walls; shakes are only used on roofs.

Shingle style a residential style popular in the late 1800s characterized by features such as towers, gables, dormers, porches, and other bulges that are uniformly covered with wood shingles. The eaves of the roof are close to the walls to enhance the homogeneous look of the shingle covering.

shiplap a configuration of boards with edges rabeted to allow an overlap from one board to another while the surface remains flush; this is often used as siding and was originally used to build ships.

short circuit when a break in an electrical circuit causes the current to find a shorter path to ground (0 volts). This shorter path usually allows too much current flow which then throws the circuit breaker.

slab a general term referring to a thin flat geometry. A slab of wood is usually a hefty plank or board milled from a log and still carrying the bark along the thin edges. A foundation slab is a concrete floor with thickened edges. A floor slab usually refers to a concrete floor above grade. A slab o'beef is what you put in your lunch box before going to the construction site. (See Figure 25.)

sleepers an array of regularly placed boards fastened over a floor or subfloor in preparation for the final flooring. Sleepers are used to provide height adjustment, insulation space, spring in the floor, a wiring chase, or simply to provide a nailing surface when wood flooring is installed over a concrete slab.

slider a glass door or window of two or more pieces that is opened by sliding one part past the other.

slump test no, not a test for hiring your crew. Rather this is a test of how much water is in the concrete mix. A bottomless metal cone is filled with concrete taken from the truck. When the supporting cone is removed, the concrete slumps in proportion to how much water is in the mix. Too much water will weaken the concrete; not enough will make it hard to work. A slump of between 3″ and 6″ is typical. The smaller the slump the stiffer the concrete. A slump of 6″ is almost soupy.

snap tie a metal rod that holds the forms together on either side of a concrete wall while it's being poured. After the concrete has set up and the forms are removed, these metal ties stick out of the wall. They are simply snapped off (thus their name) and the ends are patched over with mortar to prevent rust from migrating into the wall. (See Figure 38.)

soffit the horizontal trim on the underside of the roof overhang along the eaves. This is the trim that covers the rafter tails and in which one sees the vent strips. In the author's opinion, it is a largely overlooked opportunity for architectural expression and fun detailing. (See Figure 200d.)

soil stack the primary vertical pipe into which all branch drain pipes deposit waste water. The soil stack connects to the building trap and then the sewer or septic system. *See also* **stack vent; vent stack.**

solar, active any strategy for collecting energy from the sun that requires mechanical devices such as pumps, fans, or shutters to operate.

solar, passive a strategy for collecting energy from the sun that succeeds without the use of additional energy-consuming devices; examples are site orientation, window placement, and landscaping.

solar path finder an instrument used to assess the site for solar-heating capabilities by locating surrounding obstacles that create shade. (See Figure 10.)

soldier a masonry unit set on end with its narrow edge parallel to the wall face. (See Figure 104.)

solstice (winter, summer) the two days of the year when the sun is farthest (winter) and closest (summer) to the earth resulting in the longest and shortest days. (Northern Hemisphere only.)

spawling when sizable chunks of concrete fall away at the surface. There might be spawling if the concrete wasn't properly cured or if it froze before setting up. Spawling can also occur when water penetrates cracks in concrete and then freezes.

spec (or spec builder) spec is short for speculation. A spec builder does not build for a specific client; instead, he or she speculates that someone will buy the structure they are building.

spline a thin strip inserted into grooves on two mating pieces of material to hold them in alignment.

split lengthwise separation of the wood extending from one surface through the piece to the opposite or adjoining surface.

spring box a structure built around a spring to contain and protect the water from contamination.

stackwall a wall built from stacked cordwood with cement as a mortar. (See Figure 114.)

stack vent the short section of plastic pipe that pokes through the roof of a house and serves to vent the main soil stack. All the individual fixture vents end up in the main stack, so it should be called the *vent* stack. Right. Likewise, all the individual fixtures' drain-pipes end up in the main stack, so it should be called the *soil* stack. Right . . . maybe. Well, it turns out it's called the vent stack and the little part that sticks through the roof is called the stack vent. *See also* **soil stack.**

stadia rod used in conjunction with a transit or builder's level to establish elevations and the location of natural or man-made features. Sometimes called a "philly pole." (See Figure 3.)

stair stringer a sloping wood or steel member that supports the treads of a stair.

standing-seam roof a roofing system where sheets of metal are joined by a folded seam that runs vertically down the roof every 20″ to 24″. Before acid rain you could expect to get fifty to one hundred years of wear from a standing-seam roof, depending on the gauge and type of metal used. They are a favorite roof type in cold climates, where they are known to shed the snow and ice well.

stem wall a short, vertical concrete foundation wall.

stickered a technique for stacking and storing wood so that the air is allowed to pass freely around it. Small sticks are used as spacers between larger pieces of stacked wood.

stick frame any of a variety of building systems comprised of many small framing members fastened with nails, usually at modular intervals. Balloon frames, platform frames, and western frames are all examples of stick frames. Timber frames, picture frames, and bed frames are not. (See Figure 51.)

story pole a pole marked to measure coursing for masonry construction. (See Figure 110.)

stress-skin panel an insulated, exterior wall panel comprised of rigid foam sandwiched between two outer sheets of plywood, gypboard, masonite,

wafer board, etc. These are self-supporting, very rigid, and excellent insulation. They are so named because most of the structural stresses are accommodated by the outer skins. (See Figure 94.)

stretcher a masonry unit laid lengthwise with its edge parallel to the wall face.

strongback a vertical support member in the traditional formwork for a concrete wall. Also a quality to look for in young personnel on the crew. *See also* **waler.** (See Figure 38.)

structural ridge a ridge-beam sized to take half the load from each set of rafters without deflecting. Since the ridge now becomes structural, or load-bearing, the roof framing acts like an inclined floor rather than a truss. The rafters act like floor joists spanning from wall plate to ridge beam. Collar ties are no longer required. Structural ridge beams, like horizontal collaring beams, are used when the design won't tolerate conventional collar ties. (See Figure 125.)

substrate material used as a base, adhesive, or protection below a finish material such as tile, carpet, finish siding, or roof shingles.

summerwood denser outer portion of each annual ring, usually without easily visible pores, formed late in the growing period, not necessarily in the summer.

sustainability the quality of any thing or process to be ongoing without irrevocably depleting the resources upon which it depends. Usually referring to the environment.

swale a gentle ditch or low area that drains surface runoff. Unlike a ditch, a swale is easily walked over and usually offers a good place for grass or other plant life to grow. It is good practice to form a swale around your house when the excavator comes back to do the finish grading.

sweat in plumbing, a method of joining copper pipes and fittings using solder, flux, and a source of heat, usually a blowtorch.

synchronous inverter an electronic device that converts AC to DC, but must have another AC source for voltage and frequency reference.

task lighting lighting designed for a specific activity, i.e., desk lamp, undercabinet-counter lighting, etc.; the opposite of general lighting. (See Figure 175a.)

tempered glass a type of safety glass that is four times stronger than regular float glass and breaks into small square-edged chunks. These are relatively safe compared to the long, sharp-edged pieces that result when regular float glass shatters. For that reason, building codes require that tempered glass be used in doors, floor-to-ceiling windows near doors, and in high-wind areas.

tenon a projection at the end of a timber to be inserted into a slot or mortise to form a joint. (See Figure 49.)

tensile force a force that pulls (as distinct from those that push). Two people pulling on either end of a rope are each exerting a tensile force on the other. In building, tension always occurs in tandem with compression. *See* **compression force.**

thermal break 1: when a framing member, a rim joist for instance, is separated from the exterior sheathing by an air space or insulation to prevent the passage of warm or cold air through the member. 2: An insulating gasket used in window design to separate the outer sash surfaces from the glass and inner sash surfaces. This prevents heat loss and frost buildup.

thermal resistance, R a unit of thermal resistance used for comparing insulating values of different materials; the reciprocal of heat transfer (U-coefficient) for example, a wall with a U-coefficient of 0.25 would have a thermal resistance R of $1/0.25 = 4.0$.

thermopane a glazing consisting of two panes of glass with an air space or void between them. The space may range from $\frac{1}{2}″$ to 1″ and acts as insulation. To increase the insulating value the void is often filled with an inert gas or evacuated to a low-pressure vacuum. Thermopane glass is also referred to as double glazing or insulating glass. Different manufacturers seal the edges with a variety of technologies, from special caulks and cements to solid glass welding. (See Table 9.)

tilt-up construction a method for constructing concrete walls by tilting up concrete panels that have been cast and cured while horizontal.

timber frame, post and beam a vernacular form of wood framing using large timbers, long spans, and few joints. The joints are finely crafted and often very elaborate, requiring dowels or pegs to keep them in place. Timber framing is enjoying a vibrant renaissance in this country, led in part by the Timber Framers' Guild of North America, Box 1046, Keene, NH 03431. (See Figure 49.)

topo survey topo is short for topographic; a land survey that shows the grade or elevation changes with contour lines. (See Figure 2.)

torn grain part of the wood torn out in dressing or shaping.

tracking collectors solar collectors or photovoltaic devices mounted on a mechanism designed to keep them oriented toward the sun.

trammel set two metal points that can be attached to a long bar of wood or metal, making a beam compass. Trammel points are used to lay out distances between two points and/or to make arcs or circles. (See Figure 59.)

transit a surveying instrument that measures horizontal and vertical angles and is used to establish straight lines, horizontal and vertical distances, and elevations. Sometimes called a "full" transit, it is much the same as a builder's level, with the added feature that it tilts. This allows it to measure angles where a builder's level can't. *See also* **builder's level.** (See Figure 3.)

trap a drain fitting or device that provides a liquid seal to prevent the back draft of sewer gases

without affecting the flow of wastewater or sewage through the drain. (See Figure 163.)

triple pane a thermopane or insulated glazing comprised of three layers of glass and two air spaces. This is an effective insulator because of the extra glass and air space. (See Table 9.)

trombe wall a passive solar device consisting of glazing in front of a wall made of concrete, stone, or a phase change material. The wall absorbs and stores heat from the sun during the day and slowly releases the heat to the building at night.

true divided lites when strips of wood, known as mullions or muntons, divide a window into individual panes of glass. Untrue or false divided lites consist of a wood grid placed in front of one large piece of glass to give the appearance of many smaller panes.

truss used in both roofs and floors to span long distances and carry heavy loads. A truss consists of a triangular arrangement of structural members that reduces nonaxial forces on the truss to a set of axial forces in the members. (See Figure 68.)

Tudor an English architectural style characterized by half-timber construction, usually a timber- or cruck-type frame with straw and mud infill.

U-coefficient a unit measure of thermal conductivity; the number of BTUs per hour flowing through 1 square foot of roof, wall, floor, or other building component for a temperature difference of 1°F between the inside and outside air. It can apply to a combination of materials or to a single material such as glass. U is the reciprocal of R. *See also* **thermal resistance.**

underlayment a smooth subfloor installed prior to tiling.

undershot waterwheel a type of waterwheel powered by water as it passes under the wheel. (See Figure 176c.)

vapor barrier a layer of material intended to obstruct the passage of water vapor through a building assembly. Examples of vapor barriers include: 6 mil polyethylene, the backing on fiberglass insulation; rigid foam or drywall treated with special paint.

Van der Rohe, Ludwig Mies (1888–1969) an architect who was influential in modern skyscraper design, best known for the Pavillion in Barcelona and the Seagram Building in New York.

venting, circuit or loop venting a venting configuration where several fixtures drain into one soil pipe, which is then vented at the end.

vent stack the main vertical pipe in any DWV system. It is connected at the top to the stack vent and at the bottom to the building drain. In short, it is the main thoroughfare for all waste and venting. All the individual fixture vents end up in the main stack, so it should be called the vent stack. Right. Likewise, all the individual fixtures' drain pipes end up in the main stack, so it should be called the soil stack. Right . . . uh . . . maybe. Well, it turns out, it's called the vent stack and the little part that sticks through the roof is called the stack vent. *See also* **soil stack.**

vent system a pipe or system of pipes installed to provide a flow of air to or from a drainage system. This circulation of air protects the system from siphonage and back pressure. (See Figure 163.)

venturi a funnel-shaped tube used to produce or measure the pressure and velocity of fluids. The venturi effect is a loosely used term usually referring to the behavior of accelerated air resulting from any narrowing of the aperture through which it must pass. For a little further complexity or contradiction see Robert Venturi.

Venturi, Robert a contemporary architect, critic and author known for his book *Complexity and Contradiction in Architecture.*

vernacular architecture buildings of a particular region, time, and culture that share an architectural and constructional vocabulary. Rather than being singled out for qualities that distinguish them from one another, vernacular buildings are recognized for those qualities that they have in common. Unlike contemporary residential architecture, vernacular architecture expresses the occupant's place in a community and a context of shared values.

viga logs or beams placed horizontally to carry the roof boards and baked mud in adobe construction.

Vitruvius a Roman architect and theorist of slight importance in his own time but influential from the Early Renaissance onward. Author of a treatise on architecture in ten books, entitled *De Architettura*. This is the only complete treatise on architecture to survive from antiquity.

waler a horizontal support member in the traditional formwork for a concrete wall. Also slang for an aggressive worker. Concerning this comic usage, one might say "The waler had a good strongback." *See also* **strongback.** (See Figure 38.)

wane bark or lack of wood from some other cause on the edge or corner of a board.

warp any variation from a true or plane surface; includes bow, crook, or any combination thereof.

water-struck brick bricks resulting from molds that have been wetted prior to forming. The water prevents sticking and facilitates form removal.

watt, kilowatt unit of electrical power. Watts are the mathematical product of volts and amps;

$$watts = volts \times amps$$

This makes sense. Amps measure the rate of flow; volts measure the intensity or energy per unit of flow. Their product, watts, measures the total power used. A kilowatt is simply 1000 watts. Watts and kilowatts are the basic units for purchasing electricity. That's why your electrical bill is keyed to the watts usage. At any rate, that's watts, not Watts. Watts is the location in Los Angeles of a famous, ornate, handcrafted, owner-built tower/house. (See Figure 179.)

weep hole a small hole usually at the base of a masonry or masonry-faced wall at the level of the flashing to allow moisture to drain. (See Figure 102.)

wick 1: (noun) string part of a candle; 2: (verb) process of liquid soaking into a porous material. One might say, "Capillary action allowed the water to wick into the foundation walls." *See also* **capillary action.**

widow's walk a platform or deck on the roof of a house, usually surrounded by a railing. The widow's walk was originally used as a lookout by the wives of sailors who awaited their husbands' return from the sea.

wind data accumulator also referred to as a wind odometer; a device that measures the instantaneous speed of the wind and can be used to determine the average wind speed over a given period. (See Figure 178.)

winder a stair tread that is not in a straight run; any triangular stair tread that allows a run of stairs to turn back on itself.

wire losses a voltage drop produced by the slight resistance in the wire itself when current travels over long distances.

Wiremold a brand name for a surface-mounted raceway type of wiring. Raceway wiring is often used in renovation because the walls needn't be cut and drilled to house the cable. *See also* **raceway.**

wood pellets small regular pieces of wood used as fuel in a wood-pellet burning stove.

wythe each continuous vertical section of masonry one unit in thickness. A typical wall can be one, two, or three wythes thick.

yurt a circular tent with a cone-shaped roof developed by nomadic Mongolians in Siberia. The yurt often looks like a large, rug-covered muffin. (See Figure 72.)

zonohedra defined by Steve Baer, inventor, in his book *Zomes*, as a family of shapes similar to geodesic domes but different in that parallel edges may be stretched. (See Figure 57.)

Bibliography

Chapter 1

Alexander, Christopher. *The Timeless Way of Building.* New York: Oxford University Press, 1979.

Bachelard, Gaston. *The Poetics of Space.* Boston: Beacon Press, 1969.

Carter, Thomas, and Bernard Herman, eds. *Perspectives in Vernacular Architecture, III.* Columbia, MO: University of Missouri Press, 1989.

Fromm, Dorit. *Collaborative Communities: Cohousing, Central Living and Other Forms of Housing with Shared Facilities.* New York: Van Nostrand Reinhold, 1991.

Hubka, Thomas C. *Big House, Little House, Back House, Barn.* Hanover, NH: University Press of New England, 1987.

Jung, Carl G. *Man and His Symbols.* New York: Doubleday, 1969.

Kern, Ken. *The Owner Built Home.* New York: Charles Scribner's Sons, 1972.

Lym, Glenn R. *A Psychology of Building: How We Shape and Experience Our Structured Spaces.* Englewood Cliffs, NJ: Prentice-Hall, 1980.

Moore, Charles, Gerald Allen, and Donlyn Lyndon. *The Place of Houses.* New York: Holt, Reinhart and Winston, 1974.

Rudofsky, Bernard. *Architecture Without Architects.* New York: Doubleday, 1964.

Rybczynski, Witold. *The Most Beautiful House In the World.* New York: Penguin, 1990.

Walker, Lester. *American Shelter: An Illustrated Encyclopedia of the American Home.* Woodstock, NY: Overlook Press, 1981.

Wright, Gwendolyn. *Building the Dream: A Social History of Housing in America.* Cambridge, MA: MIT Press, 1981.

Chapter 2

Bachelard, Gaston. *The Poetics of Space.* Boston: Beacon Press, 1969.

Carter, Thomas, and Bernard Herman, eds. *Perspectives in Vernacular Architecture, III.* Columbia, MO: University of Missouri Press, 1989.

Hubka, Thomas C. *Big House, Little House, Back House, Barn.* Hanover, NH: University Press of New England, 1987.

Kern, Ken. *The Owner Built Home.* New York: Charles Scribner's Sons, 1972.

Rybczynski, Witold. *The Most Beautiful House In the World.* New York: Penguin, 1990.

Wright, Gwendolyn. *Building the Dream: A Social History of Housing in America.* Cambridge, MA: MIT Press, 1981.

Chapter 3

Alexander, Christopher. *The Timeless Way of Building.* New York: Oxford University Press, 1979.

Bloomer, Kent C., and Charles W. Moore. *Body, Memory and Architecture.* New Haven: Yale University Press, 1977.

Jung, Carl G. *Man and His Symbols.* New York: Doubleday, 1969.

Rybczynski, Witold. *The Most Beautiful House In the World.* New York: Penguin, 1990.

Walker, Les, and Jeff Milstein. *Designing Houses: An Illustrated Guide.* Woodstock, NY: Overlook Press, 1976.

Willson, Forest. *The Joy of Building: Restoring the Connection Between Architect and Builder.* New York: Van Nostrand Reinhold, 1979.

Chapter 4

Abercrombie, Stanley. *A Philosophy of Interior Design.* New York: Harper and Row, 1990.

Alexander, Christopher. *A Pattern Language.* New York: Oxford University Press, 1977.

Barnes, W. M. *Basic Surveying.* London: Butterworth, 1988.

Bloomer, Kent C., and Charles E. Moore. *Body, Memory and Architecture.* New Haven: Yale University Press, 1977.

Carter, Thomas, and Bernard Herman, eds. *Perspectives in Vernacular Architecture, III.* Columbia, MO: University of Missouri Press, 1989.

Farallones Institute. *The Integral Urban Home.* San Francisco: Sierra Club, 1979.

Fromm, Dorit. *Collaborative Communities: Cohousing, Central Living and Other Forms of Housing with Shared Facilities.* New York: Van Nostrand Reinhold, 1991.

Hubka, Thomas C. *Big House, Little House, Back House, Barn.* Hanover, NH: University Press of New England, 1987.

Jung, Carl G. *Man and His Symbols.* New York: Doubleday, 1969.

Kavanagh, Barry F., and S. J. Glenn Bird. *Surveying: Principles and Applications.* Reston, VA: Reston Publishing, 1984.

Ladau, Robert F., Brent K. Smith, and Jennifer Place. *Color in Interior Design and Architecture.* New York: Van Nostrand Reinhold, 1989.

Lym, Glenn R. *A Psychology of Building: How We Shape and Experience Our Structured Spaces.* Englewood Cliffs, NJ: Prentice-Hall, 1980.

McHarg, Ian. *Design with Nature.* New York: Doubleday, 1971.

Melaragno, Michele G. *Wind in Architectural and Environmental Design*. New York: Van Nostrand Reinhold, 1982.

Wright, Gwendolyn. *Building the Dream: A Social History of Housing in America*. Cambridge, MA: MIT Press, 1981.

Chapter 5

Alexander, Christopher. *A Pattern Language*. New York: Oxford University Press, 1977.

Barnes, W. M. *Basic Surveying*. London: Butterworth, 1988.

Farallones Institute. *The Integral Urban Home*. San Francisco: Sierra Club, 1979.

Fromm, Dorit. *Collaborative Communities: Cohousing, Central Living and Other Forms of Housing with Shared Facilities*. New York: Van Nostrand Reinhold, 1991.

Kavanagh, Barry F., and S. J. Glenn Bird. *Surveying: Principles and Applications*. Reston, VA: Reston Publishing, 1984.

Leckie, Jim, Gil Master, Harry Whitehouse, and Lily Young. *More Other Homes and Garbage*. San Francisco: Sierra Club, 1981.

McHarg, Ian. *Design with Nature*. New York: Doubleday, 1971.

Milne, Murray. *Residential Water Re-Use*. Davis, CA: California Water Resources Center, 1979.

Nichols, Herbert L., Jr. *Moving the Earth: The Workbook of Excavation*, 3rd ed. New York: McGraw-Hill Publishing, 1962.

Van der Ryn, Sim. *The Toilet Papers*. Santa Barbara, CA: Capra Press, 1978.

Chapter 6

Abercrombie, Stanley. *A Philosophy of Interior Design*. New York: Harper and Row, 1990.

Alexander, Christopher. *A Pattern Language*. New York: Oxford University Press, 1977.

Bachelard, Gaston. *The Poetics of Space*. Boston: Beacon Press, 1969.

Birren, Faber. *Color and the Human Response*. New York: Van Nostrand Reinhold, 1978.

Edwards, Betty. *Drawing on the Right Side of the Brain*. New York: St. Martin's Press, 1979.

Fromm, Dorit. *Collaborative Communities: Cohousing, Central Living and Other Forms of Housing with Shared Facilities*. New York: Van Nostrand Reinhold, 1991.

Hall, Edward T. *The Hidden Dimension*. New York: Anchor Books/Doubleday, 1966.

Ladau, Robert F., and Brent K. Smith, Jennifer Place. *Color in Interior Design and Architecture*. New York: Van Nostrand Reinhold, 1989.

Lym, Glenn R. *A Psychology of Building: How We Shape and Experience Our Structured Spaces*. Englewood Cliffs, NJ: Prentice-Hall, 1980.

Moore, Charles, Gerald Allen, and Donlyn Lyndon. *The Place of Houses*. New York: Holt, Reinhart and Winston, 1974.

Sommer, Robert. *Personal Space: The Behavioral Basis of Design*. Englewood Cliffs, NJ: Prentice-Hall, 1969.

Chapter 7

Bachelard, Gaston. *The Poetics of Space*. Boston: Beacon Press, 1969.

Edwards, Betty. *Drawing on the Right Side of the Brain*. New York: St. Martin's Press, 1979.

Hall, Edward T. *The Hidden Dimension*. New York: Anchor Books/Doubleday, 1966.

Lym, Glenn R. *A Psychology of Building: How We Shape and Experience Our Structured Spaces*. Englewood Cliffs, NJ: Prentice-Hall, 1980.

Sommer, Robert. *Personal Space: The Behavioral Basis of Design*. Englewood Cliffs, NJ: Prentice-Hall, 1969.

Chapter 8

Dowrick, David J. *Earthquake Resistant Design for Engineers and Architects*, 2nd ed. New York: John Wiley & Sons, 1977.

Nichols, Herbert L., Jr. *Moving the Earth: The Workbook of Excavation*. 3rd ed. New York: McGraw-Hill Publishing, 1962.

Olin, Harold B. *Construction: Principals, Materials and Methods*, 5th ed. New York: Van Nostrand Reinhold, 1990.

Chapter 9

Benson, Tedd. *The Timber Frame Home*. Newtown, CT: Tauton Press, 1988.

Bunting, Bainbridge, Jean Lee Booth, and William R. Simms, Jr. *Taos Adobes*. Santa Fe, NM: Fort Burgwin Research Center and Museum of New Mexico Press, 1975.

McHenry, Paul G., Jr. *Adobe and Rammed Earth Buildings: Design and Construction*. Tucson: University of Arizona Press, 1984.

McHenry, Paul G., Jr. *Adobe—Build it Yourself*. Tucson: University of Arizona Press, 1973.

Walker, Aidan, ed. *Encyclopedia of Wood*. New York: Quatro Publishing, 1989.

Chapter 10

Allen, Edward. *Fundamentals of Building Construction: Methods and Materials*, 2nd ed. New York: John Wiley & Sons, 1990.

American Institute of Timber Construction. *Timber Construction Manual*. New York: John Wiley & Sons, 1985.

J. Baldwin. *Bucky Works: Buckminster Fuller's Ideas for Today*. New York: John Wiley & Sons, 1997.

Feirer, John L., and Gilbert R. Hutchings. *Carpentry and Building Construction*, rev. Peoria, IL: Chas. A. Bennet, 1981.

Hornbostel, Caleb. *Construction Materials: Types, Uses and Applications*, 2nd ed. New York: John Wiley & Sons, 1991.

Merrilees, Doug, and Evelyn Loveday. *Low-Cost Pole Building Construction*. Charlotte, VT: Garden Way Publishing, 1975.

Olin, Harold B. *Construction: Principals, Materials and Methods*, 5th ed. New York: Van Nostrand Reinhold, 1990.

Seddon, Leigh. *Low-Cost Green Lumber Construction.* Charlotte, VT: Garden Way Publishing, 1981.

Siegele, H. H. *The Steel Square.* New York: Sterling Publishing, 1980.

Walker, Aidan, ed. *Encyclopedia of Wood.* New York: Quatro Publishing, 1989.

Chapter 11

Benson, Tedd. *The Timber Frame Home.* Newton, CT: Tauton Press, 1988.

Feirer, John L., and Gilbert R. Hutchings. *Carpentry and Building Construction,* rev. Peoria, IL: Chas. A. Bennet, 1981.

Kern, Ken. *The Owner Built Home.* New York: Charles Scribner's Sons, 1972.

Olgyay, Victor. *Design with Climate: Bioclimatic Approach to Architectural Regionalism.* Princeton: Princeton University Press, 1963.

Oliver, Alan. *Dampness in Buildings.* New York: Nichols, 1980.

Seddon, Leigh. *Low-Cost Green Lumber Construction.* Charlotte, VT: Garden Way Publishing, 1981.

Chapter 12

Allen, Edward. *Fundamentals of Building Construction: Methods and Materials,* 2nd ed. New York: John Wiley & Sons, 1990.

Beall, Christine. *Masonry Design and Detailing.* New York: McGraw-Hill, 1978.

Bunting, Bainbridge, Jean Lee Booth, and William R. Simms, Jr. *Taos Adobes.* Santa Fe, NM: Fort Burgwin Research Center and Museum of New Mexico Press, 1975.

Hornbostel, Caleb. *Construction Materials: Types, Uses and Applications,* 2nd ed. New York: John Wiley & Sons, 1991.

McDonald, Roxana. *The Fireplace Book.* London: Architectural Press, 1984.

McHenry, Paul G., Jr. *Adobe and Rammed Earth Buildings: Design and Construction.* Tucson: University of Arizona Press, 1984.

McHenry, Paul G., Jr. *Adobe—Build it Yourself.* Tucson: University of Arizona Press, 1973.

Olin, Harold B. *Construction: Principals, Materials and Methods,* 5th ed. New York: Van Nostrand Reinhold, 1990.

Orton, Vrest. *The Forgotten Art of Building a Good Fireplace.* Dublin, NH: Yankee, 1987.

Chapter 13

Gross, Marshall. *Roof Framing.* Carlsbad, CA: Craftsman Book, 1985.

Melaragno, Michele. *Simplified Truss Design.* New York: Van Nostrand Reinhold Company, 1981.

Chapter 14

Argue, Robert. *The Super-Insulated Retrofit Book.* Canada: Renewable Energy in Canada, 1981.

Bachelard, Gaston. *The Poetics of Space.* Boston: Beacon Press, 1969.

Robbins, Claude L. *Daylighting: Design and Analysis.* New York: Van Nostrand Reinhold, 1986.

Chapter 15

Air Conditioning Contractors of America. *ACCA: Manual,* 7th ed. 1513 16th St. Washington, D.C. 20036, 1986.

ASHRAE Handbook. Atlanta: American Society of Heating, Refrigerating and Air-conditioning Engineers, 1985.

Farallones Institute. *The Integral Urban Home.* San Francisco: Sierra Club, 1979.

Leckie, Jim, Gil Master, Harry Whitehouse, and Lily Young. *More Other Homes and Garbage.* San Francisco: Sierra Club, 1981.

Mayall, R. Newton, and Margaret. *Sundials: How to Know, Use and Make Them.* Cambridge, MA. Sky Publishing, 1973.

McGuiness, William J., Benjamin Stein, and John S. Reynolds. *Mechanical and Electrical Equipment for Buildings,* 6th ed. New York: John Wiley & Sons, 1980.

Seddon, Leigh. *Low-Cost Green Lumber Construction.* Charlotte, VT: Garden Way Publishing, 1981.

Waugh, Albert E. *Sundials: Their Theory and Construction.* New York: Dover Publications, 1973.

Chapter 16

ASHRAE Handbook. Atlanta: American Society of Heating, Refrigerating and Air-conditioning Engineers, 1985.

Farallones Institute. *The Integral Urban Home.* San Francisco: Sierra Club, 1979.

Leckie, Jim, Gil Master, Harry Whitehouse, and Lily Young. *More Other Homes and Garbage.* San Francisco: Sierra Club, 1981.

McGuiness, William J., Benjamin Stein, and John S. Reynolds. *Mechanical and Electrical Equipment for Buildings,* 6th ed. New York: John Wiley & Sons, 1980.

Chapter 17

BOCA National Plumbing Code. Building Officials and Code Administrators International, 1987.

Leckie, Jim, Gil Master, Harry Whitehouse, and Lily Young. *More Other Homes and Garbage.* San Francisco: Sierra Club, 1981.

Lewis, Jack R. *Support Systems for Buildings.* Englewood Cliffs, NJ: Prentice-Hall, 1986.

McGuiness, William J., Benjamin Stein, and John S. Reynolds. *Mechanical and Electrical Equipment for Buildings,* 6th ed. New York: John Wiley & Sons, 1980.

Milne, Murray. *Residential Water Re-Use.* Davis, CA: California Water Resources Center, 1979.

Van der Ryn, Sim. *The Toilet Papers.* Santa Barbara, CA: Capra Press, 1978.

Chapter 18

Davidson, Joel. *The New Solar Electric Home: The Photovoltaics How-To Handbook.* Ann Arbor, MI: aatec Publications, 1989.

Leckie, Jim, Gil Master, Harry Whitehouse, and Lily Young. *More Other Homes and Garbage.* San Francisco: Sierra Club, 1981.

Lewis, Jack R. *Support Systems for Buildings.* Englewood Cliffs, NJ: Prentice-Hall Inc., 1986.

McGuiness, William J., Benjamin Stein, and John S. Reynolds. *Mechanical and Electrical Equipment for Buildings,* 6th ed. New York: John Wiley & Sons, 1980.

Melaragno, Michele G. *Wind in Architectural and Environmental Design.* New York: Van Nostrand Reinhold, 1982.

Pacific Northwest Laboratory. *Wind Energy Resource Atlas of the United States.* Golden, CO: Solar Technical Information Program, Solar Energy Research Institute, 1986.

Park, Jack. *The Wind Power Book.* Palo Alto, CA: Cheshire Books, 1981.

Chapter 19

Abercrombie, Stanley. *A Philosophy of Interior Design.* New York: Harper and Row, 1990.

Ladau, Robert F., and Brent K. Smith, Jennifer Place. *Color in Interior Design and Architecture.* New York: Van Nostrand Reinhold, 1989.

Olin, Harold B. *Construction: Principals, Materials and Methods,* 5th ed. New York: Van Nostrand Reinhold, 1990.

Chapter 20

Alexander, Christopher. *A Pattern Language.* New York: Oxford University Press, 1977.

Allen, Edward. *The Architect's Studio Companion: Technical Guidelines for Preliminary Design.* New York: John Wiley & Sons, 1989.

Allen, Edward. *Fundamentals of Building Construction: Methods and Materials,* 2d ed. New York: John Wiley & Sons, 1990.

Bachelard, Gaston. *The Poetics of Space.* Boston: Beacon Press, 1969.

Banham, Reyner. *Age of the Masters: A Personal View of Modern Architecture.* New York: Harper and Row, 1975.

Bloomer, Kent C., and Charles W. Moore. *Body, Memory and Architecture.* New Haven: Yale University Press, 1977.

Carter, Thomas, and Bernard Herman, eds. *Perspectives in Vernacular Architecture, III.* Columbia, MO: University of Missouri Press, 1989.

Cowan, Henry J., and Peter R. Smith. *The Science and Technology of Building Materials.* New York: Van Nostrand Reinhold, 1988.

Ford, Edward R. *The Details of Modern Architecture.* Cambridge, MA: MIT Press, 1990.

Hubka, Thomas C. *Big House, Little House, Back House, Barn.* Hanover, NH: University Press of New England, 1987.

Jung, Carl G. *Man and His Symbols.* New York: Doubleday, 1969.

McHarg, Ian. *Design with Nature.* New York: Doubleday, 1971.

Moore, Charles, Gerald Allen, and Donlyn Lyndon. *The Place of Houses.* New York: Holt, Reinhart and Winston, 1974.

Orton, Andrew. *The Way We Build Now: Form Scale and Technique.* Berkshire, England: Van Nostrand Reinhold (UK), 1988.

Ramsey, Charles, and Harold Sleeper. *Architectural Graphic Standards,* the American Institute of Architects, ed., New York: John Wiley & Sons, 1988.

Rudofsky, Bernard. *Architecture Without Architects.* New York: Doubleday, 1964.

Venturi, Robert. *Complexity and Contradiction in Architecture.* New York: Museum of Modern Art, 1977.

Willson, Forest. *The Joy of Building: Restoring the Connection Between Architect and Builder.* New York: Van Nostrand Reinhold, 1979.

Appendix 1

Abercrombie, Stanley. *A Philosophy of Interior Design.* New York: Harper and Row, 1990.

Alexander, Christopher. *The Timeless Way of Building.* New York: Oxford University Press, 1979.

Bachelard, Gaston. *The Poetics of Space.* Boston: Beacon Press, 1969.

Birren, Faber. *Color and the Human Response.* New York: Van Nostrand Reinhold, 1978.

Hall, Edward T. *The Hidden Dimension.* New York: Anchor Books/Doubleday, 1966.

Jung, Carl G. *Man and His Symbols.* New York: Doubleday, 1969.

Ladau, Robert F., and Brent K. Smith, Jennifer Place. *Color in Interior Design and Architecture.* New York: Van Nostrand Reinhold, 1989.

Lym, Glenn R. *A Psychology of Building: How We Shape and Experience Our Structured Spaces.* Englewood Cliffs, NJ: Prentice-Hall, 1980.

Moore, Charles, Gerald Allen, and Donlyn Lyndon. *The Place of Houses.* New York: Holt, Reinhart and Winston, 1974.

Sommer, Robert. *Personal Space: The Behavioral Basis of Design.* Englewood Cliffs, NJ: Prentice-Hall Inc., 1969.

Appendix 3

ASHRAE Handbook of Fundamentals. Atlanta: The American Society of Heating, Refrigeration, and Air-conditioning Engineers, 1985.

Leckie, Jim, Gil Master, Harry Whitehouse, and Lily Young. *More Other Homes and Garbage.* San Francisco: Sierra Club Books, 1981.

McGuinness, William J., Benjamin Stein, and John S. Reynolds. *Mechanical and Electrical Equipment for Buildings,* 6th ed. New York: John Wiley & Sons, 1980.

Olgyay, Victor. *Design and Climate: Bioclimatic Approach to Architectural Regionalism.* Princeton: Princeton University Press, 1963.

Appendix 4

Ching, Francis D. K. *Architectural Graphics.* New York: Van Nostrand Reinhold, 1975.

Ching, Francis D. K. *Building Construction Illustrated.* New York: Van Nostrand Reinhold, 1990.

Edwards, Betty. *Drawing on the Right Side of the Brain.* New York: St. Martin's Press, 1979.

Walker, Les, and Jeff Milstein. *Designing Houses: An Illustrated Guide.* Woodstock, NY: Overlook Press, 1976.

Appendix 5

Nichols, Herbert L., Jr. *Moving the Earth: The Workbook of Excavation,* 3rd ed. New York: McGraw-Hill Publishing, 1962.

Olin, Harold B. *Construction: Principals, Materials and Methods,* 5th ed. New York: Van Nostrand Reinhold, 1990.

Appendix 6

Dowrick, David J. *Earthquake Resistant Design for Engineers and Architects,* 2nd ed. New York: John Wiley & Sons, 1977.

Nichols, Herbert L., Jr. *Moving the Earth: The Workbook of Excavation,* 3rd ed. New York: McGraw-Hill Publishing, 1962.

Appendix 7 and 8

Ambrose, James, and Harry Parker. *Simplified Design of Structural Wood.* 4th ed. New York: John Wiley & Sons, 1988.

American Institute of Timber Construction. *Timber Construction Manual.* New York: John Wiley & Sons, 1985.

Faherty, Keith F., and Thomas G. Williamson. *Wood Engineering and Construction Handbook.* McGraw-Hill, 1989.

Feirer, John L., and Gilbert R. Hutchings. *Carpentry and Building Construction.* rev. Peoria, IL: Chas. A. Bennet, 1981.

Harris, Ernest C., and Judith J. Stalnaker. *Structural Design in Wood.* New York: Van Nostrand Reinhold, 1989.

Span Tables for Joists and Rafters. Washington, D.C.: National Forest Products Association, 1977.

Appendix 9

American Institute of Timber Construction. *Timber Construction Manual.* New York: John Wiley & Sons, 1985.

Gross, Marshall. *Roof Framing.* Carlsbad, CA: Craftsman Book, 1985.

Siegele, H. H. *The Steel Square.* New York: Sterling Publishing, 1980.

Appendix 10

McDonald, Roxana. *The Fireplace Book.* London: Architectural Press, 1984.

Olin, Harold B. *Construction: Principals, Materials and Methods,* 5th ed. New York: Van Nostrand Reinhold, 1990.

Orton, Vrest. *The Forgotten Art of Building a Good Fireplace.* Dublin, NH: Yankee, 1987.

Appendix 11

Acret, James. *Architects and Engineers: Their Professional Responsibilities.* Colorado Springs, CO: McGraw-Hill, 1977.

Hageman, Jack M. *Contractor's Guide to the Building Code.* Carlsbad, CA: Craftsman Book Company, 1990.

INDEX

Accent lighting, 338
Access to property, 52–54, 63–64
Acoustics
    in domes, 146
    and wall construction, 129–31
Acrylic, 252
Active solar heat, 290
Actual maximum deflection, 408–9
Adirondeck camps, 12
Adobe construction, 184–85, 210–13
Aerobic digestion, 308
Aggregates, 193
Air Control Systems, 295
Air exchange method, 262–63, 382–84
Air heating systems
    electric baseboard, 295
    multi-zone central air, 293–94
    one zone convection, 293
    radiant floor-hot air, 294–95
Airtight drywall approach (ADA), 178, 265
All-weather wood foundation (AWWF), 98, 396
Alternating current, 330
Alternative energy, 291
Amperes, 330
Anaerobic digestion, 307
Anemometer, 344
Annular nails, 167
Aquifers, 43, 305
Architect
    fee structure for, 19–21
    functions of, 19–20
Architectural design
    complexity of, 23
    costs of, 77–79

Argon, 30, 248
Argue, R., 243
ASHRAE, 268
Asphalt, 232
Auger feed, 287
Awning, 244

Backfilling, 114–15
Baer, Steve, 146–47
Ballasts, 337
Balloon frame, 139, 187
Bamboo scaffolding, 160
Banana, 419
Bank run gravel, 43, 106
Baroque, 10, 420
Baseboard hot water heat, 296–98
Batter boards, 104
Bauhaus, 13
Beams
    bond, 211–13
    built-up, 152–55
    lateral collaring, 227–29
    and span charts, 404–7
    structural ridge, 229
Bearing capacities, 95–96
    of soils, 97
Bedroom design, 89
Beecher, Catherine, 11
Benchmark, 41
Berms, 62
Beveled glass, 241
Birdsmouth, 225–26
Black water, 61, 311

Blueboard, 356
Board and batten, 371
Bond, 199, 201
Bond beam, 211–13
Boney, 420
Bow, 420
Bowstring truss, 150
Box beam, 150
Breaker box, 331
Breast shot waterwheel, 343
Brick, 198–204
    bonds or surface patterns, 203
    modular sizes, 199
    orientation of, in the wall, 204
Brick molding, 248
British thermal unit (BTU), 260, 420
Brunberger, Ben, 215
BTU (British thermal unit), 260, 419
BTUH, 419
Bubble diagram, 81–83, 85, 87
    building walls from, 120–31
    questions for, 370
Budget, 77–79
    analysis and bid supervision, 20
Builders level, 420
Building codes, 67, 214–16, 417–18
Building envelope, thermal comfort of, 126, 257–78
Building materials, total energy embodiment in selected, 284
Built-up beams, 152–55
Butler, Lee Porter, 177
BX Cable, 332
Byzantine, 11

Cantilevers, 151–52
Capillary action, 98, 116
Cartesian grids, 41
Casement, 238, 244
Casing, 246, 251
Catalytic converter, 293
Cavity construction, 199–202, 211
Change order, 87
Chase, 173, 311, 421
Check, 421
Check damper, 421
Chimney effect, 224
Chipping, 287–88
Circuit venting, 312
Circulation pattern, 89–91
City design, 66–68
Clad windows, 244, 248
Clamp, 198
Clean out, 311
Clerestory, 241
CMUs (cementitious masonry units), 202–5
Coal, 285
Cob construction, 211
Coefficient of expansion, 243
Cold attic approach, 179, 181
Coleman, Jito, 346
Collar ties, 226–29
Colonial, 10–12
Compacting machine, 106
Composting toilets, 315–16
Compressive force, 421
Concrete, 391–94
   aggregate, 391
   mix, 391, 393
   placing and curing, 392–94
   steel-reinforced, 103, 391–92
Concrete block, 202–10
Conduction, 258–61
   heat loss by, 381–82
Connell, John, 245
Constraints, 57
Construction documents, 20
Continuous-tunnel kiln, 198
Control joint, 205

Convection, 265–66
Cooling, 242, 267, 277, 280, 288, 291–93, 300, 369
Cooling load, 267
Cooper, James Fenimore, 10
Corbel, 198
Corbusier, 13
Cordwood, 213–14
Cornice, 219
Counterfort wall, 395
Covenant, 421
Crack method, 263
Crook, 421
Crown, 421
Cruk frame, 159
Cup, 422
Curtain drain, 97, 116
Curtain wall, 119, 236
Curvilinear forms, building, 149–51

Damp-proofing, 116–17
Damper, 290, 294
Davidson, J., 348
Daylighting, 241, 338
Dead loads, 169
Decay, 422
Deciduous tree, 422
Deflection, 174–75
   actual maximum, 408–9
   maximum allowable, 409
Degree day, 275
Delta T, 259
Demand water heaters, 309
Design development, 20
Design fundamentals, importance of, 25–33
Design helix, 29–32, 57, 71, 88
Dew point, 222
Diagramming your program, 81–92
   bubble diagrams, 81–83, 85–87, 370
   metaphorical diagrams, 83–84
   steps in, 84–87, 92
   storyboard diagrams, 84, 82–88, 370–71
Digestion
   aerobic, 308
   anaerobic, 307

Dimensional lumber, 168
Dimmers, 337
Direct current, 330
Domes, 143–46
   acoustics in, 146
   geodesic, 143, 144, 146–47
   panel, 144
   problem of organizing floor plan for, 148
Doors, 249–55
   glass in, 252
   hardware for, 255
   placement of, 249–52
   placing your, 89–91
   swing of, 252, 255, 388
   and thermal security, 252
Dormers, 220
   in snow belt, 233
Double framing, 261
Double hung, 244
Double-wall masonry construction, 121
Dovetail, 136–37
Downing, Andrew Jackson, 11
Downspout, 422
Drafting conventions, 386–90
Drainage
   analysis of, 42–45
   and foundation design, 96–97
Drainage, waste, and venting (DWV) system, 311
Drain tile, 422
Dressed lumber, 167
Drilled wells, 305
Driven wells, 305
Driveways, building and maintaining, 52
Dry-laid retaining walls, 194
Dry lumber, 167
Dry press process, 198
Drywall, 187
Duct, 422
Dug wells, 305
Duplex, 332–33
Dwelling, Dymaxion, 13
Dwyer, Charles, 11

Earth-bermed architecture, 261
Earthquake-resistant construction, 401–3
    chimneys, 403
    connections, 403
    horizontal planes, 403
    fault terminology and types, 402
    masonry, 403
    openings, 402
    seismic zones, 401
    shape, 401–402
    wall design, 403
Earth-sheltered homes, 99
Easement, 55
Eave, 219, 224
Edge-grained lumber, 164
Education, 17–18
Efflorescence, 200
Electrical appliances, 353
Electrical fires, 332
Electrical symbols, list of frequently used, 334
Electrical systems, 329–54
    design, 331
        lamps and lights, 338–40
        layout, 332–37
        lighting, 337–38
        service entry, 331
        wiring, 331–32
Electric baseboard heat, 295–96
Electric power, 282–85
    generating own, 340–53
Elevations
    site, 41
    bldg, 358–59
Ell, 423
Embodied energy, 282
EMT, 332
Energy, 18
Energy distribution systems, 292–93
Energy sources, 282
    air systems
        baseboard hot water, 296–98
        electric baseboard, 295–96
        multi-zone central air, 293–94
        one zone convection, 293

Energy sources, air systems (*Cont.*)
        radiant floor, 299–300
        radiant floor-hot air, 294–95
        radiators, 298–99
    alternative energy, 291
    coal, 285
    electric power, 282–85
    fireplaces, 288, 416
    gas, 285–86
    oil, 285
    solar energy, 288–90
    wood, 286–88
Enkadrain, 116
Equinox, 423
Evergreen tree, 423
Excavation, 105
Exposure, 49

Fabric walls, 123
Face shells, 206
Families, 18
Fan coil unit, 423
Fatigue loads, 169
Fauna, 64
Fenestration. *See* Windows
Fill, 105–06
Filter fabric, 423
Finishes, 355–60
Fin-tubes, 296–98
Fire blocking, 187
Firescape, for domes, 146
Fireplaces, 288, 416
Fixture units, 312, 315
Flagg, Ernest, 195
Flat-grained lumber, 164
Float glass, 243
Floating slab, 100, 394
Flooding, resistance of pole construction to, 142
Floodplain, 43
Floodplain map, 43
Flood Plain Regulations, 59
Floor, calculating the structure for a typical, 170–75

Flooring, 356–57
Floor plan, 423
Floor register, 293
Floor trusses, 155–56
Fluorescent lamps, 339–40
Footing, 100, 106–9
Footing pour, 109–10
Footings, 394
    T-footings, 395
Foundation drain, 115–16
Foundations
    bearing capacity of, 95–96
    choosing, 100
    continuous wall, 100
    damp-proofing and waterproofing the walls, 116–17
    designbuilder attitude about, 117–18
    design guide to, 391–400
    drainage, 96–97, 115–16
    insulation, 98–99
    moisture control for, 98–99
    pier, 100
    pyramid, 194
    reinforced concrete frost wall foundation, 102–3
        considering the wall, 114–15
        fill, 105–6
        footing pour, 109–10
        footings, 106–9
        laying out and forming the wall, 111–12
        layout, 104
        wall pour, 113–14
    trench, 394
    slab, 100
    wood, 98, 396–400
Foyer, 421
Frame construction, 121, 123
Frames, 133, 156–162
    definition of, 134
    geometric flexibility, 147–48
        built-up beams, 152–55
        cantilevers, 151–52
        curves, 149–51
        domes, 143–47

Frames, geometric flexibility (*Cont.*)
    pole buildings, 140–43
      trusses, 155–58
      zomes, 146–47
    laying out rafters, 412–15
    short course on, 138
    stick, 135, 138–40, 185–88
    timber, 134–38, 142, 159–60
Framing square, 412–15
French drains, 96–98, 115–16
Frieze molding, 219
Frost heave, 97, 194
Frost line, 107–8
Frost wall, 102–3
Frozen pipes, 310
Fuel-powered generator, 341
Fuels, energy content of different, 284
Fuller, Buckminster, 13, 143

Gable, 219
Galvanized, 396
Gambrel, 219
Gang forms, 211
Garage doors, 154
Gas, 285–286
Gehner, Martin, 140
Generators, 353
Geodesic dome, 144–48
Geodetic survey maps, 38–39
Geometric flexibility, 147–48
    built-up beams, 152–55
    cantilevers, 151–52
    curves, 149–51
    domes, 143–47
    pole buildings, 140–43
    trusses, 155–58
    zomes, 146–47
GFI (Ground Fault Interrupt) components, 336
Girder
    configuration, 171
    sizing, 173–74, 405–7
Girt, 134, 142
Glazing configurations, approximate R values
    for different, 243

Global communication, 17
Glulams, 154, 157
Godey, Louis, 11
Gothic, 11, 424
Gravity walls, 395
Gray water, 61, 311
Greek revival, 11
Greenfield, 332
Greenhouse, in waste treatment, 65–66
Green lumber, 166–67
Grillo, Paul, 219
Gropius, Walter, 13
Ground fault protected, 336
Groundwater, 305
    temperature of, 260
Gypsum board, 187

Halflap, 424
Handed door, 424
Hard water, 308
Header, 149–50, 174
Heat exchanger, 262
Heat flow, 258
    analysis of, 280
    heat gain, 267–68
      windows, 268–69
    heat loss, 258
      addressing problem of, 181
      calculation of, 380–85
      conduction, 258–61
      convection, 265–66
      infiltration, 261–65
      radiation, 266–67
Heating systems
    air systems
      electric baseboard, 295
      multi-zone central air, 293–94
      one zone convection, 293
      radiant floor-hot air, 294–95
    alternative energy, 291
    coal, 285
    electric power, 282–85
    fireplaces, 288, 416

Heating systems (*Cont.*)
    gas, 285–86
    hydronic systems
      baseboard hot water, 296–98
      radiant floor, 299–301
      radiators, 298–99
    oil, 285
    solar energy, 288–90
    wood, 286–88
Heat pump, 283–84
Heat transfer factor, 423
High water table, 43–45, 60
Hollow core door, 424
Home, human quality of making, 7–9
Home base, 15
    benefits of establishing, 16
Honeycombing, 114
Hopper, 425
Hot-water leg, 309
House programs, answering questions in, 71–79,
    369–71
Houses
    building, 14–15
    costs of, 14
    impact of lifestyle on design of, 72–79
    quality of, 17
    shopping for, 12–14
Hoved, Vrinners, 346
Howard Roark Syndrome, 235–36
Humidity, 125
HVAC, 263, 280
Hydroelectric generation, 341
Hydrologic cycle, phases of, 44
Hydronic system, 293, 308–9
    baseboard hot water, 296–98
    radiators, 298–99
    radiant floor, 299–300
Hydro potential, 341–43
Hydrostat, 308

Ice dam, 181
Impact loads, 168–69
Impulse turbine, 341

Incandescent lamps, 340
Income, 17
Indirect lighting, 337–38
Infiltration, 261–65
   heat loss by, though walls, 382–85
Inglenook, 425
Inhabited basements, 99
Insolation, 289
Instantaneous boiler, 309
Insulation
   of foundation wall, 98
   of walls, 124–26, 175–88, 261–65
   of roofs, 181
   R-value, 179, 182
Irving, Washington, 10
Isolation valve, 311
Italianate, 11, 425

Jack rafter, 425
Jalousie, 425
Jamb, 425
Joinery, 134–38
Joint hanger, 425
Joists, sizing, 404–6
Jones, Fay, 159

Kahn, Lloyd, 144
Kerf, sawkerf, 150
Kern, Ken, 197
Keyway, 109–10
KISS, 425
Kitchen design, 89
Knee wall, 426
Knob and tube, 332

Lady's Book (Godey), 11
Laminated glass, 243, 426
Lateral collaring beam, 227, 230
Layout of foundation, 104
Leaching field
   location of, 64

Leaching field (*Cont.*)
   minimum absorption area for residence,
     320
   size of, 61–62, 322–23
Leads, 207, 426
Leckie, Jim, 345
Level line, 104
Levitt, William, 426
Lifestyle, impact of, on housing design, 72–79
Lighting, 337–38
   accent, 337–38
   indirect, 337–38
   lamps and lights, 338–40
Line blocks, 208
Lintel, 202, 209
Live loads, 169
Load-bearing walls, 120, 170
Loads, 168–70
   concentrated, 172
   cooling, 267
   dead, 169
   fatigue, 169
   impact, 169
   live, 169
   point, 172
   repetitive, 169
   seismic, 169
   snow, 170
   static live, 169
   total, 172
   uniform, 172
   wind, 170
Log homes, 213–14
   manufactured, 12
Look outs, 219, 426
Lot size, minimum, 52
Low-E glass, 426
Lstiburek, Joe, 177
Lumber
   abbreviations for, 169
   common dimensionals of, 167
   dimensional, 168
   dimensions of standard, stocked at lumber-
     yards, 169

Lumber (*Cont.*)
   dressed, 167
   dry, 167
   edge-grained, 164
   flat-grained, 164
   green, 167
   plane-sawn, 164
   quarter-sawn, 164
   rough-sawn, 168
   seasoned, 167
   sizes of, 72
   unseasoned, 167
   see also Wood
Lustron Home, failure of, 13

Main disconnect, 331, 426
Mansard, 219, 426
Manufactured log homes, 12
Masonry, 191–216
   adobe, 210–13
   brick, 198–202
   concrete block, 202–10
   mortar, 193–94
   slip-form stone walls, 194–98
   stone, 194
Masonry walls, 120–21
Massing, 147
Mass wall, 395
Masters, Gil, 345
Materials and methods, 92
   using local, 9, 12
Maximum allowable deflection, 409
McClintock, Mike, 197
Meadow, building in, 56
Metal roofing systems, 232
Metaphorical diagrams, 83–84
Metes and bounds, 58, 426
Meyer, Kathy, 327
Miasma, 426
Micro lams, 154
Mies van der Rohe, Ludwig, 13
Moisture, as concern in masonry construction,
   200

Moisture control, for foundation, 98–99
Moment of inertia, 408
Monadnock building, 192
Moore, Charles, 14, 74, 76–77
Mortar, 193–94
    proportions by volume, 193
Mortise, 135–38
Mound system, 62, 426
Mullions, 239
Multi-zone central air heat, 293–94
Multrum, Clivus, 316
Muntins, 239

Nail popping, 167
Narration, 84, 87
    questions for, 369–70
National Standard Plumbing Code, 308
Nearing, Helen, 197
Nearing, Scott, 197
Noise
    in site analysis, 46
    see also Acoustics
Nominal dimensions, 72
NRG Systems, 344

Oakes, George, 146
OC, 427
Oil, 285
One-hundred-year floodplain, 43, 59
Open plan, 89, 253–54
Organic roofing, 231–32
Orton, Vrest, 288
Overshot waterwheel, 342, 427
Owner/building, 15–17

Palladio, 427
Panel domes, 144
Park, Jack, 346
Passive solar heat, 290
Pattern books, 11–12
Pelletized wood, 287–88

Pencil vibrator, 114
Percolation data, 61
Percolation test, 61, 319–20
Periodic kiln, 198
Permanent wood foundation (PWF), 396
Petroleum-based products for roofing, 232
Philly pole, 41
Photovoltaic electricity (PV), 290, 341,
    346–53
Pier foundation, 100, 102
Pilaster, 427
Plane-sawed lumber, 164
Platform frame, 138
Plumbing, 303–27
Ply, 427
Pointing, 192, 208, 209
Polar grids, 41
Pole buildings, 140–43
Portland cement, 193
Post and beam, 134
Potable water, 311, 312
Power drop, 331, 427
Power Pavilion, 217–18
Prefabricated housing, 13, 123
Preliminary design and programming, 20
Primary residence, 16
Privacy, importance of, 52–53
Problem solving, 357, 359–60
Program, 71–79, 427
Program questionnaire, 369–71
Puritans, 9–10
Purlin(s), 135, 428
Pyramid foundations, 194

Quarter-sawn lumber, 164, 428

R-value, 179, 258, 428
Raceway conductors, 332, 428
Radiant floor heat, 294, 299–300
Radiation, 266–67
Radiators, 298
Radon testing, 99–100

Rafters, laying out, 138, 412–15
Railroad track, 208, 213, 428
Rain screen, 182
Rammed earth, 211, 428
Rebar—see Reinforcing steel
Reinforced concrete frost wall foundation,
    102–3
    considering the wall, 114–15
    fill, 105–6
    footings, 106–10
    layout, 104, 111–12
    wall pour, 113–14
Reinforcing steel (rebar), 103–9
Renewable fuels, 281–82
Repetitive loads, 169
Replacement field, 321, 428
Resistance heat, 283, 428
Retaining walls, 395–96
Reynolds, Michael, 213
Ridge beam, 226–29
Ringel, John, 58
Riparian laws, 45
Romex, 332, 428
Roof, 217–33
    application of theory, 224–31
    curved, 150
    materials for, 231–32
    orientation in the snow belt, 233
    shape of, and climate, 219–20
    theory behind design of, 221–24
Roof truss, 155
Rough opening, 150, 247, 428
Rough-sawn lumber, 168
Runoff, 96–97
R-value, 179, 182–83, 244
Rybczynski, Witold, 38

Sand struck bricks, 198
Sanford, Jim, 327
Scaffolding, bamboo, 160
Scale models, building, 77
Scenic views, 49–50
Screed 110–14, 428

Seasoned lumber, 167
Second home, 16
Seismic loads, 169
Seldon, Leigh, 167
Sellers, David, 154, 326
Septic system, 61–62, 307–8
Setbacks, 52, 321
Sheet-metal roofing, 232
Sheathing, 138, 139, 144, 175, 179, 182, 185,
    189, 428
Shop drawing, 155
Shoreline access, 64
Short circuit, 330, 429
Site analysis, 37–38
    access, 52–54
    reality, 54
    topography, 38–42
    scenic views, 47, 49–50
    solar views, 47, 49–50
    water, 42–45
    wind, noise, and vegetation, 45–47
    zoning, 50, 52
Site blueprints, 20
Site conditions and foundation, 95–96
Site design and development, 55–68
    access, 63–64
    city, 66–68
    constraints in, 57
    fauna, 64
    prioritizing in, 56, 57, 71
    septic considerations, 61–62
    sewage treatment, 65–66
    topography, 62
Site inspections and review, 20
Site model, building, 38
Slabs, 394, 429
Slip-form stone walls, 194–98
Slump, 113, 429
Snap ties, 111, 429
Snow belt
    dormers in, 233
    roof orientation in, 233
Snow loads, 170
Soffit, square, 415

Soft mud process, 198
Soils
    analysis of, 43, 45
    bearing capacities of, 97
Solar
    active, 290, 429
    passive, 290, 429
Solar cooling, 291–92
Solar energy, 281, 288–90
Solar heat gain factor (SHGF), 268–74
Solar Path Finder, 66, 429
Solar Site Selector, 50
Solar views, 47, 49–50
Solid walls, 201
Son Bao Vong, 7
Spawling, 103, 429
Stackwall construction, 213, 429
Stadia rod, 41, 430
Stair design, 89
Stair gauges, 413
Standing seam, 232, 430
Static live loads, 169
Stave churches, 159
Steel reinforced concrete, 103
Stem wall, 100, 430
Stepping off, 412
Stick framing, 138–40, 178, 185–87, 430
Stiff mud process, 198
Stone, 194
Stone Flower, 159
Stone walls, slip-form, 194–98
Story-board diagrams, 84, 87
    questions for, 370–71
Story pole, 110, 430
Streets, in site planning, 66–67
Stressed-skin panel, 185–88, 430
Strongbacks, 111, 430
Structural fill, 105–6
Structural ridge beam, 227, 430
Stud wall, 183
Sustainable, 281, 430
Surface water, 305
    analysis of movement of, 42–45
Surveying, 38–42, 58

Tankless water heater, 309
Task lighting, 338, 430
Tenon, 135, 428
Tent frame, 159
Test pits, 43
    digging, 47, 59
Thermal break, 261, 430
Thermal comfort of building envelope, 257–78
Thermal considerations, 175–82
Thermal Envelope House, 177
Thermodynamics, 258
Thermopane, 243, 430
Thoreau, Henry, 10
Thoroseal, 116
Timber Framers' Guild of North America, 134
Timber frames, 134–38, 148, 159, 431
Timers, 337
Title search, 58
Topographical survey, 38–42, 431
Topography, 62
Tornados, 160
Total load, 172
Trammel set, 150, 431
Transit, 39–41, 431
Trap, 312–14, 431
Trench foundation, 396
Trombe wall, 290, 431
Trusses, 155–62, 225–27, 431
Truss joists, 155–56
Tyvek, 182

U-coefficient, 258, 431
Unified Plumbing Code, 308
Uniform load, 172
Unit dimensions, 72
United States Geological Survey (USGS) map, 58
Unseasoned lumber, 167
Urban site planning, 66–68
Utilities, in site design, 52–53, 63–64

Value engineered frame, 139–40
Vapor barrier, 177, 431

Vegetation, 46–48
Venting, 312–16, 431
Venting aperture, 223
Venturi effect, 47
Vernacular architecture, 9–12, 432
Viga, 232, 432
Volts, 330

Walers, 111, 432
Wall construction, 119–20
  from bubble diagrams, 120–31
Walls
  and acoustics, 129–31
  architectural appearance of, 126–29
  heat loss by infiltration through, 382–85
  insulation for, 124–26, 182–85
  structure of, 120–24
Walsh, H. Vandervoort, 138
Warm 'N' Dry, 116
Warp, 432
Waste disposal, 61–62
  and acoustics, 129–30
Water
  hard, 308
  movement over site, 42–45
  residential consumption of, 321
  separation of black from gray, 61, 311
  treatment of, 305–6, 318–19
Water cycle, 305–8
Water heater, 306–8
  sizing your, 309
Waterproofing, 116–17
Water struck bricks, 198, 340
Water table, 45, 59, 305
Waterwheels, 342–43

Watts, 330, 340
Weather, national information on, 372–79
Weaver, Dennis, 213
Weeps, 200, 432
Well
  costs of drilling, 305
  placement of, 308
  testing water from, 306
  types of, 305
Wells, Malcolm, 175
Whitehouse, Harry, 345
White noise, 131
Wick, 98, 432
Willis, Nathaniel, 12
Wind
  impact of, on site, 45–47
  resistance of pole construction to, 142
Wind data accumulator, 345, 432
Wind generation, 341
Wind loads, 170
Windows, 235–49
  architectural composition, 244
  functions of, 236
  glass for, 239
  hardware for, 255
  and heat gain, 268–77
  installing, in curved walls, 149–50
  light access, 241–43
  orientation of, 237
  steps in designing, 245–49
  types of, 239
  for ventilation, 243–44
  view from, 47, 49, 239–41
  as weather protection, 244
Wind potential, 344–46
Wiremold, 332, 340

Wood, 164–68, 286–88. *See also* Lumber
  bending characteristics of, 406
  classification of, 164–68
  dressing of, 167
  general suitability of different, for various
    applications, 165
  methods of cutting boards, 164
  moisture content of, 164, 166–67
  pellets, 287, 432
  uses of, at different levels of dryness,
    167
Wood column design, 409–11
Wood foundation, 98, 396–400
Wythe, 432

Yestermorrow Design/Build School, 361–65
  campus for, 365
  classes offered by, 364–65
  exploring design questions at, 72–79
  graduate benefits, 174
  history and philosophy of, 19–26
    budget analysis and bid supervision, 20
    construction documents, 20
    design development, 20
    preliminary design and programming,
      20
    site inspections and review, 20
Young, Lily, 345
Yurt, 159, 432

Zero lot line, 52
Zomes, 146–47
Zoning regulations, 45, 50, 52, 53, 59, 64
Zonohedra, 146, 432

NOTES

NOTES